Fodor's 92 California

D1306279

Fodor's Travel Publications, Inc.
New York and London

Fodor's California

Editor: Larry Peterson
Editorial Contributors: Kevin Brass, Toni Chapman, Bruce
David Colen, Laura Del Rosso, Vicky Elliott, Pamela Faust,
Marie Felde, Sheila Gadsden, Sharon K. Gillenwater, Tara
Hamilton, Pamela Hegarty, Mary Jane Horton, Dan Janeck,
Marael Johnson, Jacqueline Killeen, Jane Lasky, Maria
Lenhart, Jillian Magalaner, Ellen Melinkoff, Maribeth Mellin,
David Nelson, Denise Nolty, Carolyn Price, Marcy Pritchard,
Peter Segal, Aaron Shurin, Dan Spitzer, Aaron Sugarman,
Robert Taylor, Casey Tefertiller, Julie Tomasz
Art Director: Fabrizio La Rocca
Cartographer: David Lindroth
Illustrator: Karl Tanner
Cover Photograph: Dale Baker/Photobank

Design: Vignelli Associates

Special Sales

Contents

Maps

Foreword

From sea lions barking off Monterey Peninsula and John Muir's "Range of Light," to the temperate and foggy North Coast and the extremes of snow and heat found in the southern deserts, California is diverse enough and vast enough to satisfy nearly any visitor.

This edition of *Fodor's California* covers more California sights than ever before. There are separate chapters on the Wine Country, Lake Tahoe, and the Far North and much expanded treatment of Santa Barbara and Sacramento. There are extended chapters on San Francisco, Los Angeles, and San Diego, with plenty of information for a week's stay, but this book has been written primarily for those travelers who plan to visit several regions of the state. All the writers are local, and they share their best advice on what to see and do up and down the state.

While every care has been taken to ensure the accuracy of the information in this guide, the passage of time will always bring change, and consequently, the publisher cannot accept responsibility for errors that may occur.

All prices and opening times quoted here are based on information supplied to us at press time. Hours and admission fees may change, however, and the prudent traveler will avoid inconvenience by calling ahead.

Fodor's wants to hear about your travel experiences, both pleasant and unpleasant. When a hotel or restaurant fails to live up to its billing, let us know and we will investigate the complaint and revise our entries where the facts warrant it.

Send your letters to the editors of Fodor's Travel Publications, 201 E. 50th Street, New York, NY 10022.

Highlights'92 and Fodor's Choice

Highlights '92

For the first time in 40 years, San Franciscans can stand at the foot of Market Street and gaze, without obstruction, at the sparkling waterfront and its sentinel, **The Ferry Building.** After unnerving so many parts of the city, the 1989 earthquake finally did something nice: it shook loose the foundation of the ungainly elevated Embarcadero Freeway, causing its ultimate dismantling. Standing proudly undamaged, the Ferry Building's graceful clock tower, modeled on the Seville cathedral's campanile, was left to guard the **Embarcadero** promenade. If, as planned, the freeway is replaced with a subterranean highway, San Francisco will have before it an appropriate gateway to the inner bay, with an open-air park in which a traveler can breathe in the salt air, and rest from the pressure of the downtown concrete canyons. Drivers, however, may find this area problematic for a few more years.

The city continues its tradition of imaginative redevelopment a few blocks west of the waterfront. The area known as Rincon Hill, once an enclave of English-style town houses but long since gone the way of industrial warehouses, has blossomed into a sharply contemporary living and dining complex, **Rincon Center.** The soaring towers and atrium are actually built on top of and around an old post office. The center houses two of San Francisco's finest new restaurants. **Wu Kong** has inspired three-star raves for its bustling Hong Kong ambience and spicy Shanghai cuisine. Across the way, **Etrusca** happily marries Italian regional cooking to elegant streamlined decor.

Fisherman's Wharf, nearly done in by its age-old formulas for tourist success, is also showing refreshing signs of new life. Kimco Hotels, which is responsible for a wave of small, intimate, and carefully appointed new hotels, frequently with their own fine restaurants, has just opened the **Tuscan Inn** at Fisherman's Wharf. With 199 airy rooms, many with pristine views of the bay, the Tuscan offers Old World elegance, Italian-style, and houses the **Cafe Pescatore,** a classic trattoria. A block away, the **Hyatt at Fisherman's Wharf** brings that chain's reputation to its 313 guest-friendly rooms. Both of these developments are part of a new master plan to bring comfort and spontaneity (and maybe even local residents) back to this ever-popular tourist area.

If you want to leave the city in comfort and style, you can hop the new **Sierra 49er Express** to Lake Tahoe and Reno. This luxury train has more in common with a cruise ship than a regular passenger train. Its cars include enormous panoramic windows and electrostatically cleaned air. A three-level entertainment car provides live music and dancing. Best of all, the train glides through some of the most spectacular scenery that California has to offer: the marshlands of the Sacramento delta, the Sierra foothills' Gold Country, and the majestic High Sierras. For a shorter trip, Grayline Tours can connect you with the **Napa Wine Train,** where you can enjoy lunch or dinner (and, of course, wine) while riding through the North Bay's loveliest wine-producing region.

San Francisco continues to demonstrate cultural civic pride, with ground broken for two important new sites: the new Public Library at the Civic Center, and the daringly designed **Museum of Modern Art** in the downtown Yerba Buena development in the area south of Market Street known as SoMa.

In a city noted for an abundance of restaurants, the newest place to see and be seen (as well as to eat) is the **Cypress Club** on Jackson Street, and no wonder: situated on the edge of the sober Financial District, this elegantly bizarre space seems to have dropped down from Hollywood's skies with dramatic oversized fixtures and gigantic swooping lights. It is enormously popular so if you can't get a reservation for a table, go in for a look anyway.

Long known for its sights—palm trees, the Pacific, celebrities—**Los Angeles** is increasingly recognizable by certain sounds as well: the roar of bulldozers, the pounding of steel girders, and all the auditory trademarks of rampant real-estate development. Much of the hammering and concrete-pouring comes courtesy of the travel industry, with a slew of new hotels and tourist attractions in the works.

The long-awaited redevelopment of **Hollywood** is probably causing the most noise. The area surrounding Mann's Chinese Theater on Hollywood Boulevard will continue to resemble a disaster-movie set until 1993, when the **Hollywood Promenade** rises phoenixlike from the rubble. The Promenade will house a 350-room hotel, 275,000 square feet of upscale shops and restaurants, a 19-story office tower, a state-of-the-art theater complex dubbed the American Cinematheque, and a film and broadcast museum known as the Hollywood Exposition.

In general, Los Angeles is experiencing quite a hotel boom. The first hotel to be built in Beverly Hills proper in more than two decades, the stylish **Peninsula Beverly Hills,** received quite a bit of fanfare when it made its debut in the summer of 1991 with 200 ultra-luxurious rooms. Nearby, the distinctively Japanese-influenced, 304-room **Hotel Nikko,** also in Beverly Hills, opened in late 1991 on La Cienega Boulevard's Restaurant Row. At the beach, the 195-room **Park Hyatt Santa Monica** also began operation in 1991, and in Pasadena, the Ritz-Carlton Company opened the **Ritz-Carlton Huntington Hotel,** a reincarnation of one of Southern California's most historical properties.

Always competitive, West L.A. awaits the arrival of the **J. Paul Getty Center,** set to occupy some 110 acres atop a hill that allows panoramic views of both the Pacific and the Los Angeles basin. All this is scheduled to happen sometime in the mid-1990s.

Downtown L.A. isn't exactly quiet, either. Construction is underway on the **Walt Disney Concert Hall,** the future home of the Los Angeles Philharmonic. Scheduled for completion in time for the 1995 music season, the hall is being designed by local hero Frank Gehry, although the word is that this structure will be more simple and somewhat more conservative than typical Gehry creations.

The wave of redevelopment continues in **Long Beach** as well, with a new **Hilton** hotel slated to open in 1991, joining the Sheraton and Ramada Renaissance that have gone up along Ocean Boulevard in recent years. Long Beach's revitalized downtown area now boasts a dozen-or-so restaurants that have earned high praise from food critics, and have tourists and trendy Angelenos realizing that this big town on the beach is more than just the place where the *Queen Mary* is docked. Long Beach also gained notice with the 1990 inauguration of the first completed route of the much-anticipated **Metro Blue Line trains,** a street-level commuter rail line that travels the 22 miles from downtown Long Beach to downtown Los Angeles in 60 minutes. One-way fare is $1.10, and trains leave every 10 to 15 minutes, depending on the time of day. Eventually, the 150-mile system now under construction will link far-flung parts of the Los Angeles area.

A few miles to the south, in Orange County, that classic California beach town of **Huntington Beach** added a multiplex movie theater, restaurant, and retail center called **Pierside Pavillion.** Opened in 1991, the center is on Main Street, just across the Pacific Coast Highway from the landmark and surfer's mecca, Huntington Pier.

The elements of nature—or in this case, lack thereof—caused some chaos in Southern California in 1990 and 1991. All over the Southland residents are being admonished, and efforts are being made, to conserve water in response to the ongoing and increasingly severe **drought conditions.** In Santa Barbara, water has been rationed since the summer of 1990. Some residents have taken to spray-painting their yards green to keep up the appearance of a lush lawn. Another approach is being considered by the venerable Hotel Bel-Air, which—if the drought continues to get worse—may change its landscaping from the current subtropical foliage to less-thirsty succulents and native plants. Everyone's doing their part, including Hugh Hefner, who has installed low-flow toilets in the Playboy Mansion, and now turns off the massive waterfalls at night.

Fans of the **Farmer's Market** eagerly await the mid-1990's completion of the massive renovation and expansion on this L.A. landmark. A movie theater, restaurants, and a 600-room hotel are being added to the market, which will also be enhanced by landscaping, fountains, plazas, and walkways. All of this will make the market an even more attractive place to spend some time, though the ongoing construction hasn't stopped determined shoppers.

Sailiors and crews from around the world started congregating in **San Diego** in mid-1991, gearing up for an attempt to win the America's Cup from the San Diego Yacht Club. The **America's Cup XVIII** races will be held in San Diego starting in April 1992. Preliminary challenges began in the winter of 1991, and it's a safe bet that many of those Australian, Italian, and Russian sailors will hang on through the spring of '92.

The ever-changing downtown skyline will provide the backdrop for the races, with the nautical theme echoed by the new **San Diego Convention Center,** which looks a bit like a sea creature topped with giant sails. Downtown is the center of San Diego's redevelopment energy, and the decades of planning are beginning to pay off. The waterfront **Embarcadero** area has become an exciting place to stay, thanks to the new hotels, restaurants, and nightclubs that have opened by the harbor. Major cruise lines now dock at the B Street Pier, and a seafaring taxi service sails from one waterfront hotel to another. The **San Diego Trolley's** Bayfront Line now connects the Convention Center and waterfront hotels with the center of downtown and the ever-increasing number of trolley lines running east and north into the county and south to the Mexican border.

The **San Diego Zoo** celebrated its 75th birthday in 1991 with the opening of **Gorilla Tropics,** the latest in a series of new bioclimatic exhibits that far surpass the cages of old. The zoo's animals climb, cavort, burrow, and leap in habitats that resemble their homeland haunts.

San Diego has an international airport again. **Alaska, Continental,** and **AeroCalifornia** now fly from San Diego to Mexico, and negotiations are underway for other international flights.

Fodor's Choice

No two people will agree on what makes a perfect vacation, but it's fun—and it can be helpful—to know what others think. Here, then, is a very personal list of Fodor's Choices. We hope you'll have a chance to experience some of them yourself while visiting California. We have tried to offer something for everyone and from every price category. For detailed information about each entry, refer to the appropriate chapters within this guidebook.

Lodging

Four Seasons Biltmore Hotel, Santa Barbara *(Very Expensive)*

Claremont Hotel, Oakland *(Very Expensive)*

Four Seasons Cleft Hotel, San Francisco *(Very Expensive)*

Hotel Bel-Air, Los Angeles *(Very Expensive)*

St. James Club, Los Angeles *(Very Expensive)*

Ventana Inn, Big Sur *(Very Expensive)*

Casa Del Zorro, Anza Borrego *(Moderate)*

Scenic Drives

17-mile Drive, Carmel

Highway 49, the Gold Country

I-80, San Francisco to Truckee (for a cross section of the State)

Kings Canyon Highway (Highway 180)

Mulholland Drive, Los Angeles

Historic Buildings

Coit Tower, San Francisco

General Vallejo's House, Sonoma

Hotel del Coronado, San Diego

Larkin House, Monterey

Mann's Chinese Theater, Hollywood

Mission San Carlos Borromeo, Carmel

State Capitol, Sacramento

Romantic Sites

Buena Vista Winery, Sonoma

Carnelian Room, Bank of America, San Francisco

Emerald Bay, Lake Tahoe

Griffith Observatory, Los Angeles

Highlands Inn, Carmel

Taste Treats

California wines, tasted at the wineries

Chorrizo burrito, burrito stands, Los Angeles

French-fried artichoke hearts, roadside stands, Monterey Peninsula

Fresh salmon steaks, restaurants along the North Coast

Garlic ice cream, Garlic Festival, Gilroy

Orange freeze, Merlino's, Fulton Ave., Sacramento

Ripe peaches, especially in the Central Valley

Sourdough bread and sweet butter, San Francisco

State Parks

Anza-Borrego Desert State Park, Borrego Springs

California State Railroad Museum, Sacramento

Columbia State Historic Park, Columbia

Del Norte Coast Redwoods State Park, Crescent City

Empire Mine State Historic Park, Grass Valley

Marshall Gold Discovery State Historic Park, Coloma

Point Lobos State Reserve, Carmel

San Juan Bautista State Historic Park, San Juan Bautista

Restaurants with Fabulous Atmosphere

Chateau Souverain Restaurant at the Winery, Geyserville

George's at the Cove, LaJolla

Green's at Fort Mason, San Francisco

Spago, Los Angeles

St. Orres, Gualala

Ventana Inn, Big Sur

O R E

Crescent
City

Yreka

*Redwood
National
Park* Klamath

*Mt.
Shasta*

**FAR
NORTH**

101

Arcata

Eureka

Fortuna

Redding

NORTH

Red Bluff

5

COAST

Sacramento Valley

101

Fort Bragg

Mendocino

Ukiah

505

WINE

COUNTRY

Santa Rosa

29 Vacaville

Point Arena

1

Napa

Petaluma

Fairfield

Novato

680

*Point Reyes
National
Seashore*

Concord

SAN FRANCISCO

Berkeley

Oakland

San Mateo

Fremont

Milpitas

Sunnyvale

Se

1

PACIFIC OCEAN

0   50 miles

0   75 km

Santa Cruz

OREGON

Goose
Lake

Alturas

299

395

Lassen
National
Park
Lassen
Peak

Susanville

NEVADA

Pyramid
Lake

Paradise
Chico

Oroville

99

GOLD

SIERRA

80

Truckee

Reno

50

Yuba City

Lake
Tahoe

Carson City

COUNTRY

Tahoe
Valley

395

Walker
Lake

Woodland

50

Davis   Sacramento

NEVADA

Elk Grove

88

5   Lodi

49

Stockton

Mono
Lake

120

Yosemite
National
Park

Lee
Vining

Modesto

395

San Joaquin Valley

580

Turlock

San Jose

33

99

101

Merced

152

Los Banos

Kings
Canyon
National
Park

N

Southern California

San Jose

San Luis Res.

Merced

Chowchilla

Los Banos

Madera

Fresno

SAN JOAQUIN VALLEY

Sierra National Forest

SIERRA NEVADA

Big Pine

Kings Canyon National Park

Mt. Whitney

Sequoia National Park

Santa Cruz

Castroville

Salinas

Monterey

Carmel

Soledad

Big Sur

CENTRAL COAST

Coalinga

Visalia

Porterville

Sequoia National Forest

Tulare Lake Bed

San Simeon

San Luis Obispo

Bakersfield

McKittrick

TEHACHAPI MTS.

Santa Maria

VANDENBERG AIR FORCE BASE

Tejon Pass

Lancaster

Lompoc

Solvang

Ojai

Simi Valley

Santa Barbara

Ventura

Oxnard

Burbank

Santa Barbara Channel

San Miguel

Malibu

LOS ANGELES

Santa Rosa

Santa Cruz

Long Beach

CHANNEL ISLANDS

Santa Catalina

Avalon

San Nicolas

PACIFIC OCEAN

San Clemente

N

0   50 miles

0   75 km

World Time Zones

MONDAY
SUNDAY

International Date Line

+12 +13 -9 -4 -3

25

3 -5 -4

7 14 15

4 -7 13

5 -8 8 9 17 16

6 -6

10

11 18

12

19 22

-5

20 -4 -3

23

-3

21 24

+11

+12

1

Numbers below vertical bands relate each zone to Greenwich Mean Time (0 hrs.).
Local times frequently differ from these general indications,
as indicated by light-face numbers on map.

+11 +12 - -11 -10 -9 -8 -7 -6 -5 -4 -3 -2

Algiers, **29**
Anchorage, **3**
Athens, **41**
Auckland, **1**
Baghdad, **46**
Bangkok, **50**
Beijing, **54**

Berlin, **34**
Bogotá, **19**
Budapest, **37**
Buenos Aires, **24**
Caracas, **22**
Chicago, **9**
Copenhagen, **33**
Dallas, **10**

Delhi, **48**
Denver, **8**
Djakarta, **53**
Dublin, **26**
Edmonton, **7**
Hong Kong, **56**
Honolulu, **2**

Istanbul, **40**
Jerusalem, **42**
Johannesburg, **44**
Lima, **20**
Lisbon, **28**
London (Greenwich), **27**
Los Angeles, **6**
Madrid, **38**
Manila, **57**

Mecca, **47**
Mexico City, **12**
Miami, **18**
Montreal, **15**
Moscow, **45**
Nairobi, **43**
New Orleans, **11**
New York City, **16**

Ottawa, **14**
Paris, **30**
Perth, **58**
Reykjavík, **25**
Rio de Janeiro, **23**
Rome, **39**
Saigon, **51**

San Francisco, **5**
Santiago, **21**
Seoul, **59**
Shanghai, **55**
Singapore, **52**
Stockholm, **32**
Sydney, **61**
Tokyo, **60**

Toronto, **13**
Vancouver, **4**
Vienna, **35**
Warsaw, **36**
Washington, DC, **17**
Yangon, **49**
Zürich, **31**

Introduction

Coastal California began its migration from somewhere far to the south millions of years ago. It's still moving north along the San Andreas fault, but you've plenty of time for a visit before Santa Monica hits the Arctic circle. If you've heard predictions that some of the state may fall into the Pacific, take the long-term view and consider that much of the state has been in and out of the ocean all through its history. The forces that raised the mountains and formed the Central Valley are still at work.

For a good introduction to the natural history and geology of the state, there is no better place to start than at the Oakland Museum. An impressive light and audio show over a large model of the state explains the geography. Exhibits illustrate the different ecosystems of the state; walking through the exhibit hall is like walking across the state, from the ocean across the Coast Ranges, the Central Valley, and the Sierra Nevada. On another floor, there is a fine collection of artifacts and remains of the state's human history; especially interesting are the Native American baskets, tools, and ceremonial clothing.

Those of you who can't start at the museum but who do travel through a few of California's tourist regions will see a wide variety of geography and nature. The state's history often is not as evident as its physical reality. None of the cities is much more than 200 years old (Junípero Serra didn't come to San Diego until 1769), and the immediate impression is of a 20th-century culture. Still, you will find relics of early days in San Diego, San Francisco, and Los Angeles.

The chapters here are arranged in a generally north-to-south order. When planning your trip, keep in mind the very long distances. If you drive between San Francisco and Los Angeles on Highway 1, remember that it is not only more than 400 miles but is a difficult road to drive. Scenic routes, such as Highway 1 along the coast, Highway 49 in the Gold Country, and highways 50 and 120 across the Sierra Nevada, require attention to driving and enough time to allow for frequent stops.

California's North Coast is a dramatically beautiful region whose main industries are tourism, fishing, and logging. There are no large cities, no large amusement parks, few luxury resorts. There isn't even much swimming because of a cold current that runs down the coast for most of the state (turning out to sea before it reaches Southern California beaches). And while the ocean keeps the weather temperate that doesn't mean there aren't winter storms. August is often the coldest month of the year here (as it can be in San

Francisco, too). What you will find along the North Coast
are a wonderful scenic drive (Highway 1 and U.S. 101),
many small inns (some of them quite luxurious), interesting
restaurants serving locally produced fare, some good galleries, and a number of wineries. This is primarily a region
for leisurely exploring. It shouldn't be on the itinerary of
anyone not interested in the beauties of nature, because the
main attractions are tide pools under coastal cliffs, redwood
trees, rhododendron, and banana slugs (a large yellow and
black local oddity) in the lush coastal mountains. The Russians settled this region briefly in the 19th century, and you
will find reminders of their presence here.

The two main attractions in the Far North are Mount
Shasta, a large volcano that dominates the scenery of
the northern part of the state, and Lassen Volcanic
National Park. The park is at the southern end of the Cascade Range, and is particularly interesting because of the
record of past volcanic activity and evidence of current geo-
thermal activity (such as the Sulphur Works). This region
also suits those interested in nature, even more than the
North Coast, as lodging and dining opportunities are much
more limited. Keep in mind also that much of this region can
be very hot in the summer.

The Wine Country is one of California's most popular tourist regions. There are narrow crowded highways dotted
with wineries among the vineyards and valleys of the coast
ranges north of San Francisco. Many of the wineries are
beautiful sites for meals, picnics, or tastings and there are
fine bed-and-breakfasts and restaurants in the area.

San Francisco is very much a sophisticated, urban environment. There are fine hotels and a greater concentration of
excellent restaurants than anywhere else in the state. Because it is so compact, a visitor can do very well without a
car, but this is also a fine base for tours up the coast and to
the Wine Country. If you want to drive down to Los Angeles from here, you can do it in a day (7–8 hours) if you take
I-5 down the Central Valley, but you should budget at least
two days if you want to take the coastal route. A long day's
drive down U.S. 101 will get you to Santa Barbara, but
you'll bypass Monterey and Big Sur.

The Gold Country, also known as the Mother Lode, is the
gold-mining region of the Sierra Nevada foothills. There
are many historic sites and small towns to explore, many of
them of interest to children. Most impressive are the Empire Mine in Grass Valley, the gold discovery site at Coloma,
and Columbia State Historic Park, which is a town restored
to its Gold Rush condition. As in the Wine Country, there
are many B&Bs and small inns, but this is a less expensive,
if also less sophisticated, region to visit. In the spring there
are wildflowers, and in the fall the hills are colored by
bright red berries as well as changing leaves. In the summer, the hills are golden—and hot. Visitors in that season

should probably check the weather reports: There are
many fine days, but exploring in 90-degree or hotter weather is not much fun. We've included Sacramento in the Gold
Country chapter because it is adjacent and because its history was so influenced by the Gold Rush.

Lake Tahoe is famous for its deep blue water and as the
largest alpine lake on the continent. It stands up very well
to its reputation, despite crowded areas around the Nevada
casinos. Lake Tahoe is a four-hour drive from San Francisco
along I-80; the traffic to the lake on Friday afternoons and
to San Francisco on Sundays is horrendous. If you plan a
visit in the winter, remember to carry chains in your car;
they are sometimes required even on the Interstate. In the
summer, it's generally cooler than in the foothills, but still
sometimes pretty hot. Luckily, there are lots of beaches
where you can swim.

The highlight for many travelers to California is a visit to
one of the Sierra Nevada's national parks. Yosemite is the
state's most famous park and every bit as sublime as promised. Its Yosemite-type or U-shaped valleys were formed
by the action of glaciers on the Sierra Nevada during recent
ice ages. Other examples are found in Kings Canyon and Sequoia National Parks (which are adjacent to each other and
usually visited together). At all three parks, but especially
at the latter two, there are fine groves of Big Trees *(Sequoiadendron gigantea)*, the largest living things in the
world. The parks are open year round, but large portions of
the higher backcountry are closed in winter. Yosemite Valley is only 4,000 feet high, so winter weather is mild, and
the waterfalls are beautiful when hung with ice.

The Monterey Peninsula, a two- or three-hour drive
south of San Francisco, offers some of the state's most
luxurious resorts and golf courses, interesting historic sites (Monterey was the capital during Spanish and Mexican rule and the state constitution was written here;
Junípero Serra is buried at the Carmel Mission), beautiful
coastal scenery (Point Lobos would receive many votes for
most treasured state park), and perhaps the most famous
scenic drive (the 17-Mile Drive). There are also good restaurants in Monterey and Carmel and, for those interested,
plenty of places to shop. The weather is usually mild, but
any visitor should be prepared for fog and cool temperatures.

Between Carmel and Santa Barbara is another spectacular
stretch of Highway 1, requiring concentration and nerve to
drive. This is where you'll find those bridges spanning the
cliffs along the Pacific—and Big Sur. Don't expect much in
the way of dining, lodging, shopping, or even history until
you get down to Hearst Castle. Santa Barbara flaunts its
Spanish/Mexican heritage. There's a well-restored mission,
and almost all of downtown (including some pleasant shopping areas) is done in Spanish-style architecture. The cen-

terpiece is the Courthouse, built in the 1920s and displaying some beautiful tile work and murals.

In certain lights, Los Angeles displays its own Spanish heritage, but much more evident is its cultural vibrancy as a
20th-century center on the Pacific Rim. Hollywood, the
beaches, and Disneyland are all within an hour's drive. Also
here are Beverly Hills, noted for its shops and mansions;
important examples of domestic architecture from
throughout the 20th century; and freeways. Dining options
are improving, if still not up to the range of San Francisco's
choices. Despite the city's reputation for a laidback lifestyle, a visit here can be fairly overwhelming because of the
size and variety of the region. Careful planning will help.

San Diego, at the southwestern edge of the state and the
country, is usually the first stop. Junípero Serra founded
his first mission in Alta California (as opposed to Baja California, which is still part of Mexico) here in 1769. There are
historical sites from Mexican and Victorian times, one of
the best zoos in the country, and fine beaches. The weather
is agreeable, so this is a year-round destination.

The California deserts are extensive and varied, and
usually divided into two general areas: The Mojave or
High Desert and the Colorado or Low Desert. Palm
Springs and the new cities nearby (Rancho Mirage, etc.)
are filling up with expansive new resorts sporting elaborate
gardens, waterfalls, serpentine sidewalks, and—of
course—golf courses. That area doesn't offer much of a desert experience, but it has great weather in the winter, and
you can use it as an elegant base for exploration. Joshua
Tree National Monument is a good day trip (or two trips)
from Palm Springs; the northern part is High Desert and
the southern part Low Desert, so you can see the difference. Death Valley (*see* The Mojave Desert and Death Valley) and Anza Borrego Desert Park (*see* Excursions from
San Diego in Chapter 14) are of interest to people who want
to explore the beauties of the desert landscape. Anza
Borrego is far less developed than Palm Springs, but has a
resort and a fancy golf course.

Running 400 miles down the center of the state from below
Mount Shasta to the Tehachapi Mountains, lying between
the Coast Ranges and the Sierra Nevada, is the Central
Valley. We haven't written much about the area (*see* Sacra-
mento in The Gold Country and Red Bluff and Redding in
The Far North) because this is not much of a tourist region.
You may drive across some of it on I-80 or down it on I-5, but
there isn't much to stop and see, except in the state capital.
This is, however, the most important agricultural region in
the state and the fastest growing in terms of population.

California is as varied as any state and larger than most,
and could be the subject for many visits. Don't expect to visit everything the first time, but as you travel through the

state's regions, you will get a sense of its great diversity of cultures, the ongoing pull between preservation and development, and a feel for the state's unique place in the landscapes of both geography and the imagination.

1 Essential Information

Before You Go

Visitor Information

A detailed 208-page book, *Discover the Californias*, is available free through the California Office of Tourism (tel. 800/862–2543). The term "the Californias" refers to a useful division of the Golden State into 12 segments; the book sketches in the attractions and the flavor of each area. It also includes a wide-ranging calendar of yearly events. In addition, the office of tourism can answer many questions about travel in the state. *California Office of Tourism, 801 K St., Sacramento 95814, tel. 916/322–1397.*

There are visitors bureaus and chambers of commerce throughout the state; see individual chapters for listings.

In the United Kingdom, contact the **U.S. Travel and Tourism Administration** (22 Sackville St., Longon W1X 2EA, tel. 071/439–7433).

Tour Groups

General-Interest Tours Most major airlines have sightseeing tours from San Francisco, Los Angeles, and San Diego. If you are flying into any of these cities, check with airlines about the possibilities.

Amtrak offers tours to major attractions in California. For a brochure and special information, tel. 800/872–7245, tours department, or write to **Amtrak Public Affairs** (1 California St., Suite 1250, San Francisco, CA 94111).

Other major providers of tours in California:

Domenico Tours (751 Broadway, Bayonne, NJ 07002, tel. 800/554–8687 or 201/823–8687) arranges 7- to 18-day tours of California as well as shorter tours organized around special events, such as the Rose Bowl Parade and game on New Year's Day.

Gadabout Tours (700 E. Tahquitz Way, Palm Springs, CA 92262, tel. 619/325–5556) offers more than a dozen regional tours of California, including "Death Valley Holiday," "Lake Tahoe Cooler," "Hearst Castle Rail Caper," "Big Tree Spree," and "California Wine Country."

Globus-Gateway/Cosmos (150 S. Los Robles Ave., Pasadena, CA 91101, tel. 800/556–5454 or 818/449–0919), has a nine-day "Focus on California" tour that winds its way from San Francisco to Los Angeles. Highlights include Lake Tahoe, Yosemite, Monterey, and Carmel.

Maupintour (Box 807, Lawrence, KS 66044, tel. 800/255–4266 or 913/843–1211) offers tours of the California coast from San Francisco to San Diego and north from San Francisco to Portland.

Mayflower Tours (1225 Warren Ave., Downers Grove, IL 60515, tel. 708/960–3430) also traverses the California Coast in nine days—from San Francisco to San Diego.

Talmage Tours (1223 Walnut St., Philadelphia, PA 19107, tel. 215/923–7100) hits the California highlights in nine days. The tour starts in San Diego and ends in San Francisco. Stops include Los Angeles, Monterey, and Yosemite.

Tauck Tours (11 Wilton Rd., Westport, CT 06881, tel. 800/468–2825 or 203/226–6911) offers a 10-day tour that winds its way from San Francisco to Long Beach. The Napa and Sonoma valleys are also included.

Special-Interest Tours
Gold Prospecting

Gold Prospecting Expeditions (18170 Main St., Box 974, Jamestown 95327, tel. 209/984–4653) guides clients in gold panning, dredging, and prospecting in outings that range from one hour to one to two weeks, some involving river rafting and helicopter drop-ins. Special family discount packages.

Rafting, Canoeing, Kayaking

California Rivers (10070 Old Redwood Hwy., Box 1140, Windsor 95492, tel. 707/838–7787) runs easy-water Kiwi Kayak trips lasting from a single summer evening to five days. In difficulty, they range from introducing new paddlers to the romance of paddling on easy waters to offering thrills for seasoned boaters.

O.A.R.S., Outdoor Adventure River Specialists (Box 67, Angels Camp 95222, tel. 209/736–4677) offers one- to four-day rafting trips at several gradations of difficulty in North California on the Salmon and Klamath rivers; in Central California on the three forks of the American River, the Tuolumne, and the Merced; and in South California on the Kern River. The difficulty of the trips is rated on an international scale in terms of the roughest rapid, from I (easy) to VI (unrunnable); these California trips range from II to V. Some class III trips provide overnight accommodations at bed-and-breakfast inns instead of camping. One action-packed trip combines a day of white-water rafting, an overnight at a B&B, and a morning of hot-air ballooning.

Skiing

USAir Great Escape Vacations (tel. 800/223–2929) include air flight, rental car, lodging, and an interchangeable lift ticket good at six North Tahoe resorts: Squaw Valley, Alpine Meadows, Northstar, Homewood, Ski Incline, and Mount Rose.

Wineries

Viviani Touring Company, Inc. (500 Michael Dr., Sonoma 95476, tel. 707/938–2100 or 707/226–9466) offers customized tours for one person to 600 people of the Napa, Sonoma, and Russian River wineries. Transportation, tour director, and meals are included. Lodging can be arranged at the Silverado Country Club in Napa or the Sonoma Mission Inn near Sonoma (accommodations at both are in the Very Expensive category). This company also arranges one-day shopping tours of San Francisco or Napa and Sonoma and half-day art tours of Napa Valley galleries.

Package Deals for Independent Travelers

There is a wide range of packages for independent travelers. The large casino-hotels at Lake Tahoe *(see* Chapter 8), for example, will often include a show, cocktails, and breakfast with a special lodging rate. An innovative bed-and-breakfast inn (Murphy's Inn, Grass Valley: *see* Gold Country) offers, in winter, a midweek ski package, a picnic lunch, downhill or cross-country tickets for two, and a spa to enjoy when you return; and in summer, a golf special that includes greens fees, an electric cart, and a carafe of wine.

One call to Heavenly Ski Resort (tel. 702/588–4584) can book a complete ski vacation: a four-night, four-day drive-stay-ski package or a two-night, three-day fly-stay-ski package.

Most airlines have packages that include car rentals and lodging along with your flight. Hotels in major cities often have packages for weekends or for off-season. Packages possibilities sometimes cluster around major tourist attractions; hotels and motels near Disneyland in Anaheim or Marine World/Africa in Vallejo, for instance, offer lodging and admission tickets in a package.

America Fly AAway Vacations (tel. 800/433–7300 or 817/355–1234) offers city packages with discounts on hotels and car rental in San Francisco, Anaheim, and San Diego. The airline's "Funtime Adventure" packages to Anaheim includes admission to Disneyland. Also check with **United Airlines** (tel. 800/328–6877) and **Continental Airlines** (tel. 800/634–5555) for packages. **SuperCities West** (7855 Haskell Ave., 3rd floor, Van Nuys, CA 91406, tel. 818/988–7844 or 800/556–5660) offers similar city packages.

Packages are increasing in popularity as marketing strategies. Always ask about package options as you are making reservations or thinking about making them. Often chambers of commerce or convention and visitors bureaus will have information for you. Travel agents are good sources, too.

Tips for British Travelers

Passports You will need a valid 10-year passport. You do not need a visa if you are staying for less than 90 days, have a return ticket, and are flying with a participating airline. There are some exceptions to this, so check with your travel agent or with the U.S. Embassy (Visa and Immigration Department, 5 Upper Grosvenor St., London W1A 2JB, tel. 071/499–3443). Note that the U.S. Embassy no longer accepts applications made in person.

No vaccinations are required for entry into the United States.

Customs If you are 21 or over, you can take into the U.S. (1) 200 cigarettes or 50 cigars or two kilograms of tobacco, (2) one liter of alcohol, and (3) duty-free gifts to a value of $100. You may not take in meat or meat products, seeds, plants, fruits, etc., and avoid drugs and narcotics.

Returning to Britain, you may bring home (1) 200 cigarettes or 100 cigarillos or 50 cigars or 250 grams of tobacco; (2) two liters of table wine and, in addition, (a) one liter of alcohol over 22% by volume (most spirits) or (b) two liters of alcohol under 22% by volume (fortified or sparkling wine) or (c) two more liters of table wine; (3) 60 milliliters of perfume and 250 milliliters of toilet water; and (4) other goods up to a value of £32, but not more than 50 liters of beer or 25 cigarette lighters.

Insurance We recommend that you insure yourself to cover health and motoring mishaps. **Europ Assistance** (252 High St., Croydon CR0 1NF, tel. 081/680–1234) is one company that offers this service. It is also wise to insure yourself against trip cancellations and loss of luggage. For free general advice on all aspects of holiday insurance contact the **Association of British Insurers** (Aldermary House, 10–15 Queen St., London EC4N 1TT, tel. 071/248–4477).

Tour Operators The price battle that has raged over transatlantic fares has led most tour operators to offer excellent budget packages to the United States. Among those you might consider as you plan your trip are:

Thomas Cook Ltd. (Box 36, Thorpe Wood, Peterborough, Cambridgeshire PE3 6SB, tel. 0733–330300).

Cosmosair plc (Ground Floor, Dale House, Tiviot Dale, Stockport, Cheshire SK1 1TB, tel. 061/480–5799).
Jetsave (Sussex House, London Rd., East Grinstead, West Sussex, RH19 1LD, tel. 0342–312033).
Kuoni Travel Ltd. (Kuoni House, Dorking, Surrey RH5 4AZ, tel. 0306/740500).
Premier Holidays (Premier Travel Center, Westbrook, Milton Rd., Cambridge CB4 1YQ, tel. /322634).
Speedbird (Pacific House, Hazelwick Ave., Three Bridges, Crawley, West Sussex RH10 1NP, tel. 611611).

Airfares   We suggest that you explore the current scene for budget-flight possibilities. A good source of these is the small ads found in daily and Sunday newspapers, or in the weekly magazine *Time Out*. Some of these fares can be extremely difficult to come by, so be sure to book well in advance. Also, check on APEX and other money-saving fares, since only business travelers who don't have to watch the price of their tickets fly full-price these days—and find themselves sitting right beside APEX passengers!

When to Go

Any time of the year is the right time to go to California, allowing of course for specific needs and inclinations. There won't be skiable snow in the mountains between Easter and Thanksgiving; there will usually be rain in December, January, and February in the lowlands, if that bothers you; it will be much too hot to enjoy Palm Springs or Death Valley in the summer.

San Francisco, Los Angeles, and San Diego are delightful year round; the Wine Country's seasonal variables are enticing; the coastal areas are almost always mild. You can plan an enjoyable and rewarding trip to California at any time of the year.

The climate varies amazingly in California, not only over distances of several hundred miles but occasionally within an hour's drive. A foggy, cool August day in San Francisco makes you grateful for a sweater, tweed jacket, or light wool coat. Head north 50 miles to the Napa Valley to check out the Wine Country, and you'll probably wear shirt-sleeves and thin cottons.

It's not only over distance that temperatures vary. Daytime and nighttime temperatures in some parts of the state swing widely apart, not only in the mountains where warm, sunny afternoons and cool evenings are expected but in other places as well. Take Sacramento, a city that is at sea level, but in California's Central Valley. In the summer, afternoons can be very warm indeed, in the 90s and occasionally over 100 degrees. But the nights cool down, often with a drop of 40 degrees; it makes for pleasant sleeping, and it also makes a sweater that was unnecessary at 2 PM seem welcome at 11 PM.

It's hard to generalize much about the weather in this varied state. Rain comes in the winter, and there is snow at higher elevations. Summers are dry everywhere. As a rule, if you're near the ocean, the climate will be mild year round, though as you move north, there is more fog. Inland is warmer in the summer and cooler in the winter. As you climb into the mountains, there are more distinct variations with the seasons: Winter brings snow, autumn is crisp, spring is variable, and summer is clear and warm.

Climate The following are average daily maximum and minimum temperatures for the major California cities.

Los Angeles	Jan.	64F	18C	May	69F	21C	Sept.	75F	24C
		44	7		53	12		60	16
	Feb.	64F	18C	June	71F	22C	Oct.	73F	23C
		46	8		57	14		55	13
	Mar.	66F	19C	July	75C	24C	Nov.	71F	22C
		48	9		60	16		48	9
	Apr.	66F	19C	Aug.	75C	24C	Dec.	66F	19C
		51	11		62	17		46	8

San Francisco	Jan.	55F	13C	May	66F	19C	Sept.	73F	23C
		41	5		48	9		51	11
	Feb.	59F	15C	June	69F	21C	Oct.	69F	21C
		42	6		51	11		50	10
	Mar.	60F	16C	July	69F	21C	Nov.	64F	18C
		44	7		51	11		44	7
	Apr.	62F	17C	Aug.	69F	21C	Dec.	57F	14C
		46	8		53	12		42	6

San Diego	Jan.	62F	17C	May	66F	19C	Sept.	73F	23C
		46	8		55	13		62	17
	Feb.	62F	17C	June	69F	21C	Oct.	71F	22C
		48	9		59	15		57	14
	Mar.	64F	18C	July	73F	23C	Nov.	69F	21C
		50	10		62	17		51	11
	Apr.	66F	19C	Aug.	73F	23C	Dec.	64F	18C
		53	12		64	18		48	9

Current weather information on more than 750 cities around the world is only a phone call away. Dialing **WeatherTrak** at 900/370–8725 will connect you to a computer, with which you can communicate by touch tone—at a cost of 95¢ per minute. The number plays a taped message that tells you to dial the three-digit access code for the destination in which you're interested. The code is either the area code (in the United States) or the first three letters of the foreign city. For a list of all access codes, send a stamped, self-addressed envelope to Cities, 9B Terrace Way, Greensboro, NC 27403. For further information, call 214/869–3035 or 800/247–3282.

Festivals and Seasonal Events

January **Tournament of Roses Parade and Football Game,** Pasadena. The 102nd annual parade takes place on New Year's Day 1991, with lavish floats, marching bands, and equestrian teams, followed by the Rose Bowl game. (Pasadena Tournament of Roses, 391 S. Orange Grove Blvd., Pasadena 91184, tel. 818/449–4100.)
East-West Shrine All-Star Football Classic, Palo Alto, is America's oldest all-star sports event (1651 19th Ave., San Francisco 94122, tel. 415/661–0291).
Whale Watching. Hundreds of gray whales migrate along the California coast from January through April (California Office of Tourism, 801 K St., Sacramento 95814, tel. 916/322–1397).

February **AT&T Pebble Beach National Pro-Am,** Carmel. This legendary golf tournament, formerly the Crosby begins in late January and ends in early February (Box 869, Monterey 93942, tel. 408/649–1533).

Bob Hope Chrysler Classic, Indian Wells, PGA West, La Quinta, and Bermuda Dunes (near Palm Springs). This PGA golf tournament is a celebrity-packed pro-am (Box 865, Rancho Mirage 92270, tel. 619/341–2299 or 619/346–8184).

Chinese New Year Celebration. In San Francisco, North America's biggest Chinese community celebrates for a week, ending with the Golden Dragon Parade (Visitor Information Center, Box 6977, San Francisco 94101, tel. 415/391–2000). Los Angeles also has a Chinese New Year Parade (Chinese Chamber of Commerce, 978 N. Broadway, Suite 206, Los Angeles 90012, tel. 213/617–0396).

March **Santa Barbara International Cymbidium Orchid Show.** This is a horticultural spectacular (Box 3006, Santa Barbara 93130, tel. 805/687–0766).

Monterey Wine Festival. Wine tastings, lectures and luncheons are conducted by 200 exhibiting wineries (National Restaurant Association, 150 N. Michigan Ave., Suite 2000, Chicago, IL 60601, tel. 312/853–2525).

Dinah Shore Invitational, Rancho Mirage. The finest female golfers in the world compete for the richest purse on the LPGA circuit (Nabisco Dinah Shore, 1 Raquet Club Dr., Rancho Mirage 92270, tel. 619/324–4546).

April **Ramona Pageant,** Hemet. The poignant love story of Ramona (based on the novel by Helen Hunt Jackson) is presented by a large cast on a mountainside outdoor stage (Ramona Pageant Association, 27400 Ramona Bowl Rd., Hemet 92344, tel. 714/658–3111).

Adobe Tour, Monterey. This tour covers a large number of historic adobe structures and surrounding gardens (Monterey State Historic Park, 525 Polk St., Monterey 93940, tel. 408/649–7118).

May **Jumping Frog Contest,** Angels Camp. Inspired by Mark Twain's story "The Notorious Jumping Frog of Calaveras County," this contest is for frogs and trainers who take their competition seriously (Calaveras County Convention/Visitors Bureau, Angels Camp, 753 S. Main St., Box 111, 95222, tel. 209/736–4444).

Dixieland Jazz Jubilee, Sacramento. The world's largest Dixieland festival features 100 bands from around the world (Sacramento Traditional Jazz Society, Box 15604, Sacramento 95813, tel. 916/372–5277).

June **International Bicycle Race,** Nevada City. This event is held every year on Father's Day (Nevada City Chamber of Commerce, 132 Main St., Nevada City 95959, tel. 916/265–2692).

Napa Valley Wine Auction, St. Helena. A major wine event, it features open houses, wine tasting, and the auction (Napa Valley Wine Auction, Box 141, St. Helena 94574, tel. 707/963–5246).

July **Lake Tahoe Sail Week,** South Lake Tahoe. Daily races and a lakewide gala are the highlights (Lake Tahoe Visitors Authority, Box 16299, South Lake Tahoe 95706, tel. 916/544–5050).

Carmel Bach Festival. The works of Johann Sebastian Bach are performed for three weeks; events include concerts, recitals, seminars (Box 575, Carmel 93921, tel. 408/624–1521).

August **California State Fair,** Sacramento. The agricultural showcase, with high-tech exhibits, rodeo, horse racing, carnival, big-name entertainment nightly, runs 18 days from August to Labor Day. (Box 15649, Sacramento 95815, tel. 916/924–2000). **Concours D'Elegance,** Pebble Beach. At this show you'll see more than 100 of the world's finest automobiles (Box 567, Pebble Beach 93953, tel. 408/649–8500).

September **Renaissance Pleasure Faire,** Novato. Every weekend in August and the first two weekends in September, 3,000 costumed participants stage an Elizabethan harvest festival (Living History Centre, Box B, Novato 94948, tel. 415/892–0937). **Apple Hill Festival,** Eldorado County. Fresh apples, baked goods, and family fun are available on farms between South Lake Tahoe and Sacramento. Peak season begins in September and runs throughout October. (Apple Hill Growers, Box 494, Camino 95709, tel. 916/622–9595). **Los Angeles County Fair,** Pomona. It's the largest county fair in the world (Box 2250, Pomona 91769, tel. 714/623–3111).

October **Grand National Livestock Exposition, Rodeo, and Horse Show,** San Francisco. A world-class competition, with 3,000 top livestock and horses (Cow Palace, Box 34206, San Francisco 94134, tel. 415/469–6065.).

November **Death Valley '49er Encampment,** Death Valley. Encampment at Furnace Creek commemorates historic crossing of Death Valley in 1849, with fiddlers' contest, art show (Death Valley National Monument, Box 579, Death Valley 92328, tel. 619/786–2331). **Dickens Christmas Fair,** Novato. Dickens's London presented by actors and craftspeople. Extends through December weekends (Living History Centre, Box B, Novato 94948, tel. 415/892–0937). **Southern California Grand Prix,** Del Mar. Vintage grand prix races, auto expo, and national sports car championship events are included (100 W. Broadway, Suite 760, Long Beach 90802, tel. 310/437–0341).

December **Miners' Christmas Celebration,** Columbia. The fun includes a Victorian Christmas feast, lamplight tours, Christmas theater, children's piñata, costumed carolers, and Los Posadas (Columbia Chamber of Commerce, Box 1824, Columbia 95310, tel. 209/532–4301). **The Shepherd's Play,** San Juan Bautista. The annual production by the internationally acclaimed El Teatro Campesino, is performed in the Old Mission (El Teatro Campesino, Box 1240, San Juan Bautista 95045, tel. 408/623–2444). **Christmas Boat Parade of Lights,** Newport Beach. For six nights before Christmas, 200 decorated boats parade through the harbor (1470 Jamboree Rd., Newport Beach 92660, tel. 714/644–8211).

What to Pack

Clothing The most important single rule to bear in mind in packing for a California vacation is to prepare for changes in temperature. An hour's drive can take you up or down many degrees, and the variation from daytime to nighttime in a single location is often marked. Take along sweaters, jackets, and clothes for layering as your best insurance for coping with variations in temperature. Include shorts and/or cool cottons unless you are packing for a mid-winter ski trip. Always tuck in a bathing suit. You may not be a beach lover, but the majority of overnight lodgings include a pool, a spa, and a sauna; you'll want the option of using these facilities.

While casual dressing is a hallmark of the California lifestyle, in the evening men will need a jacket and tie for many good restaurants, and women will be more comfortable in something dressier than regulation sightseeing garb.

Considerations of formality aside, bear in mind that San Francisco can be chilly at any time of the year, especially in summer, when the fog is apt to descend and stay. Nothing is more pitiful than the sight of uninformed tourists in shorts, their legs blue with cold. Take along clothes to keep you warm, even if the season doesn't seem to warrant it.

Miscellaneous Although you can buy supplies of film, sunburn cream, aspirin, and most other necessities almost anywhere in California (unless you're heading for the wilderness), it is a bother, especially if your time is limited, to have to search for staples. Take along a reasonable supply of the things you know you will be using routinely and save your time for sheer enjoyment.

An extra pair of glasses, contact lenses, or prescription sunglasses is always a good idea; the loss of your only pair can damage a vacation.

It is important to pack any prescription medications you need regularly, as well as prescriptions that are occasionally important, such as allergy medications. If you know you are prone to certain medical problems and have good, simple ways of dealing with early manifestations, take along what you might need, even though you may never use it.

Cash Machines

An increasing number of the nation's banks belong to a network of ATMs (automatic teller machines), which gobble up bank cards and spit out cash 24 hours a day in cities throughout the country. There are eight major networks in the United States, the largest of which are Cirrus, owned by MasterCard, and Plus, affiliated with Visa. Some banks belong to more than one network. These cards are not automatically issued; you have to ask for them. If your bank doesn't belong to at least one network, you should consider moving your funds, for ATMs are becoming as essential as check cashing. Cards issued by Visa and MasterCard also may be used in the ATMs, but the fees are usually higher than the fees on bank cards and there is a daily interest charge on the "loan" even if monthly bills are paid on time. Each network has a toll-free number you can call to locate machines in a given city. The Cirrus number is 800/4–CIRRUS; the Plus number is 800/THE–PLUS. Check with your bank for fees and for the amount of cash you can withdraw in a day.

Traveling with Film

If your camera is new, shoot and develop a few rolls of film before leaving home. Pack some lens tissue and an extra battery for your built-in light meter. Invest about $10 in a skylight filter and screw it onto the front of your lens. It will protect the lens and also reduce haze.

Film doesn't like hot weather. If you're driving in summer, don't store the film in the glove compartment or on the shelf under the rear window. Put it behind the front seat on the floor, on the side opposite the exhaust pipe.

On a plane trip, never pack unprocessed film in check-in luggage; if your bags get X-rayed, you can say goodbye to your pictures. Always carry undeveloped film with you through security and ask to have it inspected by hand. (It helps to isolate your film in plastic bag, ready for quick inspection.) Inspectors at American airports are required by law to honor requests for hand inspection; abroad, you'll have to depend on the kindness of strangers.

The old airport scanning machines—still in use in some Third World countries—use heavy doses of radiation that can turn a family portrait into an early morning fog. The newer models—used in all U.S. airports—are safe for anything from five to 500 scans, depending on the speed of your film. The effects are cumulative; you can put the same roll of film through several scans without worry. After five scans, though, you're asking for trouble.

If your film gets fogged and you want an explanation, send it to the **National Association of Photographic Manufacturers,** 550 Mamaroneck Avenue, Harrison, NY 10528. They will try to determine what went wrong. The service is free.

Car Rentals

All major car rental agencies serve California, though not all have outlets in every city and airport. Two important suggestions for car rentals: Compare prices, and be sure you understand all the provisions of an agreement before you sign it. Often you will have to pay extra for the privilege of picking up a car in one location and dropping it at another; know the difference in cost, and know how important it is to you. Differing requirements for filling gas tanks can change the cost of the rental. Ask questions.

It's always best to know a few essentials *before* you arrive at the car rental counter. Find out what the collision damage waiver (usually an $8 to $12 daily surcharge) covers and whether your corporate or personal insurance already covers damage to a rental car (if so, bring along a photocopy of the benefits section). More and more companies are holding renters responsible for theft and vandalism damages if they don't buy the CDW; in response, some credit card and insurance companies are extending *their* coverage to rental cars.

Here are toll-free numbers for some of the car rental agencies in California:

Agency Rent-A-Car, tel. 800/843–1143.
American International Rent a Car (AI), tel. 800/527–0202.
Avis, tel. 800/331–1212.
Budget Car and Truck Rental, tel. 800/527–0700.
Dollar Rent a Car, tel. 800/800–4000.
Hertz, tel. 800/654–3131.

National Car Rental, tel. 800/328–4567.
Thrifty Car Rental, tel. 800/367–2277.

Traveling with Children

The watchword for traveling with children is to plan ahead as much as possible. That way, the trip will be a lot more fun for all of you.

In many parts of California, bed-and-breakfast inns are growing in popularity. Small, charming, and usually old, they have a strong appeal for many people. However, if you are traveling with children, you'll have to look carefully to find one that will give you a room at the inn. It's not too surprising; most of these places are furnished with antiques and decorative accessories that are definitely not childproof. Our research shows that you can travel with children in California and occasionally stay at a B&B, but you'll have to plan ahead; look at our listings.

Motels and hotels, with few exceptions, do welcome children. Often they can stay free in the same room with their parents, with nominal charges for cribs and $5–$10 charges for an extra bed. In addition, major hotels usually have lists of baby-sitters so that parents can leave for non-child-related activities.

If you have children, you won't need anyone to tell you to have a good supply of things to keep them busy in the car, on the airplane, on the train, or however you are traveling. If you're traveling by car, you'll have the option of stopping frequently. Just getting the children out of the confines of the car for a little while has an advantage; an even bigger advantage comes when you can stop at a park and the children can run or use a playground.

When you are sightseeing, try to plan some things that will be of special interest to your children. They may tolerate a museum and even show interest in a historic building or two, but put a zoo into the itinerary when you can.

In many ways California is made to order for traveling with children: Disneyland, the San Diego Zoo, the Monterey Aquarium, the San Francisco cable cars, the city-owned gold mine in Placerville, the caverns at Lake Shasta. . . . The list could go on and on.

Publications *Family Travel Times,* an 8- to 12-page newsletter published 10 times a year by TWYCH (Travel with Your Children, 80 Eighth Ave., New York, NY 10011, tel. 212/206–0688). Subscription ($35) includes access to back issues and twice-weekly opportunities to call in for specific advice.
Great Vacations with Your Kids: The Complete Guide to Family Vacations in the U.S., by Dorothy Ann Jordon and Marjorie Adoff Cohen (E.P. Dutton, 2 Park Ave., New York, NY 10016; $12.95) details everything from city vacations to adventure vacations to child-care resources.
Places to Go with Children in Southern California, by Stephanie Kegan (Chronicle Books, 275 Fifth St., San Francisco, CA 94103, tel. 800/722–6657 or 800/445–7577 in CA; $9.95 plus $2 for shipping).
Places to Go with Children in Northern California, by Elizabeth Pomada (Chronicle Books, same as above).
Eating Out with Kids in San Francisco, by Carole Terwilliger Meyers (Carousel Press, $7.95). For Carousel Press's catalog of

100–150 family-oriented travel guides and activity books for kids, send $1 for shipping or a business-size SASE with 45¢ postage to Carousel Press, Box 6061, Albany, CA 94706.

"Kidding around in San Francisco," a free brochure available from the San Francisco Convention & Visitors Bureau (Box 6977, San Francisco 94101, tel. 415/974–6900.

Hints for Disabled Travelers

California is a national leader in providing access for handicapped people to attractions and facilities. Since 1982 the state building code has required that all construction for public use include access for the disabled. State laws more than a decade old provide special privileges, such as license plates allowing special parking spaces, unlimited parking in time-limited spaces, and free parking in metered spaces. Initia from states other than California are honored.

People with disabilities should plan ahead for travel; check with providers when you make arrangements for transportation, lodging, and special sightseeing and events. Allow plenty of time to meet bus, train, and plane schedules. Be sure your wheelchair is clearly marked if it is carried with other luggage.

Greyhound-Trailways (tel. 800/752–4841; TDD 800/345–3109) will carry a disabled person and companion for the price of a single fare.

Amtrak (tel. 800/USA–RAIL) advises that you request redcap service, special seats, or wheelchair assistance when you make reservations. Also note that not all stations are equipped to provide these services. All handicapped passengers are entitled to a 25% discount on regular discounted coach fares. A special children's handicapped fare is also available, offering qualified kids ages 2–12 a 50% discount on already-discounted children's fares. Check with Amtrak to be sure discounts are not exempt when you plan to travel. For a free copy of Amtrak's *Access Amtrak*, which outlines all its services for elderly and handicapped, write to Amtrak (National Railroad Corp., 400 N. Capitol St. NW, Washington, DC 20001, tel. 800/872–7245).

The **National Park Service** provides a Golden Access Passport free of charge to those who are medically blind or have a permanent disability; the passport covers the entry fee for the holder and anyone accompanying the holder in the same private vehicle and a 50% discount on camping and some other user fees. Apply for the passport in person at a national recreation facility that charges an entrance fee; proof of disability is required.

For additional information, write to the National Park Service (Box 37127, Washington, DC 20013–7127).

Society for the Advancement of Travel for the Handicapped (26 Court St., Penthouse, Brooklyn, NY 11242, tel. 718/858–5483 in New York; tel. 213/986–4246 in Los Angeles) is a good source for access information for the disabled. Annual membership is $45; for senior travelers and students, $25.

The Information Center for Individuals with Disabilities (Fort Point Pl., 1st floor, 27–43 Wormwood St., Boston, MA 02210, tel. 617/727–5540; TDD 617/727–5236) offers useful problem-solving assistance, including lists of travel agencies that specialize in tours for the disabled.

Travel Industry and Disabled Exchange (TIDE, 5435 Donna Ave., Tarzana, CA 91356, tel. 818/368–5648) is an industry-based organization with a $15-per-person annual membership fee. Members receive a quarterly newsletter and information on travel agencies and tours.

Moss Rehabilitation Hospital Travel Information Service (1200 West Tabor Rd., Philadelphia, PA 19141–3009, tel. 215/456–9600; TDD 215/456–9602) provides information on tourist sights, transportation, and accommodations for destinations around the world, for a small fee.

Mobility International USA (Box 3551, Eugene, OR 97403, tel. 503/343–1284) has information on accommodations, organized study, etc., around the world.

Hints for Older Travelers

Many discounts are available to older travelers: Meals, lodging, entry to various attractions, car rentals, tickets for buses and trains, and campsites are among the prime examples.

The age that qualifies you for these senior discounts varies considerably. The American Association of Retired Persons will accept you for membership at age 50, and your membership card will qualify you for many discounts. The state of California will reduce the cost of your campsite if you are at least 62.

If you are 50, our advice is to ask about senior discounts even if there is no posted notice. Ask at the time you are making reservations, buying tickets, or being seated in a restaurant. Carry proof of your age, such as a driver's license, and of course any membership cards in organizations that provide discounts for seniors. Many discounts are given solely on the basis of age, without membership requirement. A 10% cut on a bus ticket and $2 off a pizza may not seem like major savings, but they add up, and you can cut the cost of a trip appreciably if you remember to take advantage of these options.

The American Association of Retired Persons (AARP) (1909 K St. NW, Washington, DC 20049, tel. 202/662–6200). The Purchase Privilege Program offers discounts on car rentals, sightseeing, hotels, motels, and resorts. AARP also arranges group tours through **American Express Vacations** (Box 5014, Atlanta, GA 30302, tel. 800/241–1700 or 800/637–6200 in GA). These and other services are included in the annual dues of $5 per person or per couple. The AARP Motoring Plan offers emergency aid and trip routing information for an annual fee of $33.95 per couple.

Elderhostel (75 Federal St., Boston, MA 02110–1941, tel. 617/426–7788) is an innovative program for people 60 or over (only one member of a traveling couple needs to be 60 to qualify). Participants live in dorms on 1,200 campuses in the United States and around the world. Mornings are devoted to lectures and seminars, afternoons to sightseeing and field trips. The fee includes room, board, tuition, and round-trip transportation.

National Council of Senior Citizens (925 15th St. NW, Washington, DC 20005, tel. 202/347–8800) is a nonprofit advocacy group with 5,000 local clubs across the country. Annual membership is $12 per person or per couple. Members receive a monthly newspaper with travel information and an ID card for reduced-rate hotels and car rentals.

Mature Outlook (6001 N. Clark St., Chicago, IL 60660, tel. 800/336–6330), a subsidiary of Sears, Roebuck & Co., is a travel club for people over 50, with hotel and motel discounts and a bimonthly newsletter. Annual membership is $9.95 per couple. Instant membership is available at participating Holiday Inns.

September Days Club is run by the moderately priced Days Inns of America (tel. 800/241–5050). The $12 annual membership fee for individuals or couples over 50 entitles them to reduced car rental rates and reductions of 15–50% at 95% of the chain's more than 350 motels.

Greyhound-Trailways (tel. 800/752–4841; TDD 800/345–3109) and **Amtrak** (tel. 800/USA–RAIL) offer special fares for senior citizens.

Golden Age Passport is a free lifetime pass to all parks, monuments, and recreation areas run by the federal government. Permanent U.S. residents 62 and over may pick them up in person at any national park that charges admission. The passport covers the entrance fee for the holder and anyone accompanying the holder in the same private vehicle. It also provides a 50% discount on camping and various other user fees.

The California state park system includes more than 200 locations and provides a $2 discount on campsites (ask for this discount when you make advance reservations) for anyone 62 or over and others in the same private-vehicle.

Publications *The Senior Citizen's Guide to Budget Travel in the United States and Canada* is available for $4.95, including postage, from Pilot Books (103 Cooper St., Babylon, NY 11702, tel. 516/422–2225).
The Discount Guide for Travelers Over 55 by Caroline and Walter Weintz (Dutton, $7.95) lists helpful addresses, package tours, reduced-rate car rentals, etc., in the United States and abroad.

Staying in California

Shopping

In California's big cities, opportunities abound to shop for internationally famed clothing, jewelry, leather goods, and perfumes, often in shops or boutiques set up by French, Italian, British, or American designers. There are enough specialty shops and fine department stores to keep anyone "born to shop" busy and happy. *(Note:* San Francisco and Los Angeles are centers of clothing manufacture; if you're a bargain hunter, you'll want to explore the factory outlets in both cities.)

If you are shopping for something unique to California, look at the output of its artists. California is home to a great number of artists and craftspeople, and you can find their creations from one end of the state to the other in fine city galleries, in small neighborhood shops, in out-of-the-way mountain studios, at roadside stands, and at county fairs. Paintings, drawings, sculpture, wood carvings, pottery, jewelry, hand-woven fabrics, handmade baskets—the creativity and the output of California's artists and artisans seems endless. Whatever your taste and budget, you will probably have no trouble locating tempting shopping opportunities.

Another California specialty is wine. You can visit wineries in many parts of the state, not only in the Wine Country north of San Francisco. Wineries and good wine stores will package your purchases for safe travel or shipping.

Other possibilities range from antiques to souvenir T-shirts. If you're flying home from San Francisco, you can make one last purchase of the city's unique sourdough French bread at the airport.

Beaches

With almost 1,000 miles of coastline, California is well supplied with beaches. They are endlessly fascinating: You can walk on them, lie and sun on them, watch seabirds and hunt for shells, dig clams, or spot seals and sea otters at play. From December through April you can watch the migrations of the gray whales.

What you can't always do at these beaches is swim. From San Francisco north, the water is simply too cold for any but extremely hardy souls. Some beaches, even along the southern half of the coast, are too dangerous for swimming because of undertows. Look for signs and postings and take them seriously. Park rangers patrol beaches and enforce regulations, such as those on pets (dogs must be on leash at all times), alcohol, dune buggies, and fires.

Access to beaches in California is generally excellent. The state park system includes many fine beaches, and oceanside communities have their own public beaches. In addition, through the work of the California Coastal Commission, many stretches of private property that would otherwise seal off the beach from outsiders have public access paths and trails. Again, the best advice is to look for signs and obey them.

Participant Sports

Almost any participant sport you can think of is available somewhere in California at some time of the year. A great many sports know no time limits and go on year round. Skiing, of course, depends on the snow and is limited for the most part to the time between Thanksgiving and April, but golf courses and tennis courts do a thriving business all year.

Swimming and surfing, scuba diving, and skin diving in the Pacific Ocean are favorite year-round California pleasures in the southern part of the state. On the coast from San Francisco north, the seasons play a limiting role.

California has abundant fishing options: deep-sea fishing expeditions, ocean fishing from the shore, and freshwater fishing in stream, rivers, lakes, and reservoirs. There are many hunting options as well. For information on fishing and hunting licenses and regulations, check with the **California Department of Fish and Game** (1416 9th St., Sacramento 95814, tel. 916/445–3531).

Hiking, backpacking, bicycling, and sailing are popular throughout the state, and you can readily arrange for rental of equipment. River rafting, white-water and otherwise, canoeing, and kayaking are popular, especially in the northern part of the state, where there are many rivers; see individual chapters for detailed information.

Hot-air ballooning is gaining in popularity, although it is not cheap: A ride costs in excess of $100. More and more of the large, colorful balloons drift across the valleys of the Wine Country, where the air drafts are particularly friendly to this sport, and in other parts of California as well.

State and National Parks

State Parks California's state park system includes more than 200 sites; many are recreational and scenic, and some are historic or scientific. A sampling of the variety of state parks: Angel Island in San Francisco Bay, reached by ferry from San Francisco or Tiburon; Anza Borrego Desert, 600,000 acres of the Colorado Desert northeast of San Diego; Big Basin Redwoods, California's first state redwood park, with 300-foot trees, near Santa Cruz; Empire Mines, one of the richest mines in the Mother Lode in Grass Valley; Kings Beach on the shores of Lake Tahoe; Leo Carillo Beach north of Santa Monica; Pismo Beach, with surfing, clamming, and nature trails.

Reservations Most state parks are open year round. Parks near major urban areas and on beaches and lakes are often crowded, and campsite reservations are essential. MISTIX (tel. 800/444–7275) handles all state-park reservations, which may be made up to eight weeks in advance.

For information on California's state parks, contact the **California State Park System** (Dept. of Parks and Recreation, Box 942896, Sacramento 94296, tel. 916/445–6477).

National Parks National parks are administered by the Department of the Interior, and the lands within their boundaries are preserved.

There are five national parks in California: Lassen, Redwood, Sequoia and Kings Canyon, Yosemite, and the Channel Islands. National monuments include Cabrillo, in San Diego; Death Valley; Devil's Postpile, 7,600 feet up in the eastern Sierra Nevada; Lava Beds, in northeastern California; Muir Woods, north of San Francisco; and Pinnacles, in western central California.

There are three national recreation areas: Golden Gate, with 73,000 acres both north and south of the Golden Gate Bridge in San Francisco; Santa Monica Mountains, with 150,000 acres from Griffith Park in Los Angeles to the Ventura County line; and Whiskeytown-Shasta-Trinity, with 240,000 acres including four major lakes.

For information on specific parks, see the individual chapters or contact the **National Park Service** (Fort Mason, #1, San Francisco, CA 94123, tel. 415/556–2920).

Dining

Restaurants are placed in one of four categories—Inexpensive, Moderate, Expensive, and Very Expensive—according to the price of a full dinner for one person. The full dinner includes soup or salad, an entrée, vegetables, dessert, and coffee or tea. The prices does not include drinks, tax, or tip.

Dining is more expensive in major cities than in rural areas. Since price levels vary from one part of California to another, check each chapter for the dollar amount denoted by the category.

Lodging

Overnight accommodations are placed in one of four categories—Inexpensive, Moderate, Expensive, and Very Expensive—according to the amount charged for two people in one room. Since lodging costs vary from one part of the state to another, check each chapter for the dollar amount denoted by the category.

Motel, hotel, and bed-and-breakfast accommodations are listed together in each chapter. Hotels are found primarily in cities and may or may not provide parking facilities. There is usually a charge for parking. Motels have parking space but may not have some of the amenities that hotels typically have: elevators, on-site restaurants, lounges, and room service.

Except for the parking, none of these generalizations is hard and fast. Many motels have restaurants, room service, and other services. Nor is size a distinction. Some hotels are small and have few rooms; some motels have more than 200 rooms.

Bed-and-breakfast inns have become more popular in California in recent years. Most typically, an inn is a large older home, renovated and charmingly decorated with antiques, with a half-dozen guest rooms. Full breakfasts are served at a set time, at a common dining table. Baths may be private or shared. However, these are not hard and fast rules. Sometimes the breakfast is a Continental one. Sometimes the inn is a renovated hotel from the last century with a dozen rooms; occasionally it is a Victorian farmhouse with only three guest rooms.

Few B&Bs allow smoking; virtually none take pets. Antique furniture, delicate fabrics, and the elaborate decorative accessories that are typical of these inns make these restrictions understandable.

On the matter of cost, there is no reliable way of distinguishing among hotels, motels, and B&Bs. A motel may be as lavish and luxurious as a hotel, and you don't necessarily economize by staying in a B&B.

Guest ranches and dude ranches are included in lodging listings, as are resorts. Their range of recreation options is greater than the usual, and this is noted.

Credit Cards

The following credit card abbreviations are used: AE, American Express; D, Discover; DC, Diners Club; MC, MasterCard; V, Visa.

Camping

Camping facilities in the state parks are extensive, though you will need reservations. *(See* State Parks, above.) Many popular parks have all spaces reserved several weeks ahead. *California RV Park and Campground Guide* gives information about nearly 300 private parks and campgrounds throughout the state. Send $2 to **California Travel Parks Association** (Box 5648, Auburn, CA 95604).

Smoking

Limitations on smoking are more and more common; if you smoke, be sensitive to restrictions. If you do not smoke, ask for and expect accommodations for nonsmokers on airplanes, in hotels, in restaurants, and in many other public places.

Smoking is banned on all airline routes within the 48 contiguous states, within the states of Hawaii and Alaska, on flights of under six hours to and from Hawaii and Alaska, and to and from the U.S. Virgin Islands and Puerto Rico. The rule applies to both domestic and foreign carriers.

Most hotels and motels have nonsmoking rooms; in larger establishments whole floors are reserved for nonsmokers. Most B&B inns do not allow smoking on the premises.

Most eating places of any size have nonsmoking sections. Many cities and towns in California have ordinances requiring areas for nonsmokers in restaurants and many other public places.

The trend in California, a health-conscious state, is toward more "No Smoking" signs. Expect to see them in many places.

2 Portraits of California

Along the High Sierra

by Colin Fletcher

In 1958 Welsh adventurer Colin Fletcher walked the length of California, a six-month trip to "take a look at America." This essay is excerpted from his account of that traverse, The Thousand-Mile Summer. *Other works by Fletcher include* The Man Who Walked Through Time *and the* Complete Walker.

The rest of the world quite rightly sees America as a cockpit of rapacity and exploitation. But it tends to forget that America is also a land of altruistic idealism—an idealism that can give birth to magnificently generous concepts, hammer them into tangibilities, and then throw the whole thing open for the rest of humanity to enjoy.

The world is inclined to remember, for example, that early American settlers slashed and gutted the virgin forests of their new continent; that they slaughtered prodigious herds of buffalo almost into extinction; that they did, in other words, what new settlers had always done, everywhere—wage total war against a Nature that to them was the natural enemy. But the world usually ignores the reverse of this coin.

On the night of September 19, 1870, five men sat around a campfire in what was then the territory of Montana. The men were primarily speculators. To confirm rumors of rich mineral and real-estate potential, they had penetrated deep into the almost unexplored Yellowstone River wilderness. A month's journeying had shown them commercial potential beyond their wildest dreams; but it had also revealed geysers and canyons, lakes and waterfalls, forests and mountain peaks, and a teeming wildlife. Around the last campfire before they returned to civilization, these five hard-headed businessmen discussed the natural impulse to convert their discoveries into personal profit. But remembering the superb beauty they had seen, they spurned the certainty of wealth. They agreed unanimously that private ownership of the Yellowstone region should never be countenanced, and that "it ought to be set aside by the government and forever held to the unrestricted use of the people."

Back in civilization, they registered no land or minerals claims. Instead, they wrote and lectured on the wonders of Yellowstone's natural beauty. Their words swept across the country. Two years later, President Grant signed into law an act creating the world's first National Park. The revolutionary concept of conserving wilderness for its own sake has now spread to every continent. And in enlightened practice America still leads the way. James Fisher, a visiting English naturalist, recently wrote in his *Wild America*, "Never have I seen such wonders or met landlords so worthy of their land. They had, and still have, the power to ravage it; and instead they have made it a garden."

In Death Valley I had seen an attempt to preserve a part of America essentially as it was when the white man came; but

Death Valley has been opened up by roads and amenities, as have most National Parks. In Primitive or Wilderness Areas, all man's travel tools are banned: no roads, no vehicles, no boats. Only hikers and horsemen may use the narrow trails. Compared with some such reservations, the Wild Area in the summit country of the Sierra Nevada above Lake Tahoe is small and almost tame. Its highest peak reaches barely 10,000 feet above sea level. But it is beautiful country. And it is very heavily used.

Lake Tahoe itself—only a four-hour drive for the 3 million people who live around San Francisco Bay—has become northern California's most popular playground. It has something for everybody. People with money to burn flock like moths to the neon lights of the Nevada shore. There they flutter in ecstasy around the one-armed bandits that have moved in from Reno. People with simpler tastes, shorter pockets, and a yearning for suntans congregate along the California shoreline. They fish, swim, water-ski, and finally barbecue without having to move more than two drinks off the highway. People who prefer the outdoors climb up west of the lake into the Wild Area. And there they find wilderness "set aside by the government and forever held to the unrestricted use of the people."

When I climbed up into the Wild Area I found a new sample of America.

At first, it was lake country. Some of the lakes lay open and crisp and sparkling. Others brooded in retirement, like philosophers. Between the lakes, rough stepping-stones led across creeks that vanished into snowdrifts through blue-gray doorways. Sometimes, bare gray rock was the whole scenery—menacing in shadow, bright and inviting in sunlight. But usually, mile after mile, I walked through forest. And always, high above, towered snowcapped peaks.

After two days I came to the infant Rubicon River and began to follow it northward. And now, sometimes, I found myself on the edge of a meadow with a familiar look—a sunlight-and-shadow, almost-too-good-to-be-true, Silver King kind of a look.

In the week I spent wandering through the 50 miles of Wild Area, I met about half a dozen people a day. And I knew that everyone I met shared one thing with me.

All the way from Mexico, well-intentioned inquirers had been saying, "Oh, but there's an easier way than that! Why don't you take the road to So-and-So?" For them, naturally, country was something that had to be passed through on the way from one place to the next. For me, places were refueling points at the end of a stretch of country. Sometimes I had said, "Don't forget, you're interested in *getting* somewhere; I'm interested in *going*." But the idea did not always get over. Now, up in the Wild Area, I knew that everyone looked at the country with the same eyes as I did.

They had little else in common.

I met men, women, and children. Some rode horses. A few led burros—or tried to. The majority labored along under backpacks: packs that perched high on shoulders and packs that wallowed around buttocks; neat packs like bundles back from the laundry and hippopotamic packs like bundles ready to go there; little pouches as convenient as a kangaroo's and murderous millstones that buckled their bearers' knees. And the people I met were as varied as their burdens—as mixed a bunch as any cross-section of people who happen at a given time to find some common interest attracting them to Union Square, Bond Street, or Fifth Avenue.

To be accurate, I did not always quite "meet" them.

There was the evening that there floated across the Rubicon River the authentic nesting sounds of a troop of Girl Scouts.

There was the early morning, ships-that-pass-in-the-night scene beside a small lake. It was a shady, enclosed place that made me think of Walden Pond. The trail skirted one bank, and I walked slowly, trying to see down into the sunlit water. Suddenly I almost trod on a little blue tackle box. It lay open beside the trail, every compartment overflowing with spinners—red, silver, gold. Set there between two moss-covered tree boles, the box was incongruous yet friendly. I looked around. Except for the box and the narrow trail, there was no sign of man's existence. Then I glimpsed movement. A hundred yards away on the far side of the lake a fisherman stood in deep shadow, a mere silhouette against greenery. I leaned on my staff beside the tackle box, watching him. After a while he looked up. I waved. He waved back. Then I went on down the trail, and within twenty paces the lake was hidden and I was back in thick forest.

Often, though, I stopped and talked to those I met.

There was the elderly man who might have been a judge and whose voice and thoughts were quiet and contemplative but who sat astride his horse like Thor taking a weekend off from making thunder.

There were the father and 11-year-old son, engrossed in a private world, their two fly-decked caps close together as they debated which streamer was most likely to tempt the trout of Lake Aloha. We discussed this problem, and even weightier ones. Afterward, as I climbed up beyond the lake, father and son were fishing side by side at the foot of a snow-terraced rock face. They looked very much alone, very much together. Not many youngsters are so lucky, I thought. Not many fathers either.

Then there was the day I climbed a peak on the edge of the Wild Area, overlooking Lake Tahoe. For three hours the panorama had opened out below me with that slow, unfolding growth—inevitable, but full of surprises—that is one of the rewards of climbing a mountain. About noon, almost at the peak, I crossed a rocky spur. And there, 4,000 feet below, I saw the whole huge basin of Lake Tahoe.

I heard myself gasp and say out loud, "My God, what a color!"

I walked up to the peak, sat down beside the metal summit marker, and gave myself up to the blue-and-greenness of forest and lake and sky. The air was all light and space and silence. I leaned back against warm rock. The sun beat down, timelessly.

After a while a scraping sound, as of a fair-sized animal, came from just beyond the summit marker. I fixed my eyes on a ledge, less than six feet away. I had noticed that beyond it the rock sloped away quite gently. I waited, every muscle still. And then, up over the ledge, outlined against blue sky, looking straight into my eyes, appeared a boy's head. It stopped dead. It was cheerful, out of breath, and as surprised as I was. It looked very young to be at almost 10,000 feet on its own, even attached to a body.

I felt I ought to say something. "Did you come all the way up by yourself?" I asked.

"Oh no, Mommy's just behind." The boy climbed up onto the ledge. "Yes, there she is." And a little way below us appeared a tall, slim woman in shorts and a red windbreaker. She waved at her son, then stopped. "Ah, the Old Man of the Mountains!" she called out cheerfully.

She walked on up toward us. Her walk was the rare kind that goes equally well with shorts on a mountain and with an evening dress in a ballroom. As she came up close she said, "Oh no, the *Young* Man of the Mountains!" and I felt better.

She had thick, dark hair, and it was difficult to believe that the 11- or 12-year-old boy was her son.

"Isn't it a fantastic view?" she said. "Peter and I often come up. Nowadays, as you see, he gets here first." She sat down, and we discussed climbing mountains and walking from Mexico to Oregon. Her name was Jinny. I found some snow on a sheltered terrace, lit my pressure stove, and brewed tea for the three of us. Jinny provided sandwiches. Afterward I apologized for having no cigarettes to offer.

Jinny smiled. "Oh, I never seem to want to smoke out of doors anyway. I guess . . . I guess I don't really enjoy smoking much. In itself, I mean. At a party now, it's different. A cigarette takes away the taste of the liquor—and without one I'd never know what to do with my hands." She smiled again. "It's wonderful how honest a mountain makes you, isn't it?"

She got up and walked forward and stood looking out over the blueness of Lake Tahoe. Suddenly she stretched her whole body ecstatically. "Oh what a wonderful world it is!" she said. "Three weeks ago my husband and I were in Hawaii, skin-diving and climbing mountains. And now dear old Tahoe again. You know, I feel sorry for people who never discover this kind of thing. The day we left Hawaii, some friends of ours flew in. The moment they got inside the hotel they rushed for a bridge table, and we knew they'd spend their whole vacation playing bridge and drinking. What a waste! I'm afraid we Americans sometimes forget how lucky we are."

I met "Twig" just outside the Wild Area; but he was essentially a part of it. When he bounced up in his jeep, I was changing film beside an old stagecoach road that is one of the Area's boundaries. We sat and talked, looking back up the rock-bound Rubicon Valley.

"Yes, I backpack in whenever I can," said Twig. "But somehow there's not often time these days. That's why I bought this jeep. But walking's the way to travel all right. Ever since Henry Ford, we Americans have been getting soft. I can still remember my great-grandmother, and she'd crossed the United States seven times. And every time except one, when there happened to be an empty wagon, she walked."

Twig nodded up the valley, carrying the gesture far beyond the horizon. "All the way from Mexico, huh?" He sighed. "When I left school, my mother talked me into taking a degree and going into engineering. But I often wish I'd stayed a backwoods cowpuncher and taken pack trains in, like I did when I was a kid. Still, it's good to know that when the pressures build up you can get away from it all and come out to places like this."

It was then, I think, that I realized what was obvious enough really: that the Wild Area was not only a new sample of America; it was a microcosm of The Walk. It was a place where people could do for a few snatched hours or days what I was lucky enough to be doing for six months.

The realization made me more aware of all the small events that sometimes passed unnoticed because they had become part of the fabric of my life: the first clouds of the day forming over distant peaks; a scarlet snow plant sticking up through the carpet of dead leaves and looking at once succulent as strawberries and deadly as a toadstool; a very small trout following an enormous low-flying bumblebee to the river's edge and turning back at the last moment with a flounce of its tail; a turquoise-breasted hummingbird hovering ten inches from my nose and inspecting my red shirt for pollen; a lizard sunbathing on rough granite and looking me over with the critical eye of a mother-in-law elect.

There was one such moment when everything the Wild Area offered—everything The Walk stood for—came together. For three days I had been following the Rubicon River as it grew by slow degrees from brawling infancy into staid maturity. I had just waded across it and was sitting on a grassy bank, putting my boots back on. The cold river had been refreshing, and now the sun was warm. A copper-red dragonfly landed deftly on a blade of grass at the water's edge, so close I could have touched it.

And suddenly thankfulness surged through me. Thankfulness for the moment, for the day, for the freedom of The Walk, for life itself.

I sat quite still, one boot half on, holding my breath and willing memory to imprison that instant of time—to capture and hold every particle of it. I wanted the copper-red dragonfly on its blade of green grass, curving out over the blue Rubicon. I wanted the warm sunshine and the rough grassy bank. I wanted the scent of lupines and the sound of running water. I wanted the deep forest shadow on the far bank. I wanted the snowbanks that hung high above it. I even wanted the mosquitoes on my bare arms. I knew that later I would find it difficult to believe I had really wanted the mosquitoes; but at that moment I was glad for their sakes that they were alive, and I wanted them too.

The moment did not last long. The dragonfly's wings trembled; it flew away. The blade of grass straightened. I finished putting on my boots, heaved the pack onto my back, and started once more down the trail.

Before long the sun dropped behind a line of stark peaks. Down on the valley floor it was suddenly very gray. But I knew that the copper-red dragonfly beside the Rubicon had given me something I would never altogether lose. And I knew that it was for moments like these that people came to the Wild Area.

Wilderness would be worth conserving if it did nothing but make such moments possible. And as I walked I found myself wishing I could thank the five men who had sat around their Yellowstone campfire in the fall of 1870. It would have been satisfying for them to know that their altruism that night—their altruism in a cockpit of rapacity and exploitation—had done so much not only for me but for the nesting Girl Scouts and for Thor astride his horse and for the father and son fishing in Lake Aloha and for Jinny stretching ecstatically on the mountaintop and for Twig in his jeep and for millions of other Americans and for millions more, born and yet to be born, all over the world.

One evening I came down into a steep-sided little valley and found an abandoned ranch house, tucked away and forgotten. As I walked into the homestead, a herd of cattle stampeded away in panic, kicking up clouds of fine dust. The dust hung long afterward among the trees, making the place look as if it had been bombed. I lit my stove on the steps of a crumbling stone hayloft. Dusk fell. Three deer wandered past—vague brown shadows against a background of dying bracken and hanging brown dust. I walked across the farmyard and found a rusty faucet. Close by, a coyote yowled. The sound echoed up the valley.

As I filled my canteen at the faucet, I kept looking at a sage-covered bank. It was some minutes before I understood why I was doing so. Sagebrush is a sign of heat and dryness, of desert or semi-desert; and this sage was the first I had seen since I climbed up into the High Sierra. And all at once I realized that the ridges above me were lower than those I had become used to. The soil was dustier, the trees so much thinner that you almost had to call them spindly.

The mountains were tapering off.

I went back to the old hayloft, sat down beside my stove, and studied the map. The confused highland mass that lay ahead could be called a side branch of the Sierra Nevada, but its elevation was much less than I had realized. It would almost certainly be drier than what I had come to think of as Sierra country. And the foothills soon sank away. Within two days I would be out in semidesert.

Next day I found once more, as I had done when I came near to the end of the desert, that the surest way of savoring something to the full is to become aware that it is almost over.

I climbed an escarpment on the far side of the valley and came back into thick forest. And now I kept noticing, as if they were something new, little things that had become so much a part of my life since I climbed up out of the desert that I had come to take them for granted. The ground sloped gently downward, and soon there were little clearings, thick with skunk cabbage. A rivulet threaded through tall grass. Every ripple and every blade formed a part of the pattern of texture, part of the pattern of light and shade. A crimson columbine curtsied to a turquoise dragonfly. A thin brown snake, basking away its afternoon on a stone, slid off at my approach and swam down into the darkness of a pool. And always, consciously now, I was walking among trees.

All day, as I walked, I found myself listening. In the desert, the cicadas rasp and there is no doubt about it; but in the forest there is sometimes, you think, a buzzing, almost a rasping among the trees. It is a soothing and yet intriguing sound that comes from nowhere and everywhere. Sometimes it is the distorted echo of running water. Sometimes it is the wind in the treetops. And sometimes it is nothing you can name. That day I could not name it, but I heard it more clearly than ever.

All day the ground sloped away. The forest thinned. The trees grew thinner too, became undeniably spindly. The rivulet joined Sagehen Creek, and there was sagebrush again. At first it grew in isolated clumps. Then in large patches. By afternoon it stretched away, acre after acre, as far as I could see down the valley.

Late in the evening, I was almost ready to camp when I saw a man coming toward me on a parallel trail, a few feet to one side. The semi-darkness failed to hide a certain oddness about him, but I could not decide if it lay in his clothes or in his walk or in something else.

I half checked my stride, wanting to talk but not knowing quite how to begin. "Evening," I said.

"Evening," the man answered. He hesitated too, and the black-and-white collie at his heels almost ran into him. Then he resumed his slow, easy stride and vanished into the dusk.

I was still wondering about him when I camped on a dusty sagebrush flat.

While dinner cooked, I did some calculating. I knew that now the mountains were almost over, The Walk would move into a new stage. It was still two hundred miles to the Oregon border, even in a straight line. Walking, it would probably be half as far again. For various reasons—some of them quite sensible—I wanted to be at the boundary by the end of the first week in September. That left me just over three weeks. To make the border on schedule, I would on most traveling days have to walk a good twenty miles.

Before I went to sleep I made up my mind that, no matter what distractions tempted me, the next day would be the first of the 20-milers. And the most important thing was to get moving as early as possible.

I woke at dawn to the sound of bells. A large flock of sheep was browsing slowly toward me. In the center of the dust storm they created, rising up out of it like an iceberg from fog, moved a brown burro with a bell around its neck. By the time I had finished a hurried breakfast, sheep and dust surrounded me.

I had just strapped the sleeping bag onto my pack when a man appeared on the edge of the flock. I recognized him at once. The black-and-white collie still followed at his heels.

"Morning," said the man.

"Morning," I answered.

The man pushed slowly toward me through the sheep. There was indeed something old-fashioned and quaint about his much-worn tweed suit. And something old-fashioned and dignified about the way he moved and about the way he smiled, taking his time over it, as he reached me.

"I hope my sheep have not caused you inconvenience," he said. He spoke with a European accent.

"Not in the least," I said. "I was glad they woke me up."

"Good," said the man. "Very glad." He took tobacco and cigarette papers from a side pocket of his coat.

And suddenly I realized that he must be one of the Basque sheepherders I had been hoping to meet ever since I saw the blackened names on the aspens beside Silver King Creek.

We chatted about the country ahead. The Basque had herded in the Warner Mountains, up near the Oregon border, during World War I. As he talked about it, he rolled a cigarette, coaxing the tobacco into shape with the care of a potter working clay. Once or twice he smiled his slow-emerging smile. It gave him an unexpected kind of Maurice Chevalier charm.

I was settling down for a long discussion when I brought myself up short. As soon as I could do it without rudeness, I tried to explain why I had to push on. Somehow it didn't sound very convincing.

But the Basque smiled understandingly. "You are right," he said, giving his cigarette a final pat. "To start early is the only way."

I pushed through to the edge of the flock. The Basque still stood where I had left him, knee-deep in sheep and the pall of dust. I waved my staff. He waved back.

Then I turned and went down the valley. As I walked, sagebrush scratched at my legs.

Living with the Certainty of a Shaky Future

by John Burks

John Burks is a professor of journalism and humanities at San Francisco State University. He has served as editor-in-chief of two of the city's leading magazines, City *and* San Francisco Focus, *was a* Newsweek *correspondent and managing editor of* Rolling Stone, *and currently edits the quarterly* American Kite.

There's never been any question *whether* there will be another earthquake in San Francisco. The question is how soon. Even the kids here grow up understanding that it's just a matter of time, and from grade school on, earthquake safety drills become routine. *At the first rumble, duck under your desk or table or stand in a doorway,* they are instructed. *Get away from windows to avoid broken glass. When the shaking stops, walk—don't run—outdoors, as far away from buildings as possible.*

Sure as there are hurricanes along the Gulf of Mexico and blizzards in Maine, San Francisco's earthquakes are inevitable. Nobody here is surprised when the rolling and tumbling begins—it happens all the time. Just in the six months following the jarring 1989 earthquake, for instance, seismologists reported hundreds of aftershocks, ranging from the scarcely perceptible to those strong enough to bring down buildings weakened by October's jolt.

The Bay Area itself was created in upheaval such as this. Eons ago, a restless geology of shifting plates deep in the earth gave birth to the Sierra Mountains and the Pacific Coast Range. Every spring when the snows melted, the runoff rushed down from the mile-high Sierra peaks westward across what would eventually be known as California. Here, the runoff ran up against the coastal range, and a vast inland lake was formed.

The rampaging waters from the yearly thaw eventually crashed through the quake-shattered Coast Range to meet the Pacific Ocean, creating the gap now spanned by the Golden Gate Bridge. This breakthrough created San Francisco Bay, one of the world's great natural harbors, its fertile delta larger than that of the Mississippi River. What a fabulous setting for the city-to-be—surrounded on three sides by water, set off by dramatic mountainscapes to the north and south, and blessed by cool ocean breezes.

All this and gold, too. The twisting and rolling of so-called terra firma exposed rich veins of gold at and near ground level that otherwise would have remained hidden deep underground. The great upheaval pushed the Mother Lode to the surface and set the scene for the Gold Rush.

The 1906 earthquake and fire has come to define San Francisco both for itself and the outside world. In the immediate aftermath of the catastrophe, San Franciscans wondered whether they ought to believe the preachers and reformers who declared that this terrible devastation had been wrought upon their wicked city by the avenging hand of God. San Franciscans asked themselves whether, somehow, they had earned it.

But the city was quick to prove its character. Fifty years earlier, six separate fires had destroyed most of San Francisco—yet each time it was rebuilt by a citizenry not ready to give up on either the gold or the city that gold had built. Now, in 1906, heroic firefighters dynamited one of the city's main thoroughfares to prevent the inferno from spreading all the way to the Pacific. The mood of San Franciscans was almost eerily calm, their neighborliness both heartwarming and jaunty. "Eat, drink, and be merry," proclaimed signs about town, "for tomorrow we may have to go to Oakland." No sooner had the flames died than rebuilding began—true to San Francisco tradition. Forty thousand construction workers poured into town to assist the proud, amazingly resilient residents.

The 1906 earthquake provided a chance to rethink the hodge-podge, get-rich-quick cityscape that had risen in the heat of Gold Rush frenzy. City fathers imported the revered urban planner Daniel Burnham, architect of the magnificent 1893 Chicago World's Fair, to re-invent San Francisco. "Make no little plans," Burnham intoned. "They have no power to stir men's souls."

The city's new Civic Center, built under Burnham's direction, was raised to celebrate the city's comeback and is regarded as one of America's most stately works of civic architecture. It's city hall stands as a monument to the city's will to prevail—from its colonnaded granite exterior to its exuberant interior, once described by Tom Wolfe as resembling "some Central American opera house. Marble arches, domes, acanthus leaves . . . quirks and galleries and gilt filigrees . . . a veritable angels' choir of gold." The inscription found over the major's office seems to sum it all up: "San Francisco, O glorious city of our hearts that has been tried and not found wanting, go thou with like spirit to make the future thine."

In 1915, San Francisco dazzled the world with its Panama-Pacific Exposition, designed to prove not only that it was back, but that it was back bigger and better and badder than ever before. An architectural wonderland, the Expo was built on 70 acres of marshy landfill, which later became the residential neighborhood called the Marina District. When the October 1989 earthquake struck, this neighborhood was badly damaged, and became a focus as the entire nation tuned in to see how San Francisco and her people would fare this time around.

Like the gold that surfaced in the Mother Lode, the 1989 quake once again brought out the best in this region's people. Out at Candlestick Park, 62,000 fans were waiting for the start of the World Series between the San Francisco Giants and the Oakland A's when everything started shaking. They cut loose with big cheer after the temblor subsided. One San Francisco fan quickly hand-lettered a sign and held it aloft: "That was Nothing—Wait Til the Giants Bat." When it became apparent that there would be no ball played that night, the fans departed from the ballpark, just like in a grade school earthquake safety drill, quietly and in good order.

This was what millions of TV viewers across the nation first saw of the local response to this major (7.1) earthquake and, by and large, the combination of good humor and relative calm they observed was an accurate reflection of the prevailing mood around the city. San Franciscans were not about to panic. Minutes after the quake struck, a San Francisco couple spread a lace tablecloth over the hood of their BMW and, sitting in the driveway of their splintered home, toasted passersby with champagne. Simultaneously, across San Francisco Bay, courageous volunteers and rescue workers set to work digging through the pancaked rubble of an Oakland freeway in the search for survivors, heedless that they, too, could easily be crushed in an aftershock. Throughout the Bay Area, hundreds volunteered to fight the fires, clear away the mess, assist survivors, and donate food, money, and clothing.

San Francisco's city seal features the image of a phoenix rising from the flames of catastrophe, celebrating the city's fiery past and promising courage in the face of certain future calamity. The 1989 shake possessed only about one-fortieth the force of the legendary 1906 quake, and all projections point to the inevitability of another Big One, someday, on at least the scale of '06. Often people from other, more stable, parts of the world have trouble understanding how it is possible to live with such a certainty.

The *San Francisco Bay Guardian*, shortly after the 1989 quake, spoke for many Bay Area residents: "We live in earthquake country. Everybody knows that. It's a choice we've all made, a risk we're all more or less willing to accept as part of our lives. We're gambling against fate, and last week our luck ran out. It was inevitable—as the infamous bumper sticker says, Mother Nature bats last."

Former San Francisco Mayor Diane Feinstein explained it this way: "Californians seem undaunted. We [know] we'll never be a match for Mother Nature. But the principal thing that seems to arise from the ash and rubble of a quake is the strong resolve to rebuild and get on with life."

3 The North Coast

by Dan Spitzer

A history Ph.D. and resident of Northern California, Dan Spitzer is the author of four travel books based on five years' work as a journalist in Asia, Africa, and Latin America.

Within the nearly 400 miles of California coast that lie between the San Francisco Bay and the Oregon border, travelers will encounter some of the most beautiful and rugged landscapes in America. Here in the well-named Redwood Empire are primeval forests of the world's tallest trees, while just off the spectacular shoreline are secluded coves and beaches. Along this coast, you may well see gray whales migrating, seals sunning, and hawks soaring. The region is also rich in history, the domain of Native-American Miwoks and Pomos, Russian trading posts, Hispanic settlements, and more contemporary fishing folk and lumberjacks. All these diverse cultures have left a legacy that still may be experienced. For those in search of untamed natural beauty, great fishing, abundant wildlife, and elegant country inns, the vast panorama of the North Coast is a bit of heaven.

The North Coast is sparsely populated, with only 10 towns housing a population of more than 700 inhabitants. Traditionally, residents of this region made their living from fishing and timber. Today, these industries are depressed. Tourism, however, is doing well. Victorian mansions have been restored to lodge, and fine restaurants founded to feed, the increasing number of visitors.

Getting Around

By Plane **American Eagle,** linked with American Airlines (tel. 800/433–7300), has excellent regular daily service to Eureka-Arcata from San Francisco. This is by far the fastest and most convenient way to reach the redwood country. **Hertz** (tel. 800/654–3131) rents cars at the Eureka-Arcata airport.

By Car If Mendocino is your northernmost destination, the most scenic drive from San Francisco is via Highway 1. With its twists and turns, Highway 1 is slow going. You should allow a full day to drive to Mendocino. Those who wish to explore Point Reyes National Seashore en route might consider an overnight stay at Inverness or in a town along the way. You can return directly to San Francisco in about 3½ hours from Mendocino by taking Highway 1 south to Highway 128, which passes through picturesque farm and forest lands. At Cloverdale, Highway 128 intersects with U.S. 101, which continues south to San Francisco.

If Eureka or a point near the Oregon border is your destination, the quickest way to drive from San Francisco is via U.S. 101. This takes a good six to seven hours if you go straight through. Those with the time and inclination should take the scenic but slow Highway 1, which ultimately intersects with U.S. 101 at Legett. It would be backbreaking to cover the latter route in less than two days.

Although there are excellent services along Highway 1 and U.S. 101, gas stations and mechanics are few and far between on the smaller roads.

By Bicycle For the hardy rider who wishes to take in the full beauty of the North Coast by mountain bike, there are a number of rental services in San Francisco and the major North Coast towns. Some rental shops on the coast are **Point Reyes Bikes** (Hwy. 1, Point Reyes Station, tel. 415/663–1768), **Catch-a-Canoe and Bicycles Too** (Stanford Inn by the Sea, Mendocino, tel. 707/937–5615), and **Mendocino Cyclery** (45040 Main St., Mendocino, tel.

707/937–4000). If you wish to go with a group, call **Backroads Bicycle Touring** (tel. 415/527–1555 or 800/245–3874 in U.S. and Canada). There are plenty of campsites for long-distance bikers to stay at along the coast.

Important Addresses and Numbers

An excellent source of information on the North Coast is the **Redwood Empire Association.** Its San Francisco office is filled with brochures, and the staff is very knowledgeable. For $2, the association will send you its visitor's guide to the region. Write, or stop at the office (785 Market, 15th floor, San Francisco, CA 94103, tel. 415/543–8334. Open weekdays 9–5).

For **emergency services** on the North Coast, dial 911.

Exploring

Exploring the northern California coast is easiest in a car. Highway 1 is a beautiful, if sometimes slow and nerve-racking, drive. You'll want to stop frequently to appreciate the views, and there are many portions of the highway along which you won't drive faster than 30–40 mph. Even if you don't have much time, you can plan a fine trip, but be realistic and don't plan to drive too far in a day (*see* Getting Around, above).

We've arranged the exploring section for a trip from San Francisco north. The first section follows Highway 1 north past Fort Bragg to its intersection with U.S. 101. The second section follows U.S. 101 through the Redwood Empire.

The North Coast via Highway 1

Numbers in the margin correspond with points of interest on the North Coast maps.

To reach Highway 1, heading north from San Francisco, cross the Golden Gate Bridge and proceed north on U.S. 101 to the
❶ Stinson Beach/Route 1 exit. **Muir Woods** (*See* Excursions from San Francisco, Chapter 6) is an excellent side trip from this route, but be prepared for a steep, curvy descent to reach the giant trees. Because the road between Muir Woods and Stinson Beach is closed indefinitely due to earthquake and mudslide damage, you will have to climb back out again from Muir Woods, then backtrack over the mountains to Stinson Beach.

To reach Stinson Beach directly, follow the detour signs along the Panorama Highway through the redwoods to the ocean.
❷ The town of **Stinson Beach** has the most expansive sands (4,500 feet) in Marin County. Along Bolinas Lagoon, you will find the
❸ **Audubon Canyon Ranch,** a 1,000-acre wildlife sanctuary. In the spring, the public is invited to take trails to see great blue heron and great egret tree nestings. There is a small museum with displays on the geology and natural history of the region, a natural history bookstore, and a picnic area. *Tel. 415/868–9244. Donation requested. Open weekends and holidays mid–March —mid–July.*

At the northern edge of Bolinas Lagoon, a couple of miles beyond the Audubon Canyon Ranch, take the unmarked road running west from Highway 1. This leads to the sleepy town of **Bolinas.** Some residents of Bolinas are so wary of tourism that whenever the state tries to post signs, they tear them down.

④ Birders should take Mesa Road to the **Point Reyes Bird Observatory,** a sanctuary harboring nearly 225 species of bird life. *Tel. 415/868–0655. Admission free. Banding daily Apr. 1– Nov.; weekends and Wed. Dec. 1–Mar. 31. Visitor center open daily year round.*

As you drive back to Bolinas, go right on Overlook Drive and
⑤ right again on Elm Avenue until you come to **Duxberry Reef,** known for its fine tide pools.

Returning to Highway 1, you will pass a pastoral scene of horse farms. About ⅛-mile past Olema, look for a sign marking the
⑥ turnoff for **Point Reyes National Seashore's Bear Valley Visitors Center.** The center has fine exhibits of park wildlife, and helpful rangers will advise you on beaches, visits to the lighthouse for whale watching (the season for gray whale migration is mid-December through March), and hiking trails and camping. (Camping, for backpackers only, is free; reservations should be made through the visitors center.) No matter what your interests, the beauty of this wilderness is worth your time. A reconstructed **Miwok Indian Village** is a short walk from the visitors center. It provides insight into the daily lives of the first human inhabitants of this region. The lighthouse is a very pretty, 30- to 40-minute drive from the visitors center, across rolling hills that resemble Scottish heath. On busy weekends during the season, parking at the lighthouse may be difficult. If you don't care to walk down—and up—hundreds of steps, you may want to skip the descent to the lighthouse itself. You *can* see whales from the cliffs above the lighthouse, but many people will find the lighthouse view worth the effort. *Tel. 415/663–1092. Admission free. Visitor Center open weekdays 9–5, weekends 8–5.*

If you choose to stay overnight in this area, there are good country inns and decent restaurants in and around the towns of **Inverness** and **Point Reyes Station.** The architecture and cuisine of Inverness reflect the substantial Czech population here.

The Russian River empties into the Pacific at the fishing town of **Jenner.** If you are lucky, you may see seals sunning themselves off the banks of the estuary. Travelers who wish to move on to the wine-growing region from here can take Highway 116 east from Jenner.

What is perhaps the most dramatic stretch of North Coast shoreline may be seen off Highway 1 between Jenner and Gualala. The road is one series of steep switchbacks after another, so take your time, relax, and make frequent stops to enjoy the unparalleled beauty of this wild coast.

About 12 miles north of Jenner sits the very well-reconstructed
⑦ **Fort Ross,** encompassed by a state park. For history buffs, this stop is a *must*, as the state park service has painstakingly recreated the ambience of Russia's major fur-trading outpost in California, built originally in 1812. The Russians brought Aleut sea otter hunters all the way from their Alaskan bailiwicks to hunt pelts for the czar. In 1841, with the coast depleted of seal and otter, the Russians sold their post to John Sutter, later of goldrush fame. After a local Anglo rebellion against the Mexicans, the land fell under U.S. domain, becoming part of the state of California in 1850. At Fort Ross, you will find a restored Russian Orthodox chapel, a redwood stockade, officers' barracks, a blockhouse, and an excellent museum. *Fort Ross*

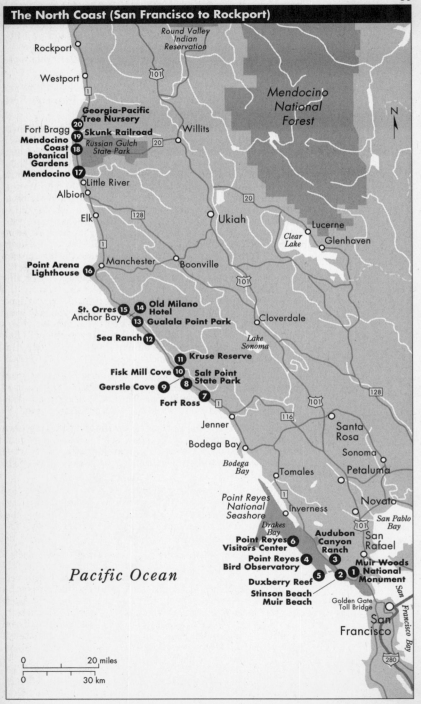

The North Coast (San Francisco to Rockport)

Round Valley Indian Reservation

Rockport

Westport

Mendocino National Forest

Georgia-Pacific Tree Nursery

Fort Bragg

Skunk Railroad

Mendocino Coast Botanical Gardens

Russian Gulch State Park

Willits

Mendocino

Little River

Albion

Elk

Ukiah

Lucerne

Clear Lake

Glenhaven

Point Arena Lighthouse

Manchester

Boonville

St. Orres

Old Milano Hotel

Anchor Bay

Gualala Point Park

Cloverdale

Sea Ranch

Kruse Reserve

Lake Sonoma

Fisk Mill Cove

Salt Point State Park

Gerstle Cove

Fort Ross

Jenner

Santa Rosa

Bodega Bay

Sonoma

Bodega Bay

Petaluma

Tomales

Novato

Point Reyes National Seashore

Inverness

San Pablo Bay

Drakes Bay

Point Reyes Visitors Center

Audubon Canyon Ranch

San Rafael

Point Reyes Bird Observatory

Muir Woods National Monument

Duxbury Reef

Stinson Beach

Muir Beach

Golden Gate Toll Bridge

Pacific Ocean

San Francisco

San Francisco Bay

0   20 miles

0   30 km

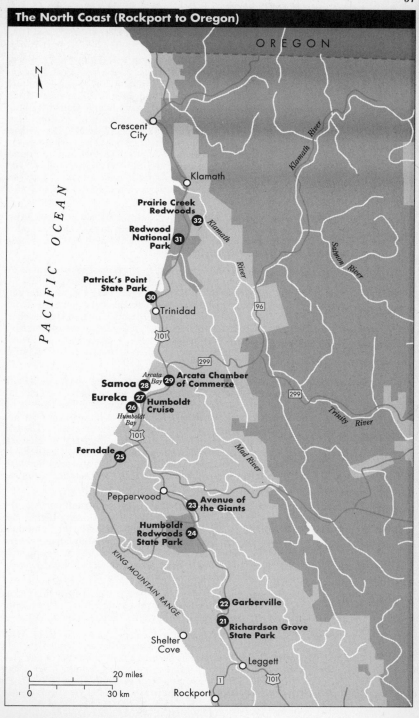

The North Coast (Rockport to Oregon)

State Historical Park, tel. 707/847-3286. Day use: $5. Open daily 10-4:30. Closed Thanksgiving, Dec. 25, and Jan. 1. No dogs allowed.

⑧ About 19 miles north of Jenner, **Salt Point State Park** offers an untamed environment well worth exploring. Visit first the **⑨** park's **Gerstle Cove,** where you probably will see seals sunning themselves off coastal rocks, and deer in the meadowlands. Note the unusual formations in the sandstone. Called "tafoni," they are the product of hundreds of years of erosion. Also, **⑩** make the *very* short drive to Salt Point's **Fisk Mill Cove,** where a five-minute walk following the trail uphill will bring you to a bench for a dramatic overview of Sentinel Rock and the pounding surf below. It's all less than a mile off Highway 1. *Tel. 707/ 847-3221. Day use: $5; camping: $16 peak season; $14 off-season, $2 discount for senior citizens. Open daily sunrise to sunset.*

⑪ Not far beyond Fisk Mill Cove, look for the sign to **Kruse Rhododendron Reserve.** In May, be certain to take this turnoff to see the towering pink flowers in this 317-acre reserve. *Admission free. Open daily.*

⑫ **Sea Ranch** is a controversial development of second homes for the affluent, consisting of 5,000 acres overlooking the Pacific about 10 miles south of Gualala. There was a great outcry by conservationists when this development was announced. To appease the critics, Sea Ranch built trails down to the beaches, which are accessible to the public. Even in the eyes of some environmentalists, the housing here is reasonably congruent with the surroundings; others find the weathered-wood buildings beautiful.

⑬ For an excellent place to watch whales, check out **Gualala Point Regional Park** (tel. 707/785-2377), where there is picnicking and camping ($10 in summer, $7 in winter). The park is off Highway 1 and is well marked. Just north of the town of Gualala **⑭** on Highway 1 are two inns worth a visit or a stay. The **Old Milano Hotel,** listed in the National Registry of Historic Places, is an elegant 1905 country inn overlooking Castle Rock. **⑮** **St. Orres,** with its Russian-style turrets, is also a premiere bed-and-breakfast inn and has one of the best restaurants on the North Coast.

⑯ For a dramatic view of the surf, take the turnoff north of the fishing village of Point Arena to the **Point Arena Lighthouse** (tel. 707/882-2777). First constructed in 1870, the lighthouse was destroyed by the earthquake that devastated San Francisco in 1906. Rebuilt, it towers 115 feet over the sea. *Tours daily 11-2:30, extended hours in summer and on holiday weekends. Admission $2 adults; 50¢ children under 12.*

As you head north to Mendocino, you will pass other fine places to stay, perched in and around the coastal cliffs of tiny former lumber ports such as Elk, Albion, and Little River.

⑰ **Mendocino** is the tourist heartbeat on the North Coast. With its stately Victorian and 19th-century flavor, coupled with its ocean views, the town has become a mecca for artists and visitors alike. See in particular the gingerbread-like **MacCallum House** (45020 Albion St.) and the **Mendocino Hotel** (45080 Main St.), overlooking the sea. There are a number of art galleries to peruse in this eminently walkable town. The **Mendocino Art**

Center (45200 Little Lake St., tel. 707/937–5818) has galleries, art classes, concerts, and a theater. A site meriting a stop is the **Kelley House Museum** (45007 Albion St., tel. 707/937–5791), a refurbished 1861 structure. The museum displays historical photographs of Mendocino's logging days, antique cameras, Victorian-era clothing, furniture, and artifacts. Open Friday–Monday 1–4. On Albion Street you will also see the **Chinese Joss Temple,** dating back to 1871. Another restored structure, the **Ford House,** built in 1854, is on Main Street and serves as the visitors center for **Mendocino Headlands State Park** (tel. 707/937–5397, open daily 10–4 in winter, 10–5 in summer). The park itself consists of the cliffs that border the town; access is free.

Off Highway 1, between Mendocino and Fort Bragg, you will
⓲ see the **Mendocino Coast Botanical Gardens.** It started as a private preserve in 1962, and the Mendocino Coast Park District acquired 17 acres of the gardens in 1982. Along 2 miles of coastal trails affording views of the sea and observation points for whale watching, you will find a splendid array of flowers, with the rhododendron season peaking from April to June and perennials in bloom from May to September. Fuchsias, heather, and azaleas are resplendent here. This is a fine place to stop for a picnic. *Tel. 707/964–4352. Admission: $5 adults, $4 senior citizens, $3 children 13–17, under 12 free. Open daily Apr.–Oct. 9–5, Nov.–Mar. 9–4. Closed Thanksgiving, Dec. 25, and Jan. 1.*

Fort Bragg is the commercial heart of Mendocino County. However, unless you are here on business, there is little reason to stay in this nondescript town. It is the headquarters for the **Skunk Train,** on which you may take scenic half- or full-day tours through redwood forests. A remnant of the old logging
⓳ days, the popular **Skunk Railroad,** dating back to 1885, travels 40 miles from Fort Bragg on the coast to the town of Willits, inland on U.S. 101. En route you pass through redwood forests that are not accessible by private car. In summer you have a choice of going partway to the Skunk's Northspur, a three-hour round trip, or making the 7½-hour journey to Willits and back. *California Western Railroad, Fort Bragg, tel. 707/964–6371. Fort Bragg-Willits: Departs daily 9:20 AM. Admission: $23 adults, $11 children. Fort Bragg-Northspur: second Sat. in June–third Sat. in Sept., departs daily 9:20 AM and 1:35 PM. Sept. 23–Dec. 4, Dec. 22–31, and March 25–June 7, departs daily 10 AM and 2 PM. Dec. 7–21 and Feb. 2–March 17, departs Sat. and Sun. 10 AM and 2 PM. Admission: $18.50 adults; $9 children.*

⓴ The **Georgia-Pacific Tree Nursery** (Main St. at Walnut St., tel. 707/964–5651) has a visitors center, picnic grounds, and a self-guiding nature trail (open daily 8–4). Those who like fishing can charter boats out of Noyo Harbor, at the southern end of town (*see* Sports, below).

Heading north on Highway 1 from Fort Bragg past the coastal mill town of **Westport,** you will find the venerable highway cut inland around the **King Range,** a stretch of mountain so rugged that road builders found it impossible to construct a major highway through it. Highway 1 joins the larger U.S. 101 at the town of Legett and continues north into the redwood country of Humboldt and Del Norte counties.

The Redwood Empire

㉑ **Richardson Grove State Park,** north of Leggett, along U.S. 101,
    marks your first encounter with the truly giant redwoods, but
    you will encounter even more magnificent stands as you head
㉒ north. A few miles below **Garberville,** perched along a lake, is
    an elegant Tudor resort, the **Benbow Inn.** Even if you are not
    staying here, stop for a drink or meal to enjoy the architecture
    and gardens.

㉓ For a treat, be certain to take the turnoff for the **Avenue of the
    Giants** just north of Garberville. Along this stretch of two-lane
    blacktop you will find yourself enveloped by some of the tallest
    trees on the planet, the coastal redwoods. The Avenue of the
㉔ Giants cuts through part of the **Humboldt Redwoods State Park,**
    51,222 acres of redwoods and waterways, as the road follows
    the south fork of the turquoise Eel River. In spring or summer,
    stop at the park visitors center near Weott (tel. 707/946–2311)
    for information on the region, its recreational opportunities,
    and its flora and fauna. The park's **Founders Grove** harbors the
    tallest tree in the park; at 362 feet, it is less than six feet short-
    er than the world's tallest tree, found in Redwood National
    Park.

㉕ Detour 5 miles west of U.S. 101 from Fortuna to **Ferndale.** This
    stately town maintains some of the most sumptuous Victorian
    homes in California, many of them originally built by 19th-cen-
    tury Scandinavian dairy farmers and timber barons. The queen
    of them all is the **Gingerbread Mansion,** 400 Berding Street, for-
    merly a hospital and now a refurbished bed-and-breakfast inn.
    Numerous shops carry a local map for self-guided tours of this
    brilliantly preserved town.

    The **Ferndale Museum** has a storehouse of antiques from the
    turn of the century. *515 Shaw Ave., tel. 707/786–4466. Admis-
    sion: $1 adults, 50¢ children 6–16. Hours vary, so call ahead.*

㉖ With 25,000 inhabitants, **Eureka** is the North Coast's largest
    town. It has gone through cycles of boom and bust, first with
    mining and later with timber and fishing. There are nearly 100
    elegant Victorian buildings in Eureka, many of them well-re-
    furbished. The most splendid is the **Carson Mansion** (at M and
    2nd Sts.), built in 1885 by the Newsom brothers for timber bar-
    on William Carson. Across the street is another Newsom ex-
    travaganza popularly known as **The Pink Lady.** For a sense that
    contemporary architects still have the skills to design lovely
    Victoriana, see the **Carter House** B&B inn (3rd and L Sts.). The
    Chamber of Commerce can provide maps of town and informa-
    tion on how to join organized tours. *2112 Broadway, tel. 707/
    442–3738. Open June–mid-Sept., weekdays 8:30–7, Sat. 9–5,
    Sun. 10–3; Sept.–May, closed weekends. Chamber of Com-
    merce Old Town Visitors Center, 123 F St. Open Mon.–Fri.
    10–6, Sat. 10–5, Sun. 10–3.*

    Old Town Eureka is one of the most outstanding existing Vic-
    torian commercial districts in California, with buildings dating
    from the 1860s to 1915. The **Clarke Museum** has an extraordi-
    nary collection of northwestern California Native American
    basketry and contains artifacts from Eureka's Victorian, log-
    ging, and maritime heritage. *240 E. St., tel. 707/443–1947. Ad-
    mission free. Open Tues.–Sat. noon–4 and Labor Day, July 4,
    and Memorial Day. Closed other major holidays.*

On the south end of Eureka stands **Fort Humboldt,** which served as an outpost to guard settlers against the Indians; now it is a state historic park. Ulysses S. Grant was once posted here. On the fort's grounds are re-creations of the logging industry's early days, with a logging museum, some ancient steam engines, and a logger's cabin. *3431 Fort Ave., tel. 707/ 445–6567. Open daily 9–5.*

㉗ Those who wish to explore the waters around Eureka can take a **Humboldt Bay Harbor Cruise.** You can observe some of the region's bird life and sail past fishing boats, oyster beds, and decaying timber mills. *The pier at C St., tel. 707/444–9440. Fare: $8.50 adults, $6.50 children 12–17, $5 children 6–11, under 6 free. Departs daily May–Sept., 1, 2:30, and 4 PM; Tues.–Sat., 5:30 PM cocktail cruise $5.50 adults, 7 PM cruise $8.50 adults.*

㉘ Across the bridge in Samoa is the **Samoa Cookhouse** (tel. 707/ 442–1659), a unique example (dating back to about the 1860s) of the lumber town cookhouses that once existed in every mill town. There is a museum displaying antique culinary artifacts, and breakfast, lunch, and dinner are served family style at long wooden tables. (*See* Dining, below.)

Just north of Eureka lies the pleasant college town of **Arcata,** home of Humboldt State University. Arcata is one of the few California burgs that retain a town square. It also has some restored Victorian structures. If you would like to take a self-
㉙ guided tour, pick up a map from the **Chamber of Commerce.** *1062 G St., tel. 707/822–3619. Open year-round, Mon.–Fri., 9–5.*

Take the turnoff to the town of **Trinidad** and follow the road a mile to one of the most splendid harbors on the West Coast. First visited by a Portuguese expedition in 1595, the waters here are now sailed by fishing boats trolling for salmon. The harbor's cove and rock formations lend a sense of untamed yet tranquil beauty to this picturesque bay.

㉚ Twenty-five miles north of Eureka sits **Patrick's Point State Park.** Set on a forested plateau almost 200 feet above the surf, the park affords good whale and sea lion watching. There are also good tide pools and a small museum with natural history exhibits. *Tel. 707/677–3570. Day use: $5 per car, $4 seniors; camping, $12.*

㉛ Those continuing north will pass through the 106,000 acres of **Redwood National Park.** After 115 years of intensive logging, this vast region of the tallest trees in the world came under government protection when Lyndon Johnson signed the park into law in 1968. Without question, this was the greatest victory won by California's environmentalists over the timber industry. The park encompasses three state parks (Prairie Creek Redwoods, Del Norte Coast Redwoods, and Jedediah Smith Redwoods) and is more than 40 miles long. *Redwood National Park Headquarters, 1111 2nd St., Crescent City, CA 95531, tel. 707/464–6101.*

Campground reservations for all state parks are usually necessary in summer. Call MISTIX 800/444–7275 (CA only) or 619/ 452–1950 (out of state) for reservations.

To gain a full sense of what Redwood National Park encompasses, stop at the **Redwood Information Center** in Orick (tel. 707/488–3461). You can drive up the steep trail to the world's tallest trees. Whale watchers will find the deck of the visitors center an excellent observation point, and birders will enjoy the nearby **Freshwater Lagoon,** a mecca for migrating waterfowl.

Drive to **Lady Bird Johnson Grove,** just off Bald Hill Road, for the short circular trail to resplendent redwoods dedicated as part of the park by the former first lady. For equally spectacular scenery, take Davison Road (often closed in winter) along a stunning seascape to **Fern Canyon.**

Wildlife lovers will see something truly special just opposite ❸❷ the entrance to Redwood's **Prairie Creek Redwoods State Park.** Extra space has been paved alongside the parklands, providing visitors with fine vantage points to observe an imposing herd of **Roosevelt elk** grazing in the adjoining meadow. Prairie Creek also has a beautiful trail fully accessible for the disabled, called **Revelation Trail.**

The route of redwoods and sea views will ultimately lead you past the Klamath River, home of the famous king salmon, to Del Norte County's largest town, **Crescent City.** Here you can get any further information you require about the national park at the headquarters (see above for address).

Travelers continuing north to the Smith River near the Oregon border will find fine trout and salmon fishing as well as a profusion of flowers. Ninety percent of America's lily bulbs are grown in this area.

Shopping

Most shops and galleries are open Monday–Saturday, 10–6. Some are open on Sunday during the summer.

In the charming town of Inverness, **Shaker Shops West** (5 Inverness Way, tel. 415/669–7256) has an exceptional array of reproduction Shaker furniture and gift items. There is a turn-of-the-century sensibility to the fine works exhibited here; open Tuesday–Saturday 11 to 5, Sunday noon–5. In Point Reyes Station, **Gallery Route One** (in the Creamery Building, tel. 415/663–1347) is a nonprofit cooperative of 24 area artists in all media, open Friday through Monday from 11 to 5.

Mendocino has earned its reputation as the artistic heart of the North Coast. So many fine artists exhibit their wares here that it is a matter of personal taste as to which galleries will curry favor with you. The few streets of this compact town are easily walkable, so look around until you see something you like. One suggestion is to visit the **Mendocino Art Center** (45200 Little Lake St., tel. 707/937–5818), where artists teach courses and display their creations.

In the Redwood Empire, the Victorian village of Ferndale is a magnet for fine painters, potters, and carpenters. Just walk down Main Street and stop in to browse at any of the stores along its three principal blocks.

Eureka has a number of fine art shops and galleries in the district running from C to I streets between 2nd and 3rd streets. One gallery of note is the **Old Town Art Guild Cooperative** (233 F St., tel. 707/445–2315). Another recommended gallery is the **Humboldt Cultural Center** (422 1st St., tel. 707/442–2611 or 707/442–0278).

Sports

The following sporting attractions and facilities are listed in a south-to-north order.

Bicycling *See* Getting Around, above.

Canoeing Among the many canoe liveries of the North Coast are **Stanford Inn by the Sea** (Mendocino, tel. 707/937–5615) and **Benbow Inn** (Garberville, tel. 707/923–2124).

Golf Among others, there are courses open to the public at **Bodega Harbour** (Bodega Bay, tel. 707/875–3538), **Little River Inn** (Little River, tel. 707/937–5667), **Benbow Inn** (nine holes, Garberville, tel. 707/923–2124), and **Eureka Golf Course** (tel. 707/443–4808).

Horseback Riding There are numerous stables and resorts that offer guided rides on the North Coast. Among them are **Five Brooks Stables** (Point Reyes, tel. 415/663–1570), **Sea Horse Guest Ranch** (Bodega Bay, tel. 707/875–2721), **Benbow Inn** (Garberville, tel. 707/923–2124), and **Lazy L Ranch** (Arcata, tel. 707/822–6736).

Fishing For ocean fishing, there are plenty of outfits from which you can charter a boat with equipment provided. Among them are **Bodega Bay Sportfishing** (tel. 707/875–3344), **Noyo Fishing Center** (Fort Bragg, tel. 707/964–7609) **Lost Coast Landing** (Shelter Cove, tel. 707/986–7624), and **Blue Pacific Charters** (Eureka, tel. 707/442–6682). You can fish for salmon and steelhead in the rivers. There's particularly good *abalone diving* around Jenner, Fort Ross, Point Arena, Westport, Shelter Cove, and Trinidad.

River & Ocean Rafting **Eel River Delta Tours** (Eureka, tel. 707/786–4187) emphasize wildlife and history.

Whale Watching There are a number of excellent observation points along the coast for watching whales during their annual migration season from December through March. Another option is a **whale-watching cruise.** Some cruises run June–Sept. to the Farallon Islands to watch the Blue and Humpback whale migration. Possibilities include: **Oceanic Society Expeditions** (San Francisco, tel. 415/474–3385), **New Sea Angler and Jaws** (Bodega Bay, tel. 707/875–3495).

Beaches

Although the waters of the Pacific along the North Coast are fine for seals, most humans find the temperatures downright arctic. Nonetheless, when it comes to spectacular cliffs and seascapes, the settings of North Coast beaches are second to none. So pack a picnic and take in the pastoral beauty of the wild coast. Explore tide pools, watch for seals, or dive for abalone. Don't worry about crowds, for on many of these beaches you will have the sands largely to yourselves. Day use is usually $5 or $6 per car, depending on the area.

The following beaches are particularly recommended and are listed in a south-to-north order:

Muir Beach. Located just off Highway 1, 3 miles from Muir Woods. Free.
Duxbury Reef. Tide pools. From Bolinas, take Mesa Road off

Olema-Bolinas Road; make a left on Overlook Drive and a right on Elm Avenue to the beach parking lot.

Point Reyes National Seashore. Limantour Beach is one of the most beautiful of Point Reyes sands. Free.

Tomales Bay State Park. Take Sir Francis Drake Boulevard off Highway 1 toward Point Reyes National Seashore, then follow Pierce Point Road to the park.

Fort Ross State Park. About 9 miles north of Jenner.

Sea Ranch Public Access Trails and Beaches. Off Highway 1 south of Gualala.

Manchester State Beach. About 9 miles north of Point Arena.

Agate Beach. Tide pools. Set within Patrick's Point State Park off U.S. 101 about 25 miles north of Eureka.

Dining

by Bruce Colen

Since 1974, Bruce David Colen has been the restaurant and food critic for Los Angeles Magazine. *He has also written on food and travel for* Town & Country, Architectural Digest, Bon Appetit, Connoisseur, Signature, *and* Endless Vacations.

For years, the better dining establishments of the North Coast specialized in fresh salmon and trout. With the growth of the tourist industry, a surprising variety of fare ranging from Mexican to Japanese to Continental haute cuisine is now being served at good restaurants charging reasonable prices. Unless otherwise noted, dress is informal. During the winter months, December to mid–March, tourism slackens on the North Coast; consequently, restaurant days and/or hours are often reduced. It is best to call ahead to check the schedule.

Highly recommended restaurants are indicated by a star ★.

Category	Cost*
Very Expensive	over $35
Expensive	$25–$35
Moderate	$15–$25
Inexpensive	under $15

*per person, not including tax, service, or drinks

Albion
Moderate–Expensive
★

The Albion River Inn. Built overlooking the site where the Albion River enters the Pacific, the glassed-in dining room offers spectacular views. The seafood, pasta, and meat dishes are better than average. *Hwy. 1, a few mi south of Mendocino, tel. 707/937–1919. MC, V. Dinner only.*

Arcata
Moderate

Crosswinds. Fine Continental cuisine is served in a comfortable dining room. Classical musicians provide the entertainment. *10th and I Sts., tel. 707/826–2133. Reservations advised on weekends. MC, V.*

Ottavio. This comfortable, polished restaurant offers Continental cuisine, from Italian *gnocchi* to Greek *spanakopita*, a spinach and cheese pie. *686 F St., tel. 707/822–4021. MC, V. Dinner only.*

Bodega Bay
Expensive

The Inn at the Tides. The town's top restaurant is best known for its fish and meat dishes. *Hwy. 1, tel. 707/875–2751. AE, MC, V. Dinner only. Closed Mon. and Tues.*

Crescent City
Moderate

Harbor View Grotto. This glassed-in dining hall overlooking the Pacific prides itself on fresh fish. *155 Citizen's Dock Rd., tel. 707/464–3815. No credit cards.*

Elk
Expensive
★

Harbor House. Continental cuisine is served in a dining room overlooking a dramatic seascape. *Rte. 1, 6 mi south of the junction with Hwy. 128, tel. 707/877-3203. Reservations recommended. No credit cards.*

Eureka
Expensive

Carter House. Comfortable, satisfying meals are served in the dining parlor of the contemporary Victorian Carter House. The accent is on California cuisine, featuring the freshest ingredients. *3rd and L Sts., tel. 707/444-8062. Reservations required. AE, MC, V. Closed lunch. Closed Mon.-Wed. dinner.*

Moderate-Expensive

★

Eureka Inn-Rib Room. In the dining hall of this Tudor manor, grilled meats are the specialty. *7th and F Sts., tel. 707/442-6441. AE, DC, MC, V.*

Lazio's. Now reopened in its new location, Lazio's has long been a premiere restaurant in Eureka, noted for its seafood. *1st and C Sts., tel. 707/443-9717. MC, V.*

Moderate

Cafe Waterfront. This restaurant serves decent seafood at reasonable prices. *102 F St., tel. 707/443-9190. MC, V.*

OH's Townhouse. This is a good choice for reasonably priced grilled meats. *206 W. 6th St., tel. 707/443-4652. MC, V. Dinner only.*

Samurai Japanese Cuisine. Decent Japanese fare at a reasonable price is served here. *621 5th St., tel. 707/442-6802. MC, V. Dinner only. Closed Sun. and Mon.*

Inexpensive

Mazzotti's. The local favorite for pizza and calzone. *305 F St., tel. 707/445-1912. No credit cards.*

Samoa Cookhouse. A local lumberman's watering hole, dating back to the early years of the century, this eatery serves three substantial family-style meals at long wooden tables. Meat dishes dominate the menu. *A short drive from Eureka, across Samoa Bridge, off Rte. 101 on Samoa Rd., tel. 707/442-1659. No credit cards.*

Fort Bragg
Moderate

The Restaurant. California cuisine is featured. The dining room doubles as an art gallery. *418 N. Main St., tel. 707/964-9800. Reservations advised. MC, V. Lunch only Thurs. and Fri. Dinner Sat.-Tues. Sun. jazz brunch. Closed Wed.*

Garberville
Moderate-Expensive
★

Benbow Inn. If you want to dine in style, this is the place. The resort's wood-paneled dining room, with fireplace ablaze, offers Continental cuisine and fresh salmon and trout. *445 Lake Benbow Dr., off U.S. 101, 2 mi south of Garberville, tel. 707/923-2124. Reservations advised. MC, V. Closed winter.*

Inexpensive-Moderate

Woodrose Cafe. This unpretentious eatery, a local favorite, serves fresh healthy food, with fish, pasta, and vegetarian specials. *911 Redwood Dr., tel. 707/923-3191. No credit cards.*

Gualala
Expensive

Old Milano. In the dining room of this house, listed in the National Registry of Historic Places, adequate country meals are served five nights a week. *Hwy. 1, tel. 707/884-3256. Reservations advised. AE, MC, V. Closed Mon.-Tues.*

★

St. Orres. From the Russian turrets that top this hotel to the hand-hewed timbers and stained-glass windows, the look and atmosphere here are very special. This is one of the best restaurants on the North Coast, with equally intriguing cuisine. You have a choice of five entrées (meat or fish), plus soup and salad, at prix fixe. *Hwy. 1, just north of Gualala, tel. 707/884-3335. Reservations recommended. No credit cards. Dinner only. Closed Wed.*

Sea Ranch Lodge Restaurant. Seafood and homemade deserts are served in a dining room overlooking the Pacific. *North of Gualala at 60 Sea Walk Dr., off U.S. 101 at Sea Ranch, tel. 707/ 785–2371. MC, V.*

Moderate **Empire Cafe.** The ocean view is a good enough reason in itself to dine here. The focus is on seafood. *Hwy. 1, tel. 707/884–4630. MC, V. Closed lunch Mon.–Fri. Closed dinner Tues. and Wed.*

Inverness **Manka's.** Excellent Czech cooking is served in a wood-paneled
Moderate–Expensive dining room warmed by a fireplace. This is the best of
★ Inverness's Eastern European restaurants. *30 Calendar Way, tel. 415/669–1034. Reservations suggested in summer. MC, V. Sun. brunch and dinner only. Closed Tues. and Wed.*

Inexpensive **Grey Whale.** A good stop-off for pizza, salad, pastries, and coffee. Open for lunch and dinner. *On Sir Frances Drake Blvd., in the center of town, tel. 415/669–1244. MC, V.*

Jenner **River's End.** The Continental/Germanic fare is very good, fea-
Moderate– turing seafood, venison, and duck dishes. Brunches are excep-
Expensive tional. *Hwy. 1, north end of Jenner, tel. 707/865–2484. MC, V. Closed Mon. and Tues., closed Nov. 30–Mar. 15.*

Little River **Heritage House.** In a plate-glass dining room overlooking the
Expensive sea, hearty American meat and fish dishes are featured at a
★ prix fixe for breakfast and dinner. *Hwy. 1, just south of Little River, tel. 707/937–5885. Reservations advised. Jacket required. No dinner. MC, V.*
Little River Restaurant. This is a tiny restaurant with the post office and gas station adjoining it, across from the Little River Inn. Appearances aside, this modest eatery serves some of the best dinners in the Mendocino area, featuring steaks and the freshest of seafood. *Hwy. 1, tel. 707/937–4945. Reservations advised. No credit cards. Closed Tues.–Thurs. Closed lunch.*

Mendocino **Cafe Beaujolais.** All the rustic charm of peaceful, backwoods
Moderate–Expensive Mendocino—with great country cooking to boot. Owner Mar-
★ garet Fox is a marvelous baker, so be sure to take home several packages of her irresistible *panforte*, made with almonds, hazelnuts, walnuts, or macadamia nuts. This is the best place in town for breakfast, and the tree house-like second-story deck is a splendid retreat for a leisurely lunch. If you don't order the delicious chicken-apple sausages, you'll never forgive yourself. *961 Ukiah St., tel. 707/937–5614. Reservations required. No credit cards. Closed dinner Mon.–Wed. Closed Jan.–Feb.*
MacCallum House Restaurant. Set within a charming, period bed-and-breakfast inn, the redwood-paneled dining room offers a Continental menu and lovely homemade desserts. *45020 Albion St., tel. 707/937–5763. Reservations advised. No credit cards. Closed Jan.–March and Mon. Closed lunch.*
Mendocino Hotel. A 19th-century ambience has been re-created in the wood-paneled dining room, fronted by a glassed-in solarium. Fine fish dishes, and the best wild berry cobblers in California are served. *45080 Main St., tel. 707/937–0511. AE, MC, V.*

Moderate **Sea Gull.** Extremely popular with the local art crowd, this unpretentious spot serves excellent fish, beef, and lamb dishes at reasonable prices. The breakfast omelets and luncheon sandwiches are also good. *On the corner of Lansing and Ukiah Sts., tel. 707/937–2100. No credit cards.*

Muir Beach
Moderate–Expensive
★

Pelican Inn. Basic English fare—from fish and chips to prime rib and Yorkshire pudding—is served with imported beers and ales. The atmosphere is wonderful: a wood-paneled dining room warmed by a great stone fireplace and a glass-encompassed solarium, ideal for sunny lunches. *Hwy. 1 at Muir Beach, tel. 415/383–6005. Reservations advised for 6 or more. MC, V. Closed Mon.*

Point Reyes Station
Moderate–Expensive

Chez Madeline. A restaurant featuring above-average French cooking and excellent seafood; its proprietor sometimes entertains by playing classical flute. *Hwy. 1, tel. 415/663–9177. MC, V. Closed Mon. Closed lunch.*

Station House Cafe. This modest local hangout serves breakfast, lunch, and dinner in a relaxing paneled dining room. Fresh fish and grilled meats highlight the dinner menu. *Hwy. 1, tel. 415/663–1515. MC, V.*

Stinson Beach
Moderate

Sand Dollar. This pleasant pub serves great hamburgers and other sandwiches for lunch and decent seafood for dinner. An added attraction is the outdoor dining deck. *Hwy. 1, tel. 415/868–0434. No credit cards.*

Trinidad
Moderate–Expensive
★

Larrupin Cafe. Actually located close to Trinidad in the town of Westhaven, Larrupin has earned a widespread reputation for Cajun ribs and fish. Dinner only. *1150 Westhaven Dr., tel. 707/677–0230. Reservations required. No credit cards. Closed Mon.–Wed.*

Moderate

Merryman's Dinner House. This is a fine oceanfront setting for hungry lovers. Fresh fish is featured. *On Moonstone Beach, tel. 707/677–3111. No credit cards. Closed weekdays in winter.*

Inexpensive–Moderate

Seascape. With a glassed-in dining room and deck for alfresco dining, this is an ideal place to take in the splendor of Trinidad Bay. Great breakfasts, substantial lunches, and good seafood dinners are served daily. *At the pier, tel. 707/677–3762. MC.*

Lodging

The North Coast offers some of the most attractive lodging in the country, with a range to fit virtually every pocketbook. You will find elaborate Victorian homes, grand old hotels, and modest motels. Many bed-and-breakfasts along the coast are sold out on weekends months in advance, so reserve early. Budget travelers will find youth hostels in Point Reyes National Seashore, Klamath, and Leggett (summer only).

Highly recommended hotels are indicated by a star ★.

Category	Cost*
Very Expensive	over $120
Expensive	$90–$120
Moderate	$50–$90
Inexpensive	under $50

double room, not including tax

Albion
Moderate–Very Expensive

Albion River Inn. Overlooking the sea, this attractive inn has sizable rooms, some with fireplaces and Jacuzzis, and provides full buffet breakfasts. *3790 No. Hwy. 1, Box 100, 95410, tel.*

707/937–1919. 20 rooms. Facilities: restaurant (dinner only), horseback riding 15 mi away. MC, V.

Arcata
Moderate—
Expensive
★

The Plough and the Stars. There's a truly Irish ambience at the Plough. It's hard to imagine a friendlier inn, as the warm hospitality of the hosts makes this former farmhouse a wonderful place to stay. The suite has a wood stove. Breakfast is included. *1800 27th St., 95521, tel. 707/822–8236. 5 rooms, 3 with bath, croquet lawn, spa. MC, V.*

Bodega Bay
Expensive–
Very Expensive

Inn at the Tides. All the rooms here have a view of the harbor and some have fireplaces. Continental breakfast is included. *800 Hwy. 1, Box 640, 94923, tel. 707/875–2751. 86 rooms. Facilities: room service (evening only), restaurant on weekends, cable TV, refrigerator, pool, sauna, Jacuzzi, laundromat. AE, MC, V.*

Crescent City
Inexpensive

Curly Redwood Lodge. True to its namesake, the lodge is built from one huge redwood tree, which produced 57,000 board feet of lumber. The rooms are a decent size, and there is a nice lobby with a fireplace. *701 Redwood Hwy. S, 95531, tel. 707/464–2137. 36 rooms. Facilities: color TV, phone. AE, DC, MC, V.*

Elk
Very Expensive

Harbor House. Constructed in 1916 by a timber company to entertain its guests, this redwood house has a dining room affording a view of the Pacific. Five of the six rooms in the main house have fireplaces. There are also four smallish cottages with wood stove and decks. Breakfast and dinner are included. *5600 S. Hwy. 1, 95432, tel. 707/877–3203. 10 rooms. No credit cards.*

Expensive–
Very Expensive
★

Elk Cove Inn. Private, romantic cottages perched on a bluff above the pounding surf. One room's shower has a full-length window that shares this magnificent view of the Pacific. Skylights, wood-burning stoves, and hand-embroidered cloths are some of the amenities. The 1883 Victorian home features three rooms with dormer windows and window seats, a private parlor and ocean-view deck. A full gourmet breakfast is included. *6300 S. Hwy. 1, Box 367, 95432, tel. 707/877–3321. 4 cabin rooms (2 with stoves) plus 3 rooms in 1883 Victorian building, all with private bath. No credit cards.*

Eureka
Expensive–
Very Expensive

Eureka Inn. This striking Tudor manor, built in 1922 and now a National Historic Landmark, oozes charm and luxury. The elegant lobby is warmed by a fireplace. *7th and F Sts., 95501, tel. 707/442–6441. 105 rooms. Facilities: color TV, phone, pool, sauna, whirlpool. AE, D, DC, MC, V.*

Moderate–
Very Expensive
★

Carter House. For elegance coupled with warmth and hospitality, it is hard to beat Carter House. With a design consonant with the Newsom architecture of the region, Mark Carter has built a truly regal Victorian structure. Most rooms have a view of the Newsom brothers' Carson Mansion as well as of the bay. There is a remarkable sense of airiness, with bay windows accenting two sizable parlors, each with a marble fireplace. On the walls, Carter exhibits fine local artwork, which blends well with the interior. The guest rooms are extraordinary, with Oriental carpets, generous windows, and fine wood furnishings. There is a two-room suite with fireplace and Jacuzzi. Four-course gourmet breakfast, voted the best in the state by *California* magazine, is included. *1033 3rd St., 95501, tel. 707/445–1390. 7 rooms. AE, MC, V.*

Hotel Carter. Situated just across from the Carter House and a block from the Carson Mansion, this tastefully appointed hotel offers a spacious, elegant ambience at reasonable cost. There are Jacuzzis in the deluxe room and suite. Gourmet Continental breakfast is included. *Gourmet dinners served Thurs.–Sun. 301 L St., 95501, tel. 707/444–8062. 20 rooms. Facilities: color TV. AE, MC, V.*

Ferndale
Expensive–
Very Expensive
★

The Gingerbread Mansion. Many visitors come expressly to stay in this spectacular Victorian home, one of the most romantic of the North Coast's bed-and-breakfast inns. The mansion's carved friezes set off its gables, and turrets dazzle the eye. Inside, the luxury continues with four comfortable parlors warmed by two fireplaces. The rooms seem designed for lovers. Some have fireplaces, some have views of the mansion's elegant English garden, and others have side-by-side bathtubs. Breakfast is included. Ask about off-season rates. *400 Berding St. Box 40, 95536, tel. 707/786–4000. 9 rooms with bath. Facilities: bicycles. MC, V.*

Fort Bragg
Moderate–
Very Expensive

Grey Whale Inn. A most comfortable, friendly abode, this inn was once a hospital but doesn't look anything like one today. Two rooms have fireplaces, four have an ocean view, and the deluxe room has a private whirlpool tub and sundeck. Breakfast is included. *615 N. Main St., 95437, tel. 707/964–0640 or 800/382–7244. 14 rooms. Facilities: phones, billiards room. AE, MC, V.*

Garberville
Moderate–
Very Expensive
★

Benbow Inn. Set alongside a beautiful lake, this three-story Tudor manor resort is the equal of any in the Redwood Empire. A magnificent fireplace warms the bar/lobby of this National Historic Landmark, and all rooms are furnished with antiques. The most luxurious rooms are under the terrace, with fine views of the Eel River; some have fireplaces. *445 Lake Benbow Dr., 95440, tel. 707/923–2124. 55 rooms. Facilities: VCR movies in lounge, 18 rooms with TV and VCR, free 250-tape library, restaurant, swimming off private beach, canoeing, tennis, golf, fishing, horseback riding. MC, V. Closed Jan. 3– Apr. 21.*

Sea Ranch
Very Expensive

Sea Ranch Lodge. South of Gualala, the lodge has ocean-view rooms, some with fireplaces and some with hot tubs. Close to beaches, trails, golf. *60 Sea Walk Dr., Box 44, 95497, tel. 707/ 785–2371. 20 rooms. AE, MC, V.*

Gualala
Moderate–
Very Expensive

Gualala Country Inn. All rooms have either ocean or river views. Some rooms have fireplaces and ocean views, two have two-person whirlpools; all have color TVs. *Hwy. 1, 95445, tel. 707/884–4343. 20 rooms. Fireplace in lounge. Sun. brunch. Ask about golf packages. MC, V.*

★ **Old Milano Hotel.** Overlooking the sea just north of Gualala, the Old Milano is one of California's premiere bed-and-breakfast inns. Established in 1905, this wonderfully rustic mansion richly deserves its listing in the National Registry of Historic Places. Set amid English gardens, the estate overlooks Castle Rock and a spectacular coast. Tastefully furnished and appointed with exceptional antiques, five of the rooms look out over the ocean, and another looks over the gardens. Those in search of something different will find a caboose with a wood-burning stove. A cottage also comes complete with wood stove. Breakfast is included, and dinners are offered Wednesday–Sunday. Note: no children, no smoking. *38300 Hwy. 1, 95445, tel. 707/884–3256. 9 rooms. Facilities: hot tub. MC, V.*

★ **St. Orres.** Located just north of Gualala, St. Orres is one of the North Coast's most eye-catching inns. Reflecting the Russian influence in the region, St. Orres's main house is crowned by two Kremlinesque towers. The carved wood is accented by balconies and leaded-glass windows. Two of the rooms overlook the sea, while the other six are set over the garden or forest. Ten wonderfully rustic cottages, built behind the main house in a tranquil woods, provide excellent alternative lodging, seven with wood stoves or fireplaces. Note: children in cottages only. Breakfast is included; for dinner, the inn's restaurant is considered one of the finest north of San Francisco. *Hwy. 1, 95445, tel. 707/884–3303. 18 rooms. Facilities: private beach, hot tub, sauna. MC, V.*

Inverness
Expensive–
Very Expensive
★

Blackthorne Inn. Rising from the base of a tranquil wooded slope is one of the most stunning North Coast bed-and-breakfasts. The Blackthorne is architecturally striking, with an octagonal wooden tower sitting above a turreted treehouse. It includes a glass-enclosed solarium and large fireplace as well as a penthouse, the Eagle's Nest, whose skylight provides a view of the stars. Breakfast is included. *266 Vallejo Ave., Box 712, Inverness Park, 94937, tel. 415/663–8621. 5 rooms, 2 with private bath. Facilities: hot tub, MC, V.*

Expensive
★

Ten Inverness Way. In a lovely old house, set on a quiet side street, you will find one of the most pleasant bed-and-breakfasts on the North Coast. The comfortable living room has a classic stone fireplace and player piano. The rooms are charming, furnished with comfortable antiques. Full breakfast is included. *10 Inverness Way, Box 63, 94937, tel. 415/669–1648. 4 rooms. Facilities: hot tub. MC, V.*

Jenner
Expensive–
Very Expensive
★

Timber Cove Inn. Set off Highway 1 about 3 miles north of the Russian fort, this attractive resort is one of the more luxurious accommodations of the North Coast. Sweeping views overlooking Timber Cove, no in-room phones, and no television anywhere have made this a popular spot for honeymooners. All but six of the rooms have both fireplaces and Jacuzzis or large sunken tubs, and the more expensive rooms have hot tubs. The bar and dining hall are festooned with flowers, and there is a Japanese pond at the entrance to the complex. There are also conference and seminar rooms. *21780 NC. Hwy. 1, 95450, tel. 707/ 847–3231. 49 rooms. AE, DC, MC, V.*

Moderate–
Very Expensive

Fort Ross Lodge. About 1½ miles north of the old Russian fort, the cabins here, most with fireplaces, afford spectacular views of the Sonoma shoreline. *20705 Hwy. 1, 95450, tel. 707/847–3333. 16 cabins, some with private hot tub on back patio, plus 7 hill suites with sauna, in-room hot tub, VCR, and fireplace. Facilities: color TV and VCR. AE, MC, V.*

Moderate–Expensive
★

Murphy's Jenner Inn. Several units of this good-value inn have been built along the edge of the Russian River; some have partial ocean views. The large suite has a full kitchen, wood stove, and loft that can accommodate up to eight. Breakfast is included. *10400 Hwy. 1, Box 69, 95450, tel. 707/865–2377. 10 rooms. Facilities: hot tub available to 3 units. AE, MC, V.*

Inexpensive–
Moderate

Stillwater Cove Ranch. Sixteen miles north of Jenner, overlooking Stillwater Cove, this former boys' school has been transformed into a pleasant, reasonably priced place to lodge. The proprietors have beautified the grounds with peacocks. *22555 Hwy. 1, 95450, tel. 707/847–3227. 7 rooms. No credit cards.*

Klamath
Inexpensive

DeMartin Redwood AYH Hostel. The California coast's northernmost hostel, this turn-of-the-century inn is a stone's throw from the ocean. It is located within Redwood National Park, so hiking begins just beyond its doors. The living room is heated by a wood stove. *14480 Hwy. 101 (at Wilson Creek Rd.), 95548, tel. 707/482–8265. No credit cards.*

Little River
Expensive–
Very Expensive
★

Heritage House. This famous resort, where the film *Same Time, Next Year* was shot, has attractive cottages overlooking a stunning seascape. There is a lovely dining room, also with fine Pacific views, serving breakfast and dinner, which are included. *Hwy. 1, 95456, tel. 707/937–5885. 70 rooms. Make reservations well in advance. MC, V. Closed Dec. and Jan.*

Moderate–
Very Expensive
★

Glendeven. For a tranquil touch of the pastoral, stay at this inn at the north end of Little River. The New England–style main house has six rooms, four with private bath, one with wood stove. The barn features a two-bedroom suite with kitchen and an exceptional art gallery. The 1986 Stevenscroft building has four rooms with fireplaces. The owners, both designers, have decorated the guest rooms with antiques, contemporary art, and ceramics. Breakfast is included. *8221 N. Hwy. 1, 95456, tel. 707/937–0083. 11 rooms. MC, V.*

Mendocino
Very Expensive
★

Stanford Inn by the Sea. For those who wish to experience the quintessence of luxury on the Mendocino coast, this is the place. In sumptuously appointed rooms, each with a deck and fireplace, you can gaze out over the Pacific and the town of Mendocino. The Stanford is adjacent to a llama farm and set along the estuary. Breakfast is included. (This was previously known as the Big River Lodge.) *Just south of Mendocino, east on the Comptche-Ukiah Rd., Box 487, 95460, tel. 707/937–5615. 25 rooms. Facilities: canoes, color TV, stereo, VCRs, coffee makers, telephones, refrigerators, state-of-the-art mountain bikes, indoor pool, hot tub. AE, DC, MC, V.*

Expensive–
Very Expensive
★

Headlands Inn. A magnificently restored Victorian building dating back to 1868, the inn combines 19th-century charm and contemporary comforts. All rooms have private baths and fireplaces; some overlook a garden and the pounding surf, others offer fine village views. There is also a private cottage on the premises. Gourmet breakfast is served in your room. *Corner of Howard and Albion Sts., Box 132, 95460, tel. 707/937–4431. 5 rooms. No credit cards.*

Moderate–
Very Expensive

Mendocino Hotel. The exterior of this fine hotel lends a sense of the Wild West; inside, an elegant atmosphere of stained-glass lamps, Remington paintings, polished wood, and Persian carpets prevails. All but 14 of the rooms have a private bath, and the 19th-century decor is appealing. There are also deluxe garden rooms with fireplaces on the property. *45080 Main St., Box 587, 95460, tel. 707/937–0511 or 800/548–0513. 51 rooms. Facilities: restaurant, bar, telephones. AE, MC, V.*

Mendocino Village Inn. This beautifully refurbished 1882 Queen Anne Victorian inn has a potpourri of motifs, with one room providing an Indian ambience, another a whaling captain's quarters, and a third a homage to Teddy Roosevelt. Many of the rooms have fireplaces, some have ocean views, and others look out on the garden. Breakfast is included. *44860 Main*

St., Box 626, 95460, tel. 707/937–0246 or 800/882–7029 in CA. 12 rooms, 10 with bath. No credit cards.

Moderate–
Expensive
★

MacCallum House. The most stunning Victorian in Mendocino, this splendid 1882 inn transports you back to another era. Its comfortable period furnishings and antiques provide a turn-of-the-century ambience. In addition to the main house, individual cottages and barn suites are set around a garden with a gazebo. Continental breakfast is included (weekends only in winter). *45020 Albion St., Box 206, 95460, tel. 707/937–0289. 21 rooms. Facilities: restaurant, bar. MC, V.*

★

Joshua Grindle Inn. This beautiful century-old Victorian inn has a reputation for friendliness. Some rooms have splendid ocean views, and some have fireplaces. Three rooms are in a water tower. There is also a two-room cottage with a Franklin stove. Full breakfast is included. *44800 Little Lake Rd., 95460, tel. 707/937–4143. 10 rooms. MC, V.*

Muir Beach
Expensive–
Very Expensive
★

Pelican Inn. A wonderfully atmospheric Tudor-style B&B house reminiscent of 16th-century England, the Pelican is a five-minute walk from splendid Muir Beach. The rooms, filled with antiques, have half-canopied two- and four-poster beds. On the ground floor, there's an Old English pub complete with dart boards and a selection of British brews. The dining quarter consists of two sections: a romantic rustic wooden hall and a glassed-in solarium, both warmed by fireplaces. Includes full English breakfast. *Hwy. 1, 94965, tel. 415/383–6000. 7 rooms. MC, V.*

Point Reyes
National Seashore
Inexpensive

Point Reyes Hostel. Located within the national seashore and a mere 2 miles from lovely Limantour Beach, this is the best deal for basic budget travelers. Lodging is dorm-style. The family room is limited to families with small children and must be reserved well in advance. *Box 247, Pt. Reyes Station, 94956, tel. 415/663–8811. Send $8 per adult per night with reservation requests; state your gender. Facilities: shared kitchen. No credit cards.*

Shelter Cove
Inexpensive–
Moderate

Beachcomber Inn. There are three good-size rooms, two with kitchenettes and wood-burning stoves, and ocean views. The inn is near the marina and it's an easy walk to the beach. *Write c/o 7272 Shelter Cove Rd., Shelter Cove, 95489, tel. 707/986–7733. 3 rooms. MC, V.*

Trinidad
Moderate–
Expensive
★

Trinidad Bed and Breakfast. Overlooking Trinidad Bay, this delightful inn gets our vote for having the most spectacular sea view on the North Coast. The innkeepers are a treasure trove of information about the nearby wilderness, beach, and fishing habitats. The living room is warmed by a crackling fireplace. Upstairs, three comfortably furnished rooms offer fabulous seascapes. Breakfast is included. *560 Edwards St., Box 849, 95570, tel. 707/677–0840. 4 rooms and 1 first-floor, 180-degree ocean-view suite with fireplace. Reserve well in advance. D, MC, V.*

Tomales Bay
Moderate

Tomales Country Inn. Secluded by trees and bordered by gardens, this Victorian house has a relaxed atmosphere. The previous owner, Byron Randall, is a painter who has filled the inn with his turn-of-the-century, European-style paintings and other local art. Expanded Continental breakfast is included. *25 Valley St., Box 376, 94971, tel. 707/878–9992. 5 rooms, 2 with bath. No credit cards.*

Westport	**Howard Creek Ranch.** This rustic redwood former ranch, built
Moderate	in 1871, has fine ocean views. It is within 300 yards of the

Howard Creek Ranch. This rustic redwood former ranch, built in 1871, has fine ocean views. It is within 300 yards of the beach. Breakfast included. *40501 Hwy. 1, Box 121, 95488, tel. 707/964–6725. 7 rooms, 4 with bath. Facilities: hot tub, sauna. MC, V.*

Nightlife

If a raucous swinging urban scene is what you are hankering for, the North Coast is not the place for you. Nonetheless, there are some watering holes favored by locals and visitors that should meet the needs of those not quite ready for a good night's sleep after exploring the forest and sea.

The following are listed alphabetically by town.

Bolinas **Smiley's Schooner Saloon.** The only nightlife in Bolinas, Smiley's has a CD sound system and live music three nights a week. *41 Wharf Rd., tel. 415/868–1311.*

Garberville **Benbow Inn.** In this elegant Tudor mansion, a pianist can be heard nightly while you are warmed by a romantic fireplace. *445 Lake Benbow Dr., tel. 707/923–2124.*

Mendocino **The Sea Gull.** Also an excellent restaurant, the Sea Gull has an upstairs bar that hosts live musical entertainment from jazz to rock Friday and Saturday evenings (summer only). *Lansing and Ukiah Sts., tel. 707/937–2100.*

Muir Beach **Pelican Inn.** Set just outside Muir Beach, this is a wonderful English pub and restaurant, with imported brews on tap, a dart board, and a stone fireplace. *Hwy. 1, tel. 415/383–6005.*

Point Reyes Station **Western Saloon.** If you are in town on the right Friday night, you can dance your jeans off at this favorite local pub. There is dancing on occasional Fridays. Other nights it's a friendly place to meet West Marinites. *Hwy. 1, tel. 415/663–1661.*

4 The Far North

While the rest of California boomed with an influx of high-tech industries, sun-seeking East Coasters, and value-conscious developers, the Far North simply hung up its "gone fishin'" sign. You won't find many hot nightspots or cultural enclaves here, but you will find some of the best hiking, fishing, and hunting the state has to offer. Some Bay area families return to the lakes of the far north year after year. Many enjoy the outdoors from their own piece of paradise—a private houseboat. A good number of retirees have chosen to live out their golden years in the area.

The towering, snow-covered Mount Shasta dominates the land. It can be seen for 100 miles, and qualifies the otherwise flat and fast trip through the valley along I–5 as a scenic drive. The 14,000-foot dormant volcano is surrounded by national and state parks. The natural and artificially created wonders include the bubbling mud pots and sulfur vents of Lassen Volcanic National Park and the immense Shasta Dam.

Almost all of the towns in the Far North are small and friendly, made up of third- and fourth-generation descendants of '49-ers who never cared to leave. Proud of their Gold Rush history, each town, no matter how small, has a museum filled with an impressive collection of artifacts donated by locals. This is the kind of place where people say hello to you as you walk down Main Street.

Getting Around

By Plane Redding Municipal Airport is served by **United Express** (tel. 800/241–6522) and **American Eagle** (tel. 800/433–7300) (which flies daily from San Francisco). Major car rental agencies are located at the airport.

By Train There are **Amtrak** stations in Redding and Dunsmuir (tel. 800/872–7245).

By Bus **Greyhound-Trailways** buses travel I–5, serving Red Bluff, Redding, Dunsmuir, and Mt. Shasta City. In Redding, a city bus system, "The Ride," serves the local area daily except Sunday (tel. 916/241–2877).

By Car I–5 runs up the center of California through Red Bluff and Redding to the Oregon border. It is an excellent four-lane divided highway. Lassen Park can be reached by Highway 36 from Red Bluff or Highway 44 from Redding; Highway 299 leads from Redding to McArthur-Burney Falls. These are very good two-lane roads that are kept open year round. If you are traveling in winter, however, always carry snow chains in your car.

Important Addresses and Numbers

Tourist Information **Mt. Shasta Convention and Visitors Bureau.** Information pavilion (300 Pine St., Mt. Shasta, 96067, tel. 916/926–4865 or 800/427–0909).

Red Bluff-Tehama County Chamber of Commerce (100 N. Main St., Box 850, Red Bluff 96080, tel. 916/527–6220).

Redding Convention and Visitors Bureau (777 Auditorium Dr., Redding 96001, tel. 916/225–4100).

Shasta Cascade Wonderland Association. Visitor information for the entire region (1250 Parkview Ave., Redding 96001, tel. 916/243–2643).

Siskiyou County Visitors Bureau (30841 Walker Rd., Horse Creek, CA 96045, tel. 800/446–7475).

Emergencies The number for emergency assistance throughout the Far North is 911. This will put you in touch with police, fire, and medical help.

Exploring

Numbers in the margin correspond with points of interest on the Far North map.

The Far North covers a large territory, from the valleys east of the coast range to the Nevada border, and from the almond and olive orchards north of Sacramento to the Oregon border. The entire state of Ohio would fit into this section of the Golden State.

Redding is the urban center of the Far North. It offers the greatest selection of restaurants and the most luxurious accommodations. You'll experience more of the true flavor of this outdoor country at motels in the smaller towns. Many visitors make the outdoors their home for at least part of their stay. Camping, houseboating, and animal pack trips into the wilderness are very popular.

We've arranged the exploring section from south to north, following the mostly flat and fast I–5 with the addition of two day-long side trips. The valley around Redding is hot, even in winter, but cooler temperatures prevail in the higher elevations to the east and north. Be aware that many restaurants and museums have limited hours and sometimes close temporarily during the off-season.

Red Bluff

The turn-off for Red Bluff will take you past a neon-lit motel row, but persevere and explore the roads to the left of the main drag to discover gracefully restored Victorian structures, a fine museum, and a Western-style downtown.

❶ The **Kelly-Griggs House Museum** is a restored 1880s Victorian dwelling with an impressive collection of antique furniture, housewares, and clothing arranged as though a refined Victorian family still resided there. An engraved silver tea server waits on the end table. A "Self Instructor in Penmanship" teaching the art of graceful, flowing handwriting sits on the desk. And eerily lifelike mannequins seem frozen in conversation in the upstairs parlor.

The museum's collection includes finely carved china cabinets, Native American basketry, and a turn-of-the-century painting by Thomas Hill, known for his western landscapes. The painting over the fireplace is by Sarah Brown, daughter of abolitionist John Brown, whose family settled in Red Bluff after his execution. Their home is on the self-guided tour map of Red Bluff Victoriana available at the museum. *311 Washington St., tel. 916/527–1129. Donation suggested. Open Thurs.–Sun. 2–4. Closed holidays.*

The Far North

OREGON

Klamath
National
Forest

CASCADE

Lava Beds
National
Monument

RANGE

Klamath National Forest

Weed ▲ Mt Shasta

**Everett
Memorial Hwy.** ⑩

McCloud

Dunsmuir

Shasta National Forest

**McArthur-Burney
Falls** ⑨

Burney

Clair
Engle
Lake

Lake
Shasta

Lassen
National
Forest

Whiskeytown-Shasta-
Trinity National
Recreation Area

⑧ **Lake Shasta
Caverns**

TO RENO

⑦ **Shasta Dam**

⑥ **Shasta**

Enterprise

Redding

Chaos Jumbles ⑤

Lassen
Volcanic
National
Park

Hot Rock ④

Drakesbad

③ **Sulphur
Works**

TO RENO

SACRAMENTO

② **Wm. B. Ide Adobe
State Historic Park**

**Kelly-Griggs
Museum** ①

Red Bluff

VALLEY

Chico

Lake
Oroville

0   20 miles

0

30 km   SACRAMENTO

TO

North of town on the banks of the Sacramento River is the
② William B. Ide Adobe State Historic Park, which is a memorial
to the man who was the first and only president of the California Republic, under the Bear Flag Party proclamation. The republic existed for 25 days in 1846 before it was occupied by the
United States. Early furnishings are displayed in an 1850s adobe. *21659 Adobe Rd., tel. 916/527–5927. Admission: $2 adults,
$1 children 6–17. Home open 11–4 in summer; park and picnic
facilities open year-round from 8 AM–sunset.*

Lassen Volcanic National Park

You'll take Highway 36 east from Red Bluff to this still-active
volcano. Except for the ski area, the park is largely inaccessible
from late October to early June because of snow. Highway 89
through the park is closed to cars in winter, but open to intrepid cross-country skiers. When it's free of snow, you can drive
Highway 89 north for a meandering 34-mile look at three sides
of the world's largest plug volcano.

In 1914 the 10,457-foot Mt. Lassen began a series of 300 eruptions that went on for seven years. Molten rock overflowed the
crater; there were clouds of smoke, and hailstorms of rocks and
volcanic cinders. Proof of the volcano's volatility becomes evi-
③ dent shortly after you enter the park at the **Sulphur Works
Thermal Area.** Boardwalks take you over bubbling mud and hot
springs, and through the nauseating sulphur stink of steam
vents. Five miles farther along the road you'll find the start of
the **Bumpass Hell Trail,** a 3-mile round-trip hike to the park's
most interesting thermal-spring area where you'll see hot and
boiling springs, steam vents, and mud pots. The trail climbs
and descends several hundred feet.

Drive on through forests and past lakes, looking out for deer
④ and wildflowers, to **Hot Rock.** This 400-ton boulder tumbled
down from the summit during the volcano's active period, and
was still hot to the touch when locals found it. Although cool
⑤ now, it's still an impressive sight. Five miles on is **Chaos Jumbles,** created 300 years ago when an avalanche from the Chaos
Crags lava domes spread hundreds of thousands of rocks 2 to 3
feet in diameter over 2 square miles.

An important word of warning: Stay on trails and boardwalks
near the thermal areas. What may appear to be firm ground can
be a thin crust over scalding mud, and serious burns can result.
Be especially careful with children!

Lassen is a unique, lovely and relatively uncrowded national
park, but services are rather sparse. You'll find a year-round
café and gift shop at the winter sports area in the southwest
corner, open during the busier ski and summer seasons; there's
another store (offering fast food and gas) at the Manzanita
Lake campground, which is open in the summer only. Admission to the park is $5 per vehicle.

There are seven campgrounds in Lassen Volcanic National
Park. Reservations are not accepted; it's first come, first
served. For campground and other information, contact Lassen
Volcanic National Park (Mineral 96063, tel. 916/595–4444).

The only other lodging in the park is a 100-year-old guest ranch
at Drakesbad, which is near its southern border, and isolated

from most of the park. Reservations should be made well in advance. *Booking office: 2150 Main St., Suite 5, Red Bluff 96080, tel. 916/529–1512. Open early June–early Oct.*

Redding

A few miles west of Redding on Highway 299 are the ruins of
6 the gold-mining town of **Shasta,** now a **state historic park** with a few restored buildings. A museum located in the old courthouse has an eclectic array of California paintings as well as memorabilia including period newspapers advertising "Gold Dust Bought and Sold," a "Prairie Traveler" guidebook with advice on encounters with Indians, and the 1860 census of the once-prosperous town. Continue down to the basement to see the iron-barred jail cells and step outside to the scaffold where the murderers were hanged. *Tel. 916/243–8194. Admission: $2 adults, $1 children 6–17. Open 10–5. Closed Jan. 1, Thanksgiving, and Dec. 25. Closed Tues. and Wed. Nov.–Feb.*

Lake Shasta

Take the Dam/Project City exit west off I–5 about 12 miles
7 north of Redding and follow the signs to **Shasta Dam.** You'll be able to see the mammoth construction from several points; this is the second-largest and the fourth-tallest concrete dam in the United States.

Whether you drive across the dam, or park at the landscaped visitors' area and walk across, you'll see three Shastas: the dam, the lake spreading before you, and the mountain presiding over it all. At twilight the sight is magical, with Mt. Shasta gleaming above the not-quite-dark water. The dam is lighted after dark, but there is no access from 10 PM to 6 AM. In addition to providing maps and brochures, the **Visitor Information Center** (tel. 916/275–4463) offers exhibits (June–Sept., weekdays 8:30–5; Oct.–May, weekdays 10–3). The coffee shop is closed in January and February.

Lake Shasta has 370 miles of shoreline and 21 varieties of fish. You can rent fishing boats, ski boats, sailboats, canoes, paddleboats, jet skis, and Windsurfer boards at one of the many marinas and resorts along the shore. But the houseboat is king on Lake Shasta, known as the houseboat capital of the world.

Houseboats come in all sizes except small. The ones that sleep 12 to 14 people are 55 feet by 14 feet; the minimum size sleeps six. As a rule these moving homes come equipped with cooking utensils, dishes, and most of the equipment you'll need to set up housekeeping on the water. (You supply the food and linens.) Renters are given a short course in how to maneuver the boats before they set out on cruises; it's not difficult.

The houseboats are slow-moving, and life aboard is leisurely. You can fish, swim, or sunbathe on the flat roof. The shoreline of Lake Shasta is beautifully ragged, with countless inlets; exploring is fun, and it's not hard to find privacy. Be aware, however, that the recent drought has considerably diminished the volume of the lake, making some areas inaccessible.

Expect to spend a minimum of $170 a day for the sleeps-six size houseboat. Contact the **Shasta Cascade Wonderland Associa-**

tion (1250 Parkview Ave., Redding, CA 96001, tel. 916/243–2643) for specifics about the 10 marinas that rent houseboats.

Stalagmites, stalactites, odd flowstone deposits, and crystals entice visitors of all ages to the **Lake Shasta Caverns.** The two-hour tour includes a ferry ride across the McCloud arm of Lake Shasta and a bus ride up Grey Rock Mountain to the cavern entrance. The caverns are a constant 58 degrees year-round, making them a cool retreat on a hot summer day. All cavern rooms are well lit, and the crowning jewel is the spectacular cathedral room. The guides are friendly, enthusiastic, and informative. *Take the Shasta Caverns Rd. exit from I–5. Tel. 916/238–2341. Admission: $12 adults, $6 children 4–12. Hourly tours May–Sept., daily 9–4; Oct.–Apr., at 10 AM, noon, and 2 PM. Closed Thanksgiving and Dec. 25.*

Burney Falls

You take the Highway 299 East exit off I–5 just north of Redding, past the town of Burney, and turn north on Highway 89 to get to **McArthur-Burney Falls Memorial State Park.** It's a two-hour round trip drive from I–5, so you may want to plan to spend the day here. Just inside the southern boundary of the park, Burney Creek wells up from the ground and divides into two cascades that fall over a 129-foot cliff into a pool below. The thundering water creates a mist at the base of the falls, often highlighted by a rainbow. Countless ribbonlike falls stream from hidden moss-covered crevices creating an ethereal backdrop to the main cascades. Each day, 100 million gallons of water rush over the falls; Theodore Roosevelt proclaimed them "the eighth wonder of the world." A self-guided nature trail descends to the foot of the falls. There is a lake and beach for swimming. A campground, picnic sites, trails, and other facilities are available. The camp store is open Memorial Day–Labor Day. *Rte. 1, Box 1260, Burney 96013, tel. 916/335–2777. Day use admission: $5 per vehicle; camping $14 per night.*

Mt. Shasta

If you drive up the valley on I–5, past the 130-million-year-old granite outcroppings of Castle Crags towering over the road, through the quaint old railroad town of Dunsmuir, you'll reach the town of Mt. Shasta, nestled at the base of the huge mountain. If you are interested in hiking on Mt. Shasta, stop at the **Forest Service Ranger Station** (204 West Alma St., tel. 916/926–4511) as you come through town for the latest information on trail conditions or call the **Fifth Season Mountaineering Shop** in Mt. Shasta City (tel. 916/926–3606) which also offers a recorded 24-hour climber/skier report (tel. 916/926–5555).

The central Mt. Shasta exit east leads out of town along the **Everett Memorial Highway.** This scenic drive climbs to almost 8,000 feet, and the views of the mountain and the valley below are extraordinary.

If you are wondering where all those eye-catching pictures of Mount Shasta reflected in a lake are shot, take the central Mt. Shasta exit west and follow the signs to **Lake Siskiyou.** This is the only lake in California created solely for recreational purposes. On the way, stop at the oldest **trout hatchery** in California. The pools there literally swarm with over 100,000 trout.

What to See and Do with Children

Almost everything we have described in the Far North of California offers something that children will enjoy: the bubbling mud at Lassen, the houseboats and caverns at Lake Shasta, and the falls at Burney. **Waterworks Park** in Redding has giant water slides, a raging river inner-tube ride, and a children's water playground. *151 N. Boulder Dr., tel. 916/246–9550. Admission: $10.95 ages 12–65, $8.95 children 4–11. Open Memorial Day–Labor Day, daily 10–8.*

Off the Beaten Track

The hand-painted sign along Main Street in **McCloud** reads "Population 1,665, Dogs 462." To reach this time-capsule town, take the Highway 89 exit east from I–5 just south of the town of Mt. Shasta. McCloud began as a lumber company town in the late 1800s, and was one of the longest-lived company towns in the country. In 1965, the U.S. Plywood Corp. acquired the town, its lumber mill, and the surrounding forest land, and allowed residents to purchase their homes. The immense mill has been cut back to a computerized operation, but the spirit of the townsfolk have kept McCloud from becoming a ghost town. Picturesque hotels, churches, a lumber baron's mansion, and simple family dwellings have been renovated, and the 60,000-pound Corliss steam engine that powered the original mill's machinery stands as a monument behind the town's small museum.

Sports

Fishing You'll need a California fishing license. State residents pay $22.60, but nonresidents must fork over $60.65 for a one-year license. Both residents and nonresidents can purchase a one-day license for $8.15. For information, contact the **Department of Fish and Game** (3211 S St., Sacramento 95816, tel. 916/739–3380).

For licenses, current fishing conditions, guides, or special fishing packages, contact **The Fly Shop** (4140 Churn Creek Rd., Redding 96002, tel. 916/222–3555), **The Fishin' Hole** (3844 Shasta Dam Blvd., Central Valley, 96019, tel. 916/275–4123), or **Shasta Cascade Wonderland Association** (1250 Parkview Ave., Redding 96001, tel. 916/243–2643).

Golf **Churn Creek Golf Course** (8550 Churn Creek Rd., Redding, tel. 916/222–6353). Nine holes, par 36. Carts.

Gold Hills Country Club (1950 Gold Hills Dr., Redding, Oasis Road exit from I–5, tel. 916/246–7867). Eighteen holes, par 72. Carts, club rentals, driving range, pro shop, restaurant.

Lake Redding Golf Course (1795 Benton Dr., Redding, in Lake Redding Park, tel. 916/243–5531). Nine holes, par 62. Pull carts, rentals.

Llama Pack Tours **Shasta Llamas** (Box 1137, Mt. Shasta 96067, tel. 916/926–3959) leads three- and five-day trips into the backcountry.

Raft and Canoe Rentals **Park Marina Watersports** (2515 Park Marina Dr., Redding, tel. 916/246–8388).

Skiing **Mt. Lassen Ski Park.** Inside the southwest entrance of Lassen Volcanic National Park is the only park facility open in winter, with three lifts. The terrain is 40% beginner, 40% intermediate, 20% advanced. Mt. Lassen's top elevation is 7,200 feet; its base, 6,600 feet; its vertical drop, 600 feet. The longest run is ¾-mile. There is a ski school and a beginner's special: lift, rentals, lessons. The Kids Are People Too program for ages 5–11 includes rentals, lunch, lesson, lifts. Facilities include a cafeteria and rental shop. *Hwy. 36 exit from I–5 at Red Bluff, tel. 916/ 595–3376. Snow phone: 916/595–4464.*

Mt. Shasta Ski Park. On the southeast flank of Mt. Shasta are three lifts on 300 acres. The terrain is 20% beginner, 60% intermediate, 20% advanced. Mt. Shasta's summit is 6,600 feet; its base, 5,500 feet; its vertical drop 1,100 feet. The longest run is 1.2 miles. Night skiing goes till 10 PM Wednesday–Saturday. There is a ski school with a beginner's special: lifts, rentals, lessons. The Powder Pups program is for ages 4–7. Lodge facilities include food and beverage, ski shop, and rentals. *Hwy. 89 exit east from I–5, just south of Mt. Shasta, tel. 916/926–8610. Snow phone 916/926–8686.*

Snowshoe Tours National Park Service rangers conduct snowshoe tours at Mt. Lassen Ski Park. A variety of natural history topics are covered. Snowshoes and instructions are free. *Tel. 916/595–4444. No reservations. Open weekends at 1:30 PM and daily through the Christmas and Easter holiday periods except Thanksgiving and Dec. 25.*

Dining

Cafés and simple, informal restaurants are ample in the far north. Most of the fast-food restaurants are clustered in Redding, though they are also found along I–5 in some of the larger communities. The restaurants listed here are of special interest because of their food and/or unique atmosphere. Dress is always casual in the Far North; reservations aren't necessary except where noted.

Highly recommended restaurants are indicated by a star ★.

Category	Cost*
Very Expensive	over $25
Expensive	$20–$25
Moderate	$15–$20
Inexpensive	under $15

per person, not including tax, service, or drinks

Lake Shasta
Inexpensive–
Moderate

Tail O' the Whale. Nautical decor distinguishes this restaurant, reminiscent of a ship's prow, overlooking the lake. Seafood, beef, poultry, and Cajun pepper shrimp are the specialties. Reservations are recommended for the Sunday brunch served during the summer. *10300 Bridge Bay Rd. (Bridge Bay exit from I–5), tel. 916/275–3021. AE, MC, V.*

Mt. Shasta
Inexpensive–
Moderate
★

Bellissimo. This bright, Mediterranean-style café has an eclectic, creative menu with generous use of fresh herbs and healthful ingredients. Specialties change, but could include curry chicken with apple-raisin chutney, parsley-garlic fettuccine with clams, ravioli with acorn squash, cheeses, and nutmeg, and decadent desserts. There's a special Sunday brunch. *204A West Lake St., tel. 916/926–4461. MC, V. Limited hours in winter.*

Inexpensive **Marilyn's.** Everyone greets each other by name at this Mayberry-esque diner where they serve 10¢ coffee. Even the local deputy orders the regular here. The former stage stop serves hearty breakfasts and sandwiches as well as Italian specialties. Complete dinners including soup or salad cost less than $7. *1136 South Mt. Shasta Blvd., tel. 916/926–2720. MC, V.*

Red Bluff **The Snack Box.** This cheerfully renovated Victorian place is
Inexpensive decorated in country-French blue and dusty rose. The carved wooden murals, like the omelets, soups and sandwiches, are homemade by the owner. *257 Main St. (1 block from Kelly-Griggs Museum), tel. 916/529–0227. No credit cards. Closed dinner.*

Redding **Misty's.** Two-story windows overlook the Red Lion Inn's pool
Moderate–Expensive area at this romantic dinner room with private booths. Special-
★ ties include steak Diane and hot rock cuisine, whisky peppercorn steak, and wild mushroom fettuccine. The meals are artistically presented, and there's a Sunday brunch. *1830 Hilltop Dr. (at the Red Lion Inn), tel. 916/221–8700. AE, D, DC, MC, V.*

Inexpensive– **J.D. Bennett's.** This open, airy garden court restaurant has a
Moderate turn-of-the-century ambience with etched glass, dark wood, and gaslight fixtures. The diverse menu offers everything from lasagna to Mexican food to filet Mignon. *1800 Churn Creek Rd. (Cypress exit east from I–5), tel. 916/221–6177. AE, MC, V. Closed Dec. 25.*
Jack's Grill. This steakhouse is usually jam-packed and noisy; it's immensely popular with the natives throughout the territory. It looks like a dive from the outside, but the 16-oz. steaks are famous. *1743 California St., tel. 916/241–9705. AE, MC, V. Closed lunch, closed Sun.*

Lodging

Motel chains, such as Best Western and Motel 6, have accommodations in many of the communities in the Far North, though Redding has the greatest selection by far. Luxury hotels are found only in Redding.

Highly recommended hotels are indicated by a star ★.

Category	Cost*
Very Expensive	over $100
Expensive	$75–$100
Moderate	$50–$75
Inexpensive	under $50

**double room, not including tax*

Dunsmuir **Railroad Park Resort.** At this railroad buff's delight, antique
Moderate cabooses have been converted to clean, playfully romantic motel rooms in honor of Dunsmuir's railroad legacy. There's also a restaurant in a restored, Orient Express-style dining car, and

a full bar in a converted railcar. The lounge now features a Karaoke machine—the popular Japanese sing-along jukebox. The nicely landscaped grounds feature a huge logging steam engine and restored water tower. *100 Railroad Park Rd., 96025, tel. 916/235–4440. 19 cabooses with bath. 4 cabins. Facilities: pool, Jacuzzi. AE, D, MC, V.*

Mt. Shasta   **Alpine Lodge.** The clean, standard motel rooms here are deco-
Inexpensive   rated in a range of colors. Amenities include in-room coffee. *908 S. Mt. Shasta Blvd., 96067, tel. 916/926–3145. 8 rooms with bath. 5 family suites. Facilities: pool, spa with Jacuzzi jets. AE, DC, MC, V.*

Redding   **Red Lion Inn.** Nicely landscaped grounds and a large, attract-
Expensive–   ive patio area with outdoor food service are the highlights here.
Very Expensive   The rooms are spacious and comfortable. Small pets are
★   allowed; notify the motel when you make reservations. *1830 Hilltop Dr., 96001. (Hwy. 44 and 299 exit east from I–5), tel. 916/221–8700 or 800/547–8010. 195 rooms with bath. Facilities: pool, wading pool, whirlpool, putting green, restaurant, coffee shop, lounge, room service, movies. AE, DC, MC, V.*

Moderate   **Vagabond Inn.** The clean, large rooms here feature a cheerful decor, with flowered drapes and spreads. Continental breakfasts and weekday papers are on the house. Pets are allowed for a $3 fee. *536 E. Cypress Ave., 96002 (Cypress exit west from I–5), tel. 916/223–1600 or 800/522–1555. 71 rooms with bath. Facilities: pool, coffee shop adjacent, movies. AE, DC, MC, V.*

Camping

There are an infinite number of camping possibilities in the Far North's national and state parks, forests, and recreation areas. You'll find every level of rusticity, too, from the well-outfitted campgrounds in McArthur-Burney State Park, with hot water, showers, and flush toilets, to isolated campsites on Lake Shasta that can be reached only by boat. For information about camping in the region, contact the **Shasta Cascade Wonderland Association** (1250 Parkview Ave., Redding, CA 96001, tel. 916/243–2643).

Nightlife

Although the larger hotels in Redding usually have weekend dance bands geared to the younger set, there's not much nightlife in this outdoors country where the fish bite early. Rock and Roll fans will enjoy the **Curiosity Club** (2655 Bechelli La., behind the bowling alley, Redding, tel. 916/223–3400), which features live music seven nights a week. There's a $2 cover charge on weekends.

5 The Wine Country

In 1862, after an extensive tour of the wine-producing areas of Europe, Count Agoston Haraszthy de Mokcsa reported to his adopted California with a promising prognosis: "Of all the countries through which I passed," wrote the Father of California's viticulture, "not one possessed the same advantages that are to be found in California. . . . California can produce as noble and generous a wine as any in Europe; more in quantity to the acre, and without repeated failures through frosts, summer rains, hailstorms, or other causes."

The "dormant resources" that Haraszthy saw in the temperate valleys of Sonoma and Napa, with their balmy days and cool nights, are in full fruition today. While its wines are savored by connoisseurs throughout the world, the area is a fermenting vat of experimentation, a crucible for the latest techniques of grape-growing and wine-making.

In the Napa Valley, it seems that every available inch of soil is combed with neat rows of vines; would-be wine-makers with very little acreage can rent the cumbersome, costly machinery needed to stem and press the grapes. Many say that making wine is one way to turn a large fortune into a small one, but this hasn't deterred the doctors, former college professors, publishing tycoons, and airline pilots who come to try their hand at the process.

Twenty years ago the Napa Valley had no more than 20 wineries; today there are almost 10 times that number. In Sonoma County, where the web of vineyards is looser, there are more than 100 wineries, and development is now claiming the cool Carneros region at the head of the San Francisco Bay, deemed ideal for growing the currently favored Chardonnay grape.

All this has meant some pretty stiff competition, and the wine makers are constantly honing their skills. They are aided by the scientific know-how of graduates of the nearby University of California at Davis, as well as by the practical knowledge of the grape-growers. They experiment with planting the vine stock closer together and with "canopy management" of the grape cluster, as well as with "cold" fermentation in stainless steel vats and new methods of fining, or filtering, the wine.

In the past the emphasis was on creating wines to be cellared, but today "drinkable" wines that can be enjoyed relatively rapidly are in demand. This has led to the celebration of dining as an art in the Wine Country. Many wineries boast first-class restaurants, which showcase excellent California cuisine and their own fine wines.

With the depredations of increased excise taxes and the health lobbyists, business has felt the pinch lately, but the stretch of highway from Napa to Calistoga rivals Disneyland as the biggest tourist draw in the state. Two-lane Highway 129 slows to a sluggish crawl on weekends throughout the year, and there are acres of vehicles parked at the picnic places, upscale gift shops, and restaurants in the area.

The pace in Sonoma County is less frenetic. While Napa is upscale and elegant, Sonoma is overalls-and-corduroy, with an air of rustic innocence. But the County's Alexander, Dry Creek, and Russian River valleys are no less productive of award-winning vintages. The Sonoma countryside also offers excellent opportunities for hiking, biking, camping, and fishing.

In addition to state-of-the-art viticulture, the Wine Country also provides a look at California's history. In the town of Sonoma, you'll find remnants of Mexican California and the solid, ivy-covered, brick wineries built by Haraszthy and his disciples. The original attraction here was the water, and the rush to the spas of Calistoga, promoted by the indefatigable Gold Rush entrepreneur Samuel Brannan in the late 19th century, left a legacy of fretwork, clapboard, and Gothic architecture. More recent architectural details can be found at the Art Nouveau mansion of the Beringer brothers in St. Helena and the latter-day neoclassical extravaganza of Clos Pegase in Calistoga.

The courting of the tourist trade has produced tensions, and some residents wonder whether projects like the *Wine Train*, finally running between Napa and St. Helena, brings the Disneyland atmosphere a little too close to home. These fears may or may not be realized, but the natural beauty of the landscape will always draw tourists. Whether in the spring, when the vineyards bloom yellow with mustard flowers, or in the fall, when fruit is ripening, this slice of California has a feel not unlike the hills of Tuscany or Provence. Haraszthy was right: This is a chosen place.

Getting Around

By Plane The San Francisco and Oakland airports are closest to the Wine Country. **Greyhound-Trailways** (tel. 415/558–6789) runs buses from the San Francisco Terminal at 7th and Mission streets to Napa (one each day), Sonoma (one each day), and Santa Rosa (three each day).

By Bus **Sonoma County Area Transit** (tel. 707/585–7516) and **The Vine** (tel. 707/255–7631), Napa's bus service, provide local transportation within towns in the Wine Country.

By Car Although traffic on the two-lane country roads can be heavy, the best way to get around the Wine Country is by private car. Rental cars are available at the airports and in San Francisco, Oakland, Santa Rosa, and Napa.

The Rider's Guide (484 Lake Park Ave., Box 255, Oakland 94610, tel. 415/653–2553) produces tapes about the history, landmarks, and wineries of the Sonoma and Napa valleys that you can play in your car. The tapes are available for $11.95, plus $2 postage at Waldenbooks, Brentanos, and Books Inc. in San Francisco, as well as at selected locations (wineries and hotels) in the Wine Country itself. Call to inquire about current availability.

Guided Tours

Full-day guided tours of the Wine Country usually include lunch and cost about $50. The guides, some of whom are winery owners themselves, know the area well and may show you some lesser-known cellars.

Gray Line Inc. (425 Mission St., San Francisco 94105, tel. 415/558–9400) has bright-red double-deckers that tour the Wine Country. Reservations are required.

Great Pacific Tour Co. (518 Octavia St., San Francisco 94102, tel. 415/626–4499) offers full-day tours, including a picnic lunch, to Napa and Sonoma, in passenger vans that seat 13.

Maxi Tours (545 Eddy St., Box 59046, San Francisco 94159, tel. 415/441–6294) provides air-conditioned van tours of the Wine Country.

Starlane Tours (416 Francisco St., San Francisco 94133, tel. 415/982–2223) provides full-day tours of Napa and Sonoma wineries; they offer group and senior-citizen rates.

Superior Sightseeing (642 Alvarado St., Suite 100, San Francisco 94114, tel. 415/550–1352) limits its full-day excursions to 20 passengers. The company offers personalized itineraries on request and provides free hotel pickup as well as group and senior-citizen rates. Reservations are required.

Wine Train (1275 McKinstry St., Napa 94559, tel. 707/253–2111, 800/427–4124 in CA, 800/522–4142 outside CA) allows you to enjoy lunch, dinner, or a weekend brunch on one of several restored 1915 Pullman railroad cars that now run between Napa and St. Helena on tracks that were formerly owned by the Southern Pacific Railroad. Round-trip fare is $29; a three-course brunch or luncheon costs $22, and a five-course dinner costs $45 (train fare is reduced to $14.50 for dinner parties of two or more). During the winter service is limited to Thursday through Sunday. There is a special car for families with children on the Saturday or Sunday brunch trip.

Horse-Drawn Vineyard Tours through the Alexander Valley are offered by Five Oaks Farm (15851 Chalk Hill Rd., Healdsburg 95448, tel. 707/433–2422). The tours run Thursday–Sunday from April through November, weather permitting, and include lunch or dinner.

Important Addresses and Numbers

Tourist Information **Redwood Empire Association** (785 Market St., 15th floor, San Francisco 94103, tel. 415/543–8334). The *Redwood Empire Visitors' Guide* is available free at the office or for $2 by mail.

Napa Chamber of Commerce (1556 1st St., Napa 94559, tel. 707/226–7455).

Sonoma Valley Visitors Bureau (453 1st St. E, Sonoma 95476, tel. 707/996–1090).

Sonoma County Convention and Visitors Bureau (10 4th St., Suite 100, Santa Rosa 95401, tel. 707/575–1191 or 800/326–7666).

Calistoga Chamber of Commerce (1458 Lincoln Ave., Calistoga 94515, tel. 707/942–6333).

Healdsburg Chamber of Commerce (217 Healdsburg Ave., Healdsburg 95448, tel. 707/433–6935 or 800/648–9922 in CA).

St. Helena Chamber of Commerce (1080 Main St., Box 124, St. Helena 94574, tel. 707/963–4456 or 800/767–8528).

Emergencies The emergency number for fire, police, ambulance, and paramedics is 911; or dial "0" for operator and ask to be connected with the appropriate agency.

Exploring

There are three major paths through the Wine Country: U.S. 101 north from Santa Rosa, Highways 12 and 121 through Sonoma County, and Highway 29 north from Napa.

From San Francisco, cross the Golden Gate Bridge and follow Highway 101 to Santa Rosa and points north. Or cross the Golden Gate, go north on Highway 101, east on Highway 37, and north on Highway 121 into Sonoma. Yet another route runs over the San Francisco Bay Bridge and along I–80 to Vallejo, where Highway 29 leads north to Napa.

If you approach the Wine Country from the east, you'll travel along I–80 and then turn northwest on Highway 12 for a 10-minute drive through a hilly pass to Highway 29. From the north, take Highway 101 south to Geyserville, turn southeast on Highway 128, and drive down into the Napa Valley.

Wineries

Choosing which of the 400 or so wineries to visit will be difficult, and the range of opportunities makes it tempting to make multiple stops. Being adventurous will pay off. The wineries along the more frequented arteries of the Napa Valley tend to charge nominal fees for tasting, but in Sonoma County, where there is less tourist traffic, fees are the exception rather than the rule. In Sonoma, you are more likely to run into a wine-grower who is willing to spend part of an afternoon in convivial conversation than you are along the main drag of Napa Valley, where the waiter serving yards of bar has time to do little more than keep track of the rows of glasses.

Unless otherwise noted, visits to the wineries listed are free.

Highway 29 The town of Napa is the gateway into the famous valley, with its unrivaled climate and neat rows of vineyards. The towns in the area are small, and their Victorian Gothic architecture adds to the self-contained and separate feeling that permeates the valley.

A few miles north of Napa is the small town of Yountville. Turn west off Highway 2 at the Veterans Home exit and then up California Drive to **Domaine Chandon,** owned by the French champagne producer Moet-Hennessy and Louis Vuitton. You can tour the sleek modern facilities of this beautifully maintained property and sample flutes of the *methode champenoise* sparkling wine. Champagne is $4 per glass, the hors d'oeuvres are complimentary, and there is an elegant restaurant. *California Dr., Yountville, tel. 707/944–2280. Restaurant closed Mon.–Tues. Nov.–Apr. No dinner Mon.–Tues. May–Oct. Tours daily 11–5 except Mon.–Tues., Nov.–Apr. Closed major holidays.*

Vintage 1870, a 22-acre complex of boutiques, restaurants, and gourmet stores is on the east side of Highway 29. The vine-covered brick buildings were built in 1870 and originally housed a winery, livery stable, and distillery. The adjacent **Vintage Cafe** is housed in the depot Samuel Brannan built in 1868 for his privately owned Napa Valley Railroad; the remodeled railroad cars of the **Napa Valley Railway Inn** accommodate guests (*see* Lodging, below).

Washington Square, at the north end of Yountville, is a new complex of shops and restaurants; **Pioneer Cemetery,** where the town's founder George Yount is buried, is across the street.

Many premier wineries lie along the route from Yountville to St. Helena.

At **Robert Mondavi,** tasters are required to take the 40–60 minute tour before they imbibe. There are concerts on the grounds during the summer. *7801 St. Helena Hwy., Oakville, tel. 707/*

The Wine Country

Beringer, **16**
Buena Vista, **26**
Charles Krug, **14**
Chateau Montelena, **9**
Christian Brothers, **15**
Clos du Bois, **4**
Clos du Val, **22**
Clos Pegase, **10**
Davis Bynum, **7**
Domaine Chandon, **20**
Freemark Abbey, **13**
Glen Ellen, **23**
Gloria Ferrer, **24**
Hans Kornell, **12**
Hop Kiln, **5**
Korbel, **8**
Lambert Bridge, **1**
Lytton Springs, **2**
Robert Mondavi, **19**
Piper Sonoma, **6**
Robert Stemmler, **3**
Rutherford Hill, **18**
Sebastiani, **25**
Stag's Leap
Winery, **21**
Sterling, **11**
V. Sattui, **17**

Geyserville

Healdsburg

River

Russian

Windsor

Mark West
Springs

Fulton

SANTA ROSA

Laguna

de
Santa Rosa

Sebastopol

Cotati

0   4 miles
0   6 km

Robert Louis
Stevenson
State Park

Pope Valley

Lake
Berryessa

9

29

Petrified Forest Trail

10

Calistoga

29

11

128

12

N A P A

13

14

St. Helena

15

16

18

17

Lake
Hennessey

128

Santa Rosa Creek

Oakmont

Sonoma Hwy.

Rutherford

Napa River

Silverado Trail

V A L L E Y

12

Kenwood

19 Oakville

Oakville Grade

21

22

23 Glen Ellen

Jack London
State Historic
Park

12

Arnold Dr.

S O N O M A   M T S.

20 Yountville

29

N A P A

Boyes Hot Springs

25 **26**

24

S O N O M A

121

963–9611. Open daily 10–4:30. Reservations advised in summer. Closed major holidays.

The **Charles Krug Winery** opened in 1861 when Count Haraszthy loaned Krug a small cider press. It is the oldest winery in the Napa Valley. Run by the Peter Mondavi family, it offers vineyard tours on Friday mornings and has a gift shop. *2800 N. Main St., St. Helena, tel. 707/963–5057. Open daily 10–5. Closed major holidays.*

The wine made at **V. Sattui** is sold only on the premises; the tactic draws crowds, as does the huge delicatessen with its exotic cheeses. Award-winning wines include Dry Johannisberg Rieslings, Zinfandels and Madeiras. *Main St. at White La., St. Helena, tel. 707/963–7774. Open daily 9–5. Tours by appointment. Closed Christmas.*

The town of St. Helena boasts many Victorian buildings; don't overlook the **Silverado Museum,** two blocks east from Main Street on Adams, with Robert Louis Stevenson memorabilia, including first editions, manuscripts, and photographs. *1490 Library La., tel. 707/963–3757. Admission free. Open Tues.–Sun. noon–4. Closed major holidays.*

Beringer Vineyards has been operating continually since 1876. Tastings are held in the Rhine House mansion, where hand-carved oak and walnut and stained glass show Belgian Art Nouveau at its most opulent. The Beringer brothers, Frederick and Joseph, built the mansion in 1883 for the princely sum of $30,000. Tours include a visit to the deep limestone tunnels in which the wines mature. *2000 Main St., St. Helena, tel. 707/963–4812. Open daily 9:30–5. Closed major holidays.*

Christian Brothers Greystone Cellars is housed in an imposing stone building, built in 1889 and recently renovated. There are tours every half hour, displays on wine-barrel making, and an unusual collection of corkscrews. *2555 Main St., St. Helena, tel. 707/967–3112. Open daily 10–5. Closed major holidays.*

Freemark Abbey Winery was founded in the 1880s by Josephine Tychson, the first woman to establish a winery in California. *3022 St. Helena Hwy. N, St. Helena, tel. 707/963–9694. Open daily 10–4:30. One tour daily at 2 PM.*

The **Hurd Beeswax Candle Factory** is next door, with two restaurants and a gift shop that specializes in handcrafted candles made on the premises.

The **Sterling Vineyards** lies on a hilltop to the east as you near Calistoga. The pristine white Mediterranean-style buildings are reached by an enclosed gondola from the valley floor; the view from the tasting room is superb. *1111 Dunaweal La., Calistoga, tel. 707/942–5151. Tram fee: $5 for adults, children under 16 free. Open daily 10:30–4:30. Closed major holidays.*

At **Clos Pegase,** neoclassicism sets the tone. The new winery, designed by architect Michael Graves, the exemplar of postmodernism, and commissioned by Jan Schrem, a publisher and art collector, pays homage to art, wine, and mythology. *1060 Dunaweal La., Calistoga, tel. 707/942–4981. Open 10:30–4:30. Closed major holidays.*

Calistoga, at the head of the Napa Valley, is noted for its mineral water, hot mineral springs, mud baths, steam baths, and massages. The Calistoga Hot Springs Resort was founded in

1859 by the maverick entrepreneur Sam Brannan, whose ambition was to found "the Saratoga of California." He tripped up over the name at a formal banquet, and it stuck. One of his cottages, preserved as the **Sharpsteen Museum,** has a magnificent diorama of the resort in its heyday. *1311 Washington St., tel. 707/942–5911. Donations accepted. Open May–Oct., daily 10–4; Nov.–Apr., daily noon–4.*

Chateau Montelena, a vine-covered building built in 1882, is set in Chinese-inspired gardens complete with a lake, red pavilions, and arched bridges. It's a romantic spot for a picnic if you reserve ahead. *1429 Tubbs La., Calistoga, tel. 707/942–5105. Open daily 10–4. Tours at 11 and 2 by appointment only.*

The **Silverado Trail,** which runs parallel to Highway 29, takes you away from the madding crowd to some distinguished wineries as you travel north from Napa:

Clos du Val. Bernard Portet, the French owner, produces a celebrated Cabernet Sauvignon. *5330 Silverado Trail, tel. 707/252–6711. Open daily 10–4:30.*
Stag's Leap Wine Cellars. The Cabernet Sauvignon was rated higher than many venerable Bordeaux wines at a blind tasting in Paris in 1976. *5766 Silverado Trail, tel. 707/944–2020. Open daily 10–4. Tours by appointment. Closed major holidays.*
Rutherford Hill Winery. The wine ages in French oak barrels stacked in more than 30,000 square feet of caves. You can tour the nation's largest such facility and picnic on the grounds. *200 Rutherford Hill Rd., Rutherford, tel. 707/963–7194. Open weekdays 10–4:30, weekends 10–5. Tours on the half hour 11:30–3:30. Cave tours at 11:30, 1, 2:30.*
Hanns Kornell Champagne Cellars. Kornell opened his winery in 1952; he still checks in on the operation run by his family. *1091 Larkmead Ln., just east of Hwy. 29, 4 mi north of St. Helena, tel. 707/963–1237. Open daily 10–4:30.*

The **Calistoga Soaring Center** will give you a bird's-eye view of the entire valley, offering rides in gliders and biplanes, as well as tandem skydiving. *1546 Lincoln Ave., tel. 707/942–5000. Fee: $70–$160. Open daily 9 AM–sunset, weather permitting.*

You don't have to be a guest at a spa to experience a mud bath. At **Dr. Wilkinson's Hot Springs** the $27 fee includes individual mineral-water showers and a mineral-water whirlpool, followed by time in the steam room and a blanket wrap. For $49, you also get a half-hour massage. Reservations are recommended. *1507 Lincoln Ave., Calistoga, tel. 707/942–4102. Open daily 8:30–3:30.*

Highway 12   Rustic Sonoma is anchored by its past. It is the site of the last and the northernmost of the 21 missions established by the Franciscan order of Fra Junipero Serra, and its central plaza includes the largest group of old adobes north of Monterey. The **Mission San Francisco Solano,** whose chapel and school labored to bring Christianity to the Indians, is now a museum that contains a collection of 19th-century watercolors. *114 Spain St. E, tel. 707/938–1519. Admission: $2 adults, $1 children 6–17; includes the Sonoma Barracks on the central plaza and General Vallejo's home, Lachryma Montis (see below). Open daily 10–5. Closed Thanksgiving, Christmas, New Year's Day.*

Time Out   The four-block **Sonoma Plaza** is the largest of its kind in California. An inviting array of shops and food stores look out onto the shady park and attract gourmets from miles around. Many pick up the makings for a first-rate picnic. The **French Bakery** (466 1st St. E) is famous for its sourdough bread and cream puffs. The **Sonoma Sausage Co.** (453 1st St. W) produces a mind-boggling selection of bratwurst, bologna, boudin, bangers, and other Old World sausages. There are good cold cuts, too. The **Sonoma Cheese Factory** (2 Spain St.), run by the same family for four generations, makes Sonoma jack cheese and a tangy new creation, Sonoma Teleme. You can peer through the glass windows at the cheese-making process: great swirling baths of milk and curds and the wheels of cheese being pressed flat to dry.

A few blocks west (and quite a hike) is the tree-lined approach to **Lachryma Montis,** which General Mariano Vallejo, the last Mexican governor of California, built for his large family in 1851. The Victorian Gothic house is secluded in the midst of beautiful gardens; opulent Victorian furnishings, including a white marble fireplace in every room, are particularly noteworthy. The state purchased the home in 1933. *Spain St. W, tel. 707/938–1578. Admission: $2 adults, $1 children 6–17. Open daily 10–5. Closed Thanksgiving, Christmas, New Year's Day.*

The **Sebastiani Vineyards,** planted by Franciscans of the Sonoma Mission in 1825 and later owned by General Vallejo, were bought by Samuele Sebastiani in 1904. The Sebastianis recently helped popularize "blush" wines, and Sylvia Sebastiani has recorded her good Italian home cooking in a family recipe book, *Mangiamo.* Tours include an unusual collection of impressive carved oak casks. *389 4th St. E, tel. 707/938–5532. Open daily 10–5. Closed major holidays.*

The landmark **Buena Vista Winery** (follow signs from the Plaza), set among towering trees and fountains, is a must-see in Sonoma. This is where, in 1857, Count Agoston Haraszthy de Mokcsa laid the basis for modern California wine making, bucking the conventional wisdom that vines should be planted on well-watered ground by planting on well-drained hillsides. Chinese laborers dug the cool aging tunnels 100 feet into the hillside, and the limestone they extracted was used for the main house. Although the wines are produced elsewhere today, there are tours, a gourmet shop, art gallery, wine museum, and great picnic spots. *18000 Old Winery Rd., tel. 707/938–1266. Open daily 10–5.*

In the Carneros region of the Sonoma Valley, south of Sonoma, the wines at **Gloria Ferrer Champagne Caves** are aged in a "cava," or cellar, where several feet of earth maintain a constant temperature. *23555 Hwy. 121, tel. 707/996–7256. Tasting $3.50. Open daily 10:30–5:30.*

The well-known **Glen Ellen Winery** uses watercolors painted by Jan Haraszthy, one of the count's descendants, on its labels. The originals hang in the tasting room. *1883 London Ranch Rd., Glen Ellen, tel. 707/935–3000. Open daily 10–4:30.*

North of Sonoma, through the Valley of the Moon and in the hills above Glen Ellen, is **Jack London State Historic Park.** The House of Happy Walls is a museum of London's effects, including his collection of South Sea artifacts. The ruins of Wolf House, which London designed and which mysteriously burned down just before he was to move into it, lie nearby, and

London is buried there. *2400 London Ranch Rd., tel. 707/938-5216. Parking: $5 per car, $4 per car driven by senior citizen. Park open daily 8–sunset, museum 10–5. Museum closed Thanksgiving, Christmas, New Year's Day.*

Highway 101 Santa Rosa is the Wine Country's largest city and your best bet for a moderately priced hotel room, especially if you haven't reserved in advance.

The **Luther Burbank Memorial Gardens** commemorate the great botanist, who lived and worked on these grounds for 50 years, single-handedly developing modern techniques of hybridization. Arriving as a young man from New England, he wrote: "I firmly believe . . . that this is the chosen spot of all the earth, as far as nature is concerned." The Santa Rosa plum, the Shasta daisy, and the lily of the Nile agapanthus are among the 800 or so plants he developed or improved. In the dining room of his house, a Webster's Dictionary of 1946 lies open to a page on which the verb "burbank" is defined as "to modify and improve plant life." *Santa Rosa and Sonoma Aves., tel. 707/524–5445. Gardens free, open daily 8–5. Home tours: $1, children under 12 free; open Apr.–Oct., Wed.–Sun. 10–3:30.*

The wineries of Sonoma County are located along winding roads and are not immediately obvious to the casual visitor; a tour of the vineyards that lie along the Russian River is a leisurely and especially bucolic experience. For a map of the area, contact Russian River Wine Road (Box 46, Healdsburg, 95448, tel. 707/433–6782).

For a historical overview, you could start at the imposing **Korbel Champagne Cellars,** with their photographic documents housed in a former stop of the North West Pacific Railway. *13250 River Rd., Guerneville, tel. 707/887–2294. Open Oct.–Apr., daily 9–4:30; May–Sept., daily 9–5.*

Traveling down the River Road east of Guerneville, turn left down Westside Road and follow it as it winds past a number of award-winning wineries.

Davis Bynum Winery, an up-and-coming label, offers a full line of varietal wines that have done well in recent competitions. *8075 Westside Rd., Healdsburg, tel. 707/433–5852. Open daily 10–5.*

The **Hop Kiln Winery** is located in an imposing hop-drying barn built during the early 1900s and used as the backdrop for such films as the 1960 *Lassie* with James Stewart. *6050 Westside Rd., Healdsburg, tel. 707/433–6491. Open daily 10–5.*

Lambert Bridge produces some superbly elegant Cabernet Sauvignons and Merlots. *4085 W. Dry Creek Rd., Healdsburg, tel. 707/433–5855. Open daily 10–4:30.*

The **Robert Stemmler Winery** draws on German traditions of wine-making and specializes in Pinot noir. There are picnic facilities on the grounds. *3805 Lambert Bridge Rd., Healdsburg (Dry Creek Rd. exit from Hwy. 101, northwest 3 mi to Lambert Bridge Rd.), tel. 707/433–6334. Open daily 10:30–4:30.*

Lytton Springs Winery produces the archetype of the Sonoma Zinfandel, a dark, fruity wine with a high alcohol content. There is still dispute over the origin of this varietal and whether it was transplanted from stock in New England, but the vines themselves are distinctive, gnarled, and stocky, many of them over a century old. *650 Lytton Springs Rd., Healdsburg, tel. 707/433–7721. Open daily 10–4.*

In Healdsburg, back on Highway 101, is **Clos du Bois,** wine-making at its most high-tech. You can tour by appointment, but you'd do better to concentrate on sampling the fine estate wines of the Alexander and Dry Creek valleys that are made here. *5 Fitch St., tel. 707/433–5576. Open daily 10–5.*

South of Healdsburg, off Highway 101, are the **Piper Sonoma Cellars,** a state-of-the-art winery that specializes in champagne. *11447 Old Redwood Hwy., Healdsburg, tel. 707/433–8843. Open daily 10–5.*

Time Out In case you've had enough wine for the day, **Kozlowski's Raspberry Farm** (5566 Gravenstein, Hwy. N. 116), in Forestville, makes jams of every berry imaginable. Also in Forestville, **Brother Juniper's** (6544 Front St., Hwy. 116, tel. 707/887–7908) makes a heavenly *Struan* bread of wheat, corn, oats, brown rice, and bran. *Open Mon.–Sat. 9–4:30.*

What to See and Do with Children

In the **Bale Grist Mill State Historic Park** there is a flour mill powered by a 36-foot overshot water wheel, erected by Dr. Edward Turner Bale in 1846 and since restored. Hiking trails lead from the access road to the mill pond. *3 mi north of St. Helena on Hwy. 29, tel. 707/942–4575. Day use: $2 adults, $1 children 7–18. Open daily 10–5.*

Old Faithful Geyser of California is a 60-foot tower of steam and vapor that erupts about every 40 minutes; the pattern is disrupted if there's an earthquake in the offing. One of just three regularly erupting geysers in the world, it is fed by an underground river that heats to 350° F. The spout lasts three minutes. Picnic facilities are available. *1299 Tubbs La., 1 mi north of Calistoga, tel. 707/942–6463. Admission: $3.50 adults, $2 children 6–11. Open daily 9–6 during daylight saving time, 9–5 in winter.*

In the **Petrified Forest** volcanic eruptions of Mount St. Helena 6 million years ago uprooted the gigantic redwoods, covered them with volcanic ash, and infiltrated the trees with silicas and minerals, causing petrification. There is a museum, and picnic facilities are available. *4100 Petrified Forest Rd., 5 mi west of Calistoga, tel. 707/942–6667. Admission: $3 adults, $2 senior citizens, $1 children 4–11. Open daily 10–6 in summer, 10–5 in winter.*

A scale steam train at **Train Town** runs for 20 minutes through a forested park with trestles, bridges, and miniature animals. *20264 Broadway, 1 mi south of Sonoma Plaza, tel. 707/938–3912. Admission: $2.40 adults, $1.80 children under 16 and senior citizens. Open mid-June–Labor Day daily 10:30–5; Sept.–mid-June, weekends and holidays 10:30–5:30. Closed Christmas.*

Howarth Memorial Park, in Santa Rosa, has a lake where canoes, rowboats, paddleboats, and small sailboats can be rented for $3–$4 an hour. The children's area has a playground, pony rides, petting zoo, merry-go-round, and a miniature train. Fishing, tennis, and hiking trails are also available. *Summer-*

field Rd. off Montgomery Rd., tel. 707/539–1499. Amusements: 25¢–50¢. Park open daily; children's area open Wed.–Sun. in summer, weekends in spring and fall.

Off the Beaten Track

You'll see breathtaking views of both the Sonoma and Napa valleys along the hairpin turns of the **Oakville Grade,** which twists along the range dividing the two valleys. The surface of the road is fine, and if you're comfortable with mountain driving, you'll enjoy this half-hour excursion. Trucks are advised not to take this route.

Robert Louis Stevenson State Park, on Highway 53, 3 miles northeast of Calistoga, encompasses the summit of Mount St. Helena. It was here, in an abandoned bunkhouse of the Silverado Mine, that Stevenson and his bride, Fanny Osbourne, spent their honeymoon in the summer of 1880. The stay inspired Stevenson's "The Silverado Squatters," and Spyglass Hill in *Treasure Island* is thought to be a portrait of Mount St. Helena. The park's 3,000 acres are undeveloped except for a fire trail leading to the site of the cabin, which is marked with a marble tablet, and then on to the summit. Picnicking is permitted, but fires are not.

Shopping

Most wineries will ship purchases. Don't expect bargains at the wineries themselves, where prices are generally as high as at retail outlets. Local residents report that the area's supermarkets stock a wide selection of local wines at lower prices. Gift shops in the larger wineries offer the ultimate in gourmet items—you could easily stock up on early Christmas presents.

Sports

Ballooning This sport has fast become part of the scenery in the Wine Country, and many hotels arrange excursions. Most flights take place soon after sunrise, when the calmest, coolest time of day offers maximum lift and soft landings. Prices depend on the duration of the flight, number of passengers, and services (some companies provide pickup at your lodging, champagne brunch after the flight, etc.). You should expect to spend about $150 per person. Companies that provide flights include **Balloons Above the Valley** (Box 3838, Napa 94558, tel. 707/253–2222 or 800/464–6824 in northern CA); **Napa Valley Balloons** (Box 2860, Yountville 94599, tel. 707/253–2224 or 800/253–2224 in CA); and **Once in a Lifetime** (Box 795, Calistoga 94515, tel. 707/942–6541 or 800/722–6665 in CA).

Bicycling One of the best ways to experience the countryside is on two wheels, and the Eldorado bike trail through the area is considered one of the best. Reasonably priced rentals are available in most towns.

Golf Though the weather is mild year-round, rain may occasionally prevent your teeing off in the winter months. Call to check on greens fees at **Fountaingrove Country Club** (1525 Fountaingrove Pkwy., Santa Rosa, tel. 707/579–4653); **Oakmont Inn and Golf Course** (7025 Oakmont Dr., Santa Rosa, tel. 707/539–0415 or 548–2454); or **Silverado Country Club** (1600 Atlas Peak Rd., Napa, tel. 707/257–0200).

Dining

by Bruce David Colen

A number of the Wine Country's kitchens are the domains of nationally prominent chefs. The emphasis everywhere on the freshest ingredients goes hand in hand with local bounty: vegetables and fruits, seafood, lamb, and poultry. While some of the restaurants are expensive (dinner at Auberge du Soleil or the Silverado Country Club may run more than $50 per person), wonderful local foods are available for picnics.

With few exceptions (which are noted), dress is informal. Where reservations are indicated to be essential, you may need to reserve a week or more ahead during the summer and early-fall harvest seasons.

The most highly recommended restaurants are indicated by a star ★.

Category	Cost*
Very Expensive	over $35
Expensive	$25–$35
Moderate	$16–$25
Inexpensive	under $16

per person, excluding drinks, service, and 6.5% sales tax

The following credit card abbreviations are used: AE, American Express; D, Discover; DC, Diners Club; MC, MasterCard; V, Visa.

Calistoga
Moderate

Calistoga Inn. With the atmosphere and appeal of a village tavern (but the talents of a big-city chef), this restaurant has nicely prepared California cuisine and excellent fish dishes. First-rate local wines are also featured. *1250 Lincoln Ave., tel. 707/ 942–4101. Reservations advised. Dress: informal. Wine and beer. MC, V.*

Alex's. This family-style restaurant features prime rib and New York steaks. If you're not in the mood for steak, try one of the several fish entrées or the daily seafood special. Don't pass up the family-recipe cheesecake. *1437 Lincoln Ave., tel. 707/ 942–6868. Full bar. AE, MC, V. Closed Mon. Dinner only.*

Geyserville
Very Expensive
★

Château Souverain Restaurant at the Winery. There is a gorgeous view of the Alexander Valley vineyards from the dining room and terrace. The California/Continental menu is imaginative: Sonoma lamb loin with soy mustard ginger glaze; black peppercorn rosemary lamb essence and Japanese eggplant; grilled marinated quail with smoked pear puree, pancetta, and basil quail essence. *400 Souverain Rd. (take Independence La. exit west from Hwy. 101), tel. 707/433–3141. Reservations advised. Jacket required at dinner. Wine. AE, MC, V. Dinner Thurs.–Sat., lunch Tues.–Sat., Sun. brunch.*

Healdsburg
Very Expensive

Madrona Manor. The chef uses a brick oven, smokehouse, orchard, and herb and vegetable garden to enhance other fresh produce and seafood on his California menus. Dinners and Sunday brunch are served in the dining room and terrace of an 1881

Victorian mansion on a hilltop west of town. À la carte and prix fixe. *1001 Westside Rd., tel. 707/433–4231. Reservations advised. Jacket required. Wines. AE, DC, MC, V.*

Moderate **Jacob Horner.** California cuisine with an emphasis on locally grown vegetables ("no more than 2 miles from the restaurant") and fresh seafood, lamb, and duck from near at hand is the focus here. An enthusiastic owner-chef has put together a comfortable, good-looking restaurant on Healdsburg's charming town plaza. There is an extensive, award-winning wine list with 17 wines served by the glass. *106 Matheson St., tel. 707/433–3939. Reservations advised. Full bar. AE, MC, V. No dinner Mon. Closed Sun.*

Plaza Grill. Mesquite-grilled meats, fresh fish (orange roughy en papillote), espresso, and cappuccino are served at a small, attractive wine bar on Healdsburg's pretty town plaza. *109–A Plaza St., tel. 707/431–8305. Reservations advised. Beer and wine. AE, MC, V. No lunch Sat. Closed Mon. and 1st week in December.*

Napa **Silverado Country Club.** There are two dining rooms and a bar
Very Expensive and grill at this large, famous resort. Vintner's Court, with California cuisine, serves dinner only; there is a seafood buffet on Friday night and a champagne brunch on Sunday. Royal Oak serves steak, seafood, and lobster for dinner; in summer, it also serves lunch. The bar and grill is open for breakfast and lunch year-round. *1600 Atlas Peak Rd., 707/257–0200. Reservations advised. Jacket preferred at dinner. Full bar. AE, DC, MC, V.*

Inexpensive **Jonesy's Famous Steak House.** This longtime institution at the Napa County Airport is popular with private pilots throughout the West and with local people. Steaks are prepared on an open grill, with large hot rocks placed on top of them while cooking. The building is nothing special: plain and businesslike. *2044 Airport Rd., tel. 707/255–2003. Reservations accepted for groups of 6 or more. Full bar. AE, MC, V. Closed Mon., Thanksgiving, a week at Christmas, New Year's Day.*

Rutherford **Auberge du Soleil.** Sitting on the dining terrace of this hilltop
Very Expensive inn, looking down across groves of olive trees to the Napa Val-
★ ley vineyards, is the closest one can get to the atmosphere and charm of southern France without needing a passport. The mood is enhanced by a menu centered around light Provençal dishes, using the fresh produce of nearby farms. The Auberge features a fine list of wines from California, France, and Italy. It is also a 48-room inn (*see* Lodging, below). *180 Rutherford Hill Rd., tel. 707/963–1211. Jacket and tie preferred. Reservations advised. Full bar. AE, MC, V.*

St. Helena **Starmont at Meadowood.** Three-course prix-fixe dinners and an
Very Expensive extensive Napa Valley wine list with some French wines are served in this elegantly casual 65-seat restaurant that turns to the outdoors, maximizing the view over the golf course and the stands of pine trees beyond. There is terrace service in warm weather and a piano bar. Lunch and Sunday brunch April–November. *900 Meadowood La., tel. 707/963–3646. Reservations required. Jacket preferred. Full bar. AE, DC, MC, V.*

Moderate– **Abbey Restaurant.** Greek specialties, seafood, beef, lamb
Expensive shanks, and pastitsio are served at lunch and dinner; next door to Freemark Abbey. *3020 N. St. Helena Hwy. (Hwy. 29), tel. 707/963–2706. Reservations accepted. Full bar, wine. V. No*

dinner Mon.–Tues. Closed Easter, Christmas, New Year's Day.

★ **Terra.** The delightful couple who own this lovely, unpretentious restaurant, in a century-old stone foundry, learned their culinary skills at the side of chef Wolfgang Puck. Hiro Sone was head chef at LA's Spago and Lissa Doumani was the pastry chef. The menu has an enticing array of American favorites, prepared with Hiro's Japanese-French-Italian finesse: addictive baked mussels in garlic butter; sautéed Miyagi oysters with jalapeño salsa; home-smoked salmon with golden caviar; grilled quail and polenta; and sweetbreads with asparagus and wild mushrooms. Save room for Lissa's desserts. *1345 Railroad Ave., tel. 707/963–8931. Reservations advised. Jacket required. Wine and beer. AE, MC, V. Closed Tues.*

Tra Vigne. This Napa Valley fieldstone building has been turned into a barn of a trattoria, serving good pizza; pastas; and traditional Italian grilled meats, fish, and fowl. Tra Vigne has terrace dining, weather permitting. This is a meeting place for locals and tourists. *1050 Charter Oak Ave., tel. 707/963–4444. Dress: casual. Reservations advised. Full bar. MC, V. Closed July 4, Thanksgiving, Christmas.*

Moderate **Fairway Grill and Bar.** California specialties include Meadowood sandwich (with chicken-apple sausage and roasted bell pepper) and roasted breast of chicken stuffed with goat cheese. This is a light, airy, casual restaurant at the Meadowood Resort, where large windows and an outdoor terrace overlook the golf course and croquet lawns. Antique croquet mallets and tennis rackets decorate the walls. *900 Meadowood La., tel. 707/963–3646. Reservations advised. Full bar. AE, DC, MC, V. No dinner in winter.*

Inexpensive **French Laundry.** Long a favorite of surrounding wine-makers
★ for its tasty blend of French and California cooking, French Laundry is one of the most attractive wine bars in the Wine Country. *Washington and Creek Sts., tel. 707/944–2380. Reservations advised. Dress: casual. Wine and beer. MC, V. Dinner only, Wed.–Sat.*

Santa Rosa **John Ash & Co.** The thoroughly regional cuisine here empha-
Expensive sizes beauty, innovation, and the seasonality of food products
★ grown in Sonoma County. In spring, local lamb is roasted with hazelnuts and honey; in fall, farm pork is roasted with fresh figs and Gravenstein apples. There are fine desserts and an extensive wine list. Two dining rooms are in a vineyard setting next to Vintner's Inn. The restaurant also offers Sunday brunch. *4330 Barnes Rd. (River Rd. exit west from Hwy. 101), tel. 707/527–7687. Reservations advised. Jacket preferred. Wine. AE, MC, V. Closed Mon.*

Moderate **Equus.** In this handsome restaurant, the equestrian theme is carried out in redwood carvings, murals, and etched glass. A gallery of Sonoma County wines features nearly 300 bottles hand-picked by their makers. *101 Fountaingrove Pkwy., tel. 707/578–6101. Reservations advised. Jacket preferred. Full bar. AE, DC, MC, V.*

Los Robles Lodge Dining Room. The elegant 120-seat dining room specializes in tableside presentations of chateaubriand, lamb, and flaming desserts. Seafood and sautéed dishes are also featured. This 28-year-old restaurant has a loyal local following. *9255 Edwards Ave. (Steele La. exit west from Hwy.*

101), tel. 707/545–6330. Reservations advised. Jacket preferred. Full bar. AE, DC, MC, V. No lunch on major holidays.

Inexpensive **Omelette Express.** At least 300 omelet possibilities are offered in an old-fashioned restaurant in historic Railroad Square. *112 4th St., tel. 707/525–1690. No reservations. Wine and beer. MC, V. No dinner. Closed Thanksgiving, Christmas.*

Sonoma **Sonoma Mission Inn.** There are two dining rooms as well as a
Expensive poolside terrace for alfresco meals at this attractive, "contemporary country" resort. The inn is also a spa, so the menu has a wide assortment of light dishes, with the accent on fresh salads, fish, and poultry, prepared in nouvelle-California style. The annual Sonoma Wine Auction is held on the inn's grounds, so the extensive wine list comes as no surprise. *18140 Hwy. 12, Boyes Hot Springs, tel. 707/938–9000. Reservations advised. Jacket preferred at dinner. Full bar. AE, DC, MC, V.*

Moderate– **L'Esperance.** The room is small and pretty, with flowered ta-
Expensive blecloths to the floor, burgundy overcloths, and burgundy
★ chairs. There is a choice of classic French entrees, such as rack of lamb, plus a "menu gastronomique" that includes hot and cold appetizers, salad, entree, dessert, and coffee. *464 1st St. E. (down a walkway off the plaza, behind the French Bakery), tel. 707/996–2757. Reservations advised. Wine and beer. AE, MC, V.*

Piatti. On the ground floor of the recently remodeled El Dorado Hotel, a 19th-century landmark building, this is the Sonoma cousin of the Napa Valley Piatti (*see* below). This very friendly trattoria features a nice selection of grilled northern Italian items. *405 1st St. tel. 707/996–3030. Dress: casual. Full bar. MC, V.*

Moderate **Gino's Restaurant and Bar.** This relaxed, friendly eating and drinking establishment on Sonoma's plaza specializes in fresh seafood and pasta. *420 1st St., tel. 707/996–4466. Reservations advised on weekends. Dress: informal. Full bar. AE, V.*

La Casa. "Whitewashed stucco, red tile, serapes, and Mexican glass" describes this restaurant just around the corner from Sonoma's plaza. There is an extensive menu of traditional Mexican food: chimichangas, snapper Veracruz, flan for dessert, sangria to drink. *121 E. Spain St., tel. 707/996–3406. Reservations advised. Full bar. AE, DC, MC, V.*

Sonoma Hotel Dining Room. Seasonal produce and homemade ingredients are featured in this restaurant with antique oak tables and stained glass. The saloon boasts a magnificent old bar of oak and mahogany. Service in garden patio in summer. *110 W. Spain St., tel. 707/996–2996. Dress: informal. Reservations advised. Full bar. AE, MC, V. Closed Tues. and Wed. in winter.*

Yountville **Domaine Chandon.** Nouvelle seafood, pasta, beef, and lamb are
Expensive– prepared imaginatively and presented beautifully. The archi-
Very Expensive tecturally dramatic dining room has views of vineyards and
★ carefully preserved native oaks. There is also outdoor service on a tree-shaded patio. *California Dr. (no number), tel. 707/ 944–2892. Reservations essential. Jacket and tie required. Wine. AE, DC, MC, V. No dinner Mon.–Tues. year-round; no lunch Mon.–Tues. Nov.–Apr.*

Anesti's Grill and Rotisserie. Rotisserie-roasted lamb, duck, and suckling pig are specialties of this small, cheerful restaurant with two mesquite grills. *6518 Washington St., tel. 707/944–1500. Reservations advised. Full bar. AE, DC, MC, V.*

California Cafe & Grill. This is the Wine Country link of a small upscale chain serving bar and grill dishes, plus roast game and a variety of good pastas and salads. Also on the menu: chicken breast with red-pepper jam, tapas, warm apple crisp, and an extensive wine list all in a large, square room with an open kitchen. There is outdoor service on the terrace. Sunday brunch is also served. *6795 Washington St., tel. 707/944–2330. Reservations accepted. Full bar. AE, DC, MC, V.*

Mama Nina's. This homey and old-fashioned restaurant serves homemade pasta and fresh grilled fish. There's a children's menu. *6772 Washington St., tel. 707/944–2112. Reservations advised. Full bar. MC, V. Lunch weekend only. Closed Easter, Thanksgiving, Christmas Eve, Christmas Day.*

★ **Mustard's Grill.** Grilled fish, hot smoked meats, fresh local produce, and a good wine list are offered in a simple, unassuming dining room. It's very popular and crowded at prime meal times. *7399 St. Helena Hwy. (Hwy. 29, 2 mi north of Yountville), tel. 707/944–2424. Reservations essential. Dress: informal. MC, V.*

Moderate–Expensive **Piatti.** A small, stylish trattoria with a pizza oven and open kitchen, this cheery place is full of good smells and happy people. Its authentic, light Italian cooking—from the antipasti to the grilled chicken to the *tiramisu*—is the perfect cure for a jaded appetite. The pastas are the best bet. *6480 Washington St., tel. 707/944–2070. Reservations advised. Jacket required at dinner. Full bar. MC, V.*

Inexpensive **The Diner.** This is probably the best-known and most-appreciated stop-off in the Napa Valley, especially for breakfast. Be sure to have the local sausages and the house potatoes. At night, many of the specials are Mexican. *6476 Washington St., tel. 707/944–2626. No reservations; expect a wait for seating. Wine and beer. No credit cards. Closed Mon.*

Lodging

Make no mistake, staying in the Wine Country is expensive. The inns, hotels, and motels are usually exquisitely appointed, and many are fully booked long in advance of the summer season. Since Santa Rosa is the largest population center in the area, it has the largest selection of rooms, many at moderate rates. Try there if you've failed to reserve in advance or have a limited budget.

Highly recommended hotels are indicated by a star ★.

Category	Cost*
Very Expensive	over $100
Expensive	$80–$100
Moderate	$50–$80
Inexpensive	under $50

All prices are for a standard double room, excluding 7% tax.

The following credit card abbreviations are used: AE, American Express; D, Discover; DC, Diners Club; MC, MasterCard; V, Visa.

Calistoga
Expensive–
Very Expensive
★

Brannan Cottage Inn. This exquisite Victorian cottage with lacy white fretwork, large windows, and a shady porch is the only one of Sam Brannan's 1860 resort cottages still standing on its original site. The restoration is excellent and includes elegant stenciled friezes of stylized wildflowers. All rooms have private entrances. Full breakfast is included. *109 Wapoo Ave., 94515, tel. 707/942–4200. 6 rooms. MC, V.*

Mount View Hotel. This refurbished 1930s hotel provides live music and dancing on weekends. Continental breakfast in the lobby is included, and the restaurant features northern Italian cuisine. *1457 Lincoln Ave., 94515, tel. 707/942–6877. 34 rooms with bath. Facilities: pool, Jacuzzi bar, restaurant. MC, V.*

Moderate–
Expensive

Dr. Wilkinson's Hot Springs. This hot springs spa resort has been in operation for more than 40 years. Reserve ahead for weekends, when there are separate fees for mud baths, massages, facials, and steam rooms. Mid-week packages include room and full spa services. *1507 Lincoln Ave., 94515, tel. 707/942–4102. 42 rooms. Facilities: 3 mineral pools. AE, MC, V.*

Moderate

Comfort Inn Napa Valley North. All the rooms in this recently opened motel have one king- or two queen-size beds, and many have vineyard views. Continental breakfast is included. There are rooms for nonsmokers and handicapped guests, and there are senior citizen discounts. *1865 Lincoln Ave., 94515, tel. 707/942–9400 or 800/228–5150. 54 rooms with bath. Facilities: natural mineral-water pool, spa sauna, steam room, movies. AE, D, DC, MC, V.*

Mountain Home Ranch. This rustic ranch, built in 1913, is set on 300 wooded acres, with hiking trails, a creek, and a fishing lake. There is just one TV, in the dining room, and no phones. Families are welcome and there are special children's rates. In summer, the modified American plan (full breakfast and dinner) is used; otherwise Continental breakfast is included. Six simple cabins without heat are available from mid-June to Labor Day. They have a separate shower facility, and you must bring your own linens. *3400 Mountain Home Ranch Rd., 94515 (north of town on Hwy. 128, left on Petrified Forest Rd., right on Mountain Home Ranch Rd., to end; 3 mi from Hwy. 128), tel. 707/942–6616. 14 rooms with bath, 6 cabins with half bath. Facilities: 2 pools, tennis. MC, V. Closed Dec.–Jan.*

Healdsburg
Very Expensive

Madrona Manor. A splendid, three-story, 1881 Gothic mansion, carriage house, and outbuildings sit on eight wooded and landscaped acres. Mansion rooms are recommended: All nine have fireplaces, and five contain the antique furniture of the original owner. The approach to the mansion leads under a stone archway and up a flowered hill; the house overlooks the valley and vineyards. Full breakfast is included, and there's a fine restaurant on the premises that serves dinner. Pets are allowed. *1001 Westside Rd., Box 818, 95448, tel. 707/433–4231 or 800/258–4003. 21 rooms with bath. Facilities: pool, restaurant. AE, DC, MC, V.*

Moderate–
Very Expensive

Healdsburg Inn on the Plaza. This renovated 1900 brick building on the attractive town plaza has a bright solarium and a roof garden. The rooms are spacious, with quilts and pillows piled high on antique beds and clawfoot tubs complete with rubber ducks. Full breakfast, afternoon coffee and cookies, and early evening wine and popcorn are included. *110 Matheson St., Box 1196, 95448, tel. 707/433–6991. 9 rooms. MC, V.*

Moderate **Best Western Dry Creek Inn.** Movies, Continental breakfast, and a complimentary bottle of wine are included at this three-story motel in Spanish Mission style. There is a 24-hour coffee shop next door. Small pets are allowed; discounts are available for senior citizens. Direct bus service from San Francisco Airport is available. *198 Dry Creek Rd., 95448, tel. 707/433–0300 or 800/528–1234; in CA, 800/222–5784. 102 rooms with bath. Facilities: pool, spa, laundry. AE, D, DC, MC, V.*

Napa **Clarion.** This modern, comfortable, and immaculately main-
Very Expensive tained motel has a restaurant and lounge on the premises, live music in the lounge, movies, and rooms for the handicapped. Pets are allowed with a $10 fee. *3425 Solano Ave., 94558 (1 block west off Hwy. 29; take Redwood-Trancas exit), tel. 707/253–7433 or 800/333–7533. 191 rooms. Facilities: pool, spa, lighted tennis courts. AE, D, DC, MC, V.*

Silverado Country Club. This luxurious 1,200-acre resort in the hills east of the town of Napa offers cottages, kitchen apartments, and one- to three-bedroom efficiencies, many with fireplaces. There are also two dining rooms, a lounge, a sundries store, seven pools, 20 tennis courts, and two championship golf courses designed by Robert Trent Jones. Fees are charged for golf, tennis, and bike rentals. *1600 Atlas Peak Rd., 94558 (6 mi east of Napa via Hwy. 121), tel. 707/257–0200 or 800/532–0500. 277 condo units. Facilities: restaurant. AE, D, DC, MC, V.*

Expensive **Chateau.** There's a French country inn atmosphere at this modern motel which provides Continental breakfast and a social hour with wine. Movies, in-room refrigerators, facilities for the handicapped, and senior citizen discounts are available. *4195 Solano Ave., 94558 (west of and adjacent to Hwy. 29; take W. Salvador Ave. exit), tel. 707/253–9300 or 800/253–6272 in CA. 115 rooms. Facilities: pool, spa. AE, D, DC, MC, V.*

Moderate– **Best Western Inn Napa.** This immaculate modern redwood mo-
Very Expensive tel with spacious rooms has a restaurant on the premises and same-day laundry and valet service. There are suites, as well as rooms for nonsmokers and the handicapped. Small pets are allowed. *100 Soscol Ave., 94558 (Imola Ave. Hwy. 121 exit east from Hwy. 29 to junction of Hwy. 121 and Soscol), tel. 707/257–1930 or 800/528–1234. 68 rooms. Facilities: pool, spa. AE, D, DC, MC, V.*

John Muir Inn. Continental breakfast and in-room coffee are included at this new, well-equipped, three-story motel that has kitchenettes, refrigerators, movies, valet service, and some whirlpool tubs. Senior citizen discounts and rooms for nonsmokers and handicapped guests are available. *1998 Trower Ave., 94558 (adjacent to Hwy. 29, east at Trower exit), tel. 707/257–7220 or 800/522–8999 in CA. 59 rooms. Facilities: pool, spa. AE, D, DC, MC, V.*

Rutherford **Auberge du Soleil.** This luxurious French country–style inn has
Very Expensive an excellent restaurant and a spectacular view over vineyards and hills. *180 Rutherford Hill Rd., 94573, tel. 707/963–1211. 48 rooms. Facilities: pool, spa, tennis, masseuse. AE, MC, V.*

Rancho Caymus Inn. Early California-Spanish in style, this inn has well-maintained gardens and large suites with kitchens and whirlpool baths. There are home-baked breads and an emphasis on decorative handicrafts, and there are unusual beehive fireplaces, tile murals, stoneware basins, and llama blankets. There is a two-night minimum stay April 1–Nov. 30. *1140 Rutherford Rd., 94573 (junction of Hwys. 29 and 128), tel. 707/ 963–1777 or 800/845–1777. 26 rooms. Facilities: restaurant. MC, V.*

St. Helena
Very Expensive

Meadowood Resort. The resort is set on 256 wooded acres, with a golf course, croquet lawns, and hiking trails. The hotel is a rambling country lodge reminiscent of turn-of-the-century Rhode Island, and separate bungalow suites are clustered on the hillside. Half of the suites and some rooms have fireplaces. *900 Meadowood La., 94574, tel. 707/963–3646 or 800/458–8080. 82 rooms. Facilities: 2 restaurants, lounge, room service, 2 pools, saunas, 9–hole and par golf courses, tennis, masseuse, wine school. AE, DC, MC, V.*

Expensive–
Very Expensive

Harvest Inn. This English Tudor inn with many fireplaces overlooks an active, 14-acre vineyard and an award-winning landscape. The furnishings are antique, but there are also wet bars, refrigerators, fireplaces, and a wine bar and dance floor in the lobby "Great Room." Dogs are allowed for a $5 fee. *1 Main St., 94574, tel. 707/963–9463 or 800/950–8466. 55 rooms. Facilities: 2 pools, 2 Jacuzzis. AE, D, MC, V.*

Hotel St. Helena. This restored 1881 stone hostelry, furnished with antiques and decorated in rich tones of burgundy, aims at Old World comfort. Continental breakfast is included. Smoking not encouraged. *1309 Main St., 94574, tel. 707/963–4388. 14 rooms with bath, 4 rooms with shared bath. AE, DC, MC, V.*

Moderate–
Expensive

Cinnamon Bear Bed and Breakfast. Built in 1904 as a wedding gift, this house is decorated with a period flavor, from the antique quilts and toys to the clawfoot tubs. Full breakfast is included. Rooms for nonsmokers are available. *1407 Kearney St., 94574 (from Main St., Hwy. 29, turn west on Adams St., then 2 blocks to Kearney), tel. 707/963–4653. 4 rooms with bath. MC, V.*

Moderate

El Bonita Motel. This old-fashioned roadside motel was recently remodeled in the Art Deco style. The decor is white and gray, with streaks of flamingo and blue; a neon calla lily graces the north side. The small rooms have soft, smart furnishings. There are 16 rooms in the main motel and six garden rooms with kitchenettes. *195 Main St., 94574, tel. 707/963–3216 or 800/541–3284. 22 rooms. Facilities: pool. AE, MC, V.*

Santa Rosa
Very Expensive

Vintner's Inn. Set in 50 acres of vineyards, this recently built inn has large rooms, French Provincial furnishings, and woodburning fireplaces. Movies and breakfast are included, and there is an excellent restaurant on the premises. Rooms for the handicapped are available, as are VCRs, for a small fee. *4350 Barnes Rd., 95403 (River Rd. exit west from Hwy. 101), tel. 707/575–7350 or 800/421–2584 in CA. 44 rooms. Facilities: spa. AE, DC, MC, V.*

Expensive
★

Fountaingrove Inn. This new, elegant, and comfortable inn boasts a redwood sculpture, *Equus III*, and a wall of cascading water in the lobby. Rooms have work spaces with modem jacks. Buffet breakfast is included, and there's an exceptional restaurant. Senior citizen discounts and rooms for nonsmokers and the handicapped are available. *101 Fountaingrove Pkwy., 95403, tel. 707/578–6101 or 800/222–6101 in CA. 85 rooms. Facilities: lap pool, spa, room service, movies. AE, DC, MC, V.*

Moderate– **Doubletree Hotel.** Many rooms in this large, modern, multi-
Very Expensive story hotel on a hilltop have views of the valley and vineyards;
the Burgundy, Cabernet, Chardonnay, Chablis, and Riesling
buildings have especially fine views. The spacious rooms have
work-size desks and functional, comfortable furnishings.
There are rooms for nonsmokers and the handicapped, and patio rooms overlooking the pool. Golf and tennis are available at
the adjacent Fountaingrove Country Club for additional fees;
there's a courtesy shuttle to Santa Rosa airport and a jogging
path. *3555 Round Barn Blvd., 95401 (Old Redwood Hwy., exit
east from Hwy. 101), tel. 707/523–7555 or 800/833–9595. 252
rooms with bath. Facilities: restaurant, bar, lounge, pool, spa,
room service, valet service. AE, D, DC, MC, V.*

Moderate– **Los Robles Lodge.** This pleasant, relaxed motel has comfort-
Expensive able rooms overlooking a grassy, landscaped pool. Rooms for
★ the handicapped and nonsmokers are available. Pets are
allowed, except in executive rooms, which have Jacuzzis. *925
Edwards Ave., 95401 (Steele La. exit west from Hwy. 101), tel.
707/545–6330 or 800/255–6330. 105 rooms. Facilities: restaurant, coffee shop, lounge with nightly entertainment, pool, outdoor Jacuzzi, laundry. AE, D, DC, MC. V.*

Inexpensive **Best Western Hillside Inn.** Some rooms at this cozy, nicely landscaped, small motel have balconies or patios. Kitchenettes and
suites are available. Pets are allowed. *2901 4th St., 95409 (at
Farmers La., 2 mi east off Hwy. 101 on Hwy. 12), tel. 707/546–
9353 or 800/528–1234. 35 rooms. Facilities: pool, restaurant,
sauna, shuffleboard. AE, DC, MC, V.*

Sonoma **Sonoma Mission Inn.** This elegantly restored 1920s resort
Very Expensive blends Mediterranean and old-California architecture. It's early Hollywood—you half expect Gloria Swanson to sweep
through the lobby. The location is unexpected, off the main
street of tiny, anything but posh, Boyes Hot Springs. The
grounds are nicely landscaped and the accommodations include
suites. This is the home of the *Spa Food* cookbook, and there are
extensive spa facilities (fee for fitness classes and treatments).
*18140 Sonoma Hwy. (Hwy. 12 north of Sonoma), Box 1447,
95476, tel. 707/938–9000 or 800/358–9022, 800/862–4945 in CA.
170 rooms. Facilities: restaurant, coffee shop, 2 bars, lounge, 2
pools, weight room, steam room, Jacuzzis, sauna, tennis. AE,
DC, MC, V.*

Moderate–Expensive **Best Western Sonoma Valley Inn.** Just one block from the town
plaza, this new motel features balconies, handcrafted furni-
ture, wood-burning fireplaces, and whirlpool baths. Continental breakfast and a complimentary split of wine are included.
Senior discounts, kitchenettes, and rooms for nonsmokers and
the handicapped are available. *550 2nd St. W, 95476, tel. 707/
938–9200 or 800/334–5784 in CA. 72 rooms. Facilities: pool,
whirlpool, laundry. AE, D, DC, MC, V.*
Sonoma Hotel. At the edge of Sonoma's plaza, this hotel, built
in 1870, has been carefully restored and each of its rooms furnished with antiques in an attempt to re-create a Victorian
country inn. There's no TV, but Continental breakfast and a
complimentary split of wine are included. The restaurant specializes in California country cuisine. *110 W. Spain St., 95476,
tel. 707/996–2996. 5 rooms with bath, 12 with shared bath. Facilities: bar. AE, MC, V.*

Windsor
Moderate

Redwood Royale Hometel. This clean, no-frills motel is a bargain for an economy-minded family. Each unit has a bedroom, bath, kitchen, and living/dining area, and the rate is the same for one to four persons. Kitchen items are available for rent. The motel is on 2½ acres, and there is secured parking for RVs. *8900 Bell Rd., 95492, tel. 707/838–9771. 80 units. Facilities: pool, laundry. AE, MC, V.*

Yountville
Very Expensive

Vintage Inn. All rooms have fireplaces, whirlpool baths, refrigerators, private verandas or patios, hand-painted fabrics, window seats, and shuttered windows in this luxurious new inn. Continental breakfast with champagne, a complimentary bottle of wine, and afternoon tea are provided. Bike rental in season and hot-air ballooning are available. *6541 Washington St., 94599, tel. 707/944–1112; 800/982–5539; in CA, 800/351–1133. 80 rooms with bath. Facilities: lap pool, spa, tennis. AE, DC, MC, V.*

Napa Valley Lodge. Spacious rooms overlook vineyards and valley in this hacienda-style lodge with tile roofs, covered walkways, balconies, patios, and colorful gardens. Freshly brewed coffee is provided in rooms, as well as Continental breakfast and the morning paper. Some rooms have fireplaces. Kitchenettes and rooms for nonsmokers and the handicapped are available. *Madison St. and Hwy. 29, Box L, 94599, tel. 707/944–2468 or 800/368–2468. 55 rooms. Facilities: exercise room, pool, spa, sauna, valet service, refrigerators. AE, D, DC, MC, V.*

Expensive

Napa Valley Railway Inn. This unusual establishment is made of nine vintage railcars on the original track of the Napa Valley Railroad. Each car is now an air-conditioned suite, with sitting area, queen-size brass beds, skylights, bay windows, and full tiled baths. Wine and coffee are provided. *6503 Washington St., 94599, tel. 707/944–2000. 9 rooms with bath. MC, V.*

The Arts and Nightlife

Galleries throughout the Wine Country display the work of local artists: painters, sculptors, potters, and jewelry makers. The **Luther Burbank Performing Arts Center** in Santa Rosa (tel. 707/546–3600, box office open Mon.–Sat. noon–6) has a full calendar of concerts, plays, and other performances, with both locally and internationally known performers. Wineries often schedule concerts and music festivals during the summer.

Nightlife in the Wine Country is best savored in a leisurely, elegant dinner at one of the restaurants for which the area is justly famous. Many of the larger hotels and motels feature live music on weekends.

6 San Francisco

The Golden Gate, sailboats on the bay, the hills and the cable cars, restored Victorian "Painted Ladies," and the whiteness of the fog—if these are your dreams, they will come to life in San Francisco. In this last decade of the 20th century, however, the city is facing some hard realities: the shift of economic power to Southern California, the recession, the AIDS epidemic, and, most recently, a reminder that the forces of nature still reign supreme—the 1989 earthquake. The quake's most lingering effect is on traffic in the area. The Embarcadero Freeway in San Francisco and Interstate 880 in Oakland had to be demolished and permanent replacements are years away, with traffic diverted onto surface roads. Visitors planning on driving to and around the area should consult the AAA or the San Francisco Convention and Visitors Bureau for the latest word on road conditions.

Arriving and Departing

By Plane
Airports and Airlines
San Francisco International Airport is just south of the city, off U.S. 101. American carriers serving San Francisco are **Alaska Air, American, Continental, Delta, Southwest, TWA, United,** and **USAir.** International carriers include **Air Canada, Canadian Pacific, Japan Air Lines, British Airways, China Airlines, Qantas, Air New Zealand, Mexicana,** and **Pan American.** Many of these same airlines serve the Oakland Airport, which is across the bay but not much farther away from downtown San Francisco (via I-880 and I-80), although traffic on the Bay Bridge may at times make travel time longer.

From the Airport to Downtown
SFO Airporter (tel. 415/495–8404) provides bus service between downtown and the airport, making the round of downtown hotels. Buses run every 20 minutes from 5 AM to midnight, from the lower level outside the baggage claim area. The fare is $5 one-way.

For $9, **Supershuttle** will take you from the airport to anywhere within the city limits of San Francisco. At the airport, after picking up your luggage, call 415/871–7800 and a van will pick you up within five minutes. To go to the airport, make reservations (tel. 415/558–8500) 24 hours in advance. The Supershuttle shops at the upper level of the terminal, along with several other bus and van transport services.

Taxis to or from downtown take 20–30 minutes and average $30.

By Train
Amtrak (tel. 800/USA–RAIL) trains (the *Zephyr,* from Chicago via Denver, and the *Coast Starlight,* traveling between San Diego and Seattle) stop at the Oakland Depot; from there buses will take you across the Bay Bridge to the Transbay Terminal at 1st and Mission streets in San Francisco.

By Bus
Greyhound-Trailways serves San Francisco from the Transbay Terminal at 1st and Mission streets (tel. 415/558–6789).

By Car
I-80 finishes its westward journey from New York's George Washington Bridge at the Bay Bridge, linking Oakland and San Francisco. U.S. 101, running north–south through the entire state, enters the city across the Golden Gate Bridge and continues south down the peninsula, along the west side of the bay.

Exploring San Francisco *(Boxes Refer to Detail Maps)*

Golden Gate Bridge
Fort Point
101

Golden Gate
National
Recreation
Area

PACIFIC OCEAN

The Presidio

*Baker
Beach*
**Land's
End**
**Palace
of the
Legion
of Honor**
*Phelan
Beach*
*Lincoln
Park*
Lake St.

SEACLIFF
Clement St.

*Point
Lobos*
43rd
34th
Geary Blvd.
25th
19th
Park Presidio Blvd.
8th Ave.
Arguello Blvd.

**Cliff
House**
Ave.
Balboa St.
Turk

Golden Gate Park
Ave.
RICHMOND
Ave.
Fulton St.

Golden Gate Park
Kennedy Dr.
Middle Dr.
Stanyan St.

Great
Lincoln Way
Judah St.
28th St.
Funston Ave.
7th Ave.
Lawton St.
1

Noriega St.
Ortega St.
19th Ave.
Clarendon Ave.
SUNSET
Quintara St.
41st Ave.
Sunset Blvd.
14th Ave.
Dewey Blvd.
*McCoppin
Square*
Taraval St.
Dr.
**Mt.
Davidson**
Vicente St.
*Larsen
Park*
Portola
Yerba Buena Ave.
Miramar
Stern Grove
Ave.
N
Monterey
Blvd.

**San Francisco
Zoo**
Sloat Blvd
Juniper Serra Blvd
Ocean Ave.
STONESTOWN
Skyline Blvd
*Harding
Park*
**San Francisco
State Univ.**
Font Blvd.
Lake Merced Blvd.
Holloway Ave.
Plymouth Ave.
Garfield St.
Lake Merced
*Brotherhood
Way*

0   1 mile
0   1 km

Marina Green
Fort Mason
Northern Waterfront
Pier 39
San Francisco Bay

MARINA
Bay St.
Fisherman's Wharf
NORTH BEACH
Downtown

Palace of Fine Arts
Lombard St.
Hyde St.
RUSSIAN HILL
Columbus
Coit Tower
TELEGRAPH HILL

San Francisco-Oakland Bay Bridge

(tunnel)

PACIFIC HEIGHTS
Broadway
Washington St.
California St.
NOB HILL
Powell St.
Great St.
FINANCIAL DISTRICT

Sacramento St.
Pine St.
Bush St.
UNION SQUARE
Post St.
Geary St.
1st St.
2nd St.
3rd St.

Presidio Ave.
Divisadero St.
Geary St.
Gough St.
Van Ness Ave.
Franklin St.
Laguna St.
Steiner
JAPAN TOWN
Turk St.
Mission St.
4th St.
5th St.
6th St.

Blvd.
Masonic Ave.
Golden Gate Ave.
Fulton St.
Market St.
SOMA

Fell St.
WESTERN ADDITION
9th St.
10th St.
Folsom
Harrison
Bryant
Brannan St.
Townsend St.
7th St.

HAIGHT-ASHBURY
Buena Vista Park
Clayton St.
Castro St.
Duboce Ave.
Central Skyway

Central Basin

17th St.
Market St.
CASTRO
Mission Dolores Park
MISSION
20th St.
Harrison St.
Patrero Ave.
Mariposa St.
POTRERO
Pennsylvania Ave.
Indiana St.
3rd St.

Twin Peaks
25th St.
Diamond St.
Dolores St.
Guerrero St.
Mission St.
Van Ness Ave.
San Francisco General Hospital
Army St.

Islais Cr. Channel

India Basin

Oakdale Ave.

Bosworth St.
Monterey Blvd.
Fwy.
Silver Ave.
Felton Ave.
Quesada Ave.
Hunter's Point

Southern
Balboa Park
San Jose Ave.
Alemany Blvd.
Mission St.
Persia Ave.
Mascow St.
GLEN PARK
Excelsior Ave.
John McLaren Park
Mansell St.
Gilman Ave.
Jamestown Ave.
3rd St.

Geneva Ave.
France Ave.
Cow Palace
South Basin
Candlestick Park

Important Addresses and Numbers

Tourist Information The **San Francisco Convention and Visitors Bureau** maintains a visitors information center on the lower level at Hallidie Plaza (Powell and Market streets), just three blocks from Union Square, near the cable car turnaround and the Powell Street entrance to BART. *Weekdays 9–5, Sat. 9–3, Sun. 10–2. Tel. 415/974–6900. Summary of daily events: tel. 415/391–2001.*

Emergencies **Police** or **ambulance,** telephone 911.

Doctors Two hospitals with 24-hour emergency rooms are **San Francisco General Hospital** (1001 Potrero Ave., tel. 415/821–8200) and the **Medical Center at the University of California, San Francisco** (500 Parnassus Ave. at 3rd Ave., near Golden Gate Park, tel. 415/476–1000).

Access Health Care provides drop-in medical care at two San Francisco locations, daily 8–8. No membership is necessary. *1604 Union St. at Franklin St., tel. 415/775–7766; and 26 California St. at Drumm St., tel. 415/397–2881.*

Pharmacies Several **Walgreen Drug Stores** have 24-hour pharmacies, including stores at 500 Geary Street near Union Square (tel. 415/673–8413) and 3201 Divisadero Street at Lombard Street (tel. 415/931–6417). Also try the Walgreen pharmacy on Powell Street near Market Street. *135 Powell St., tel. 415/391–7222. Open Mon.–Sat. 8 AM–midnight, Sun. 9 AM–8 PM. AE, MC, V.*

Getting Around

By BART **Bay Area Rapid Transit** (tel. 415/788–BART) sends air-conditioned aluminum trains at speeds of up to 80 miles an hour across the bay to Oakland, Berkeley, Concord, Richmond, and Fremont. Trains also travel south from San Francisco as far as Daly City. Wall maps in the stations list destinations and fares (85¢–$3). Trains run Mon.–Sat. 6 AM–midnight, Sun. 9 AM–midnight.

A $2.60 excursion ticket buys a three-county tour. You can visit any of the 34 stations for up to four hours as long as you exit and enter at the same station.

By Bus The **San Francisco Municipal Railway System,** or **Muni** (tel. 415/673–MUNI), includes buses and trolleys, surface streetcars, and the new below-surface streetcars, as well as cable cars. There is 24-hour service, and the fare is 85¢ for adults, 15¢ for senior citizens, and 25¢ for children ages 5–17. Exact change is always required. Free transfers are available.

A $6 pass good for unlimited travel all day ($10 for three days) on all routes can be purchased from ticket machines at cable car terminals.

By Cable Car "They turn corners almost at right angles; cross other lines, and for all I know, may run up the sides of houses," wrote Rudyard Kipling in 1889.

The Powell-Mason line (No. 59) and the Powell-Hyde line (No. 60) begin at Powell and Market streets near Union Square and terminate at Fisherman's Wharf. The California Street line (No. 61) runs east and west from Market Street near the Embarcadero to Van Ness Avenue.

Cable cars are popular, crowded, and an experience to ride: Move toward one quickly as it pauses, wedge yourself into any available space, and hold on! The views from many cars are spectacular, and the sensation of moving up and down some of San Francisco's steepest hills in a small, open-air clanging conveyance is not to be missed.

The fare is $2 for adults, $1 for children 5–17. Exact change is required.

By Taxi Rates are high in the city, although most rides are relatively short. It is unfortunately almost impossible to hail a passing cab, especially on weekends. Either phone or use the nearest hotel taxi stand to grab a cab. See the Yellow Pages for numbers of taxi companies.

By Car Driving in San Francisco can be a challenge, what with the hills, the one-way streets, and the traffic. Take it easy, remember to curb your wheels when parking on hills, and use public transportation whenever possible. On certain streets, parking is forbidden during rush hours. Look for the warning signs; illegally parked cars are towed. This is a great city for walking and a terrible city for parking. Downtown parking lots are often full and always expensive. Finding a spot in North Beach at night, for instance, may be impossible.

Guided Tours

Orientation Tours **Gray Line** offers a variety of tours of the city, the Bay Area, and northern California. Their city tour, on buses or double-decker buses, lasts 3½ hours and departs from the Trans-Bay Terminal at 1st and Mission streets five to six times daily. Gray Line also picks up at centrally located hotels. *Tel. 415/558–9400. Tours daily. Make reservations the day before. Cost: $21.50 adults, $10.75 children.*

The Great Pacific Tour uses 13-passenger vans for its daily 3½-hour city tour. Bilingual guides may be requested. They pick up at major San Francisco hotels. Tours are available to Monterey, the Wine Country, and Muir Woods. *Tel. 415/626–4499. Tours daily. Make reservations the day before, or, possibly, the same day. Cost: $25 adults, $22 senior citizens, $18 children 5–11.*

San Francisco Scenic Route. Near Escapes (Box 193005, San Francisco 94119, tel. 415/386–8687) has produced an audio cassette with music and sound effects that will take you in your own car "where the tour buses can't go." It will guide you past Fisherman's Wharf, Chinatown, Golden Gate Park, Twin Peaks, Ghirardelli Square, Mission Dolores, the Civic Center, and other tourist attractions. Another cassette offers a detailed walking tour of Chinatown; both come with route maps. They are available in a few local outlets, or you can get them mail-order for $12 (or $14 with Visa or MasterCard).

Special-Interest Tours **Near Escapes** (Box 3005-K, 94119, tel. 415/386–8687) plans unusual activities in the city and around the Bay Area. Recent tours and activities include tours of a Hindu temple in the East Bay, the Lawrence Berkeley Laboratory, the aircraft maintenance facility at the San Francisco Airport, and the quicksilver mines south of San Jose. The Julia Morgan Architectural Tour focuses on the work of one of the most prominent California architects of the early 20th century. Send $1 and a self-addressed, stamped envelope for a schedule for the month you plan to visit San Francisco.

Walking Tours

Castro District. Trevor Hailey leads a 3½-hour tour focusing on the history and development of the city's gay and lesbian community, including restored Victorian homes, shops and cafés, and the NAMES Project, home of the AIDS memorial quilt. Tours depart at 10 AM most days from Castro and Market streets. *Tel. 415/550–8110. Cost: $25, including breakfast or lunch.*

Chinese Cultural Heritage Foundation (tel. 415/986–1822) offers two walking tours of Chinatown. The Heritage Walk leaves Saturday at 2 PM and lasts about two hours. *Cost: $9 adults, $2 children under 12.* The Culinary Walk, a three-hour stroll through the markets and food shops, plus a dim sum lunch, is held every Wednesday at 10:30 AM. *Cost: $18 adults, $9 children.*

Dashiell Hammett Tour. Don Herron gives four-hour, three-mile literary walking tours designed around the life of Hammett and his character Sam Spade. Tours depart between May and August at Saturday noon from the main library at 200 Larkin Street. *Tel. 415/564–7021. Cost: $5.*

Golden Gate Park. The Friends of Recreation and Parks (tel. 415/221–1311) offer free, guided 1½- to 2-hour walking tours of the park, May–October.

Heritage Walks. The Foundation for San Francisco's Architectural Heritage, headquartered in the Hass-Lilienthal House at 2007 Franklin Street, sponsors architectural tours of nearby Pacific Heights, with excursions to Russian Hill and the Presidio. *Tel. 415/441–3004. Cost: $3.*

Exploring

Few cities in the world cram so much diversity into so little space. San Francisco is a relatively small city, with fewer than 750,000 residents nested on a 46.6-square-mile tip of land between San Francisco Bay and the Pacific Ocean.

San Franciscans cherish the city's colorful past, and many older buildings have been spared from demolition and nostalgically converted into modern offices and shops. For more than a century, the port city has been trafficking the peoples of the world. Today the city is again establishing strong commercial relations with the nations of the Pacific Rim. The unusually large number of residents with ties to other cultures flavors the cuisine, commerce, and charisma of the city. It also encourages a tolerance for deviations in customs and beliefs.

San Francisco is a maze of one-way streets and restricted parking zones. Public parking garages or lots tend to be expensive, as are the hotel parking spaces. The famed 40-plus hills can be a problem for drivers who are new to the terrain. People who know the city agree that one of the best ways to see and experience its many moods and neighborhoods is by foot. Those museums on wheels—the cable cars—or the numerous buses or trolleys can take you to or near many of the area's attractions. In the exploring tours that follow, we have often included information on public transportation.

Hills are a daily challenge to visitor and resident alike; good walking shoes are essential. Climate, too, is a consideration in deciding what to wear. There are dramatic temperature changes, especially in summer, when the afternoon fog rolls in. Winds are often a problem, both on the bay and cityside. Year-round, layered clothing are most adaptable to changing conditions; a cap or scarf and sunglasses are useful. Casual city togs are appropriate; shorts and tank tops are for southern California's climate.

Union Square Area

Numbers in the margin correspond with points of interest on the Downtown San Francisco map.

Since 1850 Union Square has been the heart of San Francisco's downtown. Its name derives from a series of violent pro-Union demonstrations staged in this hilly area just prior to the Civil War. This area is where you will find the city's finest department stores and most elegant boutiques. There are 40 hotels within a three-block walk of the square, and the downtown theater district is nearby.

The square itself is a 2.6-acre oasis planted with palms, boxwood, and seasonal flowers, peopled with a kaleidoscope of characters: office workers sunning and brown-bagging, street musicians, always at least one mime, several vocal and determined preachers, and the ever-increasing parade of panhandlers. Smartly dressed women and camera-laden tourists usually hurry past the denizens. Throughout the year, the square hosts numerous public events: fashion shows, free noontime concerts, ethnic celebrations, and noisy demonstrations. Auto and bus traffic is often gridlocked on the four streets bordering the square. Post, Stockton, and Geary are one-way, while Powell runs in both directions until it crosses Geary, where it then becomes a one-way street to Market Street. Union Square covers a convenient but costly four-story underground garage. Close to 3,000 cars use it on busy holiday shopping and strolling days.

❶ Any visitor's first stop should be the **San Francisco Visitors Information Center** (tel. 415/391–2000) on the lower level of Hallidie Plaza at Powell and Market streets. It is open daily, and the multilingual staff will answer specific questions as well as provide maps, brochures, and information on daily events. The office provides 24-hour recorded information (tel. 415/391–2001).

The **cable car terminus,** also at Powell and Market streets, is the starting point for two of the three operating lines. Before 1900 there were 600 cable cars spanning a network of 100 miles. Today there are 39 cars in the three lines, and the network covers just 12 miles. Most of the cars date from the last century, although the cars and lines had a complete $58 million overhaul during the early 1980s. There are seats for about 30 passengers, with usually that number standing or strap-hanging. If possible, plan your cable car ride for mid-morning or mid-afternoon during the week to avoid crowds. In summertime there are often long lines to board any of the three systems. (*See* Getting Around, above.)

❷ A two-block stroll north along bustling Powell Street leads to **Union Square** with its fashionable stores, fine hotels, and photogenic flower stalls. At center stage, the **Victory Monument** by Robert Ingersoll Aitken commemorates Commodore

Downtown San Francisco

Chestnut St.

Lombard St.

Octavia St.

Gough St.

Franklin St.

Van Ness Ave.

Polk St.

Larkin St.

Hyde St.

Leavenworth St.

Green

Filbert

Union

Green St.

RUSSIAN HILL

Vallejo St.

Broadway Tun

Broadway

PACIFIC HEIGHTS

Pacific St.

Jackson St.

50

Washington St.

52

53

Clay St.

Lafayette Park

Alta Plaza

51

Sacramento St.

California St.

Scott St.

Pierce St.

Steiner St.

Fillmore St.

Pine St.

Webster St.

Buchanan St.

Laguna St.

Octavia St.

Gough St.

Franklin St.

Van Ness Ave.

Polk St.

Larkin St.

Hyde St.

Leavenworth St.

Jones St.

Bush St.

Sutter St.

Post St.

JAPANTOWN

48

Geary St.

O'Farrell St.

49

Ellis St.

Eddy St.

Turk St.

Golden Gate Ave.

McAllister St.

46

45

Fulton St.

44

Alamo Square

CIVIC CENTER

47

Grove St.

Market St.

7th St.

8th St.

Hayes St.

San Francisco Bay

N

Chestnut St.
Lombard St.
Columbus Ave.
Grant Ave.
TELEGRAPH HILL
NORTH BEACH
Mason St.
Powell St.
Taylor St.
Stockton St.
Kearny St.
Montgomery St.
Sansome St.
Battery St.
Front St.
Davis St.
Front St.
Davis St.
Drumm St.
Embarcadero
Spear St.
Steuart St.
Main St.
Beale St.
Fremont St.
1st St.
NOB HILL
CHINATOWN
Halleck St.
UNION SQUARE
Maiden Ln.
New Montgomery St.
2nd St.
3rd St.
Hawthorne St.
SOMA
Market St.
Mission St.
Howard St.
4th St.
5th St.
6th St.
7th St.

George Dewey's victory over the Spanish fleet at Manila in 1898. The 97-foot Corinthian column, topped by a bronze figure symbolizing naval conquest, was dedicated by President Theodore Roosevelt in 1903 and withstood the 1906 earthquake.

After the earthquake and fire in 1906, the square was dubbed "Little St. Francis" because of the temporary shelter erected for residents of the St. Francis Hotel. The actor John Barrymore was among the guests pressed into volunteering to stack bricks in the square. His uncle, thespian John Drew, remarked, "It took an act of God to get John out of bed and the United States government to get him to work."

❸ The Westin St. Francis Hotel, on the southwest corner of Post and Powell, was built here in 1904 and was gutted by the 1906 disaster. The second-oldest hotel in the city was conceived by Charles Crocker and his associates as an elegant hostelry for their millionaire friends. Swift service and sumptuous surroundings were hallmarks of the property. A sybarite's dream, the hotel's Turkish baths had ocean water piped in. A new, larger, more luxurious residence was opened in 1907 to attract loyal clients from among the world's rich and powerful. Today you can relax over a traditional teatime or opt for champagne and caviar in the dramatic Art Deco Compass Rose lounge in the lobby. Elaborate Chinese screens, secluded seating alcoves, and soothing background music make it an ideal time-out after frantic shopping or sightseeing. For dining, before or after the theater (within walking distance), visit the award-winning Victor's. After a breathtaking ride up 30-plus stories in an outside, glass-walled elevator, guests enter a warm, wood-paneled lobby area with recessed bookshelves housing leather-bound classics. Floor-to-ceiling windows offer spectacular views of the bay and the city. Superb California cuisine is enhanced by a select list of California and French wines.

❹ Both the Geary and Curran theaters are a few blocks west on Geary Street. The **Geary** (415 Geary St., tel. 415/749–2228) is home of the American Conservatory Theatre. Now in its 26th season, A.C.T. is one of North America's leading repertory companies. The 1,300-seat house normally offers a 34-week season to 20,000 subscribers, presenting both classical and contemporary dramas. The theater was closed indefinitely as a result of the October 1989 earthquake, and currently productions are being run at the Stage Door theater (420 Mason St.) and elsewhere until repairs are complete. Its main box office **❺** remains open. The **Curran** (445 Geary St., tel. 415/474–3800) is noted for showcasing traveling companies of Broadway shows. The **San Francisco Ticket Box Office Service** (STBO, tel. 415/433–STBS) has booths on both the Stockton Street side of Union Square, opposite Maiden Lane, and in Embarcadero One. Open from noon till 7:30 PM, Tuesday through Saturday, it provides day-of-performance tickets (cash or traveler's checks only) to all types of performing arts events at half price, as well as regular full-price box-office services. Telephone reservations are not accepted.

❻ Just a dash up from STBS, the newly renovated **Grand Hyatt San Francisco** (345 Stockton St.) offers exciting city views from its lounge, the Club 36. Stop and examine sculptor Ruth Asawa's fantasy fountain honoring the city's hills, bridges, and unusual architecture plus a wonder world of real and mythical creatures. Children and friends helped Ms. Asawa shape the hundreds of tiny figures created from baker's clay and then assembled on 41 large panels from which molds were made for the bronze casting. The artist's distinctive designs decorate many public areas in the city. You can see her famous mermaid fountain at Ghirardelli Square.

⑦ Pop around the corner into **Maiden Lane,** which runs from Stockton to Kearny streets. Known as Morton Street in the raffish Barbary Coast era, this red-light district reported at least one murder a week. But the 1906 fire destroyed the brothels and the street emerged as Maiden Lane. It has since become a chic and pricey mall. The two blocks are closed to vehicles from 11 AM until 4 PM. During the day, take-out snacks can be enjoyed while resting under the gay, umbrella-shaded tables. Masses of daffodils and bright blossoms and balloons bedeck the lane during the annual spring festival. A carnival mood prevails, with zany street musicians, artsy-craftsy people, and throngs of spectators.

Note **140 Maiden Lane:** This handsome brick structure is the only Frank Lloyd Wright building in San Francisco. With its circular interior ramp and skylights, it is said to have been a model for his designs for the Guggenheim Museum in New York. It now houses the **Circle Gallery,** a showcase of contemporary artists. Be sure to study the unique limited-edition art jewelry designed by internationally acclaimed Erté. *Open Mon.–Sat. 10–6, Sun. 11–5.*

⑧ The **Crocker Galleria** (Post and Kearny Sts., tel. 415/392–0100) is an imaginatively designed three-level complex of fine dining and shopping establishments capped by a dazzling glass dome. One block north of Kearny, Sutter Street is lined by prestigious art galleries, antiques dealers, smart hotels, and noted designer boutiques. Art Deco aficionados will want to linger at the **⑨** striking medical/dental office building at **450 Sutter Street.** Handsome Mayan-inspired designs are used in both exterior and interior surfaces of the 1930 terra-cotta-colored skyscraper.

Time Out Most stores and shops here open at about 9:30–10 AM. Venturing out early and settling down to a leisurely breakfast before the day's traffic and shoppers hit in full force is a nice way to ease into a busy day of sightseeing. **Mama's** (398 Geary St.) has always been a favorite for either light or full-breakfast selections. Or blow the day's meal budget at **Campton Place Hotel.** Wonderful breads and muffins, delicious hash, and out-of-season fruits are lavishly served. *340 Stockton St., tel. 415/781–5155. Reservations advised for brunch. Open weekdays 7–11 AM, Sat. 8–11:30 AM, Sun. brunch 8 AM–2:30 PM.*

The Financial District

The heart of San Francisco's financial district is Montgomery Street. It was here in 1848 that Sam Brannan proclaimed the historic gold discovery on the American River. At that time, all the streets below Montgomery between California and Broadway were wharves. At least 100 ships were abandoned by frantic crews and passengers all caught up in the '49 gold fever. Many of the wrecks served as warehouses or were used as foundations for new constructions.

The financial district is roughly bordered by Kearny Street on the west, Washington Street on the north, and Market Street on the southeast. On workdays it is a congested canyon of soaring skyscrapers, gridlock traffic, and bustling pedestrians. In the evenings and on weekends the quiet streets allow walkers to admire the distinctive architecture. Unfortunately, the museums in corporate headquarters are closed then.

❿ The city's most photographed high rise is the 853-foot **Transamerica Pyramid** at 600 Montgomery Street, between Clay and Washington streets at the end of Columbus Avenue. Designed by William Pereira and Associates in 1972, the $34 million controversial symbol has become more acceptable to local purists as it gained San Francisco instant recognition worldwide. There is a public viewing area on the 27th floor (open weekdays 8–4). You can relax in a redwood grove along the east side of the building.

⓫ The granite and marble **Bank of America** building dominates the territory bounded by California, Pine, Montgomery, and Kearny streets. The 52-story polished red granite complex is crowned by a chic cocktail and dining restaurant. As in almost all corporate headquarters, the interiors display impressive original art, while outdoor plazas include avant-garde sculptures. A massive abstract black granite sculpture designed by the Japanese artist Masayuki in the mall has been dubbed the "Banker's Heart" by local wags.

⓬ Diagonally across Montgomery Street is the **Wells Fargo Bank History Museum** (420 Montgomery St.). There were no formal banks in San Francisco during the early years of the Gold Rush, and miners often entrusted their gold dust to saloon keepers. In 1852 Wells Fargo opened its first bank in the city, and the company established banking offices in the Mother Lode camps using stagecoaches and pony express riders to service the burgeoning state. (California's population had boomed from 15,000 to 200,000 between 1848 and 1852.) The History Museum displays samples of nuggets and gold dust from major mines, a mural-size map of the Mother Lode, original art by Western artists Charlie Russell and Maynard Dixon, mementos of the poet bandit Black Bart, and letters of credit and old bank drafts. The showpiece is the red, century-old Concord stagecoach, which in the mid-1850s carried 15 passengers from St. Louis to San Francisco in three weeks. *Admission free. Open banking days 9–5.*

⓭ The **Russ Building** (235 Montgomery St.) was called "the skyscraper" when it was built in 1927. The Gothic design was modeled after the Chicago Tribune Tower, and until the 1960s was San Francisco's tallest—at just 31 stories. Prior to the 1906 earthquake and fire, the site was occupied by the Russ House, considered one of the finest hostelries in the city.

⓮ The **Mills Building and Tower** (220 Montgomery St.) was the outstanding prefire building in the financial district. The 10-story all-steel construction had its own electric plant in the basement. The original Burnham and Root design of white marble and brick was erected in 1891–92. Damage from the 1906 fire was slight; its walls were somewhat scorched but were easily refurbished. Two compatible additions east on Bush Street were added in 1914 and 1918 by Willis Polk, and in 1931 a 22-story tower completed the design.

Ralph Stackpole's monumental 1930 granite sculptural groups, *Earth's Fruitfulness* and *Man's Inventive Genius*, flank another imposing structure, the **Pacific Stock Exchange** (which dates from 1915), on the south side of Pine Street at Sansome Street. The Stock Exchange Tower around the corner at 155 Sansome Street is a 1930 modern classic by architects Miller and Pfleuger, featuring an Art Deco gold ceiling and black marble-walled entry. *Pacific Stock Exchange, 301 Pine St., 94104, tel. 415/393–4000. Tours by 2-week advance reservation; minimum 8 persons.*

Stroll down Sansome Street and turn right on Sutter Street. The **Hallidie Building** (130 Sutter St. between Kearny and Montgomery Sts.) was built as an investment by the University of California Regents in 1918 and named for cable car inventor and university regent Andrew S. Hallidie. It is believed to be the world's first all-glass-curtain-wall structure. Architect Willis Polk's revolutionary design hangs a foot beyond the reinforced concrete of the frame. It dominates the block with its reflecting glass, decorative exterior fire escapes that appear to be metal balconies, the Venetian Gothic cornice, and horizontal ornamental bands of birds at feeders.

The Embarcadero and Lower Market Street

In one instance, the 1989 Loma Prieta earthquake changed San Francisco for the better: The Embarcadero freeway had to be torn down, making the foot of Market Street clearly visible for the first time in decades. The trademark of the port is the quaint **Ferry Building** that stands at the Embarcadero. The clock tower is 230 feet high and was modeled by Arthur Page Brown after the campanile of Seville's cathedral. The four great clock faces on the tower, powered by the swinging action of a 14-foot pendulum, stopped at 5:17 on the morning of April 18, 1906, and stayed that way for the following 12 months. The 1896 building survived the quake and is now the headquarters of the Port Authority and the World Trade Center. A waterfront promenade that extends from this point to the Oakland Bay Bridge is great for jogging, watching the sailboats on the bay (if the day is not too windy), or enjoying a picnic. Ferries from here sail to Sausalito, Larkspur, and Tiburon.

Strolling back up Market Street, one's attention is drawn to the huge **Embarcadero Center** complex. Frequently called "Rockefeller Center West," its eight buildings include over 100 shops, 40 restaurants, and two hotels, as well as high-rise residential towers and town-house condos. A three-tiered pedestrian mall links the buildings, and much attention has been given to attractive landscaping throughout the development. Louise Nevelson's dramatic 54-foot-high black-steel sculpture, "Sky Tree," stands guard over Building 3. The **Hyatt Regency Hotel** (5 Embarcadero) was designed by John Portman and is noted for its spectacular lobby and 20-story hanging garden. Just in front of the hotel is the Justin Herman Plaza. There are arts and crafts shows, street musicians, and mimes here on weekends year-round. Kite-flying is popular here. A huge concrete sculpture, the Vaillancourt Fountain, has had legions of critics since its installation in 1971; most of the time the fountain does not work, and many feel it is an eyesore.

❿ The **Old San Francisco Mint,** at 5th and Mission streets, re-opened as a museum in 1973. The century-old brick-and-stone building exhibits a priceless collection of gold coins. Visitors tour the vaults and can strike their own souvenir medal on an 1869 press. *Admission free. Open weekdays 10–4.*

The vast tract of downtown land south of Market Street along the waterfront and west to the Mission district is now known by the acronym SoMa (patterned after New York City's south-of-Houston SoHo). This is the happening place after dark. The machine shops, printers, and warehouses are losing out to res-taurants, bars, discos, and clubs.

⓴ The **Ansel Adams Center,** SoMa's first museum, operates five exhibition galleries for photography, including one always de-voted to Adams' work. It is operated by the Friends of Pho-tography, a group Adams helped establish. There is also a bookstore and a library. *250 Fourth St., tel. 415/495–7000. Ad-mission, $3 adults, $2 senior citizens and students. Open Tues.–Sun. 11–6.*

Chinatown

A city within a city, this is the largest Chinese community out-side of Asia. Approximately 100,000 Chinese live in a 24-block downtown area just south of North Beach (and in the Richmond district's "New Chinatown"). Chinatown has been revitalized by the fairly recent immigration of Southeast Asians, who have added new character and life to the neighborhood. Downtown Chinatown is officially defined as an area reaching from Bay Street south to California Street and from Sansome Street at the edge of downtown west to Van Ness Avenue; these bound-aries actually include much of Russian Hill and Nob Hill.

Visitors usually enter Chinatown through the green-tiled **㉑** dragon-crowned **Chinatown Gate** at Bush Street and Grant Av-enue. To best savor this district, explore it on foot (it's not far from Union Square), even though you may find the bustling, noisy, colorful stretches of Grant and Stockton streets north of Bush difficult to navigate. Parking is extremely hard to find, and traffic is impossible. As in Hong Kong, most families shop daily for fresh meats, vegetables, and bakery products. This street world shines with much good-luck crimson and gold; gi-ant beribboned floral wreaths mark the opening of new bake-ries, bazaars, and banks. Nighttime is as busy as the daytime around here, what with almost 100 restaurants squeezed into a 14-block area.

㉒ The handsome brick **Old St. Mary's Church** at Grant and Cali-fornia streets served as the city's Catholic cathedral until 1891. Granite quarried in China was used in the structure, which was **㉓** dedicated in 1854. Diagonally across the intersection is **St. Mary's Park,** a tranquil setting for local sculptor Beniamino (Benny) Bufano's heroic stainless-steel and rose-colored gran-ite Sun Yat Sen. The 12-foot statue of the founder of the Repub-lic of China was installed in 1937. Bufano was born in Rome on October 14, 1898, and died in San Francisco on August 16, 1970. His stainless-steel and mosaic statue of St. Francis welcomes guests at San Francisco International Airport.

Shopping surrounds the stroller on **Grant Avenue.** Much of what is offered in the countless curio shops is worthless, and discerning visitors may be dismayed by the gaudy and glittery gimcrackery. In recent years, however, a growing number of large department-store-type operations have opened. Most feature an ever-growing array of products from the People's Republic. You'll find, too, that visiting the Chinese markets, even just window-gazing, is fascinating. Note the dragon-entwined lampposts, the pagoda roofs, and street signs with Chinese calligraphy.

The city's first house was built in 1836 at the corner of Grant Avenue and Clay Street; it was later destroyed in the 1906 earthquake. Turn right here and a short walk will take you to **Portsmouth Square,** the potato patch that became the plaza for Yerba Buena. This is where Montgomery raised the American flag in 1846. Note the bronze galleon atop a nine-foot granite shaft. Designed by Bruce Porter, the sculpture was erected in 1919 in memory of Robert Louis Stevenson, who often visited the site during his 1879–80 residence. In the morning, the park is crowded with people performing solemn t'ai chi rituals.

From here you can walk to the **Chinese Cultural Center,** which frequently displays exhibits of Chinese-American artists as well as traveling exhibits of Chinese culture. The center also offers Saturday-afternoon walking tours of historic points in Chinatown. *In the Holiday Inn, 750 Kearny St., tel. 415/986–1822. Admission free. Open Tues.–Sat. 10–4.*

A short block south of the Culture Center is the **Pacific Heritage Museum,** in the Bank of Canton building. Displays illustrate the artistic, cultural, and economic history of the Pacific Basin peoples. *608 Commercial St. near Montgomery, tel. 415/ 362–4100. Admission free. Open Mon.–Fri. 10–4.*

You're now on the edge of North Beach and could easily walk over to the City Lights bookstore or other North Beach sites.

The original Chinatown burned down after the 1906 earthquake; the first building to set the style for the new Chinatown is near Portsmouth Square, at 743 Washington Street. The three-tiered pagoda called the **Old Chinese Telephone Exchange** was built in 1909.

Time Out Skip that Big Mac you've been craving; opt instead for dim sum, a variety of pastries filled with meat, fish, and vegetables, the Chinese version of a smorgasbord. Over a dozen Chinese restaurants feature this unusual lunch/brunch adventure from about 11 AM to 3 PM. In most places, stacked food-service carts patrol the premises; customers select from the varied offerings, and the final bill is tabulated by the number of different saucers on the table. Dim sum restaurants tend to be big, crowded, noisy, cheap, and friendly. Suggestions are often offered by nearby strangers as to what is inside the tempting morsels. Two favorites on Pacific Avenue, two blocks north of Washington Street, between Stockton and Powell streets, are **Hong Kong Tea House** (835 Pacific Ave.) and **Tung Fong** (808 Pacific Ave.). Many of the smaller, inexpensive Chinese restaurants and cafés do not accept credit cards; some serve beer and wine.

Waverly Place is noted for ornate painted balconies and Chinese temples. **Tien Hou Temple,** at 125 Waverly Place, was dedicated to the Queen of the Heavens and Goddess of the Seven

Seas by Day Ju, one of the first three Chinese to arrive in San Francisco in 1852.

㉙ The **Chinese Historical Society** traces the history of Chinese immigrants and their contributions to the state's rail, mining, and fishing industries. *650 Commercial St. (near Sacramento and Montgomery Sts.), tel. 415/391–1188. Admission free. Open Tues.–Sat. 12–4.*

The other main thoroughfare in Chinatown, where locals shop for everyday needs, is **Stockton Street,** which parallels Grant Avenue. This is the real heart of Chinatown. Housewives jostle one another as they pick apart the sidewalk displays of Chinese vegetables. Double-parked trucks unloading crates of chickens or ducks add to the all-day traffic jams. You'll see excellent examples of Chinese architecture along this street. Most note-

㉚ worthy is the elaborate **Chinese Six Companies** (843 Stockton St.) with its curved roof tiles and elaborate cornices. Folk-art murals grace the walls of an apartment building at Stockton Street and Pacific Avenue. Displays of jade and gold glitter from jewelry windows—the Chinese value these items above all other ornaments. It's an easy ½-hour walk back downtown

㉛ to Union Square via the **Stockton Street Tunnel,** which runs from Sacramento Street to Sutter Street. Completed in 1914, this was the city's first tunnel to accommodate vehicular and pedestrian traffic.

North Beach and Telegraph Hill

Like neighboring Chinatown, North Beach, centered on Columbus Avenue north of Broadway, is best explored on foot. In the early days there truly was a beach. At the time of the Gold Rush, the bay extended into the hollow between Telegraph and Russian hills. North Beach, less than a square mile, is the most densely populated district in the city and is truly cosmopolitan. Much of the old-world ambience still lingers in this easygoing and polyglot neighborhood. Novelist Herbert Gold, a North Beach resident, calls the area "the longest running, most glorious American bohemian operetta outside Greenwich Village."

Among the first immigrants to Yerba Buena during the early 1840s were young men from the northern provinces of Italy. By 1848, the village, renamed San Francisco, had become an overnight boomtown with the discovery of gold. Thousands more poured into the burgeoning area, seeking the golden dream. For many the trail ended in San Francisco. The Genoese started the still-active fishing industry, as well as much-needed produce businesses. Later the Sicilians emerged as leaders of the fishing fleets and eventually as proprietors of the seafood restaurants lining Fisherman's Wharf. Meanwhile, their Genoese cousins established banking and manufacturing empires.

㉜ **Washington Square** may well be the daytime social heart of what was once considered "Little Italy." By mid-morning groups of conservatively dressed elderly Italian men are sunning and sighing at the state of their immediate world. Nearby, laughing Asian and Caucasian playmates race through the grass with Frisbees or colorful kites. Multinational denim-clad mothers exchange shopping tips and ethnic recipes. Elderly Chinese matrons stare impassively at the passing parade. Camera-toting tourists focus their lenses on the adjacent Roman-

㉝ esque splendor of **Saints Peter and Paul,** often called the Italian

Cathedral. Built in 1924, its twin-turreted terra-cotta towers are local landmarks. On the first Sunday of October, the annual Blessing of the Fleet is celebrated with a mass followed by a parade to Fisherman's Wharf. Another popular annual event is the Columbus Day pageant.

The 1906 earthquake and fire devastated this area, and the park provided shelter for hundreds of the homeless. **Fior d'Italia,** facing the cathedral, is San Francisco's oldest Italian restaurant. The original opened in 1886 and continued to operate in a tent after the 1906 earthquake until new quarters were ready. Surrounding streets are packed with savory Italian delicatessens, bakeries, Chinese markets, coffeehouses, and ethnic restaurants. Wonderful aromas fill the air. (Coffee beans roasted at **Graffeo** at 733 Columbus Avenue are shipped to customers all over the United States.) You can pick up a good sandwich to go at numerous local delis.

South of Washington Square and just off Columbus Avenue is the **Church of Saint Francis of Assisi** (610 Vallejo St.). This 1860 Victorian Gothic building stands on the site of the frame parish church that served the Gold Rush Catholic community.

Over the years, North Beach has attracted creative individualists. The Beat Renaissance of the 1950s was born, grew up, flourished, then faltered in this then-predominantly Italian enclave. The Beat gathering places are gone, and few of the original leaders remain. Poet Lawrence Ferlinghetti still holds court at his **City Lights Bookstore** (261 Columbus Ave.). The face of North Beach is changing. The bohemian community has migrated up Grant Avenue above Columbus Avenue. Originally called Calle de la Fundacion, Grant Avenue is the oldest street in the city. Each June a street fair is held on the upper part of the avenue, where a cluster of cafés, boutiques, and galleries attract crowds.

Time Out The richness of North Beach lifestyle is reflected in the neighborhood's numerous cafés. Breakfast at **Caffe Roma** (414 Columbus Ave.) and create your own omelet from a list of 11 ingredients. Skip the main room with its pastel murals of cherubs and settle at one of the umbrella-shaded tables on the patio. Moviemaker Francis Ford Coppola is a regular, and the adjoining Millefiori Inn, a charming bed-and-breakfast, frequently hosts film celebrities. Across the street is **Caffe Puccini** (411 Columbus Ave.). It could be Italy: Few of the staff speak English. Their *caffe latte* (coffee, chocolate, cinnamon, and steamed milk) and strains of Italian operas recall *Roman Holiday*. A Saturday morning must is around the corner at **Caffe Trieste** (601 Vallejo St.). Get there at about 11; at noon, the Giotta family's weekly musical begins. The program ranges from Italian pop and folk music to favorite family operas. The Trieste opened in 1956 and became headquarters for the area's beatnik poets, artists, and writers. **Caffe Malvina** (1600 Stockton St.) started during the 1950s and was among the first U.S. importers of Italian-made espresso machines.

Telegraph Hill residents command some of the best views in the city, as well as the most difficult ascent to their aeries. The Greenwich stairs lead up to Coit Tower from Filbert Street, and there are steps down to Filbert Street on the opposite side of Telegraph Hill. Views are superb en route, but most visitors should either taxi up to the tower or take the Muni bus No. 39 Coit at Washington Square. To catch the bus from Union Square, walk to Stockton and Sutter streets, board the Muni No. 30, and ask for a transfer to use at Washington Square (Columbus Ave. and Union St.) to board the No. 39 Coit. Public parking is very limited at the tower, and on holidays and weekends there are long lines of cars and buses winding up the narrow road.

Telegraph Hill rises from the east end of Lombard Street to about 300 feet and is capped with the landmark Coit Tower, dedicated as a monument to the city's volunteer firemen. Early during the Gold Rush, an eight-year-old who would become one of the city's most memorable eccentrics, Lillie Hitchcock Coit, arrived on the scene. Legend relates that at age 17, "Miss Lil" deserted a wedding party and chased down the street after her favorite engine, Knickerbocker No. 5, clad in her bridesmaid finery. She was soon made an honorary member of the Knickerbocker Company, and after that always signed herself "Lillie Coit 5" in honor of her favorite fire engine. Lillie died in 1929 at the age of 86, leaving the city about $100,000 of her million-dollar-plus estate to "expend in an appropriate manner . . . to the beauty of San Francisco."

36 **Coit Tower** stands as a monument not only to Lillie Coit and the city's firemen but also to the influence of the politically radical Mexican muralist Diego Rivera. Fresco was Rivera's medium, and it was his style that unified the work of most of the 25 artists who painted the murals in the tower. The murals were commissioned by the U.S. government as a Public Works of Art Project. The artists were paid $38 a week. Some were fresh from art schools; others found no market for art in the dark depression days of the early 1930s. An illustrated brochure for sale in the tiny gift shop explains the various murals dedicated to the workers of California. There is an elevator to the top that provides a panoramic view of both the Bay Bridge and Golden Gate Bridge; directly offshore is the famous Alcatraz and just behind it, Angel Island, a hikers' and campers' paradise. Be sure to carry a camera and binoculars. There are often artists at work in **Pioneer Park,** at the foot of the tower. Small paintings of the scene are frequently offered for sale at modest prices. The impressive bronze statue of Christopher Columbus, *Discoverer of America*, was a gift of the local Italian community.

At the foot of the hill you will come to the Levi Strauss headquarters, a carefully landscaped $150 million complex that appears so collegial and serene it is affectionately known as LSU (Levi Strauss University). Fountains and grassy knolls complement the stepped-back redbrick buildings and provide a stress-reducing environment perfect for brown-bag lunches.

Nob Hill

If you don't mind climbing uphill, Nob Hill is within walking distance of Union Square. Once called the Hill of Golden Promise, it became Nob Hill during the 1870s when "the Big Four"—Charles Crocker, Leland Stanford, Mark Hopkins, and Collis Huntington—built their hilltop estates. It is still home to many of the city's elite as well as four of San Francisco's finest hotels.

In 1882 Robert Louis Stevenson called Nob Hill "the hill of palaces." But the 1906 earthquake and fire destroyed all the palatial mansions. The shell of one survived. The Flood brownstone (1000 California St.) was built by the Comstock silver baron in 1886 at a reputed cost of $1,500,000. In 1909 the property was

(37) purchased by the prestigious **Pacific Union Club.** The 45-room exclusive club remains the bastion of the wealthy and powerful. Adjacent is a charming small park noted for its frequent art shows.

Adjacent is a charming small park noted for its festive Christmas decorations and frequent art shows. It sits on the site of the Collis Huntington mansion.

(38) Neighboring **Grace Cathedral** (1051 Taylor St.) is the seat of the Episcopal Church in San Francisco. The soaring Gothic structure took 53 years to build. The gilded bronze doors at the east entrance were taken from casts of Ghiberti's *Gates of Paradise* on the baptistery in Florence. The superb rose window is illuminated at night. There are often organ recitals on Sundays at 5 PM, as well as special programs during the holiday seasons.

(39) What sets the **Fairmont Hotel** (California and Mason Sts.) apart from other luxury hotels is its legendary history. Since its dazzling opening in 1907, the opulent marble palace has hosted presidents, royalty, and local nabobs. The lobby sports as much plush red-velvet upholstery as anyone could ever want to see. The eight-room $4,000-a-day penthouse suite was used frequently in the TV series "Hotel," and the stunning Nob Hill Spa and Fitness Club is on the premises.

(40) The stately **Mark Hopkins Hotel,** across California Street, is remembered fondly by thousands of World War II veterans who jammed the Top of the Mark lounge before leaving for overseas

(41) duty. At California and Powell streets stands the posh **Stanford Court Hotel,** a world-class establishment known for service and personal attention. The structure is a remodeled 1909 apart-

(42) ment house. The **Huntington** (1075 California St.) is impeccably British in protecting the privacy of its celebrated guests.

(43) The **Cable Car Museum** (Washington and Mason Sts.) exhibits photographs, scale models, and other memorabilia from the cable car system's 115-year history. A new 17-minute film is shown continually. *Tel. 415/474–1887. Admission free. Open daily 10–5.*

Civic Center

San Francisco's Civic Center stands as one of the country's great city, state, and federal building complexes with handsome adjoining cultural institutions. It's the realization of the theories of turn-of-the-century proponents of the "City Beautiful." In recent years, it's also become the focal point for fine dining in San Francisco.

(44) Facing Polk Street, between Grove and McAllister streets, **City Hall** is a Baroque masterpiece of granite and marble, modeled after the Capitol in Washington. Its dome is even higher than the Washington version, and it dominates the area. In front of the building are formal gardens with fountains, walkways, and seasonal flower beds. Brooks Exhibit Hall was constructed under this plaza in 1958 to add space for the frequent trade shows and other events based in the Civic Auditorium on Grove Street.

San Francisco's increasing numbers of homeless people are often seen in the city's green spaces. Visitors and residents should be aware of possible danger in strolling in park areas and deserted business sectors after dark.

45 Across the plaza from City Hall on Larkin Street is the main branch of the **San Francisco Public Library.** (A new library is being built around the corner; when the library is completed, this site will become the new Asian Art Museum.) History buffs should visit the San Francisco History Room and Archives on the third floor. Historic photographs, maps, and other memorabilia are carefully documented for the layman or research scholar. *Tel. 415/557–4567. Open Tues., Fri. 12–6; Wed. 1–6; Thurs., Sat. 10–6.*

On the west side of City Hall, across Van Ness Avenue, is the **Performing Arts Center** complex which includes the Museum of Modern Art, the Opera House, and Davies Symphony Hall. The northernmost of the three is the Veterans' Building, whose **46** third and fourth floors house the **Museum of Modern Art.** The museum's permanent collection was significantly enhanced in 1991 by the $40 million Haas bequest, which features Matisse's masterpiece, *Woman in a Hat*, as well as works by Derain, Manet, Monet, and Picasso. Traveling exhibitions bring important national and international paintings, photographs, graphics, and sculpture to the Bay Area. The Museum Store has a select offering of books, posters, cards, and crafts. The Museum Cafe serves light snacks as well as wine and beer. *At McAllister St. and Van Ness Ave., tel. 415/863–8800. Admission: $4 adults, $2 senior citizens and students 13 and over with ID; free 1st Tues. of the month. Open Tues., Wed., Fri. 10–5; Thurs. 10–9, Sat., Sun. 11–5. Closed major holidays.*

South of the Veteran's Building is the opulent **War Memorial Opera House,** which opened in 1932. Lotfi Mansouri has taken over as head of the San Francisco Opera, the largest opera company west of New York. Its regular season of world-class productions runs from September through December.

South of Grove Street, still on Van Ness Avenue, is the $27.5 million home of the San Francisco Symphony, the modern 3,000-plus-seat **Louise M. Davies Symphony Hall,** made of glass and granite. *Grove St. and Van Ness Ave., tel. 415/552–8338. Cost: $3 adults, $2 senior citizens and students. Tours of Davies Hall Wed. 1:30, 2:30, Sat. 12:30, 1:30. Tours of Davies Hall and the adjacent Performing Arts Center every ½ hour Mon. 10–2:30.*

The San Francisco Opera Shop, up the street from Davies Hall, carries books, T-shirts, posters, and gift items associated with the performing arts. *199 Grove St., tel. 415/565–6414. Open weekdays 11–6, Sat. noon–6, Sun. noon–6 when there are matinees. (It frequently stays open till 8:30 during performances of the Opera and Symphony.)*

East of the Civic Center at Market and Fulton streets, the **United Nations Plaza** is the site of a bustling farmers' market on Wednesday and Sunday.

47 San Francisco's original civic center is **Mission Dolores,** founded in 1776 at what is now 16th and Dolores streets, about a mile south of city hall. The sixth of 21 missions founded by the Franciscans and the oldest building in the city, it combines Morrish, Mission, and Corinthian styles. Until the gold rush, it was surrounded by farms, and a nearby creek flowed to the bay. It retains the appearance of a small-scale outpost, dwarfed by the towers of the adjacent basilica built in 1916. There is a small museum and cemetery garden. *Tel. 415/621–8203. Donation: $1. Open daily 9–4. Public transportation: Muni Metro J-Church train to 16th St.*

Japantown

Japanese-Americans began gravitating to the neighborhood known as the Western Addition prior to the 1906 earthquake. Early immigrants arrived about 1860, and they named San Francisco Soko. After the 1906 fire had destroyed wooden homes in other parts of the stricken city, many survivors settled in the Western Addition. By the 1930s the pioneers had opened shops, markets, meeting halls, and restaurants and established Shinto and Buddhist temples. Japantown was virtually disbanded during World War II when many of its residents, including second- and third-generation Americans, were "relocated" in camps. Today **Japantown,** or "Nihonmachi," is centered on the slopes of Pacific Heights, north of Geary Boulevard, between Fillmore and Laguna streets. The Nihonmachi Cherry Blossom Festival is celebrated two weekends every April with a calendar of ethnic events. Walking in Nihonmachi is more than just a shopping and culinary treat; it is a cultural, sensory experience.

To reach Japantown from Union Square, take the Muni bus No. 38-Geary or No. 2, 3, or 4 on Sutter Street, westbound to Laguna. Remember to have exact change—fare is 85¢; free transfers are good for one direction and one change of vehicles.

We recommend visiting Japantown and the Western Addition during the day. Though the hotel, restaurant, and Kabuki movie complex are relatively safe in the evenings, it is often difficult to avoid long waits at isolated bus stops or to find a cruising cab when you want to get back to the hotel. The proximity of the often-hostile street gangs in the Western Addition could cause unpleasant incidents.

The buildings around the traffic-free **Japan Center Mall** between Sutter and Post streets are of the shoji screen school of architecture, and Ruth Asawa's origami fountain sits in the middle. (*See* Tour 1: Union Square, above, for more information on Ms. Asawa.)

48 The mall faces the three-block-long, five-acre **Japan Center.** In 1968 the multimillion-dollar development created by noted American architect Minoru Yamasaki opened with a three-day folk festival. The three-block cluster includes an 800-car public garage and shops and showrooms selling Japanese products: electronic products, cameras, tapes and records, porcelains, pearls, and paintings.

The center is dominated by its Peace Plaza and Pagoda located between the East and Kintetsu buildings. Designed by Professor Yoshiro Taniguchi of Tokyo, an authority on ancient Japanese buildings, the plaza is landscaped with traditional Japanese-style gardens and reflecting pools. A graceful *yagura* (wooden drum tower) spans the entrance to the plaza and the copper-roofed *Heiwa Dori* (Peace Walkway) at the north end connects the East and Kintetsu buildings. The five-tiered, 100-foot Peace Pagoda overlooks the plaza, where seasonal festivals are held. The pagoda draws on the tradition of miniature round pagodas dedicated to eternal peace by Empress Koken in Nara more than 1,200 years ago. It was designed by the Japanese architect Yoshiro Taniguchi "to convey the friendship and goodwill of the Japanese to the people of the United States." A cultural bridge modeled after Florence's Ponte Vecchio spans Webster Street.

Time Out At a sushi bar, sample the bite-size portions of lightly seasoned rice and seaweed topped with various kinds of seafood, usually raw. Try to manage the chopsticks, dip (don't drench) your portion into the soy sauce, and experience this typical Japanese favorite. Tea, sake, or excellent Japanese beer accompanies these morsels. One warning—the final bill is calculated by portion, and it is not unusual to run up a $20 tab per person. **Isobune,** in the Kentetsu Mall in Japan Center (tel. 415/563-1030), is unusual. The sushi chef prepares a variety of sushi, placing each small portion on a small wooden boat that floats on a "river" of water that circles the counter. The customer then fishes out a sampling.

An inexpensive and popular snack are *ramen* (noodle dishes). The noodles are either boiled and served in a broth or prepared toss-fried with bits of greens and meat added for flavor. **Mifune,** also in the Kintetsu Mall, serves both hot and cold noodles as well as either the fat strands of *udon* noodles or the buckwheat *soba*.

Walk back east on Geary Boulevard to Gough Street. This enclave of expensive high-rise residential towers is known as Cathedral Hill. The dramatic **St. Mary's Cathedral** was dedicated in 1971 at a cost of $7 million. The impressive Catholic cathedral seats 2,500 people around the central altar. Above the altar is a spectacular cascade made of 7,000 aluminum ribs. Four magnificent stained-glass windows in the dome represent the four elements: the blue north window, water; the light-colored south window, the sun; the red west window, fire; and the green east window, earth. Designed by a team of local architects and Pier Nervi of Rome, the Italian travertine church is approached through spacious plazas.

Pacific Heights

Pacific Heights forms an east–west ridge along the city's northern flank from Van Ness Avenue to the Presidio and from California Street to the bay. Some of the city's most expensive and dramatic real estate, including mansions and town houses priced at $1 million and up, are located here. Grand old Victorians, expensively face-lifted, grace tree-lined streets, although here and there glossy, glass-walled condo high rises obstruct the view.

Old money and some new, trade and diplomatic personnel, personalities in the limelight, and those who prefer absolute media anonymity occupy the city's most prestigious residential enclave. Receptions at the Gorden Getty mansion can block Broadway traffic while irate demonstrators picket the Soviet

Consulate on Green Street. Rolls-Royces, Mercedes, and security systems are commonplace.

Few visitors see anything other than the pleasing facades of Queen Anne charmers, English Tudor imports, and Baroque bastions, but strolling can still be a jackpot. The area encompasses a variety of great and small private homes. Many of the structures stand close together but extend in a vertical direction for two or more stories. A distinguishing feature of some of the grand residences is an ornate gate.

A good place to begin a tour of the neighborhood is at the corner of Webster Street and Pacific Avenue, deep in the heart of the Heights. You can get here from Union Square by taking Muni bus No. 3 from Sutter and Stockton to Jackson and Fillmore streets. Turn right and walk one block east to Webster Street.

North on Webster Street, at 2550, is the massive Georgian brick mansion built in 1896 for William B. Bourn, who had inherited a Mother Lode gold mine. The architect, Willis Polk, was responsible for many of the most traditional and impressive commercial and private homes built from the prequake days until the early 1920s. (Be sure to see his 1917 Hallidie Building, 130 Sutter Street; *see* Exploring The Financial District, above.)

Neighbors include a consulate and, on the northwest corner, two classic showplaces. **2222 Broadway** is the three-story Italian Renaissance palace built by Comstock mine heir James Flood. Broadway uptown, unlike its North Beach stretch, is big league socially. The former Flood residence was given to a religious order. Ten years later, the Convent of the Sacred Heart purchased the Baroque brick Grant house (2220 Broadway) and both serve as school quarters today. A second top-drawer school, the Hamlin (2120 Broadway), occupies another Flood property.

Go east on Broadway and at the next corner turn right onto Buchanan Street and continue south to 2090 Jackson Street. The

50 massive red sandstone **Whittier Mansion** was one of the most elegant 19th-century houses in the state, built so solidly that only a chimney toppled over during the 1906 earthquake. Next door at 2099 Pacific Avenue, is the North Baker Library of the California Historical Society. The library houses a fine collection of local historical documents but is only open to researchers, and has no public displays.

Proceed east another block to Laguna Street. The Italianate Victorians on the east side of the 1800 block of Laguna Street cost only $2,000–$2,600 when they were built during the 1870s. This block is one of the most photographed rows of Victorians in the city.

51 One block south, at Washington Street, is **Lafayette Park,** a four-block-square oasis for sunbathers and dog-and-Frisbee teams. During the 1860s a tenacious squatter, Sam Holladay, built himself a big house of wood shipped round the Horn, in the center of the park. Holladay even instructed city gardeners as if the land were his own, and defied all attempts to remove him. The house was finally torn down in 1936.

52 The most imposing residence is the formal French **Spreckels Palace** (2080 Washington St.). Sugar heir Adolph Spreckels's wife was so pleased that she commissioned architect George

Applegarth to design the city's European museum, the California Palace of the Legion of Honor in Lincoln Park.

Continue south on Gough Street (pronounced "Goff"), which runs along the east side of the park. A number of Queen Anne Victorians here have been lovingly restored. Two blocks south and one east, at the corner of California and Franklin, is an impressive twin-turreted Queen Anne–style Victorian built for a Gold Rush mining and lumber baron. North on Franklin Street, at 1735, stands a stately brick Georgian, built during the early 1900s for a coffee merchant.

53 At 2007 Franklin is the handsome **Haas-Lilienthal Victorian.** Built in 1886, at an original cost of $20,000, this grand Queen Anne survived the 1906 earthquake and fire, and is the only fully furnished Victorian open to the public. The carefully kept rooms offer an intriguing glimpse into turn-of-the-century taste and lifestyle. A small display of photographs on the bottom floor proves that this elaborate house was modest compared with some of the giants that fell to the fire. It is operated by the Foundation for San Francisco's Architectural Heritage, and tours are given by docent volunteers. *Tel. 415/441–3004. Admission: $4 adults, $2 senior citizens and children under 12. Open Wed. noon–4, Sun. 11–4:30.*

By the mid-1970s, dozens of San Francisco's shabby gingerbreads were sporting psychedelic-colored facades, and the trend continues. Renovated treasures are found not only in the Haight-Ashbury district but increasingly in the Western Addition as well as in the working-class Mission area.

The Northern Waterfront

Numbers in the margin correspond with points of interest on the Northern Waterfront map.

For the sight, sound, and smell of the sea, hop the Powell-Hyde cable car from Union Square to the end of the line. From the cable car turnaround, Aquatic Park and the National Maritime Museum are immediately to the west. If you're interested in exploring the more commercial attractions, Ghirardelli Square is behind you and Fisherman's Wharf to the east. We recommend casual clothes, good walking shoes, and a jacket or sweater for mid-afternoon breezes or foggy mists.

Or you could begin your day with one of the early-morning boat tours that depart from the Northern Waterfront piers. On a clear day (almost always), the morning light casts a warm glow on the colorful homes on Russian Hill, the weather-aged fishing boats cluttered at Fisherman's Wharf, rosy Ghirardelli Square and its fairy-tale clock tower, and the swelling seas beyond the entrance to the bay.

San Francisco is famous for the arts and crafts that flourish on the streets. Each day over 200 of the city's innovative jewelers, painters, potters, photographers, and leather workers offer their wares for sale. You'll find them at Fisherman's Wharf, Union Square, Embarcadero Plaza, and Cliff House. Be wary: Some of the items are from Mexican or other foreign factories, and some may be overpriced. If you can't live without the item, try to bargain.

❶ The **National Maritime Museum** (Aquatic Park, at the foot of Polk St.) exhibits ship models, photographs, maps, and other artifacts chronicling the development of San Francisco and the West Coast through maritime history. *Tel. 415/556–8177. Admission free. Open daily 10–5, till 6 in summer.*

❷ The museum also includes the **Hyde Street Pier** (2 blocks east), where historic vessels are moored. The *Eureka*, a sidewheel ferry, and the *C.A. Thayer*, a three-masted schooner, can be boarded. Built in 1886, she is the last of the Cape Horn fleet. *Tel. 415/556–6435. Admission: $3 adults, children and senior citizens free. Open daily 10–5, 10–6 in summer.*

The *Pampanito*, at Pier 45, is a World War II submarine. An audio tour has been installed. *Tel. 415/929–0202. Admission: $4 adults, $2 students 12–18, $1 children 6–11, senior citizens, and active military. Open Sun.–Thurs. 9–6, Fri.–Sat. 9–9, daily 9–9 in summer.*

❸ Spend some time strolling through **Ghirardelli Square,** which is across Beach Street from the National Maritime Museum. This charming complex of 19th-century brick factory buildings has been transformed into specialty shops, cafés, restaurants, and galleries. Until the early 1960s, the Ghirardelli Chocolate Company's aromatic production perfumed the Northern Waterfront. Two unusual shops deserve mention: **Light Opera** specializes in exquisite Russian lacquer boxes. (**Gump's** on Post Street also shows these sophisticated treasures, priced from about $50 to $20,000.) **Xanadu Gallery** displays museum-quality tribal art from Asia, Africa, Oceania, and the Americas. Their array of antique and ethnic jewelry is peerless.

❹ Just east of the Hyde Street Pier, **The Cannery** is a three-story structure built in 1894 to house the Del Monte Fruit and Vegetable Cannery. Now shops, art galleries, and unusual restaurants ring the courtyard. Just across the street, additional shopping and snacking choices are offered at the flag-festooned **❺** **Anchorage** mall.

❻ A bit farther down at Taylor and Jefferson streets is **Fisherman's Wharf.** Numerous seafood restaurants are located here, as well as sidewalk crab pots and counters that offer takeaway shrimp and crab cocktails. Ships creak at their moorings; sea gulls cry out for a handout. By mid-afternoon, the fishing fleet is back to port. T-shirts and sweats, gold chains galore, redwood furniture, acres of artwork—some original—beckon visitors. Wax museums, fast-food favorites, amusing street artists, and the animated robots at Lazer Maze provide diversions for all ages.

Time Out A great family spot on the wharf is **Bobby Rubino's** (245 Jefferson St.). Barbecued ribs, shrimp, chicken, and burgers—there is something tasty for everyone. A favorite with couples is crowded, noisy **Houlihan's** at the Anchorage mall. It is noted for fancy drinks, fantastic bay views, tasty pizza and pastas, plus nightly music and dancing.

Today's tourists daily have the opportunity of enjoying exhilarating cruising on the bay. Among the cruises of the **Red and White Fleet,** berthed at Pier 41, are frequent 45-minute swings under the Golden Gate Bridge and the Northern Waterfront. Advanced reservations are strongly recommended for the very

Northern Waterfront

popular Alcatraz Island tour, which enables passengers to take a self-guided tour through the prison and grounds. *Reservations for individuals from Ticketron, Box 26430, 94126, tel. 415/546–2896. Cost: $5; $7.50 with audio tour.*

The **Blue and Gold Fleet,** berthed at Pier 39, provides its passengers with validated parking across the street. The 1¼-hour tour sails under both the Bay and Golden Gate bridges. Dinner-dance cruises run April–mid-December. *Tel. 415/781–7877. Reservations not necessary. Bay Cruise: $14 adults, $7 senior citizens and children 5–18, under 5 free. Summertime dinner-dance cruise: $35 per person (group rates available). Daily departures.*

7 **Pier 39** is the newest of San Francisco's waterfront malls. Dozens of shops with fascinating but often useless merchandise will prove tempting. The myriad eateries confuse some parents seeking only a traditional soda-and-burger stop. Ongoing free entertainment, accessible validated parking, as well as nearby public transportation ensure crowds most days.

The Marina and the Presidio

8 San Francisco's rosy and Rococo **Palace of Fine Arts** is at the very end of the Marina, near the intersection of Baker and Beach streets. The palace is the sole survivor of the 32 tinted plaster structures built for the 1915 Panama-Pacific Exposition. Bernard Maybeck designed the Roman Classic beauty, and legions of sentimental citizens and a huge private donation saved the palace. It was reconstructed in concrete at a cost of $7 million and reopened in 1967. The massive columns, great rotunda, and swan-filled lagoon will be familiar from fashion layouts as well as many recent films. Recently, travelers on package tours from Japan have been using it as a backdrop for wedding-party photos, with the brides wearing Western-style finery.

The interior houses a fascinating hands-on museum, the **Exploratorium.** It has been called the best science museum in the world. The curious of all ages flock here to try to use and understand some of the 600 exhibits. Be sure to include the pitch-black, crawl-through Tactile Dome in your visit. *Tel. 415/563-7337. Prices and hours subject to change, so call ahead. Admission: $6 adults, $2 children under 17. For the Tactile Dome, reservations required, and a $6 charge includes museum admission.*

If you have a car, now is the time to use it for a drive through the **Presidio.** (If not, Muni bus No. 38 from Union Square will take you to Park Presidio; from there use a free transfer to bus No. 28 into the Presidio.) A military post for over 200 years, this headquarters of the U.S. Sixth Army may soon become a public park. De Anza and a band of Spanish settlers claimed the area in 1776. It became a Mexican garrison in 1822 when Mexico gained its independence from Spain. U.S. troops forcibly occupied it in 1846.

The more than 1,500 acres of rolling hills, majestic woods, and attractive redbrick army barracks present an air of serenity in the middle of the city. There are two beaches, a golf course, and picnic sites. The **Officers' Club,** a long, low adobe, was the Spanish commandante's headquarters, built about 1776, and is the oldest standing building in the city. The **Presidio Army Museum** is housed in the former hospital and focuses on the role played by the military in San Francisco's development. *On the corner of Lincoln Blvd. and Funston Ave., tel. 415/561-4115. Admission free. Open Tues.–Sun. 10–4.*

❾ Muni bus No. 28 will take you to the **Golden Gate Bridge** toll plaza. San Francisco celebrated the 50th birthday of the orange suspension bridge in 1987. Nearly 2 miles long, connecting San Francisco with Marin County, its Art Deco design is powerful, serene, and tough, made to withstand winds of over 100 miles per hour. Though frequently gusty and misty (walkers should wear warm clothing), the bridge offers unparalleled views of the Bay Area. The east walkway offers a glimpse of the San Francisco skyline as well as the islands of the bay. On a sunny day sailboats dot the water, and brave windsurfers test the often treacherous tides beneath the bridge. The view west confronts you with the wild hills of the Marin headlands, the curving coast south to Lands End, and the majestic Pacific Ocean. There's a vista point on the Marin side, where you can contemplate the city and its spectacular setting.

❿ **Fort Point** was constructed during the years 1853–1861 to protect San Francisco from sea attack during the Civil War. It was designed to mount 126 cannons with a range of up to 2 miles. Standing under the shadow of the Golden Gate Bridge, the national historic site is now a museum filled with military memorabilia. Guided group tours are offered by National Park Rangers, and there are cannon demonstrations. There is a superb view of the bay from the top floor. *Tel. 415/556–1693. Admission free. Open daily 10–5.*

From here, hardy walkers may elect to stroll about 3½ miles (with bay views) along the **Golden Gate Promenade** to Aquatic Park and the Hyde Street cable car terminus.

Golden Gate Park

Numbers in the margin correspond with points of interest on the Golden Gate Park map.

It was a Scotsman, John McLaren, who became manager of Golden Gate Park in 1887 and transformed the brush and sand into the green civilized wilderness we enjoy today. Here you can attend a polo game or a Sunday band concert and rent a bike, boat, or roller skates. On Sundays, some park roads are closed to cars and come alive with joggers, bicyclists, skaters, museum goers, and picnickers. There are tennis courts, baseball diamonds, soccer fields, and a buffalo paddock, and miles of trails for horseback riding in this 1,000-acre park.

Because it is so large, the best way for most visitors to see it is by car. Muni buses provide service, though on weekends there may be a long wait. On Market Street, board a west-bound No. 5-Fulton or No. 21-Hayes bus and continue to Arguello and Fulton streets. Walk south about 500 feet to John F. Kennedy Drive.

From May through October, free guided walking tours of the park are offered every weekend by the Friends of Recreation and Parks (tel. 415/221–1311).

❶ The oldest building in the park and perhaps San Francisco's most elaborate Victorian is the **Conservatory,** a copy of London's famous Kew Gardens. The ornate greenhouse was originally brought around the Horn for the estate of James Lick in San Jose. The Conservatory was purchased from the Lick estate with public subscription funds and erected in the park. In addition to a tropical garden, there are seasonal displays of flowers and plants and a permanent exhibit of rare orchids.

❷ The eastern section of the park has three museums. The **M.H. de Young Memorial Museum** was completely reorganized in 1989. It now features American art, with collections of painting, sculpture, textiles, and decorative arts from Colonial times through the 20th century. Fifteen new galleries highlight the work of American masters including Copley, Eakins, Bingham, and Sargent. Don't miss the room of landscapes, dominated by Frederic Church's moody, almost psychedelic *Rainy Season in the Tropics.* There is a wonderful gallery of American still-life and trompe l'oeil art and a small selection of classic Shaker furniture. The de Young has also retained its dramatic collection of tribal art from Africa, Oceania, and the Americas, which includes pottery, basketry, sculpture, and ritual clothing and accessories. In addition to its permanent collections, the museum hosts selected traveling shows—often blockbuster events for which there are long lines and additional admission charges.

The museum has an outstanding shop with a wide selection of art objects. The **Cafe de Young,** which has outdoor seating in the Oakes Garden, serves a complete menu of light refresh-

Golden Gate Park

PACIFIC OCEAN

Asian Art Museum, **3**
California Academy of Sciences, **4**
Conservatory, **1**
Dutch Windmill, **9**
Japanese Tea Garden, **5**

M.H. de Young Memorial Museum, **2**
Queen Wilhelmina Tulip Garden, **10**
Shakespeare Garden, **6**
Stow Lake, **8**
Strybing Arboretum, **7**

ments until 4 PM. *Tel. 415/863–3330 for 24-hour information. Admission: $4 adults, $2 senior citizens and youths 12–17, under 12 free. Free 1st Wed. and Sat. morning of the month. Note: One admission charge admits you to the de Young, Asian Art, and Legion of Honor museums on the same day. Open Wed.– Sun. 10–5.*

❸ The **Asian Art Museum** is located in galleries that adjoin the de Young. This world-famous Avery Brundage collection consists of more than 10,000 sculptures, paintings, and ceramics that illustrate major periods of Asian art. Very special are the Magnin Jade Room and the Leventritt collection of blue and white porcelains. On the second floor are treasures from Iran, Turkey, Syria, India, Tibet, Nepal, Pakistan, Korea, Japan, Afghanistan, and Southeast Asia. Both the de Young and Asian Art museums have daily docent tours. *Tel. 415/668–8921. Admission collected when entering the de Young. Open Wed.–Sun. 10–5.*

❹ The **California Academy of Sciences** is directly opposite the de Young Museum. It is one of the five top natural history museums in the country and has both an aquarium and a planetarium. Throngs of visitors enjoy its Steinhart Aquarium, with its dramatic 100,000-gallon Fish Roundabout, home to 14,000 creatures, and a living coral reef with colorful fish, giant clams, tropical sharks, and a rainbow of hard and soft corals. There is an additional charge for Morrison Planetarium shows ($2.50 adults, $1.25 senior citizens and students, tel. 415/750–7138 for daily schedule). The Space and Earth Hall has an "earthquake floor" that enables visitors to ride a simulated California earthquake. The Wattis Hall of Man presents lifelike habitat scenes that range from the icy terrain of the arctic Inuit to the lush highlands of New Guinea. Newly renovated is the Wild California Hall, with a 10,000-gallon aquarium tank showing underwater life at the Farallones (islands off the coast of northern California), life-size elephant seal models, and video information on the wildlife of the state. A stuffed great white shark, caught off the waters of Half Moon Bay, was added in 1989. The genuine 13½-foot, 1,500-pound "Jaws" is suspended in a tank. The innovative Life through Time Hall tells the story of evolution from the beginnings of the universe through the age of dinosaurs to the age of mammals. A cafeteria is open daily until one hour before the museum closes. The Academy Store offers a wide selection of books, posters, toys, and cultural artifacts. *Tel. 415/750–7145. Admission: $6 adults, $3 senior citizens and students 12–17, $1 children 6–11. Free 1st Wed. of each month. Open daily July 4–Labor Day 10–7, Labor Day–July 3 10–5.*

Time Out The **Japanese Tea Garden,** next to the Asian Art Museum, is
❺ ideal for resting after museum touring. This charming four-acre village was created for the 1894 Mid-Winter Exposition. Small ponds, streams, and flowering shrubs create a serene landscape. The cherry blossoms in spring are exquisite. The Tea House (tea, of course, and cookies are served) is popular and busy. *Tel. 415/752–1171. Admission: $2 adults, $1 senior residents of San Francisco and children 6–12. Free 1st Wed. of each month. Open daily 8:30–6:30.*

A short stroll from the Academy of Sciences will take you to the
❻ free **Shakespeare Garden.** Two hundred flowers mentioned by

the Bard, as well as bronze-engraved panels with floral quotations, are set throughout the garden.

⑦ Strybing Arboretum specializes in plants from areas with climates similar to that of the Bay Area, such as the west coast of Australia, South Africa, and the Mediterranean. There are many gardens inside the grounds, with 6,000 plants and tree varieties blooming seasonally. *9th Ave. at Lincoln Way, tel. 415/661–0668. Admission free. Open weekdays 8–4:30, weekends and holidays 10–5. Tours leave the bookstore weekdays at 1:30 PM, weekends at 10:30 AM and 1:30 PM.*

The western half of Golden Gate Park offers miles of wooded greenery and open spaces for all types of spectator and participant sports. Rent a paddleboat or stroll around **Stow Lake.** The **Chinese Pavilion,** a gift from the city of Taipei, was shipped in 6,000 pieces and assembled on the shore of Strawberry Hill Island in Stow Lake in 1981. At the very western end of the park, where Kennedy Drive meets the Great Highway, is the beautifully restored 1902 **Dutch Windmill** and the photogenic **Queen Wilhelmina Tulip Garden.**

Lincoln Park and the Western Shoreline

No other American city provides such close-up viewing of the power and fury of the surf attacking the shore. From Land's End in Lincoln Park you can look across the Golden Gate (the name was originally given to the opening of San Francisco Bay long before the bridge was built) to the Marin Headlands. From Cliff House south to the San Francisco Zoo, the Great Highway and Ocean Beach run along the western edge of the city.

The wind is often strong along the shoreline, summer fog can blanket the ocean beaches, and the water is cold and usually too rough for swimming. Carry a sweater or jacket and bring binoculars.

At the northwest corner of the San Francisco Peninsula is **Lincoln Park.** At one time all the city's cemeteries were here, segregated by nationality. Today there is an 18-hole golf course with large and well-formed Monterey cypresses lining the fairways. There are scenic walks throughout the 275-acre park, with particularly good views from **Land's End** (the parking lot is at the end of El Camino del Mar). The trails out to Land's End, however, are for skilled hikers only: There are frequent landslides, and danger lurks along the steep cliffs.

Also in Lincoln Park is the **California Palace of the Legion of Honor.** The building itself—modeled after the 18th-century Parisian original—is architecturally interesting and spectacularly situated on cliffs overlooking the ocean and the Golden Gate Bridge. Rodin's famous *Thinker* towers over the entry court and presages one of the finest Rodin collections in the world. This museum was redesigned in 1989 to present eight centuries of European art, combining painting, sculpture, and the decorative arts. Its holdings include works by Fra Angelico, Titian, El Greco, and Rembrandt, as well as four galleries of French Rococo furniture, porcelain, and paintings. The museum also features Impressionist paintings by Manet, Monet, Renoir, and Degas and houses the Achenbach Foundation for Graphic Arts, a collection of over 100,000 prints and drawings.

Legion of Honor Dr., tel. 415/863–3330. Daily docent tours. Admission: $4 adults, $2 senior citizens and youths 12–17, under 12 free. Free 1st Wed. and Sat. morning of each month. Open Wed.–Sun. 10–5. Note: One admission charge admits you to the de Young, Asian Art, and Legion of Honor museums on the same day.

Cliff House (1066 Point Lobos Ave.), where the road turns south along the western shore, has existed in several incarnations. The original, built in 1863, and several later structures were destroyed by fire. The present building has restaurants, a pub, and a gift shop. The lower dining room overlooks **Seal Rocks** (the barking marine mammals sunning themselves are actually sea lions).

An adjacent (free) attraction is the **Musée Mécanique,** a collection of antique mechanical contrivances, including peep shows and nickelodeons. The museum carries on the tradition of arcade amusement at the Cliff House. *Tel. 415/386–1170. Open weekdays 11–7, weekends 10–7.*

Two flights below Cliff House is a fine observation deck and the Golden Gate National Recreation Area **Visitors Center** (tel. 415/556–8642; open weekdays 10–4:30, weekends 10–5). There are interesting and historic photographs of Cliff House and the glass-roofed **Sutro Baths.** The baths covered three acres just north of Cliff House and comprised six enormous baths, 500 dressing rooms, and several restaurants. The baths were closed in 1952 and burned in 1966. You can explore the ruins on your own (the Visitors Center offers information on these and other trails) or take ranger-led walks on weekends.

Because traffic is often heavy in summer and on weekends, you might want to take the Muni system from the Union Square area out to Cliff House. On weekdays, take the Muni No. 38-Geary Limited to 48th Street and Point Lobos and walk down the hill. (On weekends and during the evenings, the Muni No. 38 is marked 48th Avenue.)

Time Out Cliff House has several restaurants and a busy bar. The **Upstairs Room** (tel. 415/387–5847) features a light menu with a number of omelet suggestions. The lower dining room, the **Terrace Room** (tel. 415/386–3330), has a fabulous view of Seal Rocks. Reservations are recommended, but you may still have to wait for a table, especially at midday on Sunday.

Below the Cliff House are the **Great Highway** and **Ocean Beach.** Stretching for 3 miles along the western (Pacific) side of the city, this is a beautiful beach for walking, running, or lying in the sun—but not for swimming.

At the Great Highway and Sloat Boulevard is the **San Francisco Zoo.** The zoo was begun in 1889 in Golden Gate Park. At its present home there are 1,000 species of birds and animals, over 130 of which have been designated endangered species. Among the protected are the snow leopard, Bengal tiger, red panda, jaguar, and the Asian elephant. One of the newest attractions is the greater one-horned rhino, next to the African elephants. Gorilla World, a $2 million exhibit, is the largest and most natural gorilla habitat in a zoo. The circular outer area is carpeted with natural African Kikuyu grass, while trees, shrubs, and waterfalls create communal play areas. The $5 million Primate

Discovery Center houses 16 endangered species in atriumlike enclosures. One of the most popular zoo residents is Prince Charles, a rare white tiger and the first of its kind to be exhibited in the West.

There are 33 "storyboxes" throughout the zoo that when turned on with the blue plastic elephant keys ($1.50) recite animal facts and basic zoological concepts in four languages (English, Spanish, Cantonese, and Tagalog).

The children's zoo has a minipopulation of about 300 mammals, birds, and reptiles, plus an insect zoo, a baby animal nursery, and a beautifully restored 1921 Dentzel Carousel. A ride astride one of the 52 hand-carved menagerie animals costs 75¢.

Zoo information, tel. 415/753–7083. Admission: $6 adults, $3 youths 12–15 and senior citizens, under 12 free when accompanied by an adult. Free 1st Wed. of the month. Open daily 10–5. Children's zoo admission: $1, under 3 free. Open daily 11–4.

San Francisco for Free

This is not a cheap city to live in or visit. Lodging and dining are expensive; museums, shopping, the opera, or a nightclub may set you back a bit. It is possible, however, to do much of your sightseeing very cheaply. Walking is often the best way to get around, and it's not very expensive to use the cable cars and buses. Exploring most of Golden Gate Park is absolutely free, and so is walking across the Golden Gate Bridge.

The Golden Gate National Recreation Area (GGNRA), comprising most of San Francisco's shoreline, Alcatraz and Angel islands, and the headlands of Marin County, is the largest urban park in the world. The Golden Gate Promenade's 3.5-mile footpath runs from Fort Point at the base of the bridge along the shore to Hyde Street Pier. There's also a new 8-mile-long bicycle path along Ocean beach from Cliff House south to Fort Funston, hugging sand dunes and providing constant ocean views. The GGNRA is San Francisco at its natural best.

There are also free organ concerts on Saturday and Sunday at 4 PM in the **Palace of the Legion of Honor** in Lincoln Park (tel. 415/221–4811) and free band concerts on Sunday and holiday afternoons in the **Golden Gate Park band shell,** opposite the de Young Museum (tel. 415/666–7107).

There are several venues for free concerts in San Francisco. The nation's oldest continuous free summer music festival, offering 10 Sunday afternoons of symphony, opera, jazz, pop music, and dance, takes place at **Stern Grove** (Sloat Blvd. at 19th Ave., tel. 415/398–6551) in the sunset District. Keep in mind that summer in this area near the ocean can be cool. Bring a picnic and enjoy this lovely sunken park surrounded by eucalyptus and redwoods.

What to See and Do with Children

The attractions described in the above exploring sections offer a great deal of entertainment for children as well as their families. We suggest, for example, visiting the ships at the **Hyde Street Pier** and spending some time at **Pier 39,** where there is a double-decked Venetian carousel. (*See* Exploring The Northern Waterfront, above.)

Children will find much to amuse themselves with at **Golden Gate Park,** from the old-fashioned conservatory to the expansive lawns and trails. There is another vintage carousel (1912) at the children's playground. The **Steinhart Aquarium** at the California Academy of Sciences has a "Touching Tide Pool," from which docents will pull starfish and hermit crabs for children or adults to feel. The **Japanese Tea Garden,** although crowded, is well worth exploring; climbing over the high, humpbacked bridges is like moving the neighborhood playground toys into an exotic new (or old) world.

It is also possible to walk across the **Golden Gate Bridge.** The view is thrilling and the wind invigorating, if the children (and adults) are not overwhelmed by the height of the bridge and the nearby automobile traffic. (*See* Exploring The Marina and the Presidio, above.)

Many children may enjoy walking along crowded **Grant Avenue** and browsing in the many souvenir shops. Unfortunately, nothing—not even straw finger wrestlers, wooden contraptions to make coins "disappear," shells that open in water to release tissue paper flowers, and other true junk—is as cheap as it once was. (*See* Exploring Chinatown, above.)

The **San Francisco Zoo,** with a children's zoo, playground, and carousel, is not far from **Ocean Beach.** The weather and the currents do not allow swimming, but it's a good place for walking and playing in the surf. (*See* Exploring Lincoln Park and the Western Shoreline, above.)

The **Exploratorium** at the Palace of Fine Arts is a preeminent children's museum and is very highly recommended. (*See* Exploring The Marina and the Presidio, above.)

Finally, we remind you of the **cable cars.** Try to find time for a ride when the crowds are not too thick (mid-morning or afternoon). It's usually easier to get on at one of the turnarounds at the ends of the lines. (*See* Getting Around, above.)

If you're ready to spend a day outside of the city, consider a trip to Vallejo's Marine World Africa USA Excursions, (*See* Excursions, below).

Shopping

San Francisco is a shopper's dream—major department stores, fine fashion, discount outlets, art galleries, and crafts stores are among the many offerings. Most accept at least Visa and MasterCard charge cards, and many also accept American Express, and Diner's Club. A very few accept cash only. Ask about traveler's checks; policies vary. The San Francisco *Chronicle* and *Examiner* advertise sales; for smaller innovative shops, check the San Francisco *Bay Guardian.* Store hours are slightly different everywhere, but a generally trusted rule is to shop between 10 AM and 5 or 6 PM Monday through Saturday (until 8 or 9 PM on Thursday) and from noon until 5 PM on Sunday. Stores on and around Fisherman's Wharf often have longer summer hours.

If you want to cover most of the city, the best shopping route might be to start at Fisherman's Wharf, then continue in order to Union Square and Crocker Galleria, the Embarcadero Center, Jackson Square, Chinatown, North Beach, Chestnut

Street, Union Street, Fillmore and Sacramento streets, Japan Center, Haight Street, Civic Center, and South of Market (SoMa).

Major Shopping Districts
Fisherman's Wharf

San Francisco's Fisherman's Wharf is host to a number of shopping and sightseeing attractions: **Pier 39, the Anchorage, Ghirardelli Square,** and **The Cannery.** Each offers shops, restaurants, and a festive atmosphere as well as such outdoor entertainment as musicians, mimes, and magicians. Pier 39 includes an amusement area and a double-decked Venetian carousel. One attraction shared by all the centers is the view of the bay and the proximity of the cable car lines, which can take shoppers directly to Union Square.

Union Square

San Francisco visitors usually head for shopping at Union Square first. It's centrally located in the downtown area and surrounded by major hotels, from the large luxury properties to smaller bed-and-breakfasts. The square itself is a city park (with a garage underneath). It is flanked by such large stores as **Macy's, Saks Fifth Avenue, I. Magnin,** and **Neiman Marcus. North Beach Leather** and **Gucci** are two smaller upscale stores. Across from the cable car turntable at Powell and Market streets is the **San Francisco Shopping Centre,** with the fashionable **Nordstrom** store in the top five floors of shops. Nearby is **Crocker Galleria,** underneath a glass dome at Post and Kearny streets; 50 shops, restaurants, and services make up this Financial District shopping center, which is topped by two rooftop parks.

Embarcadero Center

Five modern towers of shops, restaurants, and offices plus the Hyatt Regency Hotel make up the downtown Embarcadero Center at the end of Market Street. Like most malls, the center is a little sterile and falls short in the character department. What it lacks in charm, however, it makes up for in sheer quantity. The center's 175 stores and services include such nationally known stores as **The Limited,** and **Ann Taylor,** as well as more local or West Coast–based businesses such as the **Nature Company, Filian's European Clothing,** and **Lotus Designer Earrings.** Each tower occupies one block, and parking garages are available.

Jackson Square

Jackson Square is where a dozen or so of San Francisco's finest retail antiques dealers are located. If your passion is 19th-century English furniture, for example, there's a good chance that something here will suit. Knowledgeable store owners and staffs can direct you to other places in the city for your special interests. The shops are along Jackson Street in the Financial District, so a visit there will put you very close to the Embarcadero Center and Chinatown.

Chinatown

The intersection of Grant Avenue and Bush Street marks "the Gateway" to Chinatown; here shoppers and tourists are introduced to 24 blocks of shops, restaurants, markets, and temples. There are daily "sales" on gems of all sorts—especially jade and pearls—alongside stalls of bok choy and gingerroot. Chinese silks and toy trinkets are also commonplace in the shops, as are selections of colorful pottery, baskets, and large figures of soapstone, ivory, and jade, including netsukes (carved figures).

North Beach

The once largely Italian enclave of North Beach gets smaller each year as Chinatown spreads northward. It has been called the city's answer to New York City's Greenwich Village, although it's much smaller. Many of the businesses here tend to be small clothing stores, antiques shops, or such eccentric specialty shops as **Quantity Postcard** (1441 Grant Ave., tel. 415/986–8866), which has an inventory of 15,000 different postcards. If you get tired of poking around in the bookstores, a number of cafés dot the streets and there are lots of Italian restaurants.

Union Street Out-of-towners sometimes confuse Union Street—a popular stretch of shops and restaurants five blocks south of the Golden Gate National Recreation Area—with downtown's Union Square. (*See* above.) Nestled at the foot of a hill between the neighborhoods of Pacific Heights and Cow Hollow, Union Street shines with contemporary fashion and custom jewelry. Union Street's feel is largely new and upscale, although there are a few antiques shops and some long-term storekeepers. Shopping here is not limited to wearing apparel, but includes a good bookstore, **Solar Light Books, Union Street Graphics** for posters, and several galleries for crafts, photographs, sculpture, and serigraphs.

Japantown Unlike Chinatown, North Beach, or the Mission, the 5-acre **Japan Center** (between Geary and Post Sts.) is contained under one roof. It is actually a mall of stores filled with antique kimonos, beautiful tansu chests, and both new and old porcelains. The center always feels a little empty, but the good shops here are well worth a visit. Japan Center occupies the three-block area between Laguna and Fillmore streets, and between Geary and Post streets.

Participant Sports

One great attraction of the Bay Area is the abundance of activities. Joggers, bicyclists, and aficionados of virtually all sports can find their favorite pastimes within driving distance, and often within walking distance, from downtown hotels. Golden Gate Park has numerous paths for runners and cyclists. Lake Merced in San Francisco and Lake Merritt in Oakland are among the most popular areas for joggers.

For information on running races, tennis tournaments, bicycle races, and other participant sports, check the monthly issues of *City Sports* magazine, available free at sporting goods stores, tennis centers, and other recreational sites.

Bicycling Two bike routes are maintained by the San Francisco Recreation and Park Department (tel. 415/666–7201). One route goes through Golden Gate Park to Lake Merced; the other goes from the south end of the city to the Golden Gate Bridge and beyond. Many shops along Stanyon Street rent bikes.

Boating and Sailing **Stow Lake** (tel. 415/752–0347) in Golden Gate Park has rowboat, pedalboat, and electric boat rentals. The lake is open daily for boating, but call for seasonal hours. San Francisco Bay offers year-round sailing, but tricky currents make the bay hazardous for inexperienced navigators. Boat rentals and charters are available throughout the Bay Area and are listed under "boat rentals" in the Yellow Pages. A selected charter is **A Day on the Bay** (tel. 415/922–0227). Local sailing information can be obtained at **The Eagle Cafe** on Pier 39.

Fishing Numerous fishing boats leave from San Francisco, Sausalito, Berkeley, Emeryville, and Point San Pablo. They go for salmon outside the bay or striped bass and giant sturgeon within the bay. Temporary licenses are available on the charters. In San Francisco, lines can be cast from San Francisco Municipal Pier, Fisherman's Wharf, or Aquatic Park. Trout fishing is available at Lake Merced. Licenses can be bought at sporting goods stores. The cost of fishing licenses ranges from $5 for one day to $21.50 for a complete state license. For charters, reservations are suggested. Some selected sportfishing charters are listed. Mailing addresses are given, but you're more likely to get a response if you call.

Capt. Ron's Pacific Charters (Fisherman's Wharf. Write to 561 Prentiss St., 94110, tel. 415/285–2000).

Capt. Fred Morini (Fisherman's Wharf. Write to 138 Harvard Dr., Larkspur 94939, tel. 415/924–5575).

Muny Sport Fishing (3098 Polk St., 94109, across from Ghirardelli Sq., tel. 415/871–4445). Leaves daily from Fisherman's Wharf.

Wacky Jacky (Fisherman's Wharf. Write Jacky Douglas at 473 Bella Vista Way, 94127, tel. 415/586–9800).

Fitness **Physical fitness** activities continue to be popular, but most clubs are private and visitors could have trouble finding a workout location. **Sheraton Hotels** have arrangements with neighboring clubs, and the **Burlingame Hyatt,** near the airport, has a workout facility. **24-hour Nautilus** (1335 Sutter, tel. 415/776–2200) is open to the public for a $10 drop-in fee. **Sante West Fitness** (3727 Buchanan, tel. 415/563–6222) offers aerobics, low- impact, stretching, and other classes for a $9 drop-in fee.

Golf San Francisco has four public golf courses, and visitors should call for tee times: **Harding Park,** an 18-hole, par-72 course (at Lake Merced Blvd. and Skyline Blvd., tel. 415/664–4690); **Lincoln Park,** 18 holes, par 69 (34th and Clement Sts., tel. 415/221–9911); **Golden Gate Park,** a "pitch and putt" 9-holer (47th and Fulton Sts., tel. 415/751–8987); **Glen Eagles Golf Course,** a full-size 9-holer in McLaren Park (2100 Sunnydale Ave., tel. 415/587–2425). Another municipal course, **Sharp Park,** is south of the city in Pacifica (tel. 415/355–8546).

Tennis The San Francisco Recreation and Park Department maintains 130 free tennis courts throughout the city. The largest set of free courts is at **Dolores Park,** 18th and Dolores streets, with six courts available on a first-come, first-served basis. There are 21 public courts in **Golden Gate Park;** reservations and fee information can be obtained by calling 415/753–7101.

Spectator Sports

For the sports fan, the Bay Area offers a vast selection of events—from yacht races to rodeo to baseball.

Baseball The **San Francisco Giants** play ball at Candlestick Park (tel. 415/467–8000) and the **Oakland A's** play at the Oakland Coliseum (tel. 415/638–0500). These games rarely sell out, and game-day tickets are usually available at the stadiums. Premium seats, however, often do sell out in advance. City shuttle buses marked Ballpark Special run from numerous bus stops. Remember that Candlestick Park is often windy and cold, so take along extra layers of clothing to deal with changing weather. The Oakland Coliseum can be reached by taking BART trains to the Coliseum stop.

Basketball The **Golden State Warriors** play NBA basketball at the Oakland Coliseum Arena from October through April. Tickets are available through Ticketron (tel. 415/392–7469). Again, BART trains to the Coliseum stop are the easiest method of travel.

Football The **San Francisco 49ers** play at Candlestick Park, but the games are almost always sold out far in advance, so call first (tel. 415/468–2249).

Tennis The **Civic Auditorium** (999 Grove St.) is the site of the *Volvo Tennis/San Francisco* tournament in early February (tel. 415/239–4800). The *Virginia Slims women's tennis tour* visits the Oakland Coliseum Arena in October.

Yacht Racing There are frequent yacht races on the bay. The local papers will give you details, or you can be an uninformed but appreciative spectator from the Golden Gate Bridge or other vantage points around town.

Beaches

San Francisco's beaches are perfect for romantic sunset strolls, but don't make the mistake of expecting to find Waikiki-by-the-Metropolis. The water is cold, and the beach areas are often foggy and usually jammed on sunny days. They can be satisfactory for afternoon sunning, but treacherous currents make most areas dangerous for swimming. During stormy months, beachcombers can stroll along the sand and discover a variety of ocean treasures: glossy agates and jade pebbles, sea-sculptured roots and branches, and—rarely—glass floats.

Baker Beach Baker Beach is not recommended for swimming: Watch for larger-than-usual waves. In recent years, the north end of the beach has become popular with nude sunbathers. This is not legal, but such laws are seldom enforced. The beach is in the southwest corner of the Presidio and begins at the end of Gibson Road, which turns off Bowley Street. Weather is typical for the bay shoreline: summer fog, usually breezy, and occasionally warm. Picnic tables, grills, day-camp areas, and trails are available. The mile-long shoreline is ideal for jogging, fishing, and building sand castles.

China Beach From April to October, China Beach, south of Baker Beach, offers a lifeguard, gentler water, changing rooms, and showers. It is also listed on maps as Phelan Beach.

Ocean Beach South of Cliff House, Ocean Beach stretches along the western (ocean) side of San Francisco. It has a wide beach with scenic views and is perfect for walking, running, or lying in the sun—but not for swimming.

Dining

San Francisco probably has more restaurants per capita than any city in the United States, including New York. Practically every ethnic cuisine is represented. That makes selecting some seventy restaurants to list here from the vast number available a very difficult task indeed. We have chosen several restaurants to represent each popular style of dining in various price ranges, in most cases because of the superiority of the food, but in some instances because of the view or ambience.

Because we have covered those areas of town most frequented by visitors, this meant leaving out some great places in outlying districts such as Sunset and Richmond. The Richmond District restaurants we *have* recommended were chosen because they offer a type of experience not available elsewhere.

All listed restaurants serve dinner; they are open for lunch unless otherwise specified; restaurants are not open for breakfast unless the morning meal is specifically mentioned.

Parking accommodations are mentioned only when a restaurant has made special arrangements; otherwise you're on your own. There is usually a charge for valet parking. Validated parking is not necessarily free and unlimited; often there is a nominal charge and a restriction on the length of time.

Restaurants do change their policies about hours, credit cards, and the like. It is always best to make inquiries in advance.

The most highly recommended restaurants in each price category are indicated by a star ★.

The price ranges listed below are for an average three-course meal. A significant trend among more expensive restaurants is the bar menu, which provides light snacks—hot dogs, chili, pizza, and appetizers—in the bar for a cost that is often less than $10 for two.

Category	Cost*
Very Expensive	Over $40
Expensive	$25–$40
Moderate	$15–$25
Inexpensive	under $15

per person, excluding drinks, service, and 6.5% sales tax

The following credit card abbreviations are used: AE, American Express; DC, Diners Club; MC, MasterCard; V, Visa. Many restaurants accept cards other than those listed here, and some will accept personal checks if you carry a major credit card.

American Before the 1980s, it was hard to find a decent "American" restaurant in the Bay Area. In recent years, however, the list has been growing and becoming more diversified, with categories for Creole-Cajun, California cuisine, Southwestern, barbecue, and the all-American diner.

Civic Center
★ **Stars.** This is the culinary temple of Jeremiah Tower, the superchef who claims to have invented California cuisine. Stars is a must stop on every traveling gourmet's itinerary, but it's also where many of the local movers and shakers hang out as well as a popular place for post-theater dining—open till the wee hours. The dining room has a clublike ambience, and the food ranges from grills to ragouts to sautées—some daringly creative and some classical. Bar menu. *150 Redwood Alley, tel. 415/861–7827. Reservations accepted up to 2 weeks in advance, some tables reserved for walk-ins. Dress: informal. AE, DC, MC, V. No lunch weekends. Closed Memorial Day. Valet parking at night. Expensive.*

128

Downtown San Francisco Dining

Jefferson St.

Beach St.

North St.

Bay St.

Francisco St.

Chestnut St.

Lombard St.

Greenwich St.

Filbert St.

Union St.

Green St.

Vallejo St.

Broadway Tunnel

Pacific Ave.

Jackson St.

Pine St.

Bush St.

Sutter St.

Post St.

Geary St.

O'Farrell St.

Ellis St.

Eddy St.

Turk St.

Ave.

Hyde St.

Leavenworth St.

Columbus Ave.

Taylor St.

Mason St.

Powell St.

Stockton St.

Grant St.

Kearny St.

Montgomery St.

Sansome St.

Battery St.

Front St.

Davis St.

Embarcadero

Drumm St.

Steuart St.

Spear St.

Main St.

Beale St.

Fremont St.

1st St.

New Montgomery St.

Hawthorn St.

2nd St.

3rd St.

Market St.

4th St.

Mission St.

Howard St.

5th St.

6th St.

7th St.

Folsom St.

Harrison St.

Bryant St.

Brannan St.

Bluxome St.

Townsend St.

King St.

Mission St.

Howard St.

8th St.

9th St.

1/2 mile

500 meters

Embarcadero
★

Fog City Diner. This is where the diner and grazing crazes began in San Francisco, and the popularity of this spot knows no end. The long, narrow dining room emulates a luxurious railroad car with dark wood paneling, huge windows, and comfortable booths. The cooking is innovative, drawing its inspiration from regional cooking throughout the United States. The sharable "small plates" are a fun way to go. *1300 Battery St., tel. 415/982–2000. Reservations advised several weeks in advance for peak hours. Dress: informal. DC, MC, V. Closed Thanksgiving and Christmas. Moderate.*

MacArthur Park. Year after year San Franciscans acclaim this as their favorite spot for ribs, but the oakwood smoker and mesquite grill also turn out a wide variety of all-American fare, from steaks, hamburgers, and chili to seafood. Takeout is also available at this handsomely renovated pre-earthquake warehouse. *607 Front St., tel. 415/398–5700. Reservations advised. Dress: informal. AE, DC, MC, V. No lunch weekends. Closed Christmas. Valet parking at night. Moderate.*

Financial District

Cypress Club. Fans of John Cunin have flocked here since 1990 when Masa's long-time maître'd opened his own place, which he calls a "San Francisco brasserie." This categorizes the contemporary American cooking somewhat, but the decor defies description. It could be interpreted as anything from a pun on an ancient temple to a futuristic space war. *500 Jackson St., tel. 415/296–8555. Reservations advised. Dress: informal. AE, DC, MC, V. Valet parking at night. Expensive.*

Nob Hill

Fournou's Ovens. There are two lovely dining areas in the elegant Stanford Court Hotel. This is a multilevel room with tiers of tables; the focus of the room is the giant open hearth where many specialties—notably the rack of lamb—are roasted. The restaurant has moved away from its well-known Continental fare to more contemporary American cuisine. Some people opt for the flower-filled greenhouses that flank the hotel and offer views of the cable cars clanking up and down the hill. Wherever you sit, you'll find excellent food and attentive service. *905 California St., tel. 415/989–1910. Reservations advised. Jacket required. AE, DC, MC, V. No lunch weekends. Valet parking. Expensive.*

North Beach

Washington Square Bar & Grill. You're apt to rub elbows with the city's top columnists and writers in this no-frills saloon. Recently the restaurant broke with North Beach Italian tradition to offer lighter cooking, though pastas and seafood still dominate the menu. Basic bar fare, such as hamburgers and steaks, is also available. Pianist at night; open late. *1707 Powell St., tel. 415/982–8123. Reservations advised. Dress: informal. AE, DC, MC, V. Closed most major holidays. Validated parking at garage around the corner on Filbert St. Moderate.*

South of Market

Asta. Named after Nick and Nora's dog in "The Thin Man" series, this new spot is a time capsule of the '30s, with flicks of the famous sleuths on VCRs in the bar. The food, however, is in tune with the 1990s, with bright, creative versions of all-time American favorites and down-home desserts. *Rincon Center, 101 Spear St., 415/495–2782. Reservations accepted. Dress: informal. AE, MC, V. No lunch Sat., no dinner Mon., closed Sun. Validated parking at Rincon Center garage. Moderate.*

Union Square

Campton Place. This elegant, ultrasophisticated small hotel put new American cooking on the local culinary map. Although

opening chef Bradley Ogden is now at his own place, the Lark
Creek Inn, in Marin County, his successor at Campton Place,
Jan Birnbaum, carries on Ogden's innovative traditions with
great aplomb and has added his own touches from breakfast
and Sunday brunch (one of the best in town) through the dinner
hours. A bar menu offers some samplings of appetizers, plus a
caviar extravaganza. *340 Stockton St., tel. 415/781–5155. Reservations suggested, 2 weeks in advance on weekends. Jacket
required at dinner, tie requested. AE, DC, MC, V. Valet parking. Very Expensive.*

★ **Postrio.** Superchef Wolfgang Puck's San Francisco restaurant
debut in 1989 caused the biggest culinary commotion locally
since Berkeley chef Alice Waters reinvented the pizza, but
Puck claims to have done that in Los Angeles. Postrio has an
open kitchen (another trend started by Puck) and a stunning
three-level bar and dining area, highlighted by palm trees and
museum-quality contemporary paintings. The food is Puckish
Californian with Mediterranean and Asian overtones, emphasizing pastas, grilled seafood, and house-baked breads. A substantial breakfast and bar menu are served here, too. *545 Post
St., tel. 415/776–7825. Reservations advised. Dress: informal.
AE, DC, MC, V. Valet parking. Expensive.*

Caribbean **Miss Pearl's Jam House.** Since its opening in 1989, this Caribbe-
Tenderloin an hot spot in a Tenderloin motel has been jammed with a
younger-than-Yuppie crowd at night. But by day it's quiet and
lovely, with lunch served out by the pool. The chef draws his
inspiration from many West Indian islands, and the intense flavor of the food more than compensates for its lack of authentici-
ty. *601 Eddy St., tel. 415/775–5267. Reservations suggested.
Dress: informal. DC, MC, V. No lunch Sat. Closed Mon. Moderate.*

Chinese For nearly a century, Chinese restaurants in San Francisco
were confined to Chinatown and the cooking was largely an
Americanized version of peasant-style Cantonese. The past
few decades, however, have seen an influx of restaurants representing the wide spectrum of Chinese cuisine: the subtly seasoned fare of Canton, the hot and spicy cooking of Hunan and
Szechuan, the northern style of Peking, where meat and dumplings replace seafood and rice as staples, and, most recently,
some more esoteric cooking, such as Hakka and Chao Chow.
These restaurants are now scattered throughout the city, leaving Chinatown for the most part to the tourists.

Embarcadero **Harbor Village.** Classic Cantonese cooking, dim sum lunches,
★ and fresh seafood from the restaurant's own tanks are the hallmarks of this 400-seat branch of a Hong Kong establishment,
which sent five of its master chefs to San Francisco to supervise
the kitchen. The setting is opulent, with Chinese antiques and
teak furnishings. *4 Embarcadero Center, tel. 415/781–8833.
Reservations not accepted for lunch on weekends. Dress: informal. AE, MC, V. Free validated parking in Embarcadero Center Garage. Moderate.*

Financial District **Yank Sing.** This teahouse has grown by leaps and branches
with the popularity of dim sum. The Battery Street location
seats 300 and the older, smaller Stevenson Street site has recently been rebuilt in high-tech style. *427 Battery St., tel. 415/
362–1640. 49 Stevenson St., tel. 415/495–4510. Reservations
advised. Dress: informal. Battery-AE, MC, V. Stevenson-MC,
V. No dinner. Closed weekends. Inexpensive.*

North Beach **Hunan.** Henry Chung's first café on Kearny Street had only six tables, but his Hunanese cooking merited six stars from critics nationwide. He has now opened this larger place on Sansome Street; it's equally plain but has 250 seats. Smoked dishes are a specialty, and Henry guarantees no MSG. *924 Sansome St., tel. 415/956–7727. Reservations advised. Dress: informal. AE, DC, MC, V. Inexpensive.*

Northern Waterfront ★ **The Mandarin.** Owner Cecilia Chiang introduced San Franciscans to the full spectrum of Chinese cooking in 1961, when she opened the original Mandarin in a tiny Post Street locale. Now she holds court in a magnificent setting fit for imperial fare, decorated with paintings and embroideries from her family's palatial homes in Peking. This is one of the world's great restaurants, and its finest offerings, such as Mandarin duck, beggar's chicken cooked in clay, and the Mongolian fire pot, must be ordered a day in advance. Bay view from some tables. *Ghiradelli Sq., tel. 415/673–8812. Reservations advised. Dress: informal. AE, DC, MC, V. Closed Thanksgiving, Christmas. Validated parking in Ghiradelli Sq. garage. Moderate–Expensive.*

Richmond **Hong Kong Flower Lounge.** Many Chinaphiles swear that this outpost of a famous Asian restaurant chain serves the best Cantonese food in town. The seafood is spectacular, as is the dim sum. *5322 Geary Blvd., tel. 415/668–8998. Reservations advised. Dress: informal. AE, MC, V. Moderate.*

South of Market **Wu Kong.** Tucked away in the splashy Art Deco Rincon Center, Wu Kong features the cuisine of Shanghai and Canton. Specialties include dim sum; braised yellow fish; and the incredible vegetable goose, one of the Asian city's famous mock dishes, created from paper-thin layers of dried bean-curd sheets and mushrooms. *101 Spear St., tel. 415/957–9300. Reservations advised. Dress: informal. AE, DC, MC, V. Validated parking at Rincon Center garage. Moderate.*

Continental and Mediterranean Neither pure French nor pure Italian but a mixture of these and other European cuisines, this category includes some of San Francisco's classic establishments along with some of its brightest new spots.

Civic Center ★ **Zuni Cafe Grill.** Zuni's Italian-Mediterranean menu and its unpretentious atmosphere pack in the crowds from early morning to late evening. A balcony dining area overlooks the large bar, where both shellfish and drinks are dispensed. A second dining room houses the giant pizza oven and grill. Even the hamburgers have an Italian accent: They're served on herbed focaccia buns. *1658 Market St., tel. 415/552–2522. Dress: informal. Reservations advised. AE, MC, V. Closed Mon., Thanksgiving, Christmas. Moderate.*

Financial District **Jack's.** Little has changed in over 100 years at this bankers' and brokers' favorite. The menu is extensive, but regulars opt for the simple fare—steaks, chops, seafood, and stews. The dining room has an old-fashioned, no-nonsense aura, and private upstairs rooms are available for top-secret meetings. *615 Sacramento St., tel. 415/986–9854. Reservations advised. Jacket and tie required. AE. No lunch weekends. Closed major holidays. Moderate.*

North Beach **Julius Castle.** This turreted landmark building clings to the cliffs of Telegraph Hill and commands sweeping vistas of the bay. The food is traditional French and Italian, with an emphasis on pastas, seafood, and veal. The view and the site compensate for the lack of imagination in the cuisine. *1541 Montgomery St., tel. 415/362–3042. Reservations required. Jacket required. AE, DC, MC, V. No lunch. Closed Thanksgiving, Christmas. Valet parking. Expensive.*

French French cooking has gone in and out of vogue in San Francisco since the extravagant days of the Bonanza Kings. A renaissance of the classic haute cuisine occurred during the 1960s, but recently a number of these restaurants closed. Meanwhile, nouvelle cuisine went in and out of fashion, and the big draw now is the bistro or brasserie.

Civic Center **California Culinary Academy.** This historic theater houses one of the most highly regarded professional cooking schools in the United States. Watch the student chefs at work on the double-tiered stage while you dine on classic French cooking. Prix-fixe meals and bountiful buffets are served in the main dining room; heart-healthy à la carte lunches are served at Cyril's on the balcony level, and there's a grill on the first floor. *625 Polk St., tel. 415/771–3500. Reservations advised (2–4 weeks for Fri.-night buffet). Jacket requested. AE, DC, MC, V. Closed weekends and major holidays. Moderate–Expensive.*

Financial District **Le Central.** This is the quintessential bistro: noisy and crowded, with nothing subtle about the cooking. But the garlicky pâtés, leeks vinaigrette, cassoulet, and grilled blood sausage with crisp french fries keep the crowds coming. *453 Bush St., tel. 415/ 391–2233. Reservations advised. Dress: informal. AE, MC, V. Closed Sun. and major holidays. Moderate.*

North Beach **Amelio's.** A former speakeasy, this historic restaurant evokes turn-of-the-century San Francisco. Once known for its Italian food, the place was revitalized when the brilliant young French chef Jacky Robert became a partner. Robert's food looks as beautiful as it tastes. *1630 Powell St., tel. 415/397–4339. Reservations advised. Jacket required, tie requested. AE, DC, MC, V. Closed Sun., Mon., Christmas, New Year's Day. Very Expensive.*

★ **Ernie's.** This famous old-timer recently had a face-lift, and Alain Rondelli, one of France's most promising young chefs, is now in charge of the kitchen, preparing innovative light versions of French classics (and, at long last, has begun serving lunch). Even so, Ernie's is still steeped with the aura of Gay Nineties San Francisco. *847 Montgomery St., tel. 415/397–5969. Reservations advised. Jacket and tie required. AE, DC, MC, V. Closed major holidays. Valet parking. Very Expensive.*

Union Square **Masa's.** Chef Julian Serrano carries on the tradition of the late
★ Masa Kobayashi. In fact, some Masa regulars even say the cooking is better. The artistry of the presentation is as important as the food itself in this pretty, flower-filled dining spot in the Vintage Court Hotel. *648 Bush St., tel. 415/989–7154. Reservations should be made precisely 21 days in advance. Jacket required. AE, DC, MC, V. No lunch. Closed Sun., Mon., 1st week in July, last week in Dec., 1st week in Jan. Valet parking. Very Expensive.*

★ **Fleur de Lys.** The creative cooking of chef/partner Hubert Keller is drawing rave reviews to this romantic spot that some now consider the best French restaurant in town. The menu changes constantly, but such dishes as lobster soup with lemongrass are a signature. The intimate dining room, like a sheikh's tent, is encased with hundreds of yards of paisley. *777 Sutter St., tel. 415/673-7779. Reservations on weekends advised 2 weeks in advance. Jacket and tie required. AE, DC, MC, V. No lunch. Closed Sun., Thanksgiving, Christmas, New Year's Day. Valet parking. Expensive-Very Expensive.*

Greek and Middle Eastern
The foods of Greece and the Middle East have much in common: a preponderance of lamb and eggplant dishes, a widespread use of phyllo pastry, and an abundance of pilaf.

North Beach
Maykadeh. Here you'll find authentic Persian cooking in a setting so elegant that the modest check comes as a great surprise. Lamb dishes with rice are the specialties. *470 Green St., tel. 415/362-8286. Reservations advised. Dress: informal. MC, V. Valet parking at night. Inexpensive.*

South of Market
S. Asimakopoulos Cafe. Terrific Greek food at reasonable prices keeps the crowds waiting for seats at the counter or at bare-topped tables in this storefront café. The menu is large and varied, but lamb dishes are the stars. Convenient to Showplace Square. *288 Connecticut, Potrero Hill, tel. 415/552-8789. No reservations. Dress: informal. AE, MC, V. No lunch weekends. Closed major holidays. Inexpensive.*

Indian
The following restaurants serve the cuisine of northern India, which is more subtly seasoned and not as hot as its southern counterparts. They also specialize in succulent meats and crispy breads from the clay-lined tandoori oven.

Northern Waterfront and Embarcadero
Gaylord's. A vast selection of mildly spiced northern Indian food is offered here, along with meats and breads from the tandoori ovens and a wide range of vegetarian dishes. The dining rooms are elegantly appointed with Indian paintings and gleaming silver service. The Ghirardelli Square location offers bay views. *Ghirardelli Sq., tel. 415/771-8822. Embarcadero One, tel. 415/397-7775. Reservations advised. Dress: informal. AE, DC, MC, V. No lunch Sun. at Embarcadero. Ghirardelli closed Thanksgiving, Christmas; Embarcadero closed Labor Day, Christmas, New Year's Day. Validated parking at Ghirardelli Sq. garage and Embarcadero Center garage. Moderate.*

Pacific Heights
North India. Small and cozy, this restaurant has a more limited menu and hotter seasoning than Gaylord. Both tandoori dishes and curries are served, plus a range of breads and appetizers. Everything is cooked to order. *3131 Webster St., tel. 415/931-1556. Reservations advised. Dress: informal. AE, DC, MC, V. No lunch weekends. Parking behind restaurant. Moderate.*

International
The following restaurants are truly international in that they draw their inspiration from both Eastern and Western cuisines.

Embarcadero
★
Square One. Chef Joyce Goldstein introduces an ambitious new menu daily, with dishes based on the classic cooking of the Mediterranean countries as well as that of Asia and Latin America. The dining room, with its views of the open kitchen and the Golden Gateway commons, is an understated setting for some of the finest food in town. Bar menu. *190 Pacific Ave., tel. 415/788-1110. Reservations advised. Dress: informal. AE, DC, MC, V. No lunch weekends. Closed major holidays. Valet parking in evenings. Expensive.*

Union Square **Trader Vic's.** This is the headquarters of Vic's empire. You'll find the usual tikis, the vast array of Cantonese and Polynesian dishes, and the exotic drinks. Concentrate instead on simpler fare, such as fresh seafood and Indonesian rack of lamb. The Captain's Cabin is where the local celebs hang out, but you're not likely to get a seat there unless you're known. *20 Cosmo Pl., tel. 415/776–2232. Reservations advised. Jacket and tie required. AE, DC, MC, V. No lunch. Closed Thanksgiving, Christmas. Valet parking. Moderate–Expensive.*

Italian Italian food in San Francisco spans the "boot" from the mild cooking of northern Italy to the spicy cuisine of the south. Then there is the style indigenous to San Francisco, known as North Beach Italian—such dishes as *cioppino* (a fisherman's stew) and Joe's special (a mélange of eggs, spinach, and ground beef).

Embarcadero **Ciao.** Light, contemporary Italian food is the mainstay here: graceful appetizers, a large selection of freshly made pastas, grilled meats, and sausages. The high-tech decor of this popular trattoria is as modern as the food: all white splashed with brass and chrome. *230 Jackson St., tel. 415/982–9500. Reservations advised. Dress: informal. AE, DC, MC, V. No lunch Sun. Closed Thanksgiving, Christmas, New Year's Day. Valet parking in the evening. Moderate.*

Il Fornaio. An offshoot of the Il Fornaio bakeries, this handsome tile-floored, wood-paneled complex combines a café, bakery, and upscale trattoria with outdoor seating. The cooking is Tuscan, featuring pizzas from a wood-burning oven, superb house-made pastas and gnocchi, and grilled poultry and seafood. Anticipate a wait for a table, but once seated, you won't be disappointed—only surprised by the moderate prices. *Levi's Plaza, 1265 Battery, tel. 415/986–0100. Reservations advised. Dress:informal. MC,V. Closed Thanksgiving, Christmas. Valet parking. Moderate.*

Financial District **Blue Fox.** This landmark restaurant was revitalized in 1988 by John Fassio, son of a former owner, who redecorated the place in a low-key, formal style. The classic cooking is from the Piedmont region of northern Italy, with a seasonally changing menu. Pasta and gnocchi are made on the premises, as are the luscious desserts. *659 Merchant St., tel. 415/981–1177. Reservations required. Jacket and tie required. AE, DC, MC, V. Dinner only. Closed Sun. and major holidays. Valet parking. Expensive–Very Expensive.*

Midtown **Acquarello.** This exquisite restaurant is a new venture of the former chef and former maître 'd at Donatello. The service and food are exemplary, and the menu covers the full range of Italian cuisine, from northern Italy to the tip of the boot. Desserts are exceptional. *1722 Sacramento St., tel. 415/567–5432. Reservations advised. Dress: informal. DC, MC, V. No lunch. Closed Sun.–Mon. Validated parking across the street. Expensive.*

North Beach **Buca Giovanni.** Giovanni Leoni showcases the dishes of his
★ birthplace: the Serchio Valley in Tuscany. Pastas made on the premises are a specialty, and the calamari salad is one of the best around. The subterranean dining room is cozy and romantic. *800 Greenwich St., tel. 415/776–7766. Reservations advised. Dress: informal. AE, MC, V. No lunch. Closed Sun. and most major holidays. Moderate.*

Capp's Corner. One of the last of the family-style trattorias,

diners sit elbow to elbow at long Formica tables to feast on
bountiful six-course dinners. For the budget-minded or calo-
rie-counters, a shorter dinner includes a tureen of soup, salad,
and pasta. *1600 Powell St., North Beach, tel. 415/989–2589.
Reservations advised. Dress: informal. DC, MC, V. No lunch
weekends. Closed Thanksgiving, Christmas. Credit off meal
check for parking in garage across the street. Moderate.*

South of Market **Etrusca.** The ancient Etruscan civilization inspired this popular new showplace in Rincon Center. Onyx chandeliers cast a
warm glow on Siena gold walls, terrazzo floors and ceiling fres-
coes. The dishes from the giant wood-fired oven that dominates
the open kitchen, however, recall modern Tuscany more than
ancient Etruria. Bar menu. *Rincon Center, 101 Spear St., tel.
415/777–0330. Reservations advised. Dress: informal. MC, V.
No lunch weekends. Validated parking in Rincon Center garage. Moderate.*

Union Square **Donatello.** Much of the menu in this elegant restaurant in the
Donatello Hotel is drawn from the Emilia-Romagna region of
Italy, which is famous for its food, especially the Bolognese
pastas. The intimate dining rooms are exquisitely appointed
with silk-paneled walls, paintings, and tapestries. Service is
superb and low-keyed. Donatello also serves breakfasts that
combine typical American fare with Italian-accented dishes.
*Post and Mason Sts., tel. 415/441–7182. Reservations advised.
Jacket and tie required. AE, DC, MC, V. No lunch. Validated
parking in hotel garage. Expensive–Very Expensive.*

Kuleto's. The contemporary cooking of northern Italy, the atmosphere of old San Francisco, and an antipasti bar have made
this spot off Union Square a hit since it opened during the
1980s. Grilled seafood dishes are among the specialties. Breakfast is served, too. Publike booths and a long open kitchen fill
one side of the restaurant; a gardenlike setting with light
splashed from skylights lies beyond. *221 Powell St., tel. 415/
397–7720. Dress: informal. Reservations advised. AE, DC,
MC, V. Closed Thanksgiving, Christmas. Moderate.*

Lascaux. Despite its Gallic name (after the caves in France),
the cuisine at this smart new restaurant is primarily Mediterranean, with a contemporary Italian accent. Changing menus
offer fluffy polenta topped with steamed mussels, a torta of
sun-dried tomatoes and mascarpone, and grilled seafood with
imaginative sauces. Desserts are fabulous. A huge fireplace
cheers the romantically lit subterranean dining room. *248 Sutter St., tel. 415/391–1555. Reservations advised. Dress: informal. AE, DC, MC, V. No lunch Sat. Closed Sun.,
Thanksgiving, Christmas. Moderate.*

Japanese To understand a Japanese menu, you should be familiar with
the basic types of cooking: *yaki*, marinated and grilled foods;
tempura, fish and vegetables deep-fried in a light batter; *udon*
and *soba*, noodle dishes; *domburi*, meats and vegetables served
over rice; *ramen*, noodles served in broth; and *nabemono*,
meals cooked in one pot, often at the table. Of course sushi bars
are extremely popular in San Francisco; most offer a selection
of *sushi*, vinegared rice with fish or vegetables, and *sashimi*,
raw fish. Western seating refers to conventional tables and
chairs; *tatami* seating is on mats at low tables.

Chinatown **Yamato.** The city's oldest Japanese restaurant is by far its most
beautiful, with inlaid wood, painted panels, a meditation garden, and a pool. Both Western and tatami seating, in private

shoji-screened rooms, are offered, along with a fine sushi bar. Come primarily for the atmosphere; the menu is somewhat limited, and more adventurous dining can be found elsewhere. *717 California St., tel. 415/397–3456. Reservations advised. AE, DC, MC, V. No lunch weekends. Closed Mon., Thanksgiving, Christmas, New Year's Day. Moderate.*

Japantown **Sanppo.** This small place has an enormous selection of almost every type of Japanese food: yakis, nabemono dishes, domburi, udon, and soba, not to mention feather-light tempura and interesting side dishes. Western seating only. *1702 Post St., tel. 415/346–3486. No reservations. Dress: informal. No credit cards. Closed Mon. and major holidays. Validated parking in Japan Center garage. Inexpensive.*

Mexican In spite of San Francisco's Mexican heritage, until recently most south-of-the-border eateries were locked into the Cal-Mex taco-enchillada-mashed-beans syndrome. But now some newer places offer a broader spectrum of Mexican cooking.

Richmond District **Alejandro's.** Peruvian-Spanish dishes, especially seafood stews, are among the specialties here, although traditional Mexican combination plates are served as well. And there's an extensive tapas menu, too. The dining room is attractive—whitewashed walls and Peruvian artifacts—but noisy. *1840 Clement St., tel. 415/668–1184. Reservations advised. Dress: informal. AE, DC, MC, V. No lunch. Closed Thanksgiving, Christmas Eve, Christmas Day, New Year's Eve, New Year's Day. Moderate.*

South of Market **Chevys.** This first San Francisco branch of a popular Mexican minichain is decked out with funky neon signs and "El Machino" turning out flour tortillas. "Stop gringo food" is the motto here, and the emphasis is on the freshest ingredients and sauces. Of note are the fabulous fajitas and the grilled quail and seafood. *4th and Howard Sts., tel. 415/543–8060. Reservations accepted only for parties of 8 or more. Dress: informal. MC, V. Closed Thanksgiving, Christmas. Validated parking evenings after 5 PM and weekends at garage under bldg. (enter from Minna St.). Inexpensive.*

Union Square **Corona Bar & Grill.** The ever-changing menu offers light versions of regional Mexican dishes. Corona's paella, laden with shellfish and calamari, is sensational, as is the chocolate-coated flan. The atmosphere is a mix of old San Francisco (pressed tin ceilings and an antique bar) and old Mexico (hand-painted masks and Aztec motifs). *88 Cyril Magnin St., tel. 415/392–5500. Reservations advised. Dress: informal. AE, DC, MC, V. Closed Thanksgiving, Christmas. Moderate.*

Seafood Like all port cities, San Francisco takes pride in its seafood, even though less than half the fish served here is from local waters. In winter and spring look for the fresh Dungeness crab, best served cracked with mayonnaise. In summer, feast upon Pacific salmon, even though imported varieties are available year-round. A recent development is the abundance of unusual oysters from West Coast beds and an outburst of oyster bars.

Civic Center **Hayes Street Grill.** Eight to 15 different kinds of seafood are
★ chalked on the blackboard each night at this extremely popular restaurant. The fish is served simply grilled, with a choice of sauces ranging from tartar to a spicy Szechuan peanut concoction. Appetizers are unusual, and desserts are lavish. *320 Hayes St., tel. 415/863–5545. Reservations should be made pre-*

cisely 1 week in advance. Dress: informal. MC, V. No lunch Sat. Closed Sun. and major holidays. Moderate.

Embarcadero   **The Waterfront.** The dramatic, multilevel glass-walled dining room guarantees a bay view from every table. The food doesn't always match the fabulous view, but the fresh fish and pasta are usually above average. Very popular for weekend brunch. *Pier 7, Embarcadero, tel. 415/391–2696. Reservations required. Dress: informal. AE, DC, MC, V. Closed Christmas. Valet parking. Moderate.*

Financial District   **Sam's Grill.** Sam's and Tadich (below) are two of the city's oldest restaurants and so popular for lunch that you must arrive before 11:30 to get a table. No frills here. The aura is starkly old-fashioned; some booths are enclosed and curtained. Although the menu is extensive and varied, those in the know stick with the fresh local seafood and East Coast shellfish. *374 Bush St., tel. 415/421–0594. Reservations not accepted. Dress: informal. DC, MC, V. Closed weekends and holidays. Moderate.*

Tadich Grill. Owners and locations have changed many times since this old-timer opened during the Gold Rush era, but the 19th-century atmosphere remains, as does the kitchen's special way with seafood. Seating at the counter or in private booths; long lines for a table at lunchtime. *240 California St., tel. 415/391–2373. No reservations. Dress: informal. MC, V. Closed Sun. and holidays. Moderate.*

Pacific Heights   **Pacific Heights Bar & Grill.** This is unquestionably the best oyster bar in town, with at least a dozen varieties available each day and knowledgeable shuckers to explain the mollusks' origins. In the small dining rooms, grilled seafood and shellfish stews head the bill of fare. Paella is a house specialty. *2001 Fillmore St., tel. 415/567–3337. Reservations advised. Dress: informal. AE, MC, V. No lunch Sat. Closed Thanksgiving, Christmas. Valet parking in the evening. Moderate.*

Southeast Asian   In recent years San Franciscans have seen tremendous growth in the numbers of restaurants specializing in the foods of Thailand, Vietnam, and, most recently, Cambodia. The cuisines of these countries share many features, and one characteristic in particular: The cooking is always spicy and often very hot.

Marina   **Angkor Palace.** This is one of the loveliest Cambodian restaurants in town and also the most conveniently located for visitors. The extensive family-style menu offers such exotic fare as fish-and-coconut mousse baked in banana leaves. You'll have questions, of course, but you'll find the staff eager to explain the contents of the menu. *1769 Lombard St., tel. 415/931–2830. Reservations advised. Dress: informal. AE, MC, V. No lunch. Inexpensive.*

Richmond District   **Khan Toke Thai House.** The city's first Thai restaurant has a
★   lovely dining room, furnished with low tables and cushions, and a garden view. The six-course dinners, with two entrees from an extensive choice, provide a delicious introduction to Thai cooking. (The seasoning will be mild, unless you request it hot.) Classical Thai dancing on Sunday. *5937 Geary Blvd., tel. 415/668–6654. Reservations advised. Dress: informal. AE, MC, V. No lunch. Closed Thanksgiving, Christmas, Labor Day. Inexpensive–Moderate.*

South of Market **Manora.** When Passarin Prassl opened this homey Thai café way out on Mission Street, she named it after her daughter, Manora. Soon crowds from all over town were lined up for a table to try the extensive selection of carefully prepared dishes. Now Manora has her own spot on Folsom Street, not far from the Performing Arts Center, with the same great food. *3226 Mission St., tel. 415/550–0856. 1600 Folsom St., tel. 415/861–6224. Dress: informal. MC, V. No lunch weekends. Closed Labor Day, Thanksgiving. Inexpensive.*

Steak Houses Although San Francisco traditionally has not been a meat-and-potatoes town, the popularity of steak is on the rise. Following are some of the best steak houses, but you can also get a good piece of beef at some of the better French, Italian, and American restaurants.

Marina **Izzy's Steak & Chop House.** Izzy Gomez was a legendary San Francisco saloonkeeper, and his namesake eatery carries on the tradition with terrific steaks, chops, and seafood, plus all the trimmings—such as cheesy scalloped potatoes and creamed spinach. A collection of Izzy memorabilia and antique advertising art covers almost every inch of wall space. *3345 Steiner St., tel. 415/563–0487. Reservations accepted. Dress: informal. AE, DC, MC, V. No lunch. Closed Thanksgiving, Christmas. Validated parking at Lombard Garage. Moderate.*

Midtown **Harris'.** Ann Harris knows her beef. She grew up on a Texas
★ cattle ranch and was married to the late Jack Harris of Harris Ranch fame. In her own elegant restaurant she serves some of the best dry-aged steaks in town, but don't overlook the grilled seafood or poultry. Extensive bar menu. *2100 Van Ness Ave., tel. 415/673–1888. Reservations recommended. Dress: informal. AE, DC, MC, V. Lunch on Wed. only. Closed Christmas, New Year's Day. Valet parking. Expensive.*

Vegetarian **Greens at Fort Mason.** This beautiful restaurant with its bay
Marina views is a favorite with carnivores as well as vegetarians.
★ Owned and operated by the Tassajara Zen Center of Carmel Valley, the restaurant offers a wide, eclectic, and creative spectrum of meatless cooking, and the bread promises nirvana. Dinners are à la carte on weeknights, but only a five-course prix-fixe dinner is served on Friday and Saturday. *Bldg. A, Fort Mason, tel. 415/771–6222. Dress: informal. Reservations advised. MC, V. No dinner Sun. Closed Mon., Thanksgiving, Christmas, New Year's Day. Public parking at Fort Mason Center. Moderate.*

Vegetarians should also consider Gaylord's (*see* Indian restaurants, above), which offers a wide variety of meatless dishes from the Hindu cuisine.

Lodging

Few cities in the United States can rival San Francisco's variety in lodging. There are plush hotels ranked among the finest in the world, renovated older buildings that have the charm of Europe, bed-and-breakfast inns in the city's Victorian "Painted Ladies," and the popular chain hotels and low-rise motels that are found in most cities in the United States.

Because San Francisco is one of the top destinations in the United States for tourists as well as business travelers and con-

Downtown San Francisco Lodging

Abigail Hotel, **18**
Adelaide Inn, **25**
Amsterdam, **26**
Atherton Hotel, **17**
Aston Regis Hotel, **48**
Bed and Breakfast Inn, **5**
Bel Aire Travel Lodge, **2**
Beresford Arms, **24**

Best Western Americana, **21**
Campton Place, **41**
Cathedral Hill Hotel, **12**
Cartwright, **34**
Chancellor Hotel, **37**
Columbus Motor Inn, **28**
Essex Hotel, **16**

Fairmont Hotel and Tower, **31**
Four Season Clift, **49**
Galleria Park, **53**
Grand Hyatt, **39**
Grant Plaza, **51**
Handlery Union Square, **44**
Holiday Inn--Civic Center, **19**

Holiday Inn--Financial District, **52**
Holiday Inn--Union Square, **35**
Hotel Britton, **20**
Hotel Diva, **47**
Hotel Nikko--San Francisco, **50**
Huntington Hotel, **29**
Hyatt Regency--San Francisco, **57**

vention goers, reservations are always advised, especially during the May–September peak season.

San Francisco's geography makes it conveniently compact. No matter their location, the hotels listed below are on or close to public transportation lines. Some properties on Lombard Street and in the Civic Center area have free parking, but a car is more a hindrance than an asset in San Francisco.

Although not as high as New York, San Francisco hotel prices may come as a surprise to travelers from less urban areas. Average rates for double rooms downtown and at the wharf are in the $110 range. Motel and hotel rooms can be found for less throughout the city, especially in the Civic Center and Lombard areas. Adding to the expense is the city's 11% transient occupancy tax, which can significantly boost the cost of a lengthy stay.

An alternative to hotels, inns, and motels is staying in private homes and apartments, available through two companies: **American Family Inn/Bed & Breakfast San Francisco** (Box 349, San Francisco, CA 94101, tel. 415/931–3083) and **Bed & Breakfast International–San Francisco** (1181–B Solano Ave., Albany, CA 94706, tel. 415/525–4569 or 800/872–4500).

The **San Francisco Convention and Visitors Bureau** each year publishes a free lodging guide with a map and listing of all hotels. Send $1 for postage and handling to the SFCVB, Box 6977, San Francisco, CA 94101-6977.

If you are looking for truly budget accommodations (under $50), consider the Adelaide Inn(see Union Square/Downtown, below) and the **YMCA Central Branch**. *220 Golden Gate Ave. 94102, tel. 415/885–0460. 102 rooms, 3 with bath. Facilities: health club, pool, sauna. MC, V.*

The most highly recommended hotels are indicated by a star ★.

Lodgings are listed by geographical area and price range.

Category	Cost*
Very Expensive	over $175
Expensive	$100–$175
Moderate	$65–$100
Inexpensive	under $65

All prices are for a standard double room, excluding 11% tax.

The following credit card abbreviations are used: AE, American Express; DC, Diners Club; MC, MasterCard; V, Visa.

Civic Center/ Van Ness   The governmental heart of San Francisco has been undergoing a renaissance that has made it come alive with fine restaurants, trendy night spots, and renovated small hotels.

Expensive   **Cathedral Hill Hotel.** Guest rooms were renovated in 1988 at this popular convention hotel. *1101 Van Ness Ave., 94109, tel. 415/776–8200, 800/622–0855 in CA, 800/227–4730 nationwide. 400 rooms. Facilities: free parking, pool, 2 restaurants, lounge. AE, DC, MC, V.*

★   **Inn at the Opera.** A music or ballet lover's heart may quiver at the sight of this lovely small hotel, where musicians and singers stay when they appear at San Francisco's performing arts centers a block away. There are billowing pillows, terry-cloth robes, microwave ovens, and servibars in each room. *333 Fulton St., 94102, tel. 415/863–8400, 800/423–9610 in CA, or 800/325–2708 nationwide. 48 rooms. Facilities: classy restaurant, lounge. AE, DC, MC, V.*

Miyako. In the heart of Japantown is this elegant, recently renovated hotel. The Japanese ambience is established by a greeting from a kimono-clad hostess. Traditional Japanese rooms with tatami mats are available. *1625 Post St. at Laguna St., 94115, tel. 415/922–3200 or 800/533–4567. 208 rooms. Facilities: Japanese baths, saunas, restaurant, 2 lounges. AE, DC, MC, V.*

Moderate **★ Abigail Hotel.** A former B&B inn, this hotel retains its homey atmosphere with an eclectic mix of English antiques and mounted hunting trophies in the lobby. Hissing steam radiators and sleigh beds set the mood in the antiques-filled rooms. Room 211—the hotel's only suite—is the most elegant and spacious. *246 McAllister St., 94102, tel. 415/861–9728, 800/553–5575 in CA, or 800/243–6510 nationwide. 62 rooms. AE, DC, MC, V.*

Best Western Americania. This hotel is distinguished by its pink-and-turquoise Moorish facade. Rooms overlook inner courtyards with fountain or swimming pool. *121 7th St., 94103, tel. 415/626–0200 or 800/444–5816. 142 rooms. Facilities: outdoor pool, sauna, coffee shop, free parking, nonsmoking rooms available, evening shuttle to Union Square. AE, DC, MC, V.*

Holiday Inn–Civic Center. A 1989 renovation of the exterior, all rooms, lobby, and the restaurant has added a touch of elegance. The location is good—three blocks from the Civic Center and two blocks from Brooks Hall/Civic Auditorium. *50 8th St., 94103, tel. 415/626–6103 or 800/HOLIDAY. 390 rooms. Facilities: restaurant, lounge, outdoor pool. AE, DC, MC, V.*

★ Lombard Hotel. This is a European-style hotel with a handsome marble-floor lobby flanked on one side by the Gray Derby restaurant. Many of the rooms were refurbished in 1989 with blondwood furniture and new servibars. Quiet rooms are in the back. Complimentary evening cocktails and chauffeured limousine downtown are offered. *1015 Geary St., 94109, tel. 415/673–5232 or 800/227–3608. 100 rooms. Facilities: restaurant. AE, DC, MC, V.*

Majestic Hotel. One of San Francisco's original grand hotels, the Majestic was meticulously restored and reopened in 1985 with even more stately elegance. Romantic rooms have French and English antiques and four-poster canopy beds. Many have fireplaces and original claw-foot bathtubs. *1500 Sutter St., 94109, tel. 415/441–1100 or 800/869–8966. 60 rooms. Facilities: gourmet restaurant, lounge. AE, MC, V.*

The Mansion. This twin-turreted Queen Anne Victorian was built in 1887 and today houses one of the most unusual hotels in the city. Rooms contain an oddball collection of furnishings and vary from the tiny "Tom Thumb" room to the opulent "Josephine" suite, the favorite of such celebrities as Barbra Streisand. Owner Bob Pritikin's pig paintings and other "porkabilia" are everywhere. *2220 Sacramento St., 94115, tel. 415/929–9444. 28 rooms. Facilities: dining room, weekend concerts, Bufano sculpture, and flower garden. AE, DC, MC, V.*

New Richelieu Hotel. The Richelieu's rooms acquired new beds, furniture, and carpeting in an extensive 1988 renovation. Rooms in the back building are larger and have new bathrooms. The lobby has been spruced up with an elegant gray-and-blue color scheme. *1050 Van Ness Ave., 94109, tel. 415/673–4711 or 800/227–3608. 150 rooms. Facilities: nonsmoking rooms available, gift shop and tour desk in lobby, 24-hour restaurant adjacent. AE, DC, MC, V.*

The Phoenix Inn. Resembling more of a '50s-style beachside resort than a hotel in San Francisco's government center, the Phoenix bills itself aptly as an "urban retreat." Bungalow-style rooms, decorated with casual Filipino bamboo and original art by San Francisco artists, all face a pool courtyard and sculpture garden. *601 Eddy St., 94109, tel. 415/776–1380. 44 rooms. Facilities: free parking, lounge, heated pool; restaurant offers room service. AE, DC, MC, V.*

Inexpensive   **The Atherton Hotel.** A clean, low-price hotel with bilevel Mediterranean-style lobby. *685 Ellis St., 94109, tel. 415/474–5720 or 800/227–3608. 75 rooms. Facilities: restaurant, bar. AE, DC, MC, V.*

The Essex Hotel. New Italian marble floors in the lobby give this otherwise simple tourist hotel a touch of class. The friendliness of the Australian couple who own it is also a big plus. Popular with German and English tourists. *684 Ellis St., 94109, tel. 415/474–4664, 800/44–ESSEX in CA, or 800/45–ESSEX nationwide. 100 rooms, 52 with bath. AE, MC, V.*

★ **Hotel Britton.** This hotel is clean and comfortable, with good rates, and is close to the Civic Center. Rooms are attractively furnished, and color TVs offer in-room movies. *112 7th St. at Mission St., 94103, tel. 415/621–7001 or 800/444–5819. 80 rooms. Facilities: coffee shop. AE, DC, MC, V.*

Financial District   High-rise growth in San Francisco's Financial District has turned it into mini-Manhattan, a spectacular sight by night.

Very Expensive   **Hyatt Regency.** The stunning atrium-lobby architecture is the highlight here. Major renovations took place in late 1989 to upgrade the rooms and the lobby. *5 Embarcadero Center, 94111, tel. 415/788–1234 or 800/233–1234. 803 rooms. Facilities: 2 restaurants, coffee shop, lounge, 24-hour room service, shopping arcade. AE, DC, MC, V.*

Mandarin Oriental. The third-highest building in San Francisco's skyline is topped by a luxurious 11-story hotel on its 38th–48th floors. It's the best for spectacular views, especially from the bathrooms in the Mandarin rooms with their floor-to-ceiling windows flanking the tubs. *222 Sansome St., 94104, tel. 415/885–0999 or 800/622–0404. 160 rooms. Facilities: gourmet restaurant, lounge. AE, DC, MC, V.*

Park Hyatt. This is the Hyatt chain's candidate for competing with the ultraluxury of some of the city's best hotels. Service is highly personal and attentive and rooms are plush, with such goodies as gourmet chocolates and imported soaps. Many rooms have balconies and bay views. The hotel caters to corporate executives and the like. *333 Battery St., tel. 415/392–1234 or 800/228–9000. 360 rooms. Facilities: restaurant, lounge, library room. AE, DC, MC, V.*

Expensive   **Sheraton Palace.** One of the city's grand old hotels, the Sheraton reopened in 1991 after a $150 million reconstruction. New: air-conditioning, business center, health club, pool. Restored: the Garden Court restaurant with its leaded-glass ceiling, the

Pied Piper lounge featuring Maxfield Parrish's painting of that name. *2 New Montgomery St., 94105, tel. 415/543–0671 or 800/ 325–3535. 550 rooms. Facilities: 24-hour room service, 2 restaurants, 2 lounges, fitness center. AE, DC, MC, V.*

Fisherman's Wharf/North Beach   Fisherman's Wharf, San Francisco's top tourist attraction, is also the most popular area for accommodations, and the area is well covered by the major national hotel chains, including Marriott, Holiday Inn, Ramada, Sheraton, and TraveLodge. All are within a couple of blocks of restaurants, shops, and cable car lines. Because of city ordinances, none of the hotels exceed four stories; thus, this is not the area for fantastic views of the city or bay. Reservations are always necessary, sometimes weeks in advance during the peak summer months. Some streetside rooms can be noisy.

Moderate   **Columbus Motor Inn.** This is an attractive motel between the wharf and North Beach with suites that are ideal for families. *1075 Columbus Ave., 94133, tel. 415/885–1492. 45 rooms. Facilities: free parking. AE, DC, MC, V.*

Inexpensive   **San Remo Hotel.** This cozy hotel is reminiscent of a European-★   style pension. Renovated during recent years, its smallish rooms and narrow corridors are freshly painted and decorated with plants and antiques. It offers a good location on the border of Fisherman's Wharf and North Beach. *2237 Mason St., 94133, tel. 415/776–8688. 62 rooms, all with shared baths. Daily and weekly rates. Facilities: popular Italian restaurant. MC, V.*

Lombard Street/Cow Hollow   Lombard Street, a major traffic corridor leading to the Golden Gate Bridge, is sandwiched between two of San Francisco's poshest neighborhoods, Cow Hollow and the Marina District.

Very Expensive   **The Sherman House.** In the middle of an elegant residential dis-★   trict is this magnificent landmark mansion, the most luxurious small hotel in San Francisco. Each room is individually decorated with Biedermeier, English Jacobean, or French Second-Empire antiques, with tapestrylike canopies covering four-poster beds. Marble-top, wood-burning fireplaces and black granite bathrooms with whirlpool baths complete the picture. There is an in-house restaurant for guests only. *2160 Green St., 94123, tel. 415/563–3600. 15 rooms. Facilities: dining room, sitting rooms. AE, DC, MC, V.*

Moderate   **Bel Aire TraveLodge.** This attractive, well-kept motel is in a quiet location half a block from Lombard Street. *3201 Steiner St., 94123, tel. 415/921–5162 or 800/255–3050. 32 rooms. Facilities: free parking. AE, DC, MC, V.*

★   **Marina Inn.** Here cute B&B-style accommodations are offered at motel prices. Dainty-flowered wallpaper, poster beds, country pine furniture, and fresh flowers give the rooms an English country air. Continental breakfast is served in the cozy central sitting room. Turned-down beds and chocolates greet guests at the end of the day. No parking. *3110 Octavia St. at Lombard St., 94123, tel. 415/928–1000. 40 rooms. Facilities: lounge. AE, MC, V.*

Union Street Inn. A retired schoolteacher has transformed this 1902 Edwardian home into a cozy inn. Antiques and fresh flowers are found throughout. *2229 Union St., 94123, tel. 415/346–0424. 6 rooms with private bath. Facilities: English garden, breakfast room, free parking. AE, MC, V.*

Inexpensive **Marina Motel.** This quaint Spanish-style stucco complex is one of the oldest motels on Lombard Street, but it is well kept. Each room has its own garage. *2576 Lombard St., 94123, tel. 415/921–9406. 45 rooms, some with kitchen. Facilities: free parking. AE, MC, V.*

★ **Town House Motel.** A very attractive motel with recently redecorated rooms, this is one of the best values on Lombard Street. *1650 Lombard St., 94123, tel. 415/885–5163 or 800/255–1516. 24 rooms. Facilities: free parking. AE, DC, MC, V.*

Nob Hill Synonymous with San Francisco's high society, Nob Hill contains some of the city's best-known luxury hotels. All offer spectacular city and bay views and noted gourmet restaurants. Cable car lines that cross Nob Hill make transportation a cinch.

Very Expensive **Fairmont Hotel and Tower.** The regal "grande dame" of Nob Hill, the Fairmont has one of the most spectacular lobbies and public rooms in the city. All guest rooms are spacious and finely decorated. Those in the modern tower have the best views, while those in the old building have the stately ambience of another era. *950 Mason St., 94108, tel. 415/772–5000 or 800/527–4727. 596 rooms. Facilities: health club and spa, gift shops, 6 restaurants, 6 lounges, 24-hour room service. AE, DC, MC, V.*

★ **Huntington Hotel.** Understated class is found in this little jewel atop Nob Hill. Sumptuous rooms and suites are individually decorated. *1075 California St., 94108, tel. 415/474–5400, 800/652–1539 in CA, or 800/227–4683 nationwide. 143 rooms. Facilities: restaurant, lounge with entertainment. AE, DC, MC, V.*

Mark Hopkins Inter-Continental. Another Nob Hill landmark, "The Mark" is lovingly maintained. Rooms were redone in late 1987 in dramatic neoclassical furnishings of gray, silver, and khaki and with bold leaf-print bedspreads. Bathrooms are lined with Italian marble. Even-numbered rooms have views of the Golden Gate Bridge. *999 California St., 94108, tel. 415/392–3434 or 800/327–0200. 392 rooms. Facilities: gift shops, restaurant, lobby lounge, Top of the Mark cocktail lounge with panoramic views. AE, DC, MC, V.*

★ **Stouffer Stanford Court Hotel.** This is one of the most highly acclaimed hotels in the United States. The service is so thoughtful that the general manager recently put dictionaries in each room for guests' convenience. One of the city's finest restaurants, Fournou's Ovens, is located here. *905 California St., 94108, tel. 415/989–3500 or 800/227–4726. 402 rooms. Facilities: gift shops, 2 restaurants, 2 lounges. AE, DC, MC, V.*

Union Square/ Downtown The largest variety and greatest concentration of hotels are centered on the city's lovely downtown hub, Union Square, where hotel guests find the best shopping, the theater district, and transportation to every spot in San Francisco.

Very Expensive **Campton Place.** Steps away from Union Square is one of the
★ most highly rated and elegant hotels in San Francisco. Attentive, personal service takes off from the moment uniformed doormen greet guests outside the marble-floor lobby. *340 Stockton St., 94108, tel. 415/781–5555, 800/235–4300 in CA, or 800/647–4007 nationwide. 126 rooms. Facilities: restaurant, bar. AE, DC, MC, V.*

★ **Four Seasons Clift.** Probably San Francisco's most acclaimed hotel, this stately landmark is the first choice of many celebrities and discriminating travelers for its attentive personal service. Special attention is given to children, with fresh cookies and milk provided at bedtime. All rooms have been recently redecorated—the suites in elegant black and gray, others in bright beige and pink—in a somewhat updated contemporary style. *495 Geary St., 94102, tel. 415/775–4700 or 800/332–3442. 329 rooms. Facilities: restaurant, Redwood Room lounge. AE, DC, MC, V.*

Grand Hyatt. This hotel overlooks Union Square and Ruth Asawa's fantasy fountain in the garden. The hotel, formerly the Hyatt on Union Square, recently underwent a $20 million renovation. *345 Stockton St., 94108, tel. 415/398–1234 or 800/ 233–1234. 693 rooms. Facilities: 2 restaurants, 2 lounges, shopping arcade. AE, DC, MC, V.*

Hotel Nikko–San Francisco. Trickling waterfalls and walls of white marble set a quiet, subtle mood at this fine Japanese Airlines–owned hotel. The rooms are pink and gray contemporary with an Oriental touch. *222 Mason St., 94102, tel. 415/394–1111 or 800/NIKKO–US. 525 rooms. Facilities: indoor pool, health club and spa, 2 restaurants, lounge. AE, DC, MC, V.*

The Pan Pacific Hotel. Formerly the Portman, and reopened in June of 1990, the new management has retained much of the hotel's previous character. Attentive service is still the hotel's hallmark; personal valets and room service are available 24 hours a day. Decor is contemporary, with lots of brass and marble. Glass elevators transport guests from the atrium lobby to the room levels. Bathrooms are lined in rose-colored Italian marble. *500 Post St., 94102, tel. 415/771–8600 or 800/553–6465. 331 rooms. Facilities: restaurant, lounges, health club facilities available at nearby hotels, valet parking, meeting rooms. AE, DC, MC, V.*

Westin St. Francis. This is one of the grand hotels of San Francisco and a Union Square landmark. Rooms in the original building have been redecorated but still retain some of the 1904 moldings and bathroom tiles. Rooms in the modern tower have brighter, lacquered furniture. *335 Powell St., 94102, tel. 415/ 397–7000 or 800/228–3000. 1,200 rooms. Facilities: 5 restaurants, 5 lounges, shopping arcade. AE, DC, MC, V.*

Expensive **Aston Regis Hotel.** This is one of the finest examples of the new generation of small, renovated hotels. Rooms are large and elegant, decorated in Louis XVI–style with French and Oriental antiques and canopy beds. *490 Geary St., 94102, tel. 415/928– 7900 or 800/82–REGIS. 86 rooms. Facilities: restaurant, lounge. AE, DC, MC, V.*

Galleria Park. This very attractive hotel is convenient to the Union Square shopping district. The guest rooms were all redecorated in late 1988 in a simplified French country style. *191 Sutter St., 94104, tel. 415/781–3060, 800/792–9855 in CA, or 800/792–9636 nationwide. 177 rooms. Facilities: rooftop park and jogging track, 2 restaurants, lounge. AE, DC, MC, V.*

Holiday Inn–Union Square. This hotel enjoys a good location on the cable car line only a block from Union Square. The decor of the Sherlock Holmes Lounge is 221-B Baker Street all the way. *480 Sutter St., 94108, tel. 415/398–8900 or 800/HOLIDAY. 400 rooms. Facilities: restaurant, lounge. AE, DC, MC, V.*

Hotel Diva. This hotel attracts the avant garde set with a high-tech look that sets it apart from any other hotel in San Francisco. *440 Geary St., 94102, tel. 415/885–0200 or 800/553–1900. 125 rooms. Facilities: restaurant, lounge. AE, DC, MC, V.*

Inn at Union Square. The individually decorated rooms with goosedown pillows and four-poster beds here are sumptuous. Continental breakfast and afternoon tea are served before a fireplace in the cozy sitting areas on each floor. *440 Post St., 04102, tel. 415/397–3510 or 800/288–4346. 30 rooms. AE, DC, MC, V.*

Kensington Park. A handsome, high-ceilinged lobby sets the mood of this fine hotel, where afternoon tea and sherry are served. The rooms are decorated with English Queen Anne–style furniture. *450 Post St., 94102, tel. 415/788–6400 or 800/ 553–1900. 90 rooms. AE, DC, MC, V.*

★ **Petite Auberge.** The French countryside was imported to downtown San Francisco to create this charming bed-and-breakfast inn. Calico-printed wallpaper, fluffy down comforters, and French reproduction antiques decorate each room. Most have wood-burning fireplaces. Next door is the sister hotel, the 27-room **White Swan,** similar in style but with an English country flavor. *845 Bush St., 94108, tel. 415/928–6000. 26 rooms. Facilities: breakfast rooms, parlors. AE, MC, V.*

Sir Francis Drake. The rooms in this popular San Francisco hotel, famous for its Beefeater-costumed doormen, got a face-lift in 1986 during a multimillion-dollar renovation. They are decorated in an old English style, with mahogany furniture. The Starlight Roof is a lovely place for a drink. *450 Powell St., 94102, tel. 415/392–7755, 800/652–1668 in CA, or 800/227–5480 nationwide. 415 rooms. Facilities: restaurant, lounge, exercise room. AE, DC, MC, V.*

Moderate **The Cartwright.** This is a family-owned hotel with a friendly,
★ personal touch in an ideal location. Renovated in 1986, this hotel offers rooms with brass or wood-carved beds, small refrigerators, and newly tiled bathrooms. *524 Sutter St., 94102, tel. 415/421–2865 or 800/227–3844. 114 rooms. Facilities: coffee shop. AE, DC, MC, V.*

★ **Chancellor Hotel.** This venerable hotel has been attracting a loyal clientele since it opened in 1924. Renovated in 1986, rooms have a new, elegant appearance with polished cherry-wood furniture. One of the best buys on Union Square. *433 Powell St., 94102, tel. 415/362–2004 or 800/428–4748. 140 rooms. Facilities: restaurant, lounge. AE, DC, MC, V.*

Handlery Union Square Hotel. The former Handlery Motor Inn and Stewart Hotel were combined and refurbished at a cost of $5 million in early 1988. The suitelike Handlery Club rooms are larger and more expensive. *351 Geary St., 94102, tel. 415/781– 7800 or 800/223–0888. 378 rooms. Facilities: restaurant, outdoor heated pool, nonsmoking rooms. AE, DC, MC, V.*

★ **King George.** This charming midsize hotel was renovated in 1988 and 1989 to give it a more elegant, sophisticated look. The hotel's quaint Bread and Honey Tearoom serves traditional afternoon high tea. *334 Mason St., 94102, tel. 415/781–5050 or 800/288–6005. 144 rooms. Facilities: tearoom, lounge. AE, DC, MC, V.*

The Raphael. A favorite among repeat visitors to San Francisco, the Raphael was one of the first moderately priced European-style hotels in the city. Rooms were redecorated in 1988. The location is excellent. *386 Geary St., 94102, tel. 415/986– 2000 or 800/821–5343. 151 rooms. Facilities: restaurant, lounge, in-room HBO. AE, DC, MC, V.*

York Hotel. This very attractive, renovated old hotel is known for its Plush Room cabaret and as the site of a scene in Alfred Hitchcock's *Vertigo. 940 Sutter St., 94109, tel. 415/885–6800 or 800/227–3608. 96 rooms. Facilities: nightclub, fitness center, complimentary chauffeured limousine. AE, DC, MC, V.*

Inexpensive **Adelaide Inn.** The bedspreads may not match the drapes or carpets and the floors may creak, but the rooms are clean and cheap (under $50 for a double room) at this friendly small hotel that is popular with Europeans. Continental breakfast is complimentary. *5 Isadora Duncan Ct. (off Taylor between Geary and Post), 94102, tel. 415/441-2474. 16 rooms, all share bath. Facilities: sitting room, refrigerator for guest use. MC, V.*

Amsterdam. This European-style pension is in a Victorian building two blocks from Nob Hill. Rooms were renovated in 1988. *749 Taylor St., 94108, tel. 415/673-3277 or 800/637-3444. 30 rooms, 8 with shared bath. Facilities: cable TV in rooms, reading room, breakfast room for complimentary breakfast. AE, MC, V.*

Beresford Arms. Complimentary pastries and coffee are served in the hotel's grand old lobby. The suites with full kitchens are a good bargain for families. Standard rooms contain queen-size beds and small refrigerators. *701 Post St., 94109, tel. 415/673-2600 or 800/533-6533. 90 rooms. Facilities: some rooms have whirlpool baths. AE, DC, MC, V.*

★ **Grant Plaza.** This bargain-priced hotel at the entrance of Chinatown has small but clean and attractively furnished rooms. No restaurant, but plenty of dining nearby. *465 Grant Ave., 94103, tel. 415/434-3883, 800/472-6805 in CA, or 800/472-6899 nationwide. 72 rooms. AE, MC, V.*

Holiday Inn–Financial District. This hotel boasts excellent location in Chinatown and is five minutes from Union Square and North Beach. Rooms on 12th floor and above have city and bay views. *750 Kearny St., 94108, tel. 415/433-6600 or 800/HOLIDAY. 556 rooms. Facilities: pool, restaurant, lounge, free parking. AE, DC, MC, V.*

U.N. Plaza Hotel. This is a well-kept hotel for budget-conscious travelers who don't mind a less-than-desirable location. The large corner suites are ideal for families. Color TVs have in-room movies. *1112 Market St., 94102, tel. 415/626-5200 or 800/553-1900. 136 rooms. Facilities: tour desk in lobby. AE, DC, MC, V.*

The Arts and Nightlife

The best guide to arts and entertainment events in San Francisco is the "Datebook" section, printed on pink paper, in the Sunday *Examiner and Chronicle.* The *Bay Guardian,* a free weekly newspaper available in racks around the city, lists more neighborhood, avant-garde, and budget-priced events. For up-to-date information about cultural and musical events, call the Convention and Visitors Bureau Cultural Events Calendar (tel. 415/391-2001).

Half-price tickets to many local and touring stage shows go on sale at noon Tuesday–Saturday at the **STBS** booth on the Stockton Street side of Union Square, between Geary and Post streets. STBS is also a full-service ticket agency for theater and music events around the Bay Area (open until 7:30 PM). While the city's major commercial theaters are concentrated downtown, the opera, symphony, and ballet perform at the Civic Center. For recorded information about STBS tickets, call 415/433-7827.

The city's two charge-by-phone ticket services are **BASS** (tel. 415/762-2277), with one of its centers in the STBS booth, and **Ticketron** (tel. 415/392-7469), with a center in the Emporium

store, 835 Market Street. Other agencies downtown are the
City Box Office, 141 Kearny Street in the Sherman-Clay store
(tel. 415/392–4400) and **Downtown Center Box Office** in the
parking garage at 320 Mason Street (tel. 415/775–2021). The
opera, symphony, the ballet's *Nutcracker*, and touring hit
musicals are often sold out in advance; tickets are usually available within a day of performance for other shows.

The Arts San Francisco's "theater row" is a single block of Geary Street
Theater west of Union Square, but a number of commercial theaters are
located within walking distance, along with resident companies that enrich the city's theatrical scene. The three major
commercial theaters are operated by the Shorenstein-
Nederlander organization, which books touring plays and
musicals, some of them before they open on Broadway. The
most venerable is the **Curran** (445 Geary St., tel. 415/673–
4400), which is used for plays and smaller musicals. The **Golden
Gate** is a stylishly refurbished movie theater (Golden Gate Ave.
at Taylor St., tel. 415/474–3800), primarily a musical house.
The 2,500-seat **Orpheum** (1192 Market St. near the Civic Center, tel. 415/474–3800) is used for the biggest touring shows.

The smaller commercial theaters, offering touring shows and a
few that are locally produced, are the **Marines Memorial Theatre** (Sutter and Mason Sts., tel. 415/441–7444) and **Theatre on
the Square** (450 Post St., tel. 415/433–9500). For commercial
and popular success, nothing beats *Beach Blanket Babylon*,
the zany revue that has been running for years at **Club Fugazi**
(678 Green St. in North Beach, tel. 415/421–4222). Conceived
by imaginative San Francisco director Steve Silver, it is a lively, colorful musical mix of cabaret, show-biz parodies, and trib-
utes to local landmarks.

The city's major theater company is the **American Conservatory
Theatre (ACT)**, which quickly became one of the nation's leading regional theaters when it was founded during the mid-
1960s. It presents a season of approximately eight plays in rotating repertory from October through late spring. The ACT's
ticket office is at the **Geary Theatre** (415 Geary St., tel. 415/
749–2228), though the theater itself was closed following the
1989 earthquake. The rebuilt Geary is expected to reopen in
1993, and in the meantime, the ACT is performing at the nearby **Stage Door Theater** (420 Mason St.) and other theaters
around the city.

At the next level are several established theaters in smaller
houses and with lower ticket prices that specialize in contempo-
rary plays. The most reliable are the **Eureka Theatre** (2730 16th
St. in the Mission District, tel. 415/558–9898) and the **Magic
Theatre** (Bldg. D, Fort Mason Center, Laguna St. at Marina
Blvd., tel. 415/441–8822).

The city boasts a wide variety of specialized and ethnic theaters that work with dedicated local actors and some professionals. Among the most interesting are **The Lamplighters,** the
delightful Gilbert and Sullivan troupe that often gets better
reviews than touring productions of musicals, performing at
Presentation Theater (2350 Turk St., tel. 415/752–7755); the
Lorraine Hansberry Theatre, which specializes in plays by Afri-
can-American writers (620 Sutter St., tel. 415/474–8800); the
Asian American Theatre (405 Arguello Blvd., tel. 415/346–
8922); and the gay and lesbian **Theatre Rhinoceros** (2926 16th

St., tel. 415/861–5079). The **San Francisco Shakespeare Festival** offers free performances on summer weekends in Golden Gate Park (tel. 415/221–0642).

Music The completion of Davies Symphony Hall at Van Ness Avenue and Grove Street finally gave the San Francisco Symphony a home of its own. It solidified the base of the city's three major performing arts organizations—symphony, opera, and ballet—in the Civic Center. The symphony and other musical groups also perform in the smaller, 928-seat Herbst Theatre in the Opera's "twin" at Van Ness Avenue and McAllister Street, the War Memorial Building. Otherwise the city's musical ensembles can be found all over the map: in churches and museums, in restaurants and outdoors in parks, and in outreach series in Berkeley and on the peninsula.

San Francisco Symphony. The city's most stable performing arts organization plays from September to May, with music director Herbert Blomstedt conducting for about two-thirds of the season. Guest conductors often include Michael Tilson Thomas, Edo de Waart, and Riccardo Mutti. Guest soloists include artists of the caliber of Andre Watts, Leontyne Price, and Jean-Pierre Rampal. The symphony has stayed with the standard repertoire in recent years as Blomstedt concentrates on the ensemble's stability and focus. Special events include a Mostly Mozart festival during the spring, a Beethoven festival during the summer, a New and Unusual Music series during the spring in the more intimate Herbst Theatre, and summer Pops Concerts in the nearby Civic Auditorium. Throughout the season, the symphony presents a Great Performers Series of guest soloists and orchestras. *Davies Symphony Hall, Van Ness Ave. at Grove St., tel. 415/431–5400. Tickets at the box office or through BASS, tel. 415/762–2277.*

Opera **San Francisco Opera** (Van Ness Ave. at Grove St., tel. 415/864–3330). Founded in 1923, and the resident company at the War Memorial Opera House in the Civic Center since it was built in 1932, the Opera has expanded to a fall season of 13 weeks. Approximately 70 performances of 10 operas are given, beginning on the first Friday after Labor Day. For many years the Opera was considered a major international company and the most artistically successful operatic organization in the United States. International opera stars frequently sing major roles here, but the Opera is also well known for presenting the American debuts of singers who have made their name in Europe. In the same way, the company's standard repertoire is interspersed with revivals of rarely heard works. Ticket prices range from about $28 to a high of about $90, and many performances are sold out far in advance. Standing-room tickets are always sold, however, and patrons often sell extra tickets on the Opera House steps just before curtain time.

Dance **San Francisco Ballet** (War Memorial Opera House, Van Ness Ave. at Grove St., tel. 415/621–3838). The ballet has regained much of its luster under artistic director Helgi Tomasson, and both classical and contemporary works have won admiring reviews. The company's primary season runs February–May; its repertoire includes such full-length ballets as *Swan Lake* and a new production of *Sleeping Beauty*. The company is also intent on reaching new audiences with bold new dances, what it likes to call "cutting-edge works that will make you take a second look." Like many dance companies in the nation, the ballet presents *The Nutcracker* in December, and its recent production is one of the most spectacular.

Film The San Francisco Bay Area, including Berkeley and San Jose, is considered to be one of the nation's most important movie markets. If there is a film floating around the country or around the world in search of an audience, it is likely that it will eventually turn up on a screen in San Francisco. The Bay Area is also a filmmaking center: Documentaries and experimental works are being produced on modest budgets, feature films and television programs are shot on location, and some of Hollywood's biggest directors prefer to live here, particularly in Marin County. In San Francisco, about a third of the theaters regularly show foreign and independent films. The city is also one of the last strongholds of "repertory cinema," showing older American and foreign films on bills that change daily.

San Francisco's traditional movie theater center, downtown on Market Street, is pretty much given over to sex flicks and action films nowadays. First-run commercial movie theaters are now scattered throughout the city, although they are concentrated along Van Ness Avenue, near Japantown, and in the Marina District. All are accessible on major Muni bus routes, as are the art-revival houses. Several of the most respected and popular independent theaters have been taken over by chains recently, and their policy could change. The San Francisco International Film Festival (tel. 415/931–3456), the oldest in the country, continues to provide an extensive selection of foreign films each spring. The Pacific Film Archive in Berkeley is an incomparable source for rare American and foreign films.

Nightlife Although San Francisco is a compact city with the prevailing influences of some neighborhoods spilling into others, the following generalizations should help you find the kind of entertainment you're looking for. **Nob Hill** is noted for its plush piano bars and panoramic skyline lounges. **North Beach,** infamous for its topless and bottomless bistros, also maintains a sense of its beatnik past and this legacy lives on in atmospheric bars and coffeehouses. **Fisherman's Wharf,** while touristy, is great for people-watching and provides plenty of impromptu entertainment from street performers. **Union Street** is home away from home for singles in search of company. **South of Market** (SoMa, for short) has become a hub of nightlife, with a bevy of highly popular nightclubs, bars, and lounges in renovated warehouses and auto shops. Gay men will find the **Castro** and **Polk Street** scenes of infinite variety, while lesbian bars abound on and around **Valencia Street.**

Rock, Pop, Folk,   **Fillmore Auditorium.** Bastion of the great bands of the '60s, the
and Blues   Fillmore is being refurbished by rock promoter Bill Graham and will feature some of the hottest names on the contemporary rock scene as well as survivors of an earlier era. Headliners include Little Feet and Jimmy Cliff. *1805 Geary St., tel. 415/922–FILL. Call for show times and prices. No credit cards.*
Great American Music Hall. This is one of the great eclectic nightclubs, not only in San Francisco but in the entire country. Here you will find truly top-drawer entertainment, running the gamut from the best in blues, folk, and jazz to rock with a sprinkling of outstanding comedians. This colorful marble-pillared emporium will also accommodate dancing to popular bands. Past headliners here include Carmen McCrae, B.B. King, Tom Paxton, and Doc Watson. *859 O'Farrell St. between*

Polk and Larkin Sts., tel. 415/885–0750. Shows usually at 8 PM, but this may vary, so call. Cover: $10–$20. No credit cards.

Last Day Saloon. In an attractive setting of wooden tables and potted plants, this club offers some major entertainers and a varied schedule of blues, Cajun, rock, and jazz. Some of the illustrious performers who have appeared here are Taj Mahal, the Zazu Pitts Memorial Orchestra, Maria Muldaur, and Pride and Joy. *406 Clement St. between 5th and 6th Aves. in the Richmond District, tel. 415/387–6343. Shows 9 PM nightly. Cover: $4–$6; some weeknights free. No credit cards.*

Slim's. One of the most popular newcomers to the SoMa scene, Slim's specializes in what it labels "American roots music"—blues, jazz, classic rock, and the like. Co-owner Boz Scaggs helps bring in the crowds. *333 11th St., tel. 415/621–3330. Shows nightly 9 PM. Cover $10–$15. AE, MC, V.*

The Saloon. Some locals consider the historic Saloon the best spot in San Francisco for the blues. Headliners here include Roy Rogers. *1232 Grant St. near Columbus Ave. in North Beach, tel. 415/989–7666. Shows 9:30 PM nightly. Cover: $5–$8. No credit cards.*

The Warfield. This old Art Deco theater was completely renovated in 1988 to become a showcase for mainstream rock and roll. There are tables and chairs downstairs, and theater seating upstairs. Such contemporary acts as Robert Palmer, Simply Red, and K.D. Lang have played here recently. *982 Market St. tel. 415/775–7722. Shows most nights at 8 PM. Tickets $15–$20. V.*

Jazz **Kimball's.** Such jazz greats as Freddie Hubbard play at this club, which is also a restaurant. *300 Grove St. at Franklin St. in the Civic Center, tel. 415/861–5555. Shows 9 PM and 11 PM Wed.–Sat. Cover: $12–$15. The additional $5 minimum for food and drink is generally not enforced. AE, MC, V.*

Pasand Lounge. Features jazz and rhythm and blues. *1875 Union St., Pacific Heights, tel. 415/922–4498. Shows nightly, 7 PM–1 AM. No cover. 2-drink minimum. AE, MC, V.*

Pier 23. Pier 23 offers the best in bebop, ranging from the Brian Melvin Trio to Kitty Margolis. *At Embarcadero and Pier 23, across from the Fog City Diner, tel. 415/362–5125. Shows Tues.–Sat. 10 PM, Sun. 4–8 PM. No cover. 2-drink minimum. MC, V.*

Comedy Clubs **Cobb's Comedy Club.** Bobby Slayton, Paula Poundstone, and Dr. Gonzo are among the super stand-up comics who perform here. *In the Cannery, 2801 Leavenworth St. at the corner of Beach St., tel. 415/928–4320. Shows Mon. 8 PM, Tues.–Thurs. 9 PM, Fri.–Sat. 9 and 11 PM. Cover: $7 weeknights, $9 Fri. and Sat. 2-drink minimum Fri. and Sat. MC, V.*

Holy City Zoo. Robin Williams ascended like a meteor from an improv group that gained fame here, and terrific stand-up comics, such as local favorite Michael Prichard, headline now. The "Zoo" features comedy nightly, with an open mike for pros and would-be comedians every Tuesday. *408 Clement St. in the Richmond District, tel. 415/386–4242. Shows Sun.–Thurs. 9 PM, Fri.–Sat. 9 and 11 PM. Cover: $3 Sun.–Thurs., $8 Fri. and Sat., 2-drink minimum. MC, V.*

The Punch Line. A launching pad for the likes of Jay Leno and Whoopie Goldberg, the Punch Line features some of the top talents around—several of whom are certain to make a national impact. Note that weekend shows often sell out, and it is best to buy tickets in advance at BASS outlets (tel. 415/762–BASS).

444-A Battery St. between Clay and Washington Sts., tel. 415/ 397–PLSF. Shows Sun.–Thurs. 9 PM, Fri. 9 and 11 PM, Sat. 7, 9, and 11 PM. Cover: $7 Tues.–Thurs.; $10 Fri. and Sat.; special $5 showcases Mon. and Sun. 2-drink minimum. MC, V.

Dancing Emporiums

Cesar's Palace. Salsa-style Latin music attracts all kinds of dancers to this popular club in the city's Hispanic Mission District. *3140 Mission St., tel. 415/648–6611. Open Thurs. 8 PM–2 AM; Fri.–Sun. 9 PM–5 AM. Cover: $7.*

Club DV8. One of the largest of the trendy SoMa clubs, DV8 attracts scores of stylish young people to its 25,000 square feet (two levels) of dance floors. *540 Howard St., tel. 415/957–1730. Open Wed.–Sat. 9 PM–3 AM. Cover: $5–$10.*

Club O. This was the original SoMa crossover bar/dance club. The cover charge varies. Note: You must be 21 to enter. *278 11th St., South of Market, tel. 415/621–8119. Opens 9:30 PM.*

Firehouse 7. This popular Mission District club plays reggae, rock and roll, modern dance music, house music, and soul. Live music and open mike on Sundays. *3160 16th St., tel. 415/621– 1617. Opens at 9. Cover: $3 Mon.–Thurs.; $5 Fri. and Sat.; $1 Sun.*

Oz. The most popular upscale disco in San Francisco, the land of Oz is reached via a glass elevator. Then, surrounded by a splendid panorama of the city, you dance on marble floors and recharge on cushy sofas and bamboo chairs. The fine sound system belts out oldies, disco, Motown, and new wave. *335 Powell St. between Geary and Post Sts. on the top floor of the Westin St. Francis Hotel, tel. 415/397–7000. Open nightly 9 PM–2 AM. Cover: $8 Sun.–Thurs.; $15 Fri.–Sat.*

The Kennel Club. Alternative rock and funk rule in this small, steamy room: Everyone's dancing! On Thursdays and Saturdays this space is known as The Box, and a very gay mixed-gender, mixed-race crowd takes over. *628 Divisadero, tel. 415/931– 1914. Open nightly 9 PM–2 AM. Cover: $2–$10.*

Townsend. This big industrial space has an edgy but fashionable feel, complemented by a house mix of rock and modern dance music. *177 Townsend, near the train depot, tel. 415/974– 6020. Open Thurs. 10 PM–3 AM, Fri.–Sat. 10 PM–4AM. Cover: around $10.*

Skyline Bars

Carnelian Room. At 781 feet above the ground, enjoy dinner or cocktails here on the 52nd floor, where you may drink from the loftiest view of San Francisco's magnificent skyline. Reservations are a must for dinner here. *Top of the Bank of America Building, 555 California St., tel. 415/433–7500. Open Mon.– Fri. 3–11:30 PM; Sat. 4–11:30 PM; Sun. 10 AM–10:30 PM.*

Crown Room. Just ascending to the well-named Crown Room is a drama in itself as you take the Fairmont's glass-enclosed Skylift elevator to the top. Some San Franciscans maintain that this lounge is the most luxurious of the city's skyline bars. Lunches, dinners, and Sunday brunches are served as well as drinks. *29th floor of the Fairmont Hotel, California and Mason Sts., tel. 415/772–5131. Open daily 11 AM–1 AM.*

Equinox. What's distinctive about the Hyatt's skyline-view bar is its capacity to revolve. The Hyatt is also home to the **Other Trellis Lounge.** There is no cover charge here for music ranging from classical to jazz. *Both are open 11 AM–1:30 AM; both are in the Hyatt Regency, Embarcadero Center No. 5, tel. 415/788– 1234.*

Top of the Mark. This fabled landmark affords fabulous views in an elegant 19th-floor setting. *In the Mark Hopkins Hotel, Cali-*

*fornia and Mason Sts., tel. 415/392–3434. Open nightly 4 PM–
1:30 AM. Dress: formal.*

Gay Bars **Amelia's.** One of San Francisco's busiest lesbian bars, dancing
and a show are offered here. *647 Valencia St., tel. 415/552–
7788.*
Kimo's. This relaxed establishment affords an elegant ambience. *1351 Polk St., tel. 415/885–4535.*
The Midnight Sun. This is one of the Castro's longest-standing
and most popular bars, with giant video screens riotously pro-
grammed. *4067 18th St., tel. 415/861–4186.*
The Stud. This is a popular, jam-packed SoMa bar. *399 9th St.,
tel. 415/863–6623.*
Twin Peaks. A pleasant mirrored fern bar, Twin Peaks is a
tranquil place in which to drink and converse. *401 Castro St.,
tel. 415/864–9470.*

Excursion to Sausalito

by Robert Taylor The San Francisco Convention and Visitors Bureau describes
Sausalito's location as "the Mediterranean side of the Golden
Gate." With its relatively sheltered site on the bay in Marin
County, just 8 miles from San Francisco, it appeals to Bay Area
residents and visitors for the same reason: It is so near and yet
so far. As a hillside town with superb views, an expansive yacht
harbor, the aura of an artist's colony, and ferry service,
Sausalito might be a resort within commuting distance of the
city. It is certainly the primary excursion for visitors to San
Francisco, especially those with limited time to explore the
Bay Area. Mild weather encourages strolling and outdoor dining, although afternoon winds and fog can roll over the hills
from the ocean, funneling through the central part of town once
known as Hurricane Gulch.

There are substantial homes, including Victorian mansions, in
Sausalito's heights, but the town has long had a more colorful
and raffish reputation. Discovered in 1775 by Spanish explorers and named Saucelito (Little Willow) for the trees growing
around its springs, Sausalito was a port for whaling ships during the 19th century. In 1875, the railroad from the north connected with ferryboats to San Francisco and the town became
an attraction for the fun-loving. Even the chamber of commerce
recalls the time when Sausalito sported 25 saloons, gambling
dens, and bordellos. Bootleggers flourished during Prohibition
in the 1920s, and shipyard workers swelled the town's population during the 1940s, when tour guides divided the residents
into "wharf rats" and "hill snobs." Ensuing decades brought a
bohemian element with the development of an artists' colony
and a houseboat community. Sausalito has also become a major
yachting center, and restaurants attract visitors for the fresh
seafood as well as the spectacular views. Sausalito remains a
friendly and casual small town, although summer traffic jams
can fray nerves. If possible, visit Sausalito on a weekday—and
take the ferry.

Arriving and Departing

By Car Cross the Golden Gate Bridge and go north on Highway 101 to
the Sausalito exit, then go south on Bridgeway to municipal
parking near the center of town. The trip takes ½ hour to 45

minutes one-way. (You will need change for the parking lots' meters.)

By Bus **Golden Gate Transit** (tel. 415/332–6600) travels to Sausalito from 1st and Mission streets and other points in the city.

By Ferry **Golden Gate Ferry** (tel. 415/332–6600) crosses the bay from the Ferry Building at Market Street and the Embarcadero; **Red and White Fleet** (tel. 415/546–2896) leaves from Pier 41 at Fisherman's Wharf. The trip takes 15–30 minutes.

Guided Tours

Most tour companies include Sausalito on excursions north to Muir Woods and the Napa Valley Wine Country. Among them are **Gray Line** (tel. 415/558–9400) and **Great Pacific Tour Co.** (tel. 415/626–4499).

Exploring

Numbers in the margin correspond with points of interest on the Sausalito map.

Bridgeway is Sausalito's main thoroughfare and prime destination, with the bay, yacht harbor, and waterfront restaurants on one side, and more restaurants, shops, hillside homes, and hotels on the other. It is only a few steps from the ferry terminal to the tiny landmark park in the center of town: the **Plaza Vina del Mar**, named for Sausalito's sister city in Chile. The park features a fountain and two 14-foot-tall statues of elephants created for the 1915 Panama-Pacific International Exposition in San Francisco.

Across the street to the south is the Spanish-style **Sausalito Hotel**, which has been refurbished and filled with Victorian antiques. Between the hotel and the **Sausalito Yacht Club** is another unusual historic landmark, a drinking fountain with the invitation Have a Drink on Sally. It's in remembrance of Sally Stanford, the former San Francisco madam who later ran Sausalito's Valhalla restaurant and became the town's mayor. Actually, the monument is also in remembrance of her dog. There is a sidewalk-level bowl that suggests Have a Drink on Leland.

South on Bridgeway, toward San Francisco, there is an esplanade along the water with picture-perfect views. Farther south are a number of restaurants on piers, including—near the end of Bridgeway at Richardson Street—what was the **Valhalla** and is the oldest restaurant in Sausalito. Built in 1893 as "Walhalla," it was one of the settings for the film *The Lady from Shanghai* in the 1940s, Sally Stanford's place in the 1950s, and most recently a Chart House restaurant.

North on Bridgeway from the ferry terminal are yacht harbors and, parallel to Bridgeway a block to the west, the quieter Caledonia Street, with its own share of cafés and shops. There is a pleasant, grassy park with a children's playground at Caledonia and Litho streets, with a food shop nearby for picnic provisions.

Here and there along the west side of Bridgeway are flights of steps that climb the hill to Sausalito's wooded, sometimes rustic and sometimes lavish residential neighborhoods. The stair-

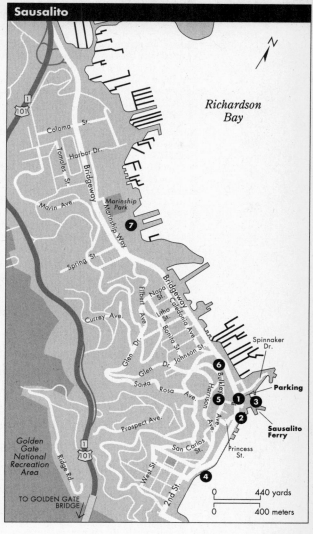

Sausalito

Richardson
Bay

Coloma St.

Harbor Dr.

Bridgeway

Marin Ave.

Marinship
Park

Marinship Way

7

Spring St.

Currey Ave.

Filbert Ave.

Napa St.

Litho St.

Bridgeway

Caledonia Ave.

Bonita St.

D. Johnson St.

Glen Dr.

Glen Dr.

Santa

Rosa Ave.

Spinnaker
Dr.

6

Bulkley Ave.

5 **1** **3**

Harrison Ave.

2

Parking

**Sausalito
Ferry**

Prospect Ave.

Golden
Gate
National
Recreation
Area

Ridge Rd.

San Carlos St.

Princess
St.

West St.

2nd St.

4

0 ____ 440 yards

0 ____ 400 meters

TO GOLDEN GATE
BRIDGE

way just across the street from Vina del Mar Park is named Excelsior, and it leads to the **Alta Mira,** a popular Spanish-style hotel and restaurant with a spectacular view. However, there are vistas of the bay from all these streets.

Where there isn't a hillside house or a restaurant or a yacht in Sausalito, there is a shop. Most are along Bridgeway and Princess Street, and they offer a wide assortment of casual and sophisticated clothing, posters and paintings, imported and handcrafted gifts, and the expected variety of T-shirts, ice cream, cookies, and pastries. The **Village Fair** (777 Bridgeway) is a four-story former warehouse that has been converted into a warren of clothing, craft, and gift boutiques. Crafts workers often demonstrate their talents in the shops, and a winding brick path—Little Lombard Street—connects various levels. The shopping complex is a haven during wet weather.

Sausalito's reputation as an art colony is enhanced by the **Art Festival** held during the three-day Labor Day weekend in September. It attracts more than 35,000 visitors to the waterfront area, and there are plans to expand the site and offer direct ferry service from San Francisco. Details are available from the Sausalito Chamber of Commerce (333 Caledonia St., 94965, tel. 415/332–0505).

➐ North on Bridgeway, within a few minutes' drive, is the **Bay Model,** a re-creation in miniature of the entire San Francisco Bay and the San Joaquin–Sacramento River delta. It is actually nearly 400 feet square and is used by the U.S. Army Corps of Engineers to reproduce the rise and fall of tides, the flow of currents, and the other physical forces at work on the bay. It is housed in a former World War II shipyard building, and there is a display of shipbuilding history. At the same site is the Wapama, a World War I–era steam freighter being restored by volunteers. *2100 Bridgeway, tel. 415/332–3871. Open Tues.–Fri. 9–4, weekends 10–6. Closed Sun. in winter.*

Along the shore of Richardson Bay, between the Bay Model and U.S. 101, are some of the 400 houseboats that make up Sausalito's "floating homes community." In the shallow tidelands, most of them float only about half the time, but they are always a fanciful collection of the rustic, the eccentric, the flamboyant, and the elegant.

Dining

Restaurants and cafés line Bridgeway, Sausalito's main street, and specialize in seafood. A variety of sandwiches, salads, and snack foods are also available. The favored restaurants are directly on the bay or on Sausalito's hillside.

Restaurants are listed according to price category.

Category	Cost*
Very Expensive	$30 and up
Expensive	$20–$30
Moderate	$10–$20
Inexpensive	under $10

per person, excluding drinks, service, and 6.5% sales tax

The following credit card abbreviations are used: AE, American Express; DC, Diners Club; MC, MasterCard; V, Visa.

Moderate–Expensive **Alta Mira.** This is a smart restaurant, with a more formal atmosphere than the downtown cafés, in a Spanish-style hotel a block above Bridgeway. The Alta Mira serves three meals a day, and the specialties are fresh scallops and Pacific salmon, grilled meats, and large crab and shrimp salads. The terrace offers one of Sausalito's best views and is popular for lunch and Sunday brunch. *125 Bulkley Ave., tel. 415/332–1350. Reservations advised. AE, DC, MC, V.*
Casa Madrona. Another restaurant in a charming hotel, this is a Victorian surrounded by a landscaped walk and newer rooms

stepping down the hill to Bridgeway. Casa Madrona serves American cuisine, with an appealing selection of breakfast and brunch dishes. *801 Bridgeway, tel. 415/331–5888. MC, V. No lunch Sat.*

Moderate **The Spinnaker.** Seafood specialties and homemade pastas are offered in a quietly contemporary building in a spectacular setting on a point beyond the harbor, near the yacht club. You may see a pelican perched on one of the pilings just outside. *100 Spinnaker Dr., tel. 415/332–1500. AE, MC, V.*

Inexpensive– **Winship Restaurant.** Here seafood, pasta, steaks, burgers, and
Moderate salads are served in a casual nautical setting directly on the Bridgeway shopping strip. *670 Bridgeway, tel. 415/332–1454. AE, DC, MC, V. No dinner Mon., Tues.*

Excursion to Muir Woods

One hundred and fifty million years ago, ancestors of redwood and sequoia trees grew throughout the United States. Today the *Sequoia sempervirens* can be found only in a narrow, cool coastal belt from Monterey to Oregon. (*Sequoiadendron gigantea* grows in the Sierra Nevada.) **Muir Woods National Monument,** 17 miles northwest of San Francisco, is a 550-acre park that contains one of the most majestic redwood groves in the world. Some redwoods in the park are nearly 250 feet tall and 1,000 years old. This grove was saved from destruction in 1908 and named for naturalist John Muir, whose campaigns helped to establish the National Park system. His response: "This is the best tree-lover's monument that could be found in all of the forests of the world. Saving these woods from the axe and saw is in many ways the most notable service to God and man I have heard of since my forest wandering began."

Arriving and Departing

By Car Take U.S. 101 north to the Mill Valley–Muir Woods exit. The trip takes 45 minutes one-way when the roads are open, but traffic can be heavy on summer weekends so allow more time.

By Bus **Golden Gate Transit** (tel. 415/332–6600) sends buses from 1st and Mission streets and other points in San Francisco to Muir Woods.

Guided Tours

Most tour companies include Muir Woods on excursions to the Wine Country, among them **Gray Line** (tel. 415/558–9400) and **Great Pacific** (tel. 415/626–4499).

Exploring

Muir Woods is a park for walking; no cars are allowed in the redwood grove itself. There are 6 miles of easy trails from the park headquarters. The paths cross streams and pass through ferns and azaleas as well as magnificent stands of redwoods such as Bohemian Grove and the circular formation called Cathedral Grove. No picnicking or camping is allowed, but snacks are available at the visitor center. The weather is usually cool and often wet, so dress warmly and wear shoes appropriate for damp trails. *Tel. 415/388–2595. Open daily 8 AM–sunset.*

Excursion to Berkeley

Berkeley and the University of California are not synonymous, although the founding campus of the state university system dominates the city's heritage and contemporary life. The city of 100,000 facing San Francisco across the bay has other interesting features for visitors. Berkeley is culturally diverse and politically adventurous, a breeding ground for social trends, a continuing bastion of the counterculture, and an important center for Bay Area writers, artists, and musicians. The city's liberal reputation and determined spirit once led detractors to describe it as the People's Republic of Berkeley. Wooded groves on the university campus, neighborhoods of shingled bungalows, and landscaped hillside homes temper the urban environment.

The city was named for George Berkeley, the Irish philosopher and clergyman who crossed the Atlantic to convert the Indians and wrote "Westward, the course of empire takes its way." The city grew with the university, which was created by the state legislature in 1868 and established five years later on a rising plain of oak trees split by Strawberry Canyon. The central campus occupies 178 acres of the scenic 1,282-acre property, with most buildings located from Bancroft Way north to Hearst Street and from Oxford Street east into the Berkeley Hills. The university has more than 30,000 students and a full-time faculty of 1,600. It is considered one of the nation's leading intellectual centers and a major site for scientific research.

Note that the telephone area code for Berkeley, Oakland, and other cities on the east side of San Francisco Bay changed from 415 to 510 in 1991.

Arriving and Departing

By Car Take I–80 east across the Bay Bridge, then the University Avenue exit through downtown Berkeley to the campus, or take the Ashby Avenue exit and turn left on Telegraph Avenue to the traditional campus entrance; there is a parking garage on Channing Way. The trip takes ½ hour one-way (except in rush hour).

By Public Transportation BART (tel. 415/788–2278) trains run under the bay to the downtown Berkeley exit; transfer to the Humphrey GoBart shuttle bus to campus. The trip takes from 45 minutes to one hour one-way.

Exploring

Numbers in the margin correspond with points of interest on the Berkeley map.

❶ The Visitors Center (tel. 510/642–5215) in **University Hall** at University Avenue and Oxford Street, is open weekdays 8–5. There are maps and brochures for self-guided walks; student-guided tours leave weekdays at 1 PM.

❷ The throbbing heart of the University of California is **Sproul Plaza,** just inside the campus at Telegraph Avenue and Bancroft Way. It's a lively panorama of political and social activists, musicians, food vendors along Bancroft Way, children, dogs,

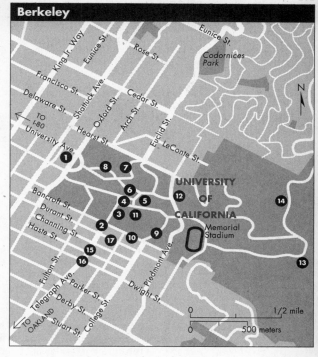

and students on their way to and from classes at this "university within a park."

The university's suggested tour circles the upper portion of the central campus, past buildings that were sited to take advantage of vistas to the Golden Gate across the bay. The first campus plan was proposed by Frederick Law Olmsted, who designed New York's Central Park, and over the years the university's architects have included Bernard Maybeck and Julia Morgan (who designed Hearst Castle at San Simeon). Beyond Sproul Plaza is the bronze **Sather Gate,** built in 1909 and the south entrance to the campus until expansion during the 1960s. Up a walkway to the right is vine-covered **South Hall,** one of two remaining buildings that greeted the first students in 1873.

Just ahead is **Sather Tower,** popularly known as the Campanile, the campus landmark that can be seen for miles. The 307-foot tower was modeled on St. Mark's tower in Venice and was completed in 1914. The carillon, which was cast in England, is played three times a day. In the lobby of the tower is a photographic display of campus history. An elevator takes visitors 175 feet up to the observation deck. *Open daily except university holidays 10–4:30. Admission: 50¢.*

Opposite the Campanile is **Bancroft Library,** with a rare-book collection and a changing series of exhibits that may include a Shakespeare first folio or a Gold Rush diary. On permanent display is a gold nugget purported to be the one that started the rush to California when it was discovered on January 24, 1848.

7 Across University Drive to the north is the **Earth Sciences Building,** with a seismograph for measuring earthquakes. The **8** building also contains the **Paleontology Museum,** which has displays of dinosaur bones and the huge skeleton of a plesiosaur. *Open when the university is in session, weekdays 8–5, weekends 1–5.*

The university's two major museums are on the south side of **9** campus near Bancroft Way. **The Lowie Museum of Anthropology,** in Kroeber Hall, has a collection of more than 4,000 artifacts. Items on display may cover the archaeology of ancient America or the crafts of Pacific Islanders. The museum also houses the collection of artifacts made by Ishi, the lone survivor of a California Indian tribe who was brought to the Bay Area in 1911. *Tel. 510/642–3681. Open Tues.–Fri. 10–4:30, weekends noon–4:30.*

10 **The University Art Museum** is a fan-shaped building with a spiral of ramps and balcony galleries. It houses a collection of Asian and Western art, including a major group of Hans Hofmann's abstract paintings, and also displays touring exhibits. On the ground floor is the Pacific Film Archive, which offers daily programs of historic and contemporary films. *2626 Bancroft Way, tel. 510/642–0808. Museum open Wed.–Sun. 11–5. Free museum admission. Film-program information, tel. 415/642–1124.*

Many of the university's notable attractions are outdoors. Just **11** south of the Campanile near the rustic Faculty Club is **Faculty Glade** on the south fork of Strawberry Creek, one of the best examples of the university's attempt to preserve a parklike atmosphere. East of the central campus, across Gayley Road, is **12** the **Hearst Greek Theatre,** built in 1903 and seating 7,000. Sarah Bernhardt once performed here; now it is used for major musical events.

Above the Greek Theatre in Strawberry Canyon is the 30-acre **13** **Botanical Garden,** with a collection of some 25,000 species. It's a relaxing gathering spot with benches and picnic tables. *Open daily 9–5, except Christmas.*

Perched on a hill above the campus on Centennial Drive is the **14** fortresslike **Lawrence Hall of Science,** which is a laboratory, a science education center, and—most important to visitors—a dazzling display of scientific knowledge and experiments. Displays are updated regularly. On weekends there are additional films, lectures, and demonstrations, especially for children. *Tel. 510/642–5132. Nominal admission charge. Open Mon.–Sat. 10–4:30, Sun. noon–5.*

Berkeley is a rewarding city to explore beyond the university. Just south of the campus on **Telegraph Avenue** is the busy, student-oriented district, full of cafés, bookstores, poster shops, and street vendors with traditional and trendy crafts items. Shops come and go with the times, but among the neighbor- **15** hood landmarks are **Cody's Books** (2454 Telegraph Ave.), with **16** its adjacent café; **Moe's** (2476 Telegraph Ave.), with a huge se- **17** lection of used books; and **Leopold Records** (2518 Durant Ave.). This district was the center of student protests during the 1960s, and on the street it sometimes looks as if that era still lives. People's Park, one of the centers of protest, is just east of Telegraph between Haste Street and Dwight Way.

Downtown Berkeley around University and Shattuck avenues is nondescript. However, there are shops for browsing along College Avenue near Ashby Avenue south of campus and in the Walnut Square development at Shattuck and Vine streets northwest of campus. Berkeley's shingled houses can be seen on tree-shaded streets near College and Ashby avenues. Hillside houses with spectacular views can be seen on the winding roads near the intersection of Ashby and Claremont avenues, around the Claremont Hotel (*see* Excursion to Oakland, below). At the opposite side of the city, there are views across the bay from the Berkeley Marina at the foot of University Avenue, west of I–80.

Dining

Berkeley's major restaurants, including those on Shattuck Avenue north of the university, are known for their innovative use of fresh local produce. There is an eclectic variety of low-cost international cafés and snack stands in the student area along Telegraph Avenue and more cafés downtown on Shattuck Avenue near the central Berkeley BART station.

Restaurants are listed according to price category.

Category	Cost*
Very Expensive	$30 and up
Expensive	$20–$30
Moderate	$10–$20
Inexpensive	under $10

per person, excluding drinks, service, and 6.5% sales tax

The following credit card abbreviations are used: AE, American Express; DC, Diners Club; MC, MasterCard; V, Visa.

Moderate–Expensive **Cafe at Chez Panisse.** Fresh and innovative light meals (lunch and dinner) are served, including pasta, pizza, salads, and light grilled dishes, upstairs from the mecca for California cuisine. *1517 Shattuck Ave., north of University Ave., tel. 510/548–5525. Same-day reservations accepted. Closed Sun. AE, DC, MC, V.*

Moderate **Spenger's Fish Grotto.** This is a rambling, boisterous seafood restaurant, with daily specials and hearty portions. *1919 Fourth St., near University Ave. and I–80, tel. 510/845–7771. Reservations for 5 or more. AE, DC, MC, V.*

Inexpensive **Kip's.** This is a student hangout but it is open to everyone, upstairs near Telegraph Avenue, with big wooden tables and burgers, pizza, and—of course—beer on tap. *2439 Durant Ave., tel. 510/848–4340. No reservations. No credit cards.*
New Delhi Junction. A popular Indian restaurant, New Delhi Junction offers Tandoori-roasted meats, curries, and regional specialties. *2556 University Ave., tel. 510/486–0477. Open daily. MC, V.*

Excursion to Oakland

Originally the site of ranches, farms, a grove of redwood trees, and, of course, clusters of oaks, Oakland has long been a warmer and more spacious alternative to San Francisco. By the end of the 19th century, Mediterranean-style homes and gardens had been developed as summer estates. With swifter transportation, Oakland became a bedroom community for San Francisco; then it progressed to California's fastest-growing industrial city. In recent decades, Oakland has struggled to redefine its identity. However, the major attractions remain: the parks and civic buildings around Lake Merritt, which was created from a tidal basin in 1898; the port area, now named Jack London Square, where the author spent much of his time at the turn of the century; and the scenic roads and parks along the crest of the Oakland-Berkeley hills. Also in the hills is the castlelike Claremont Resort Hotel, a landmark since 1915, as well as more sprawling parks with lakes and miles of hiking trails.

Arriving and Departing

By Car   Take I–80 across the Bay Bridge, then I–580 to the Grand Avenue exit for Lake Merritt. To reach downtown and the waterfront, take the I–980 exit from I–580. The trip takes 45 minutes.

By Public Transportation   Take the BART to Oakland City Center station or to Lake Merritt station for the lake and Oakland Museum. The trip takes 45 minutes one-way.

Exploring

Numbers in the margin correspond with points of interest on the Oakland map.

❶   If there is one reason to visit Oakland, it is to explore the **Oakland Museum,** an inviting series of landscaped buildings that display the state's art, history, and natural science. It is the best possible introduction to a tour of California, and its dramatic and detailed exhibits can help fill the gaps on a brief visit. The natural science department displays a typical stretch of California from the Pacific Ocean to the Nevada border, including plants and wildlife. There is a breathtaking film, *Fast Flight,* that condenses the trip into five minutes. The museum's sprawling history section includes everything from Spanish-era artifacts and a gleaming fire engine that battled the flames in San Francisco in 1906 to 1960s souvenirs of the "summer of love." The California Dream exhibit recalls a century of inspirations. The museum's art department includes mystical landscapes painted by the state's pioneers, as well as contemporary visions. There is a pleasant museum café for lunch and outdoor areas for relaxing. *1000 Oak St. at 10th St., tel. 510/834–2413. Admission free. Open Wed.–Sat. 10–5, Sun. noon–7.*

❷   Near the museum, **Lake Merritt** is a 155-acre oasis surrounded by parks and paths, with several outdoor attractions on the
❸   north side. The **Natural Science Center and Waterfowl Refuge** attracts birds by the hundreds during winter months. *At the foot of Perkins St., tel. 510/273–3739. Ope Mon. noon–5, Tues.–Sun. 10–5.*

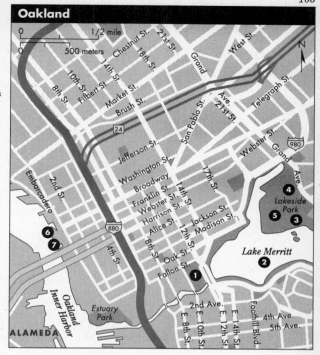

4 **Children's Fairyland** is a low-key amusement park with a puppet theater, small merry-go-round, and settings based on nursery rhymes. *Grand Ave. at Park View Terr., tel. 510/832–3609.
Open daily in summer, 10–4:30. Closed weekdays in winter.*

5 The **Lakeside Park Garden Center** includes a Japanese garden
and many native flowers and plants. *666 Bellevue Ave., tel. 510/
273–3208. Open daily 10–3 or later in summer. Closed Thanksgiving, Christmas, New Year's Day.*

Jack London, although born in San Francisco, spent his early
years in Oakland before shipping out for adventures that inspired *The Call of the Wild, The Sea Wolf, Martin Eden,* and
The Cruise of the Snark. He is commemorated with a bronze

6 bust in **Jack London Square** at the foot of Broadway. A livelier

7 landmark is **Heinhold's First and Last Chance Saloon,** one of his
hangouts. Next door is the reassembled Klondike cabin in
which he spent a winter. The square is mainly for drinking and
dining. Next door, Jack London Village has specialty shops and
restaurants. The best local collection of the author's letters,
manuscripts, and photographs is in the Jack London Room at
the Oakland Main Library (125 14th St., tel. 510/273–3134).

Oakland's downtown has been undergoing redevelopment for
many years. More stable and pleasant areas for shopping and
browsing, with a selection of cafés, can be found on Lake Shore
Avenue northeast of Lake Merritt, Piedmont Avenue near the
Broadway exit from I–580, and College Avenue west of Broadway in North Oakland. College Avenue is lined with antiques
stores, boutiques, and cafés. The neighborhood surrounds
BART's Rockridge station. Transferring there to the local No.

51 bus will take visitors to the University of California campus, about 1½ miles away in Berkeley.

Time Out
A drive through the Oakland Hills is spectacular, with open-space parks and bay views, and a stop on the way at the **Claremont Hotel** (Ashby and Domingo Aves., tel. 510/843–3000) offers fine views, a spot in which to relax, and good food. Drive north on Claremont Avenue to Ashby Avenue and on up the hill to the hotel. From a distance, this sprawling white building with towers and gables looks like a castle. Surrounded by 22 acres of lush grounds tucked into the south Berkeley hills, the Claremont is on the Oakland-Berkeley border, and for years both cities have claimed it. When a new entrance was built on a different side of the building, the address changed from Berkeley to Oakland. The 1915 hotel has been restored and refurbished and turned into a resort spa facility. The dining room is large and elegant, with pressed linen, large contemporary paintings, and views across the bay to San Francisco and the peninsula and north to Mt. Tamalpais. Meals, which fall into the Moderate–Expensive category, feature California cuisine, with seasonal fresh seafood for Sunday brunch and creative sandwiches for lunch.

The East Bay Regional Park District (tel. 510/531–9300) offers 46 parks in an area covering 60,000 acres to residents and visitors. In the Oakland hills is **Redwood Regional Park,** accessible from Joaquin Miller Road off Highway 13, to which Ashby Avenue will lead you. In the Berkeley hills is the 2,000-acre **Tilden Park,** which includes a lake and children's playground and is accessible from Grizzly Peak Boulevard off Claremont Avenue. There are scenic views of the Bay Area from roads that link the hilltop parks: Redwood Road, Skyline Boulevard, and Grizzly Peak Boulevard. Parks are open daily during daylight hours.

Dining

Oakland's ethnic diversity is reflected in its restaurants and cafés. There is a thriving Chinatown a few blocks northwest of the Oakland Museum, a number of seafood restaurants at Jack London Square, and a variety of international fare on Piedmont and College Avenues.

Restaurants are listed according to price category.

Category	Cost*
Very Expensive	over $30
Expensive	$20–$30
Moderate	$10–$20
Inexpensive	under $10

per person, excluding drinks, service, and 6.5% sales tax

The following credit card abbreviations are used: AE, American Express; DC, Diners Club; MC, MasterCard; V, Visa.

Moderate–
Expensive
The Bay Wolf. French inspiration and fresh, regional specialties mark one of the city's best restaurants, in a converted home. *3853 Piedmont Ave., tel. 510/655–6004. Reservations advised. No lunch weekends. MC, V.*

Moderate **Pacific Coast Brewing Co.** This pub/restaurant/brewery serves a fine selection of sandwiches and salads. *906 Washington St., tel. 510/836–2739. MC, V.*

Inexpensive **Ratto's.** Salads, sandwiches, soups, and pasta are served in a big, cheerful room adjacent to one of the Bay Area's best international grocery stores, in the Old Oakland Victorian Row restoration. *821 Washington St., tel. 510/832–6503. Lunch weekdays; take-out orders prepared in the deli, Mon.–Sat. No credit cards.*

Excursion to Marine World Africa USA

This wildlife theme park is one of northern California's most popular attractions. It has been a phenomenal success since moving in 1986 from a crowded site south of San Francisco to Vallejo, about an hour's drive northeast. The 160-acre park features animals of the land, sea, and air performing in shows, roaming in natural habitats, and accompanying their trainers to stroll among park visitors. Among the "stars" are killer whales, dolphins, a dozen Bengal tigers, elephants, sea lions, chimpanzees, and a troupe of human water-skiers. There are cockatoos, macaws, flamingos, cranes, and ostriches. There is a whale and dolphin show, a sea lion show, a tiger and lion show, and an elephant and chimpanzee show.

The park is owned by the Marine World Foundation, a nonprofit organization devoted to educating the public about the world's wildlife. The shows and close-up looks at exotic animals serve that purpose without neglecting entertainment. The park is a family attraction, so it's not just for youngsters. For additional sightseeing, visitors can reach the park on a high-speed ferry from San Francisco, a trip that offers unusual vistas through San Francisco Bay and San Pablo Bay. *Marine World Pkwy., Vallejo, tel. 707/643–6722. Admission: $15–$20; tickets at Ticketron outlets. Open daily 9:30–5 or later in summer; Wed.–Sun. rest of year and some school holidays.*

Arriving and Departing

By Car Take I–80 east to Marine World Parkway in Vallejo. The trip takes one hour one-way.

By Bus **Greyhound Lines** (tel. 415/558–6789) from 1st and Mission streets, San Francisco, to Vallejo, or the **BART** train (415/781–BART) to El Cerrito Del Norte Station; transfer to **Vallejo Transit** line (tel. 707/643–7663) to the park.

By Ferry **Red and White Fleet's** (tel. 415/546–2896) high-speed ferry departs mornings each day that the park is open from Pier 41 at Fisherman's Wharf. It arrives in Vallejo an hour later. Round-trip service allows five hours to visit the park. Excursion tickets are $20–$38 and include park admission.

7 The Gold Country

by Vicky Elliott

Before the Gold Rush, California looked toward the coast: The Spanish, despite their hunger for precious metal, had neglected the Sierras. When gold was discovered at Coloma in 1848, everybody headed for the hills, starting the greatest mass migration since the Crusades. It lured people from everywhere in the world, and when it was all over, California was a different place.

Today, the Gold Country lies waiting to be discovered again, once more off the beaten track and ripe with hidden treasure. You can still join a prospecting expedition and try your hand at panning for the flakes deposited by millennia of trickling streams, but the chief reward here is the chance to walk back a little into the past.

At one point in the 1850s, Nevada City was as big a place as Sacramento and San Francisco. Today, it stands out for its sophistication among its neighbors, but, like almost all the towns along Highway 49, which winds the 200-mile length of the historic mining area, its population is in the five-digit range. Time has washed over the Mother Lode; economic opportunities are limited, and consequently there is a homey, unspoiled feel to it that attracts those who are content to live modestly amidst the natural beauty of these rolling hills.

Travelers can experience that lifestyle at bed-and-breakfast inns, many in exquisite Victorian buildings that have been taken down to the studs and lovingly restored. Their sumptuous breakfasts and period atmosphere offer a comfortable and romantic base from which to explore the tumbledown villages and historic sites that speak of the 19th century.

In the frenzy of the Gold Rush, as tents and flimsy wooden buildings sprang up around promising "diggings," comfort was in short supply. During the early years, this was a man's world. After the hard journey around the Horn by ship, or the wearying trek across the continent, everyday life in the claims, under blazing sun or in freezing streams, was tough.

The saloon keepers and canny merchants realized where the real gold was to be made. Nothing came cheap. This was a market where potatoes and onions could command $1 apiece. Entrepreneurs like the storekeeper Samuel Brannan became millionaires.

The labor of panning made way for the crude wooden stamp mill and the arrastre, which were used to break up the gold-bearing rock, as well as for a host of mining techniques imported from all over the world. Hydraulic mining washed whole hillsides away, and as the industry matured, the exploitation of quartz-bearing hard-rock lodes demanded organization and capital that superseded the rough-and-tumble self-government of the first arrivals.

The story of this extraordinary episode in American history, vividly described by Mark Twain and Bret Harte, comes alive in mining towns in various stages of decay, as well as in careful reconstructions including Columbia State Historic Park. The Gold Country may be a backwater, but it repays leisurely exploration.

Getting Around

By Plane Sacramento Metropolitan Airport is the major airport closest to the Gold Country (it's an hour's drive from Placerville, and a little closer to Auburn). San Francisco International Airport is about two hours from Sacramento. Car rentals are available at both airports.

By Bus **Greyhound-Trailways** serves Sacramento, Auburn, Grass Valley, and Placerville from San Francisco. The **Sacramento Transit Authority** buses service points of major interest in downtown Sacramento.

By Car This is the most convenient way to see the Gold Country, since most of its towns are too small to provide a base for public transportation. I–80 intersects with Highway 49 at Auburn; U.S. 50 intersects with Highway 49 at Placerville.

Guided Tours

Gold Prospecting Expeditions (18170 Main St., Box 974, Jamestown 95327, tel. 209/984–4653). Specialists in the field, this outfit offers one-hour gold-panning excursions, two-week prospecting trips, and a good deal in between.

Outdoor Adventure River Specialists (O.A.R.S.) (Box 67, Angels Camp 95222, tel. 209/736–4677). A wide range of white-water rafting trips on the Stanislas, American, Merced, and Tuolumne rivers are offered from late March through early October.

Capital City Cruises (1401 Garden Hwy., Suite 125, Sacramento 95833, tel. 916/921–1111) runs two-hour narrated cruises, as well as brunch, dinner-dance, and mystery cruises on the Sacramento River year round on the *River City Queen* and the *Elizabeth Louise*.

Spirit of Sacramento (Channel Star Excursions, 1207 Front St., No. 18, Sacramento 95814, tel. 916/522–2933 or 800/433–0263). This paddlewheel riverboat offers a variety of excursions, including a happy hour, dinner and luncheon cruises, and a champagne brunch.

Important Addresses and Numbers

Tourist Information **Amador County Chamber of Commerce** (30 S. Hwy. 49–88, Box 596, Jackson 95642, tel. 209/223–0350).

Auburn Area Visitors and Convention Bureau (601 Lincoln Way, Auburn 95603, tel. 916/885–5616 or 800/427–6463 in CA).

Columbia State Historic Park (Box 151, Columbia 95310, tel. 209/532–4301 or 209/532–0150).

El Dorado County Chamber of Commerce (542 Main St., Placerville 95667, tel. 916/621–5885).

Golden Chain Council of the Mother Lode (Box 7046, Auburn 95604).

Nevada City Chamber of Commerce (132 Main St., Nevada City 95959, tel. 916/265–2692).

Nevada County Chamber of Commerce (248 Mill St., Grass Valley 95945, tel. 916/273–4667 or 800/752–6222 in CA). The Nevada County Chamber is housed in a reproduction of the home owned on this site by the notorious dancer Lola Montez when she moved to Grass Valley in the early 1850s; her bathtub is still there.)

Sacramento Convention and Visitors Bureau (1421 K St., Sacramento 95814, tel. 916/449–6711).

Old Sacramento Visitor Information Center (1104 Front St., Old Sacramento, tel. 916/442–7644).

Tuolumne County Visitors Bureau (Box 4020, 55 W. Stockton St., Sonora 95370, tel. 209/533–4420 or 800/446–1333 in CA).

Emergencies   Dial 911 for emergencies throughout the Gold Country to reach police, fire, and medical personnel.

There are several hospitals with 24-hour emergency room service in Sacramento: **Mercy Hospital of Sacramento Promptcare** (4001 J St., tel. 916/453–4424), **Sutter General Hospital** (2801 L St., tel. 916/733–3003), and **Sutter Memorial Hospital** (52nd and F Sts., tel. 916/733–1000).

Exploring

From San Francisco, I–80 runs toward the Gold Country via Sacramento; at Auburn, it intersects with Highway 49, which links many of the old Gold Rush communities. Alternatively, you can pick up U.S. 50 at Sacramento; it intersects Highway 49 at Placerville.

Today, unlike Gold Rush times, it's possible to travel the length of Highway 49 in a single day. The winding road is almost entirely two-lane, but it is excellent; there is no roughness or hardship now. It would be a spectacular outing, but on such a tight timetable, you'd miss the fun of wandering through ghost towns and exquisitely restored villages, stopping by the roadside to read historical markers, poking through antiques shops and craft stores, and visiting the foothill vineyards to sample the wines. This is an area where it pays to slow down and take your time.

Highway 49

Numbers in the margin correspond with points of interest on the Gold Country map.

1 A two-hour drive from Sacramento to the northern end of Highway 49 is **Downieville,** one of the prettiest of the Gold Rush towns. Stone, brick, and frame buildings seem to cling to the mountainsides, or hug the banks of the fast-moving Yuba River. Along the quiet streets, lovely old houses have been well-maintained or restored. The spare and elegant Methodist church, which dates from 1865, is the oldest Protestant church in continuous use in the state. Drive out Main Street past the last bridge and take a short walk past the PG&E Station to the crystal-clear Yuba River. The river forms pools as it rushes over boulders, and it's a favorite swimming spot. *An information booth in the center of town is open from May to Sept.*

2 Wind back down Highway 49 50 miles to **Nevada City,** a Gold Rush town reminiscent of New England with its white houses and picket fences. The **Nevada Theatre** on Broad Street, built in 1865, is California's oldest theater in continuous use, and when

The Gold Country

Lake Oroville

Downieville **1**

49

Tahoe National Forest

N

20

80

2 Nevada City

20

3 Grass Valley

49

65

Auburn **4**

Pilot Hill

49

Coloma

5 ▪ Marshall Gold Discovery State Park

Folsom Lake

Eldorado National Forest

50

TO LAKE TAHOE

Placerville **6**

40 99

Folsom

50

Eldorado

80

Sacramento

Plymouth 49

16

50 99

99

Dry Town

Amador City

Sutter Creek **7**

Jackson **8**

88

9 Mokelumne Hill

San Andreas

5

Murphys **11**

0   10 miles

0   15 km

Angels Camp **10**

Columbia State Historic Park **12**

49

Stockton

4

Sonora **13**

Jamestown **14**

not playing host to dramatic productions—a thriving business hereabouts—is used as a community center for the town.

Behind the theater, the **Miners Foundry,** also built in 1865, a cavernous building that now serves as a cultural center offering plays, concerts, and a wide range of events that include a Victorian Christmas fair, St. Patrick's Day, and the Spirit of John Muir celebrations, and period parties. *325 Spring St., tel. 916/ 265–5040. Open daily 10–5.*

Shopping is a draw in Nevada City. You'll find an enticing selection of antiques, brass, crystal, books, and toys. The town also has a number of good restaurants, not always the case in Gold Country communities.

Time Out **Sierra Mountain Coffee Roasters** is a cozy and appealing refreshment stop. Excellent coffee, coffee drinks, and homemade pastries are served until late afternoon. It's an informal place—there's a pile of daily papers to read in a booth or outdoors on the quiet patio. *316 Commercial St., corner of York, tel. 916/265–5282. Open until 11 PM Fri. and Sat.*

❸ South along Highway 49, **Grass Valley** is worth a full day's browsing. More than half of California's total gold production was extracted from the mines of Nevada County, and some of the area's most interesting exhibits on gold mining are to be found here.

The **Empire Mine,** which was worked from 1850 right up to 1956, was one of California's richest quartz mines, and an estimated 5.8 million ounces of gold were brought up from its 367 miles of underground passages. The mine is now a State Historic Park, and its buildings and grounds are open year round. Tours allow you to peer into the deep recesses of the mine, and to view the owner's "cottage," with its exquisite woodwork. The visitors' center has films and exhibits on mining, and you can picnic. *10791 E. Empire St. (Empire St. exit south from Hwy. 49), tel. 916/273–8522. Admission: $2 adults, $1 children 6–17. Open daily in winter, 10–5; daily in summer 9–6. Tours and lectures: winter, weekends at 1 and 2; summer, on the hour from 11–4.*

The **North Star Power House and Pelton Wheel Exhibit** boasts a 32-foot-high Pelton wheel, the largest ever built. It was used to power mining operations, and is a forerunner of the modern water turbines that generate hydroelectricity. Period mining equipment and a stamp mill are also on display, as well as one of the few operable Cornish pumps in the country, part of the legacy of the tin miners who migrated here from Cornwall in England. There are hands-on displays for children and a picnic area. *Allison Ranch Rd. and Mill St. (Empire St. exit north from Hwy. 49), tel. 916/273–4255. Donation requested. Open May–Oct. 10–5.*

Time Out A more palpable reminder of the mining past can be had at **Marshall's Pasties,** which still purveys handmade beef and potato pies like those taken down into the shafts in lunch buckets by the Cornish miners who came to work in the hard-rock mines. The apple pasties are good, too. *203B Mill St., tel. 916/272– 2844. Open Mon.–Sat. 9:30–6.*

❹ **Auburn,** at the intersection of Highway 49 and I–80 (after 49 crosses under I–80, turn right on Lincoln and follow the signs), is a small old town with narrow climbing streets, cobblestones, wooden sidewalks, and many original buildings. The **Bernhard Museum,** built in 1851 as the Traveler's Hotel, now offers a glimpse of family life in the late Victorian era. *291 Auburn-Folsom Rd., tel. 916/889–4156. Admission: $1 adults, 50¢ for children 6–16 and senior citizens over 65. Open Tues.–Fri. 11–3, weekends noon–4.*

❺ Twenty-five miles farther on is **Coloma,** where gold fever originally broke out. John Sutter erected a sawmill here on the banks of the American River, and it was in the millrace that one of his employees, James Marshall, discovered gold in January 1848. "My eye was caught with the glimpse of something shining in the bottom of the ditch," he recalled later. Unfortunately, the wagon-builder himself never found any more "color," as it came to be called.

Most of Coloma lies within **Marshall Gold Discovery State Historic Park.** Within six months of Marshall's discovery, 2,000 prospectors arrived, and Coloma became the first Gold Rush town. Its population swelled rapidly to 10,000, but as supplies of the precious metal were exhausted, the miners evaporated as quickly as they had come. A replica of Sutter's mill, based on Marshall's drawings, now stands here, with Marshall's cabin and museum; there are areas to picnic and fish. *Tel. 916/622–3470. Day use: $5 per car. Park open daily 8 AM to sunset. Museum open daily 10–5 in summer; 10:30–4:30 Labor Day–Memorial Day. Closed Dec. 25, Jan. 1, and Thanksgiving.*

❻ Follow Highway 49 south 10 miles into **Placerville,** which has shed its former name of Hangtown, a graphic allusion to the summary nature of frontier justice. Placerville today has the distinction of being one of the only cities in the world to own a gold mine. The **Gold Bug Mine** has two fully lighted shafts, one of which dead-ends at a gold-flecked vein, while the other follows an uphill trail. A shaded stream runs through the park, and there are picnic facilities. *Bedford exit north from Hwy. 49 to Gold Bug Park, tel. 916/622–0832. Admission free, 50¢ for self-guided tour of mine. Park open daily 8 AM–sunset; mine open April–Oct. and March 16–April 29, Oct. 5–Nov. 10, on weekends only.*

Placerville is the largest town on Highway 49. Driving south through rolling countryside, you'll pass villages that amount to little more than a few antiques stores and perhaps a café, with crumbling brick buildings and the ubiquitous historical markers: Plymouth, Drytown, Amador City.

❼ **Sutter Creek** is another matter, well-kept and totally unspoiled, its white homes carefully restored, with green shutters and picket fences. The stores clustered along Highway 49 are worth a closer look, and the wooden sidewalks evoke the feeling of the muddy roads of the 19th century.

A detour here along Shake Ridge Road to **Volcano** will take you past Daffodil Hill, which, from March to mid-April, comes alive with color. Dutch colonists planted the bulbs here, and the daffodils have propagated themselves riotously since. The village of Volcano, once a town of 5,000 people, with 17 hotels and 35 saloons, is a faithful reflection of a vanished age: Nothing has been tampered with, and its general store and theater are still in use, as they have been for 140 years or more.

Driving south from Sutter Creek, Highway 49 climbs sharply, twists and turns, and then rewards you with a wonderful view **8** over the mining town of **Jackson.** An old white church sits on a knoll, its small cemetery spread out around it, and from this vantage point, the brick buildings below cluster tightly. Seen up close, however, the town is a motley assortment of modern businesses and buildings in various states of repair; it has the dubious distinction of closing its bordellos only as recently as 1956.

9 Seven miles south along Highway 49 is the town of **Mokelumne Hill,** Moke Hill for short. Unlike busy Jackson, the county seat, this little village is frozen in an earlier time. Many of the buildings are constructed in light-brown rhyolite tuff, a stone common in much of the Gold Country. Where there are sidewalks, they are wooden, like the small, frail-looking houses on the hilly side streets.

10 Another 20 miles along the highway is **Angels Camp,** famed chiefly for its jumping-frog contest in May, based on Mark Twain's "The Jumping Frog of Calaveras County," one of his first stories to attract public notice. Twain was not impressed by the hospitality he experienced during his stay here in 1865; he described the coffee as "day-before-yesterday dishwater." At the north end of town is a museum with an interesting collection of minerals and early artifacts. *Tel. 209/736–2963. Open daily 10–3 March–Labor Day.*

East on Highway 4, and less than 10 miles up the road, is **11** **Murphys,** with its white picket fences and Victorian houses. In **Murphys Hotel,** opened in 1856 as the Sperry & Perry and still operating, is a guest register recording the visits of Horatio Alger and Ulysses S. Grant, who joined the 19th-century swarms who came to visit the giant sequoias in **Calaveras Big Trees State Park,** about 15 miles farther east on Highway 4. *Tel. 209/ 795–2334. Day use: $5 per car. Open daily.*

Another spectacle of nature 4 miles out of Murphys, on the Vallecito-Columbia highway, is **Moaning Cavern,** a vast underground chamber with ancient crystalline rock formations. *Tel. 209/736–2708. Admission: $5.75 adults, $2.75 children. Open 9–6 in summer, 10–5 in winter.*

Back on Highway 49 driving south, there is a breathtaking ride across the bridge over the Melones Reservoir and an indication of the rugged terrain in a part of California where the rivers have dug deep canyons. Horse-drawn wagons must have found it rough going.

12 A well-marked turnoff leads to **Columbia State Historic Park,** a pleasingly executed mix of preservation and restoration. The "Gem of the Southern Mines" comes as close to a Gold Rush town in its heyday as you can get, although there are as many ice-cream parlors than saloons today. You can still ride a stagecoach and pan for gold; street musicians give lively performances on the banjo, the fiddle, and the stump; and there is a blacksmith working at his anvil. Elegant lodging can be found at the City Hotel or Fallon House, both dating from the 1850s, and the Fallon Theater presents plays year-round. Columbia's candy store makes its own old-fashioned confectionery: licorice sticks, horehound drops, and fudge. *Exhibits and demonstrations daily 10–6. Museum open 8–5; tel. 209/532–4301.*

⑬ Highway 49 is the main street in **Sonora.** Don't miss the beautiful **St. James Episcopal Church,** built in 1860, the second-oldest frame church in California. In winter, the ski traffic passes through Sonora on the way along Highway 108 to Lake Tahoe 30 miles east.

The road turns west for a few miles out of Sonora, and heads to
⑭ **Jamestown** whose **Railtown 1897 State Historic Park** includes 26 acres of trains, a station, a roundhouse, and facilities for maintaining trains. There are slide presentations, guided tours, and train excursions on the weekends. The park is open daily from spring through fall. *Tel. 209/984–3953. Admission: $2 adults, $1.25 children; train excursions: $2.50 adults, $1.50 children; train excursions $9 adults, $4.50 children.*

Sacramento

Numbers in the margin correspond with points of interest on the Sacramento map.

A major gateway to the Gold Country, Sacramento has its own slice of Gold Rush history, as the point from which gold prospectors fanned out to seek their fortunes. Sacramento predates the Gold Rush, but came into its own as a center for financial transactions and the shipping of provisions to the prospecting fields, ultimately becoming the western terminus of the Pony Express, the transcontinental railroad, and the telegraph. One of the largest restoration projects in the United States has spruced up the old city, an airy island marooned on its plot to one side of the state capital's extravagant high rises. Today, its cobbled streets are paced by horse-drawn carts laden with visitors, and covered walkways frame magnificent commercial premises whose tall windows and high ceilings offer a revealing glimpse into 19th-century shopping.

❶ The **visitor's center** (1104 Front St., tel. 916/442–7644) is housed in a former depot for passengers and freight bound down the river to San Francisco by steamship. *Open daily 9–5.*

❷ The **Eagle Theater** (925 Front St.) was California's first, built in 1849. A reconstruction done in 1976 is in regular use now. The
❸ **Sacramento History Center** was once the nerve center of the town: mayor's offices, council chambers, jail, and policemen's quarters, among other things. It now offers a streamlined, well-presented introduction to the history of Sacramento and its surroundings, complete with gold pans that you can sift yourself, a thatched Indian hut, memorabilia from the world wars, and a colorful stack of turn-of-the-century cans of local produce. *101 I St., tel. 916/449–2057. Admission: $2.50 adults, $1 children 6–17. Open Tues.–Sun. 10–4:30. Closed Dec. 25, Jan. 1, and Thanksgiving.*

❹ Old Sacramento's biggest draw is the **California State Railroad Museum,** 100,000 square feet exhibiting 21 restored locomotives and railroad cars in perfect working order, including the Governor Stanford, the Central Pacific locomotive that steamed from Sacramento to Promontory Point to mark the completion of the transcontinental railroad. You can walk through a post-office car and peer into the cubbyholes and canvas bags of mail, or go through a sleeping car that simulates the

Sacramento

Almond Plaza, **12**

B.F. Hastings
Building, **6**

California State
Archives, **10**

California State
Railroad Museum, **4**

Crocker Art
Museum, **7**

Eagle Theater, **2**

Governor's
Mansion, **11**

Huntington, Hawkins
& Co. Store, **5**

Sacramento History
Center, **3**

State Capitol, **9**

Sutter's Fort, **13**

Towe Ford
Museum, **8**

Visitor's Center, **1**

swaying on the roadbed and the flashing lights of a passing town at night. On weekends from May through Labor Day, a steam-powered excursion train runs several miles down the river to Miller Park every hour on the hour from 10 to 5 from the depot on Front Street. *125 I St., at 2nd and I Sts., tel. 916/448–4466. Admission: $5 adults, $2 children 6–17. Open daily 10–5. Closed Dec. 25, Jan. 1, and Thanksgiving.*

⑤ The **Huntington, Hawkins & Co. Store** hardware exhibit at 111 I
⑥ Street is open daily 11–5. The **B.F. Hastings Building** (2nd and J sts.) includes the first Sacramento chambers of the California State Supreme Court, built in 1854.

⑦ The **Crocker Art Museum,** a few blocks from old Sacramento, is the oldest art museum in the West, with a collection of European, Asian, and California art, including "Sunday Morning in the Mines," a large canvas depicting the mining industry of the 1850s. The museum's lobby and magnificent ballroom retain the original 1870s woodwork, plaster moldings, and imported tiles. *216 O St., tel. 916/449–5423. Admission: $2.50 adults, and $1 children 7–17. Open Thurs. 10–9, Wed.–Sun. 10–5. Closed Dec. 25, Jan. 1, Thanksgiving, and July 4.*

⑧ A recent attraction is the **Towe Ford Museum,** a collection of more than 150 vintage cars, embracing every year and model manufactured by the Ford company for 50 years, starting in 1903. *2200 Front St., tel. 916/442–6802. Admission: $5 adults, $4.50 senior citizens, $2.50 young adults 14–18; $1 children 5–13. Open daily 10–6. Closed Dec. 25, Jan. 1, and Thanksgiving.*

⑨ The **state capitol** was built in 1869 and was extensively restored recently. The lacy plasterwork of the rotunda, 120 feet high, has the complexity and color of a Fabergé Easter egg. There are free guided tours daily every hour from 9 to 4, and there are also tours of the well-kept grounds, 2 blocks wide and 5 blocks long, whose plants and shrubs from all over the world are clearly identified. *Capitol Ave. and 10th St., tel. 916/324–0333. Admission free. Open daily 9–4 spring and summer; weekdays 9–5, 10–5 fall and winter. Closed Dec. 25, Jan. 1, and Thanksgiving.*

⑩ The **California State Archives** has a wealth of documents on the history of the state, including the oldest collection of Western newspapers, and a catalog of all those eligible to vote at the turn of the century. *1020 O St., tel. 916/445–4293. Open weekdays 8–5. Closed major holidays.*

⑪ The historic **Governor's Mansion** was originally the palatial residence of Albert Gallatin, one of the partners in the Central Pacific Railroad, and subsequently home to 13 California governors—until Ronald Reagan turned it down in 1967. *16th and H Sts., tel. 916/323–3047. Admission: $2 adults, $1 children 6–17. Tours on the hour 10–4.*

Well worth visiting also is the Blue Diamond cooperative's
⑫ **Almond Plaza,** the world's largest almond-processing factory, with tours that fill you in on the myriad uses of the almond—as butter, powder, paste and oil. The variety of almond delicacies on sale in the gift shop is amazing. *1701 C St., tel. 916/446–8409 or 800/225–NUTS. Open weekdays 9–5:30, gift shop also Sat. 10–4. Tours by appointment at 10 AM and 1 PM.*

⑬ **Sutter's Fort** is the settlement from which Sacramento grew, founded in 1839 by the Swiss immigrant John Augustus Sutter. Its thick walls now surround an adobe house and workshops for gunsmiths, blacksmiths, and candlemakers. Behind the fort is a museum displaying local Indian artifacts. *27th and L Sts., tel. 916/445-4422. Admission: $2 adults, $1 children 6-17. Open daily 10-4. Closed Dec. 25, Jan. 1, and Thanksgiving.*

Dining

Given the small population of the Gold Country (only two towns, Auburn and Placerville, approach a population of 10,000), there are a disproportionately large number of good restaurants. Many of the menus are ambitious: In addition to standard American, Italian, and Mexican fare, there is Continental, French, and California cuisine, with an emphasis on innovation and the freshest ingredients. The national fast-food chains are few and far between—the population isn't large enough to support them. It's not difficult, though, to find the makings for a good picnic in most Gold Country towns.

Sacramento is enjoying a period of prosperity and expansion, and it offers a wide range of eating places for its growing population; restaurants listed are all located in Old Sacramento or downtown. Unless otherwise noted, dress is informal.

Highly recommended restaurants are indicated by a star ★ .

Category	Cost*
Very Expensive	over $30
Expensive	$20–$30
Moderate	$10–$20
Inexpensive	under $10

per person, not including tax, service, or drinks

Auburn
Moderate
Butterworth's. Housed in a handsome Victorian mansion on a hillside overlooking Old Auburn, this restaurant features American regional cuisine with copious servings and a Sunday brunch. *1522 Lincoln Way, tel. 916/885-0249. Reservations accepted. Jacket and tie advised. AE, MC, V. Closed Mon., Tues., and Sat. lunch.*

★ **Headquarter House.** This restaurant is set on a hilltop within the Dunipace Angus Ranch, with a lounge on the top floor overlooking pine trees. Part of the view includes a nine-hole golf course, open to the public and inexpensive. The varied menu emphasizes California cuisine, with a good choice of fresh seafood. *14500 Musso Rd., tel. 916/878-1906. Reservations advised. AE, DC, MC, V.*

Moderate
Auburn Joe's. This is an informal but nicely appointed restaurant with a pleasant atmosphere, offering an American menu for lunch, dinner, and breakfast on Fridays and weekends. Beef, lamb, and seafood are emphasized, with some Italian specialties. *13480 Lincoln Way, tel. 916/885-3090. Reservations advised. AE, D, DC, MC, V.*

Cafe Delicias. Located in a picturesque building in Old Auburn, this Mexican restaurant has an extensive menu, and the helpings are generous. One dinner choice is *carne asada a la*

Tampiquena—steak grilled with spices, onions, and bell peppers, served with a cheese enchilada, rice, and beans. *1591 Lincoln Way, tel. 916/885–2050. Reservations advised. MC, V.*

Coloma **Vineyard House.** In this Victorian country inn, dating from
Expensive 1878, the small dining rooms have fireplaces or wood-burning stoves, flower-painted chandeliers, and early California memorabilia. The menu is American, with chicken, beef, seafood, and pasta. Chicken and dumplings are a house specialty. Sunday brunch is served. *Cold Springs Rd., off Hwy. 49; tel. 916/ 622–2217. Reservations advised. AE, MC, V. Closed Mon. No lunch.*

Columbia **City Hotel.** This authentically restored 1850s hotel and dining
Expensive room serves regional American cuisine, using fresh local produce stylishly prepared and served with flair. The California wine list is comprehensive and brunch is offered on weekends. An adjoining bar, also restored, is called the What Cheer Saloon, after the liquor store of that name that once operated here. *Main St. (in Columbia State Park), tel. 209/532–1479. Reservations advised. Closed Mon., and in winter, open for lunch weekends, and dinner Thurs.–Sun. AE, MC, V.*

Cool **The Nugget.** In this unassuming setting, not far from Auburn,
Inexpensive Jens Hoppe, who was born in Germany, draws on the cooking he learned at home, producing some delectable goulash and tender Wiener schnitzels. *Hwy. 49, tel. 916/823–1294. Reservations advised. No credit cards. Closed Mon. dinner.*

Downieville **Cirino's at the Forks.** This small, cheerful restaurant on the
Inexpensive– Downie River provides outdoor service on a flagstone patio at
Moderate the water's edge in summer. The menu features mainly Italian cuisine, with beef, chicken, homemade soup, salads, sandwiches, and 12 varieties of tea. There is a short, very reasonably priced California wine list. *Main St., tel. 916/289–3479 or 800/540–2099. Summer reservations advised. MC, V. Closed Mon., Tues.*

Grass Valley **Holbrook Hotel.** The recently opened restaurant in an 1851 ho-
Moderate– tel is Victorian in decor, with a saloon and some of the original
Expensive brick walls, archways, and beams. The cuisine is French-inspired and the chef's creations include salmon with light mussel sauce, blackened sea scallops nantua, and an award-winning chocolate hazelnut cake with crème anglaise. There is also an elegant Sunday brunch. *212 W. Main St., tel. 916/273– 1353 or 800/933–7077. Reservations recommended. AE, MC, V. Closed Sat. lunch, Sun. dinner.*

Jackson **Teresa's.** This long-established Italian restaurant has a local cli-
Moderate entele. The menu features daily specials, and includes homemade ravioli, fresh minestrone daily, and a fine selection of veal, scampi, and other Italian classics. *1235 Jackson Gate Rd., tel. 209/223–1786. Reservations advised. MC, V. Closed Wed.– Thurs; closed lunch Sun., dinner from 2 PM.*

Moderate **The Balcony.** This popular, unpretentious restaurant offers Continental cuisine with daily specials such as chicken marsala and veal piccata. The lunch menu includes quiches and crepes. Senior citizens receive discounts. *164 Main St., tel. 209/223– 2855. Reservations advised. AE, MC, V. Closed Tues., and dinner Mon.*

Jamestown
Moderate–
Expensive

Jamestown Hotel. Old oak sideboards, cut-glass lamps, and rocking chairs in the lobby set the tone in this restored Gold Rush hotel. The accent is on fresh seasonal produce with a country flair, including ragouts, cassoulets, and seafood dishes at dinner; salads, sandwiches, and omelets are offered at lunch. Service is in the dining room or the garden patio. Sunday brunch is served. *18153 Main St., tel. 209/984–3902. Reservations advised. AE, MC, V.*

Nevada City
Moderate–
Expensive

Country Rose Cafe. The exterior of this old brick and stone building, complete with the original iron shutters from Gold Rush days, blends well with the antiques in this French country restaurant. A lengthy menu features seafood, beef, lamb, chicken, and ratatouille. In the summer, there is outdoor service on a leafy patio. *300 Commercial St., tel. 916/265–6248. Reservations advised. AE, MC, V. Closed Sun. lunch.*

Peter Selaya's California Restaurant. Stained glass, lace curtains, antique sideboards, and old-fashioned high-back oak dining chairs set the mood in this long-established dinner house. The menu features California cuisine, with Italian and French detours and an emphasis on seafood. Desserts are a specialty. *320 Broad St., tel. 916/265–5697. Reservations advised. AE, MC, V. Closed Mon.*

Moderate

Cirino's. Fine American-Italian food in an informal, bar and grill atmosphere is offered in the popular restaurant, housed in a 19th-century building with a handsome period Brunswick back bar. The menu features seafood, pasta, and veal. *309 Broad St., tel: 916/265–2246 or 800/287–0203. Reservations advised. AE, MC, V.*

National Hotel. This is the oldest continuously operating hotel west of the Rockies (and perhaps the Mississippi), founded in 1856. The menu has a down-home Victorian feel to it, featuring prime rib, steaks, and other hearty offerings. *211 Broad St., tel. 916/265–4551. Reservations advised. AE, MC, V.*

Posh Nosh. They bake their own bread every day at this restaurant, which offers deli fare and California cuisine. Everything on the lunch menu is available for takeout: sandwiches, salads, and bagel baskets. There's a good wine list, as well as 20 varieties of imported beer, and a dozen domestic brands. Dinner features fresh seafood, including lobster, and there are vegetarian selections. You can dine on the garden patio in nice weather. *318 Broad St., tel. 916/265–6064. Reservations advised for dinner. AE, MC, V.*

Inexpensive

Trolley Junction Cafe. The expansive windows of this sparkling new restaurant take advantage of the setting beside a creek, waterfall, and waterwheel. The menu features prime rib and scampi, as well as good home food, with hearty breakfast choices and salads and sandwiches for lunch. *400 Railroad Ave., tel. 916/265–5259. Reservations advised. DC, MC, V.*

Placerville
Moderate

Smokehouse 1898. An airy two-level restaurant with garden decor offers traditional American food, including barbecued chicken, steak, and ribs, as well as Continental selections. *311 Main St., tel. 916/622–1898. Reservations advised. AE, MC, V. Closed Mon.*

Inexpensive

Apple Cafe. This light, spacious coffee shop has a superb setting, looking out over valleys and mountains. It features homemade dishes including biscuits and gravy, and soup. Breakfast is served all day. *2740 U.S. 50, tel. 916/626–8144. No reservations. No credit cards. No dinner.*

★ **Powell Bros. Steamer Co.** The decor is nautical in this seafood restaurant with old brick walls and dark wood. The menu is primarily shellfish, served in stews, pastas, chowders, cocktails, and sandwiches, and cooked in big steamers—nothing is fried. *425 Main St., tel. 916/626–1091. No reservations. MC, V.*

Sacramento **The Firehouse.** A restored firehouse, dating from 1853, this
Very Expensive luxuriously opulent restaurant offers fine cuisine, with elaborate Continental entrées. Less formal, but highly agreeable, are the outdoor lunches served in the leafy cobbled courtyard to the tinkle of fountains, weather permitting, from April through September. *1112 2nd St., tel. 916/442–4772. Reservations advised. Jacket and tie advised at dinner. AE, MC, V. Closed Sun. and major holidays.*

Moderate–Expensive **California Fat's.** The ultimate in postmodern decor, this restaurant is built on three levels with a splashy, two-story waterfall and a California Pacific menu featuring dishes from the Pacific Rim. Its banana cream pie is famous. *1015 Front St., tel. 916/441–7966. Reservations recommended. AE, MC, V. Closed Dec. 25 and Thanksgiving.*

Moderate **Fat City.** Once Sam Brannan's general merchandise store, it's now a study in art deco, incorporating the Leadville, Colorado bar behind which the unsinkable Molly Brown served before she made off on the Titanic. *1001 Front St., tel. 916/446–6768. No reservations. AE, MC, V. Closed Dec. 25, Thanksgiving.*

Los Padres. At this spacious Mexican establishment in Old Sacramento with lofty ceilings and handsome Mexican furnishings, traditional dishes from Baja California are featured. *106 J St., tel. 916/443–6376. Reservations required for groups of 10 or more. AE, D, DC, MC, V. Closed Dec. 25 and Thanksgiving.*

The Virgin Sturgeon. This restaurant is rustic and casual, and plumb on the Sacramento River; you can dine on the deck and watch the water rush by. The simple American menu offers seafood, steaks, chicken, and salads, but no desserts. *1577 Garden Hwy., tel. 916/921–2694. No reservations. MC, V. Closed Dec. 25, New Year's.*

Inexpensive **The Old Spaghetti Factory.** An old Western Pacific Railroad sta-
★ tion has been transformed into an Italian family restaurant, complete with fringed lampshades and velvet settees. Menu highlights are the pasta specialties, crusty bread, and spumoni. *1910 J. St., tel. 916/443–2862. No reservations. No credit cards. Closed for lunch weekends and Dec. 25.*

Sonora **Hemingway's Cafe Restaurant.** The menu here, starting from
Moderate Continental-Californian, is eclectic, if not downright exotic,
★ with such delicacies as Mongolian lamb chops, Cajun shrimp, gourmet pizzas, and sherry trifle: the chef does not lack for imagination. There is live music, and a dinner theater on occasion as well. The wine list features award-winning selections, and many unusual imported beers are stocked. *362 S. Stewart, tel. 209/532–4900. Reservations advised. AE, MC, V. Closed Mon. and Sun. for most of the winter.*

Sutter Creek **Pelargonium.** An old California bungalow has been reworked
Expensive into a restaurant; the walls of the small rooms are crowded with art. The California cuisine features seafood and new specials weekly, such as trout stuffed with crab, or roast lamb served

with three-cheese polenta and tomato-basil topping. *Hwy. 49 at Hanford St., tel. 209/267–5008. Reservations advised. Closed Sun. Closed lunch.*

Lodging

Among the treasures of the Gold Country today are its inns, many of them in beautifully restored buildings dating back to the 1850s and 1860s and furnished with period pieces. If you came here for the history, there's no better way to get a taste of the past. In Sacramento, the lodgings listed are all in the downtown area, close to Old Sacramento, the capitol, and Sutter's Fort. Highly recommended hotels are indicated by a star ★.

Category	Cost*
Very Expensive	over $80
Expensive	$60–$80
Moderate	$45–$60
Inexpensive	under $45

*double room, not including tax

Amador City
Moderate

Mine House Inn. On a steep hillside overlooking tiny Amador City, the headquarters of the Keystone Consolidated Mining Co., more than a century old, have been transformed into an inn furnished with original Victorian antiques. Continental breakfast is included. No pets. *Box 266, Hwy. 49, 95601, tel. 209/267–5900. 7 rooms. Facilities: pool, open from Memorial Day until the end of Sept. No credit cards.*

Angels Camp
Moderate

Gold Country Inn. This modern, air-conditioned two-story motel provides queen-size beds and a coffeemaker in each room. There is a coffee shop next door. *Box 188, 720 S. Main, Hwy. 49, 95222, tel. 209/736–4611. 40 rooms. Facilities: cable TV. AE, D, MC, V.*

Auburn
Moderate–Expensive

Auburn Inn. This beige and brown multistory inn, built in 1984, is exceptionally well-maintained. The decor is contemporary, in peach and pastel colors. There are king- and queen-size beds, suites, nonsmoking rooms, and rooms with facilities for the handicapped. *1875 Auburn Ravine Rd., 95603 (Foresthill exit north from I–80), tel. 916/885–1800 or 800/272–1444 in CA. 81 rooms. Facilities: pool, spa, laundry, cable TV. AE, DC, MC, V.*

Inexpensive–Moderate

Country Squire Inn. This three-story motel is built around a spacious central area, and has modern rooms decorated in browns and blues. Suites are available. Pets are allowed. There is a restaurant next door. *13480 Lincoln Way, 95603 (Foresthill exit south off I–80), tel. 916/885–7025. 80 rooms. Facilities: pool, spa, cable TV. AE, D, DC, MC, V.*

Coloma
Moderate–Expensive

Coloma Country Inn. A restored Victorian bed-and-breakfast that was built in 1852, this inn is set on 5 acres and offers fishing and canoeing on its own pond. The rooms have antique double beds, and private sitting areas; the decor features quilts, stenciled friezes, and fresh flowers. Country breakfasts are served. No children, pets, or smoking are allowed. Hot-air ballooning and white-water rafting can be arranged. Reservations recommended. *Box 502, 345 High St., 95613, tel. 916/622–6919. 5 rooms, 2 with shared bath. No credit cards.*

Moderate ★ **Vineyard House.** This 1878 country inn, outfitted with handsome antiques and thick carpets, is built on the site of a prizewinning winery, whose owner turned to wine-making when the Gold Rush petered out. The setting is romantic; the ruins of the wine cellars lie behind flower gardens. Continental breakfast is included. The restaurant and lounge are open every evening from May through September and closed Mondays and Tuesdays in winter. No pets. *Box 176, Cold Springs Rd., 95613 (off Hwy. 49), tel. 916/622–2217. 7 rooms with shared baths. AE, MC, V.*

Columbia Expensive **City Hotel.** The rooms in this restored 1856 hostelry are elaborately furnished with period antiques. Two balcony rooms overlook Main Street, and the four parlor rooms open onto a second-floor sitting room. Rooms have private half-baths with showers nearby; robes and slippers are provided. Continental breakfast is served in the upstairs parlor, and a dining room is open for lunch and dinner. No pets. There are weekend packages including dinner and theater tickets. *Main St. (inside Columbia State Park), Box 1870, 95310, tel. 209/532–1479. 9 rooms with half-bath. Facilities: saloon. AE, MC, V.*

Moderate– Expensive **Fallon Hotel.** The state of California recently restored this 1857 hotel to Victorian grandeur. The lobby and rooms are furnished with 1890s antiques. Each accommodation has a private half-bath; there are also men's and women's showers. Continental breakfast is served; if you occupy one of the five balcony rooms, you can sit outside with your coffee and watch the town wake up. Smoking is not allowed; one room is equipped for the handicapped. *Washington St. (inside Columbia State Park, next to the Fallon House Theater), Box 1870, 95310, tel. 209/ 532–1470. 14 rooms with half bath. AE, MC, V.*

Inexpensive **Columbia Gem Motel.** Rustic cottages and six simple airconditioned motel rooms are set among pine trees. Senior citizens receive discounts. *Columbia Hwy. (1 mi from Columbia State Park), Box 874, 22131 Parrot's Ferry Rd., 95310, tel: 209/532– 4508. 12 rooms. Facilities: cable TV. MC, V.*

Downieville Inexpensive **Saundra Dyer's Resort-Motel.** This small, cheerful, spotlessly clean motel on the Yuba River has a coffee percolator and color TV in each room; some kitchenettes are available. *9 Water St. (first right from Hwy. 49), Box 406, 95936, tel. 916/289–3308. 13 rooms. Facilities: pool. AE, MC, V.*

Grass Valley Expensive– Very Expensive ★ **Murphy's Inn.** An immaculate white house in a leafy setting (there is a giant sequoia in the back yard), this outstanding bed-and-breakfast, built in 1866, used to be the mansion of a gold mine owner. Some guest rooms have the original wallpaper, four have fireplaces, and many have the original wallpaper and gas chandeliers. The spacious veranda is festooned with ivy. There are award-winning full breakfasts; Belgian waffles and eggs Benedict are specialties. Smoking and pets are not allowed; there are kennel facilities nearby. *318 Neal St., 95945 (Colfax Hwy. 174 exit from Hwy. 49, left on S. Auburn), tel. 916/273–6873. 8 rooms. Facilities: pool, spa. AE, MC, V.*

Moderate **Best Western Gold Country Inn.** This well-kept two-story motel has contemporary rooms decorated in warm colors; 58 rooms have small refrigerators, and 16 have kitchens. Some rooms adjoin each other. Small pets are allowed. Complimentary Continental breakfast is included. *11972 Sutton Way, 95945 (Brunswick Rd. exit east from Hwy. 49), tel. 916/273–1393 or 800/528–1234. 84 rooms. Facilities: pool, spa. AE, D, DC, MC, V.*

Jackson
Moderate–
Expensive

Best Western Amador Inn. An up-to-date motel with rooms decorated in blue, rose, and light brown. Some rooms have fireplaces, and a few kitchenettes are available. No pets. *200 S. Hwy. 49, Box 758, 95642, tel. 209/223–0211 or 800/528–1234. 119 rooms. Facilities: restaurant, lounge, pool, cable TV. AE, D, DC, MC, V.*

Jamestown
Moderate–
Very Expensive

Jamestown Hotel. Each room in this old brick building with Gold Rush-era furnishings is individually decorated with comforters, iron beds, rocking chairs, flags, and other 19th-century artifacts, as well as a private Victorian bath. Continental breakfast is included. No pets. October through May is the value season with 20% discounts. *18153 Main St., Box 539, 95327, tel. 209/984–3902. 8 rooms with bath. AE, D, MC, V.*

Moderate

Sonora Country Inn. This three-story motel, opened in 1986, is decorated in subdued pastels. Continental breakfast is included. Half the rooms are for nonsmokers; there are facilities for the handicapped. *Hwy. 108 between Jamestown and Sonora, 18755 Charbroullian La., 95327, tel. 209/984–0315 or 800/847–2211 in CA. 60 rooms. Facilities: pool. AE, DC, MC, V.*

Murphys
Expensive

Dunbar House. This restored 1880 home in a pleasant setting is filled with antiques and quilts, and offers refreshments, complimentary wine, and a full country breakfast. No pets; smoking is not allowed. *271 Jones St., 95247, tel. 209/728–2897. 4 rooms. MC, V.*

Moderate

Murphys Hotel. The rooms are rustic in this restored 1855 hotel, which was visited by Mark Twain and Ulysses S. Grant. It has retained its period charm, but the modern rooms in the adjoining motel are more comfortable. Children are welcome; pets are allowed in the motel only. *457 Main St., 95247, tel. 209/728–3454. 21 rooms. Facilities: restaurant, lounge. AE, MC, V.*

Nevada City
Very Expensive

Grandmere's Bed and Breakfast Inn. This large white wedding cake of a house was built in 1856 and restored in 1985 in a country French style. The antiques, fabrics, and flower arrangements are superb, and the gardens beautifully landscaped. Full breakfast is included. Smoking is not allowed. *449 Broad St., 95959, tel. 916/265–4660. 7 rooms. MC, V.*

Expensive–
Very Expensive

The Red Castle. A state landmark, this 1860 Gothic Revival mansion stands on a hillside overlooking Nevada City. Its brick with white icicle trim, porches, and gardens add to the charm. The rooms, some of which look over the town, have antique furnishings and are elaborately decorated. A full buffet breakfast is served. No pets. *109 Prospect St., 95959, tel. 916/265–5135. 6 rooms with bath, 2 with shared bath. MC, V.*

Moderate

Northern Queen. This bright, pleasant, two-story motel has a lovely creekside setting. Accommodations include new or remodeled motel units; eight two-story chalets and eight rustic cottages with efficiency kitchens are located by a trout pond in a secluded, wooded area. Rooms have small refrigerators. Facilities for the handicapped are available. Pets are not allowed.

400 Railroad Ave., 95959 (Sacramento St. exit off Hwy. 49), tel. 916/265-5824. 85 rooms. Facilities: heated pool (year-round), spa, restaurant, cable TV. DC, MC, V.

Placerville
Expensive

Fleming Jones Homestead Bed and Breakfast. This 1883 farmhouse on 11 acres is only a few miles out of Placerville, but the atmosphere is distinctly rural. Exotic poultry and ducks wander through the rose gardens and vegetable beds; burros and ponies graze in the adjoining fields. Rooms are furnished with antiques, Victorian memorabilia, and teddy bears. A full breakfast is served. No pets; smoking is not allowed. *3170 Newtown Rd., 95667 (Hwy. 50 east from Hwy. 49, then Newtown Rd./Pt. View exit south), tel. 916/626-5840. 6 rooms with bath. No credit cards.*

Inexpensive–Moderate

Days Inn. The clean and comfortable rooms here have bright flowered bedspreads and curtains. There is a coffee shop next door and Continental breakfast is included. *1332 Broadway, 95667 (Hwy. 50 east from Hwy. 49, then Schnell School exit south), tel. 916/622-3124 or 800/325-2525. 45 rooms. Cable TV. AE, D, DC, MC, V.*

Sacramento
Very Expensive

Holiday Inn Capitol Plaza. This high-rise hotel offers fine views of the Sacramento River and the capitol building from its upper-floor rooms and top-floor restaurant and lounge. Old Sacramento is just across the road, and the capitol is 8 blocks away. The modern rooms and suites are furnished in pastels and accented with brass. Pets are allowed. *300 J St., 95814, tel. 916/446-0100 or 800/HOLIDAY. 370 rooms, 5 suites. Facilities: 2 restaurants, 2 lounges, pool, sauna, health club, garage. AE, DC, MC, V.*

Expensive–Very Expensive

Aunt Abigail's. This beautifully appointed Colonial Revival mansion near the center of town bills itself as a home-away-from-home since 1912. There is a piano, and games are available to play in the elegant living room, and the decor is soothingly Victorian. A copious breakfast includes home-baked breads and an entrée, and each bedroom has books, flowers, and an old-fashioned radio. *2120 G St., tel. 916/441-5007. 5 rooms. AE, MC, V.*

Expensive
★

Hotel El Rancho Resort. This 17-acre resort offers outstanding recreational facilities; the rooms and suites are decorated in contemporary pastels with wicker accents. There is an excellent restaurant and lounge featuring live music. *1029 W. Capitol Ave., West Sacramento, 95691 (Jefferson Blvd. exit north off Business Loop 80), tel. 916/371-6731 or 800/952-5566 in CA. 245 rooms. Facilities: room service, kitchenettes, pool, sauna, lighted tennis courts, racquetball, fitness center with aerobics, Nautilus, and free weights, 1.2-mi par course, massage. AE, D, DC, MC, V.*

Moderate

Best Western Sandman. The contemporary rooms are decorated in beige and brown at this two-story motel on the banks of the Sacramento River. The location is convenient, at a freeway exit out of Old Sacramento. Continental breakfast included. Senior citizens receive a discount. *236 Jibboom St., 95814 (Richards Blvd. exit west from I-5), tel. 916/443-6515 or 800/528-1234. 115 rooms. Facilities: restaurant, pool, therapy pool. AE, D, DC, MC, V.*

Inexpensive

Motel Orleans. This is a bright, well-maintained two-story economy hotel with simple contemporary rooms, just one freeway exit from Old Sacramento. Pets are allowed with a $5 deposit. A coffee shop is adjacent. *228 Jibboom St., 95814 (Richards Blvd. exit west from I–5), tel. 916/443–4811. 70 rooms. Facilities: pool. AE, D, DC, MC, V.*

Sonora
Expensive

Best Western Sonora Oaks Motor Hotel. This 1984 motel is located away from Sonora's crowded central area. The style is modern, with print bedspreads accenting the blue, green, or burgundy colors of the rooms and suites. *19551 Hess Ave., 95730 (3 mi east from Hwy. 49 on Hwy. 108), tel. 209/533–4400, 800/528–1234. 70 rooms. Facilities: pool, spa, restaurant, lounge. AE, D, DC, MC, V.*

Ryan House Bed and Breakfast Inn. Rose gardens and a hammock add to the pleasure of this 1855 farm homestead, furnished with country antiques. A full breakfast is served. *153 S. Shepherd St., 95370, tel. 209/533–3445. 3 rooms with private bath. AE, D, MC, V.*

Moderate

Sonora Inn. This inn stands on the site of the first hotel established by a woman in the Gold Country; its original Victorian facade was plastered over in the 1920s during the vogue of Spanish Mission architecture. The roomy lobby, restaurant, and lounge have tiled floors. There is a newer motel attached, where small pets are permitted. *160 S. Washington St., 95370, tel. 209/532–7468 or 800/321–5261. 61 rooms. Facilities: pool (unheated). AE, MC, V.*

Gunn House Bed & Breakfast. The original adobe house here was built in 1850. It was the first two-story building in town, the home of a newspaperman from Philadelphia who championed the rights of Chinese laborers. It has since been enlarged, restored, and furnished with antiques and air-conditioning. Continental breakfast is served in the old-fashioned lounge on the premises. Pets are not allowed. *286 S. Washington St., 95370, tel. 209/532–3421. 25 rooms. Facilities: pool. AE, D, MC, V.*

Sutter Creek
Very Expensive
★

The Foxes Bed & Breakfast. The rooms in this house, built in 1857, are handsome, with high ceilings, antique beds, and lofty armoires topped with floral arrangements. All rooms have queen-size beds; three have wood-burning fireplaces. A menu allows guests to select a full breakfast, brought to each room on a silver service. No pets; no smoking allowed. *Box 159, 77 Main St., 95685, tel. 209/267–5882. 6 rooms. D, MC, V.*

Expensive–
Very Expensive

Hanford House Bed & Breakfast. A modern brick building that evokes an earlier period with its California antiques and spacious rooms. The beds are queen-size, and a hearty Continental breakfast is served. No smoking. Pets are not allowed. One room offers wheelchair access, and there is a rooftop deck. *61 Hanford St., Box 1450, 95685 (Hwy. 49), tel. 209/267–0747. 9 rooms with bath. D, MC, V.*

Moderate–Very
Expensive
★

Sutter Creek Inn Bed & Breakfast. This white and green New England–style house, dating from the 1850s, is something of a legend in the bed-and-breakfast business. The rooms are comfortable and highly individual, furnished with a homey melange of antiques, wood-burning fireplaces, and unique hanging beds, suspended on chains from the ceiling. The gardens are spacious, with a variety of tables, chairs, and chaises, and the parlor is stocked with books and games. Breakfast, a communal affair, is lavish. No pets. *Box 385, 75 Main St., 95685, tel. 209/267–5606. 19 rooms. No credit cards.*

8 Lake Tahoe

With a shoreline more than 6,000 feet above sea level in the Sierra Nevada, Lake Tahoe is one of California's most spectacular natural attractions—even if a third of the lake is in Nevada. Visitors to the 482-square-mile Lake Tahoe Basin are also divided. About half of them arrive intent on sightseeing, hiking, fishing, camping, and boating, while the rest head directly for the casinos on the Nevada side of the lake where gambling is legal. During some summer weekends it seems that absolutely every tourist—100,000 at peak periods—is in a car on the 72-mile shoreline, looking for historic sites and uncrowded beaches, or parking places, restaurants, motels. But the crowds and congestion don't exist at a vantage point overlooking Emerald Bay early in the morning, or on a trail in the national forests that ring the basin, or on a sunset cruise on the lake itself, which is 22 miles long and 12 miles wide.

Placid vistas contrast with the lake's violent formation and dramatic history. About 25 million years ago the Tahoe Basin sank between the uplifting Sierra Nevada and an eastern offshoot of the Carson Range. Lava flowing from Mt. Pluto on the north blocked the basin's outlet. During the Ice Age, glaciers scoured the landscape. Now mountains rise 4,000 feet above the lake, and as much as 500 inches of snow falls in the winter at upper elevations. Sixty-three streams flow into the lake, but only the Truckee River flows out, and it never reaches the ocean. The lake's deepest point is 1,645 feet, and the brilliant blue and blue-green color can be breathtaking, but protecting its clarity is a continuing and often controversial campaign.

For centuries, before the lake was sighted by explorers Kit Carson and John C. Fremont in 1844, it was a summer gathering place and sacred site for Washoe Indians. The California gold rush lured emigrants over the treacherous Sierra north and south of the lake, and Nevada's silver bonanza enticed prospectors east from California a few years later. Hotels and resorts sprang up in the 1850s and 1860s, but the Tahoe Basin's forests were nearly stripped of trees for silver mining operations. By the turn of the century wealthy Californians were building lakeshore estates, some of which survive. Improved roads brought the less affluent in the 1920s and 1930s, when modest, rustic bungalows began to fill the wooded shoreline. The first casinos opened in the 1940s, and ski resorts also brought a development boom as the lake became a year-round attraction. Road construction and other building projects, however, washed soil and minerals into the lake, leading to a growth of algae that threatened its fabled clarity. (Objects can still be seen to a depth of 75 feet.) The environmental movement gained strength in the 1970s, resulting in a moratorium on new construction on the lakeshore and development of a master plan for future growth. A major redevelopment program has been approved that gradually will add new accommodations to the lakeshore while retaining its natural beauty.

The lake has long been a summer refuge from California's hot Central Valley and the Nevada desert. July and August daytime temperatures are in the 70s, with nighttime lows in the 40s. In the winter, the average daytime high is 36 degrees, the nighttime low 18. Ski resorts open at the end of November, sometimes with machine-made snow, and operate as late as May. Organized summer activities begin at the end of May, when the U.S. Forest Service Visitors Center opens on the south shore. Most accommodations, restaurants, and some parks are open year-round, although September and October, when crowds have thinned but the weather is still pleasant, may be the most satisfying time to visit Lake Tahoe.

Getting Around

By Plane Two airports provide good access to Lake Tahoe. **Reno Cannon International,** 58 miles northeast of the lake, is served by a number of national and regional airlines. Rental cars are available from the major agencies. There is shuttle bus service to the lake during peak travel periods, and the largest hotel/casinos offer their own transportation, for a fee. **Lake Tahoe Airport** on Hwy. 50, 3 miles south of the lake's shore, is served by **American Airlines' American Eagle service** (tel. 800/433–7300) with smaller jet planes from San Francisco, San Jose, and Los Angeles. Rental cars are also available.

By Train There is an **Amtrak** station in Truckee (tel. 800/USA–RAIL).

By Bus **South Tahoe Area Ground Express (STAGE)** (tel. 916/573–2080) runs 24 hours along U.S. 50 and through the neighborhoods of South Lake Tahoe. On the lake's west and north shores, **Tahoe Area Regional Transit (TART)** (tel. 916/581–6365 or 800/325–8278 in NV) runs between Tahoma and Incline Village daily from 6:30 AM to 6:30 PM. **Greyhound Bus** (tel. 916/587– 3822 or 702/322–4511 for 24-hour fare and schedule information) runs among Sacramento, Truckee, and Reno and between Sacramento and South Lake Tahoe. Free shuttle buses run among the casinos, major ski resorts, and motels of South Lake Tahoe.

By Car Lake Tahoe is 198 miles northeast of San Francisco, a four- to five-hour drive, depending on weather and traffic. The major route is I–80, which cuts through the Sierra Nevada about 14 miles north of the lake; from there state highways 89 and 267 reach the north shore. U.S. 50, which begins at I–80 in Sacramento, is the more direct highway to the south shore. U.S. 395 runs south toward the lake from Reno. These are all-weather highways, although there may be delays as snow is cleared during major storms. Tire chains should be carried, and are provided by rental car agencies, from October to May. Avoid the heavy traffic leaving the San Francisco area for Tahoe on Friday afternoons and returning on Sunday afternoons.

By Taxi Taxi service is plentiful in South Lake Tahoe. On the north shore, try **North Shore Taxi** (tel. 916/546–3181) and **Truckee Taxi Service** (Truckee, tel. 916/587–6336).

Guided Tours

Gray Line (2570 Pacchino, Reno 89512, tel. 702/329–1147) runs daily tours to Emerald Bay, South Lake Tahoe, Carson City, and Virginia City. Other tour providers are **Showboat Lines** (Box 12119, Zephyr Cove, NV 89448, tel. 702/588–6688) and **Tahoe Limousine Service** (Box 9909, South Lake Tahoe 95731, tel. 916/577–2727).

Important Addresses and Numbers

Tourist Information **Lake Tahoe Visitors Authority** (Box 16299, South Lake Tahoe 95706, tel. 916/544–5050 or 800/288–2463).

North Lake Tahoe Chamber of Commerce (Box 884, Tahoe City 95730, tel. 916/581–6900).

Tahoe North Visitors and Convention Bureau (Box 5578, Tahoe City 95730, tel. 916/583–3494 or 800/824–6348) for airline, car rental, and lodging reservations, as well as honeymoon and ski packages.

Ski Phone (tel. 415/864–6440) for 24-hour skiing and weather conditions.

Road Conditions (tel. 916/577–3550).

Emergencies   The emergency number throughout the Tahoe area is 911. This will put you in touch with police, fire, and medical help. Make a point of knowing your location.

Exploring

Numbers in the margin correspond with points of interest on the Lake Tahoe map.

The most common way to explore the Lake Tahoe area is to drive the 72-mile road that follows the shore, through wooded flatlands, past beaches, climbing to vistas on the rugged west side of the lake, descending to the busiest commercial developments and casinos. It takes about three hours, but it can be frustrating during peak visiting periods, such as summer holiday weekends when the population swells to 100,000. Obviously, it's best to stop at parks, picnic areas, and scenic lookouts rather than sightseeing entirely from a car. There are many hiking trails, some of them easy, paved paths; with access from the shoreline highway, they offer a quick escape from the traffic. Free maps and information are available at the U.S. Forest Service's Visitors Center (*see* below). The scenic highway around the lake is marked as Highway 28 on the north and northeast shore, U.S. 50 on the south, and Highway 89 on the southwest and west. Highway 89 may be closed at D.L. Bliss State Park when there is a heavy snowfall.

❶   We'll begin a tour around the lake at **Stateline,** actually two towns called Stateline, one on either side of the California–Nevada border. Traveling west along U.S. 50, turn left at Ski Run

❷   Boulevard and drive up to the **Heavenly Ski Resort.** Whether you're a skier or not, you'll want to ride 2,000 feet up on the 50-passenger Heavenly Tram partway up the mountain to 8,200 feet. There you'll find a memorable view of Lake Tahoe and the Nevada desert. The Top of the Tram restaurant, open daily during tram hours, offers basic American food and cafeteria service. It serves lunch, dinner, and Sunday brunch in summer, lunch only in winter. *Tram information, tel. 916/541– 1330. Dinner reservations, tel. 916/544–6263. Tram hours, June–Sept., daily 10–10; Nov.–May 9–4. Adult round-trip, $9.50, children 3–12, $5.*

Return to U.S. 50 and turn left, heading west toward South Lake Tahoe, the largest community on the lake. As the lakeshore route becomes Highway 89 in Tahoe Valley, commercial development gives way to more wooded national forest lands.

❸   You'll notice pleasant bike trails, well off the road. At **Pope-Baldwin Recreation Area,** take in the Historic Estates Tour (tel. 916/541–5227). Three grand mansions built almost 100 years ago have been restored, and are open for viewing in the summer.

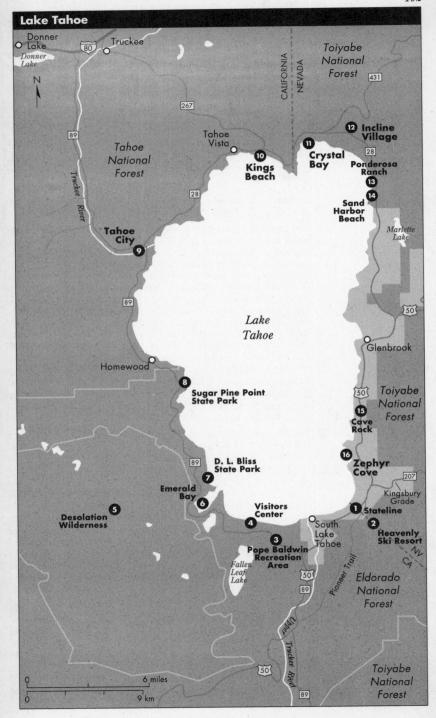

Lake Tahoe

4 The **Lake Tahoe Visitors Center** on Taylor Creek is operated by the U.S. Forest Service, and offers far more than answers to visitors' questions. This stretch of lakefront is a microcosm of the area's natural history, with the site of a Washoe Indian settlement; self-guided trails through meadow, marsh, and forest; and an underground display with windows on Taylor Creek (in the fall, you may see spawning salmon digging their nests). *Open daily June–Sept., weekends in Oct. Tel. 916/573–2674 in season; at other times of the year, 916/573–2600.*

5 To the west is the vast **Desolation Wilderness,** a 63,473-acre preserve of granite peaks, glacial valleys, subalpine forests, and more than 80 lakes. Access for hiking, fishing, and camping is by trail from outside the wilderness preserve; Meeks Bay and Echo Lake are two starting points. Permits (free) are required for access at any time of the year from the Forest Service Visitors Center or headquarters (870 Emerald Bay Rd., Suite 1, South Lake Tahoe, CA 96150, tel. 916/573–2600).

6 The winding road next takes you to **Emerald Bay,** famed for its jewellike shape and color of its waters. The road is high above the lake at this point; from Emerald Bay Lookout you can survey the whole scene, which includes Tahoe's only island. From the lookout a 1-mile trail leads down to **Vikingsholm,** a 38-room estate built in the 1920s by Lora Knight, inspired by Norwegian and Swedish castles of the 11th century. It's a rugged stone building with a partial sod roof, furnished with Scandinavian antiques and reproductions. Be forewarned that the trail leads down and that the hike back up is steep. *Tel. 916/525–7277. Admission: $2 adults, $1 children under 18. Open July–Labor Day daily 10–4.*

Another way to see Emerald Bay close up is to take one of the daily cruises across its waters. **The Tahoe Queen,** a glass-bottom sternwheeler, travels year-round on 2½-hour cruises from Ski Run Marina off U.S. 50 in South Lake Tahoe. (Tel. 916/541–3364. Daytime cruise $14 adults, $5 children under 12; sunset/dinner cruise fare: $18 adults, $9.50 children under 12. Fares do not include food or beverages.) From late April through early November the **MS Dixie** sails from Zephyr Cove Marina to Emerald Bay. (Tel. 702/588–3508. Daytime, breakfast, brunch, dinner, and cocktail cruises. Fare: $12 to $31 adults, $4 to $9.50 children 4–12, depending on type of cruise; food and beverages included in fares.) **Tahoe Cruises** offers a winter ski shuttle, including bus to ski areas, from the south shore to Tahoe City. (Tel. 916/541–3364. Fare: $18 adults, $9 children.)

7 Beyond Emerald Bay is **D.L. Bliss State Park,** which shares with the bay 6 miles of shoreline and 268 family campsites. At the north end of the park is Rubicon Point, which overlooks one of the lake's deepest spots. *Tel. 916/525–7277; day use fee: $5 per vehicle; closed in winter.*

8 The main attraction at **Sugar Pine Point State Park** is the **Ehrman Mansion,** a stately, stone-and-shingle 1903 summer home that displays the "rustic" aspirations of the era's wealthy residents. It is furnished in period style. *Tel. 916/525–7232 or 916/525–7982 in season. Open July–Labor Day, daily 11–4. Admission free. State Park day use fee: $5 per vehicle.*

9 At **Tahoe City,** Highway 89 turns north from the lake to Squaw Valley; Highway 28 continues around the lake. You'll cross the Truckee River, the lake's only outlet. Fanny Bridge is the best observation point to see the river's giant trout and the rows of visitors leaning over the railing, which gave the bridge its name. The **Gatekeeper's Log Cabin Museum** in Tahoe City provides one of the best records of the area's past, with Washoe and Paiute Indian artifacts as well as late 19th- to early 20th-century settlers' memorabilia. *130 W. Lake Blvd., tel. 916/583–1762. Admission free. Open May 15–Oct. 1 daily 11–5.*

The Museum also oversees the nearby **Watson Cabin,** a 1909 log cabin, built by Robert M. Watson and his son with turn-of-the-century furnishings and costumed docents who act out the daily life of a typical pioneer family. *560 N. Lake Blvd., tel. 916/583–8717 or 916/583–1762. Admission free. Open June 15–Labor Day daily noon–4.*

⑩ Traveling east on Highway 28 you will reach the 28-acre **Kings Beach State Recreation Area,** one of the lakeshore parks open
⑪ year-round; **Crystal Bay** just over the Nevada border, with the towering Cal-Neva hotel/casino; and the affluent residential
⑫ community of **Incline Village.**

⑬ The **Ponderosa Ranch** is east of Incline Village on Highway 28. The site of the popular television series *Bonanza* includes the Cartwrights' ranch house, a western town, and a saloon and offers free pony rides and hayrides. *Tel. 702/831–0691. Admission: $7.50 adults, $5.50 children 5–11. Open late April–Oct. daily 9:30–5.*

⑭ **Sand Harbor Beach** is one of the lake's finest, and so popular it's sometimes filled to capacity by 11 AM on summer weekends. Evenings are something else: a pop music festival in July, Shakespeare festival in August. *Festival information, tel. 916/583–9048.*

Now you meet U.S. 50 again and travel past scenic vistas. The
⑮ road passes through **Cave Rock,** through 25 yards of solid stone.
⑯ Six miles from Cave Rock, you'll come to **Zephyr Cove,** with a beach and a marina that is home to tour boats. Just ahead you see the towers of the casinos at Stateline, and you've come full circle.

What to See and Do with Children

Except for gambling and the floor shows in Nevada, most attractions and activities around the lake are family-oriented. The Forest Service is the best resource, and the Visitors Center at Taylor Creek the prime site. In the summer, the center gives discovery walks and nighttime campfires with songs and marshmallow roasts. The Stream Profile Chamber provides a peek underwater in Taylor Creek. There are Native American exhibits at the Visitors Center and at the Gatekeeper's Museum in Tahoe City. Other options range from bike rentals to flashy video arcades in many casinos.

In the winter, there is a snow play area that rents saucers at **Granlibakken** (tel. 916/583–6203), just south of Tahoe City on Highway 89. Ski areas have classes for children as young as three. **Borges Carriage and Sleigh Rides** in South Lake Tahoe (tel. 916/541–2953) and some ski resorts have sleigh rides.

Off the Beaten Track

For a new perspective that goes above the mountain trams, **CalVada Seaplanes Inc.** (tel. 916/525–7143) provides rides over the lake for $40–$72 per person, depending on the length of the trip. For a closer look at the area's scenery, **Truckin' on the Truckee** (tel. 916/583–9724) rents mountain bikes for $10 (two hours), $15 (half–day), and $20 (full day), including helmets. A 4-mile paved trail follows the Truckee River to River Ranch. A 15-mile trail runs along the lake shore. Though a prolonged drought has put a damper on river rafting, **Mountain Air Sports** (tel. 916/583–5606) offers a two- to three-hour raft trip down the Truckee River from Tahoe City to River Ranch, conditions permitting, for $15 adults, $10 children under 12.

There's never a shortage of ice at the top of Squaw Valley where the **Olympic Ice Pavillion** (tel. 916/583–6985) offers year-round ice skating with a view daily 10–9. Skate rentals are available.

A tragic reminder of the High Sierra's past is **Donner Memorial State Park** just off I–80 2 miles west of Truckee. During the ferocious winter of 1846–47 a westbound party led by George Donner was trapped here. The Pioneer Monument stands on a pedestal 22 feet high, the depth of the snow that winter. Of 89 people in the group, only 47 lived; some survived by eating animal hides and some resorted to cannibalism. The Immigrant Museum shows a film hourly about the Donner Party's plight; other displays include the history of other settlers, and railroad development through the Sierra. *Tel. 916/587–3841. Admission: $2 adults, $1 children 6–17. Open daily 10–4, closed noon–1 early Sept.–late-Nov. Closed Jan. 1, Thanksgiving, Dec. 25.*

Old West facades line the main street of nearby **Truckee.** This is a favorite stopover for people traveling from San Francisco to the north shore of Lake Tahoe. Fine art galleries and upscale boutiques are plentiful, but you also will find low-key diners, discount skiwear, and an old-fashioned five-and-dime store. For a map outlining a walking tour of historic Truckee, stop by the information booth in the Amtrak depot.

Participant Sports

For most of the popular sports at Lake Tahoe, summer or winter, you won't have to bring much equipment with you, an important factor if you're traveling by air or have limited space. Bicycles and boats are readily available for rent at Lake Tahoe. Golf clubs can be rented at several area courses. Most of the ski resorts have rental shops.

Golf   These courses in the Lake Tahoe area have food facilities, pro shops, cart rentals, and putting greens.

Edgewood Tahoe. 18 holes, par 72. Driving range. Cart mandatory. *U.S. 50 and Lake Pkwy., behind Horizon Casino, Stateline, tel. 702/588–3566. Open 7–6.*
Incline Championship. 18 holes, par 72. Driving range. Cart mandatory. *955 Fairway Blvd., Incline Village, tel. 702/832–1144. Open 6 AM–6:30 PM.*
Incline Executive. 18 holes, par 58. Cart mandatory. *690 Wilson Way, Incline Village, tel.702/832–1150. Open 7:30–5:30.*

Lake Tahoe Golf Course. 18 holes, par 71. Driving range. *U.S. 50 between South Lake Tahoe Airport and Meyers, tel. 916/ 577– 0788. Open 6 AM–8 PM.*

Northstar-at-Tahoe. 18 holes, par 72. Driving range. Cart mandatory before noon. *Hwy. 267 between Truckee and Kings Beach. Tel. 916/587–0290. Open 7:30 AM–dark.*

Skiing   The Tahoe Basin ski resorts boast the largest concentration of skiing in the country and its most breathtaking winter scenery. There are 12 downhill ski resorts and eight nordic ski centers, with more cross-country skiing available on thousands of acres of public forests and parklands. Among the resorts are Heavenly Ski Resort, the nation's largest, covering 20 square miles, and Squaw Valley, site of the 1960 Winter Olympics. There are many ski packages: lodging and lift tickets; lift tickets, rentals, and lessons; airline tickets, lodging, skiing, and auto rental. Ask questions when you are planning an excursion and you may find some bargains. Many resorts at Tahoe offer free or discounted skiing to beginners.

Free shuttle-bus service is available between most ski resorts and hotels and lodges.

Alpine Meadows Ski Area. The high base elevation and a variety of sun exposures give Alpine the longest season in Tahoe, mid-November to Memorial Day. Of its 2,000 acres, 25% are beginner, 40% intermediate, 35% advanced. Its 13 lifts handle 16,000 skiers per hour. The summit elevation is 8,637 ft.; base, 6,835 ft.; vertical drop, 1,800 ft. The longest run is 2.5 mi. There is a ski school and a children's snow school for three- to six-year-olds. The expansive day lodge has a large sun deck, restaurant, bar, cafeteria. There is an overnight RV area. *North shore, between Truckee and Tahoe City on Hwy. 89. Box 5279, Tahoe City 95730, tel. 916/583–4232. Snow information, tel. 916/583– 6914.*

Diamond Peak at Ski Incline. This north shore resort at Incline Village specializes in family skiing. The terrain is 18% beginner, 49% intermediate, 33% advanced. Its seven lifts can handle 3,700 skiers per hour. The summit is 8,540 ft.; base, 6,700 ft.; vertical drop, 1,840 ft. The longest run is 2.5 mi. Family ticket rates and special all-inclusive "Learn-to-Ski" packages are available. The Child Ski Development Center is for ages three to seven. The full-facility base lodge has a mountaintop barbecue. *1210 Ski Way, Incline Village, NV 89451, tel. 702/ 832–1177 or 800/468–2463.*

Diamond Peak Cross Country. This high-elevation cross-country ski area, opened in 1989, offers spectacular views of Lake Tahoe. Its 2,600 acres of rolling terrain are 15% beginner, 70% intermediate, 15% advanced. There are 30 km. of groomed trails and open wilderness trails. Elevation is 8,200 feet; the longest trail, 6 km. Besides a ski school, there is a beginner special that includes trail pass, rentals, and lesson. *1210 Ski Way, Incline Village, NV 89451, tel. 702/832–1177 or 800/468–2463.*

Heavenly Ski Resort. Located in the heart of the South Lake Tahoe area, this is America's largest ski resort, with nine mountain peaks and 20 square miles of ski terrain of which 25% is beginner, 50% intermediate, and 25% advanced. Its 24 lifts carry 31,000 skiers each hour. The summit is 10,100 ft.; base, 6,550 ft. (CA) and 7,200 ft. (NV); vertical drop, 3,600 ft. Its longest run is 5.5 mi. The resort has a ski school, three base lodges, and four on-mountain lodges. *Ski Run Blvd., Box 2180,*

Stateline, NV 89449, tel. 916/541–1330 or 800/243–2836. Snow information, tel. 916/541–7544.

Kirkwood Ski Resort. Thirty-five miles south of Lake Tahoe, this large resort has extensive trails and the highest base elevation in northern California. Its 2,000 acres are 15% beginner, 50% intermediate, 35% advanced. There are 11 lifts. Kirkwood's summit is 9,800 ft.; its base, 7,800 ft.; vertical drop, 2,000 ft., and longest run, 2.5 mi. Facilities include a ski school, Mighty Mountain for children 4–12, licensed child care, and two base lodges with restaurants and bars. Also available are a beginner special, shuttle bus from Lake Tahoe ($2), and hotel packages. *On Hwy. 88, Box 1, Kirkwood, CA 95646, tel. 209/258–6000. Lodging information, tel. 209/258–7000. Snow information, tel. 209/258–3000.*

Northstar-at-Tahoe. Northstar is a complete resort, with lodging and full amenities. Its 1,700 acres of tree-lined ski runs are 25% beginner, 50% intermediate, 25% advanced, with 9 lifts. The summit is 8,600 ft.; base, 6,400 ft.; vertical drop, 2,200 ft. and longest run, 2.9 mi. Northstar has a ski school; adult beginner package; all-day junior lesson program ("Starkids," for ages 5–12). It has 45 km of groomed and tracked wilderness trails for cross-country; beginner 30%, intermediate 40%, advanced 30%. The base is 6,800 ft.; vertical drop, 800 ft. and longest trail, 12 mi. Lessons, guided tours, and rentals are available. Packages may include air tickets, lodging, lifts, ski school, ski rental, child care, rental car. *Off Hwy. 267 between Truckee and North Shore. Box 129, Truckee 95734, tel. 916/562–1010 or 800/533–6787. Snow information, tel. 916/562–1330.*

Sierra Ski Ranch. This is a little farther away, but the slopes are usually uncrowded and it has spectacular views of the lake. Of 2,000 acres, 20% are beginner, 60% intermediate, 20% advanced, and there are nine lifts. The summit is 8,852 ft.; base, 6,640 ft.; vertical drop, 2,212 ft. The longest run is 3.5 mi. Ski school and children's snow school are available. Base lodge has three cafeterias, rental and retail shops; plus a lodge and café on top of mountain. Beginner specials are available. There is free shuttle bus service from South Lake Tahoe hotels. *On U.S. 50, 12 mi west of South Lake Tahoe, Box 3501, Twin Bridges 95735, tel. 916/659–7453. Snow information, tel. 916/659–7475.*

Squaw Valley USA. There are vast, open slopes here, at the site of the 1960 Winter Olympics on 8,300 acres of skiable terrain, which includes 25% beginner, 45% intermediate, 30% advanced. Its 32 lifts have an uphill lift capacity of 47,370 skiers per hour. The summit is 9,050 ft.; base, 6,200 ft.; vertical drop, 2,850 ft. and longest run, 3.5 mi. Ten Little Indians day care is available for children six months to two years; Papoose Snow School offers ski instruction for children three to five years. First-time skiers ski free midweek. Base facilities and both Gold Coast and High Camp Complex on upper mountain have a variety of food and beverages. Ski rentals and a wide range of packages are available. *Between Truckee and Tahoe City on Hwy. 89, Squaw Valley 95730, tel. 916/583–6985. Lodging reservations 800/545–4350. Snow information, tel. 916/583–6955.*

Tahoe Nordic Ski Center. This cross-country center, north of Tahoe City offers 2,000 acres, 67 km of trails, 30% beginner, 40% intermediate, 30% advanced. Its summit is 7,880 ft.; base, 6,550 ft.; vertical drop, 1,000 ft. and longest trail, 25 km. Facilities include a ski school and beginners special: trail pass, rentals, lesson. *Off Hwy. 28, north of Tahoe City, Box 1632, Tahoe City 95730, tel. 916/583-9858 or 916/583-0484.*

Swimming There are 36 public beaches ringing Lake Tahoe. Swimming is permitted at many of them, but since Tahoe is a high mountain lake with fairly rugged winters, only the hardiest will be interested, except during midsummer. Even then the water warms to only 68°F. Lifeguards are on duty at some of the swimming beaches, and yellow buoys mark safe areas where motorboats are not permitted. Opening and closing dates for beaches vary with the climate and available park service staffing. There may be a parking fee of $1 or $2.

Gambling

You don't need a roadside marker to know when you've crossed from California into Nevada. The lake's water and the pine trees may be identical, but the flashing lights and elaborate marquees of the casinos announce legalized gambling with a bang. Nevada got gambling in 1931, and nearby Reno soon proclaimed itself "the biggest little city in the world." In 1944, Harvey's Wagon Wheel Saloon and Gambling Hall, little more than a rustic cabin, brought gambling to Lake Tahoe, and competition soon flourished in the Stateline area. Now, in addition to the big casinos, visitors will find slot machines in every conceivable location, from gas stations to supermarkets.

The major casinos are also hotels and, more recently, resorts. Four are clustered on a strip of Highway 50 in Stateline, two others on the north shore at Crystal Bay and Incline Village. They are open 24 hours a day, 365 days a year, offering craps, blackjack, roulette, baccarat, poker, keno, pai gow, bingo, and vast arrays of slot machines—1,850, for instance, at Harrah's.

The hotel/casinos compete by offering celebrity entertainers in their showrooms, restaurants and lounges open around the clock, and frequent refurbishing that has transformed many of the Western settings to a more contemporary international style. Some casino restaurants are elegant settings designed to attract upscale visitors; on the other hand, Bill's Casino in Stateline has installed a McDonald's to reach a younger crowd.

Dining

Restaurants at Lake Tahoe range from rustic wood-and-rock decor to elegant French, with a stop along the way for Swiss chalet and spare modern. The food, too, is varied: delicate Continental sauces, mesquite-broiled fish, wild boar in season.

Separate listings are given here for the north and south shores. Casino restaurants are described under lodging. There are also many fast-food restaurants and coffee-shop chains in South Lake Tahoe and some in Tahoe City. Unless otherwise noted, dress is informal for all restaurants. Even the most elegant and expensive Tahoe eating places welcome customers in the casual clothes that are considered appropriate in this year-round mecca for vacationers.

Highly recommended restaurants are indicated by a star ★.

Category	Cost*
Very Expensive	over $30
Expensive	$20–$30
Moderate	$16–$20
Inexpensive	under $16

*per person, not including tax, service, or drinks

North Shore
Moderate–Expensive

Captain Jon's. The dining room is small and cozy, with linen cloths and fresh flowers on the tables and a fire burning on a raised brick hearth on chilly evenings. The lengthy dinner menu is country French, with two dozen different daily specials; the emphasis is on fish. The lounge is in a separate building on the water, with a pier where guests can tie up their boats. In summer, lunch is served in the lounge and on the deck. *7220 N. Lake Blvd., Tahoe Vista, tel. 916/546–4819. Reservations advised. Full bar. AE, DC, MC, V. Closed Mon.*

La Playa. This dinner house on the lake features a Continental menu, with outdoor service an option in the summer. Seafood is a specialty. *7046 N. Lake Blvd., Tahoe Vista, tel. 916/546–5903. Reservations advised. Full bar. AE, MC, V.*

Le Petit Pier. The decor in this lakeside dinner restaurant with fine views is French Provincial and romantic. The menu features French classics, such as roast duckling with a blueberry sauce. There is an award-winning wine list. *7250 N. Lake Blvd., Tahoe Vista, tel. 916/546–4464. Reservations advised. Full bar. AE, DC, MC, V.*

Moderate

★ **Sunnyside Restaurant and Lodge.** An expansive lakefront deck with steps down to the beach and the water fronts this handsome wooden lodge. The large lounge features rock fireplaces, comfortable sofas, a seafood bar, and snacks. The Chris Craft dining room, decorated in a nautical style in mahogany, with carpets and upholstery in maroon and blue, is trim and sleek. Seafood is a specialty of the Continental menu. *1850 W. Lake Blvd., Tahoe City, tel. 916/583–7200. Reservations accepted. Full bar. MC, V. No lunch or brunch in winter.*

★ **Wolfdale's.** An intimate dinner house on the lake, Wolfdale's offers Japanese/California cuisine. The menu changes weekly; there are a small number of imaginative entrées such as grilled Chinese pheasant with plum sauce and shitake mushrooms and baked Norwegian salmon with saffron scallop sauce. *640 N. Lake Blvd., Tahoe City, tel. 916/583–5700. Reservations advised. Full bar. MC, V. Closed Tues.*

Inexpensive–Moderate

Gar Woods Grill and Pier. This elegant but casual lakeside restaurant recalls the lake's past, with wood paneling, a river-rock fireplace, and boating photographs. It specializes in grilled foods, along with pasta and pizza. Lunch, dinner, and Sunday brunch are served daily year-round. *5000 N. Lake Blvd., Carnelian Bay, tel. 916/546–3366. Reservations accepted. MC, V.*

★ **Jake's on the Lake.** Continental food is served in spacious, handsome rooms featuring oak and glass on the water at the Boatworks Mall. There is an extensive seafood bar; the varied menu includes meat and poultry but emphasizes fresh fish. Lunch is served daily in summer. *780 N. Lake Blvd., Tahoe*

City, tel. 916/583-0188. Dress: collared shirts for men in the evening. Reservations accepted. AE, MC, V.

★ **River Ranch.** From the terrace of this old-fashioned lodge with a stellar setting beside the Truckee River you can almost get your feet wet. The food is decidedly American, with fresh fish, smoked herb chicken and barbecued ribs from a wood-burning oven, and wild game specials: pheasant, chukar partridge, rabbit, quail, goose, elk, venison, wild boar, and buffalo. The restaurant is open for dinner all year, with appetizers from 3:30 PM, and service on the terrace in summer. Lunch is served daily in summer. *Hwy. 89 between Truckee and Tahoe City, at Alpine Meadows turn, tel. 916/583-4264. Reservations accepted. Full bar. AE, MC, V.*

Tahoe House. Combining Swiss and California cuisine, this casual and somewhat rustic dinner house features an elegant menu: veal, lamb, beef, fresh pasta and seafood, fresh-baked breads, and a large selection of homemade desserts. In season, try the strawberry torte with white chocolate mousse. A children's menu is available. *625 W. Lake Blvd., Tahoe City, tel. 916/583-1377. Reservations advised. Full bar. AE, MC, V.*

Inexpensive **Cafe Cobblestone.** A basically American menu is served for breakfast and lunch (and dinner on winter weekends and during the summer high season) in a casual Tyrolean decor. Salads are a specialty; there is also a good variety of quiches, omelets, and sandwiches. *475 N. Lake Blvd., Tahoe City, tel. 916/583-2111. No reservations. Gourmet beers and wine. MC, V.*

South Shore **The Chart House.** An American menu featuring steak and sea-
Moderate- food is presented in a dinner house with a panoramic lake view.
Expensive There is a children's menu. *Kingsbury Grade, tel. 702/588-6276. Reservations accepted. Full bar. AE, MC, V.*

Christiania Inn. Located at the base of Heavenly Ski Resort's tram, this inn offers fireside dining among antiques in a Swiss country decor. The American/Continental menu emphasizes fresh seafood, prime beef, and veal. There is an extensive wine list. Midday buffets are served on holidays. Appetizers, soups, and salads are available in the lounge daily after 2 PM. *3819 Saddle Rd., South Lake Tahoe, tel. 916/544-7337. Reservations advised. Full bar. MC, V.*

Moderate **Zackary's Restaurant.** The ambience here is casual and intimate. The menu is Continental, offering fresh fish and traditional dishes. *Round Hill Mall, Zephyr Cove, tel. 702/588-2108. Full bar. AE, MC, V.*

Swiss Chalet. The Swiss decor is carried out with great consistency, making this one of the town's more attractive restaurants. The Continental menu features Swiss specialties, veal dishes, fresh seafood, and home-baked pastries. Seasonal specials change daily. There is a children's menu. *2540 Tahoe Blvd., South Lake Tahoe, tel. 916/544-3304. Reservations advised. Full bar. AE, MC, V. Closed Mon., Easter, Nov. 23-Dec. 5, Dec. 25.*

Inexpensive- **The Greenhouse.** Hanging plants, white linen cloths, a brick
Moderate fireplace, and a coppertop bar create the ambience here. The Continental menu includes veal Marsala, tournedos of lamb, and prawns à la cognac. *4140 Cedar Ave., Box RRR, South Lake Tahoe 95729, tel. 916/541-5800. Reservations advised. AE, DC, MC, V.*

Tahoe Seasons Restaurant. Located at the Tahoe Seasons Resort in Heavenly Valley, this comfortable restaurant has eight fireplaces. Breakfast is served, and at dinner the menu is Continental, with some American fare. *3901 Saddle Rd., South Lake Tahoe, tel. 916/541–6700. Reservations advised. Full bar. AE, MC, V.*

Lodging

Accommodations at Lake Tahoe are as varied as everything else at this prime vacation spot. Quiet inns on the water, motel rooms in the heart of the casino area, rooms at the casinos themselves, lodges close to the ski runs—the most deluxe of lodgings and inexpensive bases for your vacation are all here. Just remember that during the summer months and the ski season, the lake is crowded; plan in advance for a place to stay. Spring and fall give you a little more leeway and lower—sometimes significantly lower—rates. Price categories listed below reflect high-season rates. Lake Tahoe has two telephone reservation services: Tahoe North Visitors and Convention Bureau, 800/824–6348; for the south shore, Lake Tahoe Visitors Authority, 800/288–2463.

The listing of lodgings is divided between the north and south shores. The large hotel/casinos are listed at the end of each geographical section.

Highly recommended hotels are indicated by a star ★.

Category	Cost*
Very Expensive	over $100
Expensive	$75–$100
Moderate	$50–$75
Inexpensive	under $50

double room, not including tax

North Shore Hotels
Very Expensive

Hyatt Lake Tahoe Resort Hotel/Casino. This luxurious hotel on the lake was entirely renovated in 1989; some rooms have fireplaces. A children's program and rental bicycles are available. The restaurants are Hugo's Rotisserie, Ciao Mein Trattoria (Oriental/Italian), and Sierra Cafe (open 24 hours). *Lakeshore and Country Club Dr., Box 3239, Incline Village 89450. Tel. 702/831–1111 or 800/233–1234. 460 rooms. Facilities: beach, pool, spa, sauna, tennis, movies (fee), health club, laundry, valet parking lot, entertainment. AE, DC, MC, V.*

Tahoe Vista Inn & Marina. Located at the northern tip of Lake Tahoe, this small, luxurious inn has suites only. Each has a living room, fireplace, kitchen, jetted bathtub, separate bedroom, and private lanai overlooking the lake. The decor is opulently modern, with white sofas, glass coffee tables, blond wood, and fieldstone gas-jetted fireplaces. *7220 N. Lake Blvd., Tahoe Vista 95732, tel. 916/546–7662 or 800/662–3433. 7 suites. Facilities: boat slip, restaurant, lounge. AE, MC, V.*

Expensive–Very Expensive
★

Sunnyside Lodge. This modern mountain lodge is in a location that soaks up the sun. The setting features large lakefront decks and a marina. Rooms are decorated in an elegant country style with plaid bedspreads, pottery lamps, and caned chairs. Each room has its own deck and lake and mountain views. Continental breakfast is provided. *1850 W. Lake Blvd., Tahoe City*

95730, tel. 916/583–7200 or 800/822–2754 in CA. 23 rooms. MC, V.

Moderate–
Expensive

Tahoe City TraveLodge. Overlooking Lake Tahoe and the Tahoe City Golf Course, the newly refurbished motel rooms here offer king- and queen-size beds with flowered spreads, desks, and high-nap carpets; there is fresh-ground coffee in each room. A restaurant and lounge are adjacent. Senior citizens receive discount. *455 N. Lake Blvd., Box 84, Tahoe City 95730, tel. 916/ 583–3766 or 800/255–3050. 47 rooms with bath and shower/ massage. Facilities: heated pool, whirlpool on deck with lake view. AE, DC, MC, V.*

Tahoe Sands Resort. This is a pleasant older motel at a quiet spot on the lakeshore. The spacious grounds and ample play facilities make it attractive to family groups. Some rooms have wood-burning stoves and kitchenettes. *6610 N. Lake Blvd., Tahoe Vista 95732, tel. 916/546–2592. 67 rooms. Facilities: beach, pool, sauna, Jacuzzi, putting green, playground for children, laundry facilities. AE, DC, MC, V.*

★ **River Ranch.** This is a small, cozy old lodge with an exceptional setting immediately on the Truckee River, close to Alpine Meadows and Squaw Valley skiing. The rooms feature antiques and some have balconies overlooking the river. There is a good restaurant and lounge on the first floor. *Box 197, Tahoe City 95730, tel. 916/583–4264 or 800/535–9900 in CA. 21 rooms. AE, MC, V.*

North Shore
Hotel/Casinos
Expensive–
Very Expensive

Cal Neva Lodge Resort Hotel/Casino. All rooms in this remodeled hotel on Highway 28 at Crystal Bay have views of Lake Tahoe and the mountains. There is an arcade with video games for children, cabaret entertainment, and 22 cabins with living rooms. The restaurants are Lake View (coffee shop) and Sir Charles Fine Dining. *Box 368, Crystal Bay 89402, tel. 702/832– 4000 or 800/225–6382. 220 rooms. Facilities: cable tv, pool, sauna, whirlpool, tennis courts, 3 wedding chapels. AE, DC, MC, V.*

South Shore Hotels
Expensive–
Very Expensive
★

Inn by the Lake. This luxury motel across the road from the beach is far from the flashy casinos, but convenient to them by free shuttle bus. The rooms and bathrooms are spacious and comfortable, furnished in contemporary style (blond oak, pale peach, light teal blue). All rooms have balconies; some have lake views, wet bars, and kitchenettes. Continental breakfast is served each morning. Children under 12 stay free in room with parents. A senior-citizen discount is available. *3300 Lake Tahoe Blvd., South Lake Tahoe 96150, tel. 916/542–0330 or 800/ 877–1466. 100 rooms. Facilities: heated pool, 2-level spa, sauna, movies, laundry. AE, DC, MC, V.*

Tahoe Seasons Resort. Built among pine trees on the side of a mountain across from the Heavenly ski area, this resort has outfitted each room with a fireplace, spa, and minikitchen (sink, refrigerator, and microwave). Dark orange and green are the dominant colors in the contemporary decor; all beds are queen-size. *3901 Saddle Rd., South Lake Tahoe 95729, tel. 916/ 541–6700 or 541–6010. 160 rooms. Facilities: restaurant, lounge, room service, pool, whirlpool, tennis, paddleball, indoor parking, valet garage, free Lake Tahoe Airport and casino shuttle. AE, MC, V.*

Expensive
★

Best Western Station House Inn. This pleasant inn was completely remodeled in 1989, and has won design awards for its exterior and interior. The rooms are subtly decorated in mauve and are nicely appointed, with king- and queen-size beds and double vanity baths. The location is good, near a private beach and yet close to the casinos. American breakfast is complimentary October 1–May 31. A senior-citizen discount is available. *901 Park Ave., South Lake Tahoe 95729, tel. 916/542–1101 or 800/822–5953 in CA. 101 rooms. Facilities: restaurant, lounge, pool, hot tub. Shuttle service to casinos. AE, D, DC, MC, V.*

Moderate–Very Expensive
Lakeland Village Beach and Ski Resort. A town house-condominium complex located along 1,000 feet of private beach, Lakeland Village has a wide range of accommodations: studios, suites, and town houses, all with kitchens and fireplaces. *3535 Lake Tahoe Blvd., South Lake Tahoe 95705, tel. 916/541–7711 or 800/822–5969. 214 units with bath. Facilities: beach, boating and fishing pier, 2 pools, wading pool, spa, saunas, laundry. AE, MC, V.*

Moderate– Expensive
Best Western Lake Tahoe Inn. Located next to Harrah's Casino on U.S. 50, this large motel is nicely situated on 6 acres of grounds, with gardens and the Heavenly Ski Resort directly behind. Rooms are modern, decorated in pastel pinks, purple, and mauve. *Box II, South Lake Tahoe 95729, tel. 916/541–2010 or 800/528–1234. 400 rooms. Facilities: restaurants, lounge, 2 heated pools, hot tub, 1-day valet service. AE, DC, MC, V.*

Flamingo Lodge. This motel has completely refurbished rooms decorated in contemporary blues and tans, all with refrigerators and in-room fresh-ground coffee, and some with wet bars. The lodge's grounds are spacious. There is an adjacent coffee shop. *3961 Lake Tahoe Blvd., South Lake Tahoe 95729, tel. 916/544–5288. 90 rooms. Facilities: pool, steam room, sauna, hot tub, laundry. AE, D, DC, MC, V.*

Royal Valhalla Motor Lodge. On the lake at Lakeshore Boulevard and Stateline Avenue, this motel has simple modern rooms decorated in earth tones with queen-size beds. There is some covered parking. A senior-citizen discount is available. *Drawer GG, South Lake Tahoe 95729, tel. 916/544–2233. 80 rooms, 20 with kitchenettes. Facilities: pool, laundry. AE, DC, MC, V.*

Inexpensive– Moderate ★
Tahoe West Motor Lodge. A long-established motel that is proud of its repeat business, Tahoe West is 3 blocks from the beach and the downtown casinos. The exterior is rustic in appearance. The rooms are neatly furnished, and the beds are queen-size. Coffee and doughnuts are served in the lobby. *4107 Pine Blvd., South Lake Tahoe 95729, tel. 916/544–6455 or 800/522–1021. 59 rooms, 12 with kitchenettes. Facilities: pool, sauna, spa, private beach privileges. Shuttle service to casinos and ski areas. AE, DC, MC, V.*

South Shore Hotel/Casinos Very Expensive
Harrah's Tahoe Hotel/Casino. Harrah's is a luxurious 18-story hotel/casino on U.S. 50 in the casino area. All guest rooms have refrigerators, private bars, and two full bathrooms, each with a television and telephone. All rooms have views of the lake and the mountains, but the least-obstructed views are from rooms facing the back of the hotel. There is a supervised children's arcade. Harrah's has a four-star Mobil rating and a five-diamond rating from the American Automobile Association. Top-name entertainment is presented in the South Shore Room and Stateline Cabaret. There are more than 150 table games (blackjack, craps, baccarat, pai gow, keno, roulette, poker, big six, bingo), and 1,850 slot machines. Race and sports book are also available. Restaurants include The Summit (Continental), The

Forest (buffet), Cafe Andreotti (Italian bistro), Corner Deli (New York-style), Snack Bar, Friday's Station (steaks and seafood), Sierra Restaurant (24-hour breakfast, lunch, and dinner), Swensen's Ice Cream Parlor. *Box 8, Stateline, NV 89449, tel. 702/588–6606 or 800/648–3773. 534 rooms. Facilities: heated indoor pool, hot tubs, health club, valet garage, parking lot, 24-hour room and valet service, pet kennel. AE, DC, MC, V.*

Expensive–Very Expensive **Caesars Tahoe Resort.** This luxurious 16-story hotel/casino, built in 1980, is on U.S. 50 in the casino area. Each room has a view of Lake Tahoe or the encircling mountains and a massive bathtub "reminiscent of ancient Rome." There is top-name entertainment in the 1,600-seat Circus Maximus and the Cabaret. Games include dice, 21, roulette, big six, French roulette, baccarat, poker, sic bo, pai gow, and hundreds of slot machines. Race and sports book is also available. Restaurants include Empress Court (Chinese), Cafe Roma (24-hour meals), Le Posh (French-Californian, and Continental, with tableside service), Primavera (Italian), Broiler Room, and Yogurt Palace. *Box 5800, South Lake Tahoe, CA 89449, tel. 702/588–3515 or 800/648–3353 for reservations and show information. 440 rooms. Facilities: heated indoor pool, saunas, whirlpool, tennis (fee), health club (fee), movies, valet garage, parking lot. AE, DC, MC, V.*

Harvey's Resort Hotel/Casino. Today it's another luxurious mirrored 18-story hotel/casino on U.S. 50 in the casino area, but in the 1940s Harvey's was the original casino, part of a small service station at Lake Tahoe. Harvey's is the largest Tahoe resort, with well-appointed rooms, six restaurants, 10 cocktail lounges, and a complete health spa. Cabaret revues and contemporary bands perform in the Theatre Lounge. Games include blackjack, craps, roulette, baccarat, and many slot machines. Restaurants include Cafe Metro, Carriage House Restaurant, El Dorado Buffet, Sage Room Steak House, Top of the Wheel (Continental), El Vaquero (Mexican), and Seafood Grotto (seafood and Chinese). *Box 128, Stateline, NV 89449, tel. 702/588–2411 or 800/648–3361. 575 rooms. Facilities: tennis, valet parking, garage. AE, DC, MC, V.*

Lake Tahoe Horizon Casino Resort. Formerly called the High Sierra, this hotel is currently undergoing a $15 million renovation in a bid to attract upscale patrons. Rooms feature contemporary decor, and many have beautiful lake views. The casino decor follows a French Beaux Arts design, with bright molded wood and mirrors. Games include blackjack, craps, roulette, keno, mini baccarat, and many slot machines. The Grand Lake Theater showcases headliner entertainment. The Golden Cabaret features revues, magicians, and other nightclub entertainment. The Aspen Lounge presents solo entertainers. Restaurants include: Beaumont's (gourmet dining), Four Seasons (24-hour service), Gregory's (steak and seafood), Bistro (pastries, sandwiches, specialty coffees), and Le Grande Buffet. *Box C, Stateline, NV 89449, tel. 702/588–6211 or 800/322–7723 except in NV. 539 rooms. Facilities: pool, wading pool, 3 hot tubs. AE, DC, MC, V.*

Nightlife

Major nighttime entertainment is found at the casinos. The top venues are the **Circus Maximus** at Caesar's Tahoe and the **South**

Shore Room at Harrah's, each theater as large as many Broadway houses. Typical headliners are Jay Leno, Dionne Warwick, Willie Nelson, Kenny Rogers, and Johnny Mathis; their shows are more concerts than the extravaganzas of Las Vegas. The big showrooms also present performances from Broadway musicals, put on by touring Broadway companies or by casts created specifically for the casino's production.

Reservations are almost always required for superstar shows. Cocktail shows usually cost $19–$40, including Nevada's 16% sales and entertainment tax, depending on the act. Smaller casino cabarets sometimes have a cover charge or drink minimum. There are also lounges with no admission charge, featuring jazz and pop music soloists and groups. Even these performers don't try to compete all night with gambling; the last set usually ends at 2:30 or 3 AM.

Lounges around the lake may offer pop and country music singers and musicians, and in the winter the ski resorts do the same. Summer alternatives are outdoor music events, from chamber quartets to jazz bands and rock performers, at Sand Harbor and the Lake Tahoe Visitors Center amphitheater.

9 The Sierra National Parks

by Barbara Elizabeth Shannon and Pam Hegarty

Yosemite, Sequoia, and Kings Canyon National Parks are famous throughout the world for their unique sights and experiences. Yosemite, especially, should be on your "don't miss" list. Unfortunately, it's on everyone else's as well. In summer the park is very crowded—you should have advance reservations and at least several days to spend. We don't recommend any of these parks as day trips; save them for your next trip to California if you don't have time now. We also recommend that you make your plans far enough in advance so you can stay in the parks themselves, not in one of the "gateway cities" in the foothills or Central Valley. You'll probably be adjusting to a higher altitude and exercising a fair amount, so save your energy for exploring the park, not driving to and from it.

Yosemite National Park

Yosemite Valley is one of the most famous sights (or collection of sights) in California. The surrounding granite peaks and domes (El Capitan, Half Dome) rise more than 3,000 feet above the valley floor; two of the waterfalls that cascade over the valley's rim are among the world's 10 highest; and the Merced River, placid here, runs through the valley. Millions of people visit Yosemite every year. There is no arguing with the claim that especially in the summer, it's very crowded. Such extravagant praise has been written of this valley (by John Muir and others) and so many beautiful photographs taken (by Ansel Adams and others), that you may wonder if the reality can possibly measure up. For almost everyone, it does; Yosemite reminds them of what "breathtaking" and "marvelous" mean.

Yosemite Valley comprises only seven of the more than 1,000 square miles of national park here. The western boundary dips as low as 2,000 feet in the chaparral-covered foothills; the eastern boundary rises to 13,000 feet at points along the Sierra crest. Much of this country is accessible primarily to backpackers and horseback riders (and thus beyond the scope of this guide), but there are many sites to be explored by visitors who do not want to range too far from their cars. Although forest fires scorched the perimeter of the park in 1990, most of Yosemite, including the Valley, was unaffected by the blaze.

The falls are at their most spectacular in May and June. By the end of the summer, some may have dried up, or nearly so. They begin flowing again in late fall with the first storms. During the winter, they may be hung with ice. Yosemite Valley is open year round. The Vintners' Holidays in December and Chefs' Holidays in January entice "off-season" visitors with free seminars by well-known gourmets. Featured chefs present unique, although relatively pricey ($55–$65 per person), banquet dinners at the culmination of each session. Because the valley floor is only 4,000 feet high, snow does not stay long. It is possible to camp even in the winter (January highs are in the mid-40s, lows in the mid-20s). Tioga Pass Road is closed in winter (roughly from late October through May), so you can't see Tuolumne Meadows then. The road to Glacier Point beyond the turnoff for Badger Pass is also not cleared in winter.

Admission to the park is $5 per car for a week's stay; $2 per person if you don't arrive in a car. For $15, you can purchase a one-year pass to Yosemite. A Golden Eagle pass ($25) is good for a year at all national parks and monuments. The Golden Age

Passport, for seniors 62 and older, and the Golden Access Passport, for the blind and disabled, are free lifetime entrance passes for all national parks and monuments.

Getting Around

Because of the free shuttle bus that runs around Yosemite Valley (8 AM–11 PM in the summer, 10–10 the rest of the year), it is possible to visit the park without your own car. From 9–5 in the summer, another free shuttle runs from Wawona to Big Trees. Campers are not allowed on this road.

By Plane You can fly into one of the large California airports (San Francisco or Los Angeles) or one of the smaller Central Valley airports (Sacramento, Fresno) and then either rent a car or take public transportation to Yosemite.

By Bus **Yosemite Via** (tel. 209/722–0366) and **Yosemite Gray Line** (tel. 209/443–5240 or 800/640–6306 in California) run buses from Merced and Fresno, both on Highway 99, to Yosemite Valley. Both buses make connections with Greyhound and Amtrak.

By Car Yosemite is a four- to five-hour drive from San Francisco and a six-hour drive from Los Angeles. From the west, three highways come to Yosemite; all intersect with Highway 99, which runs north–south through the Central Valley. Highway 120 is the northernmost route—the one that travels farthest and slowest through the foothills. If you are exploring the Gold Country along Highway 49, you may want to come this way. The more traveled routes are Highway 140 from Merced and Highway 41 from Fresno. Highway 140 is the major route; Highway 41 provides the most dramatic first view of the valley, after you come out of the Wawona Tunnel.

If you are coming from the east, you could cross the Sierra from Lee Vining on Highway 120 (Tioga Pass). This route takes you over the Sierra crest, past Tuolumne Meadows, and down the west slope of the range. It's scenic but the mountain driving may be stressful for some, and it's only open in the summer. Carry chains at any time of the year; the eastern entrance to the park at Tioga Pass is at nearly 10,000 feet. (Road conditions, tel. 619/873–6366).

Guided Tours

California Parlor Car Tours (Cathedral Hill Hotel, 1101 Van Ness Ave., San Francisco 94109, tel. 415/474–7500 or 800/227–4250) offers several tours that include Yosemite (along with Monterey or Hearst Castle) and depart from either San Francisco or Los Angeles. Some tours are one-way. Lodging and some meals are included; you can choose to stay in either Yosemite Lodge or the Ahwahnee (there's a difference in price, of course). We recommend that you not consider any tour that leaves you less than one full day in the valley (and that is cutting it very short!).

Important Addresses and Numbers

General Information **National Park Service, Information Office** (Box 577, Yosemite National Park, CA 95389, tel. 209/372–0265; 209/372–0264 for a 24-hour recording) or **National Park Service, Fort Mason** (Bldg. 201, San Francisco, CA 94123, tel. 415/556–0560).

Reservations **Yosemite Area Road Conditions** (tel. 209/372–4605).

Camping and Recreation Information (tel. 209/372–4845).

Northern California Road Conditions (tel. 619/873–6366).

Yosemite Park and Curry Company (Central Reservations, 5410 E. Home, Fresno, CA 93727, tel. 209/252–4848).

Exploring

Numbers in the margin correspond with points of interest on the Yosemite National Park map.

Although there is certainly more to see in Yosemite National Park than the valley, this is the primary or only destination for many visitors, especially for those who won't be making backpack or pack-animal trips. Your first view of Yosemite Valley will vary, depending on the road you take. Because the valley is only 7 miles long and averages less than 1 mile wide, you can visit sites in whatever order you choose and return to your favorites at different times of the day.

At Yosemite Village, near the east end of the valley, you'll find the park headquarters, a restaurant, store, and gas station, the Ahwahnee Hotel, Yosemite Lodge, a medical clinic, and the visitors center. The **Visitors Center** is staffed by park rangers and provides information and wilderness permits (necessary for any overnight backpacking). There are exhibits on natural and human history as well as an adjacent Indian Cultural Museum, and a re-created Ahwahneechee village. *Tel. 209/372–0299. Open daily 9–5, with extended hours in summer.*

During the summer, a visitor center at Tuolumne Meadows and a Yosemite Association bookstore at Mariposa Grove are also open.

Yosemite Falls is the highest waterfall in North America and the fifth-highest in the world. The upper falls (1,430 feet), the middle cascades (675 feet), and the lower falls (320 feet) combine for a total of 2,425 feet and, when viewed from the valley, appear as one waterfall. From the parking lot there is a ⅕-mile trail to the base of the falls. (The Yosemite Falls Trail starts from Sunnyside Campground and is a strenuous 3½-mile climb that rises 2,700 feet.)

If you arrive in Yosemite via the Wawona Road, your first view of the valley (in John Muir's words "a revelation in landscape affairs that enriches one's life forever") will include **Bridalveil Fall,** a filmy fall of 620 feet that is often diverted as much as 20 feet one way or the other by the breeze. Indians called it Pohono ("puffing wind"). There is another very short (⅕-mile) trail from a parking lot on the Wawona Road to the base of the fall.

Across the valley, **Ribbon Fall** (1,612 feet) is the valley's highest single fall, but it also dries up first in the summer.

Vernal and Nevada falls are on the Merced River at the east end of the valley. **Vernal Fall** (317 feet) is bordered by fern-covered black rocks, and rainbows play in the spray at the base. **Nevada Fall** (594 feet) is the first major fall as the river comes out of the high country. Both falls can be viewed from Glacier Point or visited on foot from Happy Isles, east of Yosemite Village. The roads at this end of the valley are now closed to private cars,

Yosemite National Park

Cherry Lake

Lake Eleanor

Hetch Hetchy Reservoir ⑫

Evergreen Rd.

Mather

White Wolf

120

May Lake

Tioga Pass Rd.

Cascade Creek

Yosemite Creek

Happy Isles

Half Dome ⑧

120

Yosemite Falls ⑦ ② ① Visitors Center

El Capitan ④ Ribbon Fall

Big Oak Flat Rd.

Valley

⑨ Glacier Point

⑤ ⑥

Vernal Fall Nevada Fall

Yosemite ③ Bridalveil Fall

Glacier Point Rd.

El Portal

Merced River

140

Glacier

Badger Pass

Bridalveil Creek

Stanislaus National Forest

South Fork Merced River

41

Pioneer Yosemite History Center

⑩

South Fork Merced River

Wawona

Mariposa Grove of Big Trees

⑪

Mariposa

0   4 miles

0   6 km

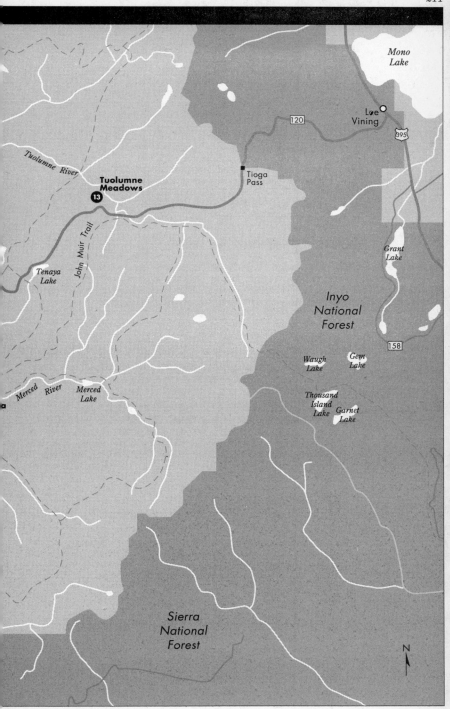

Mono Lake

Lee Vining

120

395

Tioga Pass

Tuolumne River

Tuolumne Meadows

13

John Muir Trail

Grant Lake

Tenaya Lake

Inyo National Forest

158

Waugh Lake

Gem Lake

Merced River

Merced Lake

Thousand Island Lake

Garnet Lake

Sierra National Forest

N

but a free shuttle bus runs frequently from the village. From May through September, the nature center with ecology exhibits at Happy Isles is open.

The hike on a paved trail from Happy Isles to the bridge at the base of Vernal Fall is only moderately strenuous and less than 1-mile long. It's another steep ¾-mile along the Mist Trail up to the top of the fall, and then another 2½ miles to the top of Nevada Falls. This is the beginning of the famous John Muir Trail, which leads south over 200 miles through the High Sierra to Mount Whitney.

Most famous among Yosemite's peaks are El Capitan and Half Dome. **El Capitan** is the largest exposed granite monolith in the world, almost twice the height of Gibraltar. It rises 3,593 feet above the valley, with an apparently vertical front thrust out from the valley's rim. **Half Dome** is the most distinctive rock in the region: 8,842 feet altitude, 4,733 feet above the valley floor. The west side of the dome is fractured vertically and cut away to form a 2,000-foot cliff.

Glacier Point offers what may be the most spectacular view of the valley and the High Sierra that you can get without hiking. The Glacier Point Road leaves Highway 41 about 23 miles southwest of the valley; it's then a 16-mile drive, with fine views into higher country. From the parking area, walk just a few hundred yards and you'll be able to see Nevada, Vernal, and Yosemite falls as well as Half Dome and other peaks. This road is closed beyond the turnoff for Badger Pass Ski Area in the winter.

At the **Pioneer Yosemite History Center** in Wawona (on Highway 41) are local historic buildings moved here from their original sites. A living history program in summer re-creates Yosemite's past.

Farther down the Wawona Road (36 miles from the valley) is the **Mariposa Grove of Big Trees.** This fine grove of *Sequoiadendron gigantea* can be visited on foot or on the one-hour tram rides ($5.25 adults, half-price children 12 and under, 10% discount for senior citizens) that run regularly during the summer (May–Oct. 9–6). The Grizzly Giant is the oldest tree here; its age is estimated to be 2,700 years; its base diameter is 30.7 feet, its circumference 96.5 feet, and its height 210 feet. The famous Wawona Tunnel Tree fell during the winter of 1968–69 (did anyone hear it?), but two other tunnel trees remain. A museum presents information on the big trees.

Hetch Hetchy Reservoir is about 40 miles from Yosemite Valley, via Big Oak Flat Road and Highway 120. The reservoir supplies water and power (some of which is sold at a profit) to San Francisco. Some say John Muir died of heartbreak when this beautiful valley was dammed and buried beneath 300 feet of water in 1913. Interior Secretary Donald Hodel made headlines in 1987 when he suggested that the lake might be drained and the valley restored to reduce some of the crowding in Yosemite. Not surprisingly, San Francisco politicians were irate and state environmentalists were intrigued.

The Tioga Pass Road (Highway 120) crosses the Sierra Nevada and meets U.S. 395 at Lee Vining. This scenic route (open only in summer) will take you past **Tuolumne Meadows,** the largest alpine meadow in the Sierra. There are campgrounds, a gas station, store, stables, lodge, and visitor center. This is the trailhead for many backpack trips into the High Sierra, but there are also shorter day hikes you can take. Remember, though, to give yourself time (a day or two, at least) to get acclimated to the altitude: 8,575 feet. From Yosemite Valley, it's 55 miles to Tuolumne Meadows and 74 miles to Lee Vining.

Off the Beaten Track

From early May to late October, Lee Stetson portrays noted naturalist John Muir, bringing to life Muir's wit, wisdom, and storytelling skill. Stetson's programs—"An Evening with a Tramp" and "Stickeen"—are two of the park's best-loved shows, now entering their ninth season. Locations and times are listed in the *Yosemite Guide*, the newspaper handed to you upon entering the park (and also found at the Visitors Center and at many local stores). Stetson, as John Muir, also leads free interpretive walks twice a week that meet at the Visitors Center (tel. 209/372–0299).

Sports

Bicycling If you want to bicycle around the valley, bikes can be rented at **Yosemite Lodge** or **Curry Village.**

Fishing You will have to buy a fishing license if you want to angle. State residents pay $22.60 for a year's license. Nonresidents must fork out $60.65; residents and nonresidents may purchase a one-day license for $8.15.

Hiking Hiking is the primary sport here. If you are hiking up any of the steep trails, remember to stay on the trail. Consider also the effect of the altitude on your endurance. If you plan to backpack overnight, you'll need a wilderness permit, available at visitor centers or ranger stations. At press time, there was no fee.

Rock Climbing **Yosemite Mountaineering** (tel. 209/372–1244 Sept.–May; 209/ 372–1335 June–Aug.) conducts beginner through intermediate rock climbing and backpacking classes. A one-day session includes a hands-on introduction to climbing. Classes are held April through September.

Skiing Cross-country and downhill skiing are available at **Badger Pass,** off the Glacier Point Road (tel. 209/372–1330). There is an outdoor skating rink at Curry Village.

Dining

With precious few exceptions, the best meals available in our National Parks are probably those cooked on portable grills at the various campgrounds. But, after all, one doesn't visit wilderness preserves expecting to find gourmet restaurants. Moreover, there is a snack bar in Yosemite Village, as well as coffee shops and a cafeteria at the Ahwahnee and Yosemite Lodge. Even so, if you are just there for a day, you will not want to waste precious time hunting about for food; instead, stop at a grocery store on the way in and fill up your hamper and ice chest with the makings of a picnic to enjoy under the umbrellas of giant fir trees. Price categories are based on the cost of a full dinner for one, excluding drinks, tax, and tip.

Highly recommended restaurants are indicated by a star ★.

Expensive
($15–$25)
★

Ahwahnee Hotel. With the huge sugar-pine log beams and supports, and the big roaring fireplace, you can imagine you're dining in a hunting lodge, built by one of the railroad or silver barons of the last century. Stick with what they would have eaten: steak, trout, prime rib, all competently prepared. Generations of Californians make a ritual of spending Christmas and New Year's here, so make reservations well in advance. *Yosemite Village, tel. 209/372–1489. Reservations advised. Jacket and tie required. AE, DC, MC, V.*

★ **Erna's Elderberry House.** As a special treat going to, or leaving, Yosemite, stop at this countryside gem, where the owner, Vienna-born Erna Kubin, offers bountiful Continental-California cuisine, along with dishes from the most recent country she's visited. Prix fixe, six-course dinners change nightly. *48688 Victoria La., Oakhurst, tel. 209/683–6800. Jacket advised. Reservations advised. MC, V. Sun. brunch. Closed lunch Sat.–Tues. Closed dinner Mon. and Tues.*

Moderate
($10–$20)

Mountain Room Broiler. The food becomes secondary when you see the spectacular Yosemite Falls through the dining room's window-wall. Best bets are steaks, chops, roast duck, and a fresh herb-basted roast chicken. *Yosemite Village, tel. 209/372–1281. Reservations advised. Dress: casual. AE, DC, MC, V. Dinner only.*

Inexpensive
($5–$15)

Four Seasons Restaurant. An upscale, rustic setting with high-finish natural wood tables, lots of greenery and local flora. The breakfast is hearty and all-American; dinner offerings cover the beef, chicken, and fish spectrum, plus vegetarian fare. *Yosemite Lodge, Yosemite Village, tel. 209/372–1269. Reservations advised. Dress: casual. AE, DC, MC, V. Closed for lunch.*

Lodging

If you aren't into camping, there is still a wide range of accommodation choices in Yosemite, from rustic tent cabins to the rustic luxury of the Ahwahnee Hotel. Most rooms are in the valley, but there are also tent cabins at Tuolumne Meadows and White Wolf (on Tioga Pass Road). White Wolf also has a few cabins with private baths (no electricity). Reservations should be made well in advance, especially for summer travel. At other times, you can always call and try; you might get a room for the next week.

All reservations are made through the **Yosemite Park & Curry Company** (Central Reservations, 5410 E. Home, Fresno, CA 93727, tel. 209/252–4848). Price categories are based on the cost of a room for two people.

Very Expensive
($170–$190)

Ahwahnee Hotel. This grand 1920s-style mountain lodge is constructed of rocks and sugar-pine logs, with exposed timbers and spectacular views. The Grand Lounge and Solarium are decorated in a style that is a tribute to the local Miwok and Paiute Indians. The decor in the rooms continues that motif; modern facilities include TVs. The Ahwahnee was renovated for the park's 1990 centennial. *123 rooms. Facilities: restaurant, lounge, pool, tennis. AE, DC, MC, V.*

Moderate
($22–$85)

Yosemite Lodge. The lodge has various rooms, from fairly rustic motel-style rooms with two double beds, decorated in rust and green, to very rustic cabins with no baths—all within walking distance of Yosemite Falls. *495 rooms. Facilities: restaurant, lounge, pool. AE, DC, MC, V.*

Moderate
($35)

Housekeeping Camp. These are also rustic tent cabins, set along the Merced River, but you can cook here on gas stoves rented from the front desk. These cabins are usually rented for several weeks at a time and are difficult to get; reserving at least a year in advance is advised. *282 tent cabins with no bath (maximum 4 per cabin). Toilet and shower facilities in central shower house. AE, DC, MC, V.*

Inexpensive–
Moderate
($20–$68)

Curry Village. These are plain accommodations: cabins with bath and without, tent cabins with rough wood frames and canvas walls and roofs. It's a step up from camping (linens and blankets are provided), but food or cooking are not allowed because of the animals. If you stay in a cabin without bath, the showers and toilets are centrally located, as they would be in a campground. *180 cabins, 426 tent cabins, 8 hotel rooms. Facilities: cafeteria, pool, rafting (fee), skating (fee), horseback riding (fee). AE, DC, MC, V.*

Camping

Reservations for camping are required year-round in Yosemite Valley and from spring through fall outside the valley. They are strongly recommended at any time. Reservations for all campgrounds in Yosemite are made through **Ticketron,** in person or by writing to them (Box 617516, Chicago, IL 60661–7516, tel. 800/452–1111 or 312/902–1919 for international callers). Ticketron charges a $4 handling charge for each telephone transaction, but does not charge for mail transactions. You can reserve campsites no sooner than eight weeks in advance, and should indicate the name of the park, the campground, and your first, second, and third choice of arrival dates. Campsites cost $12 per night. If space is available, you can also make reservations in person at the Campground Reservations Office in Yosemite Valley, but we strongly recommend making them ahead of time.

Sequoia and Kings Canyon National Parks

The other two Sierra national parks are usually spoken of together. The adjacent parks share their administration and their main highway. Although you may want to concentrate on either Kings Canyon or Sequoia, most people visit both parks in one trip.

Like Yosemite, Sequoia and General Grant national parks were established in 1890. The General Grant National Park, with the addition over the years of the Redwood Canyon area and the drainages of the South and Middle Forks of the Kings River, became Kings Canyon National Park. Both Sequoia and Kings Canyon now extend east to the Sierra crest. The most recent major addition was to Sequoia in 1978, to prevent the development of the Mineral King area for winter sports.

The major attractions of both parks are the big trees (*Sequoiadendron gigantea*—the most extensive groves and the most impressive specimens are found here) and the spectacular alpine scenery. These trees are the largest living things in the world. They are not as tall as the coast redwoods (*Sequoia semper-virens*), but they are much more massive and older. The exhibits at the visitors centers and the interpretive booklets that you can carry on many of the trails will explain the special relationship between these trees and fire (their thick, squishy bark protects them from fire and insects) and how they live so long and grow so big.

The parks encompass land from only 1,200 feet high to more than 14,000 feet. Mount Whitney, on the eastern side of Sequoia, is the highest mountain (14,495 feet) in the contiguous United States. The greatest portion of both parks is accessible only by foot or pack animal. The Generals Highway (46 miles from Highway 180 in Kings Canyon National Park to the Ash Mountain Entrance in Sequoia National Park) links the major groves in the two parks and is open year round.

Summer is the most crowded season, but even then it is much less crowded than at Yosemite. Fall is an especially good time to visit. The rivers will not be as full, but the weather is usually warm and calm and there are no crowds. Snow may remain on the ground in the sequoia groves into June, but is usually gone by mid-month. The flowers in the Giant Forest meadows hit their peak in July.

The entrance fee is $5 per car for a week's stay in both parks. A Golden Eagle pass ($25) will get you into all national parks and monuments for a year.

Getting Around

By Car   From the south, enter Sequoia National Park via Highway 198 from Visalia; from the north, enter Kings Canyon National Park via Highway 180 from Fresno. Both highways intersect with Highway 99, which runs north–south through the Central Valley. If you are driving up from Los Angeles, take Highway 65 north from Bakersfield to Highway 198 east of Visalia.

Highways 198 and 180 are connected through the parks by the Generals Highway, a paved two-lane road that is open year round but may be closed temporarily during heavy snowstorms (carry chains in winter). Drivers of RVs and drivers who are not comfortable with mountain driving should probably avoid the southern stretch between the Ash Mountain Entrance and Giant Forest. These 16 miles of narrow road rise almost 5,000 feet and are very twisty, but with care and without undue haste, this is a spectacular drive. Few roads up the west slope of the Sierra rise so quickly through the foothills and offer such spectacular views up into the high country. The rest of the Generals Highway is a well-graded, wide two-lane road and a pleasure to drive.

Highway 180 beyond Grant Grove to Cedar Grove and the road to Mineral King are open only in summer. Both roads, especially the latter, which is unpaved in sections, may present a challenge to inexperienced drivers. Do not expect to drive quickly, especially into Mineral King. Campers more than 30 feet long are not allowed on the Mineral King road. Trailers are not allowed in Mineral King campgrounds.

Guided Tours

For those who must see but not necessarily savor, **KOA Tours** leads one-day trips in vans from Visalia (in the Central Valley) to Giant Forest and Grant Grove. They visit Crescent Meadows, Tharp's Log, and Moro Rock and have lunch at the cafeteria at Giant Forest Village before heading on to the General Sherman Tree and Grant Grove. The tours leave at 8 AM and return at 5:30–6 PM. That's a lot of driving and a lot to see in one day, so we recommend these tours only for those who want to see the largest living things, but can't spend more than a day in the mountains. They also offer tours from Fresno for six or more people. *Tel. 209/651–0100 or 800/322–2336 in AZ, CA, OR, NV, and WA. Tours daily May–Oct., when weather permits during the rest of the year. Fare: $24.95 adults, $19.95 children 3–17.*

Within the park, you can take van tours with Sequoia Guest Services (tel. 209/561–3314) of Giant Forest ($7.95 adults, $6.95 senior citizens, $3.95 children under 12) or of King's Canyon ($19.95 adults, $16.95 senior citizens, $9.95 children). Sign up for either tour at the Giant Forest Lodge.

Important Addresses and Numbers

General Information: *Sequoia and Kings Canyon National Parks* (Three Rivers, CA 93271, tel. 209/565–3456, daily 8–4:30 or 209/565–3351, recording) or *National Park Service*, Fort Mason (Bldg. 201, San Francisco, CA 94123, tel. 415/556–0560).

Reservations: *Sequoia Guest Services* (Box 789, Three Rivers, CA 93271, tel. 209/561–3314 for both parks).

Exploring

Numbers in the margin correspond with points of interest on the Sequoia and Kings Canyon National Parks map.

If you take Highway 180 to the parks, you enter Kings Canyon National Park at the Big Stump Entrance, just southwest of Wilsonia (a private community) and **Grant Grove.** This was the grove (or what remained of a larger grove decimated by logging) that was protected as General Grant National Park in 1890. It is now the most highly developed area of Kings Canyon National Park. A walk along the 1-mile Big Stump Trail, starting near the park entrance, will demonstrate the effects of heavy logging on these groves.

At Grant Grove Village, you will find a visitor center, gas station, grocery store, campground, coffee shop, and lodging. The visitor center has exhibits on the natural (and human) history of *Sequoiadendron gigantea* and the area. Books and maps describing the region are available. Detailed maps of the trails at this and the other major areas of the two parks are available for $1 each at all the visitor centers.

A spur road leads west less than 1 mile to the General Grant Grove. A short, easy ⅓-mile trail leads through the grove and is accessible to disabled travelers. The most famous tree here is the General Grant, the nation's Christmas tree. In total mass it is not as large as the General Sherman Tree in Sequoia, but it is

Sequoia and Kings Canyon National Parks

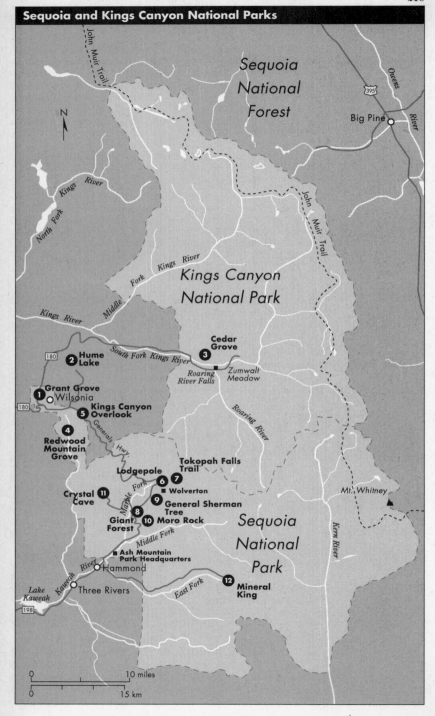

Sequoia
National
Forest

395

Owens River

Big Pine

N

John Muir Trail

North Fork Kings River

Kings River

Middle Fork Kings River

Kings Canyon
National Park

John Muir Trail

South Fork Kings River

Cedar
Grove

3

Roaring
River Falls

Zumwalt
Meadow

2 Hume
Lake

180

1 Grant Grove

Wilsonia

180

5 Kings Canyon
Overlook

Roaring River

4 Redwood
Mountain
Grove

Generals Hwy.

Tokopah Falls
Trail

Lodgepole

6 **7**

Wolverton

9 General Sherman
Tree

Mt. Whitney

Crystal
Cave **11**

Marble Fork

8

10 Moro Rock

Giant
Forest

Sequoia

Middle Fork

National

Ash Mountain
Park Headquarters

Hammond

Park

Kaweah River

Three Rivers

East Fork

12 Mineral
King

Kern River

Lake
Kaweah

198

0   10 miles

0   15 km

nearly as tall and just as wide at its base. The Gamlin Cabin is one of several pioneer cabins that can be visited in the parks. A large sequoia was cut for display at the 1876 Philadelphia Exhibition; the Centennial Stump still remains.

❷ Actually in Sequoia National Forest, **Hume Lake** is a reservoir built early this century by loggers; today it is the site of many Christian camps. There is also a public campground. This is a pretty, small lake with distant views of high mountains. If it's hot and you're desperate for a place to swim, you might want to make this side trip. It's accessible by side roads off the Generals Highway east of—or off Highway 180 north of—Grant Grove. There are fine views of Kings Canyon from either road, but the route from the Generals Highway is easier to drive.

Beyond the turnoff for Hume Lake, Highway 180 (Kings River Highway) is closed in winter (usually November–April). In the
❸ summer, you can take this for a spectacular drive to the **Cedar Grove** area, a valley along the South Fork of the Kings River. It's a one-hour drive from Grant Grove to the end of the road where you turn around for the ride back. Although it is steep in places, this is not a difficult road. Built by convict labor in the 1930s, the road clings to some dramatic cliffs along the way, and you should watch out for falling rocks. The highway passes the scars where large groves of big trees were logged at the beginning of the century, and it runs through dry foothills covered with yuccas that bloom in the summer and along the South Fork itself. There are amazing views down into what may be the deepest gorge on the continent, at the confluence of the two forks, and up the canyons to the High Sierra.

Cedar Grove, named for the incense cedars that grow there, has campgrounds and lodging, a small ranger station, snack bar, convenience market, and gas station. Horses are available and a good way to explore this country. There are also short trails (one around Zumwalt Meadow, one to the base of Roaring River Falls), and this is the trailhead for many backpackers. This is a lovely day trip if you are staying at Grant Grove or Giant Forest; pack a picnic lunch if you can.

The **Generals Highway** begins south of Grant Grove and runs through this smaller portion of Kings Canyon National Park, through a part of Sequoia National Forest, and then through Sequoia National Park to the Giant Forest and on to the southern entrance to these parks at Ash Mountain.

❹ The **Redwood Mountain Grove** is the largest grove of big trees in the world. There are several paved turnouts (about 4 miles from the beginning of the highway) from which you can look out over the grove (and into the smog of the Central Valley), but the grove is only accessible on foot or horseback. Less than 2 miles
❺ farther, on the north side of the road, a large turnout (**Kings Canyon Overlook**) offers spectacular views into the larger portion of Kings Canyon National Park (the backcountry). You can look into the deep canyons of the South and Middle Forks of the Kings River. If you drive east on Highway 180 to Cedar Grove along the South Fork, you will see these canyons at much closer range.

❻ **Lodgepole,** in a U-shape canyon on the Marble Fork of the Kaweah River, is a developed area with campground, snack bars, grocery store, gas station, and a market complex including a deli, grocery store, gift shop, ice-cream parlor, public showers, public laundry, and post office. The visitor center here has the best exhibits in the parks and a small theater for showing films about the park. The Lodgepole Nature Center is geared toward children. The trees here are lodgepole pines, not sequoia, because the canyon conducts cold air down from the high country.

A very short marked nature trail leads from behind the visitor center down to the river. Except when the river is flowing fast (be very cautious), this is a good place to rinse one's feet in cool water, because the trail runs past a "beach" of small rocks along the river.

❼ The **Tokopah Falls Trail** is a more strenuous, 2-mile hike up the river from the campground (pick up a map at the visitor center), but it is also the closest you can get to the high country without taking a long hike. This is a lovely hike, but remember insect repellent during the summer, when mosquitoes can be ferocious.

❽ Four miles beyond Lodgepole you will come to the **Giant Forest.** This is still the most developed area of the parks, with the greatest concentration of accommodations, although plans call for moving these to the Clover Creek area. In the meantime, this is a magical place to stay because of the concentration of varied trails through a series of sequoia groves. There are a grocery store, cafeteria, and two gift shops at Giant Forest Village and a wide range of accommodations at Giant Forest Lodge. The Lodge also runs a full-service dining room and a gift shop during the summer.

Whether you are staying here or elsewhere in the parks, get the map of the local trails and start exploring. The wellconstructed trails range in length from 1–5 miles. They are not paved, crowded, or lined with barricades, so you quickly get the feeling of being on your own in the woods, surrounded by the most impressive trees you are ever likely to see.

Be sure to visit one of the meadows. They are lovely (especially so in July when the flowers are in full bloom), and you can get some of the best views of the big trees across them. Round Meadow, behind Giant Forest Lodge, is the most easily accessible, with a new ¼-mile, wheelchair-accessible "Trail For All People." Crescent and Log meadows are accessible by slightly longer trails. Tharp's Log, at Log Meadow, is a very small and rustic pioneer cabin built in a fallen sequoia. There is also a log cabin at Huckleberry Meadow that children will enjoy exploring.

❾ The most famous tree here is the **General Sherman Tree.** If you aren't up for hiking at all, you can still get to this tree. There is usually a ranger nearby to answer questions, and there are benches so you can sit and contemplate the largest living thing in the world. The tree is 274.9 feet tall and 102.6 feet around at its base, but what makes this the biggest tree is the fact that it is so wide for such a long way up: The first major branch is 130 feet up.

The Congress Trail starts here and travels past a series of large trees and younger sequoias. This is probably the most popular trail in the area, and it also has the most detailed booklet, so it is a good way to learn about the ecology of the groves. You can pick up the booklet from a machine (it takes quarters) near the General Sherman Tree.

A 2½-mile spur road takes off from the Generals Highway near the village and will lead you to other points of interest in the Giant Forest area as well as to the trails to Crescent and Log meadows. The road actually goes through the Tunnel Log (there is a bypass for RVs that are too tall to fit). Auto Tree is merely a fallen tree onto which you can drive your car for a photograph (if that seems like a reasonable idea to you).

⑩ This is also the road to **Moro Rock,** a granite monolith 6,725 feet high, which rises from the edge of the Giant Forest. During the depression, the Conservation Corps built a fabulous trail up to the top. There are 400 steps and, although there is usually a railing, the trail often climbs along narrow ledges over steep drops. If the haul to the top doesn't daunt you, the view is spectacular. Southwest you look down the Kaweah River to Three Rivers, Lake Kaweah, and—on clear days—the Central Valley. Northeast you look up into the High Sierra. Below, you look down thousands of feet to the Middle Fork of the Kaweah River.

⑪ **Crystal Cave** is the only of Sequoia's many caves that is open to the public, and then only on guided tours of the stalagmites and stalactites. You'll have a ½-mile hike from the parking lot down to the cave. Bring a sweater, because the temperature is only 50 degrees. *9 mi southeast of Giant Forest on spur road of Generals Hwy. Admission: $3 adults, $1.50 children 6–11 and senior citizens. Open daily June–Aug.; Fri.–Mon. May–Sept. Tours 10–3.*

⑫ The **Mineral King** area is a recent addition to the parks. In the 1960s the U.S. Forest Service planned to have Walt Disney Productions develop a winter sports resort here, but the opposition of conservation groups led to its incorporation in Sequoia National Park in 1978. It is accessible in summer only by a narrow, twisty, and steep road that takes off from Highway 198 at Hammond. The road is only 25 miles long, but budget 90 minutes each way from Highway 198. This is a tough but exciting road to a beautiful high valley. There are campgrounds and a ranger station; facilities are limited but some supplies are available. Many backpackers use this as a trailhead, and there are a number of fine trails for strenuous day hikes.

Off the Beaten Track

Montecito-Sequoia (tel. 800/227–9900) off the Generals Highway between the two parks, offers year-round family-oriented recreation. In winter, there are 21 miles (35 kilometers) of groomed cross-country ski trails, 50 miles (84 kilometers) of backcountry trails, ski rentals, and lessons. In summer, they offer canoeing, sailing, waterskiing, horseback riding, tennis, archery, nature hikes, and a heated pool. For those who want an overnight package, there are 36 lodge rooms with private bath that hold two to six persons ($80–$90 per person, including meals and lodging). Those who do not want to stay overnight can pay for the individual activities (though package guests have priority with the facilities).

Sports

Fishing Fishing licenses are required for all anglers. State residents pay $22.60 for a year's license, nonresidents are charged $60.65. Residents and nonresidents may purchase a one-day license for $8.15.

Hiking As in Yosemite, hiking is the primary sport. Talk to the rangers at the visitor centers about which trails they recommend when you are there. Keep in mind that you will have to become acclimated to the altitude (over 6,000 feet at Giant Forest) before you can exert yourself fully.

Horseback Riding Horseback riding is available at **Grant Grove, Cedar Grove, Wolverton Pack Station** (between Lodgepole and Giant Forest), and **Mineral King.** Ask at the visitor centers for specifics.

Swimming If you get hot and need a swim, try **Hume Lake** (*see* Exploring, above). Don't try to swim in the fast-running Sierra rivers.

Winter Sports In the winter, you can ski or snowshoe. There is cross-country skiing at Grant Grove and Giant Forest. Rentals and tours are offered by **Sequoia Ski Touring Center** (209/565–3435) at Wolverton and Grant Grove.

Rangers lead snowshoe walks through Grant Grove and Giant Forest on winter weekends. You can also use the shoes on the cross-country trails at these two areas. Snowshoes can be rented from Sequoia Ski Touring at Wolverton.

Dining

Dining in Sequoia and Kings Canyon national parks is even less of a gourmet experience than in Yosemite, but acceptable food is available. Again, we suggest that you bring food (especially snacks, fresh fruit, and beverages) with you. It will give you more freedom in planning your day. There are casual places to eat at Giant Forest Village, Lodgepole, Grant Grove, and Cedar Grove. The food is not expensive and will satisfy hunger pangs. There is a restaurant at Giant Forest Lodge where you can get a more formal dinner; there is a nice salad bar and good if not inspired American food. Dinner costs $15–$20 per person.

Food should not be left overnight in cars, because bears might be tempted to break in.

Lodging

There is a range of accommodations available in the parks, but you will not find any luxurious rooms. There are hotel/motel-type accommodations at Giant Forest, Stoney Creek (on the Generals Highway), and Cedar Grove. The rooms have one or two double beds and showers but are minimally furnished. They are clean and functional. Rooms cost up to $90 a night for two.

At Giant Forest, there are cabins with private baths, showers, and electricity ($56–$82) and more rustic one- or two-room cabins with baths. At Giant Forest and Grant Grove there are extremely rustic tent-cabins, with rough wood walls, canvas roofs, and wood-burning stoves. Linen, blankets, firewood, and oil lamps are provided. There are centrally located rest rooms and showers. You can cook at these cabins; some have wood-burning cookstoves on their patios. Be sure not to leave any food outside for the animals. Cabin rates are about $35 a night for two.

All reservations should be made through **Sequoia Guest Services** (Box 789, Three Rivers, CA 93271, tel. 209/561–3314). For summer visits, make reservations well in advance. Reservations are recommended for visits at any time of the year because it's a long way out if there's no room at the inn.

Camping

Reservations are accepted only at Lodgepole Campground and only for stays between Memorial Day and Labor Day. Make reservations through **Ticketron,** in person at one of their locations or by writing (Box 617516, Chicago, IL 60661–7516, tel. 800/452–1111 or 312/902–1919 for international callers). Ticketron charges a $4 handling charge for each telephone transaction, but does not charge for mail transactions. You can reserve campsites up to eight weeks in advance, and should indicate the name of the park, the campground, and your first, second, and third choice of arrival dates. Fees vary. Some campgrounds in Sequoia National Forest (such as Landslide, a very small campground 3 miles from Hume Lake) are just about as convenient as those in the two national parks.

10 The Monterey Peninsula

by Maria Lenhart

A native of the Monterey area, Maria Lenhart lives in San Francisco and writes for magazines and newspapers, including Travel Holiday, Travel & Leisure, *and the* Christian Science Monitor.

"The interest is perpetually fresh. On no other coast that I know shall you enjoy, in calm, sunny weather, such a spectacle of ocean's greatness, such beauty of changing color or such degrees of thunder in the sound." What Robert Louis Stevenson wrote of the Monterey Peninsula in 1879 is no less true today—it still provides a spectacle that is as exciting on the first visit as on the twenty-third.

Located almost at the exact center of the California coast, the Monterey Peninsula has been blessed by nature in a number of unique ways. Here are deep green forests of Monterey cypress, oddly gnarled and wind-twisted trees that grow nowhere else. Here also is a vast undersea canyon, larger and deeper than the Grand Canyon, that supports a rich assortment of marine life from fat barking sea lions to tiny plantlike anemones.

The peninsula holds a unique place in California history that is evident in its carefully preserved adobe houses and missions. With the arrival of Father Junípero Serra and Commander Don Gaspar de Portola from Spain in 1770, Monterey became both the military and ecclesiastical capital of Alta California. Portola established the first of California's four Spanish presidios, while Serra founded the second of 21 Franciscan missions, later moving it from Monterey to its current site in Carmel.

When Mexico revolted from Spain in 1822, Monterey remained the capital of California under Mexican rule. The town grew into a lively seaport, drawing Yankee sea traders who added their own cultural and political influence. Then, on July 7, 1846, Commodore John Sloat arrived in Monterey and raised the American flag over the Custom House, claiming California for the United States.

Monterey's political importance in the new territory was short-lived, however. Although the state constitution was framed in Colton Hall, the town was all but forgotten in the excitement caused by the discovery of gold at Sutter's Mill near Sacramento. After the gold rush, the state capital moved from Monterey and the town became a sleepy backwater.

At the turn of the century, however, the Monterey Peninsula began to draw tourists with the opening of the Del Monte Hotel, the most palatial resort the West Coast had ever seen. Writers and artists also discovered the peninsula, adding a rich legacy that remains to this day.

For visitors, the decline of Monterey as California's most important political and population center can be seen as a blessing. The layers of Spanish and Mexican history remain remarkably undisturbed, while the land and sea continue to inspire and delight.

Getting Around

By Plane Monterey Peninsula Airport (tel. 408/373–3731) is 3 miles from downtown Monterey and is served by **American Eagle** (tel. 800/433–7300), **Sky West/Delta** (tel. 800/453–9417), **United Airlines** and **United Express** (tel. 800/241–6522) with daily service from San Francisco and Los Angeles. **USAir** (tel. 800/428–4322) has daily service from Los Angeles and San Francisco.

By Car Heading south from San Francisco, the drive can be made comfortably in three hours or less. The most scenic way is to follow

Highway 1 down the coast, an enjoyable ride past pumpkin and artichoke fields and the beachside communities of Half Moon Bay and Santa Cruz. Unless the drive is made on sunny weekends when locals are heading for the beach, the two-lane coast highway takes no longer than the freeway routes.

Of the freeway routes available from San Francisco, the most enjoyable is to follow I-280 south and connect with Highway 17 just south of San Jose. Taking Highway 17 south over the redwood-forested Santa Cruz mountains, the route connects with Highway 1 in Santa Cruz. The other standard route is to follow U.S. 101 in San Jose) to Highway 156 near Salinas and head east to Monterey. Traffic in San Jose can be horrendous; avoid rush hours, which start early.

From Los Angeles, the drive to Monterey can be made in less than a day by heading north on U.S. 101 to Salinas and then heading west on Highway 68. The spectacular but slow alternative is to take U.S. 101 to San Luis Obispo and then follow the hairpin turns of Highway 1 up the coast. Allow at least three extra hours if you do.

The Rider's Guide (Suite 255, 484 Lake Park Ave., Oakland 94610, tel. 415/653–2553) produces a tape you can play in your car about the history, landmarks, and attractions of the Monterey peninsula and Big Sur, for $11.95 plus $2 postage.

By Train   The closest train connection to the Monterey Peninsula is Amtrak's *Coast Starlight*, which makes a stop in Salinas during its run between Los Angeles and Seattle (tel. 800/USA–RAIL).

By Bus   From San Francisco, **Greyhound-Trailways** (tel. 415/558–6789) serves Monterey five times daily on a trip that takes up to four hours.

For getting around on the peninsula by bus, **Monterey-Salinas Transit** (tel. 408/424–7695) provides frequent service between towns and many major sightseeing spots and shopping areas for a modest fare.

Scenic Drives

17-Mile Drive   Although some sightseers balk at the $6 per car entrance fee to enter this enchanted forest, it is well worth the price to explore this 8,400-acre microcosm of the Monterey coastal landscape. The main entrance gates to the 17-Mile Drive can be found off Lighthouse Avenue in Pacific Grove and off Highway 1 and North San Antonio Avenue in Carmel.

Once inside, the drive presents a primordial nature preserve existing in quiet harmony with palatial estates. Among the natural treasures are many prime examples of the rare Monterey cypresses, trees so gnarled and twisted that Robert Louis Stevenson once described them as "ghosts fleeing before the wind." The most photographed of them all is the **Lone Cypress,** a weather-sculpted tree growing out of a rocky outcropping above the waves. A turn-out parking area makes it possible to stop for a view of the Lone Cypress, but walking out to it on the precipitous outcropping is no longer allowed. Two other natural landmarks to note are **Seal Rock** and **Bird Rock,** two islands of bird and marine life teeming with harbor seals, sea lions, cormorants, and pelicans.

As enticing as the natural scenes are along the drive, those created by man are part of the attraction as well. Perhaps no more famous concentration of celebrated golf courses exists anywhere in the world, particularly the **Pebble Beach Golf Links,** with its famous 18th hole, around which the ocean plays a major role. Even if you're not a golfer, views of impeccable greens can be enjoyed over a drink or lunch at the **Lodge at Pebble Beach** or the **Inn at Spanish Bay,** the two resorts located along the drive.

Among the stately homes, many of which reflect the classic Monterey or Spanish-Mission style that is typical of the region, the most impressive is the **Crocker Marble Palace,** a waterfront estate designed after a Byzantine castle, located not far from the Carmel entrance to the drive. The baroque-style mansion is identifiable by dozens of marble arches, and the grounds even feature a beach area with water heated by underground pipes.

Carmel Valley Road A world away from the cypress forests and tide pools of the coast are the pastoral ranchlands of Carmel Valley. The rolling meadows studded with oak trees are especially compelling during the spring, when the grass is lush, green, and blooming with bright gold California poppies and blue lupines.

Carmel Valley Road, which turns inland at Highway 1 just south of Carmel, is the main thoroughfare through this secluded enclave of horse ranchers and other well-heeled residents who prefer the valley's perpetually dry, sunny climate to the fog and wind on the coast. A pleasant two hours or so can be spent ambling up the road and back, perhaps in combination with a hike or picnic at **Garland Ranch Regional Park,** or poking around the crafts shops and art galleries in tiny Carmel Valley village.

Another popular stop along the road is the tasting room at the beautiful small **Château Julien** winery, known for its chardonnay and merlot. Personal tours of the winery can be arranged by calling ahead. *Tel. 408/624–2600. Open weekdays 8:30–5, weekends 11–5.*

An enjoyable loop drive can be made by turning off Carmel Valley Road onto **Los Laureles Grade,** a 6-mile winding road that heads over the mountains to Highway 68, ending at a point about halfway between Monterey and Salinas. Located along Highway 68 is the award-winning **Ventana Vineyards,** which has a tasting room. *Tel. 408/372–7415. Open daily noon–5.*

Guided Tours

Seacoast Safaris (tel. 408/372–1288) offers both custom tours and half-day tours of the Monterey Peninsula, which include the 17-Mile Drive, Carmel shopping, Cannery Row, and wine-tasting. Rates include minivan transportation and sightseeing with guides who are longtime area residents.

Steinbeck Country Tours (tel. 408/625–5107) offers a variety of excursions for individuals and group charters, including Scenic Highlights and Wineries of Monterey County tours. Rates include transportation and guide service.

Motorcoach tours departing from San Francisco that feature the Monterey Peninsula in their Northern California itineraries include **California Parlor Car Tours** (tel. 415/474–7500 or 800/227–4250) and **Gray Line** (tel. 415/558–9400).

PACIFIC OCEAN

N

Monterey
Bay

Pacific Grove

Ocean View Blvd. Lighthouse Ave.

Sunset Dr.

Seventeen Mile Dr.

68

Carmel-Pacific Grove Hwy.

Del Monte Blvd.

MONTEREY

Sand City
Seaside

Monterey
Peninsula
Airport

Del Rey Oaks

Pebble
Beach

1

Jacks Peak
Regional Park

Monterey -

Carmel Valley Rd.

CARMEL

Cabrillo Hwy.

Carmel River

G16

Point Lobos
Reserve
State Park

Cabrillo Hwy.

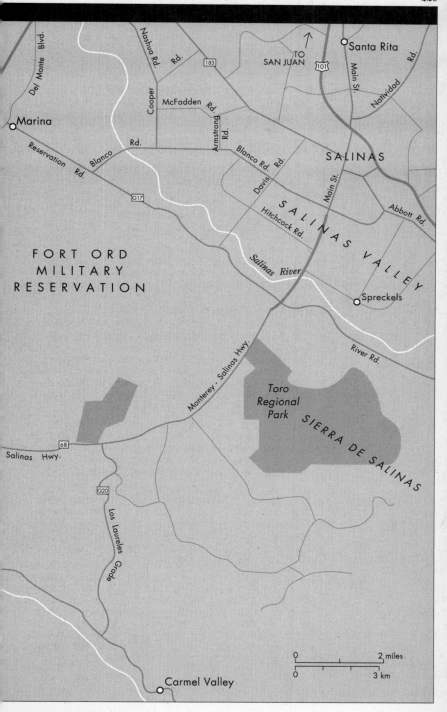

Important Addresses and Numbers

Tourist **The Monterey Peninsula Chamber of Commerce** (Box 1770, 380
Information Alvarado St., Monterey 93942, tel. 408/649–1770) and **The Salinas Chamber of Commerce** (119 E. Alisal St., Salinas 93901, tel. 408/424–7611) are both open weekdays 8:30–5.

Emergencies Dial 911 for **police** and **ambulance** in an emergency.

Doctor The **Monterey County Medical Society** (tel. 408/373–4197) will refer doctors on weekdays, 9–5. For referrals at other times, call **Community Hospital of Monterey Peninsula** (23625 Holman Hwy., Monterey, tel. 408/624–5311). The hospital has a 24-hour emergency room.

Pharmacies There are no all-night pharmacies, but for emergencies there is the Pharmacy Department at the Community Hospital of Monterey Peninsula (*see* above). **Surf 'n' Sand** in Carmel at Sixth and Junipero (tel. 408/624–1543) has a pharmacy open weekdays 9–6:30, Saturday, Sunday and holidays 9–2.

Exploring

Despite its compact size, the Monterey Peninsula is packed with many diversions, and it requires longer than a weekend to do more than skim the surface. Although most communities are situated only a few minutes' drive away from each other, each is remarkably different in flavor and in attractions.

For those with a strong interest in California history and historic preservation, the place on which to concentrate is Monterey, where you need at least two full days to explore the adobe buildings along the Path of History, a state historic park encompassing much of the downtown area. Fans of Victorian architecture will want to allow extra time in Pacific Grove, where many fine examples have been preserved and often house restaurants or bed-and-breakfast inns.

In Carmel you can shop till you drop, although a day fighting the summer and weekend hordes through boutiques, art galleries, houseware outlets, and gift shops is usually enough for most people. After that, the incomparable loveliness of the Carmel coast can restore the spirit if not the pocketbook.

The climate can also vary on the peninsula. A sweater or windbreaker is nearly always necessary along the coast, where a cool breeze is usually blowing and the fog is on the way in or out. The situation a few miles inland can be different, however, particularly during the summer, when temperatures in Salinas or Carmel Valley can be a good 15 or 20 degrees warmer than those in Carmel and Monterey.

Although a car is handy for getting from town to town, most of the Monterey Peninsula is best seen on foot. Parking is especially difficult in Carmel and in the vicinity of the Monterey Bay Aquarium on Cannery Row. Take comfortable shoes for negotiating village streets, ambling along the shoreline, and hiking through nature preserves. A good pair of binoculars is also highly recommended; you never know when a playful otter or even a migrating gray whale may splash into sight.

Carmel

Numbers in the margins correspond with points of interest on the Carmel map.

Although the community has grown quickly over the years and its population quadruples with tourists on weekends and during the summer, Carmel retains its identity as a quaint "village" where buildings have no street numbers and live music is banned in the local watering holes. Indeed, there is still a villagelike ambience for visitors wandering the side streets at their own pace, poking into hidden courtyards and stopping at a Hansel-and-Gretel-like café for tea and crumpets.

Carmel has hokey gift emporiums, but most of the wares in its hundreds of shops are distinctive and of high quality. Classic sportswear, gourmet cookware, and original art are among the best buys to be found along the main street, Ocean Avenue, and its cross streets. Just as notable is the architecture of many of the shops, a charming mishmash of ersatz English Tudor, Mediterranean, and other styles.

In recent years, the popularity of shopping in Carmel has led to the creation of several attractive, nicely landscaped shopping ❶ malls. **Carmel Plaza,** in the east end of the village proper, consists of more than 50 shops, restaurants, and small branches of ❷ ❸ major department stores. **The Barnyard** and **the Crossroads** are just southeast of the village off Highway 1.

Time Out **Patisserie Boissiere,** a Carmel Plaza café reminiscent of a country French inn, is the perfect place to take a break from shopping. Light entrées and French pastries are offered. *On Mission Ave. between Ocean and 7th Aves., tel. 408/624–5008. MC, V. Open daily except on Christmas Day.*

Before it became an art colony in the early 20th century and long before it became a shopping and browsing mecca, Carmel was an important religious center in the early days of Spanish California. That heritage is preserved in one of the state's loveliest historic sites, the Mission San Carlos Borromeo del ❹ Rio Carmelo, more commonly known as the **Carmel Mission.** Founded in 1770 and serving as headquarters for the mission system in California under Father Junípero Serra, the Carmel Mission exists today with its stone church and tower dome beautifully restored. Adjoining the church is a tranquil garden planted with California poppies and a series of museum rooms that depict an early kitchen, Father Serra's Spartan sleeping quarters, and the oldest college library in California. *Rio Rd. and Lasuen Dr., tel. 408/624–3600. Open Mon.–Sat. 9:30–4:30. Sun. 10:30–4:30. Donations suggested.*

Scattered throughout the pines in Carmel are the houses and cottages that were built for the steady stream of writers, artists, and photographers who discovered the area decades ago. ❺ Among the most impressive dwellings is **Tor House,** a stone cottage built by the poet Robinson Jeffers in 1918 on a craggy knoll overlooking the sea. The low-ceilinged rooms are filled with portraits, books, and unusual art objects, such as a white stone from the Great Pyramid in Egypt. The highlight of the small estate is Hawk Tower, a detached edifice set with stones from the Great Wall of China and a Roman villa, which served as a retreat for the poet's wife, Una, an accomplished musician. The

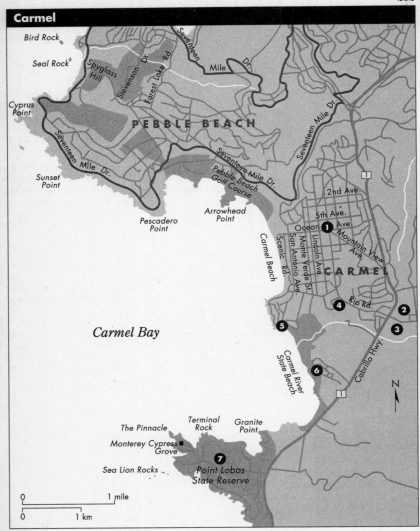

Carmel

docents who lead tours are very well-informed about the poet's work and life. His home and life present a fascinating story, even if you are not a fan of Jeffers's poetry. *26304 Ocean View Ave., tel. 408/624–1813. Admission: $5 adults, $3.50 college students, $1.50 high school students. Tours by appointment on Fri. and Sat. between 10–4.*

Carmel's greatest beauty, however, is not to be found in its historic and architectural landmarks. Nature has done the most impressive work here, particularly in forming the rugged coastline with its pine and cypress forests and countless inlets. Happily, much of the coastal area has been set aside for public enjoyment.

❻ Carmel River State Park, stretches for 106 acres along Carmel Bay. On sunny days the waters appear nearly as turquoise as those of the Caribbean. The park features a sugar-white beach with high dunes and a bird sanctuary that is a nesting ground for pelicans, kingfishers, hawks, and sandpipers. *Off Scenic Rd., south of Carmel Beach tel. 408/649–2836.*

❼ The park is overshadowed by **Point Lobos State Reserve,** a 1,250-acre headland just south of Carmel. Roads have been kept to a minimum, and the best way to explore is to walk along the extensive network of hiking trails. Especially good choices are the Cypress Grove Trail, which leads through a forest of rare Monterey cypresses clinging to the rocks above an emerald-green cove, and Sea Lion Point Trail, where sea lions, otters, harbor seals, and (during certain times of year) migrating whales can be observed. Part of the reserve is an undersea marine park open to qualified scuba divers. *Hwy. 1, tel. 408/624–4909, or 800/444–7275 to reserve for scuba diving. Admission: $5 per car, $3 if senior citizen is traveling. Open May–Sept., daily 9–7; Oct.–Apr., 9–5.*

Monterey's Path of History

Numbers in the margin correspond with points of interest on the Monterey map.

A good way to begin exploring Monterey is to start with the beginnings of the town itself—the beautifully preserved collection of adobe buildings contained in the **Monterey State Historic Park** (tel. 408/649–7118). Far from being an isolated period museum, the park facilities are an integral part of the day-to-day business life of the town, with some of the buildings serving as government offices, restaurants, banks, and private residences. Others are museums illustrating life in the raw young seaport as it developed from a colonial Spanish outpost to its brief heyday as California's political center.

The best way to enjoy the park is on a 2-mile self-guided walking tour outlined in a brochure called the "Path of History," available at the Chamber of Commerce or at many of the landmark buildings contained in the park. *Tour package for multiple sites: $4 adults, $3 children 6–17.*

❶ A logical beginning to the walking tour is at the **Custom House** across from Fisherman's Wharf. Built by the Mexican government in 1827 and considered the oldest government building west of the Rockies, this two-story adobe was the first stop for sea traders whose goods were subject to duty fees. Its grandest day in Monterey's history came in 1846, when Commodore John

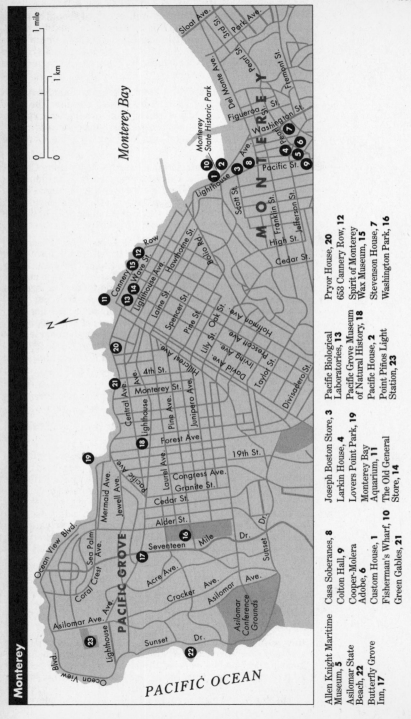

Monterey

Allen Knight Maritime Museum, **5**
Asilomar State Beach, **22**
Butterfly Grove Inn, **17**
Casa Soberanes, **8**
Colton Hall, **9**
Cooper-Molera Adobe, **6**
Custom House, **1**
Fisherman's Wharf, **10**
Green Gables, **21**
Joseph Boston Store, **3**
Larkin House, **4**
Lovers Point Park, **19**
Monterey Bay Aquarium, **11**
The Old General Store, **14**
Pacific Biological Laboratories, **13**
Pacific Grove Museum of Natural History, **18**
Pacific House, **2**
Point Piños Light Station, **23**
Pryor House, **20**
653 Cannery Row, **12**
Spirit of Monterey Wax Museum, **15**
Stevenson House, **7**
Washington Park, **16**

Sloat raised the American flag over the building and claimed California for the United States. Now the lower floor displays examples of a typical cargo from a 19th-century trading ship. *1 Custom House Plaza, tel. 408/649-7118, Admission: free. Open daily 10-4, Mar.-Oct. 10-5.*

2 The next stop along the path should be **Pacific House,** a former hotel and saloon that is now a museum of early California life. There are Gold-Rush relics, historic photographs of old Monterey, and a costume gallery with lacy Mexican shawls and tiny kid slippers from the colonial days. *10 Custom House Plaza, tel. 408/649-2907. Admission: $2, $1 for children. Open daily 10-4, Mar.-Oct. 10-5.*

3 Monterey's most historic gift shop is the **Joseph Boston Store,** located in the Casa Del Oro adobe, a tiny store that first opened for business in 1849, with woodwork from a shipwrecked Portuguese whaler. Now staffed with volunteers from the Monterey History and Art Association, the shop is stocked with antiques, tea, and a potpourri of gift items. *Scott and Oliver Sts. Open Wed.-Sat. 10-5, Sun. noon-5.*

4 Farther along the Path of History is the **Larkin House,** one of the most architecturally significant homes in California. Built in 1835, the two-story adobe with a veranda encircling the second floor is a blend of Mexican and New England influences that became known as the Monterey style. The rooms are furnished with period antiques, many of them brought from New Hampshire to Monterey by the Larkin family. *Jefferson St. and Calle Principal. Admission: $2, $1 for children. Tours on the hour Mar. 1-Nov. 1, 10-4; Nov. 1-Mar. 1, 10-3. Closed noon-1 PM and Tues.*

5 Next door, the **Allen Knight Maritime Museum** is devoted to the private collection of maritime artifacts of former Carmel mayor Allen Knight. The highlight among the exhibits of ship models, scrimshaw items, and nautical prints is the enormous multifaceted Fresnel Light from the Point Sur Lighthouse. *550 Calle Principal, tel. 408/375-2553. Open Sept. 15-June 15, Tues.-Fri. 1-4, Sat.-Sun. 2-4; June 16-Sept. 14, Tues.-Fri. 10-4, Sat.-Sun. 2-4.*

6 The largest site along the Path of History is the recently restored **Cooper-Molera Adobe,** a 4-acre complex that includes an early California house dating from the 1820s, a gift shop, a screening room where an introductory slide presentation is shown, and a large garden enclosed by a high adobe wall. The tile-roofed house is filled with antiques and memorabilia, mostly from the Victorian era, that illustrate the life of a prosperous pioneer family. *Polk and Munras Sts. Admission: $2, $1 for children. Tours on the hour 10-3, Mar.-Oct. 10-4. Closed 1-2 and Wed.*

7 For literary and history buffs, one of the path's greatest treasures is the **Stevenson House,** named in honor of Robert Louis Stevenson, author of *Treasure Island* and other classics, who boarded there briefly in a tiny upstairs room. In addition to Stevenson's room, which is furnished with items from his family's estate, there is a gallery of the author's memorabilia and several charming period rooms, including a children's nursery stocked with Victorian toys and games. *530 Houston St. Ad-*

mission: $2, $1 for children. Tours on the hour 10–3, Mar.–Oct. 10–4. Closed noon–1 PM. Closed Wed.

8 A historic house with an entirely different feel is the low-ceilinged **Casa Soberanes,** a classic adobe structure that once housed the commander of the Spanish Presidio. *336 Pacific St. Admission: $2, $1 for children. Tours on the hour 10–4, Mar.–Oct. 10–4. Closed 1–2 Tues. and Thurs.*

9 California's equivalent of Independence Hall is **Colton Hall,** a white edifice where a convention of delegates met in 1849 to draft the first state constitution. Now the historic building, which has served as a school, courthouse, and county seat, is a museum furnished as it was during the constitutional convention. The extensive grounds outside the hall also include a more notorious building, the Old Monterey Jail, where inmates languished behind thick granite walls. *Pacific between Madison and Jefferson Sts., tel. 408/375–9944. Open March–Oct., daily 10–5; Nov.–Feb., 10–4. Closed noon–1 weekends, major holidays.*

Although not on the Path of History, the **Monterey Peninsula Museum of Art** is just across the street from Colton Hall. The museum is especially strong on artists and photographers who have worked in the area, a distinguished lot that includes Ansel Adams and Edward Weston. Another focus of the museum is folk art from around the world; the collection ranges from Kentucky hearth brooms to Tibetan prayer wheels. *559 Pacific St., tel. 408/372–7591. Admission free. Open Tues.–Sat. 10–4, Sun. 1–4. $2 donation requested.*

Fisherman's Wharf and Cannery Row

Inevitably, visitors are drawn toward the waterfront in Monterey, if only because the mournful barking of sea lions that can be heard throughout the town makes its presence impossible to ignore. The whiskered marine mammals are best enjoyed while
10 walking along **Fisherman's Wharf,** an aging pier crowded with souvenir shops, fish markets, seafood restaurants, and popcorn stands.

Although tacky and touristy to the utmost, the wharf is a good place to visit, especially with children. For years, an organ grinder with a costumed monkey has entertained crowds at the entrance to the wharf. Farther down, you can buy a bag of squid to feed the sea lions that beg from the waters below.

From the wharf, a footpath along the shore leads to **Cannery Row,** a street that has undergone several transformations since it was immortalized in John Steinbeck's 1944 novel of the same name. The street that Steinbeck wrote of was crowded with sardine canneries processing, at their peak, nearly 200,000 tons of the smelly silver fish a year. During the mid-1940s, however, the sardines mysteriously disappeared from the bay, causing the canneries to close.

Over the years the old tin-roof canneries have been converted to restaurants, art galleries, and minimalls with shops selling T-shirts, fudge, and plastic otters. A recent trend, however, has been toward a more tasteful level of tourist development along the Row, including several attractive inns and hotels. The Monterey Plaza Hotel (400 Cannery Row) is a good place to relax over a drink and watch for otters.

The most important recent development on Cannery Row has
❶ been the opening of the spectacular **Monterey Bay Aquarium,**
a $50-million window on the sea waters just outside its back
doors. The aquarium has proved so popular that visitors should
expect long lines and sizable crowds on weekends, especially
during the summer. Braving the crowds is worth it, however,
especially to see the three-story Kelp Forest exhibit, the only
one of its kind in the world, and a re-creation of the sea creatures and vegetation found in Monterey Bay. Among other
standout exhibits are a bat-ray petting pool, where the flat vel-
vetlike creatures can be touched as they swim by; a 55,000-gal-
lon sea otter tank; and an enormous outdoor artificial tide pool
that supports anemones, crabs, sea stars, and other colorful
creatures. *886 Cannery Row, tel. 408/649–6466. Admission: $9
adults, $6.50 students and senior citizens, $4 children 3–12.
Tickets can be purchased ahead from Ticketron, tel. 408/247–
7469 or 415/392–7469. Open daily 10–6, 9:30–6 on holidays.
Closed Christmas. AE, MC, V.*

Although Steinbeck would have trouble recognizing the street
today, there are still some historical and architectural features
❷ from its colorful past. One building to take note of is **653 Cannery Row,** with its tiled Chinese dragon roof that dates from
1929. A weathered wooden building at 800 Cannery Row was
❸ the **Pacific Biological Laboratories,** where Edward F. Ricketts, the inspiration for Doc in Steinbeck's novel, did much of
his marine research. Across the street, the building now called
❹ **The Old General Store** is the former Wing Chong Market that
Steinbeck called Lee Chong's Heavenly Flower Grocery.

On a more kitschy note, characters from the Steinbeck novel
❺ are depicted in wax at the **Spirit of Monterey Wax Museum,**
which recently added new lighting and animation and a 25-min-
ute description of the history of the area over the past 400
years, with Steinbeck as narrator. *700 Cannery Row, tel. 408/
375–3770. Admission: $4.95 adults, $3.95 students and senior
citizens, $2.95 children 6–12. Open daily 8:45 AM–10 PM.*

Pacific Grove

If not for the dramatic strip of coastline in its backyard, Pacific
Grove could easily pass for a typical small town in the heart-
land. Beginning as a summer retreat for church groups a century ago, the town has retained some of its prim and proper
Victorian heritage in the host of tiny board and batten cottages
and stately mansions lining its streets.

Even before the church groups migrated here, however, Pacific
Grove had been receiving thousands of annual guests in the
form of bright orange and black monarch butterflies. Known as
"Butterfly Town USA," Pacific Grove is home to the monarchs
that migrate south from Canada and the Pacific Northwest and
take residence in the pine and eucalyptus groves between October and March. Seeing a mass of butterflies hanging from the
branches like a long fluttering veil is unforgettable.

Although many of their original nesting grounds have vanished, two good spots for viewing butterflies remain. The larg-
❻ est is **Washington Park** at the corner of Pine Avenue and Alder
❼ Street; the other is a grove adjoining the **Butterfly Grove Inn** at
1073 Lighthouse Avenue.

If you are in Pacific Grove when the butterflies are not, an approximation of this annual miracle is on exhibit at the **Pacific Grove Museum of Natural History.** In addition to a finely crafted butterfly tree exhibit, the museum features a collection of 400 mounted birds native to Monterey County and a film presentation about the monarch butterfly. *165 Forest Ave., tel. 408/648-3116. Admission free. Open Tues.–Sun. 10–5.*

A prime way to enjoy Pacific Grove is to walk or bicycle along its 3 miles of city-owned shoreline, a clifftop area following Ocean View Boulevard that is landscaped with succulents and native plants and has plenty of park benches on which to sit and gaze at the sea. A variety of marine and bird life can be spotted here, including colonies of cormorants that are drawn to the massive rocks rising out of the surf. **Lovers Point Park,** located midway along the waterfront, is a pleasant grassy area in which to stop and picnic.

Although it is difficult to turn away from the gorgeous coast, the other side of Ocean View Boulevard has a number of imposing turn-of-the-century mansions that are well worth your attention. One of the finest is the **Pryor House** at number 429, a massive shingled structure with a leaded and beveled glass doorway built in 1909 for an early mayor. At the corner of 5th Street and Ocean View is **Green Gables,** a romantic Swiss Gothic-style mansion, now a bed-and-breakfast inn, with steeply peaked gables and stained-glass windows.

Another beautiful coastal area in Pacific Grove is **Asilomar State Beach,** on Sunset Drive between Point Piños and the Del Monte Forest. The 100 acres of dunes, tide pools, and pocketsize beaches from one of the region's richest areas for marine life. The deep tide pools support 210 species of algae and are alive with sea urchins, crabs, and other creatures.

The oldest continuously operating lighthouse on the West Coast is also a museum open to the public, the **Point Piños Light Station.** Visitors can learn about the lighting and foghorn operations and wander through a small museum containing historical memorabilia from the U.S. Coast Guard. *Ocean View Blvd. at Point Piños, tel. 408/648-3116. Admission free. Open weekends 1–4 PM.*

Salinas

While Monterey turns its face toward the sea, Salinas, a half-hour inland and a world away in spirit, is deeply rooted as the population center of a rich agricultural valley. This unpretentious town may lack the sophistication and scenic splendors of the coast, but it is of interest to literary and architectural buffs.

The memory and literary legacy of Salinas native John Steinbeck are well-honored here. The author's birthplace, a Victorian frame house, has been converted to a lunch-only restaurant called the **Steinbeck House,** which is run by the volunteer Valley Guild. The restaurant contains some Steinbeck memorabilia and presents a menu featuring locally grown produce. *132 Central Ave., tel. 408/424-2735. Reservations required. Open weekdays for 2 sittings at 11:45 AM and 1:15 PM.*

Steinbeck did much of his research for *East of Eden*, a novel partially drawn from his Salinas boyhood, at what is now called the **Steinbeck Library.** The library features tapes of interviews with people who knew Steinbeck and a display of photos, first editions, letters, original manuscripts, and other items pertaining to the novelist. *110 W. San Luis, tel. 408/758–7311. Admission free. Open Mon.–Thurs. 10–9, Fri.–Sat. 10–6.*

Salinas's turn-of-the-century architecture has been the focus of an ongoing renovation project, much of which is centered on the original downtown area on South Main Street, with its handsome stone storefronts. One of the finest private residences from this era is the **Harvey-Baker House,** a beautifully preserved redwood house built for the city's first mayor in 1881. *238 E. Romie La., tel. 408/757–8085. Admission free. Open Sun. 1–4 PM, and weekdays by appointment.*

Of even earlier vintage is the **Jose Eusebio Boronda Adobe,** the last unaltered adobe home from Mexican California open to the public in Monterey County. Located in the meadows above the Alisal Slough, the house, which suffered some damage in the 1989 earthquake, is a treasure trove of early furniture and artifacts from the period. *333 Boronda Rd., tel. 408/757–8085. Admission free. Open weekdays 10–2, Sun. 1–4, Sat. by appointment.*

San Juan Bautista

A sleepy little hamlet tucked off U.S. 101 about 20 miles north of Salinas, San Juan Bautista is a nearly unaltered example of a classic California mission village. Protected from development since 1933, when much of it became **San Juan Bautista State Historic Park,** the village is about as close to early 19th-century California as you can get. On the first Saturday of each month, on Living History Day, costumed volunteers entertain visitors with such period events as quilting bees, making tortillas, or churning butter, and refreshments are served in the hotel's bar. *Tel. 408/623–4881. Admission: $2 adults; children 6–17 $1. Open daily 10–4:30.*

The centerpiece for the village is the wide green plaza ringed by historic buildings that include a restored blacksmith shop, a stable, a pioneer cabin, and jailhouse. Running along one side of the square is **Mission San Bautista,** a long, low colonnaded structure founded by Father Lasuen in 1797. A poignant spot adjoining it is **Mission Cemetery,** where more than 4,300 Indian converts are buried in unmarked graves.

After the mission era, San Juan Bautista became an important crossroads for stagecoach travel. The principal stop in town was the **Plaza Hotel,** a collection of adobe buildings with furnishings from the 1860s. Next door, the **Castro-Breen Adobe,** once owned by survivors from the Donner party and furnished with Spanish colonial antiques, presents a view of domestic life in the village.

More contemporary pursuits in San Juan Bautista include poking through the numerous antiques shops and art galleries lining the side streets of the village. In August the village holds a popular annual flea market.

What to See and Do with Children

Beaches. While local waters are generally too cold and turbulent for children (or adults, for that matter), the Monterey Municipal Beach east of Wharf No. 2 has shallow waters that are warm and calm enough for wading. Another good beach for kids is Lovers Point Park on Ocean View Boulevard in Pacific Grove, a sheltered spot with a children's pool and picnic area. Glass-bottom boat rides, which permit viewing of the plant and sea life below, are available during the summer.

Dennis the Menace Playground (Fremont St. and Camino El Estero, Monterey). Delightful Lake El Estero Park is the setting for this imaginative playground whose name pays tribute to one of its developers, cartoonist and longtime local resident Hank Ketcham. Among the features are a maze made from hedges, free-form play equipment, and a Southern Pacific steam locomotive. Rowboats and paddleboats can be rented on Lake El Estero, a U-shaped lake that is home to a varied assortment of ducks, mud hens, and geese.

Edgewater Packing Co. (640 Wave St., Monterey, tel. 408/649–1899). The centerpiece of this converted sardine cannery and processing plant is an antique carousel with hand-carved animals and mermaids that is as much fun to ride now as it was in 1905. A candy store and game arcade are among the other attractions.

Roller Skating. Roller skates can be rented from the old-fashioned rink at Del Monte Gardens. *2020 Del Monte Ave., Monterey, tel. 408/375–3202. Closed Mon. and Tues.*

Children will enjoy the Monterey Bay Aquarium, the Museum of Natural History, and the Point Piños Lighthouse (*see* Exploring, above). Also popular is whale-watching (*see* Participant Sports, below).

Off the Beaten Track

A few miles north of Monterey near the tiny harbor town of Moss Landing is one of only two federal research reserves in California, the **Elkhorn Slough** from the visitors' center at the National Estuarine Research Reserve at 1700 Elkhorn Road. (Hwy. 1, Moss Landing, tel. 408/728–2822). There are 2,500 acres of tidal flats and salt marshes that form a complex environment supporting more than 300 species of birds and fish. A 1-mile walk along the meandering canals and wetlands can reveal swans, pelicans, loons, herons, and egrets. You can wander at leisure or take a guided walk *on weekends at 10 AM and 1 PM and visit the heron rookery. Open Wed.–Sun. 9–5. Admission: $2.25 over 16, free for under 16.*

Shopping

Art Galleries Although few artists can afford the real estate, Carmel's heritage as a thriving art colony lives on in dozens of art galleries scattered throughout the town. A wide and eclectic assortment of art—everything from 19th-century watercolors to abstract metal sculpture—is available for browsing and purchase in galleries in Carmel and elsewhere on the peninsula.

The Coast Gallery Pebble Beach presents the work of contemporary wildlife and marine artists in forms that range from etchings to bronze sculpture. *The Lodge at Pebble Beach, 17-Mile Dr., Pebble Beach, tel. 408/624–2002. Open daily 9–5.*
The **Masterpiece Gallery** features early California Impression-

ists, Parisian street scenes and the work of local artist Roger Blum. *Dolores St. and 6th Ave., Carmel, tel. 408/624–2163. Open daily 11–5.*

Classic impressionism and traditional realism are the focus of the **Cottage Gallery.** *Mission St. and 6th Ave., Carmel, tel. 408/624–7888. Open daily 10–5.*

The **Bill W. Dodge Gallery** features one of the largest collections of contemporary folk art in the West, including Dodge's own turn-of-the-century-style paintings, posters, and prints. *Dolores St. between 5th and 6th Aves., Carmel, tel. 408/625–5636. Open daily 10–5.*

At **GWS Galleries,** which features the work of nationally recognized artists, the primary themes and styles are Western, wildlife, marine, aviation, Americana, and landscape. Museum-quality framing is offered. *26390 Carmel Rancho La., Carmel, tel. 408/625–2288. Open Mon.–Sat. 10–5:30, Sun. 11–4.*

The **Highlands Sculpture Gallery** is devoted to indoor and outdoor sculpture, primarily work done in stone, bronze, wood, and metal by West Coast artists. *Dolores St. between 5th and 6th Aves., Carmel, tel. 408/624–0535. Open Thurs.–Mon. 10:30–4:30.*

Photography West Gallery exhibits a changing spectrum of well-known 20th-century photography and features the work of Ansel Adams, who lived and worked in the region for many years. *Ocean Ave. and Dolores St., Carmel, tel. 408/625–1587. Open Mon.–Thurs. 11–5, Fri., Sat. 11–6, Sun. 10–5.*

Gift Ideas In a region known for superb golf courses, one can find the ultimate in golf equipment and accessories. At **John Riley Golf** customers can get custom-made golf clubs manufactured on the premises. *601 Wave St., Monterey, tel. 408/373–8855. Open Mon.–Sat. 9–5, Sun. noon–5.*

Unusual gifts for golfers can be found at **Golf Arts and Imports,** which features antique golf prints and clubs, rare golf books, and other golfing memorabilia. *Dolores St. and 6th Ave., Carmel, tel. 408/625–4488. Open Mon.–Sat. 10–5, Sun. 10–3.*

The illustrations of Beatrix Potter are in evidence everywhere at **Peter Rabbit and Friends,** which offers toys, nursery bedding, books, music boxes, party supplies, and other items embellished with characters and scenes from Potter's children's tales. *Lincoln Ave. between 7th and Ocean Aves., Carmel, tel. 408/624–6854. Open Mon.–Sat. 10–5, Sun. 11–5.*

One of the best places for books on marine life and attractive gifts with a marine life theme is the **Monterey Bay Aquarium Gift Shop,** which offers everything from posters and art prints to silk-screened sweatshirts and lobster-shaped wooden napkin rings. *886 Cannery Row, Monterey, tel. 408/649–6466. Open daily 10–6.*

Participant Sports

Bicycling The Monterey Peninsula is wonderful biking territory, with bicycle paths following some of the choicest parts of the shoreline, including the 17-Mile Drive and the waterfront of Pacific Grove. Bikes can be rented from **Bay Bikes** (640 Wave St., Monterey, tel. 408/646–9090). Pickup and delivery to hotels is possible in the summer season.

Adventures by the Sea (299 Cannery Row, tel. 408/372–1807) has biking packages that combine rentals with restaurant vouchers or with tickets good for the Monterey Bay Aquarium. Tour packages for groups as well as for walking tours are available.

Mopeds can be rented from **Monterey Moped Adventures** (1250 Del Monte Ave., tel. 408/373–2696). A free practice lesson is included in the rental price; a driver's license is required.

Fishing   Rock cod is a relatively easy catch in Monterey Bay, with salmon and albacore tuna also among the possibilities. Most fishing trips are a half day or a full day in duration, leave from Fisherman's Wharf in Monterey, and can include options such as equipment rental, bait, fish cleaning, and a one-day license. Boat charters for groups and trips for individuals are available.

Fishing trips in Monterey are offered by **Monterey Sport Fishing** (96 Fisherman's Wharf, tel. 408/372–2203), **Randy's Fishing Trips** (66 Fisherman's Wharf, tel. 408/372–7440), and **Sam's Fishing Fleet** (84 Fisherman's Wharf, tel. 408/372–0577).

Golf   With 19 golf courses, most of them commanding strips of choice real estate, it is not surprising that the Monterey Peninsula is sometimes called the golf capital of the world. Beginning with the opening of the Del Monte Golf course in 1897, golf has long been an integral part of the social and recreational scene in the area.

Many hotels will help with golf reservations or offer golf packages; inquire when you make lodging reservations.

Several of the courses are within the exclusive confines of the 17-Mile Drive, where the Del Monte forest and the surging Pacific help make the game challenging as well as scenic. The most famous of these courses is **Pebble Beach Golf Links** (17-Mile Dr., tel. 408/624–3811), which takes center stage each winter during the AT&T Pro-Am, known for years as the "Crosby," where show business celebrities and pros team up for what is perhaps the world's most glamorous golf tournament. Such is the fame of this course that golfers from around the world make it one of the busiest in the region, despite greens fees that are well over $100. (You do get a refund of the $5 fee for the 17-Mile Drive.) Reservations are essential.

Another famous course in Pebble Beach is **Spyglass Hill** (Spyglass Hill Rd., tel. 408/624–3811), where the holes are long and unforgiving to sloppy players. With the first five holes bordering on the Pacific, and the rest reaching deep into the Del Monte Forest, the views offer some consolation.

A newer addition to the Pebble Beach scene is **Poppy Hills** (17-Mile Dr., tel. 408/625–2035), a creation of Robert Trent Jones, Jr. that opened in 1986 and has been named by *Golf Digest* as one of the top 20 courses in the world.

The newest course in Pebble Beach is the **Spanish Bay Golf Links** (tel. 408/624–3811), which opened on the north end of the 17-Mile Drive in late 1987. Spanish Bay, which hugs a choice stretch of shoreline is designed in the rugged manner of a traditional Scottish course with sand dunes and coastal marshes interspersed among the greens.

Less experienced golfers and those who want to sharpen their iron shots can try the shortest course in Pebble Beach, the nine-hole **Peter Hay** (17-Mile Dr., tel. 408/624–3811).

Just as challenging as the Pebble Beach courses is the **Old Del Monte Golf Course** (1300 Sylvan Rd., tel. 408/373–2436) in Monterey, the oldest course west of the Mississippi. The greens fees are among the most reasonable in the region.

Another local favorite, with greens fees only a fraction of those in Pebble Beach, is **Pacific Grove Golf Links** (Asilomar Blvd., tel. 408/648–3177). Designed by Jack Neville, who also designed the Pebble Beach Golf Links, the course features a back nine with spectacular ocean views and iceplant-covered sand dunes that make keeping on the fairway a must.

Although lacking in ocean views, golf courses in Carmel Valley offer the company of deer and quail wandering across the greens. One of the choicest is **Rancho Cañada Golf Club** (Carmel Valley Rd., tel. 408/624–0111), with 36 holes, some of them overlooking the Carmel River.

Up the road a few miles is the **Golf Club at Quail Lodge** (8000 Valley Greens Dr., tel. 408/624–2770), which has a course made beautiful and challenging by several lakes incorporated into its design. The course is private but is open to guests at the adjoining Quail Lodge and by reciprocation with other private clubs.

Guests at the nearby Carmel Valley Ranch resort have access to the private Peter Dye-designed **Carmel Valley Ranch Resort** course (1 Old Ranch Rd., tel. 408/626–2510), which has a front nine running along the Carmel River and a back nine reaching well up into the mountains for challenging slopes and spectacular views.

Seven miles inland from Monterey, off Highway 68, is **Laguna Seca Golf Club** (1 York Rd., tel. 408/373–3701), a course with an 18-hole layout designed by Robert Trent Jones, Jr., and open to the public.

Horseback Riding A great way to enjoy the Del Monte Forest, which has more than 34 miles of bridle trails, is by reserving a horse from the **Pebble Beach Equestrian Center** (Portola Rd. and Alva La., tel. 408/624–2756). You can ride in a group of four people, from 10 AM to 2 PM, Tues.–Sun.

Kayaking Sea kayaking is an increasingly popular sport in Monterey Bay, giving paddlers a chance to come face to face with otters, sea lions, harbor seals, and dolphins. Kayak rentals, basic instruction, and escorted tours are offered by **Monterey Bay Kayaks** (693 Del Monte Ave., Monterey, tel. 408/373–KELP).

Scuba Diving Although the waters are cold, the marine life and kelp beds attract many scuba divers to Monterey Bay. Diving lessons, rental equipment and guided dive tours are offered at **Aquarius Dive Shops** (2240 Del Monte Ave., Monterey, tel. 408/375–1933 and 32 Cannery Row, Suite #4, tel. 408/375–6605).

Tennis Public courts are available in Monterey and Pacific Grove; information is available through **Monterey Tennis Center** (tel. 408/372–0172) and **Pacific Grove Municipal Courts** (tel. 408/648–3129). Nonmembers are eligible to play on the courts for a small fee at the **Carmel Valley Inn Swim and Tennis Club** (Carmel Valley Rd. and Los Laureles Grade, Carmel Valley, tel. 408/659–3131).

If tennis is a top vacation priority, you may want to stay at a resort where instruction and facilities are part of the scene. Among the resorts most geared for tennis are the Lodge at Pebble Beach, the Inn at Spanish Bay, Hyatt Regency Monterey, Hilton Resort of Monterey, Quail Lodge, and Carmel Valley Ranch Resort. *See* the Lodging section below for details.

Whale-watching On their annual migration between the Bering Sea and Baja California, 45-foot gray whales can be spotted not far off the Monterey coast. Although they sometimes can be spotted with binoculars from shore, a whale-watching cruise is the best way to see these magnificent mammals up close. The migration south takes place between December and March, while the migration north is from March to June. Late January is considered the prime viewing time, when their numbers in Monterey Bay peak.

Even if no whales are in sight, however, the bay cruises nearly always include some unforgettable marine-life encounter that can range from watching a cluster of sea lions hugging a life buoy to riding the waves alongside a group of 300 leaping porpoises. Whale-watching cruises, which usually last about two hours, are offered by **Monterey Sport Fishing** (96 Fisherman's Wharf, Monterey, tel. 408/372–2203), **Randy's Fishing Trips** (66 Fisherman's Wharf, Monterey, tel. 408/372–7440, and **Sam's Fishing Fleet** (84 Fisherman's Wharf, tel. 408/372–0577).

Spectator Sports

Car Racing Five major races take place each year on the 2.2-mile, 11-turn **Laguna Seca Raceway** (SCRAMP, Box 2078, Monterey 93942, tel. 408/648–5100 or 800/367–9939). They range from Indianapolis 500–style CART races to a historic car race featuring more than 150 restored race cars from earlier eras.

Rodeo One of the oldest and most famous rodeos in the West is the annual **California Rodeo** (Box 1648, Salinas 93902, tel. 408/757–2951) in Salinas, which takes place during a week of festivities starting in mid-July.

Dining

by Bruce David Colen There is no question that the Monterey area is the best and richest place to dine, along the coast, between Los Angeles and San Francisco. The surrounding waters abound with fish, there is wild game in the foothills, and the inland valleys are the vegetable basket of California, while nearby Castroville prides itself on being the Artichoke Capital of the World. The region also takes pride in producing better and better wines. San Francisco's conservative streak extends this far south, when it comes to dress—"casual" means attractive resort wear.

Highly recommended restaurants are indicated by a star ★.

Category	Cost*
Very Expensive	over $50
Expensive	$35–$50

Moderate	$20–$35
Inexpensive	under $20

per person, not including tax, service, or drinks.

Carmel
Expensive

The Covey at Quail Lodge. Continental cuisine is served in an elegant restaurant with a romantic lakeside setting. Specialties include swordfish with avocado in a curried cream sauce, black-currant duck, abalone, and sea scallop mousse. *8205 Valley Greens Dr., tel. 408/624–1581. Jacket and tie required. Reservations advised. AE, DC, MC, V. Dinner only.*

French Poodle. The service is attentive in this intimate dining room with framed maps of French wine regions on the walls. Specialties on the traditional French menu include duck breast in port. *Junipero and 5th Ave., tel. 408/624–8643. Reservations advised. Dress: informal. AE, DC. Dinner only. Closed Sun. and Wed.*

★ **Pacific's Edge.** This restaurant's dramatic views of ancient cypress trees and pounding surf combine with a staff headed by two of the nation's best chefs—Brian Whitmer and chocolatier Bruno Feldeisen—to create the most memorable dining experience along the entire California coast. *Hwy. 1, Carmel-by-the-Sea, tel. 408/624–3801. Reservations advised. Jacket required. AE, DC, MC, V.*

Raffaello. A sparkling, elegant rendezvous in one of the loveliest parts of Carmel, the menu offers very good Northern Italian dishes with French overtones. There's excellent pasta, Monterey Bay prawns with garlic butter, local sole poached in champagne, and the specialty of the house, chicken *alla Fiorentina. Mission St., between Ocean and 7th Aves., tel. 408/624–1541. Reservations recommended. Jacket and tie required. AE, DC, MC, V. Closed lunch, closed Tues.*

Moderate

Crème Carmel. This bright and airy small restaurant has a California French menu that changes according to season. Specialties include sea bass stuffed with Dungeness crab and beef tenderloin in cabernet sauce. *San Carlos St., near 7th Ave., tel. 408/624–0444. Reservations advised. MC, V.*

Flaherty's Seafood Grill & Oyster House. This is a bright blue-and-white-tiled fish house that serves bowls of steamed mussels, clams, cioppino, and crab chowder. Seafood pastas and daily fresh fish selections are also available. *6th Ave. and San Carlos St., tel. 408/624–0311. No reservations. MC, V.*

Hog's Breath Inn. Clint Eastwood's place, recently enlarged, provides a convivial publike atmosphere in which to enjoy nononsense meat and seafood entrées with sautéed vegetables. *San Carlos St. and 5th Ave., tel. 408/625–1044. Reservations advised. MC, V.*

Piatti. One more link in this chain of friendly, attractive trattorias, serving authentic, light Italian cuisine. *Junipero and Sixth Sts., tel, 408/625–1766. MC, V.*

Pine Inn. An old favorite with locals, this Victorian-style restaurant with an outdoor gazebo area for lunch offers a traditional American menu, including pork loin, roast duck, and beef Stroganoff. *Ocean Ave. and Monte Verde St., tel. 408/624–3851. Reservations advised. AE, MC, V.*

(Q) Point of Carmel. New ownership has taken over what was once the Gold Fork, changed the menu from a straight Continental to one that might best be called California/Continental, and lowered prices considerably. Featured dishes: sautéed sea scallops and Gulf prawns with basil; chicken breast, rolled and stuffed with mushrooms; pasta with the catch of the day; and rack of Sonoma lamb. *Ocean Ave. between 3rd Ave. and Delores St., tel. 408/624–2569. Reservations advised. AE, DC, MC, V. Dinner only.*

★ **Rio Grill.** The best bets in this attractive Santa Fe–style setting are meat and seafood (such as fresh tuna) cooked in an oakwood smoker. There's a good California wine list. *Hwy. 1 and Rio Rd., tel. 408/625–5436. Reservations advised. MC, V.*

Inexpensive **Friar Tuck's.** This busy wood-paneled coffee shop serves huge omelets and 17 varieties of hamburgers, including one topped with marinated artichoke hearts. *5th Ave. and Dolores St., tel. 408/624–4274. No reservations. No credit cards. No dinners.*

Shabu Shabu. Light meat and seafood dishes, cooked at the table, are the specialties in this country-style Japanese restaurant. *Ocean and 7th Aves., tel. 408/625–2828. Reservations advised. AE, MC, V.*

Swedish Restaurant. This quaint café with a fireplace and Scandinavian decor features Swedish pancakes, homemade rye bread, and meatballs for breakfast and lunch. *Dolores St. and 7th Ave., tel. 408/624–3723. No reservations. No credit cards.*

Thunderbird Bookstore and Restaurant. The Thunderbird is a very well-stocked bookstore and a good place to enjoy a light lunch or dinner and browse among the books. A hearty beef soup, sandwiches, and cheesecake are the bestsellers. *3600 The Barnyard, Hwy. 1 at Carmel Valley Rd., tel. 408/624–1803. MC, V.*

Monterey **Bindel's.** This historic old pink Sanchez adobe was recently
Expensive bought and refurbished by David Bindel, the gentleman who also owns the very successful Old Bath House (see below). The menu is Regional California with the emphasis on whatever the local fishing fleet brings back to port each day. Don't miss the crab and salmon ravioli with pesto sauce. *500 Hartnell St., tel. 408/373–3737. Reservations advised. AE, MC, V. Sun. brunch.*

Delfino. The Monterey Plaza Hotel has an elegant dining room built over the waterfront on Cannery Row. Fresh seafood, veal medallions, and angel-hair pasta with prawns are among the standouts on the California-Italian menu. *400 Cannery Row, tel. 408/646–1700. Reservations advised. AE, DC, MC, V.*

★ **Fresh Cream.** Ask the area natives where to go for pleasant, light, imaginative California cuisine, and nine out of ten will recommend this charming little restaurant in Heritage Harbor. Be sure to try the squab and quail from nearby farms. *100 Pacific St., tel. 408/375–9798. Reservations recommended. Dress: casual. MC, V. Beer and wine. Closed lunch, closed Mon.*

Sardine Factory. The interiors of an old processing plant on Cannery Row have been turned into five separate dining areas, including a glass-enclosed garden room. The decor is from the gaslight era with lots of Gay '90s touches. The menu stresses fresh seafood prepared in an elegant, Italian manner. There's a great wine list. *701 Wave St., tel. 408/373–3775. Reservations recommended. Jacket required. AE, DC, MC, V. Closed lunch.*

★ **Whaling Station Inn.** A pleasing mixture of rough-hewn wood and sparkling white linen makes this both a festive and a comfortable place in which to enjoy some of the best mesquite-grilled fish and meats in town. There are excellent artichoke appetizers and fresh salads. *763 Wave St., tel. 408/373-3778. Reservations advised. AE, DC, MC, V. Dinner only.*

Moderate **Clock Garden.** The wide-ranging eclectic decor includes a collection of antique clocks. There's a Continental menu, with a variety of fresh fish, veal, pork, lamb, and chicken dishes that can be followed by wonderful, rich desserts. *565 Abrego St., tel. 408/375-6100. Reservations advised. AE, MC, V.*

Ferrante's. Gorgeous views of both town and bay are seen from this Northern Italian restaurant at the top of the Sheraton. Pasta and seafood combinations such as spinach fettuccine with clams are especially good. *350 Calle Principal, tel. 408/649-4234. Reservations advised. AE, DC, MC, V.*

★ **The Fishery.** Popular with locals, this restaurant features a mixture of Asian and Continental influences in both food and decor. Specialties include broiled swordfish with saffron butter and fresh Hawaiian tuna with macadamia-nut butter. *21 Soledad Dr., tel. 408/373-6200. MC, V. Dinner only. Closed Sun. and Mon.*

Hammerheads. Located in what was once the town firehouse, the restaurant's main attraction is the Chocoholic Bar laden with all the desserts you can eat. There are five varieties of duck on the dinner menu. *414 Calle Principal, tel. 408/372-3463. Reservations advised. AE, DC, MC, V.*

Mara's Restaurant. Greek and Armenian dishes such as hummos, shish kebab, moussaka, and a chicken and lemon soup called *avgolemono* are featured at this family restaurant. *570 Lighthouse Ave., tel. 408/375-1919. Reservations advised. MC, V. Dinner only.*

Steinbeck Lobster Grotto. Pacific views on three sides highlight this long-established Cannery Row spot known for Maine lobster and local catches. Also good are bouillabaisse, cioppino, and seafood casseroles. *720 Cannery Row, tel. 408/373-1884. Reservations advised. AE, DC, MC, V. Dinner only.*

Surdi's. Meals at this pleasant stucco restaurant start with an impressive antipasto salad bar. Along with traditional pasta dishes, a house specialty is chicken Monterey baked with cream and artichoke hearts. *2030 Fremont St., tel. 408/646-0100. Reservations advised. Dress: casual. AE, DC, MC, V.*

Inexpensive **Abalonetti.** From a squid-lover's point of view, this casual wharfside restaurant is the best place in town. Get it served in a variety of ways: deep-fried, sautéed with wine and garlic, or baked with eggplant. *57 Fisherman's Wharf, tel. 408/375-5941. No reservations. AE.*

Beau Thai. Located across from the Monterey Bay Aquarium, this plant-filled local favorite features such dishes as beef curry with tamarind sauce and spicy noodle dishes. *807 Cannery Row, tel. 408/373-8811. Reservations advised. AE, DC, MC, V.*

Old Monterey Cafe. Breakfast, which can include fresh-baked muffins and eggs Benedict, is served all day here. It's also a good place to relax with a cappuccino or coffee made from freshly ground beans. *489 Alvarado St., tel. 408/646-1021. No reservations. MC, V.*

Sancho Panza. While the basic Mexican dishes may not be extraordinary, the atmospheric setting in this low-ceilinged 1841 Casa Gutierrez adobe along the Path of History definitely is. *590 Calle Principal, tel. 408/375-0095. AE, DC, MC, V.*

Pacific Grove
Expensive

Gernot's. The ornate Victorian Hart Mansion is a delightful setting in which to dine on seafood and game served with light sauces. California French specialties include pheasant with green peppercorns and roast venison. *649 Lighthouse Ave., tel. 408/646–1477. Reservations advised. Dress: informal. AE, MC, V. Dinner only. Closed Mon.*

★ **Old Bath House.** A romantic, nostalgic mood permeates this dining room in a converted bathhouse overlooking the water at Lovers Point. A seasonal Continental menu stresses local seafood and produce, with salmon and Monterey Bay prawns particularly worth ordering, when available. *620 Ocean View Blvd., tel. 408/375–5195. Reservations advised. Jacket required. AE, DC, MC, V.*

Moderate

Fandango. With stone walls and country furniture, this restaurant has the earthy feel of a Southern European farmhouse. Complementing it are robust flavors from southern France, Italy, Spain, Greece, and North Africa, with a menu ranging from couscous and paella to canneloni. *223 17th St., tel. 408/373–0588. Reservations advised. AE, DC, MC, V.*

Inexpensive

Peppers. This pleasant white-walled café offers fresh seafood and traditional dishes from Mexico and Latin America. The red and green salsas are excellent. *170 Forest Ave., tel. 408/373–6892. Reservations advised. AE, MC, V. Closed Tues.*

The Tinnery. The simple, clean lines of this contemporary dining room are framed by picture-window views of Monterey Bay. The eclectic menu ranges from Japanese teriyaki chicken to Mexican burritos to English fish and chips. *631 Ocean View Blvd., tel. 408/375–5195. Reservations advised. AE, DC, MC, V.*

Pebble Beach
Expensive

The Bay Club. This new restaurant decorated in pleasant pastels overlooks the coastline and golf links at the Inn at Spanish Bay. Continental specialties include truffle ravioli in lobster sauce and veal chop with rosemary butter. *2800 17-Mile Dr., tel. 408/647–7500. Reservations advised. Jacket required. AE, DC, MC, V. Dinner only.*

★ **Club XIX.** Classic French dishes are served in an intimate, cafe-style restaurant at the Lodge at Pebble Beach, with views of Carmel Bay and the 18th green. *17-Mile Dr. and Portola Rd., tel. 408/624–3811. Reservations advised. Jacket required. AE, DC, MC, V.*

Lodging

A recent hotel and resort boom on the Monterey Peninsula has given travelers a far greater choice of accommodations, especially on the most deluxe level, than ever before. The luxury resort scene is particularly flourishing in Carmel Valley and Pebble Beach, where several country clublike spreads have opened recently.

In Monterey, the trend has been toward sophisticated hotels, some with the same range of services and amenities offered by top hotels in San Francisco. Some of the newer hotels are a bit impersonal and clearly designed for conventions, but others pamper the individual traveler in grand style.

While large resorts and hotels have been opening elsewhere on the peninsula, Pacific Grove has quietly turned itself into the bed-and-breakfast capital of the region. Many of the town's landmark Victorian houses, some more than a century old, have been converted to charming inns with brass beds and breakfast buffets laden with cranberry muffins and baked pears.

Rates in the Monterey area are often as high as in a major city, especially during the April–October high season, when even modest motels may charge $100 a night for a double room.

Highly recommended hotels are indicated by a star ★.

Category	Cost*
Very Expensive	over $150
Expensive	$100–$150
Moderate	$60–$100
Inexpensive	under $60

double room, not including tax

Carmel
Very Expensive
★

Highlands Inn. The hotel's unparalleled location on high cliffs above the Pacific just south of Carmel gives it views that stand out even in a region famous for them. Accommodations are in plush condominium-style units with wood-burning fireplaces, ocean view decks; some have spa tubs and full kitchens. *Hwy. 1, Box 1700, 93921, tel. 408/624–3801 or 800/538–9525; 800/682–4811 in CA. 142 rooms. Facilities: pool, whirlpools, 2 restaurants, lounges, entertainment. AE, D, DC, MC, V.*

Tickle Pink Country Inn. Just up the road from the Highlands Inn, this small, secluded inn also features spectacular views. Simple but comfortable accommodations include Continental breakfast. *155 Highland Dr., 93923, tel. 408/624–1244 or 800/635–4774. 34 rooms. AE, MC, V.*

Expensive–Very Expensive

Carriage House Inn. This attractive small inn with a rustic wood-shingled exterior has rooms with open-beam ceilings, fireplaces, down comforters, and sunken Japanese baths. Continental breakfast, wine and hors d'oeuvres are included. *Junipero Ave. between 7th and 8th Aves., Box 1900, 93921, tel. 408/625–2585 or 800/422–4732 in CA. 13 rooms. AE, D, DC, MC, V.*

Tally Ho Inn. This is one of the few inns in Carmel's center that has good views out over the bay. There are suites and penthouse units with fireplaces and a pretty English garden courtyard. Continental breakfast and after-dinner brandy are included. *Monte Verde St. and 6th Ave., tel. 408/624–2232 or 800/624–2290 in CA. 14 rooms. MC, V.*

Expensive

Carmel Mission Inn. Located on the edge of Carmel Valley, this attractive modern inn has a lushly landscaped pool and Jacuzzi area and is close to the Barnyard and Crossroads shopping centers. Rooms are large, some with spacious decks. *Hwy. 1 and Rio Rd., 3665 Rio Rd., 92923, tel. 408/624–1841 or 800/348–9090. 165 rooms. Facilities: restaurant, bar, pool, Jacuzzi. AE, D, DC, MC, V.*

★ **Cobblestone Inn.** Recent renovations to this former motel have created an English-style inn with stone fireplaces in all the rooms and the sitting room area. Quilts and country antiques, along with a complimentary gourmet breakfast buffet and afternoon tea, contribute to the homey touch. *8th and Junipero*

Aves., Box 3185, 93921, tel. 408/625-5222. 24 rooms. AE, MC, V.

Moderate–
Expensive

Wayside Inn. Within easy walking distance of shops and restaurants, this attractive brick and wood inn has some units with fireplaces and full kitchens; all come with Continental breakfast and morning paper. *Mission St. and 7th Ave., Box 1900, 93921, tel. 408/624-5336 or 800/422-4732 in CA. 21 rooms. AE, D, DC, MC, V.*

★ **Lobos Lodge.** Pleasant pink stucco units in an oak and pine setting on the edge of the business district feature fireplaces and private brick patios. Continental breakfast is included. *Monte Verde St. and Ocean Ave., Box L-1, 93921, tel. 408/624-3874. 30 rooms. AE, MC, V.*

Pine Inn. This traditional favorite with generations of Carmel visitors features Victorian-style decor complete with grandfather clock, flocked wallpaper, and marble-topped furnishings. Located in the heart of the shopping district, the inn has its own brick courtyard of specialty shops. *Ocean Ave. and Lincoln St., Box 250, 93921, tel. 408/624-3851 or 800/228-3851. 49 rooms. Facilities: dining room. AE, DC, MC, V.*

Carmel Valley
Very Expensive

★ **Carmel Valley Ranch Resort.** This new addition to the resort scene is a stunning mix of contemporary California architecture with such down-home touches as handmade quilts, wood-burning fireplaces, and watercolors by local artists. Rooms feature cathedral ceilings, oversize decks, and fully stocked wet bars. *1 Old Ranch Rd., 93923, tel. 408/625-9500 or 800/4CARMEL. 100 suites. Facilities: restaurant, pool, golf (fee), tennis club and courts, saunas, Jacuzzis. AE, DC, MC, V.*

Quail Lodge. One of the area's most highly regarded resorts is beautifully situated on the grounds of a private country club where guests have access to golf and tennis. There are also 853 acres of wildlife preserve, including 11 lakes, frequented by deer and migratory fowl. The rooms, which are clustered in several low-rise buildings, are spacious and modern, with a mixture of Oriental and European decor. *8205 Valley Greens Dr., Carmel 93923, tel. 408/624-1581 or 800/538-9516; 800/682-9303 in CA. 100 rooms. Facilities: restaurant, 3 pools, 2 lounges, bar, Jacuzzi, putting green, golf (fee), tennis. AE, DC, MC, V.*

Stonepine. The former estate of the Crocker banking family has been converted to an ultradeluxe inn nestled in 330 pastoral acres with riding trails and an equestrian center. The main house, richly paneled and furnished with antiques, offers eight individually decorated suites and a private dining room for guests only. Less formal but still luxurious suites are also available in the ranch-style Paddock House. *150 E. Carmel Valley Rd., Box 1543, 93924, tel. 408/659-2245. 12 rooms. Facilities: dining room, pool, tennis, weight room, archery, mountain bikes, horseback riding. AE, MC, V.*

Moderate–
Expensive

Robles Del Rio Lodge. This pine-paneled charmer in a gorgeous setting of rolling meadows and oak forests dates from 1928. Rooms and cottages feature country-style decor with Laura Ashley prints, and the grounds include a large pool and sunbathing area, and hiking trails. Complimentary breakfast buffet is included. *200 Punta del Monte, 93924, tel. 408/659-3705 or 800/833-0843. 31 rooms. Facilities: restaurant, lounge, pool, tennis, sauna, hot tub. MC, V.*

Valley Lodge. In this small, pleasant inn, there are rooms surrounding a garden patio and separate one- and two-bedroom cottages with fireplaces and full kitchens. Continental breakfast and morning paper are included. *Carmel Valley Rd. at Ford Rd., Box 93, 93924, tel. 408/659–2261 or 800/641–4646. 31 rooms. Facilities: pool, Jacuzzi, sauna, small fitness center. AE, MC, V.*

Monterey
Very Expensive

Hyatt Regency Monterey. While the rooms and general atmosphere are less glamorous than at some other resorts in the region, the Hyatt does offer excellent golf and tennis facilities, two pools, and a par course jogging track. *1 Old Golf Course Rd., 93940, tel. 408/372–1234 or 800/824–2196 in CA. 579 rooms. Facilities: restaurant, lounge, entertainment, 2 pools. AE, D, DC, MC, V.*

★ **Spindrift Inn.** This elegant small hotel on Cannery Row boasts the street's only private beach and a rooftop garden overlooking Monterey Bay. Indoor pleasures include spacious rooms with sitting areas, Oriental rugs, fireplaces, canopied beds, down comforters, and other luxuries. Continental breakfast brought to the room on a silver tray and afternoon tea are included. *652 Cannery Row, 93940, tel. 408/646–8900 or 800/225–2901; 800/841–1879 in CA. 41 rooms. valet parking (fee). AE, D, DC, MC, V.*

Expensive–Very
Expensive

Doubletree Hotel. Adjacent to the downtown conference center, this hotel is geared more toward convention groups and business travelers than toward vacationers seeking local ambience. Rooms, some with good views of Fisherman's Wharf and the bay, are attractively furnished. Resort amenities include three tennis courts and a round swimming pool with adjoining Jacuzzi. *2 Portola Plaza, 93940, tel. 408/649–4511 or 800/528–0444. 374 rooms. Facilities: 2 restaurants, pool, tennis (fee), garage (fee). AE, D, DC, MC, V.*

★ **Hotel Pacific.** Unlike other new hotels in downtown Monterey that clash with the early California architecture and small-town ambience, the Hotel Pacific is an attractive adobe-style addition that fits right in. All rooms are suites, handsomely appointed with four-poster feather beds, hardwood floors, Indian rugs, fireplaces, wet bars, and balconies or patios. Continental breakfast and wine and cheese in the afternoon are included. *300 Pacific St., 93940, tel. 408/373–5700 or 800/225–2903; 800/554–5542 in CA. 104 rooms, garage, 2 Jacuzzis. AE, D, DC, MC, V.*

Monterey Hotel. Originally opened in 1904, this quaint small downtown hotel reopened in 1987 after an extensive restoration that left its oak paneling and ornate fireplaces gleaming. Standard rooms are small but well-appointed with antiques; master suites offer fireplaces and spa tubs. Complimentary Continental breakfast, afternoon tea, and wine and cheese in the evening are included. *406 Alvarado St., 93940, tel. 408/375–3184 or 800/727–0960. 45 rooms, parking (fee). AE, D, DC, MC, V.*

★ **Monterey Plaza.** This sophisticated full-service hotel commands a superb waterfront location on Cannery Row, where frolicking sea otters can be observed from the wide outdoor patio and from many of the room balconies. The architecture and decor, a blend of early California and Oriental styles that retains a little of the old cannery design, harmonizes well with the site. *400 Cannery Row, 93940, tel. 408/646–1700 or 800/631–1339; 800/334–3999 in CA. 290 rooms. Facilities: restaurant, bar, cable TV, garage (fee). AE, D, DC, MC, V.*

Monterey Sheraton. This large, convention-oriented hotel sticks out like a pale pink 9-story sore thumb in the middle of Monterey's quaint downtown. Rooms are small, but many have good views of the town and bay. *350 Calle Principal, 93940, tel. 408/649–4234 or 800/325–3535. 338 rooms. Facilities: restaurant, lounge, Jacuzzi, pool, health club, garage (fee). AE, DC, MC, V.*

Expensive **Hotel Resort.** The rooms are Monterey contemporary style, and have large private decks, some overlooking the pool area. Resort amenities include tennis courts, saunas, as well as rooms with handicapped access and a large indoor whirlpool. *1000 Aguajito Rd., 93940, tel. 408/373–6141 or 800/234–5697. 204 rooms. Facilities: restaurant, pool, tennis, sauna, Jacuzzi, putting green. AE, D, DC, MC, V.*

Victorian Inn. Under the same ownership as the Spindrift Inn, this hotel 2 blocks above Cannery Row has a more casual feel but also offers such in-room comforts as fireplaces, private balconies or patios, and Continental breakfast. A few rooms have ocean views. Wine and cheese are served in the antique-filled lobby during the afternoon. *487 Foam St., 93940, tel. 408/373–8000 or 800/225–2902; 800/232–4141 in CA. Garage, 68 rooms. AE, D, DC, MC, V.*

Moderate– **Best Western Monterey Beach.** This Best Western offers a great
Expensive waterfront location about 2 miles north of town with panoramic views of the bay and the Monterey skyline. The rooms are nondescript, but the grounds are pleasantly landscaped and feature a large pool with a sunbathing area. *2600 Sand Dunes Dr., 93940, tel. 408/394–3321 or 800/528–1234. 195 rooms. Facilities: restaurant, lounge, pool. AE, D, DC, MC, V.*

Cannery Row Inn. This is a modern small hotel on a street above Cannery Row with bay views from the private balconies of many rooms. Gas fireplaces and complimentary Continental breakfast are among the amenities. *200 Foam St., 93940, tel. 408/649–8580. 32 rooms. Facilities: Jacuzzi, garage. AE, MC, V.*

Otter Inn. This low-rise hotel with a rustic shingle exterior is 2 blocks above Cannery Row and has bay views from most of the rooms. Coffee and pastries are provided in rooms, which are spacious, with fireplaces and private hot tubs in some. *571 Wave St., 93940, tel. 408/375–2299. 31 rooms. AE, MC, V.*

Moderate **Arbor Inn.** This unusually attractive motel has a friendly, coun-
★ try-inn atmosphere. Continental breakfast is served in a pine-paneled lobby with a tile fireplace. There is an outdoor Jacuzzi, and rooms are light and airy, some with fireplaces and some with accessibility for the handicapped. *1058 Munras Ave., 93940, tel. 408/372–3381 or 800/351–8811 in CA. rooms. Facilities: hot tub. AE, D, DC, MC, V.*

★ **Monterey Motor Lodge.** A pleasant location on the edge of Monterey's El Estero park gives this motel an edge over its many competitors along Munras Avenue. Indoor plants and a large secluded courtyard with pool are other pluses. Continental breakfast is included. *55 Camino Aguajito, 93940, tel. 408/372–8057 or 800/558–1900. 45 rooms. Facilities: pool, restaurant. AE, D, DC, MC, V.*

Pacific Grove **Centrella Hotel.** A handsome century-old Victorian mansion
Very Expensive and garden cottages with clawfoot bathtubs and wicker and brass furnishings house the Centrella Hotel. Depending on the time of day, a sideboard in the large parlor is laden with

breakfast treats, cookies and fruit, sherry and wine, or hors d'oeuvres. *612 Central Ave., 93950, tel. 408/372–3372; 800/ 235–3372 outside CA. 26 rooms, 24 with bath. AE, MC, V.*

★ **Green Gables Inn.** Originally built a century ago by a Pasadena judge to house his mistress, this Swiss Gothic bed-and-breakfast retains an air of Victorian romance. Stained-glass windows framing an ornate fireplace and other details compete with the spectacular bay views. The breakfast buffet is tempting, as are afternoon hors d'oeuvres served with wine, sherry, or tea. *104 5th St., 93950, tel. 408/375–2095. 11 rooms, 7 with bath. AE, MC, V.*

Moderate– **Gosby House Inn.** This lovely yellow Victorian bed-and-break-
Expensive fast in the town center has 22 individually decorated rooms, al-
★ most all with private bath and some with fireplaces. Breakfasts and afternoon hors d'oeuvres are served in a sunny parlor or before the fireplace in the living room. *643 Lighthouse Ave., 93950, tel. 408/375–1287 or 800/527–8828. 22 rooms, 20 with bath. AE, MC, V.*

Martine Inn. While most bed-and-breakfasts in Pacific Grove are Victorian houses, this one is a pink stucco Mediterranean-style villa overlooking the water. The rooms, most of which have ocean views, are individually decorated with such unique items as a Chinese wedding bed and a mahogany bedroom set featured at the 1969 World's Fair. Full breakfast, wine, and hors d'oeuvres are included. *255 Oceanview Blvd., 93950, tel. 408/373–3388. 19 rooms. MC, V.*

Moderate– **Asilomar Conference Center.** A pleasant summer camplike at-
Inexpensive mosphere pervades this assortment of 28 rustic but comfort-
★ able lodges in the middle of a 100-acre state park across from the beach. Lodging is on the American plan. Reservations should be made at least a month before arrival. *800 Asilomar Blvd., Box 537, 93950, tel. 408/372–8016. 313 rooms. Facilities: restaurant, pool. No credit cards.*

Pebble Beach **The Inn at Spanish Bay.** Under the same management as the
Very Expensive Lodge at Pebble Beach, this 270-room resort sprawls on a breathtaking stretch of shoreline along 17-Mile Drive. The resort has a slightly more casual feel, although the 600-square-foot rooms are no less luxurious. The inn is adjacent to its own tennis courts and golf course, but guests also have privileges at all the Lodge facilities. *Box 1589, 2700 17-Mile Dr., 93953, tel. 408/647–7500 or 800/654–9300. 270 rooms. Facilities: 3 restaurants, clubhouse grill, tennis, pool. AE, DC, MC, V.*

★ **The Lodge at Pebble Beach.** A renowned resort since 1916, the Lodge features quietly luxurious rooms with fireplaces and wonderful views. The golf course, tennis club, and equestrian center are also highly regarded. Guests of the lodge have privileges at the Inn at Spanish Bay. *17-Mile Dr., Box 1418, Pebble Beach, 93953, tel. 408/624–3811 or 800/654–9300. 161 rooms. Facilities: 3 restaurants, coffee shop, lounge, pool, sauna, beach club, golf (fee), tennis (fee), riding (fee), weights, massage, bikes for rent. AE, DC, MC, V.*

The Arts and Nightlife

The area's top venue for the performing arts is the **Sunset Community Cultural Center** (San Carlos, between 8th and 10th aves., tel. 408/624–3996) in Carmel, which presents music and dance concerts, film screenings, and headline performers throughout the year. Facilities include the cathedral-domed Sunset Theater and the Forest Theater, the first open-air amphitheater built in California.

The Arts
Special Events

Performing arts festivals have a long tradition in the Monterey area, with the most famous drawing thousands of spectators. Ordering tickets as far in advance as possible is often essential. The oldest performing arts festival on the peninsula is the **Carmel Bach Festival** (Box 575, Carmel, 93921, tel. 408/624–1521), which has presented the work of Johann Sebastian Bach and his contemporaries in concerts and recitals for more than 50 years. The highlight of the three-week event, starting in mid-July, is a candlelit concert held in the chapel of the Carmel Mission Basilica.

Nearly as venerable is the celebrated **Monterey Jazz Festival** (Box JAZZ, Monterey, 93942, tel. 408/373–3366), which attracts jazz and blues greats from around the world to the Monterey Fairgrounds for a weekend of music each September.

Another popular jazz event is **Dixieland Monterey** (177 Webster St., Suite A-206, Monterey, 93940, tel. 408/443–5260), held on the first full weekend of March, which features Dixieland bands performing in cabarets, restaurants, and hotel lounges throughout Monterey, as well as a Saturday morning jazz parade downtown.

For blues fans, there is the **Monterey Bay Blues Festival** (tel. 408/394–2652), which is held in June at the Monterey Fairgrounds, featuring entertainment and soul food.

The Custom House Plaza in downtown Monterey is the setting for free afternoon performances outdoors, and, in the evenings, shows held in a tent (admission is charged) during the **Monterey Bay Theatrefest** (tel. 408/649–6852), which is held on weekend afternoons and evenings during most of the summer.

Concerts

One of the nation's most highly regarded metropolitan symphonies, the **Monterey County Symphony** (Box 3965, Carmel, 93921, tel. 408/624–8511), performs a series of concerts throughout the year in Monterey, Salinas, and Carmel. Programs range from classical to pop and often include guest artists.

The **Chamber Music Society of the Monterey Peninsula** (Box 6283, Carmel 93921, tel. 408/625–2212) presents a series of concerts featuring guest artists such as the Juilliard String Quartet and the New York Philomusica. Dance, classical music, and operatic concerts are sponsored by the **Salinas Concert Association** (318 Catharine St., Salinas, tel. 408/758–5027), which presents a series of featured artists between April and October at the Sherwood Hall in Salinas.

Film

The **Monterey Institute of Foreign Study** (440 Van Buren St., Monterey, tel. 408/626–1730) sponsors regular screenings of notable foreign films. Classic films are also shown on Thursdays once a month in the community room of the **Monterey Public Library** (625 Pacific St., Monterey, tel. 408/646–3930).

Theater

California's First Theater (Scott and Pacific Sts., tel. 408/375–4916) is home to the Troupers of the Gold Coast, who perform 19th-century melodramas year round in the state's oldest operating little theater, a historic landmark dating from 1846 on Monterey's Path of History.

Specializing in contemporary works, both comedy and drama, is the **GroveMont Theater,** an acclaimed repertory company that now has two theaters, the Grovemont Arts Center (320 Hoffman Ave., Monterey, (tel. 408/649–6852) and the newly refurbished Monterey Playhouse (425 Washington St., tel. 408/655–PLAY). Also part of the GroveMont Center is the **Poetic Drama Institute,** which often features solo dramatic performances and poetry readings.

American musicals, both old and new, are the focus of the **New Wharf Theater** (Fisherman's Wharf, Monterey, tel. 408/649–2332), where a local cast is often joined by Broadway actors, directors, and choreographers.

Nightlife   **Kalisa's** (851 Cannery Row, Monterey, tel. 408/372–8512). This
Cabaret   long-established, freewheeling café in a Cannery Row landmark building offers a potpourri of entertainment that can include belly dancing, flamenco, jazz, folk dancing, and magic.

Bars and   **Boiler Room** (625 Cannery Row, Monterey, tel. 408/373–1449).
Nightclubs   Most nights feature comedy shows, followed by dancing to live rock music. There is occasional country and western dancing and entertainment.

The Club (Alvarado and Del Monte Sts., Monterey, tel. 408/646–9244). This popular night spot has dancing to Top-40 music nightly, plus changing entertainment that includes rock bands, comedy, and male striptease.

Doc Ricketts' Lab (95 Prescott St., Monterey, tel. 408/649–4241). Live rock bands perform nightly 1 block above Cannery Row.

Doubletree Hotel (2 Portola Plaza, Monterey, tel. 408/649–4511). Popular music entertainment is offered nightly except Sundays in the Brasstree Lounge.

Highlands Inn (Hwy. 1, Carmel, tel. 408/624–3801). There is piano music nightly in the Lobos Lounge; dancing on weekends in the Fireside Lounge.

Hyatt Regency (1 Old Golf Course Rd., Monterey, tel. 408/372–1234, ext. 55). Dancing and live music are on tap in the Whispers Lounge from Monday through Saturday.

Lodge at Pebble Beach (17-Mile Dr., Pebble Beach, tel. 408/624–3811). You'll find easy listening entertainment in the Cypress Room and Terrace Lounge; there's a jazz band on Friday and Saturday evenings.

Mark Thomas Outrigger (700 Cannery Row, Monterey, tel. 408/372–8543). Top-40 dance music is played by live bands on Friday and Saturday night.

Monterey Plaza Hotel (400 Cannery Row, Monterey, tel. 408/646–1700). Piano music and a guitarist are to be heard in a romantic setting overlooking the bay in the Delfino Lounge.

Monterey Sheraton (350 Calle Principal, Monterey, tel. 408/649–4234). Live jazz is offered nightly in the Monterey Bay Club.

Sly McFlys (700 Cannery Row, Monterey, tel. 408/649–8050). This popular local watering hole has a pub atmosphere.

Discos   **Brick House** (220 N. Fremont St., Monterey, tel. 408/375–6116). There is dancing to Top-40 music with a DJ and big-screen video.

Safari Club (1425 Munras Ave., Monterey, tel. 408/649–1020). Again, dancing to Top-40 music with local DJ at the Ramada Inn. Open Friday and Saturday 9 to 2 AM.

11 The Central Coast

Introduction

The stretch of coastline between Carmel and Santa Barbara, a distance of about 250 miles, is some of the most breathtaking in California. Around Big Sur, the Santa Lucia Mountains drop down to the Pacific with dizzying grandeur. The area is sparsely populated, dotted with small towns, grazing cattle, and hillsides of wildflowers. Its inhabitants relish their isolation among the redwoods at the sharp edge of land and sea.

Traditionally, Big Sur has attracted individualists—the novelist Henry Miller comes to mind—drawn by the intractability of the terrain. Farther south, the junction of land and sea is less precipitous, there are more sandy beaches and fewer cliffs, and the facilities for tourists are better developed. The main attraction here, Hearst Castle on Enchanted Hill, was built by another famous individualist of a more gregarious bent, William Randolph Hearst.

The rolling hills in the southern part of the region support a number of wineries whose standing is rising steadily. Solvang is a popular stopover for hearty fare on the route north or south, and the artists' colony and resort town of Ojai is half an hour north of Santa Barbara. From Solvang, it is an hour's drive south to Santa Barbara, the first glimpse of the sand, surf and sun of Southern California.

The traditions of Spanish California, of unhurried hospitality and easy living, are kept alive here: Santa Barbara works hard to maintain its relaxed atmosphere and cozy scale, 90 miles from the metropolitan sprawl of Los Angeles. Wedged as it is between the Pacific and the Santa Ynez Mountains, the city never had much room for expansion. The mountains to the north protect its sunny climate, and the emphasis is on the outdoors. The focus of the town is the waterfront, with its Mediterranean feeling, its beaches, pier, and harbor. The downtown area, which retains much of its Spanish architectural heritage, is geared to the city's principal trade: tourism. Up in the hills, in Montecito and Hope Ranch, lie the expensive ranch homes of celebrities.

Highway 1, which runs through most of this region, was the first in the country to be declared a scenic highway, in 1966. Barring fog or rain, the coast is almost always in view from the road. In some sections, the waves break on rocks 11,200 feet below; in others, the highway is just 20 feet above the surf. The two-lane road is good, but it twists, and traffic, especially in the summer months, can be very slow. Allow plenty of time and sit back and enjoy the scenery.

Getting Around

By Plane **American** and **American Eagle** (tel. 800/433–7300), **Skywest/ Delta** (tel. 800/453–9417), and **United** and **United Express** (tel. 800/241–6522) fly into Santa Barbara Municipal Airport (tel. 805/967–5608), 8 miles from downtown on Marxmiller Road.

Santa Barbara Airbus (tel. 805/964–7374) runs to and from the airport and shuttles travelers between Santa Barbara and Los Angeles Airport. **Aero Airport Limousine** (tel. 805/965–2412) serves Los Angeles Airport (by reservation only). **Metropoli-**

tan **Transit District** (tel. 805/963–3364) bus #11 runs from the
airport to the downtown transit center.

By Car The only way to see the most dramatic section of the central
coast, the 70 miles between Big Sur and San Simeon, is by car.
By heading south on Highway 1, you'll be on the ocean side of
the road and get the best views. Don't expect to rush. The road
is narrow and twisting with a single lane in each direction,
making it difficult to pass slower traffic or the many lumbering
RVs that favor the route. In fog or rain, the drive can be nerve-
wracking. U.S. 101 from San Francisco to San Luis Obispo is
the quicker, easier alternative, but it misses the coast entirely.
U.S. 101 and Highway 1 join north of Santa Barbara. Both,
eventually dividing, continue south through southern California.

By Bus Major bus lines avoid Highway 1, preferring the speedier inland routes. There is, however, local service in several towns.
From Monterey and Carmel, **Monterey–Salinas Transit** (tel.
408/899–2555) operates daily bus runs to Big Sur April–
September. From San Luis Obispo, **North Coastal Transit** (tel.
805/541–BUSS) runs buses around the town and out to the
coast on regular schedules. Local service is also provided by
the Santa Barbara Metropolitan Transit District (tel. 805/963–
3364).

By Train Amtrak (tel. 800/USA-RAIL) runs the *Coast Starlight* train
along the coast from Santa Barbara to San Luis Obispo, but
there it heads inland for the rest of the route to the San Francisco Bay Area and Seattle. Local numbers are, in Santa Barbara,
tel. 805/687–6848; in San Luis Obispo, tel. 805/541–5028.

Guided Tours

California Parlour Car Tours (Cathedral Hill Hotel, 1101 Van
Ness Ave., San Francisco 94109, tel. 415/474–7500 or 800/227–
4250) offers a number of tours that include the central coast
area. Lasting three to 11 days, these are one-way trips from
San Francisco to Los Angeles (or vice versa) that travel along
the coast in 36-passenger buses, visit Hearst Castle, Santa
Barbara, and Monterey and may also include time in Yosemite
or Lake Tahoe. There are certainly advantages to such organized touring, especially in a region where driving is so demanding, but there are also disadvantages. (We recommend that you
steer clear of any tour that takes you to Yosemite for less than
one full day; readers have been disappointed in the past. Save
Yosemite for a trip when you have enough time.)

Santa Barbara Trolley Co. (tel. 805/565–1122) has five daily,
regularly scheduled runs in Santa Barbara. Motorized San
Francisco-style cable cars deliver visitors to major hotels,
shopping areas, and attractions. Stop or not as you wish and
pick up another trolley when ready to move on. All depart and
return to Stearns Wharf. *Fare: $3 adults, $2 children.*

Walking Tours Through History (tel. 805/967–9869). A longtime
Santa Barbara resident takes small groups on walking tours of
gardens and historic buildings. Mornings and afternoon tours
begin at the courthouse lobby.

Important Addresses and Numbers

Tourist Information An excellent selection of free pamphlets on accommodations, dining, sports, and entertainment is available at the **Visitors Information Center** (1 Santa Barbara St. at Cabrillo Blvd., tel. 805/965–3021. Open Mon.–Sat. 9–5, Sun. 10–4). Before arriving, contact **Santa Barbara Conference and Visitors Bureau** (510 State St., Suite A, 93101, tel. 805/966–9222).

Information on other towns along the central coast is available from:

Big Sur Chamber of Commerce (Box 87, 93920, tel. 408/667–2100).

San Luis Obispo Chamber of Commerce (1039 Chorro St., 93401, tel. 805/543–1323).

Cambria Chamber of Commerce (767 Main St., 93428, tel. 805/927–3624).

San Simeon Chamber of Commerce (Box 1, 9190 Hearst, 93452, tel. 805/927–3500).

Solvang Visitors Bureau (Box 769, 1571 Mission Dr., 93464, tel. 805/688–6144 or 800/468–6765).

California Dept. of Parks and Recreation (in Big Sur, tel. 408/667–2315.)

Emergencies Dial 911 for **police** and **ambulance** in an emergency.

Doctor Emergency care is available at **St. Francis Hospital** (601 E. Micheltorena St., Santa Barbara, tel. 805/568–5711 or 962–7661).

Road Conditions Dial 408/757–2006 for information.

Exploring

You can drive up to Santa Barbara from Los Angeles in a few hours. If you fly into town, a car is not absolutely necessary. Exploring all of California's central coast is a rewarding and memorable experience, providing you have a car and plenty of patience. For the 90 miles from Big Sur to Morro Bay, plan for three to four hours on the road. Along this stretch there are 300 turnouts offering ample opportunity to gaze out on the always changing coastline. From mid-December through January, look for migrating gray whales. In the spring, California's vibrant orange native poppy is common along the drive.

Once you start south from Carmel, there is no route off the coast until all the way to Cambria where Highway 46 connects with U.S. 101 inland. Nearly everything you want to see is right along the coastal highway, including the state parks and beaches in the Big Sur region and Hearst Castle in San Simeon. For the attractive shops and restaurants of Cambria, a short loop off of Highway 1 runs through the town's twin villages and connects again back on Highway 1 a few miles later. At Morro Bay, Highway 1 makes its move inland for 13 miles, where it connects with U.S. 101 at San Luis Obispo. From there south, in place of the dramatic coastal scenery, you are rewarded with the driving ease of U.S. 101. This passes the crowded but lively town of Pismo Beach and then travels gently rolling hills for 70 miles to the turnoff for the short drive to Solvang.

The entire 210 miles from Big Sur to Santa Barbara *can* be tackled in a long day, but that won't leave time to enjoy the drive or stop at Hearst Castle or anywhere in between. A better choice is to plan on several days, with time to explore Hearst Castle, Santa Barbara, and (if it's to your taste) Solvang. The time spent along the Big Sur coast will vary widely depending on your desire to hike or explore rocky beaches; you'll want to stop and appreciate the view, anyway.

South along Highway 1

Numbers in the margin correspond with points of interest on the Central Coast map.

If you start your coastal trip from the north, you'll be quickly treated to the quintessential view of California's coast, the elegant concrete arch of **Bixby Creek Bridge.** Just 13 miles south of Carmel, this view is every photographer's dream. There is a small parking area on the north side from which to take a photo or to start a walk across the 550-foot span.

Five miles south and you'll see the **Point Sur Light Station** atop a sandstone cliff. The century-old beacon is open to the public on ranger-led tours on Saturday at 9:30 and 1:30, and Sunday mornings at 9:30. Call the Big Sur State Park District (tel. 408/667–2315 or 625–4419) for tour times.

The small developed area of the Big Sur valley begins a few miles south. Pfeiffer Big Sur State Park, gas, groceries, hotels, and restaurants are all clustered along the highway within the next 7 miles.

One of the few places where you may actually set foot on the coastline you have been viewing from the road is at **Pfeiffer Beach.** The road to the beach is immediately past the Big Sur Ranger Station; follow it for 2 miles. The picturesque beach is at the foot of the cliffs, and a hole in one of the big sea-washed rocks lets you watch the waves break first on the sea side and then again on the beach side. The water is too cold and the surf too dangerous for swimming much of the year, however.

On the ocean side of Highway 1, a towering 800 feet above the water, is **Nepenthe,** a favorite hangout with tourists and locals. The restaurant's deck can be an excellent place to take a break from a rather stressful if very beautiful drive. Rita Hayworth and Orson Welles spent their honeymoon here. Downstairs is a craft and gift shop, displaying among other items the work of Kaffe Fassett, the famous knitting designer who grew up at Nepenthe.

A few miles south is **Julia Pfeiffer Burns State Park** (tel. 408/667–2315), where a short and popular hike is a nice way to stretch your legs. The trail leads up a small valley to a waterfall. You can go back the same (easier) way or take a loop that leads you along the valley wall, with views out into the tops of the redwood trees you were just walking among. There are picnic and camping areas as well as access to the beach.

For the next dozen miles, it is just you, the road, and the coast. At Lucia there is a gas station and the beginnings of civilization again. Among the many picnic areas and campgrounds along the way from here to San Simeon is **Jade Cove,** one of the best known areas on the coast in which to hunt for jade. Rock hunting is allowed on the beach, but you may not remove anything from the walls of the cliffs.

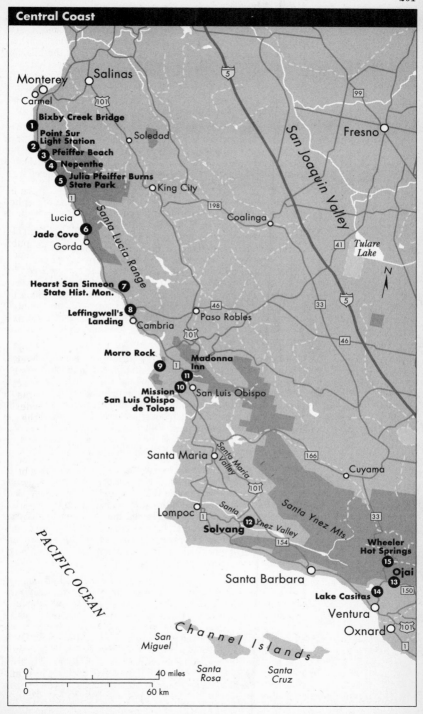

Central Coast

Monterey
Salinas
Carmel
Soledad
Bixby Creek Bridge
1
Point Sur
Light Station
2
3 **Pfeiffer Beach**
4 **Nepenthe**
5 **Julia Pfeiffer Burns**
State Park
King City
Lucia
Jade Cove **6**
Gorda
Coalinga
Fresno
San Joaquin Valley
Tulare
Lake
Santa Lucia Range
Hearst San Simeon **7**
State Hist. Mon.
Leffingwell's **8**
Landing Cambria
Paso Robles
Morro Rock
9 **Madonna**
11 **Inn**
10
Mission
San Luis Obispo
de Tolosa San Luis Obispo
Santa Maria
Santa Maria Valley
Cuyama
Santa Ynez Mts.
Lompoc
Santa
12
Solvang Ynez Valley
Wheeler
Hot Springs
15
Ojai
13
Santa Barbara
Lake Casitas **14**
Ventura
Oxnard
PACIFIC OCEAN
San
Miguel
Channel Islands
Santa
Rosa
Santa
Cruz

0   40 miles
0   60 km

❼ It is 30 miles up to the Enchanted Hill, where the **Hearst San Simeon State Historical Monument,** one of California's most popular sites for visitors, perches in solitary splendor. You may resent being herded into buses at the bottom of the hill, but that indignity is amply rewarded by the neoclassical extravagance of the millionaire's mansion at the top, with its marble halls and reflecting pools. On the way up, you may catch a glimpse of a zebra, one of the last descendants of William Randolph Hearst's magnificent private zoo.

The newspaper magnate commissioned the celebrated architect Julia Morgan to design his grandiose residence, and work began on it in 1919. Built to house his extensive entourage, not to mention houseguests from Hollywood, it was also intended as a showcase for his impressive collection of art, gathered from around the world. It was completed in 1947.

A new visitors' center offers an introduction to the life of this master of the yellow press and inspiration for Orson Welles's film *Citizen Kane.* Admission is free, but tours of the estate generally require advance reservations (tickets can be bought at the grounds, but tours fill up quickly). There is a choice of four tours, each about two hours long, and covering a considerable distance on foot. *Reservations are usually required: tel. 619/452–1950 or 800/444–7275; sometimes it is possible to gain admission directly. Tours daily 8:20 AM–3 PM (later in summer). Admission: $12 adults, $6 children 6–12, plus a $1.80 charge for booking. Closed Thanksgiving, Christmas, and New Year's Day. Reservations may be made up to 8 weeks in advance. AE, MC, V.*

Cambria, an artists' colony full of turn-of-the-century homes, is located a few minutes south of San Simeon. Moonstone Beach Drive, which runs along the coast, is lined with motels, and
❽ **Leffingwell's Landing,** a state picnic ground at its northern end, is a good place for tide-pooling and watching otters. The woodsy part of town, which boasts several fine restaurants, is divided into the newer West Village and the original East Village, each with its own shops and galleries, and many reminders of the Welsh miners who settled here in the 1890s.

You'll come to the end of the coastal ribbon of Highway 1 at Morro Bay, separated from the ocean by a 4½-mile sandspit and the causeway built in the 1930s out to the huge monolith of
❾ **Morro Rock.** You can make the quick drive out to the rock (an extinct volcano), with the sheltered harbor (home of a large fishing fleet) on one side and the crash of waves on the other. Morro Rock is a wildlife preserve to protect nesting areas of endangered peregrine falcons. The town center includes a huge chess board with human-size pieces.

San Luis Obispo, halfway between San Francisco and Los Angeles, is home to two notable institutions: California Polytechnic State University, known as Cal Poly, and the wonderfully garish Madonna Inn. A list of self-guided historic walks through the treelined downtown is available from the Chamber
❿ of Commerce. Among the places to see is the **Mission San Luis Obispo de Tolosa** (805/543–6850) at the heart of the downtown. The Ah Louis Store, 800 Palm Street, was established in 1884 to serve the Chinese laborers building the Pacific Coast and Southern Pacific railroads, and it still operates. If you happen

to be in town on Thursday night, don't miss the weekly farmers' market and street fair along Higuera Street.

⑪ Even if you don't stay at the **Madonna Inn,** drop by the café and shops for a taste of the gilt cherubs, pink bar stools, pink trash cans, pink lampposts, and all the other assorted froufrou that has made the place famous. You'll notice something is up at the "Flintstone"-like gas station made entirely of big boulders. Begun in 1958 by Alex Madonna, a local highway contractor, and his wife, Phyllis, today each of the more than 100 rooms has its own theme. The cave rooms, complete with waterfalls for showers, are among the most popular. *100 Madonna Rd. (take the Madonna Rd. exit from U.S. 101), tel. 805/543–3000.*

Avila Beach, a usually quiet beach town a short detour off Highway 1/U.S. 101, comes alive on weekends when Cal Poly students take over. A bit farther down the highway, 20 miles of wide sandy beaches begin at the town of Pismo Beach, where U.S. 101 and Highway 1 go their separate ways. The action at this busy community centers on the shops and arcades near the pier.

⑫ Leave the beach scene behind and head inland to a taste of Denmark in the town of **Solvang,** about an hour's drive south on U.S. 101 to the turnoff of Highway 246 at Buellton and then less than 5 miles east. There is no question when you've reached Solvang: Suddenly the architecture turns to half-timbered buildings, windmills, and flags galore. Clearly aimed to appeal to tourists, there is nonetheless a genuine Danish heritage here and more than two-thirds of the town is of Danish descent. The more than 200 shops selling Danish goods and an array of knickknacks and gift items are all within walking distance, many along Copenhagen Drive and Alisal Road. Stop by the narrow and jammed coffee shop attached to Birkholm's Bakery, Alisal Road, to try the Danish pastry. It is one of a half-dozen aroma-filled bakeries in town.

Everything but the palm trees outside the Bethania Lutheran Church, Atterdag Road at Laurel Avenue, is traditional; the Danish services are open to the public.

From Buellton, U.S. 101 heads back to the coast, where it joins Highway 1 again and runs east to Santa Barbara, about 30 miles away.

⑬ A half-hour drive east of Santa Barbara over the narrow and winding Highway 150 will put you in **Ojai,** a surprisingly rural town whose surroundings are reminiscent of earlier days in California. You'll see acres of ripening orange and avocado groves. Moviemaker Frank Capra used the Ojai Valley as a backdrop for his 1936 classic, *Lost Horizon.* Be aware that the valley can sizzle in the summer when temperatures reach 90 degrees.

The works of talented local artists can be seen in the Spanish-style shopping arcade along the main street. Each Sunday they display their paintings and crafts at the outdoor exhibition in the Security Bank parking lot (205 W. Ojai Ave.). The Art Center (113 S. Montgomery, tel. 805/646–0117) features art exhibits, theater, and dance.

A stroll around town should include a stop at **Bart's Books** (302 W. Matilija, tel. 805/646–3755), an outdoor store sheltered by native oaks and overflowing with used books. *Open Tues.–Sun. 10–5:30.*

⑭ Nearby **Lake Casitas** on Highway 150 offers boating, fishing, and camping. It was the venue for the 1984 Olympic rowing events.

⑮ A special draw for Ojai is a hot spring that makes use of natural mineral water in the hills nearby. The spa at **Wheeler Hot Springs** emerges like an oasis 7 miles from town on Highway 33. Its tall palms and herb gardens are fed by an adjacent stream, and natural mineral waters fill the four redwood hot tubs and a large pool at the well-kept spa. Massage is also available. A restaurant on site offers dinner Thursday through Sunday and Sunday brunch. *16825 Maricopa Hwy., tel. 805/646–8131. Open Mon. and Wed.–Fri. 10–9, Sat. 9 AM–10 PM, Sun. 9–9. Reservations advised at least a week in advance, especially for spa.*

Santa Barbara

Numbers in the margin correspond with points of interest on the Santa Barbara map.

Santa Barbara's attractions begin with the ocean, with most everything along Cabrillo Boulevard. In the few miles between the beaches and the hills, you pass the downtown and then reach the old mission and, a little higher up, the botanic gardens. A few miles farther up the coast, but still very much in Santa Barbara, is the exclusive residential district of Hope Ranch. To the east is the district called Montecito, where Charlie Chaplin built the Montecito Inn to house visiting guests during the days he was making movies in Santa Barbara before moving to Hollywood. Montecito is also where the exclusive San Ysidro Ranch is located.

Because the town is on a jog in the coastline, it faces south, making directions confusing. Up the coast is west, and down toward Los Angeles is east. The mountains are north.

Everything is so close, the 8-mile drive to the airport seems like a long trip. A car is handy, but not essential. The beaches and downtown are easily explored by bicycle or on foot. The Santa Barbara Trolley takes visitors to most of the major hotels and sights, which can also be reached on the local buses.

The Visitors Information Center publishes a free guide to a scenic drive that circles the town with a detour into the downtown. It passes the harbor, beaches, Hope Ranch, and the old mission, offers fine views on the way to Montecito, and returns to the beaches. You can pick up the drive, marked with blue "Scenic Drive" signs, anywhere along the loop. A free guide to the downtown, the "Red Tile Walking Tour," is also available free from the tourist office. It hits historical spots in a 12-block area.

The town of Goleta, the home of the University of California at Santa Barbara, is located a few miles up the coast via U.S. 101.

❶ If you decide to start at the Pacific and move inland, then one of the first spots to visit is **Stearns Wharf** on Cabrillo Boulevard at the foot of State Street. You can drive out and park on the pier, then wander through the shops or stop for a meal at the wharf's restaurants or snack bar. The **Sea Center,** a recent addition to

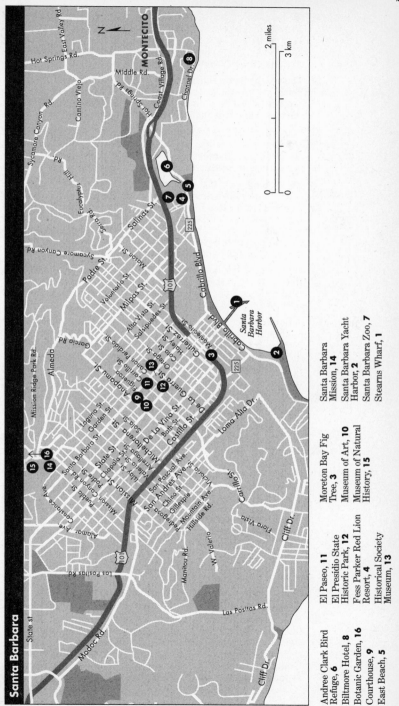

Santa Barbara

Andree Clark Bird Refuge, **6**
Biltmore Hotel, **8**
Botanic Garden, **16**
Courthouse, **9**
East Beach, **5**

El Paseo, **11**
El Presidio State Historic Park, **12**
Fess Parker Red Lion Resort, **4**
Historical Society Museum, **13**

Moreton Bay Fig Tree, **3**
Museum of Art, **10**
Museum of Natural History, **15**

Santa Barbara Mission, **14**
Santa Barbara Yacht Harbor, **2**
Santa Barbara Zoo, **7**
Stearns Wharf, **1**

the pier, is a branch of the Museum of Natural History that specializes in exhibits of marine life. First built in 1872, then rebuilt in 1981 after a fire, the wharf extends 3 blocks into the Pacific. It is a fine place to look back on the city for a sense of its size and general layout.

2 The nearby **Santa Barbara Yacht Harbor** is sheltered by an artificial breakwater at the west end of Cabrillo Boulevard. You can take a ½-mile walk along the paved breakwater, check out the tackle and bait shops, or hire a boat from here.

3 Planted in 1877, the **Moreton Bay Fig Tree,** at Chapala Street and Highway 101, is so huge it reportedly can provide shade for 10,000 people. In recent years the tree has become a gathering place for an increasing number of homeless people.

Back along Cabrillo, sandy beaches stretch for miles. The sprawling reddish Spanish-style hotel across from the beach is

4 the **Fess Parker Red Lion Resort.** Parker, the actor who played Davy Crockett and Daniel Boone, owned the oceanfront acreage and spent years trying to convince city fathers to allow him to develop a hotel. He finally did, and the hotel opened in 1987 as the largest in Santa Barbara.

5
6 Just beyond the hotel is the area's most popular beach, **East Beach,** at the east end of Cabrillo. Nearby is the **Andree Clark Bird Refuge,** a peaceful lagoon and gardens. *1400 E. Cabrillo Blvd. Admission free.*

7 Adjoining the lagoon is the **Santa Barbara Zoo,** a small lushly landscaped home to big-game cats, elephants and exotic birds. *500 Ninos Dr., tel. 805/962–6310. Admission: $4 adults, $2 senior citizens and children 2–12. Open daily in winter 10–5; daily in summer 9–6.*

8 Where Cabrillo Boulevard ends at the lagoon, Channel Drive picks up and, a short distance east, passes the **Biltmore Hotel,** now owned by the Four Seasons chain. For more than 60 years, the rich have come here to indulge in quiet elegance.

9 To reach the downtown area, return to Cabrillo and head inland along State Street. **The Courthouse,** in the center of downtown, has all the grandeur of a Moorish palace. In fact, as you wander the halls, admiring the brilliant hand-painted tiles and spiral staircase, you forget you are in a public courthouse until a handcuffed group of juvenile offenders marches through. This magnificent building was completed in 1929 at the height of the city's cultural reawakening. An elevator to the tower takes visitors to a panoramic view of the city and a fine place to take photos. The second-floor supervisors' ceremonial chambers contains murals painted by the artist who did backdrops for Cecil B. DeMille's silent films. *1100 block of Anacapa St., tel. 805/962–6464. Open weekdays 8–5, weekends 9–5. Free 1-hour guided tours Tues.–Sat. 2 PM, Wed. and Fri., 10:30 AM.*

10 Continue one block down Anapamu Street past the Spanish-style **Public Library** to the **Santa Barbara Museum of Art.** This fine small museum houses a permanent collection featuring ancient sculpture, Oriental art, a collection of German expressionist paintings, and a sampling of American artists such as Grandma Moses. *1130 State St., tel. 805/963–4364. Admission: $3 adults, $1.50 children 6–16. Open Tues.–Sat. 11–5 (9 PM*

*Thurs. eve.), Sun. noon–5. Tours are led Tues.–Sat. at 2 PM,
Sun. at 1 PM.*

⑪ Walking south you'll pass **El Paseo,** a shopping arcade built
around an old adobe home. There are several such arcades in
this area and many small art galleries. A few blocks north is the
⑫ **El Presidio State Historic Park.** Built in 1782, the presidio was
one of four military strongholds established by the Spanish
along the coast of California. The guardhouse, El Cuartel, is
one of the two original adobe buildings that remain of the complex and is the oldest building owned by the state. *123 E. Cañon Perdido St., tel. 805/966–9719. Admission free. Open daily
10:30–4:30.*

⑬ A block away is the **Historical Society Museum,** with an array of
items from the town's past, including a silver-clad riding saddle
and a collection of fancy ladies' fans. *136 E. De la Guerra St.,
tel. 805/966–1601. Admission free. Open Tues.–Sat. 10–5,
Sun. noon–5.*

A short distance from downtown (take State St. north and
⑭ make a right on Los Olivos) at the base of the hills is the **Santa Barbara Mission,** the gem of the chain of 21 missions established in California by Spanish missionaries in the late 1700s.
One of the best preserved of the missions, it still functions as a
Catholic church. *Laguna St., tel. 805/682–4713. Admission:
adults $1, children under 16 free. Open daily 9–5.*

⑮ Continuing north a block you pass the **Museum of Natural His-
⑯** **tory,** 2559 Puesta del Sol, and then the **Botanic Garden,** 1½
miles north of the mission. The 60 acres of native plants are particularly beautiful in the spring. *1212 Mission Canyon Rd., tel.
805/682–4726. Admission $3 adults. Open 8 AM–sunset.
Guided tours (10:30 AM and 2 PM) Thurs., Sat., and Sun.*

What to See and Do with Children

Santa Barbara Zoo. Youngsters particularly enjoy the scenic
railroad and barnyard petting zoo (*see* Exploring, above).

Beach playground. For children who tire of the beach quickly,
there is an elaborate jungle gym play area at Santa Barbara's
East Beach, next to the Cabrillo Bath House.

Whale bones. Outside the Museum of Natural History in Santa
Barbara is the skeleton of a blue whale, the world's largest
creature. Kids are dwarfed by the bones and invited to touch
them (they just can't climb on them) (*see* Exploring, above).

Off the Beaten Track

Channel Islands Hearty travelers will be rewarded with a day visit or overnight
camping trip to one of the five Channel Islands that often ap-
pear in a haze off the Santa Barbara horizon. The closest of the
islands and the most often visited is Anacapa Island, 11 miles
off the coast. The islands' remoteness and unpredictable seas
protected them, providing a nature enthusiast's paradise—
both underwater and on land. In 1980 the islands became the
nation's 40th national park, and the water a mile around each is
protected as a marine sanctuary.

On a good day, you'll view seals, sea lions, and an array of bird
life. From December through March, migrating whales can be

seen close up. On land, tide pools alive with sea life are often accessible. Underwater, divers view fish, giant squid, and coral. Off Anacapa Island, scuba divers can see the remains of a steamship that sank in 1853. Frenchy's Cove, on the west end of the island, has a swimming beach and fine snorkeling.

A visit to the islands can be a rugged trip, often in rough waters. You can charter a boat and head out on your own, if you wish, but most visitors make the 40-minute drive south to the Ventura Harbor. There, a park-district concessionaire carries small groups to the islands for day hikes, barbecues, and primitive overnight camping.

Boat trips. *Island Packers* provide day trips to the islands and overnight camping to three of them. Boats link up with National Park naturalists for hikes and nature programs. A limited number of visitors is allowed on each island and unpredictable weather can limit island landings. *Reservations are essential in the summer. 1867 Spinnaker Dr., Ventura 93001, tel. 805/642–7688.*

Wineries Centered around the Solvang area is a California wine-making region with much of the variety but none of the glitz of the famed Napa Valley in Northern California. Most of the region's 30 wineries are located in the rolling hills in either the Santa Maria or Santa Ynez valleys. A leisurely tour of the entire area can easily take all day, but many wineries are no more than a short detour off U.S. 101. These are generally small wineries. Only some offer guided tours, but most have tasting rooms run by helpful staff, and wine makers will often act as your tour guide. You can arrange your tour to assure you are in town for lunch, but why not pack a lunch and take advantage of the picnic areas provided at many of the wineries?

Pamphlets with detailed maps and listings of each winery are readily available at motels and tourist centers all along the coast. A map for a self-guided driving tour is available free from the Santa Barbara County Vintners' Association (Box 1558, Santa Ynez, 93460, tel. 805/688–0881).

Shopping

Antiques A dozen antiques and gift shops are clustered in restored Victorian buildings on Brinkerhoff Avenue, 2 blocks west of State Street at West Cota Street, in Santa Barbara.

Arcade In all, 32 shops, art galleries, and studios share the courtyard and gardens of El Paseo, a shopping arcade rich in history. Lunch at the outdoor patio is a nice break from a downtown tour. *Between State and Anacapa Sts. at Cañon Perdido St. in Santa Barbara.*

Beach Wear If you want to go home with the absolute latest in California beach wear, stop by **Pacific Leisure,** which specializes in volleyball fashions, shorts, tops, and beach towels. *808 State St., Santa Barbara, tel. 805/962–8828. Open Mon.–Sat. 10–6, Sun. noon–5.*

Beaches

Santa Barbara's beaches don't have the big surf of beaches farther south, but neither do they have the crowds. A short walk from the parking lot can usually find you a solitary spot. Be aware that fog often hugs the coast until about noon in May and June.

East Beach. At the east end of Cabrillo Boulevard, this is *the* beach in Santa Barbara. There are lifeguards, volleyball courts, a jogging and bike trail, and the Cabrillo Bath House with a gym, showers, and changing rooms open to the public.

Arroyo Burro Beach. Located a little west of the harbor on Cliff Drive at Las Positas Road, this state beach has a small grassy area with picnic tables and sandy beaches below the cliffs. The Brown Pelican Restaurant on the beach is nice for breakfast.

Goleta Beach Park. To the north in Goleta, this is a favorite with the college kids from the nearby University of California campus. The easy surf makes it perfect for beginning surfers and families with young children.

State Beaches. West of Santa Barbara on Highway 1 are *El Capitan*, *Refugio*, and *Gaviota* state beaches with campsites, picnic tables, and fire pits. East of the city is the state beach at *Carpinteria*, a sheltered, sunny and often crowded beach.

Participant Sports

Bicycling All through Solvang you'll see people pedaling along in quadricycles, or four-wheel carriages. Those and other bikes are available at **Surrey Cycle Rental** (486 1st St., tel. 805/688–0091 and 2164 Center St., tel: 805/653–0449).

Camping There are many campsites along Highway 1, but they can fill up early any time but winter. In Big Sur, campsites are at Pfeiffer Big Sur and Julia Pfeiffer Burns state parks. Near Hearst Castle, camping is available at several smaller state parks (San Simeon, Atascadero, Morro Bay, and Montana de Oro). Most of the sites require advance reservations from MISTIX reservation service (tel. 800/444–7275 or 619/452–1950).

Fishing There is access to freshwater- and surf-fishing spots all along the coast. For deep-sea trips, **Virg's Fish'n** (tel. 805/772–1222) offers day trips out of Morro Bay all year. Also in Morro Bay is **Bob's Sportfishing** (tel. 805/772–3340).

Glider Rides Rides of 15–20 minutes are offered weekends, 10–5, at the Santa Ynez Airport near Solvang (tel. 805/688–8390).

Hiking There are miles of hiking trails in the Ventana Wilderness, with trailheads at state parks and picnic areas on Highway 1 from Big Sur to San Simeon. Twelve miles east of Solvang is Cachuma Lake, a jewel of an artificial lake offering hiking as well as fishing and boating.

Santa Barbara Sports

Bicycling Santa Barbara's waterfront boasts the level, two-lane Cabrillo Bike Lane. In just over 3 easy miles, you pass the city zoo, bird refuge, beaches, and harbor. There are restaurants along the way, or you can stop for a picnic along the palm-lined path looking out on the Pacific. Rent bikes from **Beach Rentals** (8 W. Cabrillo Blvd., tel. 805/963–2524; open 8 AM to sunset in winter, and 8 AM–11 PM in summer). It also has roller skates for hire. Bikes and quadricycles can also be rented from the **Cycles 4 Rent** concession near the pool at Fess Parker's Red Lion Resort (633 E. Cabrillo, tel. 805/564–4333, ext. 444).

Boating Charter or rent 14- to 50-foot sailboats and powerboats from **Sailing Center of Santa Barbara,** which also has a sailing school (Breakwater near the harbor, tel. 805/962–2826 or 800/350–9090).

Fishing Surface and deep-sea fishing are possible all year. Fully equipped boats leave the harbor area for full- and half-day trips, dinner cruises, island excursions, and whale-watching from **SEA Landing** (Cabrillo Blvd. at Bath, tel. 805/963–3564).

Golf Play nine or 18 holes at the **Santa Barbara Golf Club** (Las Positas Rd. and McCaw Ave., tel. 805/687–7087). **Sandpiper Golf Course,** 15 miles west in Goleta, offers a challenging course that used to be a stop on the women's professional tour. (7925 Hollister Ave., Goleta, tel. 805/968–1541).

Horseback Riding San Ysidro Ranch hotel offers trail rides for parties of no more than six into the foothills by the hour (900 San Ysidro La., Montecito, tel. 805/969–5046. Reservations advised; hotel guests only on Sat.).

Tennis Many hotels have their own courts, but there are also excellent public courts. Day permits, for $3, are available at the courts. **Las Positas Municipal Courts,** 1002 Las Positas Road, has six lighted courts. Large complexes are also at the **Municipal Courts,** near Salinas Street and Highway 101, and **Pershing Park,** Castillo and Cabrillo.

Volleyball The east end of East Beach has more than a dozen sandlots. There are some casual, pickup games, but be prepared—these folks play serious volleyball.

Spectator Sports

Polo The public is invited to watch the elegant game at the **Santa Barbara Polo Club,** 7 miles east in Carpinteria. *Take the Santa Claus La. exit from Hwy. 101, turn left under the freeway and then left again onto Via Real. The polo grounds are ½-mi farther, surrounded by high hedges. Tel. 805/684–6683. April–Oct., Sun. Modest admission.*

Dining

by Bruce David Colen

Although you will find some chain restaurants in the bigger towns, the Central Coast from Big Sur to Solvang is far enough off the interstate rush to assure that each restaurant and café has its own personality—from chic to down-home and funky. You'll find a few burger places, but they won't come with golden arches. In almost all cases, the restaurants will be right off Highway 1.

There aren't many restaurants along the coast from Big Sur until you reach Hearst Castle, where there is a large, new snack bar in the visitors center. From there south, however, the commercial fishing industry assures daily fresh fish in many of the restaurants. The stretch of Highway 1 in and around San Simeon is a popular tour-bus route, and restaurants catering to large groups offer solid, if routine, American fare. Generous quantities of prime rib for dinner and bacon and eggs for breakfast can always be found. Cambria, true to its British-Welsh flavor, provides a taste of English cooking complete with peas and Yorkshire pudding, but the offerings range far beyond that. In Solvang, where the tone turns to Danish, count on traditional smorgasbord and sausages.

The variety of good food in Santa Barbara is astonishing for a town its size. Menu selections range from classic French to Cajun to fresh seafood, and the dining style from tie-and-jacket and reservations necessary to shorts-and-T-shirt hip. A leisurely brunch or lunch will take the best advantage of the beach and harbor views afforded by many restaurants and cafes. At the Biltmore's acclaimed and expensive Sunday brunch, however, all attention is on the spread of fresh fruits, seafood, and pastries. Served in the hotel's airy glass-roof courtyard, it is a perfect choice for special occasions.

But a tasty and satisfying meal certainly doesn't have to cost a fortune. If it is good, cheap food with an international flavor you are after, follow the locals to Milpas Avenue on the east edge of downtown. A recent count there found three Thai restaurants, a Hawaiian, a Greek, and a New Mexican food place. Freshly made tortillas are easily found in the markets on Milpas, particularly at La Super Rica, one of Julia Child's favorites for a quick, authentic Mexican snack.

Highly recommended restaurants are indicated by a star ★ . Casual dress is acceptable, unless otherwise noted.

Category	Cost*
Very Expensive	over $50
Expensive	$40–$50
Moderate	$15–$40
Inexpensive	under $15

per person, without tax, service, or drinks

The following abbreviations for credit cards have been used: AE, American Express; D, Discover Card, DC, Diners Club; MC, MasterCard; V, Visa.

Big Sur **Ventana Restaurant.** The low, wide, modern/rustic stone and
Expensive wood dining room is attractive; the terrace, with views over
★ golden hills down to the ocean, is spectacular. Even if it's foggy along the highway, it may be sunny and warm up here. Noted for its handling of the light touches of California cuisine, the menu features grilled veal chops, sliced duck, occasional and unexpected game dishes, and some creative sandwiches. Weekend brunches on the patio are a real event. *Off Hwy. 1, near the south end of town, tel. 408/667-2331. Reservations advised on weekends. AE, DC, MC, V.*

Moderate **Deetjen's Big Sur Inn.** The restaurant is in the main house of the old, funky inn. There are four small dining rooms, none with more than four tables. Classical music enhances the stylish fare that includes roast duckling for dinner and wonderfully light and flavorful whole-wheat pancakes for breakfast (there is no lunch). *Hwy. 1, south end of Big Sur, tel. 408/667-2377. No credit cards.*

Glen Oaks Restaurant. Food critics praise the originality of the food served in this small, simply decorated dining room. The restaurant, owned by a husband and wife team, emphasizes fresh ingredients, mesquite grilling, fish, and pasta. *Hwy. 1, north end of town, tel. 408/667-2623. MC, V. No lunch Mon.*

Inexpensive–
Moderate
★

Nepenthe. You'll not find a more spectacular coastal view between Los Angeles and San Francisco. The 800-foot-high cliff site, overlooking lush meadows to the ocean below, was once owned by Orson Welles and Rita Hayworth. The food is adequately average—from roast chicken with sage to sandwiches and hamburgers—so it is the one-of-a-kind location, in the one and only magnificent Big Sur, that rates the star. An outdoor café serves lunch until nightfall. *Hwy. 1, south end of town, tel. 408/667-2345. Reservations for large parties only. AE, MC, V. No breakfast. Full bar.*

Cambria
Moderate

Brambles Dinner House. This is the best-known restaurant in Cambria, but it can be hit-or-miss. Specialties include fresh salmon cooked over a seasoned oak fire, blackstrap molasses bread, prime rib, and Yorkshire pudding. *4005 Burton Dr., tel. 805/927-4716. Reservations advised. AE, MC, V. No lunch.*

Sylvia's Rigdon Hall. Delicate pink floral china sets the tone for this dinner house with a British flavor. The Spencer steak marinated in Jack Daniels is a favorite; also featured are a chicken curry mulligatawny soup and prime rib. *4022 Burton Dr., tel. 805/927-5125. MC, V. Dinner only. Closed Christmas Day.*

Inexpensive–
Moderate
★

The Hamlet at Moonstone Gardens. This is in the middle of a plant nursery. The enchanting patio garden is perfect for lunch. The upstairs dining room—sleek chrome and lavender with fireplace and grand piano—looks over the Pacific or the gardens. Service can be slow, but no one seems to mind. Fish of the day comes poached in white wine; other entrées range from hamburgers to rack of lamb. Downstairs is the Central Coast Wine Center, where you can taste wines from more than 50 wineries. *East side Hwy. 1, tel. 805/927-3535. Reservations accepted. MC, V. Closed Dec.*

Mustache Pete's. This lively, upbeat place with overhead fans and baskets of flowers features Italian food, with seafood, pasta, and poultry selections. *4090 Burton Dr., tel. 805/927-8589. AE, MC, V.*

Morro Bay
Moderate–
Expensive

Dutch's Fine Dining. In a house built of stone quarried from the big Morro Rock, the restaurant features crab *quo vadis* (with artichoke hearts and button mushrooms) and lobster thermidor, as well as steaks and fresh fish. *2738 N. Main St., tel. 805/772-8645. DC, MC, V. Dinner only.*

Moderate

Dorn's. This very pleasant seafood café overlooks the harbor and main square. It looks like a Cape Cod cottage, with blue walls, wainscoting, awnings, and bay windows. Breakfast, lunch, and dinner are served; dinner features excellent fish and native abalone. *801 Market St., tel. 805/772-4415. No credit cards.*

Inexpensive
★

Margie's Diner. This clean and attractive, Mom-and-Pop type diner-cafe, serves generous portions of All-American favorites: ham or steak and eggs, three-egg omelets, chili, nine versions of hamburger, hot and cold sandwiches, fried chicken steak, and deep dish apple pie. You name it, but don't forget the milkshakes. Top quality produce is used and service is excellent. *1698 N. Main St., tel. 805/772-2510. No credit cards.*

Ojai
Moderate

Wheeler Hot Springs Restaurant. The menu changes weekly but always features herbs and vegetables grown in the spa's garden. In Ojai, 6 miles north on Highway 33. The restaurant serves brunch on Sunday. *16825 Maricopa Hwy., tel. 805/646–8131. AE, MC, V. Dinner only. Closed Mon.–Wed.*

San Luis Obispo
Inexpensive–
Moderate

Madonna Inn. This visual Disneyland has to be seen to be believed. It is the ultimate in kitsch, from rococo bathrooms to pink-on-pink, frou-frou dining areas. You come to ogle, not necessarily to dine, although the latter is perfectly adequate, stop-by cooking, with decor-matching desserts. *100 Madonna Rd., tel. 805/543–3000. Dress: informal. No credit cards.*

San Simeon
Moderate

Europa. A Hungarian touch brings egg dumplings and paprika to the unexpected menu in an area of traditional fare. Crisp linen tablecloths brighten the small dining room. Steaks are featured as well as specialties from Italy and Vienna. Weekend brunch is served. *9240 Castillo Dr. (Hwy. 1), tel. 805/927–3087. MC, V. Closed Sun. Dinner only.*

Inexpensive–
Moderate

San Simeon Restaurant. This restaurant makes the most of its proximity to Hearst Castle, with a mind-boggling decor of imitation Greek columns, statues, and tapestries. There is a standard American menu; prime rib is the big draw. The dark dining room opens to views of the Pacific across the highway. *East side Hwy. 1, tel. 805/927–4604. Reservations advised in summer. AE, MC, V. Open daily breakfast, lunch, and dinner.*

Santa Barbara
Expensive
★

Downey's. Chef-owner John Downey was the first to introduce Santa Barbara to the assorted pleasures of *nouvelle*-California cooking, and local admirers have kept this charming little restaurant crowded ever since. Try the in-house cured prosciutto, the local mussels with a chile sauce, fresh sea bass and asparagus, or grilled duck or lamb, with local wild mushrooms. *1305 State St., tel. 805/966–5006. Reservations required. Dress: casual. Closed Mon. dinner, and lunch Tues.–Fri. MC, V.*

El Encanto. Sitting on the awninged dining terrace of this hilltop hotel, one has a marvelous view of Santa Barbara's red-tiled roofs stretching down to the harbor below. It is like being on the French or Italian Riviera, and chef James Sly provides the matching cuisines, from bouillabaisse to pasta with lobster sauce. There's also an abundance of fresh, local salads. *1900 Laseun Rd., tel. 805/687–5000. Reservations required. Jacket required. AE, DC, MC, V.*

★

Michael's Waterside. Started with the financial help of the Roux brothers, who own London's Waterside Inn and the three-star LeGavroche, this beautiful Victorian house, facing a bird sanctuary, is a romantic gem. And there is nothing about chef Michael Hutchings's *haute*-California cuisine to spoil the mood: "cultured" abalone, mushroom mousse with escargot, gruyère cheese soufflé; baked king salmon, Santa Barbara prawns and ranch-bred squab, and lovely rich desserts. *50 Los Patos Way, tel. 805/969–0307. Reservations required. Jacket and tie required. AE, DC, MC, V. Open for dinner Wed.–Sun., and Sun. brunch.*

Moderate–
Expensive

The Harbor Restaurant. This place tops annual surveys on where locals like to take out-of-town guests. The lovely seascape makes it particularly pleasant for breakfast or lunch. The restaurant specializes in fresh seafood, local catches, and Maine lobster; and there is an oyster bar on the second floor. *210 Stearns Wharf, tel. 805/963–3311. Dress: casual; jackets required in Santa Barbara Room. AE, MC.*

★ **The Stonehouse.** This farmhouse restaurant, part of the San Ysidro Ranch, features the best light French-California cuisine in Santa Barbara. For lunch order chef Marc Ehrler's Mediterranean-style pizza while sitting on the tree-shaded deck. At night, the cooking gets more serious, with game, roasts, and fresh fish entrées. *900 San Ysidro La., 805/969–5046. Reservations required. Jacket required. MC, V.*

Moderate **The Palace Cafe.** This stylish and lively restaurant has won acclaim for its Cajun and Creole food. If the dishes aren't spicy enough, each table has its own bottle of hot sauce. Only dinner is served, and be prepared for a wait. It's lots of noisy fun. *8 E. Cota St., tel. 805/966–3133. Dress: informal. Reservations accepted for 5:30 PM seating only. MC, V.*

Pane & Vino. This is a tiny trattoria, with an equally small sidewalk dining terrace, in one of Santa Barbara's tree-shaded, flower-decked shopping centers. The cold antipasto is very good, as are grilled meats and fish, pastas and salads. There's a nearby water trough and hitching post for the visiting horsey set. *1482 E. Valley Rd., tel. 805/969–9274. Reservations advised. Closed Sun. No credit cards.*

Inexpensive **Castagnola Bros. Fish Galley.** Here's an unassuming spot a quick 2 blocks from the beach where wonderfully good, fresh fish comes served on paper plates. Most of the tables are outside on the patio, but a few fast-food style booths share the interior with the fish market, the other half of this enterprise. *205 Santa Barbara St., tel. 805/962–8053. No credit cards. Closes at 6 PM, 9 PM on weekends.*

East Beach Grill. Watch the waves break and the world go by at a surprisingly pleasant outdoor café right on the beach. It's a step above the usual beach stand with friendly table service, real plates, and cutlery. Basic breakfast fare is followed by hot dogs and burgers for lunch. *At the Cabrillo Bath House, East Beach, tel. 805/965–8805. No credit cards. Closed 3:30 daily.*

Joe's Cafe. The vinyl checked tablecloths and simple round stools at the hefty wooden counter tell the story: nothing fancy, but solid American cafe fare in generous portions. A popular hangout and drinking spot, particularly for the younger crowd. The martinis are great. *536 State St., tel. 805/966–4638. AE, MC, V. Closed Sun. lunch.*

Solvang **Danish Inn.** The smorgasbord is popular, but there are also *Moderate–* steaks and many Continental-style items to choose from. Din-*Expensive* ing is more formal here than in most Solvang restaurants. Atmosphere: lace curtains and a cozy fireplace. *1547 Mission Dr., tel. 805/688–4813. Reservations advised. AE, MC, V.*

Inexpensive– **Restaurant Mollenroen.** A busy upstairs dining room serves *Moderate* smorgasbord and other Danish specialties. It has a cheerful, light setting, with fresh flowers on the tables and booths. The local folks come here for a good meal at good prices. *435 Alisal Rd., tel. 805/688–4555. AE, DC, MC, V.*

★ **Royal Scandia Restaurant.** Despite the size (there are three dining rooms), this restaurant is decorated like an old Danish cottage, with vaulted ceilings, rafters, and lots of brass and frosted glass. You can dine on the patio protected by glass and brick. The menu caters to traditional American tastes, with a few Danish items. *420 Alisal Rd., tel. 805/688–8000. AE, DC, MC, V. Dinner only.*

Inexpensive **Little Belgium Inn.** This café with outdoor patio does a booming breakfast and lunch business. Waffles of all kinds and grilled Danish sausage are among the offerings. Inside, the café is sunny and pleasant, though it can get crowded. *475 1st St., tel. 805/688-0095. MC, V.*

Lodging

The lodging choices in Big Sur, though few in number, range from the dramatic Ventana Inn to the rustic and funky Deetjen's Big Sur Inn. Neither cater to children, but the Big Sur Lodge is the perfect place for them. You won't find many hotels or motels between Big Sur and San Simeon. In castle country—from San Simeon to San Luis Obispo—there are many moderately priced hotels and motels, some nicer than others, but mostly just basic lodging. Only the Madonna Inn, the all-pink, one-of-a-kind motel in San Luis Obispo, is worthy of a stay for its own sake. Be sure you make reservations ahead of time, well ahead in the summer. Remember that there may not be another town just down the road with more lodging options.

Bargain lodging is hard to come by in Santa Barbara, where high-end resorts are more the style. Long a favorite getaway for congestion-crazed Los Angeles residents, the resorts promise, and usually deliver, pampering and solitude in romantic settings. The beach area is certainly the most popular locale for lodging. It is also where you will find the largest concentration of moderately priced motels. Many places offer discounts in the winter season. Come summer weekends, when 90% of the town's 46,000 motel and hotel rooms are filled, reservations well in advance are strongly advised.

Highly recommended lodgings are indicated by a star ★.

Category	Cost*
Very Expensive	over $150
Expensive	$100–$150
Moderate	$60–$100
Inexpensive	under $60

for a double room, not including tax

Big Sur **Ventana Inn.** A getaway that is essential California chic—restful and hip. Rooms, scattered in clusters on a hillside above the Pacific, are done in natural woods, and the floors are cool tile. Activities here are purposely limited to sunning at poolside—there is a clothing-optional deck—and walks in the hills nearby. Rates include an elaborate Continental breakfast and afternoon wine and cheese (featuring California wines). *Hwy. 1, 93920, tel. 408/667-2331 or 800/628-6500 in CA. 59 rooms. Facilities: 2 pools, spa, restaurant, gift shop. Minimum stay 2 nights on weekends, 3 on holidays. AE, D, DC, MC, V.*

Very Expensive ★

Moderate **Big Sur Lodge.** Located inside Pfeiffer Big Sur State Park, this is the best place in Big Sur for families. Motel-style cottages are set around a meadow surrounded by redwood and oak trees. Some have fireplaces, some kitchens. *Hwy. 1, Box 190,*

93920, tel. 408/667–2171. 61 rooms. Facilities: pool, sauna. MC, V.

Deetjen's Big Sur Inn. Built in bits and pieces in the '20s and '30s, this place is charming, but also rustic and not always comfortable. There are no locks on the doors (except from the inside), the heating is by wood-burning stove in half of the rooms, and your neighbor is often heard through the walls. Still, it's a special place, set among redwood trees with each room individually decorated and given a name like "Château Fiasco." *Hwy. 1, south end of town, 93920, tel. 408/667–2377. 19 rooms, 13 with bath. Facilities: restaurant. No credit cards.*

Cambria
Moderate
★

Best Western Fireside Inn. This modern motel has spacious rooms decorated in cream and peach, with sofas and upholstered lounge chairs (plus refrigerators and coffee makers). Some have whirlpools. Ask for a room with a fireplace and an ocean view. Continental breakfast is served in a room adjacent to the pool. The landscaping is very attractive, and the inn is just across from the beach, with fishing nearby. *6700 Moonstone Beach Dr., 93428, tel. 805/927–8661 or 800/528–1234. 46 rooms. Facilities: heated pool, spa. AE, D, DC, MC, V.*

Cambria Pines Lodge. The lodge's buildings are set among 25 acres of pine trees above the town, with peacocks wandering the grounds. There is a big stone fireplace in the lounge, and all the furnishings—new and old—fit the decor of the 1920s, when the lodge was built. *2905 Burton Dr., 93428, tel. 805/927–4200 or 800/445–6868. 125 rooms. Facilities: bar, restaurant, pool, Jacuzzi, weight room. MC, V.*

★ **San Simeon Pines Resort Motel.** There is a quiet lodgelike feel here, directly across from Leffingwell's Landing, a state picnic area on the rocky beach. Areas are set aside for adults and families. *7200 Moonstone Beach Dr., Box 117, San Simeon 93452, tel. 805/927–4648. 60 rooms. Facilities: children's playground, nine hole golf, pool, shuffleboard. AE, MC, V.*

Inexpensive

Bluebird Motel. Located between the east and west villages, this older motel was recently fully redecorated, and includes a homey lounge for hanging out. *1880 Main St., 93428, tel. 805/927–4634. 31 rooms. AE, D, MC, V.*

Morro Bay
Moderate

The Breakers. Rooms in this motel, ½-block from the waterfront, are decorated in pastels—each with a different wallpaper—and traditional furniture. Most have ocean views, some have fireplaces, all have coffee makers and refrigerators. *Morro Bay Blvd. at Market, Box 1447, 93443, tel. 805/772–7317. 25 rooms. Facilities: heated pool, spa, cable TV. AE, D, DC, MC, V.*

Ojai
Very Expensive
★

Ojai Valley Inn and Country Club. Reopened in January 1988 after a $40 million renovation, the hotel is set in landscaped grounds lush with flowers. The enormously peaceful setting comes with hillside views in nearly all directions. Some of the nicer rooms are in the original adobe building, where the best of the old—like huge bathrooms—is enhanced with contemporary touches. The suites in cabanas are more expensive. Interesting works by celebrated local artists are featured throughout the resort. *Country Club Rd., 93023, tel. 805/646–5511 or 800/422–OJAI. 218 units. Facilities: championship golf course, lighted tennis courts, 2 pools, men's and women's sauna and steam room, complimentary bicycles, 2 restaurants, bar. AE, D, DC, MC, V.*

Expensive **Oaks at Ojai.** Well-known, comfortable spa with a solid fitness program that includes lodging, three nutritionally balanced, low-calorie meals (surprisingly good), complete use of spa facilities, and 16 optional fitness classes. *122 E. Ojai Ave., 93023, tel. 805/646–5573. Facilities: complete spa, including pool, Jacuzzis, sauna. D, MC, V.*

Inexpensive **Los Padres Inn.** This is a modern hotel on the main street of town across from the Soule Park Golf Course. *1208 E. Ojai Ave. 93023, tel. 805/646–4365 or 800/228–3744 in CA. 31 units. Facilities: pool, whirlpool. AE, D, DC, MC, V.*

San Luis Obispo
Moderate–Expensive
★ **Apple Farm.** No effort has been spared to make this the exemplar of the modern, country-style hotel, decorated to the hilt with sprigged bedspreads and wallpaper, and with watercolors by local artists. Each room is decorated individually, though all include canopy beds and cozy window seats. Complimentary coffee is served in the rooms. The adjoining restaurant serves such hearty country fare as chicken with dumplings and smoked ribs, and the breakfasts are copious. *2015 Monterey St., 93401, tel. 805/544–2040 or 800/255–2040 in CA. 101 rooms. Facilities: bakery, gift shop, adjacent Mill House. AE, MC, V.*

★ **Madonna Inn.** A designer's imagination gone berserk, this place is as much a tourist attraction as a place to stay. Each room is unique. "Rock Bottom" is all stone, even the bathroom. The "Safari Room" is decked out in animal skins. "Old Mill" features a waterwheel that powers cuckoo clock-like figurines. *100 Madonna Rd., 93405, tel. 805/543–3000 or 800/543–9666. 109 rooms. Facilities: ballroom, 2 restaurants, wine cellar, 2 gift shops, gourmet shop, and bakery. No credit cards.*

Inexpensive **Motel Inn.** If it is nostalgia rather than comfort you seek, this place, built in 1925, bills itself as the world's first motel. Small bungalows with stucco exterior and flat red-tile roofs make you feel like you are on the set of an old B movie. Although they are old, the rooms are kept clean and the grounds are nicely lush. *2223 Monterey St., 93401, tel. 805/543–4000. Facilities: pool, bar. AE, MC, V.*

San Simeon
Moderate
  Holiday Inn. This is a newish 2-story motel with comfortable rooms opening on an interior corridor. The rooms are standard Holiday Inn-style, decorated in blue and rust. *9070 Castillo Ave. (Hwy. 1), 93452, tel. 805/927–8691 or 800/465–4329. 100 rooms. Facilities: heated pool, restaurant, lounge, room service. AE, D, DC, MC, V.*

Inexpensive **San Simeon Lodge.** Built in 1958, the exterior looks its age, but the modernized rooms have nice touches, like matching spreads and curtains. *9520 Castillo Dr. (Hwy. 1), 93452, tel. 805/927–4601. 63 rooms. Facilities: pool, restaurant, bar, lounge. AE, DC, MC, V.*

Santa Barbara
Very Expensive
  Four Seasons Biltmore. Santa Barbara's grande dame has been spruced up with a $15 million face-lift by its new owners. A decor featuring muted pastels and bleached woods gives the cabanas a light, airy touch without sacrificing the hotel's reputation for understated elegance. It's a bit more formal than elsewhere in Santa Barbara, with lush gardens and palm trees galore. *1260 Channel Dr., 93108, tel. 805/969–2261 or 800/332–3442. 236 rooms. Facilities: 2 Olympic pools, whirlpool, croquet, shuffleboard, racquet ball, health club, casino, putting green, tennis courts, 2 restaurants, bar. AE, DC, MC, V.*

San Ysidro Ranch. At this luxury "ranch" you can feel at home in jeans and cowboy boots, but be prepared to dress for dinner. A hideout for the Hollywood set, this romantic place hosted John and Jackie Kennedy on their honeymoon. Guest cottages, some with antique quilts and all with wood-burning stoves or fireplaces, are scattered among 14 acres of orange trees and flower beds. There are 500 acres more left in open space to roam at will on foot or horseback. The hotel welcomes children and pets. *900 San Ysidro La., Montecito, 93108, tel. 805/969–5046. 45 rooms. Facilities: pool, tennis courts, horseback riding, croquet, badminton, restaurant. AE, DC, MC, V. Minimum stay: 2 days on weekends, 3 days on holidays.*

Expensive– **Fess Parker's Red Lion Resort.** This is a sprawling resort com-
Very Expensive plex with a slightly Spanish flair. Two- and three-story stucco
★ buildings are located directly across the street from the beach. This is Santa Barbara's newest luxury hotel and, with its huge and lavishly appointed lobby, a showplace for the chain. Spacious rooms, all with either private patio or balcony, and many with ocean views, are furnished with pastels and light wood. *633 E. Cabrillo Blvd., 93103, tel. 805/564–4333 or 800/879–2929. 360 rooms. Facilities: pool, sauna, tennis courts, exercise room, Jacuzzi, gift shop, lounge with dance floor, 2 bars, 2 restaurants. AE, D, DC, MC, V.*

Moderate– **Ambassador by the Sea.** Near harbor and Stearns Wharf, this
Expensive place has a real California beach feel. Sun decks overlook the ocean and bike path. *202 W. Cabrillo Blvd., 93101, tel. 805/965–4577. 32 units. Facilities: pool, 2 units with kitchenettes. AE, D, DC, MC, V.*

Old Yacht Club Inn. Built in 1912 as a private home near the beach, the inn was one of Santa Barbara's first bed-and-breakfasts with rooms featuring period antiques and Oriental rugs. Guests receive complimentary breakfast and evening wine, along with the use of bikes and beach chairs. No smoking. *431 Corona del Mar Dr., 93103, tel., 805/962–1277. 9 rooms. Facilities: dining room, airport pickup service. AE, D, MC, V.*

Pacific Crest Inn. A block from East Beach on a quiet residential street, this motel has clean and comfortable rooms, without the austerity of some budget operations. Kitchens are available. *433 Corona Del Mar Dr., 93103, tel. 805/966–3103. 26 rooms. Facilities: pool, laundromat. AE, D, DC, MC, V. Minimum stay: 2 nights on weekends, 3 on holidays.*

Santa Barbara Inn. There is a new Mediterranean decor at this three-story motel, directly across the street from East Beach. Many rooms have ocean views, but the lower-price ones with mountain views also look over the parking lot. *901 E. Cabrillo St., 93103, tel. 805/966–2285 or 800/231–0431. 71 rooms. Facilities: pool, whirlpool, restaurant. AE, D, DC, MC, V.*

Villa Rosa. The atmosphere is of a private home. Housed in a 50-year-old Mediterranean house a block from the beach, the rooms and intimate lobby are decorated with a southwestern style. Rates include Continental breakfast and wine and cheese in the afternoon. *15 Chapala St., 93101, tel. 805/966–0851. 18 rooms. Facilities: pool, spa. AE, MC, V.*

Inexpensive **Motel 6.** Low price and great location near the beach are the pluses for this no-frills place. Reserve well in advance all year. *443 Corona Del Mar Dr., 93103, tel. 805/564–1392 or 505/891–6161. 52 units. Facilities: heated pool. AE, D, DC, MC, V.*

Solvang
Moderate–
Very Expensive

Chimney Sweep Inn. All the rooms are pleasant, but it is the cottages in the backyard that are extra special (and expensive). Built in a half-timbered style, they were inspired by the C. S. Lewis's children's book, *The Chronicles of Narnia.* The cottages have kitchens and fireplaces. In the garden are a waterfall and fish pond. Complimentary Continental breakfast includes hot apple cider. *1554 Copenhagen Dr., 93463, tel. 805/ 688–2111 or 800/824–6444. 28 rooms. Facilities: spa, garden. AE, MC, V.*

Moderate **Sheraton Royal Scandinavian Inn.** This member of the chain follows the Danish theme of the town. The rooms—in Danish decor, of course—have nice touches, like handpainted furniture. The large, brick, and darkly timbered lobby has a fireplace and overstuffed chairs. *400 Alisal Rd., 93463, tel. 805/688–8000 or 800/624–5572. 133 rooms. Facilities: restaurant, lounge, pool, Jacuzzi. AE, D, DC, MC, V.*

Inexpensive **Solvang Gaard Lodge.** This was Solvang's first motel and is still as comfortable and friendly as you could want. Some of the old-Danish-style rooms are rented to full-time residents, others to repeat visitors who come to spend a week or more in a quiet place, just beyond the center of things. *293 Alisal Rd., 93463, tel. 805/688–4404. 21 units. AE, MC, V.*

The Arts and Nightlife

The Arts Santa Barbara prides itself on being a top-notch cultural center. It supports its own professional symphony and chamber orchestra and an impressive art museum. The proximity to the University of California at Santa Barbara assures an endless stream of visiting artists and performers.

The performing arts find a home in two theaters that are themselves works of art. The enormous Moorish-style **Arlington Theater** on State Street is home to the Santa Barbara Symphony. You can also catch a first-run movie there. The **Lobero**, a state landmark, at the corner of Anacapa and Cañon Perdido streets, shares its stage with community theater groups and touring professionals.

The works housed in the **Museum of Art** range from Greek and Roman collections to Grandma Moses's vistas. There's also a fine collection of antique dolls. *1130 State St., tel. 805/963–4364. Admission $3 adults, $1.50 children 6–16. Open Tues.– Sat. 11–5, Sun. noon–5, Thurs. 11–9. Tours are led Tues.–Sat. 2 PM, Sun. 1 PM.*

For a more casual art experience, catch the beachfront display of wares from local artists and craftspeople each Sunday from 10 AM to dusk along Cabrillo Boulevard.

The **Santa Barbara Arts Council** (1236 Chapala St., tel. 805/ 966–7022) provides information on performances and events and also has a gallery space for emerging local artists.

Music Since 1971, the **San Luis Obispo Mozart Festival** (Box 311, San Luis Obispo, 93406, tel. 805/543–4580) has been held early in August. The settings include the Mission San Luis Obispo de Tolosa and the Cal Poly Theater. There are afternoon and evening concerts and recitals—by professionals and well-known visiting artists—as well as seminars and workshops. Not all the music is Mozart; you'll hear Haydn and other composers. The Festival Fringe offers free concerts outdoors.

Theater Boo and hiss the villains year-round at the **Great American Melodrama** (Hwy. 1, tel. 805/489–2499) in the small town of Oceano, south of San Luis Obispo.

The **Pacific Conservatory of the Performing Arts** (Box 1700, Santa Maria, 93456, tel. 805/922–8313, or 800/221–9469 in CA) presents a full spectrum of theatrical events, from classical to contemporary, with a few musicals thrown in, in different theaters in Solvang and Santa Maria. The Solvang Festival Theater has open-air performances.

Film The **Santa Barbara International Film Festival,** (1216 State St. #201, tel. 805/963–0023) held in March, draws the celebrity crowd, with premieres and screenings of American and international films.

Nightlife Most of the major hotels offer nightly entertainment during the summer season and live weekend entertainment all year. To see what's scheduled at the hotels and many small clubs and restaurants, pick up a copy of the free weekly *Santa Barbara Independent* newspaper for an extensive rundown.

Dancing **Zelo.** This is a high-energy restaurant that doubles as a progressive rock and punk dance club featuring offbeat videos and innovative lighting. *630 State St., tel. 805/966–5792. Closed Mon.*

by Jo

You're preparing for your trip to Los Angeles. You're psyching up with Beach Boys cassettes on your car radio or perhaps some Hollywood epics on the VCR. You've pulled out your tropical Hawaiian shirts and tennis shorts. You've studied the Mexican menu at Taco Bell. Maybe you're even doing a crash regimen at your local tanning salon and aerobics studio so you won't *look* like a tourist when you hit the coast.

Well, relax. *Everybody's* a tourist in LaLa Land. Even the stars are star-struck (as evidenced by the celebrities watching the other celebrities at Spago). Los Angeles is a city of ephemerals, of transience, and above all, of illusion. Nothing there is quite real, and that's the reality of it all. That air of anything-can-happen—and it often does—is what keeps thousands moving to this promised land each year and millions more vacationing in it. Not just from the East or Midwest, mind you, but from the Far East, Down Under, Europe, and South America. It's this influx of cultures that's been the lifeblood of Los Angeles since its Hispanic beginning.

We cannot predict what *your* Los Angeles will be like. You can laze on a beach or soak up some of the world's greatest art collections. You can tour the movie studios and stars' homes or take the kids to Disneyland, Magic Mountain, or the *Queen Mary/Spruce Goose*. You can shop luxurious Beverly Hills' Rodeo Drive or browse for hipper novelties on boutique-lined Melrose Avenue. The possibilities are endless—rent a boat to Catalina Island, watch the floats in Pasadena's Rose Parade, or dine on tacos, sushi, goat cheese pizza, or just plain hamburgers, hot dogs, and chili.

None of this was imagined when Spanish settlers founded their Pueblo de la Reina de Los Angeles in 1781. In fact, no one predicted a golden future for desert-dry Southern California until well after San Francisco and Northern California had gotten a good head start with their own gold rush. The dusty outpost of Los Angeles eventually had oil and oranges, but the golden key to its success came on the silver screen: the movies. If the early pioneers of Hollywood—religiously conservative fruit farmers—had gotten their way, their town's name would never have become synonymous with cinema and entertainment.

In mid-century, the U.S. automakers and oil companies lobbied against an urban mass transit system in Southern California in order to sell more cars and gasoline. Free-spirited Californians drove blithely on, indulging their independence until one day, sometime in the late 1950s, the smog got thick enough to kill. Mandatory emission controls have helped clear up that problem. Nevertheless, check the papers daily to ascertain the air quality. Because the 700 miles of freeways are so full, a metro subway system is finally being dug, offering a possible solution to the smog problem someday. Perhaps not too little, but already too late: The first phase of the system won't be ready until sometime in the mid-1990s.

No city embraces the romance of the automobile as does Los Angeles. Cars themselves announce the wealth, politics, and taste of their drivers. Vanity license plates, a California innovation, condense the meaning of one's life into seven letters (MUZKBIZ). Sun roofs, ski racks, and cardboard windshield visors sell better here than anywhere else. You are what you drive—a thought worth remembering when you rent a car. Yes, Lamborghinis are available, even by the hour.

The distance between places in Los Angeles explains the ethnic enclaves that do not merge, regardless of the melting-pot appearance of the city. It would be misleading of us to gloss over the tensions among racial groups learning to share Los Angeles. More notable for visitors, however, is the rich cultural and culinary diversity this mix of peoples creates.

Arriving and Departing

By Plane   The new, improved Los Angeles International Airport or LAX (tel. 213/646–5252) is the largest airport in the area. It was revamped for the 1984 Olympics as a two-level airport, with departures on the upper level and arrivals on the lower level. Over 85 major airlines are serviced by LAX, the third largest airport in the world in terms of passenger traffic.

Airlines   Among the major carriers that serve LAX are Air Canada (tel. 800/422–6232), America West (tel. 800/228–7862), American (tel. 800/433–7300), Braniff (tel. 800/752–4556), British Airways (tel. 800/247–9297), Continental (tel. 800/525–0280), Delta (tel. 800/221–1212), Japan Airlines (tel. 800/525–3663), Northwest (tel. 800/225–2525), Southwest (tel. 800/531–5601), TWA (tel. 800/221–2000), United (tel. 800/241–6522), and USAir (tel. 800/428–4322).

From the Airport to   A dizzying array of ground transportation is available from
the Hotels   LAX to all parts of Los Angeles and its environs. A taxi ride to downtown Los Angeles can take 20 minutes—*if* there is no traffic. But in Los Angeles, that's a big if. Visitors should request the flat fee ($24 at press time) to downtown or choose from the several ground transportation companies that offer set rates.

SuperShuttle offers direct service between the airport and hotels. The trip to downtown hotels runs about $11. The seven-passenger vans operate 24 hours a day. In the airport, phone 213/417–8988 or use the SuperShuttle courtesy phone in the luggage area; the van should arrive within 15 minutes. To be picked up anywhere in the Los Angeles area, phone 213/338–1111. **L.A. Top Shuttle** (9100 S. Sepulveda Blvd., #128, tel. 213/670–6666) features door-to-door service and low rates ($10 per person from LAX to hotels in the Disneyland/Anaheim area).

The following limo companies charge a flat rate for airport service, ranging from $65 to $75: **Jackson Limousine** (tel. 213/734–9955), **West Coast Limousine** (tel. 213/756–5466), and **Dav-El Livery** (tel. 213/550–0070). Many of the cars have bars, stereos, televisions, and cellular phones.

Flyaway Service (tel. 818/994–5554) offers transportation between LAX and the eastern San Fernando Valley for around $5. For the western San Fernando Valley and Ventura area, contact **The Great American Stage Lines** (tel. 800/287–8659). **RTD** (tel. 213/626–4455) also offers limited airport service.

Other Airports   The greater Los Angeles area is served by several other local airports. **Ontario Airport** (tel. 714/988–2700), located about 35 miles east of Los Angeles, serves the San Bernardino–Riverside area. Domestic flights are offered by Air LA, Alaska Airlines, American, America West, Continental, Delta, Northwest, PSA, SkyWest, Southwest, TWA, United, United

Exploring Los Angeles *(Boxes Refer to Detail Maps)*

SAN FERNANDO

Foothill Fwy.

CANOGA PARK

RESEDA

Ventura Fwy

Sepulveda Dam Recreation Area

VAN NUYS

NORTH HOLLYWOOD

BURBANK

GLENDALE

Golden State Fwy.

Mulholland Dr.

SHERMAN OAKS

SANTA MONICA MTS.

Topanga State Park

Griffith Park

Hollywood

WEST HOLLYWOOD

Santa

Monica Blvd.

HOLLYWOOD

BEVERLY HILLS

WESTWOOD

Monica Blvd.

Sunset Blvd.

Wilshire Blvd.

Westside

Downtown

MALIBU

TOPANGA BEACH

Santa Monica and Venice

SANTA MONICA

Santa

Santa Monica Fwy.

CULVER CITY

San Diego Fwy.

Slauson Ave.

VENICE

MARINA DEL REY

Los Angeles International Airport

INGLEWOOD

EL SEGUNDO

Imperial Hwy.

Sepulveda

Hawthorne Blvd.

Western Ave.

Harbor Fwy.

MANHATTAN BEACH

HERMOSA BEACH

TORRANCE

San Diego

REDONDO BEACH

Pacific Coast Hwy.

PACIFIC OCEAN

PALOS VERDES ESTATES

RANCH PALOS VERDES

SAN PEDRO

N

0   5 miles

0   5 km

Palos Verdes, San Pedro, and L

Express, and USAir. Ground transportation possibilities include Super-shuttle as well as Inland Express (tel. 714/626–6599), Empire Airport Transportation (tel. 714/884–0744), and Southern California Coach (tel. 714/978–6415).

Burbank Airport (tel. 818/840–8847) serves the San Fernando Valley with commuter, and some longer, flights. Alaska Airlines, Alpha Air, USAir, American, America West, TWA, United, Delta, LA Helicopter, SkyWest, States West, and United Express are represented.

John Wayne Airport, in Orange County (tel. 714/252–5006), is served by Jet America, TWA, SkyWest, American, Northwest, Alaska, American West, Continental, Delta, United, USAir, and States West.

By Car Three main interstate routes take drivers into the Los Angeles area. I-5 runs from Canada to Mexico, through Seattle, Sacramento, and San Diego. It is known as the Golden State or Santa Ana Freeway here. I-10 crosses the country from Florida to Los Angeles and is known locally as the Santa Monica Freeway. I-15 comes into the area from the northeast, from Montana through Las Vegas and San Bernardino.

By Train Los Angeles can be reached by Amtrak (tel. 800/USA–RAIL). The *Coast Starlight* is a superliner that travels along the spectacular California coast. It offers service from Seattle-Portland and Oakland–San Francisco down to Los Angeles. Amtrak's *San Joaquin* train travels a route through the Central Valley from Oakland to Bakersfield, where passengers transfer to an Amtrak bus that takes them to Los Angeles. The *Sunset Limited* goes to Los Angeles from New Orleans, the *Eagle* from San Antonio, and the *Southwest Chief* and the *Desert Wind* from Chicago.

Union Station in Los Angeles is one of the grande dames of railroad stations. The Spanish Mission–style station is a remnant of the glory days of the railroads. It is located at 825 North Alameda Street.

By Bus The Los Angeles **Greyhound/Trailways** terminal (tel. 800/237–8211) is located at 208 East 6th Street, on the corner of Los Angeles Street.

Getting around Los Angeles

By Bus A bus ride on the **Southern California Rapid Transit District (RTD)** (tel. 213/626–4455) costs $1.10, with 25¢ for each transfer.

By Taxi You probably won't be able to hail a cab on the street in Los Angeles. Instead, you should phone one of the many taxi companies. The metered rate is $1.60 per mile. Two of the more reputable companies are **Independent Cab. Co.** (tel. 213/385–8294 or 385–TAXI) and **United Independent Taxi** (tel. 213/653–5050). United accepts MasterCard and Visa.

By Limousine Limousines come equipped with everything from a full bar and telephone to a hot tub and a double bed—depending on your needs. Reputable companies include **Dav-El Livery** (tel. 213/550–0070), **First Class** (tel. 213/476–1960), and **Le Monde Limousine** (tel. 213/271–9270 or 818/887–7878).

By Car It's almost a necessity to have a car in Los Angeles. Rental agencies are listed in Planning Your Trip. The accompanying map of the freeway system should help you. If you plan to drive extensively, consider buying a *Thomas Guide*, which contains detailed maps of the entire county. Despite what you've heard, traffic is not always a major problem outside of rush hours (7–9 AM and 3–7 PM).

To the Airport **Supershuttle** (tel. 213/338–1111) will pick you up at your hotel or elsewhere and take you to the Los Angeles airport. The cost varies; it's about $11 from downtown. **Funbus Airlink Airport Service** (tel. 800/962–1976 in CA or 800/962–1975 nationwide) provides regular service from hotels to LAX. From the Valley, try **Flyaway Service** (Van Nuys, tel. 818/994–5554) or the **Great American Stage** (Woodland Hills, Thousand Oaks, Oxnard, Van Nuys, tel. 800/287–8659).

If you're driving, leave time for heavy traffic; it really can't be predicted.

Important Addresses and Numbers

Tourist Information **Visitor Information Center.** Arco Plaza, Level B, 6th and S. Flower streets, 90071, tel. 213/689–8822. Open Mon.–Sat. 8–5. **Los Angeles Visitor and Convention Bureau.** 515 S. Figueroa, 90071, tel. 213/624–7300.
Beverly Hills Visitors and Convention Bureau. 239 S. Beverly Dr., 90212, tel. 213/271–8174. Open weekdays 8:30–5.
Long Beach Area Convention and Visitors Council (1 World Trade Center, Suite 300, Long Beach 90831, tel. 213/436–3645).
Santa Monica Visitors Center. 1400 Ocean Ave. (in Palisades Park), tel. 213/393–7593. Open daily 10–4. Write to 2219 Main St., 90405.
Hollywood Visitors Center. 6541 Hollywood Blvd., 90028, tel. 213/461–4213. Open Mon.–Sat. 9–5.
Pasadena Convention and Visitors Bureau. 171 S. Los Robles Ave., 91101, tel. 818/795–9311. Open weekdays 9–5, Sat. 10–4.

Emergencies Dial 911 for **police** and **ambulance** in an emergency.

Doctor **Los Angeles Medical Association Physicians Referral Service,** tel. 213/483–6122. Open weekdays 8:45–4:45. Most larger hospitals in Los Angeles have 24-hour emergency rooms. A few are: **St. John's Hospital and Health Center** (1328 22nd St., tel. 213/829–5511), **Cedar-Sinai Medical Center** (8700 Beverly Blvd., tel. 213/855–5000), **Hollywood Presbyterian Medical Center** (1300 N. Vermont Ave., tel. 213/413–3000).

24-Hour Pharmacies **Horton and Converse Pharmacy** (6625 Van Nuys Blvd., Van Nuys, tel. 818/782–6251).
Bellflower Pharmacy (9400 E. Rosecrans Ave., Bellflower, tel. 213/920–4213).
Horton and Converse (11600 Wilshire Blvd., tel. 213/478–0801, and 3875 Wilshire Blvd., tel. 213/382–2236). Open until 2 AM.

Surf and Weather Report: Tel. 213/451–8761.

Guided Tours

Orientation Tours Los Angeles is so spread out and has such a wealth of sightseeing possibilities that an orientation bus tour may prove useful. The cost is about $25.

Los Angeles Freeways

Gray Line (1207 W. 3rd St., 90017, tel. 213/856–5900), one of the best-known tour companies in the country, picks passengers up from more than 140 hotels. There are more than 24 tours to Disneyland, Universal Studios, the *Queen Mary*, Catalina Island, and other attractions.

All tours are fully narrated by a driver-guide. Reservations must be made in advance. Many hotels can book them for you.

StarLine Sightseeing Tours (6845 Hollywood Blvd., Hollywood 90028, tel. 213/463–3131) has been showing people around Los Angeles since 1935, with an emphasis on the homes of the stars.

Casablanca Tours (Roosevelt Hotel, 7000 Hollywood Blvd., Cabana 4, Hollywood 90028, tel. 213/461–0156), offers an insider's look at Hollywood and Beverly Hills. The four-hour tour, which can be taken in the morning or afternoon, starts in Hollywood or in centrally located hotels. Tours are in minibuses with a maximum of people, and prices are equivalent to the large bus tours—about $25. Guides are college students with a high-spirited view of the city.

Special-Interest Tours So much of Los Angeles is known to the world through Hollywood, it is fitting that many of the special-interest tours feature Hollywood and its lore.

Grave Line Tours (Box 931694, Hollywood 90093, tel. 213/469–3127) digs up the dirt on notorious suicides and visits the scenes of various murders, scandals, and other crimes via a luxuriously renovated hearse. A clever, definitely off-the-beaten-track tour in the true sensationalist spirit of Hollywood. Tours daily at noon for two hours; $30 per person reserved, $25 standby.

Hollywood Fantasy Tours (1651 N. Highland, Hollywood 90028, tel. 213/469–8184) has one tour that takes you through Beverly Hills, down Rodeo Drive, around Bel Air, and up and down colorful Sunset Strip, then on to exclusive Holmby Hills, home of *Playboy* magazine's Hugh Hefner. If you're only interested in Hollywood, ask about a tour of that area, pointing out television and film studios as well as famous stores, such as Frederick's of Hollywood.

The Next Stage (Box 35269, Los Angeles 90035, tel. 213/939–2688) takes from four to 46 people, on buses or vans, in search of ethnic L.A., Victorian L.A., Underground L.A. (in which all the places visited are underground), and so on. The Insomniac Tour visits the flower market and other places in the wee hours of the morning. Marlene Gordon, who is a member of the L.A. Conservancy and the California Historical Society, also plans some spectacular tours outside of Los Angeles. Among them are a bald eagle tour to Big Bear with a naturalist; a whale-watching and biplane adventure; and a glorious garlic train, which tours Monterey and Carmel, and takes in the Gilroy Garlic Fest.

LA Today Custom Tours also has a wide selection of offbeat tours, some of which tie in with seasonal and cultural events, such as theater, museum exhibits, and the Rose Bowl. Groups range from 8 to 50, and prices from $6 to $50. The least expensive is a walking tour of hotel lobbies in downtown Los Angeles. The two-hour tour costs $6. For further information contact Elinor Oswald (LA Today, 14964 Camarosa Dr., Pacific Palisades 90272, tel. 213/454–5730).

Architecture in Los Angeles is rich and varied. Guided and self-guided tours of the many design landmarks are becoming increasingly popular. Buildings run the gamut from the Victorian Bradbury Building in the downtown core, to the many fine examples of Frank Lloyd Wright's works—the Ennis-Brown House, Hollyhock House, and Snowden House among them. On the last Sunday of April each year the Los Angeles County Museum of Art (tel. 213/857–6500) holds a fund-raising tour of a selection of special houses in the city.

Personal Guides Perhaps the best way to see Los Angeles, or any city, is with a guide who knows the city well and can gear sightseeing to your interests. One such service, **Tour Elegante** (15446 Sherman Way, Van Nuys, tel. 818/786–8466), offers the perk of a personal guide without the usual expense (under $50 per person). Tours run from three to six hours.

Elegant Tours for the Discriminating (tel. 213/472–4090) is a personalized sightseeing and shopping service for the Beverly Hills area. Joan Mansfield offers her extensive knowledge of Rodeo Drive to one, two, or three people at a time. Lunch is included.

Judith Benjamin Personally Designed Sightseeing (2210 Wilshire Blvd., #754, Santa Monica 90403, tel. 213/826–8810) also matches your interests with sightseeing outings. Judith will design architectural tours, museum tours, shopping tours, visits to jazz nightclubs—anything you might want to see or do in the area.

L.A. Nighthawks (Box 10224, Beverly Hills 902, tel. 213/392–1500) will arrange your nightlife for you. For a rather hefty price, you'll get a limousine, a guide, a gourmet dinner, as well as immediate entry into L.A.'s hottest night spots. For a group of eight, prices come down considerably because vans or tour buses are used. Nighthawks proprietor Charles Andrews, a music writer and 20-year entertainment-business veteran, has been featured on "Eye on LA" and other television shows for this innovative approach to nighttime entertainment.

Exploring Los Angeles

In a city where the residents think nothing of a 40-mile commute to work, visitors have their work cut out for them. To see the sites—from the Huntington Library in San Marino to the *Queen Mary* in Long Beach—requires a decidedly organized itinerary. Be prepared to put miles on the car. It's best to view Los Angeles as a collection of destinations, each to be explored separately, and not to jump willy-nilly from place to place. In our guide, the major sightseeing areas of Los Angeles have been divided into seven major tours: Downtown; Hollywood; Wilshire Boulevard; the Westside; Santa Monica, Venice, Pacific Palisades, and Malibu; Palos Verdes, San Pedro, and Long Beach; Highland Park, Pasadena, and San Marino.

Each takes visitors to the major sites, augmented with bits of history and comments on the area, and occasional Time Out suggestions for meals. These main attractions are listed and numbered on the accompanying maps, and followed by short sections describing an assortment of other attractions, things to do for free, and things to see and do with children.

Downtown Los Angeles

Numbers in the margin correspond with points of interest on the Downtown Los Angeles map.

All those jokes about Los Angeles being a city without a downtown are simply no longer true. They might have had some ring of truth to them a few decades ago when Angelenos ruthlessly turned their backs on the city center and hightailed to the suburbs. There *had* been a downtown, once, when Los Angeles was very young, and now the city core is enjoying a resurgence of attention from urban planners, real estate developers, and intrepid downtown office workers who have discovered the advantages of living close to the office. During the day, downtown is relatively safe and quite interesting. A tour of downtown cuts through more than a century of history and colorful ethnic neighborhoods.

Downtown Los Angeles can be explored on foot or better yet, on DASH (Downtown Area Short Hop). This minibus service travels in a loop past most of the attractions listed here. Every ride costs 25¢, so if you hop on and off to see attractions, it'll cost you every time. But the cost is worth it, since you can travel quickly and be assured of finding your way. Whether you begin your tour at ARCO, as suggested, or decide to start at Olvera Street in Chinatown, DASH will get you around. The bus stops every two blocks or so. DASH (tel. 213/689–8822) runs weekdays 6:30–6:30, Saturday 9–5.

Begin your walk in the Los Angeles of today. The new downtown is a collection of east-side streets, paralleling the Harbor Freeway. Your walk will take you from the most modern buildings back in time past Art Deco movie palaces to the very oldest adobe in the city.

ARCO Plaza is hidden directly under the twin ARCO towers. This subterranean shopping mall is jam-packed with office workers during the week, nearly deserted on weekends. The **❶ Los Angeles Visitor and Convention Bureau** is nearby. It offers free information about attractions as well as advice on public transportation. *699 S. Figueroa at 7th St., tel. 213/689–8822. Open weekdays 9–5.*

One block from the ARCO Plaza, at the corner of Flower and 7th streets, is the downtown L.A. terminus of the Metrorail Blue Line trains that run from here to Long Beach.

❷ Just north of ARCO, the **Westin Bonaventure Hotel** (404 S. Figueroa St., tel. 213/624–1000) is unique in the L.A. skyline: five shimmering cylinders in the sky, with not a 90 degree angle in sight. Designed by John Portman in 1974, it remains a science fiction fantasy. Nonguests can use only one elevator, which rises through the roof of the lobby to soar through the air outside to the revolving restaurant and bar on the 35th floor. Food is expensive here. A better bet is to come for a drink (still overpriced) and nurse it for an hour as Los Angeles makes a full circle around you.

In the 19th century, Bunker Hill was the site of many stately mansions. Thanks to bulldozers, there's not much of a hill left, but this downtown area is being redeveloped, and two major sites here showcase visual arts (painting, sculpture, and environmental work) and media and performing arts.

Downtown Los Angeles

Biltmore Hotel, **12**
Bradbury Building, **10**
Chinatown, **5**
El Pueblo State
Historic Park, **6**
Garment District, **13**
Grand Central
Market, **11**

Greater Los Angeles
Visitor and Convention
Bureau, **1**
Little Tokyo, **9**
Los Angeles City
Hall, **8**
Museum of
Contemporary Art, **3**
Music Center, **4**
Union Station, **7**
Westin Bonaventure
Hotel, **2**

❸ The **Museum of Contemporary Art** houses a permanent collection of international scope, representing modern art from 1940 to the present. Included are works by Mark Rothko, Franz Kline, and Susan Rothenberg. The red sandstone building was designed by one of Japan's renowned architects, Arata Isozaki, and opened in late 1986. Pyramidal skylights add a striking geometry to the seven-level, 98,000-square-foot building. Don't miss the gift shop or the lively Milanese-style cafe. *250 S. Grand Ave., tel. 213/626–6222. Admission: $4 adults, children under 12 free; free to all Thurs. and Fri. after 5 PM. Open Tues., Wed., Sat., and Sun. 11–6, Thurs. and Fri. 11–8.*

❹ Walk north to the **The Music Center,** which has become the cultural center for Los Angeles since it opened in 1969. For years, it was the site of the Academy Awards each spring: The limousines arrived at the Hope Street drive-through and celebrities whisked through the crowds to the Dorothy Chandler Pavilion, the largest and grandest of the three theaters. It was named after the widow of the publisher of the Los Angeles *Times,* who was instrumental in fund-raising efforts to build the complex. The round, center building, the Mark Taper Forum, seats only 750 and seems almost cozy. Most of its offerings are of an experimental nature, many of them on a pre-Broadway run. The Ahmanson, at the north end, is the venue for many musical comedies. The plaza has a fountain and sculpture by Jacques Lipchitz. *First St. and Grand Ave., tel. 213/972–7211. Free 1-hr, 10-min tours are offered Tues.–Sat. 10–1:30. Call for reservations.*

❺ L.A.'s **Chinatown** runs a pale second to San Francisco's Chinatown but it still offers visitors an authentic slice of life, beyond the tourist hokum. The neighborhood is bordered by Yale, Bernard, Alameda, and Ord, and the main street is North Broadway, where, every February, giant dragons snake down the center of the pavement during Chinese New Year celebrations. More than 15,000 Chinese and Southeast Asians (mostly Vietnamese) actually live in the Chinatown area, but many times that regularly frequent the markets (filled with exotic foods unfamiliar to most Western eyes) and restaurants (dim sum parlors are currently the most popular).

❻ **El Pueblo State Historic Park** preserves the "birthplace" of Los Angeles (no one knows exactly where the original 1781 settlement was), the oldest downtown buildings, and some of the only remaining pre-1900 buildings in the city. The state park, comprising 44 acres and including the Plaza and Olvera Street, is bounded by Alameda, Arcadia, Spring, and Macy streets. *The Visitors Center is in Sepulveda House, 622 N. Main St., tel. 213/628–1274. Open weekdays 10–3, Sat. 10–4:30. Most shops and restaurants in the park are open daily 10–9.*

Olvera Street is the heart of the park and one of the most popular tourist sites in Los Angeles.

With its cobblestone walkways, pinatas, mariachis, and authentic Mexican food, Olvera Street should not be dismissed as a mere approximation of Old Mexico, a gringo version of the real thing. Mexican families come here in droves, especially on weekends and Mexican holidays—to them it feels like the old country.

Begin your walk of the area at the Plaza, between Main and Los Angeles streets, a wonderful Mexican-style park with shady trees, a central gazebo, and plenty of benches and walkways for strolling. On weekends there are often mariachis and folkloric dance groups here. You can have your photo taken in an oversize velvet sombrero, astride a stuffed donkey (a take-off of the zebra-striped donkeys that are a tradition on the streets of Tijuana).

Head north up Olvera Street proper. Mid-block is the Sepulveda House, which houses the Visitors Center and is now undergoing renovations. The Eastlake Victorian was built in 1887 as a hotel and boardinghouse. Pelanconi House, built in 1855, was the first brick building in Los Angeles and has been used by La Golondrina restaurant for more than 50 years. During the 1930s, famed Mexican muralist David Alfaro Siquieros was commissioned to paint a mural on the south wall of the Italian Hall building. The patrons were not prepared for the anti-imperialist mural depicting the oppressed workers of Latin America held in check by a menacing American eagle; it was whitewashed into oblivion. It remains, under the paint, to this day, as preservationists from the Getty Conservation Trust work on ways of restoring the mural. (Ask to see copies of the mural at the Visitors Center.)

Walk down the east side of Olvera Street to mid-block, passing the only remaining sign of Zanja Ditch (mother ditch), which supplied water to the area in the earliest years. Avila Adobe (open weekdays 10–3), built in 1818, is generally considered the oldest building still standing in Los Angeles. This graceful, simple adobe is designed with the traditional interior courtyard. It is furnished in typical 1840s fashion.

On weekends, the restaurants are packed, and there is usually music in the plaza and along the street. Two Mexican holidays, Cinco de Mayo (May 5) and Independence Day (September 16), also draw huge crowds—and long lines for the restaurants. To see Olvera Street at its quietest and perhaps loveliest, visit on a late weekday afternoon. The long shadows heighten the romantic feeling of the street and there are only a few strollers and diners milling about.

South of the plaza is an ambitious area that has undergone recent renovation but remains largely underutilized. Except for docent-led tours, these magnificent old buildings remain closed, awaiting some commercial plan (à la Ghiradelli Square in San Francisco) that never seems to come to fruition. Buildings seen on tours include the Merced Theater, Masonic Temple, Pico House, and the Garnier Block—all ornate examples of the late 19th-century style. Under the Merced and Masonic Temple are the catacombs, secret passageways and old opium dens used by Chinese immigrants. Tours depart Tuesday–Saturday 10–1, on the hour. Meet at the Old Firehouse (south side of plaza), an 1884 building that contains early fire-fighting equipment and old photographs.

Time Out   The Olvera Street dining ranges from fast-food stands to comfortable, sit-down restaurants. The most authentic food is at **La Luz del Dia**, at the southwest corner of the street. Here they serve traditional Mexican favorites like barbecued goat and pickled cactus as well as standbys such as tacos and enchiladas. Best of all are the handmade tortillas. You haven't tasted real tortillas until you've tried handmade ones like these (the only ones on the street), which are patted out in a practiced rhythm by the women behind the counter. **La Golondrina** and **El Paseo** restaurants, across from each other in mid-block, have delightful patios and extensive menus.

7 **Union Station** (800 N. Alameda St.), directly east of Olvera Street across Alameda, is one of those quintessentially Californian buildings that seemed to define Los Angeles to moviegoers all over the country in the 1940s. Built in 1939, its Spanish Mission style is a subtle combination of Streamline Moderne and Moorish. The majestic scale of the waiting room is definitely worth a walk over. Imagine it in its heydey, as Carole Lombard or Groucho Marx or Barbara Stanwyck might alight from a train and sashay through.

8 **Los Angeles City Hall** is another often-photographed building. It's been used in "Dragnet," "Superman," and other television shows. Opened in 1928, the 27-story City Hall remained the only building to break the 13-story height limit (earthquakes, you know) until 1957. Although other buildings (e.g., the Bonaventure) may offer higher views, City Hall offers a 45-minute tour and ride to the top-floor observation deck. *200 N. Spring St., tel. 213/485–4423. Tours are by reservation only, weekday mornings at 10 and 11.*

9 **Little Tokyo** is the original ethnic neighborhood for Los Angeles's Japanese community. Most have deserted the downtown center for such suburban areas as Gardena and West Los Angeles, but Little Tokyo remains a cultural focal point. Nisei (the name for second-generation Japanese) Week is celebrated here every August with traditional drums, obon dancing, a carnival and huge parade. Bound by First, San Pedro, Third, and Los Angeles streets, Little Toyko has dozens of sushi bars, tempura restaurants, trinket shops, and even an eel-only restaurant. The Japanese American Cultural and Community Center presents such events as kabuki theater straight from Japan.

Broadway between First and Ninth is one of Los Angeles's busiest shopping streets. The shops and sidewalk vendors cater to the Hispanic population with bridal shops, immigration lawyers, and cheap stereos. First-floor rental space is said to be the most expensive in the city, even higher than in Beverly Hills. It can be an exhilarating slice-of-life walk, past the florid old movie theaters like the Mayan and the Million Dollar and the still-classy-no-matter-what Bradbury Building.

10 The five-story **Bradbury Building** (304 S. Broadway, tel. 213/624–2378) remains a marvelous specimen of architecture, serenely anchoring the southeast corner of Third and Broadway and keeping its nose above the hustle and bustle of the street like a real lady. Once the site of turn-of-the-century sweatshops, it now houses genteel law offices. The interior courtyard with its glass skylight and open balconies and elevator is picture perfect—and naturally another popular movie locale. The building is only open during the week, and its owners prefer that you not wander too far past the lobby.

11 **Grand Central Market** is the most bustling market in the city, and a testimony to the city's diversity. The block-through market of colorful and exotic produce, herbs, and meat draws a faithful clientele from the Hispanic community, senior citizens on a budget, and money-is-no-object Westside matrons seeking rare foodstuffs for their recipe adventures. Even if you don't plan to buy even one banana, Grand Central Market is a delightful place in which to browse. The produce stalls are piled high with the ripest, reddest tomatoes. The herb stalls promise remedies for all your ills. Mixed among them are fast-food stands (one Chinese but most Mexican). *317 S. Broadway. Open Mon.–Sat. 9–6, Sun. 10–4.*

⓬ The **Biltmore Hotel** (515 S. Olive St.) rivals Union Station for sheer majesty in the Spanish Revival tradition. The public areas have recently been restored; the magnificent, hand-painted wood beams brought back to their former glory.

⓭ The **Garment District** (700–800 blocks of Los Angeles St.) is an enclave of jobbers and wholesalers that sell off the leftovers from Los Angeles's considerable garment industry production. The Cooper Building (860 S. Los Angeles St.) is the heart of the district and houses several of what local bargain-hunters consider to be the best pickings.

Hollywood

Numbers in the margin correspond with points of interest on the Hollywood map.

Hollywood. The name once defined movie stars, glamour, the Big Time. The big studios were here; starlets lived in sorority-like buildings in the center of town; the latest movies premiered at the Chinese and the Pantages theaters.

Those days are gone. Paramount is the only major studio left; some celebrities may live in the Hollywood Hills, but certainly not in the "flats." Hollywood is no longer "Hollywood." These days it is, even to its supporters, a seedy town that could use a good dose of urban renewal (some projects are, in fact, finally under way). Why visit? Because the legends of the golden age of the movies are heavy in the air. Because this is where "they" were: Judy Garland lived here and so did Marilyn Monroe and Lana Turner. Because visitors are able to look past the junky shops and the lost souls who walk the streets to get a sense of yesterday. Even today, no visit to Los Angeles is truly complete without a walk down Hollywood Boulevard.

❶ Begin your tour of Hollywood simply by looking to the **Hollywood sign** in the Hollywood Hills that line the northern border of the town. Even on the smoggiest days, the sign is visible for miles. It is north of Beachwood Canyon, which is approximately 1 mile east of Hollywood and Vine. The sign was erected in 1923 as a promotional scheme for a real estate development called Hollywoodland. (The sign originally read "Hollywoodland"; "land" was taken down in 1949.) Standing high on Mount Lee, the 50-foot-high letters seem to be an ongoing lure for vandals and pranksters. There has been only one known suicide off the letters (in 1932), but every year there are several alterations (dopers turning it into "Hollyweed," right wingers into "Ollywood" during the Iran-Contra hearings).

❷ **Hollywood and Vine** was once considered the heart of Hollywood. The mere mention of the intersection inspired thoughts of stars, starlets, and movie moguls passing by, on foot and in snazzy convertibles. These days, Hollywood and Vine is far from the action. Pedestrian traffic is—well, pedestrian. No stars, no starlets, not even any moguls. The big Broadway department store on the southwest corner has been closed for sev-

Hollywood

Capitol Records Building, **3**

Frederick's of Hollywood, **7**

Hollywood Bowl, **10**

Hollywood High School, **12**

Hollywood Memorial Cemetery, **13**

Hollywood sign, **1**

Hollywood Studio Museum, **11**

Hollywood and Vine, **2**

Hollywood Walk of Fame, **6**

Hollywood Wax Museum, **8**

Mann's Chinese Theater, **9**

The Palace, **4**

The Pantages Theater, **5**

eral years, and the intersection these days is little more than a place for visitors to get their bearings.

❸ Capitol Records Building. When Capitol decided to build its headquarters just north of Hollywood and Vine, at 1756 N. Vine Street, two big Capitol talents of the day (singer Nat King Cole and songwriter Johnny Mercer) suggested that it be done in the shape of a stack of records. It opened in 1956, the very picture of '50s chic. These days, it doesn't seem so odd.

❹ The Palace, just across the street at 1735 N. Vine Street, was opened in 1927 as the Hollywood Playhouse. It has played host to many shows over the years, from Ken Murray's *Blackouts* to Ralph Edwards's *This Is Your Life.* It is now the site of rock concerts and *The Sunday Comics* TV show.

❺ The Pantages Theater, at 6233 Hollywood, just east of Vine, opened in 1930, the very height of movie-theater opulence. From 1949 to 1959, it was the site of the Academy Awards.

❻ The Hollywood Walk of Fame is at every turn as you make your way through downtown Hollywood on foot. The sidewalks of Hollywood feature dark gray terrazzo circles embedded by pink-colored stars, with the name of a Hollywood legend in brass in the center. The first eight stars were unveiled in 1960 at the northwest corner of Highland Avenue and Hollywood Boulevard. Some names have stood the test of time better than others: the eight were Olive Borden, Ronald Colman, Louise Fazenda, Preston Foster, Burt Lancaster, Edward Sedgwick, Ernest Torrence, and Joanne Woodward. In the more than 30 years since, 1,800 others have been added. Being walked on, day after day, may be a celebrity's dream but it does not come cheap. The personality in question (or, for instance, the record company) must pay for the honor: $3,500. Walk a few blocks and you'll quickly find that not all the names are familiar. Many are stars from the earliest days of Hollywood. To aid in the identification, celebrities are identified by one of five logos: a motion picture camera, a radio microphone, a television set, a record, or theatrical masks. Here's a guide to a few of the more famous stars on the Walk of Fame: Marlon Brando at 1765 Vine, Charlie Chaplin at 6751 Hollywood, W.C. Fields at 7004 Hollywood, Clark Gable at 1608 Vine, Marilyn Monroe at 6774 Hollywood, Rudolph Valentino at 6164 Hollywood, and John Wayne at 1541 Vine.

❼ Frederick's of Hollywood (6608 Hollywood Blvd., tel. 213/466–8506) is one of Hollywood's more infamous spots. Until 1989, a gaudy lavender building, Frederick's was finally restored to its original understated Art Deco look. Inside houses the famous name in trashy lingerie plus a bra museum, featuring undergarments of living and no longer living legends—a very popular tourist spot, if only for a good giggle.

❽ Hollywood Wax Museum. It's not the same as seeing them in the flesh, but the museum can offer visitors sights that real life no longer can (Mary Pickford, Elvis Presley, and Clark Gable) and a few that even real life never did (Rambo and Conan). A short film on Academy Award winners is shown daily. *6767 Hollywood Blvd., tel. 213/462–8860. Admission: $7 adults, $6 senior citizens, $5 children. Children under 6 admitted free if accompanied by an adult. Open Sun.–Thurs. 10 AM–midnight, Fri.–Sat. 10 AM–2 AM.*

❾ It took the residents quite a few years to stop calling **Mann's Chinese Theater** (6925 Hollywood Blvd., tel. 213/464–8111) "Grauman's Chinese," but now the new owners seem to have a firm hold on the place in the public's eye. The theater opened in 1927 with the premiere of Cecil B. DeMille's *King of Kings*. The architecture is a fantasy of Chinese pagodas and temples as only Hollywood could turn out. Although you'll have to buy a movie ticket to appreciate both the interior trappings and the exterior excess, the famous courtyard is open for browsing. You'll see the famous cement hand- and footprints. The tradition is said to have begun at the premiere itself, when actress Norma Talmadge accidentally stepped in the wet cement. Now more than 160 celebrities have added their footprints, handprints, even a few oddball prints like Jimmy Durante's nose. Space has pretty much run out and, unlike the Walk of Fame on the sidewalks, these cement autographs are by invitation only.

❿ Summer evening concerts at the **Hollywood Bowl** have been a tradition since 1922, although the shell has been replaced several times. The 17,000-plus seating capacity ranges from boxes (where local society matrons put on incredibly fancy alfresco preconcert meals for their friends) to cement bleachers in the rear. Some people prefer the back rows of the bleachers for their romantic appeal.

The official concert season begins in early July and runs through mid-September with performances on Tuesdays, Thursdays, and weekends. The program ranges from jazz to pop to classical. Evenings can be chilly (even on 90-degree days), so bring a sweater and wear comfortable shoes. A night at the Bowl involves considerable walking. *2301 N. Highland Ave., tel. 213/850–2000. Grounds open daily summer, 9–sunset. Call for program schedule.*

⓫ The **Hollywood Studio Museum** sits in the Hollywood Bowl parking lot, east of Highland Boulevard. The building, recently moved to this site, was once called the Lasky–DeMille Barn and it was where Cecil B. DeMille produced the first feature-length film, *The Squaw Man*. In 1927, the barn became Paramount Pictures, with the original company of Jesse Lasky, Cecil B. DeMille, and Samuel Goldwyn. The museum shows the origin of the motion picture industry. There's a re-creation of DeMille's office, with original artifacts and a screening room offering vintage film footage of Hollywood and its legends. A great gift shop sells such quality vintage memorabilia as autographs, photographs, and books. *2100 N. Highland Ave., tel. 213/874–2276. Admission: $3.50 adults, $2.50 children. Open weekends 10–4.*

⓬ Such stars as Carol Burnett, Linda Evans, Rick Nelson, and Lana Turner attended **Hollywood High School** (1521 N. Highland Ave.), Today the student body is as diverse as Los Angeles itself, with every ethnic group represented.

⓭ Many of Hollywood's stars, from the silent-screen era on, are buried in **Hollywood Memorial Cemetery,** a few blocks from Paramount Studios. Walk from the entrance to the lake area and you'll find the crypt of Cecil B. DeMille and the graves of Nelson Eddy and Douglas Fairbanks, Sr. Inside the Cathedral Mausoleum is Rudolph Valentino's crypt (where fans, the press, and the famous Lady in Black turn up every August 23, the anniversary of his death). Other stars interred in this section are Peter Lorre and Eleanor Powell. In the Abbey of Palms Mausoleum, Norma Talmadge and Clifton Webb are buried. *6000 Santa Monica Blvd., tel. 213/469–1181. Open daily 8–5.*

Wilshire Boulevard

Wilshire Boulevard begins in the heart of downtown Los Angeles and runs west, through Beverly Hills and Santa Monica, ending at the cliffs above the Pacific Ocean. In 16 miles it moves through poor immigrant neighborhoods and middle-class ones and on through a corridor of the highest priced high-rise condos in the city. Along the way (within a few blocks of each other) are many of Los Angeles's top architectural sites, museums, and shops.

This linear tour can be started at any point along the way but to really savor a true cross-section of the city, it takes a Bullocks-west-to-the-sea approach. It would be better to skip Koreatown and Larchmont and pare down the museum time than to do only one stretch. All these sites are on Wilshire or within a few blocks north or south.

"One" Wilshire is just another anonymous office building in downtown Los Angeles. Begin, instead, a few miles westward. As Wilshire Boulevard moves from its downtown genesis, it quickly passes through neighborhoods now populated by recent Central American immigrants. In the early years, however, this area was home to many of the city's wealthy citizens, as the faded Victorian houses on the side streets attest.

As the population crept westward, the distance to downtown shops began to seem insurmountable and the first suburban department branch store, **I. Magnin Wilshire** (3050 Wilshire Blvd., tel. 213/382–6161), was opened in 1929. It remains in excellent condition today and is still operating. To appreciate the real splendor of the store, enter from the rear door. The behind-the-store parking lot was quite an innovation in 1929 and the first accommodation a large Los Angeles store made to the automobile age. Look up at the ceiling of the porte cochere, where a mural depicts early 20th-century history. Inside, the store remains a well-preserved monument to the Art Deco age. The walls, the elevators, and the floors are the height of late 1920s style.

Koreatown begins almost at I. Magnin Wilshire's backdoor. Koreans are one of the latest and largest groups in our ethnically diverse city. Arriving from the old country with generally more money than most immigrant groups do, Koreans nevertheless face the trauma of adjusting to a new language, new alphabet, and new customs. Settling in the area south of Wilshire Boulevard, along Olympic Boulevard between Vermont and Western avenues, the Korean community has slowly grown into a full-fledged enclave with active community groups and newspapers. The area is teeming with Asian restaurants (not just Korean but also Japanese and Chinese, because Koreans are fond of those cuisines). Many of the signs in this area are in Korean only.

At the southwest corner of Wilshire and Western Avenue sits **Wiltern Theater,** one of the city's best examples of Art Moderne. The 1930s zigzag design has been recently restored to its splendid turquoise hue. Inside, the theater is magnificently opulent, in the grand tradition.

Continuing west on Wilshire, the real estate values start to make a sharp climb. The mayor of Los Angeles has his official residence in **Getty House** (605 S. Irving Blvd.), one block north of Wilshire in the Hancock Park district. This is one of the city's most genteel neighborhoods, remaining in vogue since its development in the 1920s. Many of L.A.'s old monied families live here in English Tudor homes with East Coast landscaping schemes that seem to defy the local climate and history. The white-brick, half-timber Getty House was donated to the city by the Getty family.

Miracle Mile, the strip of Wilshire Boulevard between La Brea and Fairfax avenues, was so dubbed in the 1930s as a promotional gimmick to attract shoppers to the new stores. The buildings went into a decline in the '50s and '60s, but the area is now enjoying a strong comeback. Exceptionally strong Art Deco buildings like the Darkroom (5370 Wilshire) and the El Rey Theater (5519 Wilshire) stand out as examples of period design. In the Callender's Restaurant (corner of Wilshire and Curson), there are recent murals and old photographs that effectively depict life on the Miracle Mile during its heyday.

Across Curson Avenue is Hancock Park (not to be confused with Hancock Park, the residential neighborhood). The park is home to two of the city's best museums as well as the city's only world-famous fossil source, the **La Brea Tar Pits.** Despite the fact that *la brea* means "tar" in Spanish and to say "La Brea Tar Pits" is redundant, the name remains firm in local minds. These tar pits were known to the earliest inhabitants of the area and were long used to seal leaky boats and roofs. In the early 20th century, geologists discovered that the sticky goo contained the largest collection of Pleistocene fossils ever found at one location. More than 200 varieties of birds, mammals, plants, reptiles, and insects have been discovered here. The statues of mammoths in the big pit near the corner of Wilshire and Curson depict how many of them were entombed: Edging down to a pond of water to drink, animals were caught in the tar and unable to extricate themselves.

The pits were formed about 35,000 years ago when deposits of oil rose to the Earth's surface, collected in shallow pools, and coagulated into sticky asphalt. Over 100 tons of fossil bones have been removed in the 70 years since excavations began here. There are several pits scattered around Hancock Park. They are a reminder of nature's superiority over man. Construction in the area has had to accommodate these oozing pits, and in nearby streets and along sidewalks, little bits of tar ooze up, unstoppable.

Also in Hancock Park, the **George C. Page Museum of La Brea Discoveries** is a satellite of the Los Angeles County Museum of Natural History. The Page Museum is situated at the tar pits, and set, bunkerlike, half underground; a bas-relief around four sides depicts life in the Pleistocene era. The museum has over one million Ice Age fossils. Exhibits include reconstructed, life-size skeletons of mammals and birds whose fossils were recovered from the pits: saber-tooth cats, mammoths, wolves, sloths, eagles, and condors. Several large murals and colorful dioramas depict the history of the Pleistocene period. The glass-enclosed Paleontological Laboratory permits observation of the ongoing cleaning, identification, and cataloguing of fossils excavated from the nearby asphalt deposits. *The La Brea Story* and *Dinosaurs, the Terrible Lizards* are short documentary films shown every 15–30 minutes as museum traffic requires. A hologram magically puts flesh on "La Brea Woman," and a tar contraption shows visitors just how hard it would be to free oneself from the sticky mess. An excellent gift shop offers nature-oriented books and trinkets. *5801 Wilshire Blvd., tel. 213/936–2230. Admission: $3 adults, 75¢ children; free the second Tues. of the month. Open Tues.–Sun. 10–5.*

The **Los Angeles County Museum of Art,** also in Hancock Park and the largest museum complex in Los Angeles, has grown considerably in the past few years with generous donations from local patrons who are determined to put Los Angeles on the map, art-wise. The original buildings (Ahmanson Gallery, Frances and Armand Hammer Wing, and Leo S. Bing Center) have been joined by the Robert O. Anderson Building and the Pavilion for Japanese Art. The museum's new Wilshire Boulevard facade sports spiffy glass tile.

The Ahmanson Gallery, built around a graceful central atrium, houses a permanent collection of paintings, sculptures, graphic arts, costumes, textiles, and decorative arts from a wide range of cultures and periods, prehistoric to present. Included are works by Picasso, Rembrandt, Veronese, Durer, Hals, de la Tour, and Homer. One of the Western world's largest collections of Indian, Nepalese, and Tibetan art is housed here. Major changing exhibitions are presented in the Frances and Armand Hammer Wing.

The 115,000-square-foot Robert O. Anderson Building houses 20th-century art from the museum's permanent collection and traveling exhibits. The new Pavilion for Japanese Art houses the Sinen-Kan collection of over 300 Japanese scroll paintings and screens.

The Leo S. Bing Center contains the Art Rental Gallery, the Bing Theater, Art Research Library, and the indoor/outdoor cafeteria-style Plaza Cafe. The museum offers the community many cultural activities, including film series, concerts, lectures, tours of the collections, and student programs. The Museum Shop features a selection of books, magazines, postcards, posters, antiquities, jewelry, and gifts.

The museum, as well as the adjoining Page Museum and Hancock Park itself, is brimming with visitors on warm weekend days. Although crowded, it can be the most exciting time to visit the area. Mimes and itinerant musicians ply their trades. Street vendors sell fast-food treats and there are impromptu soccer games on the lawns. To really study the art, though, a quieter weekday visit is recommended. *5905 Wilshire Blvd., tel. 213/857–6111. Open Tues.–Fri. 10–5, weekends 10–6. Admission: $5 adults, $3 children ($2 for special exhibits).*

The **Craft and Folk Art Museum,** across Wilshire, offers consistently fascinating exhibits of both contemporary crafts and folk crafts from around the world. The museum's collections include Japanese, Mexican, American, and East Indian folk art, textiles, and masks. Six to eight major exhibitions are planned each year. The museum's library and media resources center are open to the public. The museum shop carries displays of merchandise relating to each current exhibition as well as quality work by expert craftspeople, folk art from around the world, original postcards, and educational materials. *5814 Wilshire Blvd., tel. 213/937–5544. Admission free. Open Tues.– Sat., 10–5; Sun. 11–5.*

Continue west on Wilshire a few blocks to the corner of Fairfax Avenue. On the northeast corner is the May Co. department store, another 1930s landmark with a distinctive curved corner.

Head north on Fairfax a few blocks to the **Farmer's Market.** Thanks to tour bus operators and its own easygoing, all-year-outdoor setting, the Farmer's Market is a popular stop of L.A. city tours. When it first opened in 1934, the market sold farm-direct produce at bargain prices. These days, the produce is still tantalizing but definitely high-priced. No longer farm-direct, the stands offer out-of-season peppers and tiny seedless champagne grapes from Chile at top prices. In addition to produce stands, there are dozens of cooked-food stalls offering Cajun gumbos, Mexican enchiladas, fish-and-chips, frozen yogurt, pizza, and hamburgers. *6333 W. 3rd St., tel. 213/933–9211. Open Mon.–Sat. 9–6:30, Sun. 10–5. Open later during summer.*

Time Out **Kokomo** is not only the best eatery in the Farmer's Market, it's got some of the best new-wave diner food anywhere in L.A. Lively, entertaining service is almost always included in the reasonable prices. *Located on the Third St. side of the market, tel. 213/933–0773. Reservations. No credit cards. Open Mon.– Sat. to 7 and Sun. to 6 during summer.*

North of the market, Fairfax becomes the center of Los Angeles's Jewish life. The shops and stands from Beverly Boulevard north are enlivened with friendly conversations between shopkeepers and regular customers. Canter's Restaurant, Deli, and Bakery (419 N. Fairfax, tel. 213/651–2030) is the traditional hangout.

The Westside

Numbers in the margin correspond with points of interest on the Westside map.

The Westside of Los Angeles, which to residents means from La Brea Avenue westward to the ocean, is where the rents are the most expensive, the real estate values sky high, the restaurants (and the restaurateurs) the most famous, the shops the most chic. It's the good life Southern California style and to really savor the Southland, spend a few leisurely days or half days exploring the area. Short on such traditional tourist attractions as musement parks, historic sites, and museums, it more than makes up for those gaps with great shopping districts, exciting walking streets, outdoor cafes, and lively nightlife.

The Westside can be best enjoyed in at least three separate outings, allowing plenty of time for browsing and dining. Attractions #1 through #4 are in the West Hollywood area; #5 through #8 in Beverly Hills; and #9 through #10 in Westwood. But the Westside is small enough that you could pick four or five of these sites to visit in a day, depending on your interests.

West Hollywood is a glitzy section of Los Angeles. Once an almost forgotten parcel of county land surrounded by the city of L.A. and Beverly Hills, it became an official city in 1984. The West Hollywood attitude—trendy, stylish, plenty of disposable income—spills over beyond the official city borders.

❶ Melrose Avenue, which isn't exactly in West Hollywood, nevertheless remains firmly fixed in residents' minds as *very* West Hollywood. If you're entertained by post-punk fashion plates and other people in spiked hairdos, just about the most outlandish ensembles imaginable, Melrose is the place for you. Would-be rock stars and weekend punkers hang out and provide a wonderful show for the ordinary folks. The busiest stretch of Melrose is between Fairfax and La Brea avenues. Here you'll find one-of-a-kind boutiques and small, chic restaurants for more than a dozen blocks. Park on a side street (the parking regulations around here are vigorously enforced: a rich vein for the city's coffers) and begin walking. The quintessential Melrose shops are Soap Plant and Wacko, on the same block near Martel Avenue. Gaudy both inside and out and offering the most bizarre trinkets and books, these shops are just plain fun. Other busy shops: War Babies (clothes from the armies of the world) and Rene's (offbeat records and a local skateboarders' hangout as well).

Time Out Melrose has no shortage of great eateries. Part of any visit here is trying to pick one from the dozens of choices: Thai, Mexican, sausages, yogurt, Italian, and more. The ultimate Melrose "joint" is **Johnny Rocket's** (7507 Melrose Ave., tel. 213/651–3361), a very hip '50s-style diner near the corner of Gardner Street. It's just stools at a counter, the best of old-time rock and roll on tape, and great hamburgers, shakes, and fries—and almost always crowded, with people lined up behind the stools to slip in the moment they are vacated. Off-hours are best.

---

❷ Beverly Center (8500 Beverly Blvd. at La Cienega, Los Angeles, tel. 310/854–0070) is that hulking monolith dominating the corner of La Cienega and Beverly Boulevard. Designed as an all-in-one stop for shopping, dining, and movies, it has been a boon to Westsiders—except those who suffer the congestion by living too close. Parking is on the second through fifth floors, shops on the sixth and seventh, and movies and restaurants on the eighth. The first floor features Irvine Ranch Market, a state-of-the-art gourmet grocery that is a booby trap for impulse buyers who love to try new foods. At the northwest corner, the Hard Rock Cafe (look for the vintage green Cadillac imbedded in the roof) always has a line of hungry customers (salivating for both burgers and a chance to see celebrities who often come here). Upstairs in the center proper are two major department stores, dozens of upscale clothing boutiques, 14 movie theaters, and a wide variety of restaurants (Mandarin Cove, Siam Orchid, Tea Room St., Petersburg plus cookie shops, pizza parlors, and hamburger stands).

West Hollywood is the center of Los Angeles's thriving interior decorating business. **The Pacific Design Center** (8687 Melrose Ave., West Hollywood, tel. 310/657–0800) has been dubbed the "Blue Whale" by residents. The all-blue-glass building designed by Cesar Pelli in 1975 houses to-the-trade-only showrooms filled with the most tempting furnishings, wallpapers,

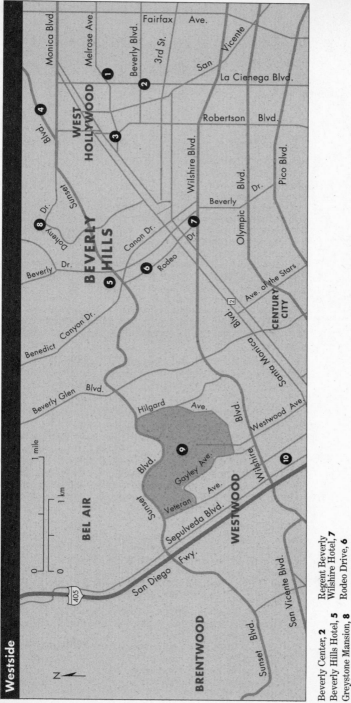

Westside

N

1 mile

1 km

0

0

Monica Blvd

Melrose Ave.

Fairfax Ave.

Beverly Blvd.

3rd St.

San Vicente

La Cienega Blvd.

WEST HOLLYWOOD

Blvd.

Robertson Blvd.

Sunset

Dr.

Doheny

Beverly Dr.

BEVERLY HILLS

Canon Dr.

Rodeo

Wilshire Blvd.

Beverly Blvd.

Dr.

Olympic

Pico Blvd.

Dr.

Ave. of the Stars

CENTURY CITY

Benedict Canyon Dr.

Santa Monica Blvd.

BEL AIR

Beverly Glen Blvd.

Hilgard Ave.

Blvd.

Westwood Ave.

Wilshire

Blvd.

Gayley Ave.

Veteran Ave.

Sunset

Sepulveda Blvd.

WESTWOOD

San Diego Fwy.

San Vicente Blvd.

BRENTWOOD

Sunset Blvd.

405

1

2

4

3

8

5

6

7

9

10

Beverly Center, **2**
Beverly Hills Hotel, **5**
Greystone Mansion, **8**
Melrose Avenue, **1**
Pacific Design
Center, **3**

Regent Beverly
Wilshire Hotel, **7**
Rodeo Drive, **6**
Sunset Strip, **4**
University of
California at
Los Angeles, **9**
Westwood Memorial
Park, **10**

and accessories. In 1988, the center added a second building by Pelli, this one clad in green glass. Most of the showrooms discourage casual browsers, but the building is open and anyone can stroll the halls and rubberneck in the windows.

The same rules apply for "Robertson Boulevard," the name given to the outside-PDC showrooms that surround the Blue Whale. They are not confined to Robertson Boulevard but are well represented on Beverly Boulevard and Melrose Avenue. This section is exceptionally walkable, and residents often walk their dogs here in the evening (even driving them to the area to do their walking) so they can browse the well-lit windows. A few of the showrooms will accommodate an occasional retail buyer, so if you see something to die for, it's worth a timid inquiry inside.

❹ **Sunset Strip** was famous in the '50s, as in "77 Sunset Strip," but it was popular even in the 1930s when nightclubs like Ciro's and Mocambo were in their heyday. This winding, hilly stretch is a visual delight, enjoyed both by car (a convertible would be divine) or on foot. Drive it once to enjoy the hustle-bustle, the vanity boards (huge billboards touting new movies, new records, new stars), the dazzling shops. Then pick a section and explore a few blocks on foot. The Sunset Plaza section is especially nice, with very expensive shops and a few outdoor cafes (Tutto Italia, Chin Chin) that are packed for lunch and on warm evenings. At Horn Street, Tower Records (a behemoth of a record store with two satellite shops across the street), Book Soup (finally, a literary bookstore in L.A.!), and Spago (tucked a half block up the hill on Horn) make a nice browse, especially in the evening.

The glitz of the Strip ends abruptly at Doheny Drive, where Sunset Boulevard enters the famous and glamorous city of Beverly Hills. Suddenly the sidewalk street life gives way to expansive, perfectly manicured lawns and palatial homes, all representative of what the name Beverly Hills has come to mean.

❺ West of the Strip a mile or so is the **Beverly Hills Hotel** (9641 Sunset Blvd., Beverly Hills, tel. 310/276–2251). Dubbed the "Pink Palace," its quiet Spanish Colonial Revival architecture and soft pastel exterior belie the excitement inside, where Hollywood wheelers and dealers have meetings over margaritas in the Polo Lounge and where many stars keep permanent bungalows as second homes.

It is on this stretch of Sunset, especially during the daytime, that you'll see hawkers peddling maps of stars' homes. Are the maps reliable? Well, that's a matter of debate. Stars do move around, so it's difficult to keep any map up to date. But the fun of looking at some of these magnificent homes, regardless of whether they're owned by a star at (or of) the moment, makes many people buy such maps and embark on tours.

Beverly Hills was incorporated as a city early in the century and has been thriving ever since. As a vibrant, exciting city within the larger city, it has retained its reputation for wealth and luxury, an assessment with which you will agree as you drive along one of its main thoroughfares, Santa Monica Boulevard (which is actually two parallel streets at this point: "Big Santa Monica" is the northern street; "Little Santa Monica," the southern one).

Within a few square blocks in the center of the city are some of the most exotic, not to mention high-priced, stores in Southern California. Here one can find such items as $200 pairs of socks wrapped in gold leaf and stores that take customers only by appointment. A fun way to spend an afternoon is to stroll famed
6 **Rodeo Drive** between Santa Monica and Wilshire boulevards. Some of the Rodeo (pronounced ro-DAY-o) shops may be familiar to you since they supply clothing for major network television shows and their names often appear among the credits. Others, such as Gucci, have a worldwide reputation. Fortunately, browsing is free (and fun), no matter how expensive the store is. Several nearby restaurants have outside patios where you can sit and sip a drink while watching the fashionable shoppers stroll by.

7 The **Regent Beverly Wilshire Hotel** (9500 Wilshire Blvd., tel. 310/275–5200) anchors the south end of Rodeo Drive, at Wilshire. Opened in 1928, and vigorously expanded and renovated since, the hotel is often home to visiting royalty and celebrities, who arrive amid much fanfare at the porte cochere in the rear of the old structure. The lobby is quite small for a hotel of this size and there is little opportunity to meander; you might stop for a drink or meal in one of the hotel's restaurants.

8 The **Greystone Mansion** was built by oilman Edward Doheny in 1923. This Tudor-style mansion, now owned by the city of Beverly Hills, sits on 16 landscaped acres and has been used in such films as *The Witches of Eastwick* and *All of Me*. The gardens are open for self-guided tours and peeking in the windows (only) is permitted. *905 Loma Vista Dr., Beverly Hills, tel. 310/550–4796. Admission free. Open daily 10–5.*

One of Beverly Hills' mansions opens its grounds to visitors. The **Virginia Robinson Gardens** are 6.2 terraced acres on the former estate of the heir to the Robinson Department Store chain. A guide will take you on an hour tour of the gardens and the exquisite exteriors of the main house, guest house, servants' quarters, swimming pool, and tennis court. A highlight of the tour is the collection of rare and exotic palms. Since the gardens' administration is trying to keep a low profile to avoid congestion in the cul-de-sac where the gardens are situated, visitors must call for reservations and be told the address and directions. *Tel. 310/276–5367. Admission: $3. Tours Tues.–Thurs. 10 AM and 1 PM, Fri. 10 AM.*

Westward from Beverly Hills, Sunset continues to wind past
9 palatial estates and passes by the **University of California at Los Angeles**. Nestled in the Westwood section of the city and bound by LeConte, Sunset, and Hilgard, the parklike UCLA campus is an inviting place for visitors to stroll. The most spectacular buildings are the original ones, Royce Hall and the library, both in Romanesque style. In the heart of the north campus is the Franklin Murphy Sculpture Garden, with works by Henry Moore and Lachaise dotting the landscaping. For a gardening buff, UCLA is a treasure of unusual and well-labeled plants. The Mildred Mathias Botanic Garden is located in the southeast section of campus and is accessible from Tiverton Avenue. Maps and information are available at drive-by kiosks at major entrances, even on weekends. Free 90-minute, guided walking tours of the campus are offered on weekdays. The campus has several indoor and outdoor cafes, plus bookstores that sell the very popular UCLA Bruins paraphernalia. *Tours (tel.*

310/825–4574) weekdays at 10:30 AM and 1:30 PM. Meet at 10945 LeConte St., room 1417, on the south edge of the campus, facing Westwood.

The **Hannah Carter Japanese Garden,** located in Bel Air just north of the campus, is owned by UCLA and may be visited by making phone reservations two weeks in advance (tel. 310/825–4574).

Directly south of the campus is Westwood, once a quiet college town and now one of the busiest places in the city on weekend evenings—so busy that during the summer, many streets are closed to car traffic and visitors must park at the Federal Building (Wilshire and Veteran) and shuttle over. However you arrive, Westwood remains a delightful village filled with clever boutiques, trendy restaurants, movie theaters, and colorful street life.

The village proper is delineated on the south by Wilshire Boulevard, which is now a corridor of cheek-by-jowl office buildings whose varying architectural styles can be jarring, to say the least. Tucked behind one of these behemoths is **Westwood Memorial Park** (1218 Glendon Ave.). In this very unlikely place for a cemetery is one of the most famous graves in the city. Marilyn Monroe is buried in a simply marked wall crypt. For 25 years after her death, her former husband Joe DiMaggio had six red roses placed on her crypt three times a week. Also buried here is Natalie Wood.

Santa Monica, Venice, Pacific Palisades, and Malibu

Numbers in the margin correspond with points of interest on the Santa Monica and Venice map.

The towns that hug the coastline of Santa Monica Bay reflect the wide diversity of Los Angeles, from the rich-as-can-be Malibu to the cheek-by-jowl Yuppie/seedy mix of Venice. Life is lived outdoors here and the emphasis is on being out in the sunshine, always within sight of the Pacific. Visitors might savor the area in two sections: Santa Monica to Venice in one day and Pacific Palisades to Malibu in another.

From Santa Monica to Venice Santa Monica is a sensible place. It's a tidy little city, 2 miles square, whose ethnic population is largely British (there's an English music hall and several pubs here), attracted perhaps by the cool and foggy climate. The sense of order is reflected in the economic/geographic stratification: The most northern section has broad streets lined with superb, older homes. Driving south, real estate prices drop $50,000 or so every few blocks.

Begin exploring at **Santa Monica Pier,** located at the foot of Colorado Avenue and easily accessible for beach-goers as well as drive-around visitors. Cafes, gift shops, a psychic advisor, bumper cars, and arcades line the pier. The 46-horse carousel, built in 1922, has seen action in many movie and television shows, most notably the Paul Newman/Robert Redford film *The Sting. Tel. 310/394–7554. Rides: 50¢ adults, 25¢ children. Carousel open in summer, Tues.–Sun. 10–9; in winter, weekends 10–5.*

Palisades Park is a ribbon of green that runs along the top of the cliffs from Colorado Avenue to just north of San Vicente Boule-

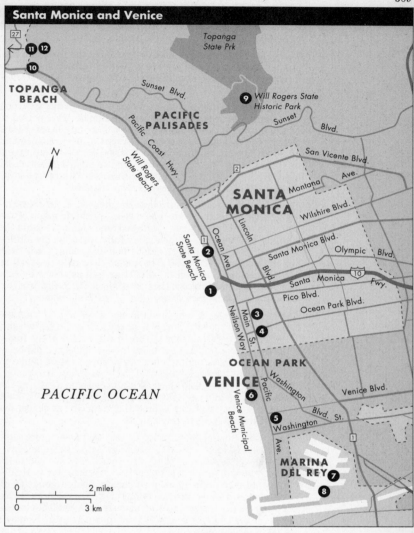

Santa Monica and Venice

Topanga
State Prk

TOPANGA
BEACH

⑪ ⑫
⑩

Sunset   Blvd.

PACIFIC
PALISADES

⑨ Will Rogers State
Historic Park

Sunset   Blvd.

Pacific Coast Hwy.

Will Rogers
State Beach

San Vicente Blvd.

②

SANTA
MONICA

Montana   Ave.

Wilshire Blvd.

Lincoln

Santa Monica State Beach

① Ocean Ave.

②

Santa Monica Blvd.

Olympic   Blvd.

Blvd.

Santa Monica   ⑩ Fwy.

①

Pico Blvd.

Neilson Way

③ Main St.

Ocean Park Blvd.

④

OCEAN PARK

VENICE

Pacific

Washington

Venice Blvd.

PACIFIC OCEAN

⑥

Venice Municipal Beach

Blvd.   St.

⑤ Washington

Washington   Ave.

①

MARINA
DEL REY   ⑦

⑧

0   2 miles
0   3 km

Adamson House , **11**   Palisades Park, **2**
Burton Chase Park, **7**   Santa Monica Heritage
Fisherman's Village, **8**   Museum, **4**
J.Paul Getty   Santa Monica Pier, **1**
Museum, **10**   Santa Monica Museum
Malibu Lagoon State   of Art, **3**
Park, **12**   Venice Boardwalk, **6**
Pacific Ave./Venice   Will Rogers State
Blvd. Canals, **5**   Park, **9**

vard. The flat walkways are usually filled with casual strollers as well as joggers who like to work out with a spectacular view of the Pacific as company. It is especially enjoyable at sunset.

The Visitor Information Center is located in the park, at Santa Monica Boulevard. It offers bus schedules, directions, and information on Santa Monica–area attractions. *Tel. 310/393–7593. Open daily 10–4.*

Santa Monica has grown into a major center for the L.A. art community, and the **Santa Monica Museum of Art** is poised to boost that reputation. Designed by local architect Frank Gehry, the museum presents the works of performance and video artists and exhibits works of lesser-known painters and sculptors. *2437 Main St., Santa Monica, tel. 310/399–0433. Open Wed. and Thurs. 11–8, Fri.–Sun. 11–6. Admission: $3 adults, $1 artists, students, and senior citizens.*

The **Santa Monica Heritage Museum**, housed in an 1894-vintage, late-Victorian home once owned by the founder of the city, was moved to its present site on trendy Main Street in the mid-1980s. Three rooms have been fully restored: the dining room in the style of 1890 to 1910; the living room, 1910–1920; and the kitchen, 1920–1930. The second-floor galleries feature photography and historical exhibits as well as shows by contemporary Santa Monica artists. *2612 Main St., Santa Monica, tel. 310/392–8537. Open Thurs.–Sat. 11–4, Sun. noon–4.*

The museum faces a companion home, another Victorian delight moved to the site that is now the Chronicle restaurant. These two dowagers anchor the northwest corner of the funky Main Street area of Santa Monica. Several blocks of old brick buildings here have undergone a recent rejuvenation (and considerable rent increases) and now house galleries, bars, cafes, omelet parlors, and boutiques. With its close proximity to the beach, parking can be tight on summer weekend days. Best bets are the city pay lots behind the Main Street shops, between Main and Neilsen Way.

Venice was a turn-of-the-century fantasy that never quite came true. Abbot Kinney, a wealthy Los Angeles businessman, envisioned this little piece of real estate, which then seemed so far from downtown, as a romantic replica of Venice, Italy. He developed an incredible 16 miles of canals, floated gondolas on them, and built scaled-down versions of the Saint Marks Palace and other Venice landmarks. The name remains but the connection with the Old World Venice is as flimsy as ever. Kinney's project was plagued by ongoing engineering problems and disasters and drifted into disrepair. Three small **canals** and bridges remain and can be viewed from the southeast corner of Pacific Avenue and Venice Boulevard. Gone are the amusement park, swank seaside hotels, and the gondoliers.

What's left is a colorful mishmash of street life: the liveliest waterfront walkway in Los Angeles, known as both Ocean Front Walk and the **Venice Boardwalk.** It begins at Washington Street and runs north. Save this visit for a weekend. There is plenty of action year-round: bikini-clad rollerskaters gather a crowd around them as they put on impromptu demonstrations, vying for attention with the unusual breeds of dogs that locals love to prance along the walkway. A local body-building club works out on the adjacent beach, and it's nearly impossible not to stop to ogle at the pecs as these strong men lift weights.

At the south end of the boardwalk, along Washington Street, near the Venice Pier, roller skates and bicycles (some with baby seats) are available for rent.

Time Out   The boardwalk is lined with fast-food stands, and food can then be brought a few feet away to be enjoyed as a beachy picnic. But for a somewhat more relaxing meal, stand in line for a table at **Sidewalk Cafe** (1401 Ocean Front Walk, tel. 310/399–5547). Wait for a patio table, where you can watch the free spirits on parade. Despite their flamboyant attire, they seem like Sunday wild ones, and it's amusing to imagine them in their sedate Monday-go-to-work suits.

Just south of Venice is a quick shift of the time frame. Forget Italy of the Renaissance, or even the turn of the century. Marina del Rey is a modern and more successful, if less romantic, dream than Venice. It is the largest man-made boat harbor in the world, with a commercial area catering to the whims of boat owners and boat groupies.

❼ For boatless visitors, the best place from which to savor the marina is **Burton Chase Park,** at the end of Mindinao Way. Situated at the tip of a jetty and surrounded on three sides by water and moored boats, this small, six-acre patch of green offers a cool and breezy spot from which to watch boats move in and out of the channel, and it's great for picnicking.

❽ **Fisherman's Village** is a collection of cute Cape Cod clapboards housing shops and restaurants. It's not much of a draw unless you include a meal or a snack or take one of the 45-minute marina cruises offered by Hornblower Dining Outs that depart from the village dock. *13755 Fiji Way, tel. 310/301–6000. Tickets: $5 adults, $3.50 senior citizens, $4 children. Open in summer, daily 11 AM–4 PM; in winter, weekends 11–4. Cruises leave every hour, weekdays 12–3, weekends 11–5.*

A Tour of Pacific Palisades and Malibu   The drive on Pacific Coast Highway north of Santa Monica toward Malibu is one of the most pleasant in Southern California, day or evening. The narrow-but-expensive beachfront houses were home to movie stars in the 1930s.

❾ Spend a few hours at **Will Rogers State Historic Park** in Pacific Palisades and you will understand why America fell in love with this cowboy/humorist in the 1920s and 1930s. The two-story ranch house on Rogers's 187-acre estate is a folksy blend of Navajo rugs and Mission-style furniture. Rogers's only extravagance was raising the roof several feet (he waited till his wife was in Europe to do it) to accommodate his penchant for practicing his lasso technique indoors. The nearby museum features Rogers memorabilia. The short films showing his roping technique will leave even sophisticated city slickers breathless, and hearing his homey words of wisdom can be a real mood elevator.

Rogers was a polo enthusiast, and in the 1930s, his front-yard polo field attracted such friends as Douglas Fairbanks for weekend games. The tradition continues, with free games scheduled most summer weekends. The park's broad lawns are excellent for picnicking. For postprandial exercise, there's hiking on miles of eucalyptus-lined trails. Those who make it to the top will be rewarded with a panoramic view of the mountains and ocean. Neighborhood riders house their horses at the stable up the hill and are usually agreeable to some friendly chatter (no rental horses, alas). *14253 Sunset Blvd., Pacific Palisades, tel. 310/454-8212. Call for polo schedule.*

🔟 The **J. Paul Getty Museum** contains one of the country's finest collections of Greek and Roman antiquities (also a few items of uncertain provenance). The building is a re-creation of a 1st-century Roman villa. The main level houses sculpture, mosaics, and vases. Of particular interest are the 4th-century Attic stelae (funerary monuments) and Greek and Roman portraits. The newly expanded decorative arts collection on the upper level features furniture, carpets, tapestries, clocks, chandeliers, and small decorative items made for the French, German, and Italian nobility, with a wealth of royal French treasures (Louis XIV to Napoleon). Richly colored brocaded walls set off the paintings and furniture to great advantage.

All major schools of Western art from the late 13th century to the late 19th century are represented in the painting collection, which emphasizes Renaissance and Baroque art and includes works by Rembrandt, Rubens, de la Tour, Van Dyck, Gainsborough, and Boucher. Newly added are Old Master drawings, and medieval and Renaissance illuminated manuscripts.

The museum itself has a fascinating history. Getty began collecting art in the 1930s, concentrating on the three distinct areas that are represented in the museum today: Greek and Roman antiquities, Baroque and Renaissance paintings, and 18th-century decorative arts. In 1946 he purchased a large Spanish-style home on 65 acres of land in a canyon just north of Santa Monica to house the collection. By the late 1960s, the museum could no longer accommodate the rapidly expanding collection and Getty decided to build an entirely new museum, which was completed in 1974. Getty's estimated $1.3 billion bequest upon his death in 1976 has appreciated to $2.1 billion with the 1984 takeover of Getty Oil by Texaco.

The bookstore carries art books, reproductions, calendars, and a variety of scholarly and general-interest publications. A self-service lunch is available in the indoor/outdoor Garden Tea Room. There are no tours, but docents give 15-minute orientation talks. Summer evening concerts (reservations are required) are given on an irregular basis, with the lower galleries open at intermission. Parking reservations are necessary, and there is no way to visit the museum without using the parking lot unless you are dropped off or take a tour bus. They should be made one week in advance by telephoning or writing to the museum's Reservations Office. *17985 Pacific Coast Hwy., Malibu, tel. 310/458-2003. Admission free. Open Tues.–Sun. 10–5.*

⓫ **Adamson House** is the former home of the Rindge family, which owned much of the Malibu Rancho in the early part of the 20th century. Malibu was quite isolated then, with all visitors and supplies arriving by boat at the nearby Malibu Pier (and it can still be isolated these days by rock slides that close the highway). The Moorish-Spanish home, built in 1928, has been recently opened to the public and may be the only chance most visitors get to be inside a grand Malibu home. The Rindges led an enviable Malibu lifestyle, decades before it was trendy. The house is right on the beach (high chain-link fences keep out curious beach-goers). The family owned the famous Malibu Tile Company and their home is predictably encrusted with some of the most magnificent tilework in rich blues, greens, yellows, and oranges. Even an outside dog shower, near the servants' door, is a tiled delight. Docent-led tours help visitors to envision family life here as well as to learn about the history of Malibu and its real estate (you can't have one without the other). *23200 Pacific Coast Hwy., Malibu, tel. 310/456–8432. Admission: $2 adults; $1 children. Open Wed.–Sun. 11–3.*

⑫ Adjacent to Adamson House is **Malibu Lagoon State Park** (23200 Pacific Coast Hwy., Malibu), a haven for native and migratory birds. Visitors must stay on the boardwalks so that the egrets, blue herons, avocets, and gulls can enjoy the marshy area. The signs that give opening and closing hours refer only to the parking lot; the lagoon itself is open 24 hours and is particularly enjoyable in the early morning and at sunset. Luckily, street-side parking is available then (but not midday).

Palos Verdes, San Pedro, and Long Beach

Numbers in the margin correspond with points of interest on the Palos Verdes, San Pedro, and Long Beach map.

Few local residents take advantage of Long Beach's attractions. If they should take a day to see the *Queen Mary* when their in-laws are here from Michigan, they are astounded to discover Long Beach's impressive skyline, the string of fine hotels along Ocean Boulevard, the revitalized downtown area, and the city's close proximity to the rest of L.A. and Orange County. How could this big city, the fifth largest in the state, be right here and they never knew about it? Allow a generous half day or more to explore the *Queen Mary* complex. Plump up the itinerary with a glorious drive through Palos Verdes and a few short stops at local historic sites and parks.

The drive on Pacific Coast Highway around the water's edge takes you soaring high above the cliffs. An aerial shot of this area was used in the original opening of television's "Knots Landing." The real estate in these small peninsula towns, ranging from expensive to very expensive, are zoned for stables and you'll often see riders along the streets (they have the right of way).

① **Wayfarers Chapel** was designed by architect Frank Lloyd Wright in 1949. He planned his modern glass church to blend in with an encircling redwood forest. The redwoods are gone (they couldn't stand the rigors of urban encroachment), but another forest has taken their place and the breathtaking combination of ocean, trees, and structure remains. This "natural church" is a popular wedding site. *5755 Palos Verdes Dr. S. Rancho Palos Verdes, tel. 310/377–1650. Chapel open during odd-numbered hours 9–5 (weddings are held on even-numbered hours); grounds open 7 AM–8 PM.*

San Pedro shares the peninsula with the Palos Verdes towns, but little else. Here, the cliffs give way to a hospitable harbor. The 1950s-vintage executive homes give way to tidy 1920s-era white clapboards, and horses give way to boats. San Pedro (the locals ignore the correct Spanish pronunciation—it's "San Pee-dro" to them) is an old seafaring community with a strong Mediterranean and Eastern European flavor. There are enticing Greek and Yugoslavian markets and restaurants throughout the town.

Palos Verdes, San Pedro, and Long Beach

PACIFIC OCEAN

San Pedro Bay

0   2 miles
0   3 km

Banning Residence
Museum and Park, **4**
Cabrillo Marine
Museum, **2**
Naples, **11**

Ports O'Call Village, **3**
Queen Mary, **5**
Rancho Los
Alamitos, **10**
Rancho Los Cerritos, **9**
Shoreline Aquatic
Park, **8**

Shoreline Village, **7**
South Coast Botanic
Gardens, **12**
Spruce Goose, **6**
Wayfarers Chapel, **1**

2 **Cabrillo Marine Museum** is a gem of a small museum dedicated to the marine life that flourishes off the Southern California coast. Recently moved from a nearby boathouse to a modern Frank O. Gehry–designed building right on the beach, the museum is popular with school groups because its exhibits are especially instructive as well as fun. The 35 saltwater aquariums include a shark tank, and a see-through tidal tank gives visitors a chance to see the long view of a wave. On the back patio, docents supervise as visitors reach into a shallow tank to touch starfish and sea anemones. *3720 Stephen White Dr., San Pedro, tel. 310/548–7546. Parking $5.50. Admission free. Open Tues.– Fri. noon–5, weekends 10–5.*

If you're lucky enough to visit at low tide, take time to explore the tide pool on nearby Cabrillo Beach (museum staff can direct you).

3 **Ports O' Call Village** is a commercial rendition of a New England shipping village, an older version of Fisherman's Village in Marina del Rey, with shops, restaurants, and fast-food windows. *Berth 77, San Pedro, tel. 310/831–0996. Fare: $7 adults, $3 children. 1-hr cruises depart from the village dock. Whale-watching cruises, $10. Call for schedule.*

4 **Banning Residence Museum and Park,** in Wilmington, is a pleasant, low-keyed stop before the razzle-dazzle of the *Queen Mary*. In order to preserve transportation and shipping interests for the city of Los Angeles, Wilmington was annexed in the late 19th century. A narrow strip of land, mostly less than a half mile wide, follows the Harbor Freeway from downtown south to the port.

General Phineas Banning was an early entrepreneur in Los Angeles, and is credited with developing the harbor into a viable economic entity and naming the area Wilmington (he was from Delaware). Part of the estate has been preserved in a 20-acre park that offers excellent picnicking possibilities. A 100-year-old wisteria, near the arbor, blooms in the spring. *401 E. M St., Wilmington, tel. 310/548–7777. Admission: $2. The interior of the house can only be seen on docent-led tours, Tues.–Thurs., Sat., and Sun. 12:30–3:30 on the half hour.*

Long Beach began as a seaside resort in the 19th century and during the early part of the 20th century was a popular destination for Midwesterners and Dust Bowlers in search of a better life. They built street after street of modest wood homes.

At the corner of 1st St., and Long Beach Ave., is the terminus of the new Metrorail system's Blue Line trains that run between Long Beach and downtown Los Angeles.

5 The first glimpse of the *Queen Mary,* the largest passenger ship ever built, as she sits so smugly in Long Beach Harbor is disarming. What seemed like sure folly when Long Beach officials bought her in 1964 has turned out to be an attention-getting and money-making bonanza that has put the city on the proverbial map. She stands permanently moored at Pier J.

The 50,000-ton *Queen Mary* was launched in 1934, a floating treasure of Art Deco splendor. It took a crew of 1,100 to minister to the needs of 1,900 demanding passengers. This most luxurious of luxury liners is completely intact, from the extensive wood paneling to the gleaming nickel- and silver-plated handrails and the hand-cut glass. Tours through the ship are available (the "Myths and Legends" tour takes you into rarely seen sections of the ship as a guide, aided by special effects, tells spooky tales of mysterious and gruesome goings-on from the ship's years at sea), and guests are invited to browse the 12 decks and witness close-up the bridge, staterooms, officers' quarters, and engine rooms. There are several restaurants and shops on board, and visitors may even spend the night in the first-class cabins, now the Queen Mary Hotel. *Pier J, Long Beach, tel. 310/435–3511. Admission: $17.50 adults, $9.50 children for an all-day combination ticket to both the Queen Mary and the Spruce Goose. Guided 90-min tours are $5 and leave every half hour beginning at 10:30 AM. Open July 4–Labor Day, daily 9–9; rest of year, daily 10–6.*

❻ Just a short walk away from this most amazing ship is a most amazing plane, the **Spruce Goose,** housed in a 12-story aluminum dome. The *Spruce Goose* was Howard Hughes's folly. It is the largest wooden aircraft ever built, with a 320-foot wingspan. Designed by Hughes in 1942, it made its first and only flight on November 2, 1947. Multimedia displays surround the plane explaining its history. Howard Hughes memorabilia is also on view. New under the *Spruce Goose* dome is *Time Voyager,* "a multi-sensory entertainment journey," with a narration aimed at children, in which passengers board a 100-seat flight module to experience time periods past and present. Free with admission. *See Queen Mary for times and prices.*

❼ **Shoreline Village** is the most successful of the pseudo–New England harbors here. Its setting, between the Long Beach skyline and the *Queen Mary*, is reason enough to stroll here, day and evening (when visitors can enjoy the lights of the ship twinkling in the distance). In addition to gift shops and restaurants there's a 1906 carousel with bobbing giraffes, camels, and horses. *Corner of Shoreline Dr. and Pine Ave., tel. 310/590–8427. Rides: $1. The carousel is open daily 10–10 in summer, 10–9 the rest of the year.*

❽ **Shoreline Aquatic Park** (205 Marina Dr.) is literally set in the middle of Long Beach Harbor (another inspired landfill project) and is a much-sought-after resting place for RVers. Kite-flyers also love it, because the winds are wonderful here. Casual passersby can enjoy a short walk, where the modern skyline, the quaint Shoreline Village, the *Queen Mary*, and the ocean all vie for attention like four clamoring children. One at a time, please! The park's lagoon is off-limits for swimming, but aquacycles and kayaks can be rented during the summer months. Contact **Long Beach Water Sports** (730 E. 4th St., Long Beach, 90802, tel. 310/432–0187) for information on sea kayaking lessons, rentals, and outings.

❾ **Rancho Los Cerritos** is a charming Monterey-style adobe built by the Don Juan Temple family in 1844. Monterey-style homes can be easily recognized by two features: They are always two-storied and have a narrow balcony across the front. Imagine Zorro here, that swashbuckling hero of the rancho era, jumping from the balcony to rescue Don Juan Temple's lovely daughter. The 10 rooms have been furnished in the style of the period and are open for viewing. Don't expect a Southwest fantasy with primitive Mexican furniture and cactus in the garden. The Temple family shared the prevalent taste of the period. They might live in Southern California, but the East Coast and Europe still set the style, emphasizing fancy, dark woods and frou-frou Victorian bric-a-brac. The gardens here were designed in the 1930s by well-known landscape architect Ralph Cornell and have been recently restored. *4600 Virginia Rd., Long Beach, tel. 310/424–9423. Open Wed.–Sun. 1–5. Self-guided tours on weekdays. Free 50-min guided tours on weekends hourly 1–4.*

⑩ **Rancho Los Alamitos** is said to be the oldest one-story domestic building still standing in the county. It was built in 1806 when the Spanish flag still flew over California. There's a blacksmith shop in the barn. *6400 E. Bixby Hill Rd., Long Beach, tel. 310/431–3541. Open Wed.–Sun. 1–5. Hour-long, free tours leave every half hour.*

⑪ The **Naples** section of Long Beach is known for its pleasant and well-maintained canals. Canals in Naples, you ask? You're right, this is a bit of a misnomer. But better misnamed and successful in Naples than aptly named and a big bust in Venice, a few miles north. Naples is actually three small islands in man-made Alamitos Bay. It is best savored on foot. Park near Bay-shore Drive and Second Street and walk across the bridge, where you can begin meandering the quaint streets with very Italian names. This well-restored neighborhood boasts eclectic architecture—vintage Victorians, Craftsman bungalows, and Mission Revivals. You may spy a real gondola or two on the canals. You can hire them for a ride but not on the spur of the moment. Gondola Getaway offers one-hour rides, usually touted for romantic couples, although the gondolas can accommodate up to four people. *5437 E. Ocean Blvd., Naples, tel. 310/433–9595. Rides: $50 a couple, $10 for each additional person. Reservations essential, at least 1 to 2 wks in advance.*

⑫ **South Coast Botanic Gardens** began life ignominiously—as a garbage dump–cum-landfill. It's hard to believe that as recently as 1960, truckloads of waste (3.5 million tons) were being deposited. With the intensive ministerings of the experts from the L.A. County Arboreta department, the dump soon boasted lush gardens with plants from every continent except Antarctica. The gardens are undergoing an ambitious five-year reorganization at the end of which all the plants will be organized into color groups. Self-guided walking tours take visitors past flower and herb gardens, rare cacti, and a lake with ducks. Picnicking is limited to a lawn area outside the gates. *26300 Crenshaw Blvd., Rancho Palos Verdes, tel. 310/544–6815. Open daily 9–4:30. Admission: $3 adults, $1.50 children.*

Highland Park, Pasadena, and San Marino

Numbers in the margin correspond with points of interest on the Highland Park, Pasadena, San Marino map.

The suburbs north of downtown Los Angeles have much of the richest architectural heritage in Southern California as well as several fine museums. The Highland Park area can be explored in a leisurely afternoon. Pasadena could take a full day, more if you want to savor the museums' collections.

A Tour of Highland Park To take advantage of the afternoon-only hours of several sites here, and to enjoy a relaxed Old California patio lunch or dinner, this tour is best scheduled in the afternoon.

Once past Chinatown, the Pasadena Freeway (110) follows the curves of the arroyo (creek bed) that leads north from downtown. It was the main road north during the early days of Los Angeles where horses-and-buggies made their way through the chaparral-covered countryside to the small town of Pasadena. In 1942, the road became the Arroyo Seco Parkway, the first freeway in Los Angeles, later renamed the Pasadena Freeway. It remains a pleasant drive in nonrush-hour traffic, with the freeway lined with old sycamores and winding up the arroyo like a New York parkway.

Highland Park, midway between downtown Los Angeles and Pasadena, was a genteel suburb in the late 1800s, where the Anglo population tried to keep an Eastern feeling alive in their architecture despite the decidedly Southwest landscape. The streets on both sides of the freeway are filled with faded beauties, classic old clapboards that have gone into decline in the past half century.

❶ **Heritage Square** is the ambitious attempt by the Los Angeles Cultural Heritage Board to preserve some of the city's architectural gems of the 1865–1914 period from the wrecking ball. During the past 20 years four residences, a depot, a church, and a carriage barn have been moved to this small park from all over the city. The most breathtaking building here is Hale House, built in 1885. The almost-garish colors of both the interior and exterior are not the whim of some aging hippie painter, but rather a faithful re-creation of the palette that was actually in fashion in the late 1800s. The whitewashing we associate with these old Victorians was a later vogue. The Palms Depot, built in 1886, was moved to the site from the Westside of L.A. The night the building was moved, down city streets and up freeways, is documented in photomurals on the depot's walls. *3800 Homer St., Highland Park, off Ave. 43 exit, tel. 818/449–0193. Admission: $4.50 adults, $3 children 12–17. Open Wed.–Sun. 12–4. Tours begin at 12:15, 1:15, 2:15, 3:15 on Sun. only.*

❷ **El Alisal** was the home of eccentric Easterner-turned-Westerner-with-a-vengeance Charles Lummis. This Harvard graduate was captivated by Indian culture (he founded the Southwest Museum), often living the lifestyle of the natives, much to the shock of the staid Angelenos of the time. His home, built from 1898 to 1910, is constructed of boulders from the arroyo itself, a romantic notion until recent earthquakes made the safety of such homes questionable. The Art Nouveau fireplace was designed by Gutzon Borglum, the sculptor of Mount Rushmore. *200 E. Ave. 43, Highland Park, tel. 213/222–0546. Admission free. Open Thurs.–Sun. 1–4.*

❸ **The Southwest Museum** is the huge Mission Revival building that stands halfway up Mount Washington and can be seen from the freeway. It contains an extensive collection of Native American art and artifacts, with special emphasis on the people of the Plains, Northwest Coast, Southwest U.S., and Northern Mexico. The basket collection is outstanding. *234 Museum Dr., Highland Park, off the Ave. 43 exit, tel. 213/221–2163. Admission: $4 adults, $1 children. Open Tues.–Sun. 11–5.*

❹ **Casa de Adobe** is a satellite of the Southwest Museum and is located directly below it at the bottom of the hill. What appears to be the well-preserved, authentically furnished hacienda of an Old California don is actually a 1917 re-creation of a 19th-century rancho. The central courtyard plan is typical. *4605*

Casa de Adobe, **4**
El Alisal, **2**
Gamble House, **7**
Heritage Square, **1**
Huntington Library,
Art Gallery, and
Botanical Gardens, **14**
Kidspace, **12**
Lawry's California
Center, **5**
Norton Simon
Museum, **8**
Old Town Pasadena, **9**
Pacific Asia
Museum, **11**
Pasadena Historical
Society, **10**
Ritz Carlton,
Huntington Hotel, **13**
Rose Bowl, **6**
Southwest Museum, **3**

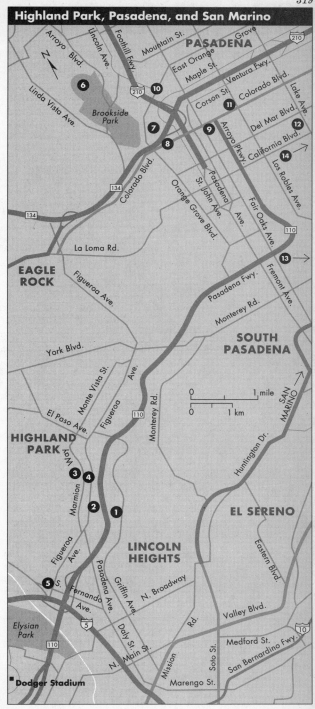

Highland Park, Pasadena, and San Marino

Figueroa St., Highland Park, tel. 213/221–2163. Admission free. Open Tues.–Sun. 11–5.

Time Out
⑤
Lawry's California Center is a more recent attempt to capture the romance of Old Mexico—Zorro and Ramona all rolled up in one—but this one leaves no doubt that it is a recent construction. It is *Sunset* magazine come to life, with bougainvillea-covered patios and flowers in pots at every turn, winter and summer. A spice-blending company, Lawry's offers free tours of its plant on weekdays, but the best reason to come here is to enjoy a patio meal. Lunches, both cafeteria-style and full service, are served year-round 11–3. Fiesta dinners are served (May–Oct.) nightly under the stars to the accompaniment of strolling mariachis. Wine and gourmet shops stay open late for after-dinner browsing. *570 W. Ave. 26, Los Angeles, tel. 213/ 225–2491. Open daily.*

Pasadena and San Marino

Although now absorbed into the general Los Angeles sprawl, Pasadena was once a distinctly defined, and refined, city. Its varied architecture, augmented by lush landscaping, is the most spectacular in Southern California. With only a few hours to spend, visitors should consider driving past the Gamble House, through Old Town, and then on to the grand old neighborhood of the Huntington Library, spending most of their time there.

⑥ **The Rose Bowl** (991 Rosemont Ave., Pasadena) is set at the bottom of a wide area of the arroyo in an older wealthy neighborhood that must endure the periodic onslaught of thousands of cars and party-minded football fans. The stadium is closed except for games and special events such as the monthly Rose Bowl Swap Meet. Held the second Sunday of the month, it is considered the granddaddy of West Coast swap meets.

⑦ **Gamble House,** built by Charles and Henry Greene in 1908, is the most spectacular example of Craftsman-style bungalow architecture. The term "bungalow" can be misleading, since the Gamble House is a huge two-story home. To wealthy Easterners such as the Gambles, who commissioned the Greenes to build a vacation home for them, this type of home seemed informal compared with their accustomed mansions. What makes visitors swoon here is the incredible amount of hand craftsmanship: the hand-shaped teak interiors, the Greene-designed furniture, the Louis Tiffany glass door. The dark exterior has broad eaves, with many sleeping porches on the second floor. *4 Westmoreland Pl., Pasadena, tel. 818/793–3334. Open Thurs.– Sun. noon–3. Admission: $4 adults, children free. Tours are given Tues. and Thurs. approximately every hour, Sun. noon– 12:45.*

⑧ **The Norton Simon Museum** will be familiar to television viewers of the Rose Parade. The TV cameras position themselves to take full advantage of the sleek, modern building as a background for the passing floats. Like the more famous Getty Museum, the Norton Simon is a tribute to the art acumen of an extremely wealthy businessman. In 1974, Simon reorganized the failing Pasadena Museum of Modern Art and assembled one of the world's finest collections, richest in its Rembrandts,

Goyas, Degas, and Picassos—and dotted with Rodin sculptures throughout.

Also strong are the museum's collections of Impressionists (van Gogh, Matisse, Cézanne, Monet, Renoir, et al.) and Cubists (Braque, Gris). Older works range from Southeast Asian artworks from 100 BC, bronze, stone, and ivory sculptures from India, Cambodia, Thailand, and Nepal.

The museum's wealth of Early Renaissance, Baroque, and Rococo artworks could fill an art history book. Church works by Raphael, Guariento, de Paolo, Filippino Lippi, and Lucas Cranach give way to robust Rubens maidens and Dutch landscapes, still lifes, and portraits by Frans Hals, Jacob van Ruisdael, and Jan Steen. And a magical Tiepolo ceiling highlights the Rococo period. The most recent addition to the collection are seven 19th-century Russian paintings.

The bookstore has posters, prints, and postcards. There are no dining facilities. *411 W. Colorado Blvd., Pasadena, tel. 818/ 449–6840. Admission: $4 adults, $2 students and senior citizens. Open Thurs.–Sun. noon–6*

9 Half a mile east of the museum, **Old Town Pasadena** is an ambitious, ongoing restoration. Having fallen into seedy decay in the past 50 years, the area is being revitalized as a blend of restored brick buildings with a Yuppie overlay. Rejuvenated buildings include bistros, elegant restaurants, and boutiques. On Raymond Street, the Hotel Green, now the Castle Apartments, dominates the area. Once a posh resort hotel, the Green is now a faded Moorish fantasy of domes, turrets, and balconies reminiscent of the Alhambra but with, true to its name, a greenish tint. Holly Street, between Fair Oaks and Arroyo, is home to several shops offering an excellent selection of vintage '50s objects, jewelry, and clothes. This area is best explored on foot. Old Town is bisected by Colorado Boulevard, where on New Year's Day throngs of people line the street for the Rose Parade.

Time Out If browsing the Holly Street shops leaves you both nostalgic and hungry, walk down Fair Oaks Avenue to the **Rose City Diner**. Classic diner fare, from chicken-fried steak and eggs to macaroni and cheese, is served in an *American Graffiti* setting. Bebop singers roam the joint from 11 AM to 3 PM every Sunday for added '50s flavor. *45 S. Fair Oaks Ave., tel. 818/793–8282. Open daily 6:30 AM–2 AM.*

10 The **Pasadena Historical Society** is housed in Fenyes Mansion. The 1905 mansion still holds the original furniture and paintings on the main and second floors; in the basement, the focus is on the history of the city. There are also four acres of well-landscaped gardens. *170 N. Orange Grove Blvd., Pasadena, tel. 818/795–3002. Historical Society Museum, 470 W. Walnut St., tel. 818/577–1660. Admission: $3 adults, children free. Open Tues., Thurs., and Sun. 1–4.*

11 The **Pacific Asia Museum** is the gaudiest Chinese-style building in Los Angeles outside of Chinatown. Designed in the style of a Northern Chinese imperial palace with a central courtyard, it is devoted entirely to the arts and crafts of Asia and the Pacific Islands. Most of the objects are on loan from private collections and other museums, and there are usually changing special exhibits that focus on the objects of one country. A bookstore and the Collectors Gallery shop sell fine art items from members' collections. The extensive research library can be used by appointment only. *46 N. Los Robles Dr., Pasadena, tel. 818/449–2742. Admission: $3 adults, children free. Open Wed.–Sun. noon–5.*

⑫ **Kidspace** is a children's museum housed in the gymnasium of an elementary school. Here kids can talk to a robot, direct a television or radio station, dress up in the real (and very heavy) uniforms of a fire fighter, an astronaut, a football player, and more. A special "Human Habitrail" challenges children by changing architectural environments, and "Illusions" teases one's ability to perceive what is real and what is illusion. *390 S. El Molino Ave., Pasadena, tel. 818/449–9144. Admission: $3. Open during the school year, weekends noon–4, Wed. 2–5; longer hours during summer and other school vacation periods.*

⑬ **The Ritz-Carlton, Huntington Hotel** (1401 S. Oak Knoll Ave., Pasadena, tel. 818/568–3900) is situated in Pasadena's most genteel neighborhood of Oak Knoll, close to San Marino. Although all the original buildings were closed in 1986 because of an inability to conform to earthquake regulations, this hotel, built in 1906, reopened in 1991, preserving its original design, including the Japanese and Horseshoe Gardens. Don't miss the historic Picture Bridge with its murals depicting scenes of California along its 20 gables. Features include the Japanese Garden and the Picture Bridge. You can still make reservations here, but only for the 106 newer rooms.

⑭ The **Huntington Library, Art Gallery, and Botanical Gardens** is the area's most important site. If there's only time for a quick drive through the area and one stop, this should be it. Railroad tycoon Henry E. Huntington built his hilltop home in the early 1900s. It has established a reputation as one of the most extraordinary cultural complexes in the world, annually receiving more than a half million visitors. The library contains six million items, including such treasures as a Gutenberg Bible, the earliest known edition of Chaucer's *Canterbury Tales*, George Washington's genealogy in his own handwriting, and first editions by Ben Franklin and Shakespeare. In the library's hallway are five tall hexagonal towers displaying important books and manuscripts.

The art gallery, devoted to British art from the 18th and 19th centuries, contains the original "Blue Boy" by Gainsborough, "Pinkie," a companion piece by Lawrence, and the monumental "Sarah Siddons as the Tragic Muse" by Reynolds.

The Huntington's awesome 130-acre garden, formerly the grounds of the estate, now includes a 12-acre Desert Garden featuring the largest group of mature cacti and other succulents in the world, all arranged by continent. The Japanese Garden offers traditional Japanese plants, stone ornaments, a moon bridge, a Japanese house, a bonsai court, and a Zen rock garden. Besides these gardens, there are collections of azaleas and 1,500 varieties of camellias, the world's largest public collection. The 1,000-variety rose garden displays its collection historically so that the development leading to today's roses can be observed. There are also herb, palm, and jungle gardens plus a Shakespeare garden, where plants mentioned in Shakespeare's plays are grown.

Because of the Huntington's vastness, a variety of orientation options is available for visitors. They include: a 12-minute slide show introducing the Huntington; an hour-and-a-quarter guided tour of the gardens; a 45-minute audio tape about the art gallery (which can be rented for a nominal fee); a 15-minute introductory talk about the library; and inexpensive, self-guided tour leaflets.

In 1980, the first major facility constructed on the Huntington grounds in more than 60 years opened. The $5 million Huntington Pavilion offers visitors unmatched views of the surrounding mountains and valleys and houses a bookstore, displays, and information kiosks as well. Both the east and west wings of the pavilion display paintings on public exhibition for the first time. The Ralph M. Parsons Botanical Center at the pavilion includes a botanical library, a herbarium, and a laboratory for research on plants. No picnicking or pets. A refreshment room is open to the public. *Oxford Rd., San Marino, tel. 818/405–2100. Open Tues.–Sun. 1–4:30. Reservations required Sun. Donation requested.*

Other Places of Interest

Burbank Studios. Warner Brothers and Columbia Studios share this lot where a two-hour guided walking tour is available. Because the tours involve a lot of walking, you should dress comfortably and casually. This tour is somewhat technical, centered more on the actual workings of filmmaking than the one at Universal. It varies from day to day to take advantage of goings-on on the lot. Most tours see the backlot sets, prop construction department, and sound complex. *400 Warner Blvd., Burbank, tel. 818/954–1008. Tours given weekdays at 10 and 2. Admission: $22. No children under 10 permitted. Reservations essential, 1 wk in advance.*

Exposition Park (Figueroa St. at Exposition Blvd., Los Angeles). This beautiful park was the site of the 1932 Olympics and the impressive architecture still stands. Adjoining the University of Southern California, Exposition Park is the location of two major museums: the California Museum of Science and Industry and the Natural History Museum (*see* Museums, above). Also included in the 114-acre park is the Los Angeles Swimming Stadium (home of Los Angeles aquatic competitions), which is open to the public in summer, and the Memorial Coliseum, the site of college football games. There are plenty of picnic areas on the grounds as well as a sunken rose garden.

Forest Lawn Memorial Park–Hollywood Hills. Just west of Griffith Park on the north slope of the Hollywood Hills, this 340-acre sister park to Forest Lawn Glendale is dedicated to the ideal of American liberty. Featured are bronze and marble statuary, including Thomas Ball's 60-foot Washington Memorial and a replica of the Liberty Bell. There are also reproductions of Boston's Old North Church and Longfellow's Church of the Hills. The film *The Many Voices of Freedom* is shown daily and Revolutionary War documents are on permanent display. Among the famous people buried here are Buster Keaton, Stan Laurel, Liberace, Charles Laughton, and Freddie Prinze. *6300*

Forest Lawn Dr., Hollywood, tel. 213/254-7251. Open daily 8-5.

Gene Autry Western Heritage Museum. The American West, both the movie and real-life versions, is celebrated via memorabilia, artifacts, and art in a structure that draws on Spanish mission and early Western architecture. The collection includes Teddy Roosevelt's Colt revolver, Buffalo Bill Cody's saddle, and Annie Oakley's gold-plated Smith and Wesson guns, alongside video screens showing clips from old Westerns. *4700 Zoo Dr., Los Angeles, tel. 213/667-2000. Admission $5.50 adults, $4 senior citizens, $2.50 children 2-12. Open Tues.-Sun. 10-5.*

Griffith Park Observatory and Planetarium. Located on the south side of Mount Hollywood in the heart of Griffith Park, the planetarium offers dazzling daily shows that duplicate the starry sky. A guide narrates the show and points out constellations. One of the largest telescopes in the world is open to the public for free viewing every clear night. Exhibits display models of the planets with photographs from satellites and spacecraft. A Laserium show is featured nightly, and other special astronomy shows are offered frequently. The Observatory sits high above Los Angeles and from the outside decks and walkways offers a spectacular view of the city, very popular on warm evenings. *Griffith Park, tel. 213/664-1191. Enter at the Los Feliz Blvd. and Vermont Ave. entrance. Hall of Science and telescope are free. Planetarium shows: $3.50 adults, $1.50 children. Laserium show: $6 adults, $5 children. Call for schedule. Open Tues.-Fri. 2-10, weekends 12:30-10.*

Hollyhock House. Frank Lloyd Wright designed a number of homes in the Los Angeles area. Hollyhock House was his first, built in 1921 and commissioned by heiress Aline Barnsdall. It was done in the pre-Columbian style Wright was fond of at that time. As a unifying theme, he used a stylized hollyhock flower, which appears in a broad band around the exterior of the house and even on the dining room chairs. Now owned by the city, as is Barnsdall Park, where it is located, Hollyhock House has been restored and furnished with original furniture designed by Wright and reproductions. His furniture may not be the comfiest in the world, but it sure looks perfect in his homes. *4800 Hollywood Blvd., Hollywood, tel. 213/662-7272. Admission: $1.50 adults, children free. Tours conducted Tues.-Thurs. at 10, 11, noon, and 1; Sat. and the 1st, 2nd, and 3rd Sun. of the month at noon, 1, 2, and 3.*

Mulholland Drive. One of the most famous streets in Los Angeles, Mulholland makes its very winding way from the Hollywood Hills across the spine of the Santa Monica Mountains west almost to the Pacific Ocean. Driving its length is slow, but the reward is sensational views of the city, the San Fernando Valley, and the expensive homes along the way. For a quick shot, take Benedict Canyon north from Sunset Boulevard, just west of the Beverly Hills Hotel, all the way to the top and turn right at the crest, which is Mulholland. There's a turnout within a few feet of the intersection, and at night, the view of the valley side is incredible.

NBC Television Studios are also in Burbank, as any regular viewer of *The Tonight Show* can't help knowing. Tours of the facilities were suspended in early 1991, and at press time it was not known when, or if, they would be resumed. For those who wish to be part of a live studio audience, however, tickets are still being made available for tapings of the various NBC shows that are done here. *3000 W. Alameda Ave., Burbank, tel. 818/ 840–3537.*

Universal Studios is the best place in Los Angeles behind the scenes of the movie industry. The five- to seven-hour Univeral tour is an enlightening and amusing (if a bit sensational) day in the world's largest television and movie studio, complete with live shows based on "Miami Vice," *Conan the Barbarian,* and "Star Trek." The complex stretches across more than 400 acres, amny of which are traversed during the course of the tour by trams featuring witty running commentary provided by enthusiastic guides. Visitors experience the parting of the Red Sea, an avalanche, and a flood, and have the opportunity to meet a 30-foot-tall version of the legendary King Kong, as well as Kit, the talking car from the NBC television series "Knightrider." They live through an encounter with a runaway train and an attack by the ravenous killer shark of *Jaws* fame and endure a confrontation by aliens armed with death rays— all without ever leaving the safety of the tram. And now, thanks to the magic of Hollywood, visitors can experience the perils of The Big One—an all-too-real simulation of an 8.3 earthquake, complete with collapsing earth, deafening train wrecks, floods, and other life-threatening amusements. There is a New England village, an aged European town, and a replica of an archetypal New York street. The newest exhibits are *The Riot Act,* a show of over 100 action-packed Hollywood stunts; Steven Spielberg's *An American Tale,* a fantasy adventure for children with oversize props and sets; and *The Animal Actors Stage Show,* featuring performances by movie and TV animals, including Lassie. Visitors relax in the snack bar and picnic area, before going on to the Entertainment Center, the longest and last stop of the day, where they stroll around to enjoy various shows. In one theater animals beguile you with their tricks. In another you can pose for a photo session with the Incredible Hulk. Visit Castle Dracula and confront a variety of terrifying monsters. At the Screen Test Theater, visitors may find themselves being filmed as extras in films already released and recut to include them. *100 Universal Pl., Universal City, tel. 818/508–9600. Box office open daily 9:30–3:30. Admission: $22.50 adults, $17 senior citizens and children 3–11.*

Watts Towers (1765 E. 107th St.). This is the folk-art legacy of an Italian immigrant tile-setter, Simon Rodia, and one of the great folk-art structures in the world. From 1920 until 1945, without helpers, this eccentric and driven man erected three cement towers, using pipes, bed frames, and anything else he could find, and embellished them with bits of colored glass, broken pottery, sea shells, and assorted discards. The tallest tower is 107 feet. Plans are under way to stabilize and protect this unique monument, often compared to the 20th-century architectural wonders created by Barcelona's Antonio Gaudi. Well worth a pilgrimage for art and architecture buffs (or anyone else, for that matter).

Los Angeles for Free

In Los Angeles, every day is a free event in terms of nature; the sun, sand, and ocean alone can fill a vacation. But there are plenty of other free activities, events, and cultural attractions to keep even those with limited budgets busy.

Christmas Boat Parades. During December, many local marinas celebrate Christmas in a special way. Boat owners decorate their boats with strings of lights and holiday displays and then cruise in a line for dockside visitors to see. Call for specific dates (Marina del Rey, tel. 213/823–0905; Port of Los Angeles, tel. 213/519–3508).

Rose Parade. Seen from the streets (rather than the bleachers), the Rose Parade is as free as it is on television. Arrive before dawn and dress warmly. Thousands of residents prefer to watch on television and then go out to East Pasadena a day or two later to view the floats, which are parked there for a few days for observation. *Corner of Sierra Madre Blvd. and Washington St., Pasadena. Call for viewing hours, tel. 818/ 449–7673.*

Santa Monica Mountains Nature Walks. The rangers and docents of the many parks in the Santa Monica Mountains offer an ambitious schedule of walks for all interests, ages, and levels of exertion. These include wildflower walks, moonlight hikes, tidepool explorations, and much more. Several outings are held every day. For updated information, call the National Park Service (tel. 818/597–9192).

What to See and Do with Children

The youngsters of Los Angeles have plenty going for them: their own museums, our museums, a world-class zoo, children's theater every weekend, nature walks, pony rides, art classes, and much more.

In addition to the attractions listed here, check the Parks and Gardens section, below, for more places to take children. Also, the Los Angeles *Times* provides ideas for the upcoming week in two regular columns: "54 Hours," which runs on Thursdays in the View section, and "Family Spots," which runs on Saturdays in View. *L.A. Parent*, a monthly tabloid devoted to family life, has a monthly calendar.

Los Angeles Children's Museum was the first of several strictly-for-kids museums now open in the city. All the exhibits here are hands-on, from Sticky City (where kids get to pillow fight with abandon in a huge pillow-filled room) to a TV studio (where they can put on their own news shows). *310 N. Main St., tel. 213/687–8800. Admission: $4. Open during school sessions Wed.–Thurs. 2–4 and weekends 10–5; during summer vacations, open weekdays 11:30–5, weekends 10–5.*

Long Beach Children's Museum. Recently moved to expanded quarters in a Long Beach mall, the museum features the regulation-issue children's-museum exhibits such as The Art Cafe and Granny's Attic. All exhibits welcome curious minds and eager hands. *445 Long Beach Blvd. at Long Beach Plaza, Long Beach, tel. 310/495–1163. Admission: $2.95. Open Thurs.–Sat. 10–4.*

Magic Mountain. The only real amusement park actually in Los Angeles County, Magic Mountain offers 260 acres of rides, shows, and entertainments. The roster of major rides is headlined by Viper, the world's largest looping roller coaster. The first drop is 18 stories high, and three vertical loops turn you upside down seven times. There's also the Roaring Rapids, a simulated white-water wilderness adventure complete with whirlpools, waves, and real rapids; the Colossus, the largest dual-track wood roller coaster ever built, offering two "drops" in excess of 100 feet and experiencing speeds of up to 62 miles per hour; and the Revolution, a steelcoaster with a 360-degree, 90-foot vertical loop. On the Z-Force ride, passengers ride upside down, and recent addition Ninja is a suspended roller coaster. Children's World is a minipark with scaled-down rides, such as the Red Baron's Airplane and the Little Sailor Ride. Other attractions at the park include a puppet theater, celebrity musical revues, Dixieland jazz, rock concerts, and the Aqua Theater high-diving shows. Spillikin's Handcrafters Junction is a 4-acre compound in which craftsmen exhibit skills and wares from blacksmithing to glassblowing. *26101 Magic Mountain Pkwy., off I–5, Valencia, tel. 818/992–0884. Admission: $23 adults, $11 senior citizens, $14 children 4 ft tall and under. Open daily May 19–Labor Day 10–10 (later on weekends); rest of the year, open weekends and holidays.*

Griffith Park **Los Angeles Zoo.** The zoo, one of the major zoos in the United States, is noted for its breeding of endangered species. Koala bears and white tigers are the latest additions. The 113-acre compound holds more than 2,000 mammals, birds, amphibians, and reptiles. Animals are grouped according to the geographical areas where they are naturally found—Africa, Australia, Eurasia, North America, and South America. A tram is available for stops at all areas. Seeing the zoo calls for a lot of walking, seemingly all uphill, so strollers or backpacks are recommended for families with young children. The zoo is beautifully landscaped and areas for picnicking are available. Not-to-be-missed features at the zoo include Adventure Island, a new children's zoo offering interactive exhibits and featuring animals of the American Southwest; a walk-through bird exhibit with more than 50 different species from all over the world; and a koala area, where the furry creatures live amid eucalyptus trees in an environment resembling their native Australia. *Junction of the Ventura and Golden State freeways, Griffith Park, tel. 213/666–4090. Admission: $6 adults, $2.75, children under 12, $5 senior citizens. Open daily 10–5.*

Merry-Go-Round in Griffith Park. Just up the road from the real pony rides, this 1926-vintage carousel offers safe and melodic rides for families. The broad lawn nearby was the scene of some of the most colorful love-ins of the 1960s.

Pony Rides. Most youngsters in Los Angeles (and their parents before them) had their first pony ride at the track in Griffith Park. Two-year-olds are routinely strapped on and paraded around on the slowest of old nags, and these days, the event is dutifully recorded on video camera. The ponies come in three versions: slow, medium, and fast. The slow ones are the best, for all ages. The faster ones are jarring, and the children seem disappointed. To round out an eventful morning (the lines are long in late afternoon), there are stagecoach rides and a miniature train ride that makes a figure eight near the pony rides. *Crystal Springs Dr., Griffith Park, tel. 213/664–3266. Use entrance near Golden State Freeway (I–5) and Los Feliz Blvd. Pony rides $1 for two rounds; stagecoach rides $1; miniature train rides $1.50 adults, $1.25 children. Open in summer,* *weekdays 10–5:30, weekends 10–6:30; rest of year, Tues.–Fri. 10–4:30, weekends 10–5.*

Travel Town. Fifteen vintage railroad cars are resting here, all welcoming the onslaught of climbing and screaming children, who love to run from car to car, jump in the cab, run through the cars, and jump off the high steps. The collection includes a narrow-gauge sugar train from Hawaii, a steam engine, and an old L.A. trolley. Travel Town goes beyond just trains with a collection of old planes such as World War II bombers. There's also an old fire engine, milk wagon, buggies, and classic cars. A miniature train takes visitors on a ride around the area. *5200 Zoo Dr., Griffith Park, tel. 213/662–5874. Admission free. Open weekdays 10–4, weekends 10–6.*

Off the Beaten Track

The Flower Market. Just east of the downtown high rises, in the 700 block of Wall Street, is a block-long series of stores and stalls that open up in the middle of the night to sell wholesale flowers and house plants to the city's florists, who rush them to their shops to sell that day. Many of the stalls stay open until late morning to sell leftovers to the general public at the same bargain prices. And what glorious leftovers they are: Hawaiian ginger, Dutch tulips, Chilean freesia. The public is welcome after 9 AM and the stock is quickly depleted by 11 AM. Even if you don't buy, it's a heady experience to be surrounded by so much fragile beauty.

Laurel and Hardy's Piano Stairway. One of the most famous scenes in the history of movies is one in *The Music Box* where Laurel and Hardy try to get a piano up an outdoor stairway. This Sisyphean tale was filmed in 1932 at 923–927 Vendome Street (where the stairway remains today much as it was then), in the Silverlake section of Los Angeles, a few miles northeast of downtown.

Pig Murals (3049 E. Vernon Ave., Vernon). Vernon Avenue is the heart of Los Angeles's meat-packing industry and to be stuck in traffic on Vernon Avenue on a hot summer afternoon is an odorific experience not soon forgotten. Nevertheless, for aficionados of offbeat sites and/or street murals, the Pig Murals on the outside walls of the Farmer John Company are great fun. Probably the first public murals in Los Angeles, they were originally painted by Leslie Grimes, who was killed in a fall from the scaffolding while painting. They depict bucolic scenes of farms and contented pigs, rather an odd juxtaposition to what goes on inside the packing plant.

Beaches

The beach scene is very much a part of the Southern California lifestyle. There is no public attraction more popular in L.A. than the white, sandy playgrounds of the deep blue Pacific.

From the L.A. Civic Center, the easiest way to hit the coast is by taking the Santa Monica Freeway (I–10) due west. Once you reach the end of the freeway, I–10 turns into the famous Highway 1, better known in Southern California as the Pacific Coast Highway (PCH), and continues up to Oregon. Other basic routes from the downtown area include Pico, Olympic, Santa Monica, or Wilshire boulevards, which all run east–west through the city. Sunset Boulevard offers a less direct but more scenic drive to the beaches, starting near Dodger Stadium, passing through Hollywood, Beverly Hills, and Pacific Palisades, and eventually reaching the Pacific Ocean 1 mile south of Malibu. The RTD bus lines, L.A.'s main form of public transportation until the new Metro Rail is completed, runs every 20 minutes to and from the beaches along each of these boulevards.

Los Angeles County beaches (and the state beaches operated by the county) have lifeguards. Public parking (for a fee) is available at most. The following beaches are listed in north-south order. Some are excellent for swimming, some for surfing (check with lifeguards for current conditions for either activity), others better for exploring.

Leo Carillo State Beach. This beach along a rough and mountainous coastline is most fun at low tide, when a spectacular array of tide pools blossom for all to see. Rock formations on the beach create some great secret coves for picnickers looking for solitude. There are hiking trails, sea caves, and tunnels, and whales, dolphins, sea lions, and otters are often seen swimming in the offshore kelp beds. The waters here are rocky and best for experienced surfers and scuba divers; fishing is good. Picturesque campgrounds are set back from the beach. *36000 block of PCH, Malibu, tel. 818/706–1310. Facilities: parking, lifeguard, rest rooms, showers, fire pits.*

Zuma Beach County Park. This is Malibu's largest and sandiest beach, and a favorite spot for surfing. It's also a haven for high school students who've discovered NautilusPlus. *30050 PCH, Malibu, tel. 213/457–9891. Facilities: parking, lifeguard, rest rooms, showers, food, playground, volleyball.*

Westward Beach/Point Dume State Beach. Another favorite spot for surfing, this half-mile-long sandy beach has tide pools and sandstone cliffs. *South end of Westward Beach Rd., Malibu, tel. 213/457–9891. Facilities: parking, lifeguard, rest rooms, food.*

Paradise Cove. With its pier and equipment rentals, this sandy beach is a mecca for sport-fishing boats. Though swimming is allowed, there are lifeguards during the summer only. *28128 PCH, Malibu, tel. 213/457–2511. Facilities: parking, rest rooms, food.*

Surfrider Beach/Malibu Lagoon State Beach. The steady 3- to 5-foot waves make this beach, just north of Malibu Pier, a great long-board surfing beach. The International Surfing Contest is held here in September. Water runoff from Malibu Canyon forms a natural lagoon, a sanctuary for many birds. Take a romantic sunset stroll along the nature trails. *23200 block of PCH, Malibu, tel. 818/706–1310. Facilities: parking, lifeguard, rest rooms, picnicking, visitor center.*

Las Tunas State Beach. Las Tunas is small (1,300 feet long, covering a total of only two acres), narrow, and sandy, with some rocky areas, set beneath a bluff. Surf fishing is the biggest attraction here. There is no lifeguard, and swimming is not encouraged because of steel groins set offshore to prevent erosion. *19400 block of PCH, Malibu, tel. 213/457–9891. Facilities: parking, rest rooms.*

Topanga Canyon State Beach. The rocky beach stretches from the mouth of the canyon, which is great for surfing, down to Coastline Drive. Catamarans dance in these waves and skid onto the sands of this popular beach, where dolphins sometimes come close enough to shore to startle sunbathers. *18500 block of PCH, Malibu, tel. 213/394–3266. Facilities: parking, lifeguard, rest rooms, food.*

Will Rogers State Beach. This wide, sandy beach is several miles long, with an even surf. Parking is limited at the Castle Rock section, but there is plenty of beach, volleyball, and bodysurfing parallel to the pedestrian bridge. *15100 PCH, Pacific Palisades, tel. 213/394–3266. Facilities: parking, lifeguard, rest rooms.*

Santa Monica Beach. This is one of L.A.'s most popular beaches. In addition to a pier and a promenade, a man-made breakwater just offshore has caused the sand to collect and form the widest stretch of beach on the entire Pacific coast. Wider beaches mean more bodies! If you're up for some sightseeing on land, this is one of the more popular gathering places for L.A.'s young, toned, and bronzed. All in all, the 2-mile-wide beach is well equipped with bike paths, facilities for the disabled, playgrounds, and volleyball. *West of PCH, Santa Monica, tel. 213/394–3266. Facilities: parking, lifeguard, rest rooms, showers.*

Venice Municipal Beach. While the surf and sands of Venice are fine, the main attraction here is the boardwalk. Venice combines the pure beef of some of L.A.'s most serious bodybuilders with the productions of lively crafts merchants and street musicians. There are roller skaters and break dancers to entertain you and cafes to feed you. You can rent bikes at Venice Pier Bike Shop (21 Washington St.) and skates at Roller Skates of America (64 Windward Ave.) or Skatey's (102 Washington St.). *1531 Ocean Front Walk, Venice, tel. 213/394–3266. Facilities: parking, rest rooms, showers, food, picnicking.*

Playa Del Rey. South of Marina Del Rey lies a beach not quite as famous as its neighbors, but known to its nearby residents as one of the more underrated beaches in Southern California. Its sprawling white sands stretch from the southern tip of Marina Del Rey almost two miles down to Dockweiler Beach. The majority of the crowds that frequent these sands are young.

One of the more attractive features of this beach is an area called Del Rey Lagoon. Located right in the heart of Playa Del Rey, this grassy oasis surrounds a lovely pond inhabited by dozens of ducks, and it offers picnickers barbecue pits and tables to help stave off starvation on afternoon outings. *6660 Esplanade, Playa Del Rey. Facilities: Parking, lifeguard, rest rooms, food.*

Dockweiler State Beach. There are consistent waves for surfing at this beach, and it is not crowded, due to an unsightly power plant with towering smokestacks parked right on the beach. While the plant presents no danger to swimmers in the area, its mere presence, combined with the jumbo jets taking off overhead from L.A.'s International Airport, makes this beach a better place for working out than for lying out. There is firewood for sale for barbecues on the beach; beach fires are legal in this area as long as they are contained within the special pits that are already set up along the beach. *Harbor Channel to Vis-*

*ta Del Mar and Grand Ave., Playa Del Rey, tel. 213/322–5008.
Facilities: parking, lifeguard, rest rooms, showers.*

Manhattan State Beach. Here are 44 acres of sandy beach for
swimming, diving, surfing, and fishing. Polliwog Park is a
charming, grassy landscape a few yards back from the beach.
Ducks waddle around a small pond, picnickers enjoy a full
range of facilities including grills and rest rooms, and there is
even a series of rock and jazz concerts held here in the summer.
*West of Strand, Manhattan Beach, tel. 213/372–2166. Facili-
ties: parking, lifeguard, rest rooms, showers, food.*

Redondo State Beach. The beach is wide, sandy, and usually
packed in summer; parking is limited. The Redondo Pier marks
the starting point of the beach area, which continues south for
more than 2 miles along a heavily developed shoreline community. Storms have damaged some of the restaurants and shops
along the pier, but plenty of others are still functioning. Excursion boats, boat launching ramps, and fishing are other attractions. *Foot of Torrance Blvd., Redondo Beach, tel. 213/372–
2166. Facilities: parking, lifeguard, rest rooms, showers, food.*

Shopping

by Jane E. Lasky   Most Los Angeles shops are open from 10 to 6 although many
remain open until 9 or later, particularly at the shopping centers, on Melrose Avenue, and in Westwood Village during the
summer. Melrose shops, on the whole, don't get moving until
11 AM but are often open on Sundays, too. At most stores
around town, credit cards are almost universally accepted and
traveler's checks are also often allowed with proper identification. If you're looking for sales, check the *Los Angeles Times*.

Shopping Districts   When asked where they want to shop, visitors to Los Angeles
inevitably answer, "Rodeo Drive." This famous thoroughfare is
not only high-high-end—and therefore somewhat limited—it
is also only one of many shopping streets Los Angeles has to
offer. Visitors should also consider other shopping districts
within this huge metropolitan area. Remember that distances
between each can be vast, so don't choose too many different
stops in one day. If you do, you'll spend more time driving than
shopping.

Downtown   Although downtown Los Angeles has many enclaves to explore, we suggest that the bargain hunter head straight for the
Cooper Building (860 S. Los Angeles St., tel. 213/622–1139).
Eight floors of small clothing and shoe shops (mostly for wom-
en) offer some of the most fantastic discounts in the city. Grab a
free map in the lobby, and seek out as many of the 82 shops as
you can handle. Nearby are myriad discount outlets selling
everything from shoes to suits to linens.

Near the Hilton Hotel, **Seventh Street Marketplace** (tel. 213/
955–7150) was erected in 1986 and is worth a visit. It's an in-
door/outdoor multilevel shopping center with an extensive
courtyard that boasts many busy cafes and lively music. The
stores surrounding this courtyard include **G.B. Harb** (tel. 213/
629–5051), a fine menswear shop, and **Bullocks** (tel. 213/624–
9494), a small version of the big department store geared to the
businessperson.

Melrose Avenue   West Hollywood, especially Melrose Avenue, is where young
shoppers should try their luck, as should those who appreciate

vintage styles in clothing and furnishings. The 1½ miles of intriguing, one-of-a-kind shops and bistros stretch from La Brea to a few blocks west of Crescent Heights; it is definitely one of Los Angeles's hottest shopping areas. A sampling of the stores that operate there: **Betsey Johnson** (7311 Melrose) offers vivid, hip women's fashions; **Ecru** (7428 Melrose) displays finely designed clothing, including lines by Ana Salazar, John Galliano, and Uomo; **Industrial Revolution** (7560 Melrose) has high-tech furniture and furnishings; **Modern Living** (8125 Melrose) for top 20th-century home design from Phillippe Starck, Ettore Sottsass, and Massino Isosaghini; **A Star Is' Worn** (7303 Melrose) sells secondhand clothing once worn by celebrities; **Wacko** (7416 Melrose) is a wild space crammed with all manner of blow-up toys, cards, and other semiuseless items that make good Los Angeles keepsakes.

The Beverly Center and Environs

The **Beverly Center** (tel. 213/854–0070), bound by Beverly Boulevard, La Cienega Boulevard, San Vicente Boulevard, and Third Street, covers more than seven acres and contains some 200 stores. Many European designers—Daniel Hechter, Rodier, and others—have opened retail outlets here, as have unusual American shops. The shopping center is anchored by the Broadway department store on one end, and Bullocks on the other. Inside, there are also some interesting restaurants (like the Kisho-an, a Japanese restaurant known for its fine sushi, and The Hard Rock Cafe) and one of Los Angeles's finest cineplexes with 14 individual movie theaters. It's worthwhile to venture outside the confines of the Beverly Center to discover some very interesting shops.

The **Pacific Design Center** (corner of Melrose Ave. and San Vicente Blvd., tel. 213/657–0800) is where leading interior designers find the best in home furnishings and accessories for clients who aim to impress. Set in two startlingly big colored-glass buildings—known to locals as the Blue Whale and the Green Giant—the PDC's exclusive showrooms sell only to the trade. If you would like to do more than look here, contact LA Design Concepts, an interior-design shopping service (8811 Alden Dr., tel. 213/276–2109). A design professional will guide you through the PDC for $15 an hour, offer advice, and order items for you at less than half the standard industry markup of 33%.

Century City

Century City Shopping Center & Marketplace (tel. 213/277–3898) is set among gleaming steel office buildings. Here, in the center of a thriving business atmosphere, is a city kind of mall—open-air. Besides The Broadway and Bullocks, both department stores, you'll find **Sasha of London** for trendy shoes and bags; **Ann Taylor** for stylish but not outlandish clothing and Joan & David shoes; and **The Pottery Barn** for contemporary furnishings at comfortable prices. **Card Fever** is a whimsical boutique with fun and funky messages to send. **Go Sport** is a gigantic European sporting goods store. **Brentano's** is one of the city's largest bookstores. You'll find California wines, a great gift to take home, at **Gelson's,** a gourmet food market. Besides dozens of stores, there are five restaurants on the premises—which, incidentally, used to be Twentieth Century Fox Film Studios' backlot. Among them are Langan's Brasserie, the offspring of a famous London dining spot, and Stage Deli, the kind of New York–style deli that previously was hard to find in L.A. Also at Century City is the AMC Century 14 Theater Complex.

West Los Angeles The **Westside Pavilion** (tel. 213/474–6255) is a pastel-colored postmodern mall on Pico and Overland boulevards. The two levels of shops and restaurants run the gamut from high-fashion boutiques for men and women to a store devoted solely to travelers' needs. Among them are **Muppet and Stuff,** filled with novelties commemorating these familiar characters; **The May Company** and **Nordstrom,** two full-scale department stores; **Mr Gs for Kids,** a good place for children's gifts; **The Cashmere People,** filled with fine woolens; and **Victoria's Secret,** a lingerie boutique. Worth visiting even if you're not here to shop is **Sisley Italian Kitchen,** which serves California-Italian dishes, pizzas, and terrific salads.

Santa Monica Another worthwhile and multifaceted area, farther west and next to the ocean, offers both malls and street shopping. **Santa Monica Place Mall** (315 Broadway, tel. 213/394–5451) is a three-story enclosed mall that's nothing special. Next door, **Santa Monica Promenade** (tel. 213/393–8355) is an open-air arena of shops with pedestrian walkways and a landscaped island. A light, airy atrium views all three floors of the mall at once, and from particular points you can see the Pacific in the background. Robinson's and The Broadway are department stores in this complex.

Montana Avenue is a stretch of a dozen blocks that has evolved into an L.A. version of New York City's Columbus Avenue. Boutique after boutique of quality goods can be found along Montana from 7th to 17th streets. The stretch of **Main Street** leading from Santa Monica to Venice (Pico Blvd. to Rose Ave.) makes for a pleasant walk, with a collection of quite good restaurants, unusual shops and galleries, and an ever-present ocean breeze.

Beverly Hills We've saved the most famous section of town for last. **Rodeo Drive** is often compared to famous streets such as Fifth Avenue in New York and the Via Condotti in Rome. Along the several blocks between Wilshire and Santa Monica boulevards, you'll find an abundance of big-name retailers—but don't shop Beverly Hills without shopping the streets that surround illustrious Rodeo Drive. There are plenty of treasures to be purchased on those other thoroughfares as well.

Some of the many shops, boutiques, and department stores in Beverly Hills: **Alfred Dunhill of London** (201 N. Rodeo Dr., tel. 213/274–5351) is an elegant shop selling British-made suits, shirts, sweaters, and slacks. Pipes, tobacco, and cigars, however, are this store's claim to fame; **Ann Taylor** (357 N. Camden Dr., tel. 213/858–7840) is the flagship shop of this chain of women's clothing stores, offering the epitome of the young executive look, and a good selection of casual clothing and Joan & David shoes as well; **Bijan** (420 N. Rodeo Dr., tel. 213/273–6544) is a store where you shop by appointment only. Bijan claims that many Arabian sheiks and other royalty shop here, along with some of the wealthiest men in the United States. Many designs are created especially by the owner; **Carroll and Co.** (466 N. Rodeo Dr., tel. 213/273–9060) is a conservative man's shop that's been in business for nearly a decade. It's known for quality, service, and its professional and celebrity clientele; **Fred Hayman** (273 N. Rodeo Dr., tel. 213/271–3000).

At this illustrious store, one does not merely shop for glitzy American and European clothing, accessories, and footwear; one also refreshes oneself at the stunning Oak Bar that separates the women's from the men's clothes; **Polo/Ralph Lauren** (444 N. Rodeo Dr., tel. 213/281–7200) serves up a complete presentation of Lauren's all-encompassing lifestyle philosophy; **Torie Steele** boutiques (414 N. Rodeo Dr., tel. 213/271–5150) is a collection of six designers, including Valentino, Fendi, Maud Frizon, Luciano Soprani, and Krizia. Artisans were flown in from Europe to paint the stone-textured trompe l'oeil facade.

Even Beverly Hills has a shopping center, though owners wouldn't dare call their collection of stores and cafes a mall. It's the **Rodeo Collection** (tel. 213/276–9600) located between Brighton Way and Santa Monica Boulevard, and it's the epitome of opulence and high fashion. Many famous European designers who have never had freestanding stores on the West Coast have opened their doors in this piazzalike area of marble and brass.

Department Stores

The Broadway (The Beverly Center, 8500 Beverly Blvd., tel. 213/854–7200). This complete department store offers merchandise in the moderate price range, from cosmetics, to housewares, to linens, to clothing for men and women. There are stores throughout Los Angeles.

Bullocks (Citicorp Plaza, 925 W. 8th St., downtown, tel. 213/624–9494). More upscale than The Broadway, Bullocks carries an extensive collection of clothing for men and women, as well as housewares and cosmetics. Stores are throughout Southern California, with the flagship store at the Beverly Center (8500 Beverly Blvd., tel. 213/854–6655).

I. Magnin (Wilshire District, 3050 Wilshire Blvd., tel. 213/382–6161). This large store with many designer labels for men and women and a good handbag and luggage department has stores throughout Southern California. The flagship store (I. Magnin Wilshire) is an Art Deco landmark.

The May Company (Downtown at 6067 Wilshire Blvd., tel. 213/938–4211). Modestly priced clothing and furniture without glitz or glitter are offered in these stores throughout Southern California.

Nordstrom (Westside Pavilion at 500 N. Pico Blvd., in West Los Angeles, tel. 213/470–6155). This Seattle-based department store infiltrated Southern California within the past decade and has brought with it a wide selection of clothing for men and women as well as a reputation for fine customer service, a huge shoe department, and the entertainment of popular music played on the store's grand piano.

Robinson's (9900 Wilshire Blvd., Beverly Hills, tel. 213/275–5464). This high-end department store has many women's selections, a few men's selections, a good housewares department, and stores throughout Southern California.

Saks Fifth Avenue (9600 Wilshire Blvd., Beverly Hills, tel. 213/275–4211). The Los Angeles version of this New York store isn't as impressive as the one you'll find next to St. Patrick's in Manhattan. Still, the buyers have good taste.

Participant Sports

If you're looking for a good work-out, you've come to the right city. Los Angeles is one of the major sports capitals in the United States. Whether your game is basketball, golf, billiards, or bowling, L.A. is a dream town for athletes. Not only does the near-perfect climate allow sports enthusiasts to play outdoors almost year-round, but during some seasons it's not impossible to be surfing in the morning and snow skiing in the afternoon . . . all in the same city!

Bicycling   In the last few years, Los Angeles has made a concerted effort to upgrade existing bike paths, and to designate new lanes along many major boulevards for cyclists' use. Perhaps the most famous bike path in the city, and definitely the most beautiful, can be found on the beach. The path starts at Temescal Canyon, and works its way down to Redondo Beach. San Vicente Boulevard in Santa Monica has a nice wide lane next to the sidewalk for cyclists. The path continues for about a five-mile stretch. Balboa Park in the San Fernando Valley is another haven for two-wheelers. For more information about other bike trails in the city, contact the **L.A. Bicycle Club Association** (tel. 213/806–4646).

All of the cycling areas mentioned above are also excellent for roller skating, even though cyclists still have the right of way. Venice Beach is the skating capital of the city.

Fishing   Shore fishing is excellent on many of the beaches. Pier fishing is another popular method of hooking your dinner. The Malibu, Santa Monica, and Redondo Beach piers each offer nearby bait-and-tackle shops, and you can generally pull in a healthy catch. If you want to break away from the piers, however, the **Malibu Pier Sport Fishing Company** (23000 Pacific Coast Hwy., tel. 213/456–8030) and the **Redondo Sport Fishing Company** (233 N. Harbor Dr., tel. 213/372–2111) have half-day and full-day charters. Half-day charters, 8 AM–1 PM, run about $18 per person, while a full day goes for about $55. You can rent a pole for $6.50. Sea bass, halibut, bonita, yellowtail, and barracuda are the usual catch.

For something with a little more bite, there are a number of fishing charters out of Marina Del Rey, like **Twenty Second Street Landing** (141 W. 22nd St., San Pedro, tel. 213/832–8304). Since you can't see the fish anyway, this night charter is perfect because at least it affords you a look at the stars while waiting for a bite. Complete with bunk beds and full galley, these boats leave at 11 PM and dock at 5 AM. Price is $50 per person. Day charters available as well, at $37.

The most popular and most unique form of fishing in the L.A. area involves no hooks, bait, or poles. The great **grunion runs,** which take place March–August, are a spectacular natural phenomenon in which hundreds of thousands of small silver fish wash up on Southern California beaches to spawn and lay their eggs in the sand. The Cabrillo Museum in San Pedro (tel. 213/548–7562) has entertaining and educational programs about grunion during most of the runs. In certain seasons, touching grunion is prohibited, so it's advisable to check with the Fish and Game Department (tel. 213/590–5132) before going to see them wash ashore.

Golf The Department of Parks and Recreation lists seven public 18-hole courses in Los Angeles. **Rancho Park Golf Course** (10460 W. Pico Blvd., tel. 213/838–7373) is one of the most heavily played links in the entire country. Rancho is a beautifully designed course with enough towering pines to make those who slice or hook want to forget they ever learned how to play golf. There's a two-story driving range, a nine-hole pitch'n'put (tel. 213/838–7561), a snack bar, and a pro shop where you can rent clubs.

Perhaps the most concentrated area of golf courses in the city can be found in **Griffith Park.** Here you'll find two splendid 18-hole courses along with a challenging nine-hole course. **Harding Golf Course** and **Wilson Golf Course** (both on Crystal Springs Dr., tel. 213/663–2555) are located about a mile and a half inside the Griffith Park entrance at Riverside and Los Feliz. Peaceful bridle paths surround the outer fairways, as the San Gabriel Mountains make up the rest of the gallery in a scenic background. The nine-hole **Roosevelt Course** (tel. 213/665–2011) can be found by entering Griffith Park at the Hillhurst Street entrance.

Yet another course in the Griffith Park vicinity (where there usually is no wait) is the nine-hole **Los Feliz Pitch'n'Put** (3207 Los Feliz Blvd., tel. 213/663–7758). Other pitch'n'put courses in Los Angeles include **Holmby Hills** (601 Club View Dr., West L.A., tel. 213/276–1604) and **Penmar** (1233 Rose Ave., Venice, tel. 213/396–6228).

Health Clubs Many movies, TV shows, and songs have depicted the L.A. body as some kind of mythological creature possessing the secret of the three *T*s: tanning, toning, and tightening! Well, those chiseled muscles don't just grow on you when you get off the plane at LAX . . . it involves hard work!

There are dozens of health-club chains in the city that offer monthly and yearly memberships. **Nautilus Plus** and **Holiday Spa Health Clubs** are the most popular chains. The Holiday Club located south of Hollywood Boulevard (1607 Gower St., tel. 213/461–0227) is the flagship operation. This place has everything, including racquetball courts, indoor running tracks, pools, men's and women's weight and aerobics rooms, and a juice bar. **Sports Club L.A.** (1835 Sepulveda Blvd., West L.A., tel. 213/473–1447) is a hot spot, attracting such diverse celebrities as James Woods, Magic Johnson, and Princess Stephanie of Monaco. Probably the most famous body-pumping facility of this nature in the city is **Gold's Gym** (360 Hampton Dr., Venice, tel. 213/392–6004). This is where all the "incredible hulks" pump themselves into modern art. For $10 a day or $35 a week, several tons of weights and Nautilus machines can be at your disposal.

Horseback Riding Although horseback riding in Los Angeles is extremely popular, stables that rent horses are becoming an endangered species. Of the survivors, **Bar "S" Stables** (1850 Riverside Dr., in Glendale, tel. 818/242–8443) will rent you a horse for $13 an hour. Riders who come here can take advantage of over 50 miles of beautiful trails in the Griffith Park area. **Sunset River Trails** (on Rush St., at the end of Peck Rd., in El Monte, tel. 818/444–2128) offers riders the nearby banks of the San Gabriel River to explore. **Los Angeles Equestrian Center** (480 Riverside Dr., Burbank, tel. 818/840–8401) rents pleasure horses—both English and Western—for riding along bridle paths throughout the Griffith Park hills. Horses cost $13 per hour. **Sunset Stables** (at the end of Beachwood Dr. in Hollywood, tel. 213/469–5450) offers a $25 "dinner cruise." Riders take a trail over the hill into Burbank at sunset where they park their horses and have a feast at a Mexican restaurant.

Jogging Most true joggers don't care where they run, but if you've got the time to drive to a choice location to commence your leg-pumping exercises, here are a few suggestions: First of all, just about every local high school and college in the city has a track. Most are public and welcome runners, and the private schools usually don't give a hoot who jogs on their tracks between 5 AM and 8 AM. A popular scenic course for students and downtown workers can be found at Exposition Park. Circling the Coliseum and Sports Arena is a jogging/workout trail with pull-up bars, and other simple equipment spread out every several hundred yards. San Vicente Boulevard in Santa Monica has a wide grassy median that splits the street for several picturesque miles. Griffith Park offers several thousand acres of grassy hills for a course with more challenging terrain. Of course, the premium spot in Los Angeles for any kind of exercise can be found along any of the beaches.

Tennis And on the eighth day, God created the tennis court! At least, it seems that way when you drive around most L.A. neighborhoods. If you want to play tennis, you'll have no problem finding a court in this town—although you might have to wait a while when you get there. Many public parks have courts that require an hourly fee. **Lincoln Park** (Lincoln and Wilshire Blvd., Santa Monica), **Griffith Park** (Riverside and Los Feliz), and **Barrington Park** (Barrington just south of Sunset in L.A.), all have well-maintained courts with lights.

For a full rundown of all the public tennis courts in Los Angeles, contact the L.A. Department of Recreation and Parks (tel. 213/485–5515) or the **Southern California Tennis Association** Los Angeles Tennis Center, UCLA Campus (Box 240015, Los Angeles 90024, tel. 213/208–3838).

Hotels with If you're just in town for a few days and you don't have time to *Tennis Courts* drive around looking for a court, you may very well be staying at a hotel that has facilities. The Century Plaza in Beverly Hills (tel. 213/277–2000) has eight rooftop courts overlooking the city; the Sheraton Town House (2961 Wilshire Blvd., tel. 213/382–7171) has four courts; and downtown, the L.A. Bonaventure (tel. 213/624–1000) has eight courts for their guests. *See* Lodging for other details on these hotels.

Spectator Sports

If you enjoy watching professional sports, you'll never hunger for action in this town. Los Angeles is the home of some of the greatest franchises in pro basketball, football, and baseball.

Baseball The **Dodgers** will try to muster up the old glory of "Dodger Blue," in another eventful season at the ever-popular Dodger Stadium. For ticket information, call 213/224–1400. Down the freeway a bit in Anaheim, the **California Angels** continue their race for the pennant in the American League West. For Angel ticket information, contact Angel Stadium: tel. 213/625–1123.

Basketball While the great American pastime may be baseball, in the town where the perennial world champion **Los Angeles Lakers** display what they call "showtime," basketball is king. The Lakers' home court is the Fabulous Forum in Inglewood. Ticket information: tel. 213/419–3182. L.A.'s "other" team, the **Clippers,** make their home at the L.A. Sports Arena downtown next to the Coliseum. Ticket information: tel. 213/748–6131.

Football In 1991, Al Davis proclaimed his Raiders an official L.A. team, so the L.A. Coliseum (3911 S. Figueroa, downtown, tel. 213/747–7111) continues to be refurbished to the team's specifications. The **Los Angeles Rams** will continue their struggle to get back to the Super Bowl this year. The team plays out of Anaheim Stadium. Ticket information: tel. 213/625–1123.

Hockey The **L.A. Kings** put their show on ice at the Forum, November–April. Ticket information: tel. 213/419–3182.

Horse Racing **Santa Anita Race Track** (Huntington Dr. and Colorado Pl., Arcadia, tel. 818/574–7223) is still the dominant site for exciting Thoroughbred racing. You can always expect the best racing in the world at this beautiful facility. **Hollywood Park** (tel. 213/419–1500) is another favorite racing venue. Since the completion of the Cary Grant Pavilion, a sense of class and style that has been lacking from this once-great park for some time has been restored. The track is next to the Forum in Inglewood, off Century Boulevard. Open late April–mid-July. For harness racing, **Los Alamitos** (tel. 213/431–1361) has both day and night racing.

Dining

by Bruce David Colen

This past decade has seen Los Angeles emerge as a top gastronomic capital of the world. It has been an amazing and delicious transformation. Where once the city was only known for its chopped Cobb salad, Green Goddess dressing, drive-in hamburger stands, and outdoor barbecues, today it is home to many of the best French and Italian restaurants in the United States, plus so many places featuring international cuisines that listing them all would sound like a roll call at the United Nations. Actually, there are so many new, *good* dining establishments opening every week that, currently, there are more chairs, banquettes, and booths than there are bodies to fill them. Net result? The fierce competition among upscale restaurateurs has made L.A. one of the least expensive big cities—both here and abroad—in which to eat well.

The natives tend to dine early, between 7:30 and 9 PM, a holdover from when this was a "studio" town, and film-making started at 6 AM. Advance reservations are essential at the "starred" restaurants, and at almost all restaurants on weekend evenings.

Highly recommended restaurants are indicated by a star ★.

Category	Cost*
Very Expensive	over $70
Expensive	$40–$70

Downtown Los Angeles Dining and Lodging

Dining

Checkers, **8**
The Chronicle, **17**
Engine Co. #28, **7**
Horikawa, **14**
Lawry's California Center, **18**
Mon Kee's Seafood Restaurant, **15**
Pacific Dining Car, **1**
Rex Il Ristorante, **10**

Seventh Street Bistro, **2**
Vickman's, **16**

Lodging

The Biltmore Hotel, **9**
Checkers Hotel, **8**
Figueroa Hotel, **5**
Holiday Inn L.A. Downtown, **3**
Hyatt Regency L.A., **6**
The New Otani and Garden, **13**
Orchid Hotel, **4**
Sheraton Grande Hotel, **12**
The Westin Bonaventure, **11**

Beverly Hills and Hollywood Dining and Lodging

Dining

Antonio's Restaurant, **47**
The Bistro, **19**
The Bistro Garden, **22**
Border Grill, **45**
Cafe Blanc, **58**
California Pizza Kitchen, **14**
Carnegie Deli, **20**

Cha Cha Cha, **57**
Champagne, **5**
Chan Dara, **51**
Chasen's, **28**
Chopstix, **48**
Citrus, **50**
Columbia Bar & Grill, **52**
The Dining Room, **15**
Ed Debevic's, **44**
El Cholo, **62**

Greenblatt's, **36**
The Grill, **17**
Hard Rock Cafe, **41**
Harry's Bar & American Grill, **4**
Jimmy's, **13**
Katsu, **55**
L.A. Nicola, **56**
L'Ermitage, **39**

L'Orangerie, **38**
La Toque, **35**
Le Chardonnay, **43**
Le Dome, **30**
Locanda Veneta, **29**
The Mandarin, **16**
Nate 'n Al's, **18**
The Palm, **25**
Prego, **10**
Primi, **1**
Restaurant Katzu, **54**

RJ's the Rib Joint, **21**
Spago, **26**
Tommy Tang's, **46**
Trader Vic's, **11**
Trumps, **40**
The Windsor, **60**
Lodging
Beverly Hills
Comstock, **7**
Beverly Hills Hotel, **9**
The Beverly
Hilton, **11**

Beverly House
Hotel, **12**
Century City Inn, **2**
Century Plaza Hotel, **6**
Château Marmont
Hotel, **34**
Four Seasons Los
Angeles, **24**
Hollywood Holiday
Inn, **49**
Hollywood
Roosevelt, **37**

Hyatt on Sunset, **32**
Hyatt Wilshire, **61**
J W Marriott Hotel at
Century City, **3**
L'Ermitage Hotel, **23**
Le Bel Age Hotel, **27**
Le Mondrian Hotel, **31**
Ma Maison Sofitel
Hotel, **42**
Peninsula Beverly
Hills, **8**

Regent Beverly
Wilshire, **15**
Saint James's
Club, **33**
Sheraton Towne
House, **59**
Sunset Dunes
Motel, **53**

Dining

Lodging

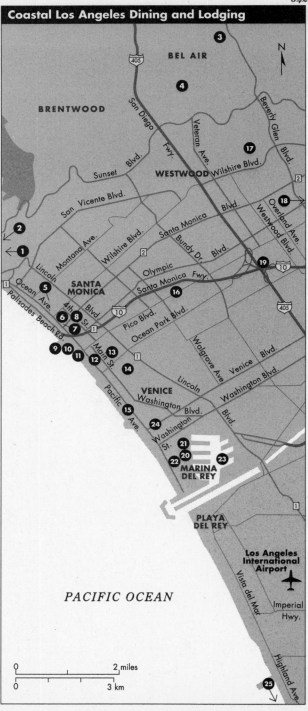

Coastal Los Angeles Dining and Lodging

Moderate	$20–$40
Inexpensive	under $20

per person, without tax (6.5%), service, or drinks

American
Beverly Hills
★

The Grill. The closest Los Angeles comes in looks and atmosphere to one of San Francisco's venerable bar and grills, with their dark wood paneling and brass trim. The food is basic American, cleanly and simply prepared, and includes fine steaks and chops, grilled fresh salmon, corned beef hash, braised beef ribs, and a creamy version of the Cobb salad. *9560 Dayton Way, tel. 213/276–0615. Reservations required. Dress: casual. AE, DC, MC, V. Valet parking eve. Closed Sun. Moderate.*

Ed Debevic's. This is a good place to take the kids and yourself, if you are yearning for the nostalgia of youth. Old Coca-Cola signs, a blaring juke box, gum-chewing waitresses in bobby sox, and meat loaf and mashed potatoes will take you back to the diners of the '50s. *134 N. La Cienega, tel. 213/659–1952. No weekend reservations; weekday reservations advised. Dress: casual. No credit cards. Valet parking. Inexpensive.*

RJ'S the Rib Joint. There is a large barrel of free peanuts at the door, sawdust on the floor, and atmosphere to match. The outstanding salad bar has dozens of fresh choices and return privileges, and there are big portions of everything—from ribs, chili, and barbecued chicken, to mile-high layer cakes—at very reasonable prices. *252 N. Beverly Dr., tel. 213/274–RIBS. Reservations advised. Dress: casual. AE, DC, MC, V. Valet parking eve. Inexpensive.*

Downtown

Pacific Dining Car. This is one of L.A.'s oldest restaurants, located in a 1920s railroad car that has been expanded over the years. Best known for well-aged steaks, rack of lamb, and an extensive California wine list at fair prices, it's a favorite haunt of politicians and lawyers around City Hall, and of sports fans after the Dodger games. *1310 W. 6th St., tel. 213/483–6000. Reservations advised. Dress: casual. MC, V. Valet parking. Moderate–Expensive.*

Engine Co. #28. The ground floor of this National Historic Site was recently refurbished and refitted; now it's a very polished, "uptown" downtown bar and grill. It has been crowded from day one. Reason? All-American food carefully prepared and served with obvious pride. Don't miss the corn chowder, "Firehouse" chili, grilled pork chop, smoked rare tenderloin, and grilled ahi tuna. And there's a great lemon meringue pie. *Corner of Figueroa St. and Wilshire Blvd., tel. 213/624–6966. Reservations required. Dress: Jacket and tie suggested for lunch; casual for dinner. AE, MC, V. Valet parking. Closed weekend lunches. Moderate.*

Lawry's California Center. What out-of-towners envision when they think of dining under the stars in the Big Orange: a terraced courtyard lush with flowers, ferns, and palm trees. There is a strolling mariachi band and, on weekends, a jazz group. The food is not special, but the entrees—charbroiled New York steak, swordfish, grilled salmon, and hickory-smoked chicken—come with the works: a garden fresh salad, freshly baked herb bread, corn on the cob, steamed vegetables, and a tortilla casserole. *570 West Ave. 26, tel. 213/225–2491. Reservations advised for dinner. Dress: casual. AE, MC, V. Parking.*

Vickman's. Located next to the L.A. Produce Market, this bustling cafeteria opens at 3 AM to accommodate fleets of truck drivers, restaurant and hotel buyers, stall owners, curious night-people, and customers at the nearby flower mart. The dishes are simple, hearty, and bountiful: ham and eggs, grits, stuffed pork chops, giant sandwiches, and a famous fresh strawberry pie. It's a fun place to go to if you can't sleep. *1228 E. 8th St., tel. 213/622–3852. No reservations. Dress: casual. No credit cards. Closed 3 PM–3 AM. Inexpensive.*

Eastside **The Chronicle.** You will think you are in San Francisco's Sam's or the Tadish Grill, both very good places to be. The Chronicle's steaks, chops, prime rib, oysters and other shellfish are excellent, and it has one of the best California wine lists south of the Napa Valley. *897 Granite Dr., tel. 818/792–1179. Reservations advised. Jacket and tie required. AE, MC, V. Valet parking. Moderate.*

Hollywood **Columbia Bar & Grill.** Located front and center in the heart of Tinsel Town, this comfortably contemporary restaurant, with Jasper Johns and David Hockneys on the walls, is the daytime mecca for people from the surrounding television and film studios. The food is definitely above par. Don't pass up the crab cakes; Caesar salad; or the fish, fowl, and meats grilled over a variety of flavor-filled woods. *1448 N. Gower St., tel. 213/461–8800. Reservations required. Dress: casual. AE, DC, MC, V. Closed Sun. Valet parking. Moderate–Expensive.*

L.A. Nicola. Owner/chef Larry Nicola spent his early years in his family's produce market. His appreciation for fresh vegetables, greens, and meats is evident in all his offerings, as is his penchant for off-beat American cooking, utilizing the bounty from California's farms and waters. Nicola raises the lowly hamburger to a place of eminence. And don't miss the grilled shark, veal chop with capers, or the appetizer of fried artichoke hearts. Perhaps the nicest thing about this California-style bistro, with its white walls and huge pails of fresh flowers, is its hideaway atmosphere. It is a place with style but no pretensions. *4326 Sunset Blvd., tel. 213/660–7217. Reservations advised. Dress: casual. AE, DC, MC, V. Valet parking. Closed Sun. Moderate.*

West Hollywood **Chasen's.** It may no longer be Hollywood's "in" spot, but the clublike rooms are full of nostalgia and have a quaintly formal charm. The dishes that Alfred Hitchcock, Gary Cooper, and Henry Fonda loved—and George Burns still does—are as good as ever: hobo steak, double-rib lamb chops, boiled beef with matzo dumplings, and the late Dave Chasen's famous chili. For the finales, try the sensational banana shortcake or frozen éclair. This is a place for special celebrations. *9039 Beverly Blvd., tel. 213/271–2168. Weekend reservations advised. Jacket and tie required. No credit cards. Valet parking. Closed Mon. and lunch. Expensive.*

The Palm. If you don't mind the roar of the jocks, or having the New York–style waiters rush you through your Bronx cheesecake, this is where you'll find the biggest and best steamed Maine lobster, good steaks and chops, great french-fried onion rings, and paper-thin potato slices. If you have the roast beef hash for lunch, you'll have to skip dinner. A three-deep bar adds to the noise. *9001 Santa Monica Blvd., tel. 213/550–8811. Reservations advised. Dress: casual. AE, DC, MC, V. Valet parking. Closed weekend lunches. Expensive.*

The Hard Rock Cafe. Big burgers, rich milkshakes, banana splits, BLTs and other pre-yuppie food delights, along with loud music, have made this '50s-era barn of a cafe the favorite of local teenagers. There is a large and busy bar for curious adults, many of whom are parents watching the kids. The place drew national attention—and spawned other Hard Rocks—for its fish-tail Cadillac jutting out of the roof, Fonzie's leather jacket on the wall, and Elvis's motorcycle. *8600 Beverly Blvd., tel. 213/276–7605. No reservations. Dress: casual. AE, DC, MC, V. Valet parking. Inexpensive.*

Westside **West Beach Cafe.** It seems that owner Bruce Madder can do no ★ wrong. Ten years ago, he opened this upscale restaurant within a Frisbee toss of all the voyeur action on the Venice Beach strand. Next came **Rebecca's,** just across the street, where Mexican food is treated as semi-*haute cuisine* and idolized by the yuppie set. Then came **DC-3,** a 21st-century architectural extravaganza at the Santa Monica Airport, followed by his most recent hit, the **Broadway Deli** in Santa Monica. Best at the West Beach are: Caesar salad, filet mignon taco, braised lamb shank, ravioli with port and radicchio, fisherman's soup and what many consider the best hamburger and fries in all of Los Angeles. There's also a fabulous selection of French wines and after-dinner liqueurs. *60 N. Venice Blvd., tel. 310/823–5396. Reservations advised. Dress: casual. AE, DC, MC, V. Valet parking. Moderate–Expensive.*

Gilliland's. While Gerri was teaching cooking in her native Ireland, she took a vacation in Southern California—and never went back. She created this charming restaurant, which offers the best of both culinary worlds, and showcases her fascination with Mediterranean dishes. The soda bread, Irish stew, and corned beef and cabbage are wonderful; and marvelous is the only word for her bitter lemon tart. The place is warm and friendly, just like its owner. *2424 Main St., Santa Monica, tel. 310/392–3901. Reservations advised. Dress: casual. AE, MC, V. Moderate.*

Gladstone's 4 Fish. This is undoubtedly the most popular restaurant along the entire California coast, serving well over a million beachgoers a year. Perhaps the food is not the greatest in the world, but familiar seashore fare is prepared adequately and in large portions, and the prices are certainly right. Best bets: crab chowder, steamed clams, three-egg omelets, hamburgers, barbecued ribs, and chili. And then there's the wonderful view, especially from the beach-side terrace—ideal for whale-, porpoise-, and people-watching. *17300 Pacific Coast Hwy. (corner of Sunset Blvd.), Pacific Palisades, tel. 310/ GL4–FISH. Dress: casual. Reservations advised. AE, DC, MC, V. Valet parking. Moderate.*

Cajun **Orleans.** Jambalaya and gumbo dishes are hot—in more ways **Westside** than one—at this spacious eatery, where the cuisine was created with the help of New Orleans chef Paul Prudhomme. The blackened redfish is probably the best catch on the menu. *11705 National Blvd., W. Los Angeles, tel. 310/479–4187. Reservations advised. Dress: casual. AE, DC, MC, V. Moderate.*

California **The Bistro Garden.** The flower-banked outdoor dining terrace **Beverly Hills** makes this the quintessential Southern California luncheon experience. It's chic and lively without being pretentious or "Hollywood." There's excellent smoked salmon, fresh cracked crab, steak tartare, calves' liver with bacon, and a unique apple pancake. *176 N. Canon Dr., tel. 213/550–3900. Reservations re-*

quired. *Jacket and tie required at dinner. AE, DC, MC, V. Valet parking. Closed Sun. Moderate–Expensive.*

★ **The Dining Room.** Located in the remodeled Regent Beverly Wilshire, this elegant, European-looking salon is the best thing to happen to L.A. hotel dining in decades. Wonderful California cuisine, plus splendid service at surprisingly non-posh prices. Adjoining is an equally attractive, sophisticated cocktail lounge, with romantic lighting and a show-tune pianist. *9500 Wilshire Blvd., tel. 213/275–5200. Reservations advised. Jacket and tie required. AE, DC, MC, V. Valet parking. Moderate–Expensive.*

California Pizza Kitchen. The place to go if you hanker for a good pizza at a fair price but don't feel like the usual pizza-parlor surroundings. There's an immaculate, pleasingly modern dining room, plus counter service by the open kitchen, and a wide, rather esoteric choice of pizza toppings. The pastas are equally interesting and carefully prepared. The few sidewalk tables are in great demand. *207 S. Beverly Dr., tel. 213/272–7878. No reservations. Dress: casual. AE, MC, V. Inexpensive–Moderate.*

West Hollywood

★ **Citrus.** Tired of being known only as one of the country's greatest pastry chefs, Michel Richard opened this contemporary restaurant to display the breadth of his talent. He creates superb dishes by blending French and American cuisines. You can't miss with the delectable tuna burger, the thinnest angel-hair pasta, or the deep-fried potatoes, sautéed foie gras, rare duck, or sweetbread salads. Best get your doctor's permission before even looking at Richard's irresistible desserts. *6703 Melrose Ave., tel. 213/857–0034. Reservations advised. Jacket required. AE, MC, V. Valet parking. Closed Sun. Moderate–Expensive.*

★ **Spago.** This is the restaurant that propelled owner/chef Wolfgang Puck into the national and international culinary spotlights. He deserves every one of his accolades for raising California cuisine to an imaginative and joyous gastronomic level, using only the finest West Coast produce. The proof is in the tasting: grilled baby Sonoma lamb, pizza with Santa Barbara shrimp, thumbnail-size Washington oysters topped with golden caviar, grilled free-range chickens, and, from the North Pacific, baby salmon. As for Puck's incredible desserts, he's on Weight Watchers' Most Wanted List. This is the place to see *People* magazine live, but you'll have to put up with the noise in exchange. Be safe: Make reservations at least two weeks in advance. *1114 Horn Ave., tel. 213/652–4025. Reservations required. Jacket required. AE, DC, MC, V. Valet parking. Closed lunch. Moderate–Expensive.*

Trumps. A smartly designed contemporary adobe building, with striking abstract art on the pure-white walls. But the best artist in the house is chef/co-owner Michael Roberts, an imaginative young American who takes special pleasure in combining off-beat flavors that result in a delectable whole: brie-and-apple bisque, salmon tartare with tomatillo, corn pancakes with mussels, duck breast and pickled pumpkin, and gingersnap cheesecake. This is the perfect cure for jaded appetites, and a popular rendezvous for L.A.'s tastemakers. It serves the best afternoon tea in town. *8764 Melrose Ave., tel. 213/855–1480. Reservations advised. Jacket required. AE, DC, MC, V. Closed weekend lunches. Moderate–Expensive.*

Westside **Hotel Bel-Air.** Even if the food were terrible, one would not
★ care, since the romantic, country-garden setting is so satisfying. But the California-Continental cooking is first-rate, be it
breakfast, lunch, or dinner. A meal at the Bel-Air is a not-to-
be-missed experience. *701 Stone Canyon Rd., Bel Air, tel. 310/
472–1211. Reservations advised. Jacket and tie required. AE,
DC, MC, V. Valet parking. Expensive.*

Caribbean **Cha Cha Cha.** When the Cajun food craze cooled off among L.A.
Hollywood foodies, Caribbean cooking became the trend, and this small
shack of a place became the hottest spot in town. There's corn-
meal chicken, spicey swordfish, fried banana chips, and assorted flans. This is a hangout for celebrities gone slumming.
*656 N. Virgil Ave., tel. 213/664–7723. Reservations required,
but expect to wait. Dress: casual. AE, DC, MC, V. Valet parking. Moderate.*

Chinese **The Mandarin.** Who said you only find great Chinese food in
Beverly Hills hole-in-the-wall places with oilcloth tabletops? Here is a good-
★ looking restaurant with the best crystal and linens, serving an
equally splendid mixture of Szechuan and Chinese country-
cooking dishes. Minced squab in lettuce-leaf tacos, Peking
duck, a superb beggars chicken, scallion pancakes, and any of
the noodle dishes are recommended. *430 N. Camden Dr., tel.
213/272–0267. Reservations required. Jacket required. AE,
DC, MC, V. Valet parking. Closed weekend lunches. Moderate.*

Downtown **Mon Kee Seafood Restaurant.** The name says it all—except how
good the cooking is and how morning-fresh the fish are. The delicious garlic crab is addictive; the steamed catfish is a masterpiece of gentle flavors. In fact, almost everything on the menu
is excellent. This is a crowded, messy place; be prepared to wait
for a table. *679 N. Spring St., tel. 213/628–6717. No reservations. Dress: casual. MC, V. Pay parking lot. Inexpensive–
Moderate.*

West Hollywood **Chopstix.** Never underestimate the ability of Californians to
adopt, and adapt, an ethnic-food vogue. In this case it is dim
sum, subtly doctored for non-Oriental tastes. The result is
nouvelle Chinese junk-food served in a mod setting, at high-
stool tables or at a dinerlike counter. The dishes are appetiz-
ing, but don't expect a native Chinese to agree. *729 Melrose
Ave., tel. 213/935–2944. No reservations. Dress: casual. AE,
DC, MC, V. Inexpensive.*

Continental **The Bistro.** The kitchen is not quite as good as Jimmy's (*see* be-
Beverly Hills low), but nobody has ever questioned that this replica of a Parisian boîte is one of the most stylish dining rooms west of
Europe. The original owner, director Billy Wilder, was responsible for the interior design: mirrored walls, etched-glass par-
titions, giant bouquets of fresh flowers, and soft lighting. The
food is more American bistro than French. There is a delicious,
juicy chopped steak, good veal medallions, Eastern lobster on
tagliatelli and, most likely, the greatest chocolate soufflé
you've ever tasted. *246 North Canon Dr., tel. 310/273–5633.
Reservations required. Jacket and tie required. AE, DC, MC,
V. Valet parking. Closed Sat. lunch and Sun. Expensive.*

Century City **Jimmy's.** When the Beverly Hills C.E.O.s are not entertaining,
they head here or to the Bistro (*see* above). Owner Jimmy Murphy provides the warmth in this expensive, decorator-elegant
restaurant. The best dishes on the broad menu include smoked

Scottish salmon, prawns with herbs and garlic, saddle of lamb, Chateaubriand, and pheasant breast with wild blueberry sauce. There's steak tartare at lunch. *201 Moreno Dr., tel. 310/ 879–2394. Reservations required. Jacket and tie required. AE, DC, MC, V. Valet parking. Expensive.*

Mid-Wilshire **The Windsor.** This is what an upscale L.A. restaurant was like 40 years ago: a dark, quiet retreat with red-leather booths and banquettes, where captains prepare dishes table-side. Talk about the old days, the menu even has Baked Alaska and Crepes Suzette. Stick with the steak and chop entrees and the Caesar salad. *3198½ West 7th St., tel. 213/382–1261. Reservations required. Jacket and tie required. AE, DC, MC, V. Valet parking. Moderate.*

Westwood **Dynasty Room.** This peaceful, elegant room in the Westwood Marquis Hotel has a European flair and tables set far enough apart for privacy. Besides well-handled Continental fare, there is a *cuisine minceur* menu for calorie counters. Best of all, an especially lavish, excellent Sunday brunch. *930 Hilgard Ave., tel. 310/208–8765. Reservations required. Jacket and tie required. AE, DC, MC, V. Valet parking. Closed lunch. Moderate.*

Deli **Carnegie Deli.** Marvin Davis, the oil millionaire, got tired of
Beverly Hills jetting cheesecake, pastrami, and lox back from the parent Carnegie in New York City, so he financed a Beverly Hills taste-alike to challenge Nate 'n Al's preeminence. His big guns are corned beef and pastrami sandwiches that are 4½ inches high, cheese blintzes under a snowcap of sour cream, and wonderfully creamy cole slaw. *300 N. Beverly Dr., tel. 213/275–3354. No reservations. Dress: casual. AE, DC, MC, V. Inexpensive.*
Nate 'n Al's. A famous gathering place for Hollywood comedians, gag writers, and their agents. Nate 'n Al's serves first-rate matzo-ball soup, lox and scrambled eggs, cheese blintzes, potato pancakes, and the best deli sandwiches west of Manhattan. *414 N. Beverly Dr., tel. 213/274–0101. No reservations. Dress: casual. DC. Free parking. Inexpensive.*

West Hollywood **Greenblatt's.** Who ever heard of a deli famous for its extensive wine list? This one also serves wood-smoked ribs, rotisserie chicken, and 20 different salads, along with the usual sandwiches. *8017 Sunset Blvd., tel. 213/656–0606. No reservations. Dress: casual. MC, V. Parking lot. Inexpensive.*

French **Champagne.** Patrick Healy, another young American who
Century City trained under some of the best chefs in France, has opened this
★ attractive restaurant, where cuisine, not people-watching, keeps patrons returning week after week. They have their choice of contemporary or traditional French dishes and spa cuisine selections. Two specialties include a three-layered eggplant and crayfish cake, plus a real farmhouse cassoulet. The desserts are light and lovely. *10506 Santa Monica Blvd., tel. 310/470–8446. Reservations required. Jacket and tie required. AE, DC, MC, V. Valet parking. Closed Mon. Moderate.*

Downtown **Seventh Street Bistro.** Set in a landmark Art Deco office build-
★ ing, this ground-floor restaurant is full of light and beautifully designed. It has all the sophistication and panache of a townhouse in Paris or Manhattan. The nouvelle Franco-Californian cuisine is splendid. The menu changes monthly, but the enthusiasm of the bistro's loyal customers is a constant. *811 W. 7th*

*St., tel. 213/627–1242. Reservations advised. Jacket and tie re-
quired. Valet parking eve. Closed Sat. lunch and Sun. Moderate–Expensive.*

Hollywood   **Cafe Blanc.** It appears to be only a small storefront restaurant
in a scruffy part of town, but inside you'll discover what is probably the most beautifully prepared, tastiest Franco-Japanese
cuisine in Los Angeles. And, almost as tantalizing as owner/
chef "Tommy" Harase's lamb chops with truffles or the sautéed
foie gras on a poached pear are the cafe's reasonable prices,
with a consummate dinner for two costing between $50 and $65.
*3706 Beverly Blvd., tel. 213/380–2829. Reservations suggested.
Dress: informal. MC, V. Closed Sun., and Sat. lunch. BYOB.
Inexpensive.*

West Hollywood   **L'Ermitage.** Although they are served in a sedate, French
★   country-house setting, there's nothing imitative about chef
Michel Blanchet's three-star classic French-California dishes.
Specialties include escargot pancake, smoked salmon ravioli
with leeks and caviar, sea bass in a pastry crust, sweetbread
stew, salmon tartare, and fabulous desserts. *730 N. La Cienega
Blvd., tel. 213/652–5840. Reservations required. Jacket and tie
required. AE, DC, MC, V. Valet parking. Closed lunch and
Sun. Very Expensive.*

★   **L'Orangerie.** For sheer elegance and classic good taste, it would
be hard to find a lovelier restaurant in this country. And the
cuisine, albeit nouvelle-light, is as French as the l'orangerie at
Versailles. Specialties include coddled eggs served in the shell
and topped with caviar, squab with foie gras, pot-au-feu, rack
of lamb for two, and an unbeatable apple tart served with a jug
of double cream. *903 N. La Cienega Blvd., tel. 213/652–9770.
Reservations required. Jacket and tie required. AE, DC, MC,
V. Valet parking. Closed lunch. Expensive.*

La Toque. Amid the hurly-burly of Sunset Strip is this small,
unassuming, one-story building. Step through the door, and
you'll imagine you've entered a French country inn. The charming hideaway is the province of Ken Frank, one of the nation's
best American, French-cooking chefs. Each day some new delight graces the menu: raviolis stuffed with foie gras and pheasant, fettuccine with egg and black truffle, venison seared with
Armagnac, or grilled duck breast in a calvados sauce. Be sure
to order the roasted, shredded potato pancake with golden caviar and crème fraîche. *8171 Sunset Blvd., tel. 213/656–7515.
Reservations required. Jacket required. AE, DC, MC, V. Valet
parking. Closed Sat. lunch, Sun. Moderate–Expensive.*

Le Chardonnay. The interiors are Art Deco in this unabashed
copy of a famous Left Bank bistro, circa 1920. Despite the high
noise level, it's a most romantic rendezvous, with comfortable,
cozy booths. Specialties include warm sweetbread salad, goat
cheese ravioli, roast venison, grilled fish, Peking duck with a
ginger and honey sauce, and lots of lush desserts. *8284 Melrose
Ave., tel. 213/655–8880. Reservations required. Jacket required. AE, MC, V. Valet parking. Closed Sat. lunch, Sun.
Moderate.*

Le Dome. For some reason, local food critics have never given
this brasserie the attention it deserves. Perhaps they are in-
timidated by the hordes of show- and music-biz celebrities that
keep the place humming. By and large the food is wonderful,
honest, down-to-earth French: cockles in white wine and shal-
lots, veal ragout, marvelous veal sausage with red cabbage,
and a genuine, stick-to-the-ribs cassoulet. *8720 Sunset Blvd.,*

tel. 213/659–6919. Reservations required. Dress: casual. AE, DC, MC, V. Valet parking. Closed Sun. Moderate.

Westside   **Fennel.** Ocean Avenue has often been compared to a sea bluff
★   boulevard on the French Riviera; and Fennel is the closest you
can come to the latest true Parisian cooking in California. It is
very, very trendy with L.A.'s Francophiles. Call in advance
to find out which of three French chefs is in residence. *1535
Ocean Ave., tel. 310/394–2079. Reservations required. Jacket
required. AE, DC, MC, V. Valet parking. Closed weekend
lunches in winter. Expensive.*

★   **Chinois on Main.** The second of the Wolfgang Puck pack of restaurants, this one is designed in tongue-in-cheek kitsch by his
wife, Barbara Lazaroff. Both the look of the place and Puck's
merging of Chinese and French cuisines for contemporary
tastes are great good fun. A few of the least resistible dishes on
an irresistible menu include Mongolian lamb with eggplant,
poach-curried oysters, whole catfish garnished with ginger
and green onions, and rare duck with a wondrous plum sauce.
The best desserts are three differently flavored *crèmes brû-
lées*. This is one of L.A.'s most crowded spots—and among the
noisiest. Bring earplugs. *2709 Main St., Santa Monica, tel.
310/392–9025. Reservations required for dinner. Dress: casual. AE, DC, MC, V. Valet parking, evenings. Closed Sat.–Tues.
lunch. Moderate–Expensive.*

Beaurivage. A charming, romantic restaurant designed in the
fashion of an auberge on the Cote D'Azur, this is the best of the
Malibu dining places with a view of the beach and ocean. The
menu complements the Provençal atmosphere: roast duckling
Mirabelle, pasta with shellfish, mussel soup, filet mignon with
a three-mustard sauce and, in season, wild game specials. It's a
satisfying getaway. *26025 Pacific Coast Highway, tel. 310/
456–5733. Reservations required. Dress: casual. Parking lot.
Open Mon.–Sat. 5–11, Sun. 11–4 and 5– 11. Moderate.*

Italian   **Primi.** Valentino's younger, less expensive brother, with a
Beverly Hills   menu that features a wide variety of appetizer-size portions of
Northern Italian treats, including pasta and salad selections.
This is a cheerful, contemporary setting, with a pleasant out-
side terrace. *10543 W. Pico Blvd., tel. 310/475–9235. Reserva-
tions advised. Jacket required. AE, DC, MC, V. Valet parking.
Closed Sun. Moderate.*

Prego. This is a super bargain in the highest of high-rent districts. The baby lamb chops, large broiled veal chop, and Flor-
entine rib steak are among the best, dollar for dollar, in town.
The baked in-house bread sticks are great. *362 N. Camden Dr.,
tel. 310/277–7346. Reservations advised. Dress: casual. AE,
DC, MC, V. Valet parking at night. Closed Sun. lunch. Inexpensive–Moderate.*

Century City   **Harry's Bar & American Grill.** A more private, posh, uptown
version of Prego, run by the same management. The decor and
selection of dishes are acknowledged copies of Harry's Bar in
Florence. But you'll find that for first-rate food—paper-thin
carpaccio, excellent pastas, grilled fish and steaks, along with
a fine hamburger—the check will be far lower than in Italy.
This is the best place to dine before or after seeing a movie in
the area. *2020 Ave. of the Stars, tel. 310/277–2333. Reservations advised. Jacket required. AE, DC, MC, V. Valet parking.
Closed Sun. lunch. Moderate.*

Downtown ★ **Rex Il Ristorante.** Owner Mauro Vincenti probably knows more about Italian cuisine than any other restaurateur in this country. The Rex is the ideal showcase for his talents: Two ground floors of a historic Art Deco building were remodeled to resemble the main dining salon of the circa-1930 Italian luxury liner *Rex*. The cuisine is equally special, the lightest of *cucina nuevo*. Be prepared for small and costly portions. *617 S. Olive St., tel. 213/627–2300. Reservations required. Jacket and tie required. AE, DC, MC, V. Valet parking. Lunch Thurs. and Fri., closed Sun. Very Expensive.*

West Hollywood ★ **Locanda Veneta.** The food may be more finely wrought at one or two other spots, but the combination of a splendid Venetian chef, Antonio Tomassi, and a simpatico co-owner, Jean Louis de Mori, have re-created the atmospheric equivalent of a genuine Italian trattoria, *at reasonable* prices. Specialties include fried white-bait, risotto with porcini mushrooms, veal chop, ricotta and potato dumplings, linguini with clams, lobster ravioli with saffron sauce, and pear tart. *8638 W. 3rd St., tel. 213/274–1893. Reservations required. Jacket required. AE, DC, MC, V. Valet parking. Closed Sat. lunch and Sun. Moderate.*

Tuttobene. If Silvio de Mori, Jean Louis's older brother, served nothing more than peanut-butter sandwiches, his place would be doing SRO business. But this best-loved restaurateur, a genuinely gracious, caring host, happens to provide some of the most delectable trattoria dishes west of Tuscany. There are different, freshly baked breads every day, superb down-to-earth pastas and gnocci, luscious risotto with wild mushrooms, picked-that-morning arugula salad—all at very fair prices. *945 N. Fairfax Ave., tel. 213/655–7051. Reservations required. Dress: casual. AE, MC, V. Valet parking. Moderate.*

Westside ★ **Valentino.** Rated among the best Italian restaurants in the nation, Valentino is generally considered to have the best wine list outside Italy. Owner Piero Selvaggio is the man who introduced Los Angeles to the best and lightest of modern-day Italian cuisine, and the natives have loved him ever since. There's superb prosciutto, bresola, fried calamari, lobster canneloni, fresh broiled porcini mushrooms, and osso buco. *3115 Pico Blvd., Santa Monica, tel. 310/829–4313. Reservations required. Jacket required. AE, DC, MC, V. Valet parking. Closed Sat.–Thur. lunch and Sun. Expensive.*

La Scala Malibu. Malibu's most celebrity-crowded hangout has moved to brand-new, cheerful quarters, and, in the process, the Northern Italian food has greatly improved, and the prices have come down a notch. You can't quite see the ocean, but, "There's Cher over there talking to Olivia Newton-John and Jack Lemmon, next to the table with Larry Hagman and Walter Matthau." *3874 Cross Creek Rd., tel. 310/456–1979. Reservations advised. Dress: casual. AE, MC, V. No lunch weekends. Moderate.*

Japanese Downtown **Restaurant Horikawa.** A department store of Japanese cuisines including sushi, teppan steak tables, tempura, sashimi, shabu-shabu, teriyaki, and a $50-per-person *kaiseki* dinner. All are good or excellent, but the sushi bar is the best. The decor is traditional Japanese, with private sit-on-the-floor dining rooms for 2 to 24. *111 S. San Pedro St., tel. 213/680–9355. Reservations advised. Jacket and tie required. AE, DC, MC, V. Valet parking. Closed weekend lunches. Moderate–Expensive.*

Los Feliz **Restaurant Katsu.** A stark, simple, perfectly designed sushi
★ bar with a small table area, serving the most exquisite and delicious delicacies in all of Southern California. This is a treat for
eye and palate. *1972 N. Hillhurst Ave., tel. 213/665–1891. No
lunch reservations, dinner reservations advised. Dress: casual. AE, MC, V. Valet parking. Closed Sat. lunch. Moderate.*

Mexican **El Cholo.** This progenitor of the present-day, upscale South-
Hollywood land chain, has been packing them in since the '20s. It serves
good bathtub-size margaritas, a zesty assortment of tacos,
make-your-own tortillas, and, from June to September, green-
corn tamales. It's friendly and fun, with large portions at peso
prices. *1121 S. Western Ave., tel. 213/734–2773. Reservations
advised. Dress: casual. AE, MC, V. Parking lot. Inexpensive.*

West Hollywood **Border Grill.** This is a very trendy, very loud storefront place,
owned by two women chefs with the most eclectic tastes in
town. The menu ranges from crab tacos to vinegared-and-pep-
pered grilled turkey to pickled pork sirloin. It's worth dropping by, if you don't mind the noise while you're there. *7407 ½
Melrose Ave., tel. 213/658–7495. Reservations advised. Dress:
casual. AE, MC, V. Moderate.*
Antonio's Restaurant. Don't let the strolling mariachis keep
you from listening to the daily specials, the true Mexico City
dishes that put this unpretentious favorite several cuts above
the ubiquitous taco-enchilada cantinas. The *chayote* (squash)
stuffed with ground beef; ricotta in a spicy tomato sauce; pork
ribs in a sauce of pickled chipotle peppers; veal shank with garlic, cumin, and red pepper; and chicken stuffed with apples, ba-
nanas and raisins are definitely worth trying. Have the flan for
dessert. *7472 Melrose Ave., tel. 213/655–0480. Dinner reservations advised. Dress: casual. AE, MC, V. Valet parking. Inexpensive–Moderate.*

Polynesian **Trader Vic's.** Sure, it's corny, but this is the most restrained
Beverly Hills and elegant of the late Victor Bergeron's South Sea extravaganzas. Besides, who says corn can't be fun—and tasty, too.
The crab Rangoon, grilled cheese wafers, skewered shrimp,
grilled pork ribs, and the steaks, chops, and peanut-butter–
coated lamb cooked in the huge clay ovens, are just fine. As for
the array of exotic rum drinks, watch your sips. *9876 Wilshire
Blvd., tel. 310/274–7777. Reservations required. Jacket and tie
required. AE, DC, MC, V. Valet parking. Closed lunch. Moderate–Expensive.*

Thai **Chan Dara.** Here you'll find excellent Thai food in a bright and
Hollywood shiny Swiss chalet! Try any of the noodle dishes, especially
those with crab and shrimp. There is noise here, but it's bear-
able. *310 N. Larchmont Blvd., tel. 213/467–1052. Reservations
advised for parties of more than 4. Dress: casual. AE, MC, V.
Inexpensive.*

West Hollywood **Tommy Tang's.** A very "in" grazing ground for yuppies and celebs alike. So much people-watching goes on, nobody seems to
notice the small portions on their plates. The kitchen features
crisp duck marinated in ginger and plum sauce, blackened sea
scallops, and a spinach salad tossed with marinated beef. There
is also a sushi bar. *7473 Melrose Ave., tel. 213/651–1810. Reservations advised. Dress: casual. AE, DC, MC, V. Valet parking. Closed for lunch. Moderate.*

Lodging

by Jane E. Lasky

You can find almost any kind of accommodation in Los Angeles, from a simple motel room that allows you to park right in front of your room to a posh hotel like the Beverly Hills, where an attendant will park your car and whisk you off to a spacious room or to your own bungalow.

Because L.A. is so spread out—it's actually a series of suburbs connected by freeways—it's a good idea to select a hotel room not only for its ambience, amenities, and price, but also for a location that is convenient to where you plan to spend most of your time. West Hollywood and Beverly Hills are trendy and central, while Hollywood itself has lost much of its legendary glamour. Westwood and Santa Monica are attractive but less accessible locations, and more recently developed Century City offers new hotels and a large shopping mall.

It's best to plan ahead and reserve a room; many hotels offer special prices for weekend visits and offer tickets to amusement parks or plays. A travel agent can help in making your arrangements.

Hotels are listed in categories, determined first by location: Downtown, Mid-Wilshire, Hollywood/West Hollywood, Beverly Hills/Bel Air, West Los Angeles, Santa Monica, Marina del Rey, and South Bay Beach Cities. They are further divided, under location, into categories determined (roughly) by the price of a room for two people, on the European plan.

The most highly recommended accommodations are indicated by a star ★.

Category	Cost*
Very Expensive	over $155
Expensive	$110–$155
Moderate	$70–$110
Inexpensive	under $70

for a double room

Downtown
Very Expensive

The Biltmore Hotel. Since its 1923 opening, the Biltmore has hosted such notables as Mary Pickford, J. Paul Getty, Eleanor Roosevelt, Princess Margaret, and several U.S. presidents. Now a historic landmark, it was renovated in 1986 for $35 million, with modern, updated guest rooms decorated in pastels. The lobby ceiling was painted by Italian artist Giovanni Smeraldi; imported Italian marble and plum-color velvet grace the Grand Avenue Bar, which features excellent jazz nightly. Bernard's is an acclaimed Continental restaurant. The private, swank health club has a Roman bath motif. Banquet and meeting rooms serve up to 1,200; the special club floor boasts a library, wide-screen TV, and pocket billiards room. *506 S. Grand Ave., 90071, tel. 213/624–1011, or 800/245–8673. 704 rooms. Facilities: restaurants, lounge, entertainment, health club (fee). AE, DC, MC, V.*

Checkers Hotel. With its excellent pedigree and smaller scale, the brand-new Checkers is a sophisticated, welcome addition to the downtown hotel scene. Set in one of downtown's few remaining historic buildings—opened as the Mayflower Hotel in 1927—Checkers boasts the same management as the acclaimed Campton Place in San Francisco (one of the nation's top hotels). Rooms are furnished with oversize beds, upholstered easy chairs, writing tables, and minibars. A library is available for small meetings or tea. *535 S. Grand Ave., 90071, tel. 213/624–0000 or 800/628–4900. 190 rooms. Facilities: restaurant, rooftop spa and lap pool, exercise studio. AE, DC, MC, V.*

Hyatt Regency, Los Angeles. The Hyatt is located in the heart of the "new" downtown financial district, minutes away from the Convention Center, Dodger Stadium, and the Music Center. Each room has a wall of windows with city views. The Regency Club has a private lounge. The hotel is part of the Broadway Plaza, comprising 35 shops. Nearby tennis and health club facilities are available at an extra cost. *711 S. Hope St., 90017, tel. 213/683–1234 or 800/233–1234. 485 rooms. Facilities: restaurant, coffee shop, lounge, entertainment. AE, DC, MC, V.*

★ **Sheraton Grande Hotel.** Opened in 1983, this 14-story, 550-room mirrored hotel is near Dodger Stadium, the Music Center, and downtown's Bunker Hill District. Rooms have dark wood furniture, sofas, minibars; colors are aqua or copper; baths are marble. Butler service on each floor. Stay in the penthouse suite if you can afford it. Limousine service is available, and there are privileges at a local health club. *333 S. Figueroa St., 90071, tel. 213/617–1133 or 800/325–3535. 469 rooms. Facilities: restaurants, nightclub, outdoor pool, 23 meeting rooms, 4 movie theaters. AE, DC, MC, V.*

The Westin Bonaventure. This is John Portman's striking masterpiece: a 35-story, circular-towered, mirrored-glass high rise in the center of downtown. Rooms have a wall of glass, streamlined pale furnishings, and comfortable appointments. The outside elevators provide stunning city views; there are also 5 acres of ponds and waterfalls in the lobby, several restaurants, including Beaudry's Gourmet, and the Bona Vista revolving lounge at the top of the hotel. The grand ballroom seats 3,000. A popular Sunday brunch is served in the atrium lobby. Parking is expensive. *404 S. Figueroa St., 90071, tel. 213/624–1000 or 800/228–3000. 1,474 rooms. Facilities: restaurant, lounge, entertainment, pool, and 5-level shopping arcade. AE, DC, MC, V.*

Expensive–
Very Expensive
★
The New Otani and Garden. East meets west in L.A., and the exotic epicenter downtown is this 21-story, ultramodern hotel surrounded by Japanese gardens and waterfalls. The decor combines a serene blend of Westernized luxury and Japanese simplicity. Each room has a refrigerator, an alarm clock, color TV, and phone in the bathroom, and most provide a kimono. For the ultimate Little Tokyo experience, book a Japanese suite. These suites are so authentic that guests sleep on futons on mats on the floor. Concrete walls give great noise control. A Thousand Cranes offers classic Japanese cuisine; Commodore Perry's, steak and lobster. There is a large conference center and a relaxing piano bar. *120 S. Los Angeles St., 90012, tel. 213/629–1200, 800/252–0197 in CA, or 800/421–8795 nationwide. 448 rooms. Facilities: restaurants, nightclubs, sauna and massage (fee), parking (fee). AE, DC, MC, V.*

Moderate **Figueroa Hotel.** This hotel has managed to keep its charming Spanish style intact as it enters its second half-century. There's a poolside bar. The hotel is on the Gray Line sightseeing tour route and there is airport service every hour to LAX. *939 S. Figueroa St., 90015, tel. 213/627–8971, 800/421–9092 nationwide, or 800/331–5151 in CA. 280 rooms. Facilities: restaurants, coffee shop, lounge, pool, free parking. AE, DC, MC, V.*

Holiday Inn L.A. Downtown. This offers Holiday Inn's usual professional staff and services, and standard room decor. Pets are allowed, and there is plenty of free parking. It's close to the Museum of Contemporary Art and Dodger Stadium. *750 Garland Ave., 90017, tel. 213/628–5242 or 800/465–4329. 204 rooms. Facilities: restaurant, lounge, pool, parking. AE, DC, MC, V.*

Inexpensive **Orchid Hotel.** One of the smaller downtown hotels, this is very reasonably priced. There are no frills, but the standard rooms are clean. Note that there is no parking at the hotel, but public lots are close by. *819 S. Flower St., 90017, tel. 213/624–5855. 66 rooms. Facilities: color TV, coin-operated laundry. AE, DC, MC, V.*

Mid-Wilshire **Hyatt Wilshire.** One of Wilshire Boulevard's largest hotels, this
Expensive– 12-story building's interior was renovated in 1987. There's a
Very Expensive grand piano and concert pianist in the lobby. The rooms have views of either Hollywood or downtown. The Hyatt's corporate clients often use the large banquet and meeting rooms for up to 400 people. *3515 Wilshire Blvd., 90010, tel. 213/381–7411 or 800/233–1234. 397 rooms. Facilities: restaurant, cafeteria, lounge, disco, room service, laundry service, parking (fee). AE, DC, MC, V.*

Sheraton Towne House. Howard Hughes slept (and lived) here. A great example of L.A.'s best Art Deco architecture, this hotel, built in the 1920s, retains its original charm and elegance. Marble fireplaces, antiques, and cedar-lined closets enhance the country-estate tone. It's convenient to Bullocks Wilshire shopping. *2961 Wilshire Blvd., 90010, tel. 213/382–7171 or 800/325–3535. 300 rooms. Facilities: restaurants, coffee shop, pool, tennis, parking (fee). AE, DC, MC, V.*

Hollywood/West **Le Bel Age Hotel.** This is a wonderful location for an all-suite,
Hollywood European-style hotel with a distinctive restaurant, which fea-
Very Expensive tures fine Russian meals with an elegant French flair. There
★ are many extravagant touches, like three telephones with five lines in each suite, original art, private terraces, and courtesy limousine service. Ask for a suite that faces south for terrific views looking out as far as the Pacific over the L.A. skyline. The decor is French country style. *1020 N. San Vicente Blvd., West Hollywood 90069, tel. 213/854–1111 or 800/424–4443. 190 suites. Facilities: 2 restaurants, lounge, pool. AE, DC, MC, V.*

Le Mondrian Hotel. This giant structure is a monument to the Dutch artist after whom the hotel takes its name. The outside of the 12-story hotel is actually a giant surrealistic mural; inside there's fine artwork. Accommodations are spacious, with pale wood furniture and curved sofas in the seating area. Ask for south-corner suites; they tend to be quieter than the rest. A chauffeured limo is placed at each guest's disposal. Nouvelle cuisine is served at Mondrian Cafe. The hotel is convenient to major recording, film, and TV studios. *8440 Sunset Blvd., West Hollywood 90069, tel. 213/650–8999 or 800/424–4443. 243 suites. Facilities: restaurant, pool, health club, parking. AE, DC, MC, V.*

★ **The Saint James's Club/Los Angeles.** Located on the Sunset Strip, this is the latest in the prestigious group of St. James's Clubs, and the first in the United States. The building has been around since the 1930s; today all the furnishings are exact replicas of Art Deco masterpieces, the originals of which are in New York's Metropolitan Museum of Art. Ask for a city or mountain view. Both are great, but the cityside accommodations are more expensive. The hotel also features a 1930s-style supper club (California cuisine) with piano entertainment, a club bar, and a lounge. *8358 Sunset Blvd., West Hollywood 90069, tel. 213/654–7100 or 800/225–2637. 63 rooms. Facilities: restaurant, health center, sauna, pool, secretarial services, small meeting facilities. AE, DC, MC, V.*

Expensive **Chateau Marmont Hotel.** Although planted on the Sunset Strip amid giant billboards and much Hollywood glitz, this castle of Old World charm and French Normandy design still promises its guests a secluded hideaway close to Hollywood's hot spots. A haunt for many show-biz personalities and discriminating world travelers since it opened in 1927, this is the ultimate in privacy. All kinds of accommodations are available, including fully equipped cottages, bungalows, and a penthouse. *8221 Sunset Blvd., Hollywood 90046, tel. 213/656–1010 or 800/ CHATEAU. 62 rooms. Facilities: dining room, gardens, pool, patios. AE, MC, V.*

Hollywood Roosevelt. This hotel across from Mann's Chinese Theater was considered state-of-the-art Hollywood glamour and luxury before it gradually fell into disrepair. But in true Hollywood fashion, this site of the first Academy Awards ceremony made a comeback in 1985, thoroughly restored right down to the ornate Art Deco lobby and elegant courtyard. Highlights are the Olympic-size pool decorated by artist David Hockney and the Tropicana Bar in the courtyard. *7000 Hollywood Blvd., Hollywood 90028, tel. 213/466–7000, or 800/950–7667. 320 rooms plus 90 poolside cabanas. Facilities: restaurants, lounge, rental cars, airport transportation, valet parking. AE, DC, MC, V.*

Hyatt on Sunset. In the heart of the Sunset Strip, this Hyatt is a favorite of music-biz execs and rock stars. There are penthouse suites, some rooms with private patios, and a rooftop pool. The rooms are decorated in peach colors and modern furniture; some rooms even have aquariums. *8401 W. Sunset Blvd., West Hollywood 90069, tel. 213/656–4101 or 800/233–1234. 262 rooms. Facilities: restaurant, lounge, entertainment, pool, parking (fee). AE, DC, MC, V.*

Moderate **Hollywood Holiday Inn.** You can't miss this hotel, one of the tallest buildings in Hollywood. It's 23 stories tall, topped by Windows, a revolving restaurant-lounge. The rooms are decorated in light gray and rose in standard Holiday Inn fashion. There is a safekeeping box in each room. The hotel is only minutes from the Hollywood Bowl, Universal Studios, and Mann's Chinese Theater, and it's a Gray Line Tour Stop. *1755 N. Highland Ave., Hollywood 90028, tel. 213/462–7181 or 800/465–4329. 468 rooms. Facilities: restaurant, coffee shop, pool, coin laundry, parking. AE, DC, MC, V.*

Inexpensive **Sunset Dunes Motel.** Across the street from two TV stations, this hotel with Spanish-style rooms is a popular stop for studio folk. Its Dunes restaurant is open until 10 PM and the family-oriented Spaghetti Factory is nearby. *5625 Sunset Blvd., Hol-*

lywood 90028, tel. 213/467–5171. 56 rooms. Facilities: restaurant, lounge, free parking. AE, DC, MC, V.

Beverly Hills
Very Expensive
★

Beverly Hills Hotel. This is a California landmark: 12 acres of beautiful grounds in a quiet location with tropical plants. The lovely rooms are all different, decorated with traditional furniture and overstuffed chairs and sofas. For the full flavor of this Beverly Hills legend, book a bungalow by the pool. Movie stars often take the bungalows and congregate in the famous Polo Lounge. Breakfast and lunch are served in the Dining Room overlooking the heated pool. *9641 Sunset Blvd., Beverly Hills 90210, tel. 310/276–2251 or 800/283–8885. 268 units. Facilities: restaurants, pool, wading pool, exercise room, parking. AE, DC, MC, V.*

The Beverly Hilton. This large hotel complex has a wide selection of restaurants and shops. Most rooms have balconies overlooking Beverly Hills or downtown. Trader Vic's and L'Escoffier are two of the city's better restaurants. There is a theater ticket desk, limo service, and free coffee in the lobby for hotel guests. *9876 Wilshire Blvd., Beverly Hills 90210, tel. 310/274–7777 or 800/445–8667. 592 rooms. Facilities: restaurants, pool, wading pool, exercise room, refrigerators, parking. AE, DC, MC, V.*

★ **L'Ermitage Hotel.** L'Ermitage features Old World charm with modern conveniences. Opened in 1976, it's one of the few hotels on the West Coast to garner a Mobil Four Star Award. The property is near Beverly Hills' elegant shopping, and Twentieth Century Fox. The suites have balconies and sunken living rooms with fireplaces. The best is the split-level town-house suite. The fine Cafe Russe is reserved exclusively for hotel guests. Complimentary Continental breakfast; chauffeured limo within Beverly Hills. *9291 Burton Way, Beverly Hills 90210, tel. 310/278–3344 or 800/424–4443. 114 rooms. Facilities: restaurant, pool, whirlpool, spa, private solarium, parking. AE, DC, MC, V.*

★ **Four Seasons Los Angeles.** This new hotel combines the best in East and West Coast luxury. Formal European decorative details are complemented by outpourings of flora from the porte cochere to the rooftop pool deck. There is an outstanding restaurant and a great shopping location within five minutes of Rodeo Drive and trendy Melrose Avenue. Many of the suites come with French glass doors and a walk-out balcony. *300 S. Doheny Dr., Los Angeles 90048, tel. 310/273–2222 or 800/332–3442. 285 rooms. Facilities: restaurant, 1-hr pressing service, pool, exercise equipment. AE, DC, MC, V.*

Ma Maison Sofitel Hotel. This fine hotel offers first-class service and an intimacy usually reserved for small European-style hotels. The country-French guest rooms are done in terracotta and blues, with small prints. The hotel is next to some of L.A.'s best shopping, restaurants, and boutiques. It also faces a large brick wall; insist on a northern view. *8555 Beverly Blvd., Los Angeles 90048 (on the fringe of Beverly Hills), tel. 213/278–5444 or 800/221–4542. 311 rooms. Facilities: 2 restaurants, 24-hr room service, pool, sauna, fitness center, parking. AE, DC, MC, V.*

The Peninsula Beverly Hills. Located in the heart of Beverly Hills, this luxury hotel was the first new property to open in this prestigious Los Angeles enclave in more than two decades when it made its debut in 1991. Surrounded by flowered hedges, poplar trees, and elephant ears, a circular motorcourt greets guests in rare style. The hotel's appearance is classic, done in French Renaissance architecture with contemporary overtones. Rooms are decorated in a residential motif, with antiques, rich fabrics, and marble floors. Minibars and refrigerators can be found behind French doors in all rooms, and all suites are equipped with compact disc players, fax machines, and individual security systems. *9882 Santa Monica Blvd., Beverly Hills, 90212, tel. 310/273–4888; 800/462–7899 (nationwide). 200 rooms. Facilities: business center, rooftop gardens, lap pool, health club, poolside cabanas, restaurants, bars, 24-hour valet parking, voice-mail. AE, DC, MC, V.*

Regent Beverly Wilshire. This famous hotel facing Rodeo Drive and the Hollywood Hills reopened in 1989 after a major renovation (and under new management). It remains stylish, with personal service and extras to match. There are great restaurants, limo service to the airport, and a multilingual staff. *9500 Wilshire Blvd., Beverly Hills 90212, tel. 310/275–5200; 800/427–4354 (nationwide). 401 rooms. Facilities: restaurants, pool, health spas, parking (fee). AE, DC, MC, V.*

Expensive **Beverly Hills Comstock.** Because this is a low-rise hotel (only three floors), guests need not walk through long corridors to reach their rooms. All the suites are situated off the pool. Furnishings are smart, some in Early American style and some contemporary; all feature kitchen/living room, one bedroom, and bath. *10300 Wilshire Blvd., Beverly Hills 90024, tel. 310/275–5575 or 800/343–2184. 150 rooms. Facilities: restaurant, pool, Jacuzzi, garage. AE, DC, MC, V.*

Moderate **Beverly House Hotel.** This is a small, elegantly furnished, Euro-
★ pean-style bed-and-breakfast hotel. Even though it's near busy areas of L.A. (Century City and Beverly Hills shopping), this hotel is quiet and actually quaint. *140 S. Lasky Dr., Beverly Hills 90212, tel. 310/271–2145 or 800/432–5444. 50 rooms. Facilities: laundry, free parking. AE, DC, MC, V.*

West Los Angeles **Century Plaza Hotel.** This 20-story hotel (on 14 acres of tropical
Very Expensive plants and reflecting pools) features a new 30-story tower,
★ which is lavishly decorated with signature art and antiques; it's furnished like a mansion, with a mix of classic and contemporary appointments. Each room has a refrigerator and balcony with ocean or city view. Complimentary car service is provided to Beverly Hills. There are four excellent restaurants: award-winning La Chaumiere for California/French cuisine, the Terrace for American/Continental, the Garden Pavilion for spa cuisine, and the Cafe Plaza, a French-style cafe. *2025 Ave. of the Stars, Century City 90067, tel. 310/277–2000 or 800/228–3000. 1,072 rooms. Facilities: restaurants, 2 pools, whirlpools, parking. AE, DC, MC, V.*

★ **J W Marriott Hotel at Century City.** This hotel, which opened in 1988, is the West Coast flagship for the multifaceted Marriott chain. Its elegant, modern rooms are decorated in soft pastels and equipped with minibars, lavish marble baths, and facilities for the handicapped. Ask for accommodations that overlook Twentieth Century Fox's back lot. The hotel offers complimentary limo service to Beverly Hills and boasts the 2,000 sq. ft. Presidential Suite and excellent service. *2151 Ave. of the Stars, Century City 90067, tel. 213/277–2777 or 800/228–9090. 375 rooms. Facilities: restaurant, indoor and outdoor pools, whirlpools, fitness center. AE, DC, MC, V.*

Moderate **Century City Inn.** This hotel is small but well designed for comfort. Rooms have refrigerators, microwave oven, remote control TV, and VCR, as well as a 10-cup coffee unit with fresh gourmet-blend coffee and tea. Baths have whirlpool tubs and a phone. Complimentary breakfast is served as an added plus. *10330 W. Olympic Blvd., Los Angeles 90064, tel. 310/553–1000 or 800/553–1005. 46 rooms. Facilities: rental cars, parking. AE, DC, MC, V.*

Coastal Los Angeles
Very Expensive

Hotel Bel-Air. This is a charming, secluded hotel (and celebrity mecca) with lovely gardens and a creek complete with swans. The rooms and suites are decorated individually in peach and earth tones. All are villa bungalow style with Mediterranean decor. For their quietest accommodation, ask for a room near the former stable area. The Bel-Air has a 5 star rating from the Mobil Guide, and 5 diamonds from AAA. *701 Stone Canyon Road, Bel Air 90077, tel. 310/472–1211 or 800/648–4097 outside CA. 60 rooms, 32 suites. Facilities: pool, restaurant, lounge, parking. AE, DC, MC, V.*

Westwood Marquis. This hotel near UCLA is a favorite of corporate and entertainment types. Each individualized suite in its 15 stories has a view of Bel Air, the Pacific Ocean, and downtown L.A. Ask for a suite that overlooks the pool and garden. Breakfast and lunch are served in the Garden Terrace, which is also famous for its Sunday brunch. The award-winning Dynasty Room features Continental cuisine plus special Minceur spa diet menu. European teas are served in the afternoon in the Westwood Lounge. *930 Hilgard Ave., Los Angeles 90024, tel. 310/208–8765 or 800/692–2140. 258 suites. Facilities: 2 pools, sauna, phones in bathrooms, banquet and meeting rooms, pay parking. AE, DC, MC, V.*

Inexpensive **Best Western Royal Palace Hotel.** This small hotel located just off I–405 has all suites, decorated with conservative, homey prints. In-room morning coffee and tea are complimentary, as is parking to hotel guests. Suites have kitchenettes. *2528 S. Sepulveda Blvd., West Los Angeles 90064, tel. 310/477–9066 or 800/528–1234. 58 rooms. Facilities: pool, Jacuzzi, exercise room and billiard room, laundry facilities. AE, DC, MC, V.*

Santa Monica
Very Expensive

Loews Santa Monica Beach Hotel. Set on the most precious of L.A. real estate—beachfront—the Loews opened mid-1989 just south of the Santa Monica Pier. Most of the contemporary rooms have ocean views and private balconies, and all guests have private access to the beach. Its restaurant, Riva, serves Northern Italian cuisine with an emphasis on seafood. *1700 Ocean Ave., 90401, tel. 310/458–6700 or 800/223–0888. 350 rooms, including 35 suites. Facilities: restaurant, cafe, fitness center, indoor/outdoor pool, valet parking.*

Miramar Sheraton. This hotel, "where Wilshire meets the sea," is close to all area beaches, across the street from Pacific Palisades Park, and near deluxe shopping areas and many quaint eateries. The landscaping incorporates the area's second-largest rubber tree. Many rooms have balconies overlooking the ocean. The decor in some rooms is very contemporary, with bleached wood, marble, granite, glass, and brick. A new wing has traditional furnishings. *101 Wilshire Blvd., 90403, tel. 310/ 394–3731 or 800/325–3535. 305 rooms. Facilities: 3 restaurants, lounge, entertainment, pool. AE, DC, MC, V.*

Moderate **Pacific Shore.** Formerly the Royal Inn of Santa Monica, this modern building is a half block from the beach and many restaurants. The attractive rooms are decorated with contemporary fabrics and modern furniture; some have ocean views. *1819 Ocean Ave., 90401, tel. 310/451–8711, or 800/622–8711. 169 rooms. Facilities: restaurant, lounge, pool, sauna, therapy pool, Jacuzzi, laundry facilities, Avis Rent-a-Car, gift shop, free parking. AE, MC, V.*

Inexpensive **Carmel Hotel.** This charming hotel from the 1920s is one block from the beach and the new Santa Monica Shopping Plaza, as well as from movie theaters and many fine restaurants. Electric ceiling fans add to the room decor. There is a Mexican-American restaurant on the premises. *201 Broadway, 90401, tel. 310/451–2469. 110 rooms. Facilities: restaurant, parking (overnight fee). AE, DC, MC, V.*

Palm Motel. This quiet, unceremonious motel has old-fashioned rooms. The decorative highlight is the color TVs, but the motel does offer complimentary coffee, tea, and cookies at breakfast. It's only a short drive away from several good restaurants. *2020 14th St., 90405, tel. 310/452–3822. 26 rooms. Facilities: self-service laundry, free parking. MC, V.*

Marina del Rey
Very Expensive
★
The Doubletree Inn (formerly the Marina Beach Hotel). This luxurious nine-story high-rise hotel has high-tech design softened by a pastel decor accented in brass and marble. Ask for upper-floor rooms that face the marina. There are lovely touches, such as a gazebo in the patio and rooms with water views. The restaurant Stones is known for its fresh seafood. The hotel offers 24-hour free transportation to and from LAX. All of the rooms are decorated in pastels and have a safe for valuables. *4100 Admiralty Way, 90292, tel. 310/301–3000, 800/528–0444 nationwide, or 800/862–7462 in CA. 386 rooms. Facilities: restaurant, lounges, pool, pay parking. AE, DC, MC, V.*

Expensive–
Very Expensive
Marina International Hotel. Directly across from an inland beach, this hotel is unique for its village-style decor. The rooms are done in earth tones with California-style furniture. Each of the very private rooms offers a balcony or patio that faces the garden or the courtyard. Ask for a bungalow—they're huge. The Crystal Fountain restaurant has Continental cuisine. Boat charters are available for up to 200 people. *4200 Admiralty Way, 90292, tel. 310/301–2000, 800/528–0444 nationwide, or 800/862–7462 in CA. 110 rooms, 25 bungalows. Facilities: restaurant, lounge, pool, airport transportation, free parking. AE, DC, MC, V.*

The Ritz-Carlton, Marina del Rey. Opened in 1990, this sumptuous property sits on some prime real estate at the northern end of a basin, offering a resplendent panoramic view of the Pacific. The extremely attractive rooms have marble baths, honor bars, and plenty of amenities—from maid service twice a day to plush terry robes. *4375 Admiralty Way, Marina del Rey 90292, tel. 310/823–3656. 306 rooms. Facilities: pool, sun deck, fitness center, tennis courts, boutiques, complimentary transportation to LAX. AE, DC, MC, V.*

Moderate **Marina Pacific Hotel & Suites.** This hotel faces the Pacific and one of the world's most vibrant boardwalks; it's nestled among art galleries, shops, and elegant, offbeat restaurants. The marina is just a stroll away. The Spanish-style rooms are all decorated in pink. Comfortable accommodations include suites, conference facilities, full-service amenities, and a delightful sidewalk cafe. For the active traveler, there are ocean swimming, roller skating along the strand, racquetball, and tennis nearby. *1697 Pacific Ave., Venice 90291, tel. 310/399–7770, 800/421–8151 nationwide, or 800/826–2474 in CA. 125 rooms. 1-bedroom apartments available. Facilities: restaurant, laundry. AE, DC, MC, V.*

South Bay Beach Cities
Expensive–Very Expensive

Sheraton at Redondo Beach. Opened in 1987, this swank five-story hotel, located across the street from the Redondo Beach Pier, overlooks the Pacific. There are plenty of amenities, including indoor and outdoor dining and a nightclub. The rooms are decorated in a seaside theme of light woods and bright colors. *300 N. Harbor Dr., Redondo Beach 90277, tel. 310/318–8888 or 800/325–3535. 339 rooms. Facilities: restaurant, lounge, entertainment, pool, exercise room, game room, sauna, whirlpool, tennis, pay parking. AE, DC, MC, V.*

Moderate
★

Barnaby's Hotel. Modeled after a 19th-century English inn, with four-poster beds, lace curtains, and antique decorations, Barnaby's also has an enclosed greenhouse pool. Rosie's Bar resembles a cozy pub, with live entertainment; Barnaby's Restaurant features Continental cuisine and curtained private booths. Afternoon tea is a highlight. An adjacent health club charges $10 per day. Weekend packages are available. *3501 Sepulveda Blvd., at Rosecrans, Manhattan Beach, tel. 310/545–8466 or 800/552–5285. 128 rooms. Facilities: restaurants, lounge, pool. AE, DC, MC, V.*

Airport
Expensive–Very Expensive

Sheraton Plaza La Reina. A luxurious 15-story hotel befitting its name of "Plaza of the Queen," this is in a perfect setting for business and leisure travelers alike. The contemporary rooms are decorated in muted shades of mauve, brown, green, and purple. Ninety-six meeting rooms, with in-house audiovisual equipment, can accommodate groups up to 1,000. There are two restaurants: Plaza Brasserie, a coffee shop open from 6 AM to midnight, and Landry's, for steak and lobster, with an excellent sushi bar, open till 10 PM. 48 of the rooms are especially designed for the disabled. *6101 W. Century Blvd., Los Angeles 90045, tel. 310/642–1111. 852 rooms. Facilities: restaurants, lounges, live entertainment, multilingual concierge, room service, currency exchange, direct international dialing from guest-room telephones. AE, DC, MC, V.*

Expensive

Hyatt Hotel-LAX. Earth tones and brass decorate this elegant 12-story building, the hotel closest to LAX, Hollywood Park, the Forum, and Marina del Rey. The Hyatt keeps business travelers in mind, and it offers large meeting rooms with ample banquet space. The hotel's staff is bilingual and a concierge is on duty 24 hours a day. *6225 W. Century Blvd., 90045, tel. 310/670–9000 or 800/233–1234. 596 rooms. Facilities: restaurant, coffee shop, lounge, entertainment, pool, sauna, exercise room, pay parking. AE, DC, MC, V.*

★

Stouffer Concourse Hotel. This is a good place to stay if you're looking for pampering near the airport. Rooms and suites are decorated in soft pastels and some deeper colors to complement the contemporary decor; many suites have private outdoor spas. The expansive, luxurious lobby is decorated in earth tones and brass. The Trattoria Grande restaurant features pasta and seafood specialties. *5400 W. Century Blvd., Los Angeles 90045, tel. 310/216–5858 or 800/468–3571. 750 rooms. Facilities: 2 restaurants, lounge, entertainment, pool, sauna, fitness center, pay parking. AE, DC, MC, V.*

Moderate **Holiday Inn-LAX.** This recently decorated, international-style
hotel is ideal for families and business types. The hotel features
standard Holiday Inn rooms in such colors as beige, burgundy,
pink, orange, or green. Other amenities include the well-
known restaurant and cocktail lounge, Wings; multilingual
telephone operators; and tour information. *9901 La Cienega
Blvd., Los Angeles 90045, tel. 310/649–5151 or 800/238–8000.
403 rooms. Facilities: restaurant, pool, free parking. AE, DC,
MC, V.*

Pacifica Hotel. Just three miles north of LAX and a few minutes from Marina del Rey, this deluxe Spanish American–style
hotel is convenient for business types. There is both elegant
and casual dining. The Culver's Club Lounge has lively entertainment and dancing. Extra special is the Shalamar Suite,
with beautiful decorations and its own indoor pool. Package
rates are available. *6161 Centinela Ave., Culver City 90230,
tel. 310/649–1776 or 800/542–6082. 368 rooms. Facilities: restaurant, lounge, entertainment, pool, sauna, health club, free
parking. AE, DC, MC, V.*

The Arts

For the most complete listing of weekly events, get the current
issue of *Los Angeles* or *California* magazine. The Calendar section of the *Los Angeles Times* also offers a wide survey of Los
Angeles arts events, as do the more irreverent free publications the *L.A. Weekly* and the *L.A. Reader.*

Most tickets can be purchased by phone (with a credit card)
from **Teletron** (tel. 213/410–1062), **Ticketmaster** (tel. 213/480–
3232), **Ticketron** (tel. 213/642–4242), **Good Time Tickets** (tel.
213/464–7383), or **Murray's Tickets** (tel. 213/234–0123).

Theater Even small productions might boast big names from "the Business" (the Los Angeles entertainment empire). Many film and
television actors love to work on the stage between "big" projects as a way to refresh their talents or regenerate their creativity in this demanding medium. Doing theater is also an
excellent way to be seen by those who matter in the more glitzy
end of show business. Hence there is a need for both large houses—which usually mount productions that are road-company
imports of Broadway hits or, on occasion, are the place where
Broadway-bound material begins its tryout phase—and a host
of small, intimate theaters for the talent that abounds in this
city.

The following sampling includes some of the major houses in
the area.

Ahmanson Theater. With 2,071 seats, this is the largest of the
three-theater Music Center complex (with the Dorothy Chandler Pavilion and the Mark Taper Forum), and productions include both classics and new plays. The list of artists who have
worked at this theater reads like a Who's Who of stage and
screen. *135 N. Grand Ave., tel. 213/972–7211. Tickets:
$37–$50. AE, DC, MC, V.*

Mark Taper Forum. Also part of the Music Center, this house
boasts 742 seats, excellent acoustics, and an intimate setting.
The theater, under the direction of Gordon Davidson, is com-
mitted to new works and to the development of a community of
artists. Many of its plays, including *Children of a Lesser God,*

have gone on to Broadway. *135 N. Grand Ave., tel. 213/972–7353. Tickets: $17.50–$30. AE, DC, MC, V.*

Westwood Playhouse. An acoustically superior theater with great sightlines, the 498-seat playhouse showcases new plays, primarily musicals and comedies in the summer. Many productions come in from Broadway; two—*Perfectly Frank* and *Passionate Ladies*—went on to Broadway. Jason Robards and Nick Nolte got their starts here. *10886 Le Conte Ave., Westwood, tel. 310/208–6500 or 213/208–5454. Tickets: $17.50–$30. AE, DC, MC, V.*

Wilshire Theater. The interior of this newly renovated, 1,900-seat house is Art Deco–style; musicals from Broadway are the usual fare. *8440 Wilshire Blvd., Beverly Hills, tel. 310/642–4242. Tickets: $14.50–$27.50. MC, V.*

Concerts Los Angeles is not only the focus of America's pop/rock music recording scene, after years of being regarded as a cultural invalid, but now also a center for classical music and opera.

The following is a list of Los Angeles's major concert halls:

Dorothy Chandler Pavilion (135 N. Grand Ave., tel. 213/972–7211). Part of the Los Angeles Music Center and—with the Hollywood Bowl—the center of L.A.'s classical music scene, the 3,200-seat Pavilion is the home of the Los Angeles Philharmonic and the showcase for the Los Angeles Master Chorale Group, the Los Angeles Civic Light Opera, and, in the fall, the Joffrey Ballet. *AE, MC, V.*

The Greek Theater (2700 N. Vermont Ave., tel. 213/410–1062). This open-air auditorium near Griffith Park offers some classical performances in its mainly pop/rock/jazz schedule from June to October. Its Doric columns evoke the amphitheaters of ancient Greece. *AE, MC, V.*

The Hollywood Bowl (2301 Highland Ave., tel. 213/850–2000). Open since 1920, the Bowl is one of the world's largest outdoor amphitheaters, located in a park surrounded by mountains, trees, and gardens. The L.A. Philharmonic spends its summer season here. Concert goers usually arrive early, bringing or buying picnic suppers. There are plenty of picnic tables, and box-seat subscribers can reserve a table right in their own box. Restaurant dining is available on the grounds (reservations recommended, tel. 213/851–3588). The seats are wood, so you might bring or rent a cushion—and bring a sweater. A convenient way to enjoy the Hollywood Bowl experience without the hassle of parking is to take one of the Park-and-Ride buses, which leave from various locations around town; call the Bowl for information. *MC, V.*

Royce Hall (405 N. Hilgard, tel. 310/825–9261). Internationally acclaimed performers are featured in this 1,800-seat auditorium at UCLA. The university's **Schoenberg Hall,** smaller but with wonderful acoustics, also hosts a variety of concerts. *MC, V.*

The Shrine Auditorium (665 W. Jefferson Blvd., tel. 213/749–5123). Built in 1926 by the Al Malaikah Temple, the auditorium's decor could be termed Basic Baghdad and Beyond. Touring companies from all over the world, along with assorted gospel and choral groups, appear in this one-of-a-kind, 6,200-seat theater. *AE, MC, V.*

Wiltern Theater (Wilshire Blvd. and Western Ave., tel. 213/380–5005 or 213/380–5031). Reopened in 1985 as a venue for the Los Angeles Opera Theater, the building was constructed in

1930, is listed in the National Register of Historic Places, and is a striking example of Art Deco in its green terra-cotta glory. *MC*, *V*.

Dance Los Angeles offers not only its own Bella Lewitsky and the Los Angeles Chamber Ballet, but also yearly visiting dance companies including the Joffrey, American Ballet Theatre, Martha Graham, and Paul Taylor, to name a few. Most dance events in Los Angeles will be listed each Sunday in the *Los Angeles Times* Calendar section. The **Dance Resource Center of Greater Los Angeles** (tel. 213/281–1918) also offers current dance information.

The Music Center (135 N. Grand, tel. 213/972–7211). At the western home of the late Robert Joffrey's bicoastal ballet company, you'll find (in spring and fall) the company dancing a range of works from the elegant *pas de trois Monotones* to the full production of *Romeo and Juliet*. The yearly Folk Dance Festival is held in March. *AE*, *MC*, *V*.

The Shrine Auditorium (665 W. Jefferson, tel. 213/749–5123). This is host of the American Ballet Theatre (ABT) in March. ABT's repertoire includes Baryshnikov's *Cinderella* and Saint Leon's classic *Coppelia*. *AE*, *MC*, *V*.

UCLA Center for the Arts (405 N. Hilgard, tel. 310/825–9261) attracts masters of modern dance, jazz, and ballet, along with its own UCLA Dance Company. Rush tickets priced at $7 are available on the night of the performance for full-time students and senior citizens. *MC*, *V*.

Nightlife

Nightlife in Los Angeles has come to mean anything from catching a stand-up routine at the Comedy Store to frenetic disco dancing at Chippendale's. This city offers a potpourri of specialized entertainment, not only in the hub of the city but also in the outlying suburbs.

Despite the high energy level of the nightlife crowd, Los Angeles nightclubs aren't known for keeping their doors open until the wee hours. This is an early-to-bed city, and it's safe to say that by 2 AM, most jazz, rock, and disco clubs are closed for the night. Perhaps it's the temperate climate and the sports orientation of the city: Most Angelenos want to be on the tennis court or out jogging first thing in the AM, so a late-night social life is out of the question.

Dress codes vary depending on the place you visit. Jackets are expected at cabarets and hotels. Discos are generally casual, although some will turn away the denim-clad. The rule of thumb is to phone ahead and check the dress code, but on the whole, Los Angeles is oriented toward casualwear.

Consult *Los Angeles* and *California* magazines for current listings. The Sunday *Los Angeles Times* Calendar section, the *Herald Examiner* Style section, and the free *L.A. Weekly* and *L.A. Reader* also provide listings.

Jazz **The Baked Potato.** A tiny club where they pack you in like sardines to hear a powerhouse of jazz. The featured item on the menu is, of course, baked potatoes; they're jumbo and stuffed with everything from steak to vegetables. *3787 Cahuenga Blvd. W, North Hollywood, tel. 818/980–1615. AE, MC, V.*

Birdland West. This is the place to come for contemporary jazz,

Art Deco decor, and great happy hours. *105 W. Broadway, Long Beach, tel. 213/436–9341. Open daily. AE, DC, MC, V.*

Jax. An intimate club serving a wide variety of food, from sandwiches to steak and seafood. Live music is an added draw. *339 N. Brand Blvd., Glendale, tel. 818/500–1604. AE, MC, V. No cover.*

The Lighthouse. One of Los Angeles's finest offers a broad spectrum of music, from reggae to big band. Jam sessions are often held on weekends. Freddie Hubbard, Woody Herman, and Jimmy Witherspoon all have played here. The decor is wood, brass, and brick, with a lot of plants. Dine on fettuccine, appetizers, or steaks while listening to, the sounds. *30 Pier Ave., Hermosa Beach, tel. 310/372–6911 or 213/376–9833. MC, V with a $5 minimum. No cover.*

Nucleus Nuance. This Art Deco restaurant features vintage jazz every night. *7267 Melrose Ave., West Hollywood, tel. 213/939–8666. AE, DC, MC, V.*

Vine Street Bar and Grill. This elegant club in the heart of Hollywood (across the street from the James Doolittle Theater) features two shows nightly. Past performers have included Eartha Kitt, Cab Calloway, and Carmen McRae. Italian food is served. *1610 N. Vine St., Hollywood, tel. 213/463–4375. AE, MC, V.*

Folk/Pop/Rock

Blue Saloon. For rock 'n roll, this is the place to go. (You'll also catch a smattering of country and blues, at times, too.) If your seat gets tired listening to music, rustle up a game of billiards or darts. This is the friendliest club around. *4657 Lankershim Blvd., North Hollywood, tel. 818/766–4644. Open noon–2 AM. No credit cards.*

The Central. A musician's hangout. Road crews, pop-act managers, and famous guitarists alike come to hear live music in the pop, soul, and jazz/fusion genres. Many celebrity musicians attend the Tuesday night jam sessions. *8852 Sunset Blvd., West Hollywood, tel. 213/855–9183. AE.*

Club Lingerie. One local describes it as "clean enough for the timid, yet seasoned quite nicely for the tenured scenester." Best of all is its mix of really hot bands. *6507 Sunset Blvd., Hollywood, tel. 213/466–8557.*

Gazzarri's. A Sunset Strip landmark offering pure rock and roll with a 19–early 20s age group. Dress is casual. *9039 Sunset Blvd., West Hollywood, tel. 213/273–6606. No credit cards.*

Madame Wong's West. In a nutshell: a young crowd, local bands, dancing, and video games. Over 21 only. *2900 Wilshire Blvd., Santa Monica, tel. 213/829–7361.*

The Palace. The "in" spot for the upwardly mobile. It's plush Art Deco—truly a palace—and boasts live entertainment, a fabulous sound system, full bar, and dining upstairs. TV comedy/variety shows are filmed here. Patrons dress to kill. *1735 N. Vine St., Hollywood, tel. 213/462–3000 or 213/462–6031. AE, MC, V.*

The Roxy. The premier Los Angeles rock club, classy and comfortable, offers performance art as well as theatrical productions. Many famous Los Angeles groups got their start here as opening acts. *9009 Sunset Blvd., West Hollywood, tel. 213/276–2222. AE, DC, MC, V.*

The Strand. This major concert venue covers a lot of ground, hosting hot new acts, or such old favorites as Asleep at the Wheel, bluesman Albert King, rock vet Robin Trower, and Billy Vera, all in the same week. Who says you can't have it all?

1700 S. Pacific Coast Hwy., Redondo Beach, tel. 310/316–1700. AE, MC, V.

The Troubador. In the early '70s this was one of the hottest clubs in town for major talent. Then business entered a shaky phase for a few years as the music industry changed its focus, but now it's rolling again, this time with up-and-coming talent. The adjoining bar is a great place in which to see and be seen. *9081 Santa Monica Blvd., West Hollywood, tel. 213/276–6168. No credit cards.*

Disco/Dancing **Bar One.** Celebrities such as Warren Beatty and Charlie Sheen enjoy this restaurant and bar. A hot, hip place for dancing, this is L.A.'s club of the moment. There's also a pool table and comfortable lounging areas. *9229 Sunset Blvd., Beverly Hills, tel. 213/271–8355.*

Circus Disco. A gay-owned and -operated club, featuring funk, rock, and exclusively new wave on Thursday nights. Open nightly. *6655 Santa Monica Blvd., Hollywood, tel. 213/462–1291. AE, MC, V.*

Crush Club. If the 1960s is a decade that appeals to you, stop by this happening dance club. After all, there's nothing like some golden Motown to get you moving. *1743 Cahuenga Ave., Hollywood, tel. 213/461–9017. Open Thurs.–Sat. 9 PM–2 AM. $5–$7 cover. MC, V.*

DC3. Hip and uptown, this club/restaurant in the Santa Monica Airport plays pop music until 2 AM. Look for an older, upscale crowd and sophisticated lighting effects. *2800 Donald Douglas Loop North, Santa Monica, tel. 310/399–2323.*

20/20. Once the Playboy Club, this night spot is where the beautiful people party, with plenty of mirrors for checking themselves out. Music runs from oldies to Top 40. *2020 Ave. of the Stars, Century City, tel. 310/933–2020. Open Thurs., Fri., and Sat.*

Vertigo. A New York–style club with restricted entrance policy, large dance floor, balcony bar, and restaurant. Open Friday and Saturday until 4 AM, which is unusual for this city. *303 S. Boylston, Los Angeles, tel. 213/747–4849. MC, V.*

Country **The Palomino.** There's occasionally a wild crowd at this premier country showcase in Los Angeles. Good old boys and hip cowboys meet here, and everybody has a good time. *6907 Lankershim Blvd., North Hollywood, tel. 818/764–4010. AE, DC, MC, V.*

Comedy and Magic

Comedy and Magic Club. This beachfront club features many magicians and comedians seen on TV and in Las Vegas. The Unknown Comic, Elayne Boosler, and Pat Paulsen have all played here. Reservations are suggested. The menu features light American fare and many appetizers. *1018 Hermosa Ave., Hermosa Beach, tel. 310/372–1193. Closed Mon. AE, MC, V.*

Comedy Store. Los Angeles's premier comedy showcase for over a decade. Many famous comedians, including Robin Williams and Steve Martin, occasionally make unannounced appearances here. The cover varies. *8433 Sunset Blvd., Hollywood, tel. 213/656–6225. AE, MC, V.*

Igby's Comedy Cabaret. You'll see familiar television faces as well as up-and-coming comedians Tuesday through Saturday. Cabaret fare includes cocktails and dining in a friendly ambience. Reservations are necessary. *11637 Tennessee Place, Los Angeles, tel. 213/477–3553. AE, DC, MC, V.*

The Improvisation. The Improv is a transplanted New York establishment. Comedy is showcased, with some vocalists. The Improv was the proving ground for Liza Minnelli and Richard Pryor, among others. Reservations are recommended. *8162 Melrose Ave., West Hollywood, tel. 213/651–2583 and 321 Santa Monica Blvd., Santa Monica, tel. 213/394–8664. MC, V for food and drinks only.*

Merlin McFly Magical Bar and Grill. If you're seeing double here, it might not be the drinks: Magical illusions are featured nightly until midnight. Ladies, watch out for the powder room; lights will dim there, and you'll see a Houdini-like figure with a crystal ball in the mirror. *2702 Main St., Santa Monica, tel. 310/392–8468. AE, DC, MC, V.*

Comedy Act Theater. Comedy by and for the black community. Recent performers have been *Hollywood Shuffles'* Robert Townsend and "Night Court's" Marcia Warfield. *3339 W. 43rd St., near Crenshaw, tel. 213/677–4101. No credit cards. Open Tues.–Sat.*

Excursion to Santa Catalina Island

When you approach Catalina Island through the typical early morning ocean fog, it's easy to wonder if perhaps there has been some mistake. What is a Mediterranean island doing 22 miles off the coast of California? Don't worry, you haven't left the Pacific—you've arrived at one of the Los Angeles area's most popular resorts.

Though lacking some of the sophistication of a European pleasure island, Catalina offers virtually unspoiled mountains and canyons, coves and beaches. It is Southern California without the freeways, a place to relax and play golf or tennis, go boating, hiking, diving, or fishing, or just lay on the beach. Avalon is the island's only "city," a charming old-fashioned beach community. Yachts are tied up in neat rows in the crescent-shape bay, palm trees rim the main street, and there are plenty of restaurants and shops to attract the attention of day-trippers out strolling in the sunshine.

Of course, life was not always this leisurely on Catalina. Discovered by Juan Rodriguez Cabrillo in 1542, the island has sheltered many dubious characters, from sun-worshiping Indians, Russian fur trappers (seeking sea-otter skins), slave traders, pirates, and gold miners, to filmmakers and movie stars. Avalon was named in 1888 after the island of Avalon in Tennyson's *Idylls of the King*. In 1919, William Wrigley, Jr., the chewing-gum magnate, purchased controlling interest in the company developing the island. Wrigley had the island's most famous landmark, the Casino, built in 1929, and he made Catalina the site of spring training for his Chicago Cubs baseball team. The Santa Catalina Island Conservancy, a nonprofit foundation, acquired about 86% of the island in 1974 to help preserve Catalina's natural resources.

A wide variety of tours offer samples of those resources, either by boat along the island's coast or by bus or van into Catalina's rugged interior country. Depending on which route you take, you can expect to see roving bands of buffalo, deer, goats, and boar or unusual species of sea life, including such oddities as electric perch, saltwater goldfish, and flying fish. The buffalo originally came to the island in 1924 for the filming of *The Vanishing American;* apparently, they liked it well enough to stay.

Although Catalina can certainly be done in a day, there are several inviting romantic hotels that promise to make it worth extending your stay for one or more nights. Between Memorial Day and Labor Day we strongly suggest you make reservations *before* heading out to the island. After Labor Day, rates drop dramatically and rooms are much easier to find.

Arriving and Departing

By Boat Boats to Catalina run from San Pedro and Long Beach. **Catalina Express** (tel. 310/519–1212) makes the hour-long run from Long Beach to Avalon; round-trip fare is $34 for adults, $25 for children 2–11. **Catalina Cruises** (tel. 800/888–5939) is a bit slower, taking two hours, and cheaper, charging about $27. Service is also available from Newport Beach through **Catalina Passenger Service** (tel. 714/673–5245), leaving from Balboa Pavilion. Catalina Express launches regularly scheduled service from San Pedro ($28 round-trip) and Long Beach ($32 round-trip). Advance reservations for all lines are recommended.

By Plane **Helitrans** (tel. 310/548–1314 or 800/262–1472) offers helicopter service from San Pedro's Catalina Island Terminal to Pebbly Beach, five minutes by van from Avalon. **Island Express** (tel. 213/491–5550) flies from San Pedro and Long Beach. The trip takes about 14 minutes and costs $57 one-way, $99 round-trip. Commuter air service is available from Long Beach Airport and John Wayne Orange County Airport to Catalina's Airport in the Sky. Call **Allied Air Charter** (tel. 310/510–1163) for schedules and fares.

Guided Tours

The major tour operators on the island are the **Santa Catalina Island Co.** (tel. 213/510–2000 or 800/428–2566). Tours include: inland motor tour, Skyline Drive, coastal cruise to Seal Rocks (summer only), the Flying Fish boat trip (evenings, summer only), casino tour, Avalon scenic tour, and the glass-bottom boat tour. Advance reservations are highly recommended for the first four tours; the other three are offered several times daily. Costs range from $4.50 for the casino tour (adults) to $17 for the four-hour inland motor tour; discounts are available for children under 12 years and senior citizens over 55. Catalina Adventure Tours also offers para-sailing, fishing, and diving options.

The Catalina Conservancy (tel. 310/510–1421) offers walks led by knowledgeable docents.

Exploring

Catalina Island is one of the very few places in the L.A. environs where walking is considered quite acceptable. In fact, you cannot bring a car onto the island or rent one once you get there. If you are determined to have a set of wheels, rent a bicycle or golf cart along Crescent Avenue as you walk in from the docks. To hike into the interior of the island you will need a permit, available free from the L.A. County Department of Parks and Recreation (Island Plaza, Avalon, tel. 310/510–0688).

The **Visitors Center** and the **Chamber of Commerce Visitors Bureau** are good places to get your bearings, check into special events, and plan your itinerary. The Visitors Center (tel. 310/510–2000) is located on the corner of Crescent Avenue and Catalina Avenue, across from the Green Pier; the Chamber's Visitors Bureau is on the pier.

Housed on the northwest point of Crescent Bay is the **Casino.** The round structure is an odd mixture of Spanish, Moorish, and Art Deco modern style, with Art Deco murals on the porch as you enter. In the Casino are an art gallery, museum, movie theater (tel. 310/510–0179), and ballroom. Guided tours are available.

The **Wrigley Memorial and Botanical Garden** is 2 miles south of Avalon via Avalon Canyon Road. Wrigley's family commissioned this monument to Wrigley, replete with grand staircase and Spanish mausoleum with Art Deco touches. Despite the fact that the mausoleum was never used by the Wrigleys, who are buried in Los Angeles, the structure is worth a look, and the view from the mausoleum is worth even more. The garden is small but exceptionally well planted. Tram service between the memorial and Avalon is available daily between 8 AM and 5 PM. There is a nominal entry fee of 50¢.

If modern architecture interests you, be sure to stop by the **Wolfe House** (124 Chimes Rd.). Built in 1928 by noted architect Rudolph Schindler, its terraced frame is carefully set into a steep site, affording extraordinary views. The house is a private residence, rarely open for public tours, but you can get a good view of it from the path below it and from the street.

El Rancho Escondido is a ranch in Catalina's interior, home to some of the country's finest Arabian horses. The ranch can be visited on the Inland motor tour *(see* Guided Tours, above).

Dining

American **The Sand Trap.** Omelets are the specialty at this local favorite
Inexpensive located on the way to Wrigley Botanical Garden. *Bird Park*
(under $10) *Rd., tel. 213/510–1349. No credit cards.*

Italian **Cafe Prego.** This restaurant features an intimate setting on the
Moderate ($10–$20) waterfront, several good pasta dishes, and a hearty minestrone. *603 Crescent Ave., tel. 310/510–1218. AE, MC, V. Dinner only.*

Inexpensive **Antonio's Pizzeria.** You'll find spirited atmosphere, decent piz-
(under $10) za, and appropriately messy Italian sandwiches. *2 locations: 230 Crescent Ave., tel. 310/510–0008, and 114 Sumner, tel. 213/510–0060. MC, V.*

Seafood **Pirrone's.** This restaurant has a bird's-eye view of the bay, and
Moderate ($10– $20) serves fresh seafood. *417 Crescent Ave., tel. 310/510–0333. MC, V. Open Mon.–Sat. for dinner and for Sun. brunch in winter, daily for lunch and dinner in summer.*

Lodging

Very Expensive
($190–$580)

Inn on Mt. Ada. The former Wrigley Mansion is now the island's most exclusive hotel. There are only six rooms, the views spectacular, the grounds superbly planted. *Box 2560, Avalon 90704, tel. 310/510–2030. 6 rooms. AE, MC, V.*

Moderate–Very
Expensive
($100–$325)

Glenmore Plaza Hotel. This striking Victorian hotel dating from 1891 has hosted the likes of Clark Gable, Teddy Roosevelt, and Amelia Earhart. Located near the beach, the hotel offers complimentary breakfast and suites with whirlpool or Jacuzzi. *120 Sumner Ave., Avalon 90704, tel. 310/510–0017. 50 rooms. AE, MC, V.*

Moderate–
Expensive
($85–$160)

Hotel Villa Portofino. This is a Mediterranean-style waterfront hotel with a sun deck, an art gallery, and an ambitious Italian restaurant. *111 Crescent Ave., Avalon 90704, tel. 310/510–0555. 34 rooms. AE, MC, V.*

Moderate
($70– $110)

Hotel Catalina. A renovated Victorian, half a block from the beach, the Catalina offers a choice of rooms and cottages. Extra touches include an attractive sun deck with Jacuzzi and free movies every afternoon. *129 Whittley Ave., Avalon 90704, tel. 310/510–0027. 32 rooms, 4 cottages. AE, MC, V.*

Zane Grey Pueblo Hotel. The former home of the famous American novelist, this hotel offers a stunning harbor view from its hilltop perch. Built in 1926 in Hopi Indian pueblo style, the Zane Grey offers such amenities as eccentric decor, a swimming pool, and a courtesy bus. No phones or TVs in rooms; no children allowed. *199 Chimes Tower Rd., Avalon 90704, tel. 213/510–0966. 18 rooms. AE, MC, V.*

Inexpensive
($44–$60)

Atwater Hotel. This family-oriented hotel is a half-block from the beach. *Box 737, Avalon 90704, tel. 310/510–1788. 84 rooms. AE, DC, MC, V.*

Excursion to Antelope Valley

The most memorable parts of a trip are often its surprises—the places and people you stumble onto when you least expect to. Antelope Valley, which makes up the western corner of the Mojave Desert, holds several unexpected pleasures. A sudden turn along a desert road reveals a riot of flaming orange poppies on acres of rolling hills nestled between barren rises and desolate flatlands. In the late summer and fall, after the flowers have faded, you can pick your own cherries, peaches, and pears at nearby orchards incongruously set in the desert. Head east and you can hike to the top of Saddleback Butte for a spectacular view of where the desert ends and the San Gabriel Mountains begin, their snow-capped peaks a beautiful contrast to the arid valley.

Another surprise is the valley's wildlife. No, don't look for the hoary antlers of the antelope that lent their name to the area. Once practically overrunning the region, the antelope went into decline with the arrival of the railroad in 1876. They apparently refused to cross the tracks that blocked the route to their traditional grazing grounds and many starved to death. A severe winter in the 1880s and the growth of ranching and farming in the early 1900s spelled the end for the few that had survived.

What you can see on an Antelope Valley safari are the eminently amusing and increasingly rare desert tortoises. Thanks to preservationists, a safe haven has been created for California's official state reptile. Visiting the tortoise in its natural habitat is a great opportunity for budding photographers—not noted for their speed, the tortoises make willing subjects. If birds are more your fancy, there is also a 40-acre wildlife sanctuary in the valley noted for its winged inhabitants.

Man, of course, has also made his mark in Antelope Valley. You'll find gold mines and historic railroad towns that still evoke the spirit of the Old West. Some $40 million in gold and silver has been taken out of the hills between Rosemond and Mojave since a Mr. Hamilton hit pay dirt on what is now called Tropico Hill in the 1890s. The Burton Mining Company believes there is still some gold to be found in Tropico and is today still excavating the same hill Hamilton made his fortune on.

Arriving and Departing

By Car Heading north from Los Angeles, I–5 will lead you to Highway 14, which runs north through Palmdale, Lancaster, Rosamond, and Mojave. It should take about 90 minutes to reach Palmdale and another hour between Palmdale and Mojave. To reach the Antelope Valley California Poppy Reserve, take the Avenue I exit in Lancaster off Highway 14 and head west about 10 miles. Rosemond and the Tropico Mine are just north of Lancaster on Highway 14. Take the Rosamond Boulevard exit and go west for 3 miles to Mojave-Tropico Road; turn north here and you will see the mine shortly. For the Desert Tortoise Natural Area, take Highway 14 about 4 miles past Mojave and then turn east on California City Boulevard through California City; turn left on Randsburg-Mojave Road and follow signs about 5 miles to the preserve. Take Avenue J (Rte. N5) east from Lancaster for about 19 miles to get to Saddleback Butte State Park. To reach the Devil's Punchbowl Natural Area Park and nearby Hamilton Preserve, take Highway 138 southwest from Palmdale; just past Pearblossom turn south on Route N6 (Longview Rd.) and go about 8 miles. On Highway 138, you can continue southeast along the San Gabriel Mountains, pick up I–15 south through Cajon Pass, and return to Los Angeles via I–10 heading west.

Exploring

You can't miss the **Antelope Valley California Poppy Reserve**— its orange glow with dots of purple lupine and yellow goldfields and fiddleneck can be seen long before you reach the reserve itself. The best time to visit is between March and May, peak flower time. There are four short (between a mile and 2 miles) walking trails leading through the fields, some reaching wonderful viewpoints. While there is a perfectly serviceable picnic area by the parking lot, a snack on the bench atop Kitanemuk Vista (an easy five-minute stroll up a well-marked trail) offers much finer scenery. Do take a few minutes to walk through the visitor center. The uniquely designed building is burrowed into a hill to keep the building cooler during the summer and warmer during the winter. You can pick up trail maps and other useful information. *Visitor Center open Mar.–May, daily 9–3. State Park day-use fee: $3 per car. For more information and schedules of guided tours, call the California Dept. of Parks and Recreation, tel. 805/942–0662.*

You will find the area's orchards along State Highway 138 in the communities of **Littlerock** and **Pearblossom,** and in **Leonia,** just to the southwest of Lancaster. Harvesting season starts in June. Contact the Lancaster Chamber of Commerce and Visitors Center (44335 Lowtree, Lancaster 93534, tel. 805/948–4518) for more information.

A short drive north of Lancaster to **Rosamond** will take you back a long way in years. Gold was first discovered in Tropico Hill in 1894 and Burton's Tropico Mine and Mill, hanging awkwardly against the hill, looks just as it did during the height of the gold rush. Unfortunately, the high cost of liability insurance put an end to mine tours and led to the closing of an informative museum, but you can still get a close look at the old buildings and let your imagination fill in the sights and sounds of a turn-of-the-century mining town.

The **Desert Tortoise Natural Area** is a good place in which to commune with nature. Cars must be left behind as you stroll through the preserve's peaceful and picturesque landscape. Be sure to do two things: look around and consider the fact that there isn't a sign of civilization to be seen; and breathe deeply, because you won't find air this fresh too often in and around Los Angeles or any urban center. The best time of the year for viewing the tortoises is generally March through June, but avoid the midafternoon. The tortoises sensibly stay cool during the heat of the day by retiring to their shallow burrows. Two warnings about the natural area: The road into the area is wide and flat, but not paved, so your car is bound to get a bit dusty; also, there is no water available at the preserve. The preserve is open land, there is no admission, and you may feel free to roam about whenever you like. For more information and to arrange guided tours, call the California City Recreation Department (tel. 619/373–4278).

East of Lancaster is **Saddleback Butte State Park,** a favorite among hikers and campers. A 2½-mile trail leads to the 3,651-foot summit of the butte the park is named for, which offers some grand views. Throughout the park there is a great deal of typical high-desert plant and animal life—stands of Joshua trees, desert tortoises, golden eagles, and many other species of reptiles, mammals, and birds. Near park headquarters is a picnic area with tables, stoves, and rest rooms. The Los Angeles County Department of Parks and Recreation (tel. 805/259–7721) offers a fact sheet on the various wildlife sanctuaries near the park. Information on camping at Saddleback Butte is available from the State Department of Parks (tel. 805/942–0662).

Farther south is another popular spot for hikers—**Devils Punchbowl Natural Area Park**. Once at the bottom of an ocean, and currently nestled between the active San Andreas and San Jacinto faults, the park offers a network of well-planned trails. The nearby **Hamilton Preserve** consists of 40 acres of pinyon-juniper woodland sheltering numerous bird species.

Antelope Valley is also home to **Edwards Air Force Base** and the **NASA Ames-Dryden Flight Research Facility** (off State Hwy. 14, northeast of Lancaster). Tours of the facility are available, with a film describing the history of flight test programs, a walk through a hangar, and a look at experimental aircraft. This is the place to see the space shuttle land. *Free tours weekdays 10:15 AM and 1:15 PM. Call ahead (tel. 805/258–3446), as the base is occasionally closed for security reasons.*

Dining

Antelope Valley is not known for its fine dining. There are several fast-food and very average roadside restaurants in Lancaster, Palmdale, and Mojave. You might be better off packing a gourmet picnic basket before you leave Los Angeles and dining alfresco at one of the many scenic spots you will come across throughout the valley.

13 Orange County

Sometime during the recessions of the 1970s, Middle America packed up its bags and moved west, settling comfortably in Orange County. Stretching between two major cities—Los Angeles and San Diego—Orange County is essentially one vast suburb. It is perhaps America's foremost suburb, a place where Mickey Mouse rules, the median home costs more than $200,000, and finding the right wave and beach volleyball action are daily concerns among the younger set. The county's affluence continues to attract an ever-growing number of exclusive shopping malls, new performing arts arenas, and luxurious oceanfront resorts—along with traffic jams, slow-growth initiatives, and an occasional metallic haze to the sky. Orange County is a proverbial land of contrasts: It is beach and city, conservative and hedonistic, old society and high technology. It is a region some travelers love and others love to hate, but when it comes to theme parks, shopping, and beach life, few places do it better than Orange County.

Served by convenient airports and only an hour's drive from Los Angeles, Orange County is both a destination on its own and a very popular excursion from Los Angeles.

Getting Around

By Plane Several airports are accessible to Orange County. **John Wayne Orange County Airport** (tel. 714/755–6500) is the county's main facility; it is 14 minutes from Anaheim and centrally located within the county. It is serviced by Alaska Airlines (tel. 800/426–0333); America West Airlines (tel. 800/AWA–WEST); American (tel. 800/433–7300); Delta (tel. 800/221–1212); TWA (tel. 800/221–2000); United (800/241–6522).

Los Angeles International Airport is only 35 miles from Anaheim and from **Ontario Airport,** 30 miles. LAX is still the destination of some nonstop transcontinental flights.

Long Beach Airport (tel. 213/421–8295) is another good choice for Orange County visits. It is about 20 minutes by coach from Anaheim. Airlines flying into Long Beach include America West, American Airlines, Delta, TWA, and United.

Airport Coach (tel. 800/772–5299 in CA or 800/491–3500 nationwide) services LAX to Anaheim, Long Beach, and Pasadena. Fare from the airport to Anaheim is $14 one-way, $20 round-trip.

Prime Time Airport Shuttle (tel. 213/558–1606 or 818/901–9901) offers door-to-door service to LAX, Burbank Airport, and San Pedro Harbor. The company's motto is "We're on time or you don't pay." The fare is $12 from Anaheim hotels to LAX. Children under 2 ride free.

SuperShuttle (tel. 213/338–1111) provides 24-hour door-to-door service from all the airports to all points in Orange County. Fare to the Disneyland district is $12 a person from any airport. Phone for other fares and reservations.

By Car Two major freeways, I–405 and I–5, run north and south through Orange County. Past Laguna they merge into I–5. Try to stay away from these during rush hours (7–9 AM and 4–6 PM) when they can slow for miles. Coming off I–405 is I–605, another major Orange County route. Highways 22, 55, and 91 go west to the ocean and east to the mountains: Take Highway 91 or Highway 22 to inland points (Buena Park, Anaheim) and take Highway 55 to Newport Beach.

Pacific Coast Highway (Highway 1) allows easy access to beach communities, and it is the most scenic route. It follows the entire Orange County coast, from Huntington Beach to San Clemente.

By Train Amtrak (800/USA–RAIL) has several stops in Orange County: Santa Ana, San Juan Capistrano, San Clemente, Anaheim, and Fullerton. There are six departures daily. A special motorcoach also takes people to Disneyland from the Fullerton station.

By Bus In Southern California, relying on public transportation is usually a mistake, unless you have plenty of time and patience. The **Los Angeles RTD** has limited service to Orange County. At the downtown Los Angeles terminal, on 6th Street, you can get the No. 460 to Anaheim; it goes to Knott's Berry Farm and Disneyland.

The **Orange County Transit Department** (tel. 714/636–7433) will take you virtually anywhere in the county, but, again, it will take time; OCTD buses go from Knott's Berry Farm and Disneyland to Huntington and Newport beaches. The No. 1 bus travels south along the coast.

Greyhound/Trailways (tel. 213/394–5433) as well has scheduled bus service to Orange County. For **Gray Line's** schedule and fare information, call 213/856–5900.

Pacific Coast (tel. 714/978–8855) provides transportation from Orange County hotels to the San Diego Zoo, Tijuana, the *Queen Mary/Spruce Goose*, and Knott's Berry Farm.

Scenic Drives Winding along the seaside edge of Orange County on the **Pacific Coast Highway** is an eye-opening experience. Here, surely, are the contradictions of Southern California revealed—the powerful, healing ocean vistas and the scars of commercial exploitation; the appealingly laid-back, simple beach life and the tacky bric-a-brac of the tourist trail. Oil rigs line the road from Long Beach south to Huntington Beach, suddenly giving way to pristine stretches of water and dramatic hillsides. Prototypical beach towns like Laguna Beach, Dana Point, and Corona del Mar serve as casual stopping points irregularly arrayed along the route. This is a classic coastline drive.

For a scenic mountain drive, try **Santiago Canyon Road,** which winds through the Cleveland National Forest in the Santa Ana Mountains. Tucked away in the mountains are Modjeska Canyon, Irvine Lake, and Silverado Canyon, of silver mining lore. The terrain is rugged and you hardly feel as if you are anywhere near urban civilization.

Guided Tours

General-Interest Tours **Gray Line** (tel. 213/856–5900) has all-day tours to Disneyland and Knott's Berry Farm, as well as a combination tour of Knott's and Movieland Wax Museum.

For those who want specialized sightseeing services for small-group or personal tours, **The Orange County Experience** (tel. 714/680–3556) has been showing groups around the county for many years. Owner Louis Reichman is the author of *The Orange County Experience.* Stories behind Disneyland, Knott's

Berry Farm, and some of Orange County's most interesting cities make up these insiders' tours. The Crystal Cathedral, Mission San Juan Capistrano, and many local beaches can be part of the tour. A special tour, "From Orange to Wine," visits the Callaway Winery in scenic Rainbow Gap via the old Butterfield Stage Route.

Boat Tours At the **Cannery** in Newport Beach, you can hop a boat and go for a brunch cruise around the harbor on Sundays. Cruises last two hours and depart at 10 AM and 1:30 PM. Champagne brunches cost $25 per person. For more information call 714/675–5777.

Catalina Passenger Service (tel. 714/673–5245) at the Balboa Pavilion offers a full selection of sightseeing tours and fishing excursions to Catalina and around Newport Harbor. The 45-minute narrated tour of Newport Harbor, at $5, is the least expensive. Whale-watching cruises (Dec.–Mar.) are especially enjoyable. Narrated by a speaker from the American Cetacean Society, the tours follow the migration pattern of the giant gray whales.

Hornblower Yachts (tel. 714/646–0155) offers a number of special sightseeing brunch cruises. Whale-watching brunches (Jan.–Apr.) are scheduled each Saturday and Sunday; special cruises take place on such holidays as Valentine's Day, Easter, Halloween, Thanksgiving, and Christmas.

Walking Tours If you want to walk in Orange County, you're going to have to drive somewhere first. For a respite from suburban sprawl and urban smog, the **Tucker Wildlife Preserve** in Modjeska Canyon (tel. 714/649–2760), 17 miles southeast of the city of Orange, is worth the effort. The preserve is a haven for more than 140 bird species, including seven varieties of hummingbird—bizarre creatures that are surprisingly amusing to watch.

Free walking tours of **Mission San Juan Capistrano** are offered every Sunday at 1 PM, whether the swallows are in town or not. The tours take in the ruins of the Great Stone Church, destroyed by an earthquake in 1812, the Serra Chapel, the Mission's courtyards and fountains, and other historical sights.

Shopping Tours Several shopping shuttles help visitors make their own shopping tours. Six days a week, **South Coast Plaza's Shuttle Service** (tel. 714/241–1700) furnishes free round-trip transportation from many coastal-area hotels to this ritzy shopping area. Santa Ana's **Main Place** (tel. 714/547–7800), a newly improved shopping center, offers several shuttles a day from Anaheim hotels. One-way fare is $2 adults and $1 children under 13. **The City Shopper** offers transportation to the Crystal Cathedral, the City Shopping Center in Orange, and local hotels for $1 one-way. Information is available at hotels.

Important Addresses and Numbers

Tourist Information The main source of tourist information is the **Anaheim Area Convention and Visitors Bureau,** located at the Anaheim Convention Center (800 West Katella Ave., 92802, tel. 714/999–8999). The **Guest Information Hot Line** (tel. 714/635–8900) offers information on entertainment, special events, and sightseeing tours in Orange County. This recording also describes amusement park hours and major attractions.

Other area chambers of commerce and visitors bureaus are generally open Monday–Friday 9–5 and will help with information. These include the following:

Buena Park Visitors Bureau (6280 Manchester Blvd., 90261, tel. 714/994–1511).

Newport Harbor Chamber of Commerce (1470 Jamboree Rd., 92660, tel. 714/644–8211).

Huntington Beach Chamber of Commerce (Seacliff Village, Suite 32, 2213 Main St., 92648, tel. 714/536–8888).

Laguna Beach Chamber of Commerce (357 Glenneyre, 92651, tel. 714/494–1018).

Dana Point Chamber of Commerce (Box 12, 92629, tel. 714/496–1555).

San Juan Capistrano Visitors Center (inside the mission, 31882 Camino Capistrano, tel. 714/493–1424), **San Juan Capistrano Visitors Bureau** (31682 El Camino Real, 92675, tel. 714/493–4700).

San Clemente Tourism Bureau (1100 N. El Camino Real, 92672, tel. 714/492–1131).

Emergencies Dial 911 for **police** and **ambulance** in an emergency.

Doctor Orange County is so spread out and comprises so many different communities that it is best to ask at your hotel for the closest emergency room. Here are a few: **Anaheim Memorial Hospital** (1111 W. La Palma, tel. 714/774–1450), **Western Medical Center** (1025 S. Anaheim Blvd., Anaheim, tel. 714/533–6220), **Hoag Memorial Hospital** (301 Newport Blvd., Newport Beach, tel. 714/645–8600), **South Coast Medical Center** (31872 Coast Hwy., South Laguna, tel. 714/499–1311).

Exploring Orange County

Residents have long battled the popular belief that Orange County's borders start and end at Disneyland. We take the more enlightened view that there are two sides to the county—the theme parks that dominate the inland area (of which Disneyland is certainly first and foremost), and the coastline. Our Exploring section is therefore divided in two.

As the county lacks any definitive center, day trips will typically be destination-oriented rather than open explorations. If you're traveling with children, you can easily devote several full days to the theme parks: a day or two for Disneyland, a day for Knott's Berry Farm, perhaps a day driving between some of the area's lesser-known attractions. To rent a sailboard or other water-sports paraphernalia, you'll have to head to the beach towns. For cultural fare, you'll need to drive to the Orange County Performing Arts Center. Only on the coastline is there any real wandering to be done. Beach days can be a mix of sunning, studying surf culture, and browsing the small shops native to the beach communities.

Inland Orange County

Numbers in the margin correspond with points of interest on the Orange County map.

Anaheim is indisputably the West's capital of family entertainment. With Disneyland, Knott's Berry Farm, and Movieland Wax Museum all nearby, there are as many rides and attractions, color and merriment, as anyone could want. The Anaheim Convention Center attracts almost as many conventions as Disneyland attracts children. For many visitors to Anaheim, a family trip to Disneyland may be an added attraction of an Anaheim meeting.

❶ Perhaps more than any other attraction in the world, **Disneyland,** the first Disney theme park, and the lasting physical evidence of Walt Disney's dream, is a symbol of the enduring child in all of us, a place of wonder and enchantment—also an exceptionally clean and imaginatively developed wonder. Decades ago, when the Yippies staged a small demonstration there, the papers reported that a woman stepped from behind a stroller to remind them that there were children present. There always are—plus many adults who find they can't help enjoying themselves.

Disney built the park in 1955, and new attractions are added every year. As a matter of fact, when Disneyland opened there were 18 major attractions, and now there are 60. An entire troupe of both new and older, more familiar characters, including the Gummi Bears, Chip and Dale, and Launchpad McQuak, found a home when **"Disney Afternoon Live at Disneyland"** arrived at the Magic Kingdom. These stage shows present mixed-media, live-action, and animation extravaganzas at the newly expanded and transformed Videopolis, Disneyland's large-scale entertainment area.

Also new in 1991 was the "Great American Celebration." This state fair-type celebration features hometown parades, autograph sessions with baseball greats, and garden dance parties. In the summer, new daytime entertainment is offered every year, as well as the evening's "Fantasy in the Sky" fireworks and the ever-popular Main Street Electrical Parade.

Set in the park's **Critter Country** area, **Splash Mountain** is the newest large-scale attraction, added in 1989. The highlight here is an eight-passenger flume ride inspired by the Disney film *Song Of The South.* The combination thrill-and-show ride features more than 100 of Disney's signature robotic characters, including Brer Fox, Brer Rabbit, and Brer Bear. At one point the flume drops 52 feet at 40 miles an hour; the longest, fastest flume ride anywhere, according to sources at Disney.

The adventure also features the largest animated prop ever. The showboat in the finale scene is 50 feet wide, 30 feet high, and carries 21 animated characters singing "Zip-A-Dee-Doo-Dah," which has, over the years, become somewhat of a Disney anthem.

Star Tours, also one of the newer attractions, opened in 1987, is based on the popular movie *Star Wars,* and is guided by the robots C3PO and R2D2. Developed by George Lucas and the Disney Imagineers, the robots take riders on a trip with them and find themselves in a battle between rebel and imperial forces. The ride uses very convincing flight simulator technology.

Along with the new additions, all of the old standbys in Disneyland are still going strong. Disney's idealized turn-of-the-century Main Street is what first greets visitors; through it are Tomorrowland, Frontierland, Fantasyland, New Orleans Square, Adventureland, and Critter Country.

Orange County

PACIFIC OCEAN

0   10 miles

0   15 km

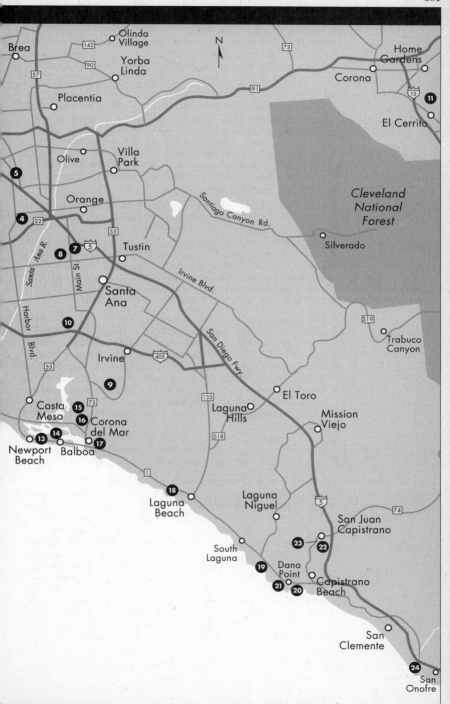

At the entrance, **Main Street, USA** has remained largely as it was built in 1955. Horse-drawn streetcars make their way down the colorful street, which is lined with the Main Street Cinema, the Penny Arcade, as well as snack shops and restaurants. This is also where you hop on the Disneyland Railroad, which tours the perimeter of the park and serves as transportation to New Orleans Square and Tomorrowland.

Tomorrowland is the site of Star Tours as well as the popular *Captain Eo*, the Michael Jackson 3-D movie directed by Francis Ford Coppola. Space Mountain is perhaps one of the scariest rides in the park; it is a high-speed journey into outer space. The Monorail, which was added to the park in 1959, is still transporting guests today, although Disney was, as usual, ahead of his time when he predicted this mode of transportation would be widely used.

Fantasyland is the favorite domain of kids: Pinocchio's Daring Journey takes the rider through this puppet's escapades. One exciting element of Peter Pan's Flight is a fly-through waterfall. And in Snow White's Scary Adventure unassuming logs turn into crocodiles. Dumbo the Flying Elephant, Mad Tea Party, and King Arthur Carousel are also part of this area. A three-dimensional ride depicting more than 500 singing children from 100 countries around the world, "It's a Small World," originally appeared at the 1964 New York World's Fair.

Frontierland takes visitors back to the Wild West. Big Thunder Mountain Railroad, one of the newer rides, is a runaway mine-car roller coaster. For a more relaxing ride, the Mark Twain and Columbia River vessels take passengers on an exploration of the river, complete with Tom Sawyer's Island. Big Thunder Ranch, set on nearly two acres, is a re-creation of an 1880s working horse ranch with a blacksmith shop, a harness-making shop, draft horses, and a petting barnyard with baby animals. A barbecue restaurant is also on hand, and serves guests from chuck wagons.

Time Out   **Blue Bayou,** featuring Creole food, is a great place to eat. It is located in the entrance to the Pirates of the Caribbean, so you can hear the antics in the background.

Adventureland's Jungle Cruise is an ever-popular water-based ride, with jungle sounds and realistic snapping crocodiles. New Orleans Square is the setting for The Pirates of the Caribbean, a swashbuckling adventure with cannonballs flying overhead to the accompaniment of a catchy pirate tune. **New Orleans Square** also has the elegant Crescent City with winding streets, quaint shops, and restaurants. **The Haunted Mansion,** populated by 999 ghosts and spirits, is one of the park's most popular attractions. *1313 Harbor Blvd., Anaheim, tel. 714/ 999–4565. Admission: $27.50 adults, $22.50 children 3–11; this allows entrance to all the rides and attractions. In summer, open Sun.–Fri. 9 AM–midnight, Sat. 9 AM–1 AM; in fall, winter, and spring, open Mon.–Fri. 10–6, weekends 9–midnight. Hours subject to change.*

❷ Knott's Berry Farm, another family tradition, is located in nearby Buena Park. Several decades ago, people used to come to a 10-acre fruit patch here for Mrs. Knott's home cooking and the re-created ghost town. Now Knott's is a 150-acre complex with more than 60 eating places, 60 shops, attractions. The recently opened Boomera with six loops—it moves slow to fast, giving that you're falling out. Recent addition Wild water... ness, set in a California river wilderness park of the early 1900s, has a raging white-water river, cascading waterfall, and geysers, landscaped with indigenous California trees. Bigfoot Rapids, a white-water rafting ride, incorporates the legend of Bigfoot; the ride itself is more than a third of a mile long. Floating rafts pass towering cliffs, race under waterfalls, and shoot the rapids. Bigfoot memorabilia—photos, footprints, etc.—are on hand in the "ranger's station."

Time Out   Don't forget what made Knott's famous, Mrs. Knott's fried chicken dinners and boysenberry pies at **Mrs. Knott's Chicken Dinner Restaurant,** just outside the park in Knott's Marketplace.

The other themed areas at Knott's include Camp Snoopy, a children's wonderland set in California's High Sierras; Ghost Town, an authentic 1880s Old West town; and Fiesta Village, a salute to California's Spanish heritage. Knott's is known for its daring thrill rides. "Montezooma's" Revenge accelerates from 0 to 55 mph in less than five seconds. The Corkscrew is the world's first upside-down roller coaster, featuring two 360-degree loops. And the Parachute Sky Jump falls 20 stories. *8039 Buena Park Blvd., Buena Park, tel. 714/220–5200. Admission: $21.95 adults, $15.95 children 3–11, senior citizens, expectant mothers, and disabled visitors. Open in summer, weekdays 10 AM–11 PM, Sat. 9 AM–midnight, Sun. 9 AM–midnight; in winter, weekdays 10 AM–6 PM, Sat. 10 AM–10 PM, Sun. 10 AM–7 PM. Times and prices subject to change.*

❸ Visitors will find 70 years of movie magic immortalized at **Movieland Wax Museum** in 240 wax sculptures of Hollywood's greatest stars. Realistic movie sets are the backdrop for such celebs as George Burns, Clint Eastwood, Mel Gibson, and Roger Moore. The Black Box is the newest attraction here; it takes visitors through scary scenes from *Alien, Halloween,* and *Altered States. 7711 Buena Park Blvd., one block north of Knott's, tel. 714/522–1155. Admission: $11.95 adults, $6.95 children. Open daily in summer 9 AM–10 PM; daily in winter 10 AM–8 PM.*

❹ Garden Grove, a community adjacent to Anaheim and Buena Park, is the site of one of the most impressive churches in the country, the **Crystal Cathedral.** The domain of television evangelist Robert Schuller, the glass edifice resembles a four-pointed star. More than 10,000 panes of glass cover the weblike steel truss to form translucent walls. The feeling as you enter is nothing less than mystical. A *Newsweek* writer called the building, designed by the renowned architect Philip Johnson, "the most spectacular religious edifice in the world." In addition to tours of the cathedral, two pageants are offered yearly—"The Glory of Christmas" and "The Glory of Easter." These dramas, which include live animals in the cast, flying angels, and other special effects, are seen by more than 200,000 people each year. *12141 Lewis St., Garden Grove, tel. 714/971–4013. Admission free. Usually open for self-guided tours Mon.–Sat. 9–3:30, Sun. 1:30–3:30. For reservations for the Easter and Christmas productions, call 714/54–GLORY.*

5 Several unique museums fill the inland area. The **Anaheim Museum,** which recently moved to the Carnegie Library Building, circa 1908, explores the prehistory and geology of the area as well as Anaheim's wine-producing story. *133 S. Anaheim Blvd., tel. 714/778–3301. Suggested admission: $1.50 adults, $1 senior citizens. Open Wed.–Fri. 10–4, Sat. noon–4. Closed Sun.*

6 The **Museum of World Wars and Military History** will fascinate history buffs. Included in the $2 million collection are military field equipment, armor, uniforms, posters, and armored vehicles. *7884 E. La Palma Ave. (at Beach Blvd.), Buena Park, tel. 714/952–1776. Admission: $1 adults. Open Mon.–Sat. 11–6, Sun. noon–6.*

7 The **Bowers Museum** presents cultural arts of the Americas, the Pacific Rim, and Africa. Each year it does exhibitions of international, national, and regional scope. Expansion and renovation due to be completed by mid-1992. *2002 N. Main St., Santa Ana, tel. 714/972–1900. Admission free. Open Tues.–Sat. 10–5, Sun. noon–5.*

8 Santa Ana, the county seat, is undergoing a dramatic restoration in its downtown area. Gleaming new government buildings meld with turn-of-the-century structures to give a sense of where the county came from and where it is going. The **Fiesta Marketplace** is a new downtown development that has been recognized as a grass-roots effort involving businessmen and government. The Spanish-style, four-block project brings life to one of the traditionally most successful Hispanic marketplaces in Southern California.

9 Known for its forward-looking concept of community planning, Irvine is also a center for higher education. The **University of California at Irvine** was established on land donated by the Irvine Company in the mid-1950s. The Bren Events Center, Fine Art Gallery on campus sponsors exhibitions of 20th-century art (free, Tues.–Sat. 10–5). Tree lovers will be enthralled by the campus; it's an arboretum with more than 11,000 trees from all over the world. *Take the San Diego Frwy. (I–405) to Jamboree Rd. Go west to Campus Dr. S.*

10 It is no small irony that the Costa Mesa/South Coast Metro area is known first for its posh shopping mall and then for its performing arts center. **South Coast Plaza** (3333 South Bristol St., Costa Mesa) attracts more than 20 million visitors a year, making it the busiest mall in southern California. This is Adventureland for the credit card set, built around attractions with names like Polo/Ralph Lauren, Charles Jourdan, Godiva Chocolates, and Courreges. The adjacent **Orange County Performing Arts Center,** (600 Town Center Dr., tel. 714/556–2787), is a world-class complex, hosting such notables as the Los Angeles Philharmonic, the Pacific Symphony and the New York Opera. *California Scenario,* a 1.6 acre sculpture garden designed by artist Isamu Noguchi, connects the arts center and the mall, completing this unusual union of art and upscale consumerism. Noguchi uses sandstone, running water, concrete, and native plants to evoke different aspects of the California environment.

Time Out For a quick, healthful meal during a South Coast Plaza visit, try **Forty Carats** on the lower level between Saks and Bullocks.

This spin-off of a restaurant in Bloomingdale's has a selection of tasty natural muffins, carrot and pumpkin among them.

After you have sightseen yourself to exhaustion, you might want to try the ultimate in the California spa experience at **(11) Glen Ivy Hot Springs.** Thirty-five miles east of Anaheim, the spa is a day-use-only resort. It features an Olympic-size mineral water pool, seven outdoor whirlpool baths, and a pool designed for tanning. The highlight is California's only European-style clay bath. Certified massage therapists are on duty. *Take Hwy. 91 east to I–15 south. Continue 8 mi to Temescal Canyon Rd. and exit. Make 2 immediate rights and take Glen Ivy Rd. to its end. Tel. 714/277–3529. Admission: $14.75 Sat., Sun., and holidays; $12.50 weekdays. Open daily 10–6.*

The Coast

To explore Orange County's coast you need four things: a car, the Pacific Coast Highway, comfortable walking shoes, and a fair supply of sun block. The highway serves as the main thoroughfare for all the beach towns along the coast. Small in scale, these communities are eminently walkable, so park the car to have a look about. We'll start our tour in the north and head south.

(12) You won't find surfers at the **Bolsa Chica Ecological Reserve,** but you may well encounter a great blue heron, light-footed clapper rail, or harlequin duck. Close to 200 different species of birds have been sighted at the 300-acre salt marsh located off the Pacific Coast Highway, between Warner Avenue and Golden West Street. On the first Saturday of each month, October through March, the Amigos de Bolsa Chica offer guided tours of the reserve. *Tel. 714/897–7003. Call for a schedule.*

A popular surfer hangout, **Huntington Beach** is practically a living museum of Southern California beach life. Each September, surfers from around the world converge on the city for its annual surfing competition. **The Huntington Pier,** the best place from which to observe the sporting and social scene, has been undergoing a major renovation and is scheduled to open in mid-1992. The face-lift also includes a new theater, restaurant, and shopping complex, called Pierside Pavilion, located across the Pacific Coast Highway from the pier.

Newport Beach is the county's bastion of high society. Yacht clubs and country clubs thrive and host one gala party after the next. The community got its start as a commercial shipping center, but now it has become one of the county's most popular recreation and shopping areas.

In this Beverly-Hills-by-the-sea community, boats are as vital as BMWs; nearly 10,000 of them bob gently on the swells in **(13) Newport Harbor.** During the Christmas season the boats are decorated with more lights than most homes, making for a lively, definitely showy, boat parade. In June, the annual Flight of the Snowbirds is held in the harbor. An exceptionally popular race featuring small, Snowbird-class boats, this regatta was first run in 1926.

The U-shaped harbor, with the mainland along one leg and Balboa Peninsula along the other, shelters eight small islands. The

⑭ most visited is **Balboa Island,** connected to the peninsula by a three-car ferry. You can drive directly to the island (via Jamboree, off the Pacific Coast Highway), but the ferry—one of the few remaining in the state—offers significantly more character. The **Victorian Balboa Pavilion** is the architectural jewel of the peninsula. Built in 1902 as a bath and boat house, the pavilion was a haven for the big band sound in the 1940s. Today it hosts boating facilities for harbor cruises, a sport-fishing fleet, whale-watching boats (December through February), and a restaurant. The Newport Pier is older still, dating to 1888.

Time Out | **Irvine Ranch Farmer's Market** in Fashion Island Shopping Center sells a vast array of fresh produce, deli fare, and any other exotic food that you can imagine. It is best to visit off-hours; the place is mobbed at lunchtime.

Near the pier is a section called the Fun Zone. It has a carnival feel with an old-fashioned Ferris wheel, arcades, and novelty concessions. And you can get a notorious Balboa Bar (chocolate-covered frozen banana) here without going to Balboa Island.

To get to the Balboa Peninsula, take Hwy. 55 (Newport Frwy.) southwest until it becomes Newport Blvd. At the end, bear left onto Balboa Blvd.

⑮ The **Newport Harbor Art Museum** is internationally known for its impressive collection of works by California artists. The emphasis is on contemporary art, and there are many changing exhibits. Snacks are available in the Sculpture Garden Cafe. *850 San Clemente Dr., tel. 714/759–1122. A donation is requested. Open Tues.–Sun. 10–5.*

⑯ **Fashion Island** is another Newport Beach signature venue. Atrium Court, a Mediterranean-style plaza, is especially popular with upscale shoppers. Splash and Flash, with trendy swimwear; Amen Wardy, with the most haughty of women's fashions; and Posh, a unique men's store, are just some of the entries. In the first-floor court, you can relax to the sounds of a a grand piano. A recent expansion and renovation has added several new stores. *On Newport Center Dr. between Jamboree and MacArthur Blvds., just off Pacific Coast Hwy.*

Just south of Newport Beach, **Corona del Mar** is a small jewel of a town with an exceptional beach. You can walk clear out onto the bay on a rough-and-tumble rock jetty. The town itself stretches only a few blocks along the Pacific Coast Highway, but some of the fanciest stores and ritziest restaurants in the **⑰** county are located here. **Sherman Library and Gardens,** a lush botanical garden and library specializing in Southwest flora and fauna, offers diversion from sun and sand. Colorful seasonal flowers adorn the grounds, and you can have pastries and coffee in the tea garden. *2647 E. Coast Hwy., Corona del Mar, tel. 714/673–2261. Admission: $2. Open daily 10:30–4.*

If Newport is a seaside Beverly Hills, Laguna Beach is the SoHo of the surf. Some 60 art galleries peacefully coexist with the endless volleyball games and parades of people on Main Beach. Local shops offer crafts and current fashion in addition to canvases and sculptures. In the true spirit of the '60s, when Timothy Leary and his hippie cronies used to hang out in Laguna's fast-food joints along Pacific Coast Highway, the artistic style here can best be described as anything goes. Expect to see placid dune and ocean watercolors as well as shocking neon colored works and out of the ordinary assemblages of found objects.

⑱ The **Laguna Beach Museum of Art** has two locations. In Laguna Beach (307 Cliff Dr., tel. 714/494–6531), right near Heisler Park, the museum offers exhibits of historical and contemporary American art. The smaller gallery near the Carousel Court at South Coast Plaza (tel. 714/662–3366) offers smaller scale exhibits in the same vein.

In front of the Pottery Barn on the Coast Highway is a bit of local nostalgia—a life-size statue of Eiler Larson, the town greeter. For years he stood at the edge of town saying hello and goodbye to visitors.

Laguna's many festivals are what give it a worldwide reputation in the arts community. During July and August, the Sawdust Festival and Art-a-Fair, the Festival of the Arts, and the **Pageant of the Masters** take place. The Pageant of the Masters (tel. 714/494–1147) is Laguna's most impressive event, a blending of life and art. Live models and carefully orchestrated backgrounds are arranged in striking mimicry of famous paintings. Participants must hold a perfectly still pose for the length of their stay on stage. It is an impressive effort, requiring hours of training and rehearsal by the 400 or so residents who volunteer each year.

Going to Laguna without exploring its beaches would be a shame. To get away from the hubbub of Main Beach, go north to Woods Cove, off the Coast Highway at Diamond Street; it's especially quiet during the week. Big rock formations hide lurking crabs. As you climb the steps to leave, you'll see a stunning English-style mansion. It was once the home of Bette Davis. At the end of almost every street in Laguna, there is another little cove with its own beach.

⑲ **The Ritz-Carlton, Laguna Niguel** is the classiest hotel for miles and has become a watering hole for the movers and shakers of Orange County. Gleaming marble and stunning antiques fill this posh hotel, and traditional English tea is served each afternoon to the strains of live piano music. *33533 Ritz Carlton Dr., Laguna Niguel, tel. 714/240–2000.*

⑳ Although it's been a popular port town for some 150 years, it's only recently that **Dana Point** has started to boom. New shops, restaurants, and hotels appear regularly. The town's main attraction is its harbor, set on a secluded cove surrounded by steep, jagged cliffs. Boats can be rented at Dana Wharf Sportsfishing (tel. 714/496–5794) for fishing or recreation. The beach here is quite good. In the summer, it's not unusual to see the adventurous parasailing above the sun worshipers; come winter, attention typically turns to whale watching (for information, call 714/496–5794). Mariners Village is the harbor's shopping area, a nautically themed, not terribly original, affair.

㉑ The **Orange County Marine Institute** is a unique educational facility that helps adults and children explore the ocean environment. A 65-foot diesel sportsfishing boat is a floating laboratory; hands-on opportunities allow you to study marine life. Anchored near the institute is *The Pilgrim*, a full-size replica of the square-rigged vessel on which sailed Richard Henry Dana, the author of *Two Years Before the Mast*, for whom the town is named. Tours of *The Pilgrim* are offered one Sunday each month. *Dana Point Harbor Dr. and Del Obispo, tel. 714/ 496–2274. Open daily 10 AM–10:30 PM.*

San Juan Capistrano is best known for its Mission, and, of course, for the swallows that migrate here each year from their winter haven in Argentina. The arrival of the birds on St. Joseph's Day, March 19, launches a week of celebration. After summering in the arches of the old stone church, the swallows head home on St. John's Day, October 23.

㉒ Founded in 1776 by Father Serra, **Mission San Juan Capistrano** was the major Roman Catholic outpost between Los Angeles and San Diego. Although the original Great Stone Church lies in ruins, the victim of an 1812 earthquake, many of the mission's adobe buildings have been restored, and the grounds are well kept. The impressive Serra Chapel is believed to be the oldest building still in use in California. The knowledgeable staff in the mission's visitors center can help you with a self-guided tour. *Camino Capistrano and Ortega Hwy., tel. 714/ 493–1111. Admission: $3 adults, $1.50 children 11 and under. Open daily 8:30 AM–5 PM.*

㉓ Near the mission is the postmodern **San Juan Capistrano Library,** built in 1983. Architect Michael Graves mixed classical design with the style of the mission for a striking effect. It has a courtyard with private places for reading as well as a running water fountain. *31495 El Camino Real, tel. 714/493–3984. Open Mon.–Thurs. 10–9, Fri.–Sat. 10–5.*

Time Out The **Capistrano Depot** (26701 Verdugo St., tel. 714/496–8181) is not only a train station for Amtrak but also a restaurant and jazz spot. White tablecloths, linen napkins, and flowers grace the restaurant, which specializes in rack of lamb, prime rib, and combinations of filet mignon and scampi for dinner. It's a perfect way to see San Juan if you are based in Los Angeles—a train ride, a meal, and then a little sightseeing.

The southernmost city in Orange County, San Clemente, is probably best remembered as the site of the Western White House during the Nixon years. Casa Pacifica made the news often in those years. The house, on a massive 25.4-acre estate, is visible from the beach; just look up to the cliffs.

More infamous—at least locally—than Nixon's house is the
㉔ **San Onofre Nuclear Power Plant,** a controversial installation lending an eerie feeling to the nearby beach, where surfers surf undaunted. Off the Coast Highway, the San Onofre Nuclear Information Center is a must for those who want to know more about the mechanics of nuclear energy.

San Clemente also offers a wide selection of activities that make Southern California the playground that it is: swimming, surfing, sailing, fishing, and picnicking. San Clemente State Beach is one of the least crowded and most beautiful of the state beaches.

In the summer, San Clemente is awhirl for nine days during La Christianita Pageant. The three-act play commemorates the first baptism of an Indian in California. (This may or may not be an event you feel needs honoring. Christianized Indians throughout the state died in very large numbers.) The pageant is presented in La Christianita Bowl, three miles from a wilderness clearing where it was first presented. Soldiers, priests, Indian rites, and singing make up the colorful production.

For avid bicycle riders, the next 20 miles south of San Clemente is prime terrain. Camp Pendleton welcomes cyclists to use its roads. But don't be surprised if you see a troop helicopter taking off right beside you. This is the country's largest Marine Corps base. Training involves off-shore landings; overland treks are also conducted on the installation's three mountain ranges, five lakes, and 250 miles of roads.

What to See and Do with Children

Disneyland and Knott's Berry Farm are the prime attractions *(see* Inland Orange County, above), but there are many other amusements designed for children and families.

Raging Waters is a water theme park sure to please the whole family. It's actually in southeast Los Angeles County, but not far from Anaheim. Clean beaches and river rapids (man-made), water slides, and safe water fun for the smallest of children are found here. *111 Via Verde, San Dimas, where I–10 and I–210 meet (take the Raging Waters Blvd. exit), tel. 714/592–6453. Admission: $15.95 adults, $8.95 children 42–48 inches, children under 42 inches free, reduced rates for senior citizens and nonsliders. Open May and June, weekends 10–6; the rest of the summer Mon.–Thurs. 10–9, weekends 9–10.*

Wild Rivers is Orange County's newest water theme park. It has more than 40 rides and attractions. Among them: a wave pool, several daring slides, a river inner-tube ride, and several places at which to eat and shop. *8800 Irvine Center Dr., Laguna Hills (just off I–405 at Irvine Center Dr.), tel. 714/768–WILD. Admission: $15.95 adults, $11.95 children 3–9, 2 and under free; discounts after 4 AM. Open mid-May–Sept. Call for hours.*

Golf-n-Stuff offers unusual family golfing fun. This miniature golf and arcade center is near Disneyland. Colored lights sparkle on geyser fountains amid windmills, castles, and waterfalls. *1656 S. Harbor Blvd., 714/994–2110. Admission: $5 children 6 to adult, 5 and under free. Special family rates. Open Sun.–Thurs. 10 AM–10 PM, Fri. and Sat. 10 AM–midnight.*

Hobby City Doll and Toy Museum houses antique dolls and toys from around the world in a replica of the White House. It is one of the world's largest hobby, crafts, and collector centers. *1238 S. Beach Blvd., Anaheim, tel. 714/527–2323. Open daily 10 AM–6 PM.*

La Habra Children's Museum features all kinds of diversions for children. The restored 1923 railroad depot has a beehive, railroad cars, and several touchable displays. *301 S. Euclid St., tel. 213/905–9793. Admission: Adults $2, children 2–16 and senior citizens, $1.50. Open Mon.–Sat. 10 AM–4 PM.*

Laguna Moulton Playhouse has a special children's theater with changing fare. *606 Laguna Canyon Rd., tel. 714/494–0743.*

Off the Beaten Track

If you find time to visit any of these spots during your trip to Orange County, you can term yourself local. These are some of the "in" spots that natives know well.

Lido Island. This beautiful island in Newport Harbor is the location of some of the most elegant homes in Orange County. It's an inviting spot for a walk and a great view of the boats. *Take Hwy. 55 to Pacific Coast Hwy. in Newport Beach. Turn left at the signal onto Via Lido and follow this street onto the island.*

Orange County Swapmeet. This is no ordinary flea market. With a huge collection of items at big discounts, it's truly a Southern Californian way to spend the day, enjoying some beer and hot dogs in the sun. There are more than 1,000 vendors every Saturday and Sunday. Good bargains to look for include stereo equipment, plants, and artwork. *Orange County Fairgrounds, 88 Fair Dr., Costa Mesa (off Hwy. 55), tel. 714/751–3247.*

C'est Si Bon. This little cafe resembles quaint sidewalk cafes in Paris. It offers the best selection of coffee and croissants anywhere around; there is also a great selection of cheeses and pâtés. *Riverside Ave., off Pacific Coast Hwy. in Newport Beach, tel. 714/645–0447. Open Mon.–Fri. 6:30–6, Sat. 8–5, Sun. 8:30 AM–1:30 PM.*

Shopping

Shopping is Orange County's favorite indoor sport, and the region has the facilities to prove it. Some of the most exclusive shopping areas in the world fill the Newport Beach area, and South Coast Plaza in Costa Mesa is the second-largest mall in the country. Following is just a small selection of the shopping available in the county.

South Coast Plaza (Bristol and Sunflower Sts.) 270 stores offer everything from tires to ball gowns. Saks Fifth Avenue, Nordstrom, Neiman Marcus, Bullocks, I. Magnin, May Company, Sears, the Broadway, and Robinson's are the department stores anchoring the mall. For literary buffs, there is a branch of the famous Rizzoli's International Bookstore.

Fashion Island on Newport Center Drive in Newport Beach sits on the top of a hill, so shoppers enjoy a distinct ocean breeze. It is an open-air, single-level mall of more than 120 stores. Don't miss the Irvine Ranch Farmers Market, on the first level of the Atrium Court. This awesome market is a high-quality specialty gourmet store, surrounded by international eateries—a salsa bar, Italian bakery, and gourmet chocolate stand to name a few.

The **City Shopping Center,** in Orange, is an enclosed mall enhanced with attractive landscaping. May Company and J.C. Penney are the department stores. **Buena Park Mall,** near Disneyland and Knott's, has more than 160 stores.

If you can look past the inflatable palm trees, unimaginative T-shirts and other tourist novelties, there is some good browsing to be done in Laguna Beach. This is Main Street USA shopping, with the sort of antiques dealers and craftsmen you won't find in a generic shopping mall. Dozens of art and custom jewelry shops dot the streets. There are more jewelers per capita in Laguna than in any other town in the country. Some of the more unusual Laguna stores include: **Chicken Little Emporium,** Coast Highway, with whimsical gifts and clothing; **From Laguna,** 241 Forest Avenue, for unique fashions; **Khyber Pass,** 384 Forest Avenue, with gifts from the Middle East and Afghanistan; and **Toni's Kids Closet,** Coast Highway, with designer children's clothing and handcrafted wooden toys.

Beaches

Huntington Beach State Beach runs for miles along Coast Highway (take Beach Blvd. if you are coming from inland). There are changing rooms, concessions, and lifeguard vigilance on the premises. **Bolsa Chica State Beach,** down the road and across from the Bolsa Chica Ecological Reserve, has facilities for barbecues and picnics.

Lower Newport Bay provides an enclave sheltered from the ocean. This area, off Coast Highway on Jamboree, is a 740-acre preserve for ducks and geese. **Newport Dunes Aquatic Park,** nearby, offers picnic facilities, changing rooms, and a place to launch boats.

Just south of Newport Beach, **Corona del Mar State Beach** has a tide pool and caves waiting to be explored. It also sports one of the best walks in the county—a beautiful rock pier jutting into the ocean.

The county's best place for scuba diving is in the **Marine Life Refuge,** which runs from Seal Rock to Diver's Cove in Laguna. Farther south, in South Laguna, **Aliso County Park** is a recreation area with a pier for fishing.

Doheny State Park, near the Dana Point Harbor, has food stands and shops nearby. Camping is permitted here; there are also picnic facilities and a pier for fishing. **San Clemente State Beach** is one of the least crowded. It has ample camping facilities and food stands. Boogie boards and small boats can be rented nearby as well.

Participant Sports

Orange County is a sportsperson's playground; from surfing to walking, from sailing to biking, there is something for everyone who wants to be active.

Bicycling Bicycles and roller skates are some of the most popular means of transportation along the beaches. Again, most beaches have rental stands. A bike path spans the whole distance from Marina del Rey all the way to San Diego, with some minor breaks. In Laguna, try the **Laguna Cyclery** (tel. 714/552–1798); in Huntington Beach, **Two Wheel Transit Authority** (tel. 714/536–8841).

Golf Golf is one of the most popular sports in Orange County, and owing to the climate, almost 365 days out of the year are perfect golf days. Here is a selection of golf courses:

Anaheim Hills Public Country Club (tel. 714/637–7311); **Costa Mesa Public Golf and Country Club** (tel. 714/540–7500); **Mile**

Square Golf Course, Fountain Valley (tel. 714/545–3726); **Mead-owlark Golf Course,** Huntington Beach (tel. 714/846–1364); **Rancho San Joaquin Golf Course,** Irvine (tel. 714/786–5522); **Costa del Sol Golf Course,** Mission Viejo (tel. 714/581–0940); **Newport Beach Golf Course** (tel. 714/852–8681); **San Clemente Municipal Golf Course** (tel. 714/361–8278); **San Juan Hills Country Club,** San Juan Capistrano (tel. 714/837–0361); **Aliso Creek Golf Course,** South Laguna (tel. 714/499–1919).

Snorkeling   Corona del Mar is off-limits to boats; this fact—along with its two colorful reefs—makes it a great place for snorkeling. Laguna Beach is also a good spot for snorkeling and diving; the whole beach area of this city is a marine preserve.

Surfing   Orange County's signature sport may be too rough-and-tumble for some; you can get the same feel with a boogie board. Rental stands are found at all beaches. Body surfing is also a good way to start. Huntington Beach is popular for surfers and spectators. "The Wedge" at Newport Beach is one of the most famous surfing spots in the world. Don't miss the spectacle of surfers, who look tiny in the middle of the waves, flying through this treacherous place. San Clemente surfers are usually positioned right across from the San Onofre Nuclear Reactor.

Swimming   All of the state, county, and city beaches in Orange County allow swimming. Make sure there is a manned lifeguard stand nearby and you are safe. Also keep on the lookout for posted signs about undertow as it can be mighty nasty in certain places.

Tennis   Most of the larger hotels have tennis courts. Here are some other choices; try the local Yellow Pages for further listings.

Huntington Beach   **Edison Community Center** (21377 Magnolia St., tel. 714/960–8870) has four courts available on a first-come, first-served basis, or reservations can be made. The **Murdy Community Center** (70000 Norma Dr., tel. 714/960–8895) requires reservations.

Laguna Beach   Eight metered courts can be found at **Laguna Beach High School,** on Park Avenue. On Monday, Wednesday, and Friday, courts are also available at the **Irvine Bowl,** Laguna Canyon Road.

Newport Beach   Call the recreation department at 714/644–3151 for information about court use at **Corona del Mar High School,** 2102 East Bluff Street. There are eight courts for public use.

San Clemente   There are four courts at **San Luis Rey Park,** on Avenue San Luis Rey. They are offered on a first-come, first-served basis. Call the recreation department at 714/361–8200 for further information.

Water Sports   Rental stands for surfboards, windsurfers, small power boats, and sailboats can almost always be found near most of the piers. Here are some of the more well-known rental places: **Hobie Sports** has three locations for surfboard and boogie board rentals—two in Dana Point (tel. 714/496–2366 or 714/496–1251) and one in Laguna (tel. 714/497–3304).

In the biggest boating town of all, Newport Beach, you can rent sailboats and small motorboats at **Balboa Boat Rentals** in the harbor (tel. 714/673–1320; open Fri.–Sun. 9 AM–sundown). Sailboats rent for $25 an hour, and motorboats for $26 an hour.

You must have a driver's license, and some knowledge of boating is helpful; rented boats are not allowed out of the bay.

In Dana Point, power and sailboats can be rented at **Embarcadero Marina** (tel. 714/496–6177), near the launching ramp at Dana Point Harbor. Boat sizes vary—sailboats range from $12 to $50 for two hours, motorboats are $17 an hour.

Spectator Sports

Orange County has some of the best, unplanned, casual spectator sports; besides the surfers, you are bound to catch a volleyball or basketball game at any beach on a weekend. Professional sports in Orange County include the following:

Baseball The **California Angels** (tel. 714/634–2000) play at the Anaheim Stadium from April through October.

Football The **Los Angeles Rams** (tel. 714/937–6767) have called Anaheim Stadium their home since 1980. The season runs from August through December.

Horse Racing The **Los Alamitos Race Course** (tel. 714/995–1234) has quarter horse racing and harness racing on a ⅝-mile track. Thoroughbred racing is part of the fare here as well.

Horse Shows Twice monthly at the **Orange County Fair Equestrian Center** (714/641–1328) show jumping is featured. Admission is free.

Dining

by Bruce David Colen

Orange County seems to prove that nothing improves the quality of restaurants quite so much as being in a high-rent district. Since the region became one of the most costly places to buy a home, the dining scene is vastly improved. Restaurant prices, however, are not as high as in the upscale communities of Los Angeles and San Francisco; perhaps high mortgage payments have made the natives dining-dollar wary. The growing number of luxury hotels, with dining rooms to match, has also broadened gastronomic choices. The French cuisine at Le Meridien, for example, in Newport, is the best of any California hotel. At each of these restaurants, it is safest to call ahead for reservations.

The most highly recommended restaurants are indicated by a star ★.

Category	Cost*
Very Expensive	over $40
Expensive	$30–$40
Moderate	$15–$30
Inexpensive	under $15

**per person, without tax (7%), service, or drinks*

Anaheim
Expensive

JW's. You would never guess you were in a hotel—the dining room looks like a French country inn, complete with a fireplace. The food is well prepared classic French, featuring roasted saddle of lamb, venison, and wild boar. *Marriott Hotel, 700 W. Convention Way, tel. 714/750–8000. Reservations re-*

quired. Jacket required. AE, DC, MC, V. Valet parking. Dinner only. Closed Sun.

Moderate **Bessie Wall's.** Citrus rancher John Wall built this house for his bride-to-be in 1927. It has been restored, and the rooms have been converted into dining areas decorated with Wall memorabilia. Bessie's favorite chicken-and-dumplings recipe is on the menu, which features Southern California–Mexican dishes. The place is nostalgic fun. *1074 N. Tustin Blvd., tel. 714/630–2812. Reservations advised. Jacket advised. AE, DC, MC, V. Closed Sat. lunch.*

Overland Stage. A dining Disneyland of sorts. The theme here is California in its Wild West days. There's a stagecoach over the entrance, and all sorts of Western bric-a-brac within. The daily specials are intriguing: wild boar, buffalo, rattlesnake, bear, and elk. *1855 S. Harbor Blvd., tel. 714/750–1811. Reservations advised. Jacket advised. AE, DC, MC, V. Closed for lunch weekends.*

Corona del Mar
Expensive **Trees.** The contemporary look, atmosphere, and menu of this upscale restaurant are among the most appealing in Orange County. The three dining rooms, with walls and table appointments done in shades of pink, surround a glassed-in atrium planted with towering ficus trees. Each room has its own fireplace. Satisfying cooking matches the setting: Maryland crab cakes, roast turkey dinners on Sunday; Chinese chicken salad, potstickers and spring rolls; veal sweetbreads in puff pastry. Don't pass up the apricot mousse dessert. There's also a piano bar. *440 Heliotrope Ave., tel. 714/673–0910. Reservations required. Jacket required. AE, DC, MC, V. Closed for lunch.*

Moderate
★ **The Five Crowns.** A surprisingly faithful replica of Ye Old Bell, England's oldest inn. The barmaids and waitresses are costumed in Elizabethan dress; there's a wide array of British ales and, of course, Guinness stout. The roast beef with Yorkshire pudding and the rack of lamb are very good, as are the fish dishes, all at reasonable prices. *3801 E. Pacific Coast Hwy. tel. 714/760–0331. Reservations required. Jacket advised. AE, DC, MC, V. Closed lunch; open for Sun. brunch.*

Costa Mesa
Moderate–Expensive **Alfredo's.** Northern Italian dishes served in an attractive, multi-level dining room, beneath a huge skylight. There's lots of cheerful greenery with service to match. Menu suggestions include mozzarella marinara, scampi sautéed with garlic and white wine, chicken and spinach cannelloni, and a fine seafood salad. Brunch is served on Sunday. *666 Anton Blvd., tel. 714/540–1550. Reservations advised. Jacket required. AE, DC, MC, V. Closed Sat. lunch and Sun. dinner.*

Inexpensive **Mandarin Gourmet.** Dollar for bite, owner Michael Chang provides what the critics and locals consider the best Chinese cuisine in the area. His specialties include: a crisp-yet-juicy Peking duck, cashew chicken, and seemingly everyone's favorite, mu-shu pork. Very good wine list. *1500 Adams Ave., tel. 714/540–1937. Reservations accepted. Dress: casual. AE, DC, MC, V.*

Dana Point
Expensive **Watercolors.** This light, cheerful dining room gives a clifftop view of the harbor and an equally enjoyable Continental/California menu, along with low-calorie choices. Try the baked breast of pheasant, roast rabbit, grilled swordfish, and either the Caesar or poached spinach salad. *Dana Point Resort, tel.*

714/661–5000. Reservations suggested. Dress: resort casual. AE, DC, MC, V. Valet parking.

Moderate **Chart House.** This is one of the most popular of the small chain of steak-and-seafood houses in Southern California. Mud pie is the dessert everyone asks for. This particular location has a sensational view of the harbor from most of the tables and booths. *34442 Green Lantern, tel. 714/493–1183. Reservations advised. Jacket advised. AE, DC, MC, V. Closed lunch; open for Sun. brunch.*

Delaney's Restaurant. Seafood from nearby San Diego's fishing fleet is what this place is all about. Your choice is prepared as simply as possible. If you have to wait for a table, pass the time at the clam and oyster bar. *25001 Dana Dr., tel. 714/496–6196. Reservations advised. Dress: casual. AE, DC, MC, V.*

Fullerton **The Cellar.** And it is just that, a subterranean dining room,
Expensive with beamed ceiling and stone walls, wine casks and racks. The
★ list of wines from Europe and California is among the best in the nation. The classic French cuisine is lightened for the California palate. *305 N. Harbor Blvd., tel. 714/525–5682. Reservations required. Jacket and tie advised. AE, DC, MC, V. Closed lunch and Sun. and Mon.*

Huntington Beach **MacArthur Park.** Modeled after the popular San Francisco res-
Moderate taurant, this casual eatery has a view of Huntington Harbor. Contemporary art hangs on brick walls. Standouts on the California menu are smoked filet mignon appetizers and sweet potatoes with tequila-and-lime sauce. *16390 Pacific Coast Hwy., tel. 714/846–5553. Weekend reservations advised. Jacket advised. AE, MC, V.*

Inexpensive **Texas Loosey's Chili Parlor & Saloon.** This place serves up Tex-Mex cooking with hot fixings, plus steaks, ribs, and burgers. Country-and-western music is played at night. *14160 Beach Blvd., tel. 714/898–9797. Dress: informal. MC, V.*

Irvine **Chanteclair.** This Franco-Italian country house is a lovely,
Moderate–Expensive tasteful retreat in an island of modern high-rise office buildings. French Riviera–type cuisine is served; Chateaubriand for two and rack of lamb are recommended. *18912 MacArthur Blvd., tel. 714/752–8001. Reservations advised. Jacket required. AE, DC, MC, V. Closed Sat. lunch; open for Sun. brunch.*

Moderate **Gulliver's.** Jolly old England is the theme of this groaning board. Waitresses are addressed as "wenches" and busboys as "squires." Prime rib is the specialty. *18482 MacArthur Blvd., tel. 714/833–8411. Reservations advised. Jacket advised. MC, V.*

Pavilion. Excellent Chinese food is offered in what resembles a formal eating hall in Chef Hu's native Taiwan. Specialties include steamed whole fish, ginger duck, and Hunan lamb. *14110 Culver Drive, 714/551–1688. Reservations advised. Dress: casual. AE, MC, V.*

Prego. A much larger version of the Beverly Hills Prego, this one is located in an attractive approximation of a Tuscan villa, with an outdoor patio. A favorite of Orange County's Yuppies, who rave about the watch-the-cooks-at-play open kitchen and the oak-burning pizza oven. Try the spit-roasted meats and chicken, or the charcoal-grilled fresh fish. Also try the California or Italian wines. *18420 Von Karman Ave., tel. 714/553–*

1333. Dress: casual. AE, MC, V. Valet parking. Closed for lunch weekends.

Laguna Beach
Expensive

The Ritz-Carlton. The Dining Room in this ocean-side resort hotel serves rather pretentious pseudo-nouvelle cuisine, but the lavish Sunday brunch, served in The Cafe, is considered the best in Southern California. Be sure to make reservations several days in advance and ask for a table on the terrace, overlooking the swimming pool. *33533 Ritz-Carlton Dr., Niguel, tel. 714/240–2000. Reservations required. Dress: casual but neat. AE, DC, MC, V.*

Moderate

Las Brisas. A longtime coastal favorite with a spectacular view of the rugged coastline from the clifftop terrace, wonderful margaritas, addictive guacamole, and nouvelle Mexican dishes. The first three compensate for the last. *361 Cliff Dr., tel. 714/ 497–5434. Reservations advised. Dress: casual. AE, DC, MC, V.*

Partners Bistro. Beveled glass, antiques, and lace curtains adorn this neighborhood hangout. Fresh fish and tournedos of beef are featured on the Continental menu. *448 S. Coast Hwy., tel. 714/497–4441. Reservations advised. Dress: casual. MC, V.*

The White House. Bing Crosby and Cecil B. DeMille dined at this local hangout. The broad American menu has everything from bagels and lox to Mexican favorites. There's also a salad bar, for while you're making up your mind. *340 S. Coast Hwy., tel. 714/494–8088. No reservations. Dress: casual. AE, DC, MC, V.*

Inexpensive

The Beach House. A Laguna tradition, the Beach House has a white-water view from every table. Fresh fish, lobster, and steamed clams are the drawing cards. *619 Sleepy Hollow La., tel. 714/494–9707. Reservations advised. Jacket advised. AE, MC, V.*

The Cottage. The menu is heavy on vegetarian dishes, and the price is right. Specialties include fresh fish, Victoria Beach scallops, and chicken Alfredo. *308 N. Pacific Coast Hwy., tel. 714/494–3023. Weekend reservations advised. Dress: casual. AE, MC, V.*

Tortilla Flats. This hacienda-style restaurant specializes in first-rate chile relleno, carne Tampiquena, soft-shell tacos, and beef or chicken fajitas. There's a wide selection of Mexican beers and tequilas. *1740 S. Coast Hwy., tel. 714/494–6588. Dinner reservations advised. Dress: casual. AE, MC, V. Sun. brunch.*

Newport Beach
Expensive

Antoine's. This lovely, candle-lit dining room is made for romance and quiet conversation. It serves the best French cuisine of any hotel in Southern California; the fare is nouvelle, but neither skimpy nor tricky. *4500 MacArthur Blvd., tel. 714/ 476–2001. Reservations advised. Jacket and tie required. Closed lunch; open for brunch Sun.* ★

★ **The Ritz.** One of the most comfortable Southern California restaurants—the bar area has red leather booths, etched glass mirrors, and polished brass trim. Don't pass up the smorgasbord appetizer, the roast Bavarian duck, or the rack of lamb from the spit. This is one of those rare places that please everyone. *880 Newport Center Dr., tel. 714/720–1800. Reservations advised. Jacket required. AE, DC, MC, V. Lunch Sat., closed Sun.*

★ **Pascal.** If it weren't in a shopping center, once inside this bright and cheerful bistro, you'd think you were dining in St-Tropez. One taste of Pascal Olhat's light Provençal cuisine, the best in Orange County, and you'd *swear* you were in the south of France. Try the sea bass with thyme, the rack of lamb, and the lemon tart. *1000 Bristol Street, tel. 714/752–0107. Reservations suggested. Jacket advised. AE, MC, V.*

Moderate **Le Biarritz.** Newport Beach natives have a deep affection for this restaurant, with its country French decor, hanging greenery, and skylit garden room. There's food to match the mood: a veal-and-pheasant pâté, seafood crepes, boned duckling and wild rice, sautéed pheasant with raspberries, and warm apple tart for dessert. *414 N. Newport Blvd., tel. 714/645–6700. Reservations advised. Dress: casual. AE, DC, MC, V. Closed Sun. lunch.*

Bubbles Balboa Club. This whimsical take-off on a 1930s nightclub has cigarette girls and canned music from the Big Band Era. While you're taking in the scene, order a steak or the grilled lamb chops. *111 Palm St., tel. 714/675–9093. Reservations advised. Dress: casual. AE, DC, MC, V.*

Cannery. The building was a cannery, and it has wonderful wharf-side views. The seafood entrees are good, and the sandwiches at lunch are satisfying, but the location and lazy atmosphere are the real draw. *3010 Lafayette Ave., tel. 714/675–5777. Reservations advised. Dress: casual. AE, DC, MC, V.*

Marrakesh. In a casbah setting straight out of a Bob Hope road movie, diners become part of the scene—you eat with your fingers while sitting on the floor or lolling on a hassock. Chicken *b'stilla*, rabbit couscous, and skewered pieces of marinated lamb are the best of the Moroccan dishes. It's what-the-heck fun. *1100 Pacific Coast Hwy., tel. 714/645–8384. Reservations advised. Dress: casual. AE, DC, MC, V. Closed lunch.*

Inexpensive **Crab Cooker.** If you don't mind waiting in line, this shanty of a place serves fresh fish grilled over mesquite at low-low prices. The clam chowder and cole slaw are good, too. *2200 Newport Blvd., tel. 714/673–0100. No reservations. Dress: casual. No credit cards.*

★ **El Torito Grill.** Southwestern cooking incorporating below-the-border specialties is the attraction here. The just-baked tortillas with a green pepper salsa, the turkey mole enchilada, and the blue-corn duck tamalitos are good choices. The bar serves 20 different tequila brands and hand-shaken margaritas. *951 Newport Center Dr., tel. 714/640–2875. Reservations advised. Dress: casual. AE, DC, MC, V.*

Orange **The Hobbit.** This is the place for a feast, if you can make reser-
Expensive vations two to three months in advance. The six- to eight-course French-Continental meal starts in the wine cellar at 7:30 and ends about three hours later. *2932 E. Chapman Ave., tel. 714/997–1972. Reservations required far in advance. Jacket and tie required. DC, MC, V. One seating only. Closed Mon.*

Moderate **La Brasserie.** It doesn't look like a typical brasserie, but the varied French cuisine fits the name over the door. One dining room in the multifloor house is done as an attractive, cozy library. There's also an inviting bar-lounge. *202 S. Main St., tel. 714/978–6161. Reservations advised. Dress: casual. AE, DC, MC, V. Closed Sat. lunch and Sun.*

San Clemente **Andreino's.** Pasta is the key word at this Italian restaurant dec-
Moderate orated with antiques, flowers, and lace curtains. *1925 S. El
Camino Real, tel. 714/492-9955. Reservations advised. Jacket
advised. AE, MC, V. Dinner only, Tues.-Sat.*
Carlos O'Malley. As the name hopes to suggest, here you will
find a mixture of Mexican and Irish cooking. You'll have more
fun with the latter: Finnegan's stew, Irish whiskey chicken,
and Irish pot roast with stuffed cabbage. *111 W. Palizada, tel.
714/498-6072. Dress: casual. AE, MC, V.*
Etienne's. Smack-dab in the center of town, this restaurant is
housed in a white stucco historical landmark. There is outdoor
seating in a terra-cotta patio with fountains. Indoors, the decor
is French château. Only fresh fish is served; chateaubriand,
frogs' legs, and other French favorites are on the menu, along
with flaming desserts. *215 S. El Camino Real, tel. 714/492-
7263. Reservations advised. Jacket advised. AE, DC, MC, V.
Dinner only. Closed Sun.*

San Juan **El Adobe.** President Nixon memorabilia fills the walls in this
Capistrano Early American–style eatery serving Mexican-American food.
Moderate Mariachi bands play Wednesday–Sunday. *31891 Camino Capistrano, tel. 714/830-8620. AE, MC, V.*
L'Hirondelle. There are only 12 tables at this charming French
inn. Duckling is the specialty, prepared three different ways.
*31631 Camino Capistrano, tel. 714/661-0425. Reservations
necessary. MC, V. Dinner and Sun. brunch. Closed Mon. and
Tues.*

Inexpensive **Swallow Inn.** The food is Mexican, but the atmosphere is American West, complete with sawdust on the floor. Live entertainment Tuesday–Sunday. *31786 Camino Capistrano, tel. 714/
493-3188. No credit cards.*

Santa Ana **Saddleback Inn.** The decor here takes Orange County back in
Inexpensive time to hacienda days, blending Old Spain and Mission California. Slow-cooked barbecued roast beef is the house specialty;
filet of sole amandine, barbecued baked chicken, and filet mignon with bordelaise sauce are other possibilities. *1660 E. 1st
St., tel. 714/835-3311. AE, V. Closed Sun. lunch.*

Lodging

Like cuisine, hotels have also come a long way in Orange County. Sophistication seems to grow with each new hotel opening.
The beaches are the most expensive for lodging; family areas,
like Anaheim, are full of more inexpensive, simpler motels,
which are too numerous to list. Categories here are based on
prices for summer; winter rates tend to be lower. Be sure to ask
about discounted promotional and weekend rates, which can be
as much as 50% below standard "rack" rates.

The most highly recommended lodgings in each price category
are indicated by a star ★.

Category	Cost*
Very Expensive	over $110
Expensive	$80–$110

Moderate	$60–$80
Inexpensive	under $60

for a double room

Anaheim
Very Expensive
★

Anaheim Hilton and Towers. This hotel is one of the largest on the West Coast. It is truly a city unto itself complete with its own post office. The lobby is dominated by a bright, airy atrium, and rooms are decorated in pinks and greens with lightwood furniture. *777 Convention Way, 92702, tel. 714/750–4321 or 800/445–8667. 1,600 rooms. Facilities: 4 restaurants, several lounges and shops, outdoor pool, fitness center, sun deck, concierge. AE, DC, MC, V.*

Anaheim Marriott. With outstanding meeting facilities, this hotel caters to convention attendees. A total renovation was recently completed; sunlight streaming in from the huge windows fill the expanded lobby's gleaming marble. Rooms, decorated with pastels, have balconies. *700 W. Convention Way, 92802, tel. 714/750–8000. 1,039 rooms. Facilities: gift shops, beauty salon, 2 heated swimming pools, Jacuzzi, weight rooms, video games, 2 restaurants, lounge, and entertainment. AE, DC, MC, V.*

Disneyland Hotel. Always bustling with activity, this hotel is connected to Disneyland by monorail. It encompasses a 60-acre resort that carries on the fun atmosphere of its neighbor. The biggest refurbishment in the hotel's 35-year history was completed in 1991. New towers and tropical village make for unique accommodations; rooms, decorated in contemporary colors, all have balconies with views of Disneyland or the hotel marina. *1150 W. Cerritos Ave., 92802, tel. 714/778–6600 or 800/MICK-EY–1. 1,132 rooms. Facilities: waterfront bazaar with wares from all over the world, tennis courts, pool, marina with playland and pedalboats, 6 restaurants, 5 lounges. AE, DC, MC, V.*

Pan Pacific Anaheim. This hotel is geared toward the business traveler. Its distinctive atrium lobby has glass-enclosed elevators. Contemporary graphics fill the rooms. Nonsmoking rooms are available. *1717 S. West St., 92802, tel. 714/999–0990 or 800/821–8976. 502 rooms. Facilities: 2 restaurants, pool, sun deck, and Jacuzzi. AE, DC, MC, V.*

Expensive

Anaheim Holiday Inn. Large glass chandeliers greet the visitor to this establishment one block south of Disneyland. *1850 S. Harbor Blvd., 92802, tel. 714/750–2801. 312 rooms. Facilities: heated pool, sauna, suites, dining room, lounge, and coffee shop. AE, DC, MC, V.*

Anaheim Plaza Resort. Soft pastels and plants fill the lobby of this hotel near Disneyland. Wheelchair units and suites are available. *1700 S. Harbor Blvd., 92602, tel. 714/772–5900 or 800/228–9000. 300 rooms. Facilities: heated pool, restaurant. AE, DC, MC, V.*

Grand Hotel. Lobby and rooms are decorated in a pleasant plum–teal green combination. This property is adjacent to Disneyland and offers a free shuttle. Each room in the nine-story high rise has a balcony. *7 Freedman Way, 92802, tel. 714/772–7777. 242 rooms. Facilities: pool, gift shop, dining room, coffee shop, the Grand Dinner Theater. AE, DC, MC, V.*

Inn at the Park. Mountains of all kinds can be seen from private balconies—the man-made Matterhorn at Disneyland and the Santa Ana Mountains. *1855 S. Harbor Blvd., 92802, tel. 714/*

*750–1811. 500 rooms. Facilities: heated pool, exercise room,
suites, restaurant, coffee shop, lounge with entertainment.
AE, DC, MC, V.*

Sheraton-Anaheim Motor Hotel. This Tudor-style hotel offers a
free shuttle to Disneyland. *1015 W. Ball Rd., 92802, tel. 714/
778–1700 or 800/325–3535. 500 rooms. Facilities: dining room,
coffee shop, deli, heated pool, suites, game room, and bar.
Wheelchair units. AE, DC, MC, V.*

Moderate **Quality Hotel and Conference Center.** A large, open, red-tile
lobby is filled with mirrors, plants, and flowers; rooms are decorated in greens and yellows. The hotel is close to Disneyland.
*616 Convention Way, 92802, tel. 714/750–3131. 284 rooms. Fa-
cilities: suites, heated pool, gift shop, bar, 2 restaurants, game
room, beauty parlor. AE, DC, MC, V.*

Ramada Hotel Maingate. A clean, reliable, new member of the
worldwide chain. Located across the street from Disneyland,
with free shuttle service to the park. *1460 S. Harbor Blvd.,
92802, tel. 714/772–6777. 467 rooms. Facilities: pool, restaurant. AE, MC, V.*

Inexpensive **Hampton Inn.** Basic lodging at a basic price. *300 E. Katella
Way, 92802, tel. 714/772–8713. 136 rooms. Facilities: pool, cable TV. AE, MC, V.*

Buena Park **Buena Park Hotel and Convention Center.** A spiral staircase
Expensive leading to the mezzanine centers a lobby of marble, brass, and
glass. Sleeping rooms are done in blues, greens, and peaches.
*7675 Crescent Ave., 90620, tel. 714/995–1111. 328 rooms. Facil-
ities: heated pool, dining rooms, lounge, coffee shop. AE, DC,
MC, V.*

Costa Mesa **Westin South Coast Plaza.** The lobby lounge dominates a sunk-
Very Expensive en lobby here; rooms are all decorated in a different style. This
is the perfect hotel for die-hard shoppers, who only have to
cross the street to get to South Coast Plaza, one of the poshest
shopping centers in the country. Special weekend rates are
available. *666 Anton Blvd., 92626, tel. 714/540–2500. 400
rooms. Facilities: volleyball, shuffleboard, tennis courts, 2
restaurants, 3 bars, live entertainment, gift shop. AE, DC,
MC, V.*

Dana Point **Dana Point Resort.** This resort, built in 1988, brings Cape Cod
Very Expensive to Southern California in pleasant shades of sea-foam green
★ and peach. The lobby is filled with large palm trees and original
artwork. It is casual yet elegant; every room has an ocean view.
Several package deals include assorted land and water recreational possibilities. *25135 Park Lantern Ave., 92629, tel. 714/
661–5000. 350 rooms. Facilities: 2 pools, 3 spas, health club,
restaurant, and lounge. AE, DC, MC, V.*

Expensive **Marina Best Western.** Set right in the marina, this hotel is accessible to many restaurants and shops. All rooms have balconies and vary in size from a basic room to a family suite with
kitchen and fireplace. *24800 Dana Point Dr., 92629, tel. 714/
496–1203. 135 rooms. Facilities: pool. AE, DC, MC, V.*

Huntington Beach **The Waterfront Hilton.** This new oceanfront hotel rises 12 stor-
Very Expensive ies above the surf. The Mediterranean-style resort is decorated
in soft mauves, beiges, and greens and offers a panoramic
ocean view from each guest room. *21100 Pacific Coast Hwy.,
92648, tel. 714/960-SURF or 800/HILTONS. 300 rooms. Facilities: concierge level, 2 restaurants, lounge, tennis courts, pool*

and Jacuzzi, car-rental desk, boutique, gift shop. AE, DC, MC, V.

Expensive **Best Western Huntington Beach Inn.** This inn, decorated in light green and mauve, is right across from the ocean. *21112 Pacific Coast Hwy., 92648, tel. 714/536–1421. 94 rooms. Facilities: restaurant, pool, coffee shop, lounge, gift shop, 3-par golf course. AE, DC, MC, V.*

Moderate **Huntington Shore Motor Hotel.** Also across from the ocean,
★ some rooms at this small hotel have ocean views. The cozy lobby is set off with a fireplace. The extra-large rooms are decorated in earth tones. Complimentary Continental breakfast is offered. *21002 Pacific Coast Hwy., 92648, tel. 714/536–8861. 50 rooms. Facilities: heated pool. AE, MC, V.*

Irvine **Hyatt Regency Irvine.** This beautiful hotel has all the amenities
Very Expensive of a first-class resort. It is elegantly decorated in pale earth tones; the marble lobby is flanked by glass-enclosed elevators. Weekend rates are a great deal. *17900 Jamboree Rd., 92714, tel. 714/863–3111. 536 rooms. Facilities: pool, Jacuzzi, tennis, workout room, entertainment, 2 restaurants, 2 cocktail lounges, concierge. AE, DC, MC, V.*

Irvine Marriott. Peach and teal fill this contemporary hotel, and flower arrangements beautify the lobby. *1800 Von Karman, 92715, tel. 714/553–0100. 502 rooms. Facilities: restaurant, indoor-outdoor pool, tennis courts, sports-oriented bar, massage room, concierge floors, American Airlines and Hertz Rent-a-Car desks. AE, DC, MC, V.*

Moderate **Airporter Inn Hotel.** To cater to businesspeople, all rooms here have a work area and are decorated in earth tones. One deluxe suite even has its own private pool. *18700 MacArthur Blvd., 92715, tel. 714/833–2770. 213 rooms. Facilities: Heated pool, dining room, coffee shop, cocktail lounge, suites. AE, DC, MC, V.*

Laguna Beach **Inn at Laguna.** This Southwest-style inn has recently been ren-
Very Expensive ovated and enlarged. It's got one of the best locations in town—
★ close to Main Beach and Las Brisas restaurant and bar, one of Laguna's most popular watering holes, yet far enough away to be secluded. The inn is decorated in peacock blue and peach and overlooks the ocean from a high bluff. *211 No. Coast Hwy., 92651, tel. 714/497–9722. 70 rooms, Facilities: VCRs in the rooms, heated pool, Jacuzzi, complimentary Continental breakfast in the rooms. AE, DC, MC, V.*

Surf and Sand Hotel. The largest hotel in Laguna, the Surf and Sand is right on the beach. Newly done rooms sport soft sand colors and wooden shutters; they feature private balconies and honor bars. *15555 S. Coast Hwy., 92651, tel. 714/497–4477. 157 rooms. Facilities: private beach, pool, lounge, concierge, 2 restaurants, entertainment, gift shop. AE, DC, MC, V.*

Expensive– **The Carriage House.** This New Orleans–style bed-and-break-
Very Expensive fast is surrounded by a lush garden. Complimentary family-style breakfast is offered daily. Fresh fruit and wine gifts welcome guests. *1322 Catalina St., 92651, tel. 714/494–8945. 6 suites. No credit cards. 2-night minimum on weekends.*

Expensive **Eiler's Inn.** A light-filled atrium centers this newly remodeled B&B. All rooms are unique and decorated with antiques. Outdoor breakfast is served; in the afternoon there's wine and cheese, often to the accompaniment of live music. With only 12 rooms, you'll need to book well in advance. *741 S. Coast Hwy., 92651, tel. 714/494–3004. 12 rooms. AE, MC, V.*

Hotel Laguna. This downtown landmark, the oldest hotel in Laguna, was totally redone recently. Lobby windows look out on manicured gardens, and a patio restaurant overlooks the ocean. *425 S. Coast Hwy., 92651, tel. 714/494–1151. 65 rooms. Facilities: 2 restaurants, private beach, lounge, entertainment. AE, DC, MC, V.*

Laguna Niguel
Very Expensive
★

The Ritz-Carlton, Laguna Niguel. One of the only Mobil five-star and AAA five-diamond hotels in California, this has become *the* place for the county's haute society. The Mediterranean architecture and extensive landscaping make it feel like an Italian country villa. *33533 Ritz Carlton Dr., 92677, tel. 714/240–2000. 393 rooms. Facilities: beach access, health club, tennis courts, 2 pools, 3 restaurants, 3 lounges and a club with entertainment, concierge. Adjacent to an ocean-view 18-hole golf course. AE, DC, MC, V.*

Newport Beach
Very Expensive
★

Four Seasons Hotel. This hotel lives up to the quality of its fellow chain members. Marble and antiques fill the airy lobby; all rooms—decorated with beiges, peaches, and other southwestern tones—have spectacular views. *690 Newport Dr., 92660, tel. 714/759–0808. 285 rooms. Facilities: pool, whirlpool, lighted tennis courts, health club, 2 restaurants, lounge, concierge. AE, DC, MC, V.*

Hotel Meridien Newport Beach. An eye-catching cantilevered design is the trademark of this ultramodern hotel in Koll Center. Decor is Southern Californian with striking pastels. Special weekend rates are available. *4500 MacArthur Blvd., 92660, tel. 714/476–2001. 435 rooms. Facilities: restaurant, cafe, lounge, health club with Jacuzzi, pool, tennis courts, complimentary bicycles, concierge. AE, DC, MC, V.*

Expensive

The Hyatt Newporter Resort. Terra-cotta reigns supreme at this recently redecorated and expanded resort. Upper Newport Bay is an added attraction for soothing walks or invigorating runs. Guests have access to the John Wayne Tennis Club right next door. *1107 Jamboree Rd., 92660, tel. 714/644–1700. 410 rooms. Facilities: par-3, 9-hole golf course, jogging paths, exercise room, 3 pools, 2 restaurants, lounge, entertainment, concierge. AE, DC, MC, V.*

Marriott Hotel and Tennis Club. Arriving guests' first view of the hotel's interior is the distinctive fountain surrounded by a high, plant-filled atrium. Location is directly across the street from Fashion Island shopping center. *900 Newport Center Dr., 92660, tel. 714/640–4000 or 800/228–9290. 600 rooms. Facilities: pools, adjacent golf course, tennis courts, Jacuzzi, 2 restaurants, lounge, entertainment. AE, DC, MC, V.*

Sheraton Newport Beach. Bamboos and palms decorate the lobby in this Southern California beach–style hotel. Vibrant teals, mauves, and peaches make up the color scheme. Complimentary morning paper, buffet breakfast, and cocktail parties are offered daily. *4545 MacArthur Blvd., 92660, tel. 714/833–0570. 358 rooms. Facilities: pool, Jacuzzi, tennis courts, restaurant, lounge, entertainment. AE, DC, MC, V.*

Orange
Very Expensive

Doubletree Inn. This hotel has a dramatic lobby of marble and granite with silent waterfalls cascading down the walls. The oversize guest rooms come equipped with a small conference table. Location is near the popular shopping center called The City. *100 The City Dr., 92668, tel. 714/634–4500. 450 rooms.*

Facilities: 2 concierge floors, 2 restaurants, bar, heated pool, 2 tennis courts, spa. AE, DC, MC, V.

Inexpensive **Best Western El Camino.** This motel is close to Knott's Berry Farm and Disneyland. The large lobby is comfortably decorated with overstuffed sofas. Complimentary Continental breakfast is offered. *3191 N. Tustin Ave., 92665, tel. 714/998-0360. 56 rooms. Facilities: heated pool. AE, DC, MC, V.*

San Clemente **San Clemente Inn.** Located in the secluded southern part of San
Expensive Clemente, this inn is adjacent to the state beach. Refurbished each year in soft earth tones, all the condo units are equipped with bars and kitchens. *2600 Avenida del Presidente, 92672, tel. 714/492-6103. 96 units. Facilities: large pool, tennis, exercise equipment, restaurant. MC, V.*

Moderate **Ramada San Clemente.** This four-year-old Mission-style hotel is beautifully set on a lush hillside. The lobby has a dramatic vaulted ceiling. A private patio or balcony is part of each room. *35 Calle de Industrias, 92672, tel. 714/498-8800. 110 rooms. Facilities: pool, restaurant with American cuisine, lounge, cable TV, HBO in rooms. AE, DC, MC, V.*

San Juan **Country Bay Inn.** Built in the 1930s, all the rooms here are dec-
Capistrano orated with antiques of brass, wood, and rattan. The rooms in
Moderate this cozy inn also all have a wood-burning fireplace. It is right
★ across from the beach, and some rooms have balconies or patios. Continental breakfast is complimentary; champagne is served on arrival during the weekend. *34862 Pacific Coast Hwy., 92624, tel. 714/496-6656. 28 rooms. Facilities: Jacuzzi. AE, MC, V.*

The Arts

The biggest draw on the arts scene is the **Orange County Performing Arts Center** (600 Town Center Dr., tel. 714/556–ARTS) in Costa Mesa. Among the groups that perform here are the American Ballet Theatre and the New York City Ballet, the Opera Pacific, and symphony orchestras from around the country.

Concerts The **Irvine Meadows Amphitheater** (8800 Irvine Center Dr., tel. 714/855–4515) is an open-air structure offering musical events from May through October.
Anaheim Stadium (2000 State College Blvd., tel. 714/254–3000) hosts a variety of musical events throughout the year.
The **Pacific Amphitheater** (Orange County Fairgrounds, Costa Mesa, tel. 714/634–1300) offers musical entertainment and stages plays from April through October.

Theater **South Coast Repertory Theater** (655 Town Center Dr., tel. 714/957–4033), near the Orange County Performing Arts Center in Costa Mesa, has been a tradition in the county for the last 24 years. Twelve productions are offered each year on two different stages. A resident group of actors forms the nucleus for this facility's innovative productions.
La Mirada Theater for the Performing Arts (14900 La Mirada Blvd., tel. 714/994–6150) presents a wide selection of Broadway shows, concerts, and film series.
Muckenthaler Cultural Center (1201 W. Malvern Ave., tel. 714/738–6595) often presents cabaret theater. Located in a beautiful Spanish house, the center was a gift to the city of Fullerton by the Muckenthaler family.

Nightlife

Bars **The Cannery** (3010 Layfayette Ave., tel.714/721–0100) and the **Warehouse** (3450 Via Osporo, tel. 714/673–4700) are two crowded Newport Beach bars. The **Studio Cafe** (100 Main St., on the Balboa Peninsula, tel. 714/675–7760) presents jazz musicians every night.

In Laguna Beach, the **Sandpiper** (1183 Coast Hwy., tel. 714/494–4694) is a tiny dancing joint that attracts an eclectic crowd. And **Laguna's White House** (340 Coast Hwy., tel. 714/494–8088) has nightly entertainment that runs the gamut from rock to motown, reggae to pop.

Comedy **The Improvisation** (4255 Campus Dr., Irvine, tel. 714/854–5455) is probably the funniest place in the county. From well known to lesser known, comedians try out their acts nightly.

Country **Bandstand** (1721 S. Manchester, Anaheim, tel. 714/956–1410) offers live country music Sunday, Tuesday, and Thursday. On Friday and Saturday Top 40s are featured with a DJ, and hard rock is offered on Wednesday. Six dance floors and four bars are part of the complex.

Dinner Theater Several night spots in Orange County serve up entertainment with dinner. **Tibbie's Music Hall** (16360 Coast Hwy., Huntington Beach, tel. 714/840–5661) offers rowdy musical revues along with prime rib, fish, or chicken.

Medieval Times Dinner and Tournament (7662 Beach Blvd., tel. 714/521–4740) is a new Buena Park attraction that takes guests back to the days of knights and ladies. Knights on horseback compete in medieval games, sword fighting, and jousting. Dinner, all of which is eaten with your hands, includes vegetables, roast chicken, potatoes, pastry, and cocktails.

Other area dinner theaters include **The Grand Dinner Theater** (Grand Hotel, Anaheim, tel. 714/772–7777), **Curtain Call** (690 El Camino Real, Tustin, tel. 714/838–1540).

Nightclubs **Crackers** (710 Katella Ave., Anaheim, tel. 714/978–1828) is a zany restaurant and nightclub where waiters and waitresses double as on-stage performers. The live entertainment seven days a week varies, with music from the '40s to the '90s.
The Righteous Brothers' Hop (18774 Brookhurst St., Fountain Valley, tel. 714/963–2366) is a 1950s–1960s-style diner/nightclub owned by—you guessed it—the Righteous Brothers. Nostalgia fills this fun place, which has a basketball court-dance floor and a '56 Chevy attached to the front of the DJ booth. Only music circa 1950–60 is played.

14 San Diego

*by Maribeth
Mellin*

Each year, San Diego absorbs thousands of visitors who are
drawn by the climate: sunny, dry, and warm nearly year-
round. They swim, surf, and sunbathe on long beaches facing
the turquoise Pacific, where whales, seals, and dolphins swim
offshore. They tour oases of tropical palms, sheltered bays
fringed by golden pampas grass, and far-ranging parklands
blossoming with brilliant bougainvillaea, jasmine, ice plant,
and birds of paradise. They run and bike and walk for hours
down wide streets and paths planned for recreation among the
natives, who thrive on San Diego's varied health, fitness, and
sports scenes.

San Diego County is the nation's seventh largest—larger than
nearly a dozen U.S. states—with a population of over 2 million.
It sprawls east from the Pacific Ocean through dense urban
neighborhoods to outlying suburban communities that seem to
sprout overnight on canyons and cliffs. The city of San Diego is
the state's second largest, behind Los Angeles. It serves as a
base for the U.S. Navy's 11th Naval District and a port for
ships from many nations. A considerable number of its residents were stationed here in the service and decided to stay
put. Others either passed through on vacation or saw the city in
movies and TV shows and became enamored with the city and
its reputation as a prosperous Sunbelt playground. From its
founding San Diego has attracted a steady stream of prospectors, drawn to the nation's farthest southwest frontier.

Tourism is San Diego's third largest industry, after manufacturing and the military. San Diego's politicians, business leaders, and developers have set the city's course toward a steadily
increasing influx of visitors—which gives residents some
pleasant attractions and not-so-enjoyable distractions. With
growth comes congestion, even in San Diego's vast expanse.

Arriving and Departing

By Plane There are regularly scheduled nonstop flights to San Diego
from many U.S. and Mexican cities. San Diego is served by
AeroCalifornia (tel. 800/258–3311), Alaska Airlines (tel. 800/
426–0333), America West (tel. 619/560–0727), American (tel.
619/232–4051), Braniff (tel. 619/231–0700), Continental (tel.
800/525–0280), Delta (tel. 619/235–4344), Northwest (tel. 619/
239–0488), Skywest (tel. 800/453–9417), Southwest (tel. 619/
232–1221), Trans World Airlines (tel. 619/295–7009), United
(tel. 619/234–7171), and USAir (tel. 800/428–4322).

*From the Airport to
Center City* All flights arrive at Lindbergh Field, just three miles northwest of downtown. **San Diego Transit** Route 2 buses leave every
20–30 minutes, from 5:30 AM–midnight, from the center traffic
aisle at the East Terminal and at the traffic island at the far
west end of the West Terminal. The buses go to 4th and Broadway, downtown. Fare is $1 per person. Bus fares are projected
to rise in 1992. Taxi fare is $5–$6, plus tip, to most center-city
hotels. **The Super Shuttle Airport Limousine** (tel. 619/278–5800
or 800/722–9455) will take you directly to your destination, often for less than a cab would cost. Numerous hotels and motels
offer complimentary transportation to their guests. If you have
rented a car at the airport, follow the signs to I-5 and go south
for about three miles to downtown.

By Car I-5 stretches from Canada to the Mexican border and bisects
San Diego. I-8 provides access from Yuma, Arizona, and points

east. Drivers coming from Nevada and the mountain regions beyond can reach San Diego on I-15. Avoid rush-hour periods when the traffic can be jammed for miles.

By Train **Amtrak** trains (tel. 800/USA–RAIL) from Los Angeles arrive at Santa Fe Depot, at Kettner Boulevard and Broadway, near the heart of downtown. There are additional stations in Del Mar and Oceanside, both located in north San Diego County. Eight trains operate daily in either direction.

By Bus **Greyhound-Trailways** (tel. 619/239–9171) operates frequent daily service between the downtown terminal at 120 W. Broadway and Los Angeles, connecting with buses to all major U.S. cities. Many buses are express or nonstop; others make stops at coastal towns en route.

Getting Around

Many attractions, such as the Gaslamp Quarter, Balboa Park, and La Jolla, are best seen on foot. A variety of public transportation can be incorporated to reach any major tourist and shopping area, but it is best to have a car for exploring more remote coastal and inland regions. The International Information Center in Horton Plaza, at the corner of 1st Avenue and F Street, provides maps of the city.

By Bus Fares on **San Diego Transit** buses are $1, $1.25 on express buses; senior citizens pay 50¢ on any bus. Bus fares are expected to rise in 1992. A free transfer is included in the fare, but it must be requested upon boarding. Buses to most major attractions leave from 4th or 5th and Broadway. San Diego Transit Information Line (tel. 619/233–3004) is open daily, 5:30 AM–8:30 PM. Call for precise details on getting to any location.

By Taxi Taxi fares are regulated at the airport—all companies charge the same rate—and the average fare from Lindbergh Field to the downtown area is $5–$6. Fares vary between companies on other routes, however, including the ride back to the airport. Cab companies that serve most areas of the city are **Yellow Cab** (tel. 619/234–6161), **Orange Cab** (tel. 619/291–3333), **La Jolla Cab** (tel. 619/453–4222), **Co-op Silver Cabs** (tel. 619/280–5555), **Coast Cab** (tel. 619/226–8294), and **Coronado Cab** (tel. 619/435–6211).

By Trolley The **San Diego Trolley** travels from downtown to within 100 feet of the United States–Mexican border, stopping at 21 suburban stations en route. Basic fare is 50¢–$1.50, one way (expected to rise in 1992). The trolley also travels from downtown to La Mesa and El Cajon in East County. Ticket vending machines, located at each station, require exact change. Tickets must be purchased before boarding. Trolleys operate daily, approximately every 15 minutes, 5 AM–1 AM. The new Bayside line serves the Convention Center and Seaport Village; a line to Old Town is under construction.

By Ferry The San Diego–Coronado Ferry leaves from the Broadway Pier daily, every hour on the hour, 10 AM–10 PM. Fare is $1 each way. **The Harbor Hopper** (tel. 619/229–8294) is a water-taxi service that shuttles passengers from one side of the San Diego Harbor to another, with 87 possible pick-up points. The fare is $5 each way.

By Limousine Limousine companies provide chauffeured service for business or pleasure. Some offer airport shuttles and customized tours. Rates vary and are per hour, per mile, or both, with some minimums established. Companies offering a range of services include **A Touch of Class** (tel. 619/698–6301), **Olde English Livery Service** (tel. 619/232–6533), **La Jolla Limousines** (tel. 619/459–5891), and **Presidential Limousine** (619/291–2820).

Important Addresses and Numbers

Tourist Information **The International Information Center** is in Horton Plaza, at the corner of 1st Avenue and F Street, tel. 619/236–1212. Open daily 8:30–5. Closed Thanksgiving and Christmas.

Recorded visitor information (tel. 619/236–1212).

Mission Bay Visitor Information Center is located at 2688 East Mission Bay Drive, off I–5 at the Mission Bay side of the Clairemont Drive exit, tel. 619/276–8200. Open Mon.–Sat. 9–5, Sun. 9:30–4:30.

Balboa Park Information Center is at 1549 El Prado, in Balboa Park, tel. 619/239–0512. Open daily, 9:30–4.

Beach Report (tel. 619/225–9492).

Weather Forecast (tel. 619/289–1212).

Emergencies **Police, Ambulance,** and **Fire** departments can all be reached by dialing 911. For the **Poison Control Center,** call 619/543–6000.

Doctor Hospital emergency rooms, with physicians on duty, are open 24 hours. Major hospitals are **UCSD Medical Center** (225 Dickinson, tel. 619/543–6400), **Mercy Hospital and Medical Center** (4077 5th Ave., tel. 619/260–7000), **Scripps Memorial Hospital** (9888 Genesee Ave., La Jolla, tel. 619/457–6150), **Veterans Administration Hospital** (3350 La Jolla Village Dr., La Jolla, tel. 619/453–7500).

Guided Tours

Orientation Tours Both **Gray Line Tours** (tel. 619/491–5011) and **San Diego Mini Tours** (tel. 619/234–9044) offer daily four-hour sightseeing excursions. Gray Line uses 45-passenger buses; San Diego Mini Tours uses 25-passenger tour buses. Cost: $20–$50 depending on the length of the tour and the attractions visited. **Champagne Cowboy Tours** (tel. 619/283–0220) escorts smaller groups of 12 in minibuses or vans. Each of the companies provides pickup at major hotels. Tour prices start at $20. **Old Town Trolley** (tel. 619/298–8687) travels to almost every attraction and shopping area on open-air trackless trolleys. Drivers double as tour guides. You can take the full 90-minute, narrated city tour or get on and off as you please at any of the 10 stops. An all-day pass costs only $14 for adults, $7 for children 5–12. The trolley carries 34 passengers and operates daily 9–5. Free one-hour bus tours of the downtown redevelopment area, including the Gaslamp Quarter, are hosted by **Centre City Development Corporation** (tel. 619/696–3215). Groups of 43 passengers leave from 119 W. F Street, downtown, every Saturday at 10 AM. Reservations are necessary. The tour may be cancelled if there aren't enough passengers.

Special-Interest Tours **Golflink** (tel. 800/356–4653) arranges golf tournaments and golf-related tours.

Holidays on Horseback (tel. 619/445–3997) offers horseback riding excursions in the back country.

Pied Piper Tours (tel. 619/224–7455) offers customized shopping trips for individuals or groups, specializing in excursions to the Los Angeles garment district.

Flight Trails Helicopters also known as Civic Helicopters (tel. 619/438–8424) has helicopter tours starting at $65 per person per ½ hour.

San Diego Harbor Excursion (tel. 619/234–4111) and **Invader Cruises** (tel. 619/234–8687) sail with more than 100 passengers on narrated cruises of San Diego harbor. Both vessels have snack bars. One-hour cruises depart several times daily from the Broadway Pier. San Diego Harbor Excursion offers a two-hour tour each day at 2 PM. Reservations are not necessary for any of the tours. Cost: $9 for a one-hour tour; $12 for a two-hour tour.

Mariposa Sailing Cruises (tel. 619/542–0646) offers morning and afternoon sailing tours of the harbor and San Diego Bay on the 35-foot cutter, *Mariposa*.

Whale-Watching Tours   The California gray whale migrates south to Mexico and back north from mid-December to mid-March. Up to 200 whales pass the San Diego coast each day, coming within yards of tour boats. Some tour companies will give a free second trip to any passenger who fails to sight a whale. *The Avanti* (tel. 619/222–0391), a 70-foot, luxury motor yacht, and California Cruisin's 180-passenger *Fast Cat* (tel. 619/235–8600), are two of the fastest boats in the harbor. Both offer 2½-hour narrated tours twice a day during the week, three times a day on weekends. **H&M Landing** (tel. 619/222–1144) and **Seaforth Boat Rentals** (tel. 619/223–1681) have daily whale-watching trips in large party boats. An intimate tour is conducted by **Sail San Diego** (tel. 619/548–4227) on a 38-foot Bristol sailing yacht. A full lunch and an informative lecture are provided for a maximum of six persons. Early booking is recommended because of space limitations.

Walking Tours   **The Gaslamp Foundation** (410 Island Ave., tel. 619/233–5227) leads 1½-hour guided walks of the restored downtown historic district, highlighting the Victorian architecture. Groups meet at the foundation office, near Horton Plaza, Saturday at 10 AM and 1 PM. A donation is requested. Self-guided tour brochures are available at the office weekdays 8:30–5.

Free walking tours exploring the gardens, architecture, and history of Balboa Park are given every Saturday at 10 AM by **Offshootours** (tel. 619/525–8200). Also offered are guided botanical tours through more than 7,000 species of exotic fauna and flora at the San Diego Zoo. The tour is free with zoo admission and is offered on the last Sunday of each month.

Old Town Walking Tours (tel. 619/296–1004) leads strolls through 200 years of history in San Diego's original city center. Groups leave from 3977 Twiggs St., daily, on the hour, 10–5. Cost: $1, and reservations are suggested.

Exploring San Diego

Exploring San Diego is an endless adventure, limited only by time and transportation constraints, which, if you don't have a car, can be considerable. San Diego is more an endless chain of separate communities than a cohesive city. Many of the major

Exploring San Diego *(Boxes Refer to Detail Maps)*

N

Torrey Pines
State Beach

N. Torrey
Pines Rd.
S21

Mira Mesa Blvd.

Genessee Ave.

805

Miramar

Rd.

MIRAMAR

**MIRAMAR
NAVAL AIR
STATION**

Gilman Dr.

La Jolla

Torrey Pines

Ardath Rd.

52

Clairemont

Mesa

Blvd.

163

La Jolla Blvd.

5

Clairemont Dr.

Balboa Ave.

Genessee Ave.

Aero Dr.

Cabrillo Fwy

805

**PACIFIC
BEACH**

Grand Ave.

**Mission
Bay**

**LINDA
VISTA**

Mission Blvd.

Ingraham St.

*Mission
Bay*

**MISSION
BEACH**

Linda Vista Rd.

Friars Rd.

San Diego River

Mission Bay Dr.

■ Sea World

Old Town

8

163

Adams Ave.

**OCEAN
BEACH**

Nimitz Blvd.

Sunset Cliffs Blvd.

Catalina Blvd.

Rosecrans

Pacific Hwy.

University

**Balboa
Park**

9

Harbor Dr.

209

**POINT
LOMA**

DOWNTOWN

Imperial

Cabrillo Memorial Dr.

North Island
**U.S. NAVAL
AIR STATION**

Harbor Dr.

75

Natl

*Coronado
Beach*

San Diego Bay

Central San Diego

Strand Blvd.

PACIFIC OCEAN

*Silver Strand
State Beach*

NAVAL RESERVATION
SYCAMORE CANYON
ANNEX

EL CAJON

Broadway

Main St.

Chase Ave.

Navajo Rd.

Lake Murray Blvd.

Lake Murray

Fletcher Pkwy.

LA MESA

Mission Gorge Rd.

Waring Rd.

Montezuma Rd.

El Cajon Blvd.

College Rd.

Campo Rd.

Avocado Blvd.

Jamacha Rd.

Magnolia Ave.

Escondido Fwy.

Murphy Canyon Rd.

Fairmount Ave.

Euclid Ave.

47th St.

Imperial Ave.

Jamacha Blvd.

Sweetwater Reservoir

Paradise Valley Rd.

South Bay Fwy.

Proctor Valley Rd.

Upper Otay Reservoir

National City

8th St.

18th St.

CHULA VISTA

E St.

Highland Ave.

City Blvd.

Montgomery Blvd.

Broadway

Hilltop Dr.

J St.

Otay Lakes Rd.

Canyon

Otay Lakes Rd.

Telegraph

Otay Reservoir

Chula Vista
Wildlife
Reserve

attractions are 15 miles or so away from each other—a half-hour or more apart under the best circumstances. The streets are fun for getting an up-close look at how San Diegans live, and if you've got a car, be sure to drive through Mission and Pacific beaches along Mission Boulevard for a good view of the vibrant beach scene. But true Southern Californians use the freeways, which crisscross the county in a sensible fashion. Interstate 5 runs a direct north–south route through the county's coastal communities to the Mexico border. Interstates 805 and 15 do much the same inland, with Interstate 8 as the main east–west route. Highways 163, 52, and 94 act as connectors.

If you are going to drive around San Diego, study your maps before you hit the road. The freeways are convenient and fast most of the time, but if you miss your turnoff or get caught in commuter traffic, you'll experience a none-too-pleasurable hallmark of Southern California living—freeway madness. Southern California drivers rush around on a complex freeway system with the same fervor they use for jogging scores of marathons each year. They particularly enjoy speeding up at interchanges and entrance and exit ramps. Be sure you know where you're going before you join the freeway chase. Better yet, use public transportation or tour buses from your hotel and save your energy for walking in the sun.

Downtown and the Embarcadero

Numbers in the margin correspond with points of interest on the Central San Diego map.

Long ignored by the local populace, downtown San Diego, just three miles south of the international airport, is changing and growing rapidly, gaining status as a cultural and recreational center for the county's residents and visitors alike.

Downtown's natural attributes were easily evident to its original booster, Alonzo Horton, who arrived in San Diego in 1867. Horton looked at the bay and the acres of flatland surrounded by hills and canyons and knew he had found San Diego's center. Though Old Town, under the Spanish fort at the Presidio, had been settled for years, Horton knew it was too far away from the water to take hold as the commercial center of San Diego. He bought 960 acres along the bay at 27½¢ per acre and literally gave away the land to those who would develop it or build houses. Within months, he had sold or given away 226 city blocks of land, and settlers were camping on their land in tents as their houses and businesses rose. In 1868, Horton and other city fathers staked out 1,400 acres surrounding a mesa overlooking the harbor and created a permanent greenbelt overlooking downtown. That acreage officially became Balboa Park in 1911.

The transcontinental train arrived in 1885, and the grand land boom was on. The population soared from 5,000 to 35,000 in less than a decade—a foreshadowing of San Diego's future. In 1887, the tile-domed Santa Fe Depot was constructed at the foot of Broadway, two blocks from the water. Freighters chugged in and out of the harbor, and by the early 1900s, the navy had discovered this perfect West Coast command center. Today, the navy has a strong presence in the harbor and on Point Loma and Coronado Island and is an integral part of the cityscape.

As downtown grew into San Diego's transportation and commercial hub, residential neighborhoods blossomed along the beaches and inland valleys. Downtown's business district gradually moved farther away from the original heart of downtown, at Fifth and Market, past Broadway, up toward the park. Downtown's waterfront fell into bad times during World War I, when sailors, gamblers, prostitutes, and boozers were drawn like magnets to each other and the waterfront bars.

But Alonzo Horton's modern-day followers, city leaders intent on prospering while preserving San Diego's natural beauty, have reclaimed the waterfront. Replacing old shipyards and canneries are hotel towers and waterfront parks, which surround the new San Diego Convention Center. The $160 million, 760,000-square-foot center hosted its first events in early 1990, and since then downtown has been lively even when the offices and banks are closed. Hotels, restaurants, shopping centers, and housing developments are rising on every square inch of available space as downtown San Diego comes of age.

❶ Your first view of downtown, no matter what your mode of transportation, will likely include the **Embarcadero,** a waterfront walkway lined with restaurants and cruise-ship piers along Harbor Drive. Though the entire waterfront has become a major tourist attraction, as yet there is no tourist office on the Embarcadero. Your closest access to maps and brochures is at **❷** the recently restored **Santa Fe Depot,** just two blocks away, at the corner of Broadway and Kettner Boulevard. There is a tourist information booth inside the station, with bus schedules, maps, and a Traveler's Aid booth. The depot's unmistakable blue tile dome will soon be overshadowed by the Great American Plaza, a massive office tower under construction that will include a transit center linking the train, trolley, and bus systems. For now, the depot is the city's transit hub. Tour buses to Mexico depart from here, and the Greyhound bus station is just a few blocks away at 120 West Broadway. The bright red **San Diego Trolley** departs a block from the depot, at the corner of India and C streets. The trolley runs through San Diego's south coastal communities—Chula Vista, National City, and Imperial Beach—to the Tijuana border.

Begin your Embarcadero tour at the foot of Ash Street on Harbor Drive, where the harbor's collection of houseboats, ferries, cruise ships, naval destroyers, tour boats, and a fair share of seals and seagulls begins. The *Star of India,* a beautiful windjammer built in 1863, is docked at the foot of Grape Street on Harbor Drive, across from the Spanish-style San Diego County Administration Center. The *Star of India* is part of the **❸** **Maritime Museum,** a collection of three ships that have been restored and are open for tours. *The Maritime Museum headquarters is located in the* Berkeley *paddle-wheeler boat by the B Street Pier, tel. 619/234-9153. Admission: $5 adults, $4 senior citizens and students, $10 families. Ships open daily 9–8.*

A cement pathway runs from the *Star of India* along the water, past restaurants and fish markets to the docks for harbor tour boats and whale-watching trips (which are scheduled in January and February during the grand migration of the gray whales from the Pacific Northwest to southern Baja). This section of the Embarcadero, at Harbor Drive and the foot of Broadway, has become a tourists' gathering spot. A cluster of streetfront windows sell tickets for tours; those waiting for

Central San Diego

their boats grab a beer or ice cream at the diner-style Bay Cafe and sit on the upstairs patio or on benches along the busy pathway and watch the sailboats, paddle-wheelers, and yachts vie for space.

❹ The pink and blue **B Street Pier** has become a central loading zone for catamaran trips to the island of Catalina, about three hours northeast, and cruise trips to Ensenada, Mexico's harborfront city about 80 land miles south of San Diego. Major cruise lines use San Diego's pier as both a port of call and a departure point for cruises to San Juan, Vancouver, and the Panama Canal. The cavernous pier building has a cruise-information center and a small, cool bar and gift shop. There is a huge public parking lot ($3 a day) along the south side of the pier building. Since much of the parking along Harbor Drive is limited to two-hour meters, this lot is good if you're planning to tour the harbor for the day. One of the newest, yet most traditional, boat trips is the **Bay Ferry** to Coronado Island, which runs hourly from 10 AM to 10 PM.

Back along the Embarcadero are other traditional craft, some housing gift shops, some awaiting restoration. The navy's Eleventh Naval District has control of the next few waterfront blocks, and a series of destroyers, submarines, and carriers cruise in and out, some staying for weeks at a time. The navy occasionally offers tours of these floating cities.

A steady stream of joggers, bicyclists, and serious walkers pick up speed where the Embarcadero pathway passes the Tuna Harbor, where San Diego's tuna boats once gathered. A new Fish Market Restaurant has opened over the water at the end of the pier, offering spectacular views of the harbor and downtown.

❺ **Seaport Village** (tel. 619/235–4013) is next. This stretch of prime waterfront connects the harbor with the newly rising hotel towers and convention center. Seaport Village is a privately developed and operated 14-acre shopping, dining, and recreational outdoor mall of sorts. The village's clapboard and stucco buildings house a seemingly unending series of specialty shops, snack bars, and restaurants—each with an independent theme. The **Broadway Flying Horses Carousel,** whose hand-carved animals rose and fell at Coney Island during the turn of the century, has been transplanted to the other coast, and is now surrounded by inexpensive ethnic cafes and take-outs and a video parlor for those who prefer their fun in the shade. The tables here fill up quickly, but there is a long concrete wall by the water where you can sit and dine alfresco. Beside the wall is Seaport Village's official symbol, the 45-foot-high Mulkilteo Lighthouse, modeled after an 80-year-old lighthouse in Everett, Washington. The San Diego Pier Cafe, an on-the-water seafood restaurant, occupies the lighthouse.

Seaport Village spreads from Harbor Drive to the waterfront. The parking lots along Harbor Drive also fill up quickly, but there is additional parking up Market Street and Kettner Boulevard. Stay away from parking meters if you're planning to stay for awhile, since they are patrolled frequently. Seaport Village's shops are open daily from 10 to 9, with restaurants closing closer to midnight.

❻ The mirrored towers of the **San Diego Marriott Hotel and Marina** mark the end of Seaport Village. The waterfront walkway continues past the hotel's marina, where hotel guests moor their enormous, extravagant yachts. Farther on is a large park with a fishing pier and walking paths. Just past the Marriott is

7 the new **San Diego Convention Center.** The architecture is striking, especially against the blue sky and sea. The Center often holds trade shows that are open to the public.

To reach the heart of downtown, walk up Market Street from Seaport Village or up Broadway from the B Street Pier. The

8 **Olde Cracker Factory,** at Market and State streets, houses antiques and collectibles shops.

Walking up Broadway, you'll pass the Santa Fe Depot and a dwindling collection of dive bars and tattoo parlors. Lower Broadway has long been a headache for downtown's boosters, but the businesses along here are ever-popular with sailors and fishermen back from weeks at sea. Several high-rise office buildings have been erected in the area, and more are in the planning stages. A few blocks farther, at the corner of First and Broadway, is where downtown comes alive. Here you'll

9 pass the **Spreckels Theater,** a grand old stage that now presents pop concerts and touring plays.

10 The grand **U.S. Grant Hotel,** built in 1910, is across the street. Far more elegant and formal than most San Diego hotels, the U.S. Grant has massive marble lobbies, with gleaming chandeliers and hospitable doormen. The Grant Grill is the prime watering hole for San Diego's old guard. One block away is

11 **Westgate Hotel,** another deluxe hostelry for visiting celebrities and royalty. The Westgate is French Provincial in style and has a piano bar on the main floor and an elegant French restaurant, Le Fontainebleau, at the top.

The theme of shopping in adventureland carries over from Sea-

12 port Village to downtown San Diego's centerpiece, **Horton Plaza.** Completed in 1985, this shopping, dining, and entertainment mall fronts Broadway and G Street from First to Fourth avenues and covers more than six city blocks. Designed by Jon Jerde, whose touch you might have seen in views from the 1986 Summer Olympics in Los Angeles, Horton Plaza is far from what one imagines a shopping center, or city center, to be. A collage of pastel colors with elaborate, colorful tilework marking benches and stairways, sculptures marking entrances and banners hanging everywhere, it rises in uneven, staggered levels to six floors and has great views of all downtown, from the harbor to Balboa Park and beyond. The 450-room Omni Hotel is connected to Horton Plaza and often hosts special events in conjunction with the plaza.

The **International Visitor Information Center** was opened in Horton Plaza by the San Diego Convention and Visitors Bureau in 1985, and it has become the traveler's best resource for information on all San Diego. The staff members and volunteers who run the center speak an amazing array of languages and are well acquainted with the myriad needs and requests of tourists. They dispense information on hotels, restaurants, and tourist attractions, including Tijuana. Photos of San Diego's landmarks decorate the walls, and a wealth of brochures and pamphlets in many languages are neatly arrayed by the counters. *11 Horton Plaza, street level at the corner of First and F Sts., tel. 619/236–1212. Open daily 8:30–5:30.*

Long before Horton Plaza became the bright star on downtown's redevelopment horizon, the **Gaslamp Quarter** was gaining attention and respect. A 16-block National Historic District, centered on Fifth and Fourth avenues, from Broadway to Market Street, the quarter contains most of San Diego's Victorian-style commercial buildings from the late 1800s, when Market Street was the center of early downtown. At the farthest end of the redeveloped quarter, the **Gaslamp Quarter Association** is headquartered in the William Heath Davis house (410 Island Ave., tel. 619/233–5227), a restored 19th-century saltbox house. Walking tours of the historic district leave from here on Saturdays at 10 and 1. A $2 donation is suggested. If you can't make the tour, stop by the house and pick up a brochure and map.

The William Heath Davis house is located in the heart of Alonzo Horton's New Town, so-called to distinguish it from Old Town. At the turn of the century, downtown's business district moved farther west, and many of San Diego's first buildings fell into disrepair. The quarter became known as the Stingaree district, where hookers picked up sailors in lively taverns and dance halls. Crime flourished, and the blocks between Market Street and the waterfront were considered to be seedy, dangerous, and best left alone. As the move for downtown redevelopment emerged, there was talk about destroying the buildings in the quarter, but in 1974 history buffs, developers, architects, and artists formed the Gaslamp Quarter Council, bent on preserving the district. Beaten down flophouses are now choice office buildings. The brick sidewalks are lined with trees and benches, and the shops and restaurants tend toward individuality.

Across the street from the Gaslamp Quarter Association's headquarters, at the corner of Island and Third streets, is the 100-year-old **Horton Grand Hotel,** restored and operated in turn-of-the-century style. The hotel's central courtyard has become a popular wedding and party site. The 110 rooms are decorated with period furnishings, lace curtains, and gas fireplaces—some even have legendary ghosts. A small Chinese Museum serves as a tribute to the surrounding Chinatown district, which is nothing more than a collection of modest homes that once housed Chinese laborers and their families.

Many of the quarter's landmark buildings are located on Fourth and Fifth avenues, between Island and Broadway. Among the nicest are the Backesto Building, the Keating Building, the Louis Bank of Commerce, and the Mercantile Building, all on Fifth. The Golden Lion Tavern, at the corner of Fourth and F, is a magnificently restored turn-of-the-century tavern with a 12-foot mahogany bar and a spectacular stained-glass domed ceiling.

Coronado

Coronado Island is a charming, peaceful community, essentially left alone for decades to grow at its characteristically slow pace. It is a city unto itself, ruled by its own municipal government. Longtime residents live in grand Victorian homes handed down by their families for generations. The streets are wide, quiet, and friendly, with lots of neighborhood parks where young families mingle with the island's many senior citizens. Grand old homes face the waterfront and the Coronado Municipal Golf Course, with its lovely setting under the bridge, across the water from Seaport Village. Community celebrations, live band concerts, and the Fourth of July fireworks take place in the park next to the golf course. North Island Naval Air Station was established in 1911 on the island's north end, across from Point Loma, and was the site of Charles Lindbergh's departure on his flight around the world. Today, high-tech air- and seacraft arrive and depart continuously from North Island, providing a real-life education in military armament. Coronado's long relationship with the navy has made it an enclave of sorts for retired military personnel.

Coronado is visible from downtown and Point Loma and accessible via the arching blue 2.2-mile-long San Diego–Coronado Bridge, a landmark just beyond downtown's skyline. There is a $1 toll for crossing the bridge into Coronado, but cars carrying two or more passengers may enter through the free car-pool lane. The bridge handles more than 20,000 cars each day, and rush hour tends to be slow, which is fine, since the view of the harbor, downtown, and the island is breathtaking, day and night. Until the bridge was completed in 1969, visitors and residents relied on the Coronado Ferry, which ran across the harbor from downtown. When the bridge was opened, the ferry closed down, much to the chagrin of those who were fond of traveling at a leisurely pace. In 1987, the ferry returned, and with it came the island's most ambitious development in decades.

⓯ The Bay Ferry runs from the B Street Pier at downtown's Embarcadero to the **Old Ferry Landing,** which is actually a new development on an old site. Its buildings resemble the gingerbread domes of the Hotel Del Coronado, long the island's main attraction. The Old Ferry Landing is similar to Seaport Village, with small shops and restaurants and lots of benches facing the water. Nearby, the elegant Le Meridien Hotel accommodates many wedding receptions and gala banquets. The Bay Ferry is located at the B Street Pier, at Broadway and Harbor Drive. Boats depart hourly from 10 to 10. The fare is $1.50 each way.

A trackless trolley runs from the landing down Orange Avenue, the island's version of a downtown, to the Hotel Del Coronado. Coronado's residents and commuting workers have quickly adapted to this traditional mode of transportation, and the ferry has become quite popular with bicyclists who shuttle their bikes across the harbor and ride the island's wide, flat boulevards for hours.

⓰ The **Hotel Del Coronado** is the island's most prominent landmark. Selected as a National Historic Site in 1977, the Del (as natives say) celebrated its 100th anniversary in 1988. Celebrities, royalty, and politicians marked the anniversary with a weekend-long party that highlighted the hotel's colorful history. *1500 Orange Ave., tel. 619/435–6611. Free guided tours from the lobby Sat. 1 PM.*

The hotel is integral to the island's history. In 1884, two wealthy financiers, Elisha Spurr Babcock, Jr., and H. L. Story, stopped hunting grouse and rabbits on the undeveloped island long enough to appreciate the long stretches of virgin beaches, the view of San Diego's emerging harbor, and the island's potential. They decided to build a luxurious resort hotel, formed the Babcock-Story Coronado Beach Company and purchased the 4,100-acre land parcel for $110,000 in 1885, and in 1886 sold lots and shares in the new hotel.

It took only one year to build the 400-room main hotel, though it was a mighty effort that employed hundreds of Chinese laborers racing against the clock. All materials and laborers had to be ferried to the island and transported up Orange Avenue on the Babcock-Story Railroad, which was capable of transporting private railroad cars popular with industrial tycoons. The hotel was completed in 1888, and Thomas Edison himself threw the switch as the Del became the world's first electrically lighted hotel. It has been a dazzling sight ever since.

The hotel's gingerbread architecture is recognized all over the world, for it has served as a set for many movies, political meetings, and extravagant social happenings. The Duke of Windsor met Wally Simpson here. Eight presidents have stayed here. The film *Some Like It Hot*, starring Marilyn Monroe, was filmed here. The hotel's underground corridors are lined with historic photos from the days when the hotel was first built. Of particular interest are the photos of the enormous tent city that was built during a major remodeling project in 1902. The tent city was so popular with guests that it was reerected every summer until 1939.

Coronado's other main attraction is its 86 historic homes and sites. Many of the homes are turn-of-the-century mansions. The **Glorietta Bay Inn,** across the street from the Del, was the home of John Spreckels, original owner of North Island and the property on which the Hotel Del Coronado now stands. Nearby is the **Boat House,** a small replica of the hotel that once served as the launching point for deep-sea fishing craft, which now houses a Chart House restaurant. The Boat House is a great spot for watching the sails in the harbor and watching the sun set over downtown. **Star Park,** on Loma Avenue, acts as a hub for five streets all designated as historic sites. Among the homes here is the Meade House, where L. Frank Baum wrote *The Wizard of Oz*. Coronado Touring (tel. 619/435–5892 or 619/435–5993) has historical tours of the homes that leave from the Glorietta Bay Inn on Tuesday, Thursday, and Saturday mornings at 11; the cost is $5 per person.

Point Loma, Shelter Island, and Harbor Island

Point Loma curves around the San Diego Bay west of downtown and the airport, protecting the center city from the Pacific's tides and waves. Though its main streets are cluttered with hotels, fast-food shacks, and military installations, Point Loma is an old and wealthy enclave of stately family homes for military officers, successful Portuguese fishermen, and political and professional leaders. Its bayside shores front huge estates, with sailboats and yachts packed tightly in private marinas.

⓱ Cabrillo National Monument, named after the Portuguese explorer Juan Rodríguez Cabrillo, sits at the very tip of Point Loma. Cabrillo was the first European to discover San Diego, which he called San Miguel, in 1542. In 1913 the monument grounds were set aside to commemorate his discovery. Begin your tour at the Visitor Center, where films and lectures about the monument, the sea-level tidal pools, and the gray whales migrating offshore are presented frequently. Signs along the walkways that edge the cliffs explain the views, with posters picturing the various navy, fishing, and pleasure craft that sail into and fly over the bay. A new statue of Cabrillo overlooks downtown from the next windy promontory, where visitors gather to admire the stunning panorama over the bay, from the snow-capped San Bernardino Mountains, some 200 miles northeast, to the hills surrounding Tijuana. Rest rooms and water fountains are plentiful along the paths that climb to the monument's various view points, but there are no food facilities. Exploring the grounds consumes time and calories; bring a picnic and rest on a bench overlooking the sailboats headed to sea. *1800 Cabrillo Memorial Dr., tel. 619/557–5450. Admission: $1; $3 for parking. Open daily 9–5:15.*

The oil lamp of the **Old Point Loma Lighthouse** was first lit in 1855. The light, sitting in a brass and iron housing above a painstakingly refurbished white wooden house, shone through a state-of-the-art lens from France and was visible from the sea for 25 miles. Unfortunately, it was too high above the cliffs to guide navigators trapped in Southern California's thick offshore fog and low clouds. In 1891 a new lighthouse was built on the small shore under the slowly eroding 400-foot cliffs. The old lighthouse is open to visitors, and the Coast Guard still uses the newer lighthouse and a mighty foghorn to guide boaters through the narrow channel leading into the bay.

⑱ Shelter Island sits in the narrow channel between Point Loma's eastern shore and the west coast of Coronado. In 1950 the port director thought there should be some use for the soil dredged to deepen the ship channel. Why not build an island?

His hunch paid off. Shelter Island's shores now support towering mature palms, a cluster of mid-range resorts, restaurants, and side-by-side marinas. It is the center of San Diego's yacht-building industry, and boats in every stage of construction are visible in the yacht yards. A long sidewalk runs from the landscaped lawns of the **San Diego Yacht Club** (tucked down Anchorage Street off Shelter Island Drive), past boat brokerages to the hotels and marinas, which line the inner shore, facing Point Loma. On the bay side, fishermen launch their boats or simply stand on shore and cast. Families relax at picnic tables along the grass, where there are fire rings and permanent barbecue grills, while strollers wander to the huge Friendship Bell, given to San Diegans by the people of Yokohama in 1960.

⑲ Harbor Island, made from 3.5 million tons of rock and soil from the San Diego Bay, forms a peninsula adjacent to the airport. Again, hotels and restaurants line the inner shores, but here, the buildings are many stories high, and the views from the bayside rooms are spectacular. The bay shore has pathways and gardens and picnic spots for sightseeing or working off the calories from the island restaurants' fine meals. On the west point Tom Ham's Lighthouse restaurant has a coast guard-approved beacon shining from its tower.

⑳ Sunset Cliffs Park is at the western side of Point Loma near Ocean Beach. The cliffs are aptly named, since their main attraction is their vantage point as a fine sunset-watching spot. The dramatic coastline here seems to have been carved out of ancient rock. Certainly the waves make their impact, and each year more sections of the cliffs sport caution signs. Don't climb around on the cliffs when you see these signs. It's easy to lose your footing and slip in the crumbling sandstone, and the surf can get very rough. Small coves and beaches dot the coastline and are popular with surfers drawn to the pounding waves and locals from the neighborhood who name and claim their special spots. The homes along Sunset Cliffs Boulevard are lovely examples of Southern California luxury, with pink stucco mansions beside shingle Cape Cod-style cottages. To reach the cliffs from Cabrillo Monument, take Catalina Boulevard to Hill Street. Turn left and drive straight to the cliffs. Sunset Cliffs Boulevard intersects Hill Street and runs through Ocean Beach to Interstate 8.

Balboa Park

Numbers in the margin correspond with points of interest on the Balboa Park map.

If it were on the ocean, Balboa Park would encompass all that is wonderful about San Diego. But you can see the ocean, or the bay at least from many points in the park's 1,400 acres of cultural, recreational, and environmental delights. Many of the park's ornate Spanish-Moorish buildings were intended to be temporary structures housing exhibits for the Panama–California International Exposition of 1915 and the California Pacific International Exposition of 1935–36. Most of San Diego's museums are located in the park, making it San Diego's cultural center. The museums offer free admission on a rotating basis on Tuesdays.

The Laurel Street Bridge, also known as Cabrillo Bridge, is the park's official gateway, leading over a vast canyon, filled with downtown commuter traffic on Highway 163, to El Prado which, beyond the art museum, becomes the park's central pedestrian mall. At Christmas the bridge is lined with colored lights; bright pink blossoms on rows of peach trees herald the coming of spring. The 100-bell carillon in the California Tower tolls the hour. Figures of California's historic personages decorate the base of the 200-foot spire, and a magnificent blue-tiled dome shines in the sun.

❶ **The Museum of Man** sits under the California Tower and houses the extensive collection of archaeological and anthropological exhibits first assembled for the 1915 exposition. One of that fair's primary cultural highlights was the "Story of Man Through the Ages" display, with artifacts culled from expeditions throughout the world. Over the years the museum has amplified that original theme and is now one of the finest anthropological museums in the country. Exhibits focus on Southwestern, Mexican, and South American cultures, and the museum sponsors expeditions and research in South America. *Tel. 619/239-2001. Admission: $3 adults, $1 children 13–18. Open daily 10–4:30.*

❷ The **Simon Edison Center for the Performing Arts** (tel. 619/239-2255) sits beside the Museum of Man under the California Tower. It includes the Cassius Carter Centre Stage, the Lowell Davies Festival Theatre, and the Old Globe. Beside the center is the **Sculpture Garden,** an outdoor exhibit of traditional and modernistic sculptures. The Sculpture Garden Cafe, with tables set amid the art, is open for lunch.

Balboa Park

Botanical Building, **5**
Hall of Champions, **7**
House of Pacific Relations, **12**
Museum of Man, **1**
Museum of Photographic Arts, **8**

Natural History Museum, **9**
Organ Pavilion, **11**
Park Information Center, **6**
Reuben H. Fleet Space Theater and Science Center, **10**

San Diego Aerospace Museum, **13**
San Diego Museum of Art, **3**
San Diego Zoo, **14**
Simon Edison Center for the Performing Arts, **2**
Timken Art Gallery, **4**

❸ The **San Diego Museum of Art** faces the central parking lot, where an empty parking space is rarer than any painting. Traffic is diverted from the rest of El Prado here, with the roadway leading toward the park's southern circle of museums. Be sure to check out the Museum of Art's special shows, which can be quite adventurous. Recent shows have included the paintings of Dr. Seuss and Maurice Sendak, giving the kids something to appreciate while the grownups admire the old masters. *Tel. 619/232-7931. Admission: $5 adults, $4 seniors, $2 children 6–18. Open Tues.–Sun. 10–4:30.*

❹ The **Timken Art Gallery,** next to the museum, is a private gallery housing works of European masters and a collection of Russian icons. The Putnam Foundation operates the gallery, which is the only privately owned building in the park. *Tel. 619/239-5548. Admission free. Open Tues.–Sat. 10–4:30, Sun. 1:30–4:30. Closed Sept.*

The action gets lively in the next section of El Prado, where mimes, jugglers, and musicians perform on long lawns beside ❺ the Lily Pond, in front of the graceful **Botanical Building.** Built for the 1915 exposition, the latticed, open-air nursery houses over 500 types of tropical and subtropical plants. The orchid collection is stunning, and there are benches beside cool, miniature waterfalls for resting away from the sun. The Lily Pond is filled with giant koi fish and blooming water lilies and is a popular spot for taking photographs. *Admission free. Open Tues.–Sun. 10–4:30.*

❻ The **Park Information Center** (tel. 619/239–0512), open daily 9–4:30, is located in the **House of Hospitality,** across El Prado from the pond. The office has maps and booklets on Balboa Park, and sells the Passport to Balboa Park, which offers reduced-price coupons to the museums. Many cultural groups also have offices in this building, which surrounds a peaceful patio and Spanish fountain. Next door, the Cafe Del Rey Moro serves drinks, lunch, and dinner. The flowering grotto, hidden by eucalyptus trees behind the restaurant, is a favorite spot for weddings.

❼ The **Hall of Champions,** a sports museum with a vast collection of memorabilia honoring local athletes and sports history, is next in line. San Diego, sometimes called the Sports Center of the United States, has nurtured the talents of many famous athletes. *Tel. 619/234-2544. Admission: $2 adults, 50¢ children 6–17. Open daily 10–4:30.*

❽ The **Museum of Photographic Arts,** in the **Casa de Balboa,** is one of few museums in the country dedicated solely to photography. MOPA exhibits the works of world-renowned and relatively obscure photographers, ranging from themes that highlight human tragedies to celebrations. *Tel. 619/239-5262. Admission: $2.50. Open daily 10–5, Thurs. 10–9.*

Below MOPA in the basement of the Casa de Balboa is the **San Diego Model Railroad Museum.** The room is filled with the sounds of chugging engines, screeching brakes, and shrill whistles when the six model-train exhibits are in operation. *Tel. 619/696-0199. Admission: $1 adults, 50¢ children. Open Wed.–Fri. 11–4, weekends 11–5.*

The short flight of steps leading to the park's main fountain is another gathering spot for talented street performers. On one

❾ side of the fountain is the **Natural History Museum,** with displays on the plants and animals of Southern California and Mexico. Children seem particularly impressed by the dinosaur bones, while amateur geologists, gemologists, and jewelers admire the collection of gems, including beautiful rose-colored tourmaline crystals mined in San Diego County. *Tel. 619/232–3821. Admission: $5 adults, $1 children 6–18. Open daily 10–4:30.*

❿ The **Reuben H. Fleet Space Theater and Science Center** is on the other side of the fountain. The Omnimax theater has a domed overhead screen on which fantastic films about nature, space, and life seem to lift the viewer into the action. Films are shown regularly throughout the day, and are informative and exhilarating. The science center is like a giant laboratory playground, where clever interactive exhibits teach children and adults about basic and complex scientific principles. The center's gift shop is akin to a museum, with toys and gadgets that inspire the imagination. The Laserium has laser shows set to rock music at night. *Tel. 619/238–1168. Science Center admission: $2.25 adults, $1 children 5–15 or included with price of theater ticket. Theater tickets: $5.50 adults, $3 children 5–15; laser shows: $6 adults, $3.50 children 6–17. Open Sun.–Thurs. 9:30–9:30, Fri.–Sat. 9:30 AM–10:30 PM.*

El Prado ends in a bridge that crosses over Park Boulevard to a perfectly tended rose garden and a seemingly wild cactus grove. From here you can see across the canyon to even more parkland, with picnic groves, sports facilities, and acres of ranging chaparral. Back along El Prado, roads and pathways lead to even more sights.

The main road off El Prado goes south from the parking lot by the Museum of Art.˙ A long island of flowers divides the road

⓫ curving around the **Organ Pavilion** and the 5,000-pipe Spreckels Organ, believed to be the largest outdoor organ in the world. Much of the time it is locked up on a stage before rows of benches where wanderers rest and regroup. Concerts are sometimes given on Sunday afternoons, and the organ is amazing to hear. On summer evenings local military bands, gospel groups, and barbershop quartets give concerts in the pavilion. At Christmas the park's massive Christmas tree and life-size nativity display turn the Organ Pavilion into a seasonal wonderland.

⓬ The **House of Pacific Relations,** across from the pavilion, is really a cluster of stucco cottages representing various foreign countries. The buildings are open on Sunday, and individual cottages often present celebrations on their country's holidays. A large parking lot sits just behind the pavilion and is a good place to find a space, particularly if you're attending an evening cultural event.

⓭ This southern road ends at the Pan American Plaza and the **San Diego Aerospace Museum and International Aerospace Hall of Fame.** The building is unlike any other in the park. The Ford Motor Company commissioned the building for the 1935 exposition, when sleek, streamlined design was all the rage. A thin line of blue neon outlines the round building at night, giving it the appearance of a landlocked UFO. Exhibits about aviation and aerospace pioneers line the rotunda, and a collection of real and replicated aircraft fill the center. *Tel. 619/234–8291. Admission: $4 adults, $1 children 6–17. Open daily 10–4:30.*

One of the newest museums in Balboa Park is the **San Diego Automotive Museum.** It maintains a large collection of classic cars and has an ongoing restoration program. *Tel. 619/231–2886. Admission: $3.50 adults, $1 children 6–16. Open daily 10–4:30.*

⑭ The **San Diego Zoo** is Balboa Park's most famous attraction. It ranges over 100 acres fronting Park Boulevard and is surely one of the finest zoos and tropical gardens in the world. Over 3,200 animals of 777 species roam in expertly crafted habitats that spread down into, around, and above the natural canyons. Equal attention has been paid to the flora and the fauna, and the zoo is an enormous botanical garden with one of the world's largest collections of subtropical plants. From the moment you walk through the entrance and face the swarm of bright pink flamingos and blue peacocks, you know you've entered a rare pocket of natural harmony. Exploring the zoo fully takes the stamina of a healthy hiker, but there are open-air trams running throughout the day on a three-mile tour of 80% of the zoo's exhibits. The Skyfari ride soars 170 feet above ground, giving a good overview of the zoo's layout and a marvelous panorama of the park, downtown San Diego, the bay, and the ocean, far past the Coronado Bridge. *Tel. 619/234–3153. Admission (including unlimited access to the Skyfari ride and the Children's Zoo): $10.75 adults, $4 children 3–15. Deluxe package (bus tour, Skyfari ride, and Children's Zoo): $13.75 adults, $6.50 children. Gates open daily 9–4; visitors may remain until 5 PM. Summer hours are 9–5; visitors may remain until 6.*

Old Town

Numbers in the margin correspond with points of interest on the Old Town San Diego map.

San Diego's Spanish and Mexican history and heritage are best evident in Old Town, just north of downtown at Juan Street, near the intersection of interstates 5 and 8. It wasn't until 1968 that Old Town became a state historic park. Fortunately, private efforts kept the area's history alive until then, and many of San Diego's oldest structures remain in good shape.

Though Old Town is often credited as being the first European settlement in Southern California, the true beginnings took **①** place overlooking Old Town from atop **Presidio Park.** There, Father Junipero Serra established the first of California's missions, called San Diego de Alcalá, in 1769. San Diego's Indians, called the San Diegueños by the Spaniards, were forced to abandon their seminomadic lifestyle and live at the mission. In 1774 the hilltop was declared a Royal Presidio, or fortress, and the mission was moved to its current location along the San Diego River, six miles east of the original site. The Indians lost more of their traditional grounds and ranches as the mission grew along the riverbed. In 1775 the Indians attacked and burned the mission, destroying religious objects and killing Franciscan Padre Luis Jayme. Their later attack on the presidio was less successful, and their revolt was short lived. By 1800, around 1,500 Indians were living on the mission's grounds, receiving religious instruction and adapting to the Spanish way of life.

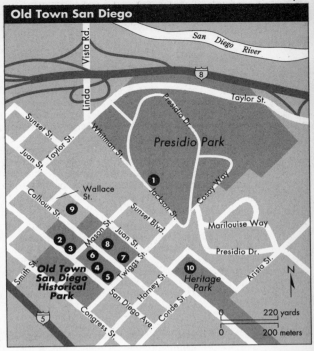

Old Town San Diego

The pioneers living within the presidio's walls were mostly
Spanish soldiers, poor Mexicans, and mestizos of Spanish and
Indian ancestry, all unaccustomed to farming San Diego's arid
land. They existed marginally until 1821, when Mexico gained
independence from Spain, claimed its lands in California, and
flew the Mexican flag over the presidio. The Mexican government, centered some 2,000 miles away in Monterrey, stripped
the Spanish missions of their landholdings, and an aristocracy
of landholders began to emerge. At the same time, settlers
were beginning to move down from the presidio to what is now
called Old Town.

A rectangular plaza was laid out along today's San Diego Avenue to serve as the settlement's center. In 1846, during the war
between Mexico and the United States, a detachment of marines raised the U.S. flag over the plaza on a pole said to have
been a main ship mast. The flag was torn down a time or two,
but within six months, Mexico had surrendered California, and
the U.S. flag remained. In 1850 San Diego became an incorporated city, with Old Town as its center.

Old Town's historic buildings are clustered around the main
plaza, called **Old Town Plaza,** with a view of the presidio from
behind the cannon by the flagpole. The plaza today serves much
the same purpose as it did when it was first laid out. It is a
pleasant place to rest and regroup as you plan your tour of Old
Town and watch other visitors stroll by. Art shows often fill the
lawns around the plaza, and lounging and strolling are encouraged. San Diego Avenue is closed to traffic here, and the cars

are diverted to Juan and Congress streets, both of which are lined with shops and restaurants. There are plenty of free parking lots on the outskirts of Old Town, which is best seen by foot. Shopping and eating are essential for a true Old Town tour, so bring your wallet and an appetite.

❸ The **Old Town State Historic Park** office is located in the **Robinson-Rose House,** on the south side of the plaza. Free guided tours of the park are available from here at 2 PM daily, and there is a good booklet for sale that provides a brief history and self-guided tour map for the 12-acre park. The Robinson-Rose House was the original commercial center of old San Diego, housing railroad offices, law offices, and the first newspaper press; one room has been restored and outfitted with period furnishings. Park rangers now show films and distribute information from the living room. *San Diego Ave. and Mason St., tel. 619/237–6770. Open 10–5 daily. Free walking tour of the park at 2 PM daily.*

The historic section of Old Town includes a collection of adobe
❹ and log houses in a subdued Mexican-colonial style. **La Casa de Pedrorena,** a hacienda-style home built in 1869, is currently
❺ closed for renovation. **La Casa de Altamirano** serves as the **San Diego Union Newspaper Historical Building.** A wood-frame structure prefabricated in Maine and shipped around Cape Horn in 1851, the building has been restored to replicate the newspaper's offices of 1868, when the first edition of the *San Diego Union* was printed.

❻ **La Casa de Estudillo,** across Mason Street from the plaza, is an original Old Town adobe built in 1827. The house has been restored to its former grandeur as the home of the prestigious
❼ Estudillo family, and it is now open for tours. The **Seeley Stables** became San Diego's stagecoach stop in 1867 and was the hub of Old Town until near the turn of the century, when the tracks of the Southern Pacific Railroad passing by the south side of the settlement became the favored route. The stables now house a collection of horse-drawn vehicles, Western memorabilia, and Indian artifacts. There is a $1 admission fee to tour the stables, where a slide show on San Diego history is presented three times a day.

❽ **La Casa de Bandini,** next to the stables, is one of the loveliest haciendas in San Diego. Built in 1829 by a Peruvian, Juan Bandini, the house served as Old Town's social center during Mexican rule. After Bandini lost his financial, political, and social standing through various political and business schemes, he lost the house in the 1850s. Albert Seeley, the stagecoach entrepreneur, purchased the home in 1869, built a second story, and turned it into the Cosmopolitan Hotel, a comfortable way station for travelers on the day-long trip south from Los Angeles. Surely it must have been a lovely hotel, with rooms overlooking the huge central gardens and patio. Casa Bandini's colorful gardens and main-floor dining rooms now house a good Mexican restaurant run by the owners of other highly successful Old Town businesses.

❾ The unofficial center of Old Town is the **Bazaar del Mundo,** a shopping and dining enclave built to represent a colonial Mexican square. The central courtyard is always in blossom with magenta bougainvillaea, scarlet hibiscus and irises, poppies, and petunias in season. Ballet Folklorico and flamenco dancers perform in the outdoor gazebo on weekend afternoons, and the bazaar frequently holds arts and crafts exhibits and Mexican festivals in the courtyard. Colorful shops specializing in Latin American crafts and unusual gift items border the courtyard, beyond a shield of thick bushes and huge birdcages with cawing macaws and toucans.

10 **Heritage Park,** up the Juan Street hill east of the Seeley Stables, is the headquarters for SOHO, the Save Our Heritage Organization. The climb up to the park is a bit steep, but the view of the harbor is great. SOHO has moved several grand Victorian homes and a temple from other parts of San Diego to the park, where they have been restored. The homes are now used for offices, shops, and restaurants. The Heritage Park Bed & Breakfast Inn is housed in a particularly fine Queen Anne mansion and is a peaceful spot to stay, away from traffic and noise.

Mission Bay and Sea World

Numbers in the margin correspond with points of interest on the Mission Bay Area map.

Mission Bay is San Diego's monument to sports and fitness. Action and leisure are the main themes of this 4,600-acre aquatic park, 75% of which is public land. Admission to its 27 miles of bayfront beaches and 17 miles of ocean frontage is free. All you need for a perfect day is a bathing suit, shorts, and the right selection of playthings.

When explorer Juan Rodriguez Cabrillo first spotted the bay in 1542, he called it "Baja Falso." The ocean-facing inlet led to acres of swampland, inhospitable to boats and inhabitants. In the 1960s the city planners decided to dredge the swamp and build a man-made bay with acres of beaches and lawns for play. Only 25% of the land would be used for commercial property, and now just a handful of resort hotels break up the natural landscape. Kite flying has become a fine art on the lawns facing Interstate 5, where the sky is flooded with the bright colors of huge, intricately made kites.

1 The **Visitor Information Center,** at the East Mission Bay Drive exit from Interstate 5, is an excellent tourist resource for the bay and all of San Diego. Leaflets and brochures for most of the area's attractions are provided free, and information on transportation, reservations, and sightseeing is offered cheerfully. The center is a gathering spot for the runners, walkers, and exercisers who take part in group activities. From the low hill outside the building, you can easily appreciate the bay's charms. *2688 E. Mission Bay Dr., tel. 619/276–8200. Open Mon.–Sat. 9–5, Sun. 9:30–4:30.*

A five-mile-long pathway runs through this section of the bay from the trailer park and miniature golf course, south past the high-rise Hilton Hotel to Sea World Drive. Playgrounds and picnic areas abound on the beach and low grassy hills of the park. Group gatherings, company picnics, and birthday parties are common along this stretch. On weekend evenings, the path is filled with a steady stream of exercisers jogging, speed walking, biking, and skating, releasing the stress from a day at the office. The water is filled with bathers, water-skiers, fishermen, and boaters, some in single-man kayaks, others in crowded powerboats. Swimmers should note signs warning

Mission Bay Area

about water pollution; certain areas of the bay are chronically polluted, and bathing is strongly discouraged.

② **Fiesta Island,** off Mission Bay Drive and Sea World Drive, is a smaller, man-made playground popular with jet- and water-skiers. In July the annual Over-the-Line Tournament, a local variety of softball, attracts thousands of players and oglers drawn by the teams' raunchy names and outrageous behavior.

③ Ingraham Street is another main drag through the bay, from the shores of Pacific Beach to Sea World Drive. **San Diego Princess Resort** on Vacation Isle, is the focal point of this part of the bay, with its lushly landscaped grounds, model yacht pond, and bayfront restaurants. Ducks and cottontail bunnies are as common as tourists, and the village is a great family playground.

④ West Mission Bay Drive runs from the ocean beyond Mission Boulevard to Sea World Drive. The pathways along the Mission Beach side of the bay are lined with vacation homes, many for rent by the month. Those fortunate to live here year-round have the bay as their front yards, with wide sandy beaches, volleyball courts, and an endless stream of sightseers on the sidewalk. **Belmont Park,** once an abandoned amusement park at the corner of Mission Boulevard and West Mission Bay Drive, is now a shopping, dining, and recreation area between the bay and the Mission Beach boardwalk. Twinkling lights outline the old, but recently refurbished Belmont Park roller coaster where screaming thrill-seekers can once again ride the coaster's curves. Nearby, younger riders enjoy the antique carousel, beside a stand selling fresh cotton candy. The Plunge, an indoor fresh-water swimming pool has also been renovated, and is open to the public making Belmont Park a focal point for the beach area.

⑤ Sea World is Mission Bay's grandest attraction, on the shore along Sea World Drive. The world's largest marine-life park, Sea World is an ocean-oriented amusement park set amid tropical landscaping along the bay. The Sky Tower's glass elevator takes you to the top, where the views of San Diego County from the ocean to the mountains are nicest in early morning and late evening.

The traditionally favorite exhibit is the Shamu show, with giant killer whales performing in a newly constructed stadium. The Penguin Encounter has a moving sidewalk passing by a glass-enclosed arctic environment, where hundreds of emperor penguins slide over glaciers into icy waters. The shark exhibit, with fierce-looking sharks of a variety of species, is especially popular with imaginative youngsters.

Sea World spreads over 100 acres of bayfront land, where a cool breeze seems always to rise off the water. A sky tram travels between Sea World and the Atlantis Hotel across Mission Bay. *Sea World is located on Sea World Dr. at the western end of I–8, tel. 619/226–3901. Admission: $22.95 adults, $16.96 children 3–11. Gates open 9–3; park open until 5 PM and later during summer.*

La Jolla

Numbers in the margin correspond with points of interest on the La Jolla map.

La Jollans have long considered their village to be the Monte Carlo of California, and with good cause. Its coastline curves into natural coves backed by verdant hillsides and covered with lavish homes, now worth millions as housing values soar. Though La Jolla is considered part of San Diego, it has its own postal zone and a coveted sense of class. Movie stars and royalty frequent established hotels and private clubs, and the social scene is the stuff gossip columns are made of.

The Indians called it "La Hoya," meaning "the cave," referring to the caves dotting the shoreline. The Spaniards changed the name to La Jolla, meaning "the jewel," and its residents have cherished the name and its allusions ever since. Though development and construction have radically altered the town's once-serene and private character, it remains a haven for the elite, a playground for those who can afford lavish luxuries.

To reach La Jolla from Interstate 5, take the Ardath Road exit if you're traveling north and drive slowly down this long hill so you can appreciate the breathtaking view. Traveling south, take the La Jolla Village Drive exit. If you enjoy meandering, the best way to reach La Jolla from the south is to drive through Mission and Pacific beaches on Mission Boulevard, past the crowds of roller skaters, bicyclists, and sunbathers headed to the beach. The clutter and congestion eases up as the street becomes La Jolla Boulevard, where quiet neighborhoods with winding streets lead down to some of the best surfing beaches in San Diego. The boulevard here is lined with expensive restaurants and cafes and a few take-out spots.

1 La Jolla's coastal attraction is **Ellen Browning Scripps Park** at the **La Jolla Cove.** Towering palms line the sidewalk along Coast Boulevard, where strollers in evening dress are as common as Frisbee throwers. The **Children's Pool,** at the south end of the park, is aptly named for its curving beach and shallow waters protected by a seawall from strong currents and waves.

2 The **La Jolla Caves** are at the far northern point of the cove, under the La Jolla Cave and Shell Shop. A trail leads down from the shop into the caves, with some 133 steps down to the largest, Sunny Jim Cave. For claustrophobic types, there are photos of the caves in the shop, along with a good selection of shells and coral jewelry. *1325 Coast Blvd., tel. 619/454–6080. Admission to caves $1 adults, 50¢ children 3–11. Open Mon.–Sat. 10–5, Sun. 11–5.*

Prospect Street, La Jolla's main boulevard, overlooks the cove from one block up. The street is lined with excellent restaurants, expensive boutiques, and a recent proliferation of office buildings and two-story shopping complexes. Many of the restaurants on the west side of the street have great views of the cove. At the corner of Prospect and Girard streets sits the **3** charming pink **La Valencia Hotel.** Its grand lobby with floor-to-ceiling windows overlooking the cove is a popular weding spot, and its Whaling Bar is the main hangout for La Jolla denizens. The hotel exudes a certain snobbish stuffiness, and as Prospect Street grows ever more crowded, lines of Mercedes and Jaguars crowd the valet stand at the hotel's entrance. Pretend you are visiting nobility and wander through the lobby to the outdoor balcony—the view is worth the deception.

Like Prospect Street, Girard Street is lined with expensive shops, where the wares are lovely to look at, even if they are unaffordable. The shopping and dining district has spread to Pearl and other side streets, with a steady parade of amblers and sightseers strolling about, chatting in many languages. Wall Street, a quiet tree-lined boulevard, was once the financial heart of La Jolla, but banks and investment houses can now be found throughout town. The nightlife scene is an active one here, with jazz clubs, piano bars, and watering holes for the elite younger set coming and going with the trends. Though the village has lost some of its charm and its close-knit community feeling, it has gained a cosmopolitan air that makes it a popular vacation resort for the international set.

4 The **San Diego Museum of Contemporary Art** is the village's cultural center, housed in a remodeled Irving Gill home. The museum has a permanent collection of post-1950 art and often exhibits shows of contemporary art, furnishings, and design. Film series and lectures are held frequently in Sherwood Hall. An excellent bookstore adjacent to the museum has a good collection of art books and magazines. *700 Prospect St., tel. 619/454–3541. Admission: $4 adults, $2 children 12–18, $1 children under 12; free after 5 PM on Wed. Open Tues. and Thurs.–Sun. 10–5, Wed. 10–9.*

North of the cove on La Jolla Shores Drive is the La Jolla Beach and Tennis Club, host of many tennis tournaments. **La Jolla Shores'** beaches are some of the finest in San Diego, with long **5** stretches allotted to surfers or swimmers. The **Scripps Institute of Oceanography,** up the hill from the shore, has a fine aquarium with more than 20 huge tanks filled with colorful saltwater fish and helpful exhibits on how tides affect the shoreline. The fish are most active during feeding time, at 1:30 on Wednesday and Sunday. An outdoor tidal-pool exhibit is filled with starfish, sea anemones, lobsters, crabs, and myraid sea creatures that inhabit the local shoreline. The bookstore has a nice selection of illustrated books and cards. There are paths leading down from the institution's buildings to the beaches at La Jolla Shores. The beach north of the Scripps Pier is a great tidal-pool spot, where you can find all sorts of sea creatures. If you plan to stay at the beach, be sure not to park at a meter. A new aquarium building is scheduled to open in 1992. *8602 La Jolla Shores Dr., tel. 619/534–6933. Suggested admission by donation: $3 adults, $2 children 12–18, $1 children 3–11. Open daily 9–5.*

San Diego for Free

San Diego's main attractions are its climate and natural beauty, which are accessible to all, free of charge. The 70 miles of beaches are free—no boardwalks with admission fees, no high-priced parking lots. All you need is a swimsuit and a towel. You can easily while away a week or two just visiting a different beach community each day, from the opulence of La Jolla to the laid-back hippie style of Ocean Beach. Nearly all San Diego's major attractions in our Exploring section are situated amid huge parks, gardens, and waterfronts, with plenty of natural wonders to keep you amused.

Mission Bay is a massive playground for all ages, with beaches for sunning and swimming, playgrounds and picnic tables, and fire rings for nighttime bonfires. **Balboa Park** is similarly entrancing, with its gorgeous gardens and recreational areas. **Seaport Village** hosts a popular series of pops concerts on summer nights, complete with fireworks displays, all for free. **Sea World** has fireworks as well, which are visible from Mission Bay and Ocean Beach.

What to See and Do with Children

As if swimming, roller-skating, biking, and hiking weren't enough, San Diego has plenty of additional activities to keep kids happy. The **San Diego Zoo** and **San Diego Wild Animal Park** both have children's petting zoos, where the animals are content to play nicely with curious kids. The zoo's animal nursery is a lot of fun for the little ones, who can spot baby chimps and antelopes playing with the same brightly colored plastic toys that all kids enjoy.

Many of **Balboa Park's** museums have special exhibits for children. Kids seem particularly entranced by the Museum of Man's "Lifestyles and Ceremonies" exhibit; teens delight in the small collection of mummies. The Natural History Museum's dinosaurs are always a hit. But best of all is the Science Center at the Reuben H. Fleet Space Theater, where the gadgets and hands-on experiments are fascinatingly clever and educational.

Sea World's Cap'n Kids' World is an imaginative, no-holds-barred playground that captures kids and occupies their energy and time for hours on end. The play equipment is designed for various ages—the little ones like tumbling in huge pools of plastic balls, while older kids like racing all over the rope swings and balconies. The playground is so popular that San Diegans often get yearly passes to Sea World so they can bring their kids and have some time to sit peacefully in the sun while the kids play.

Mission Bay and many of the beaches have large playgrounds by the water. In **Old Town,** Geppetto's toy store is a must-see for its inexpensive gadgets imported from Europe. The carousels at Balboa Park and the zoo are good for burning up some energy. **Belmont Park** in Mission Beach is a mini-amusement park by the sea, with a renovated 1925 rollercoaster, a carousel, a photo booth where you can pose on a surfboard inside a plastic wave, and a life-size gyroscope ride.

Off the Beaten Track

Don't think you've finished seeing San Diego once you've hit all the main attractions. The real character of the place doesn't shine through until you've hit a few neighborhoods and mingle with the natives. Then you can say you've seen San Diego.

Mission Hills is an older neighborhood near downtown that has the charm and wealth of La Jolla and Point Loma, without the crowds. The prettiest streets are above Presidio Park and Old Town, where huge mansions with rolling lawns resemble eastern estates. Drive along Fort Stockton Drive up from the Presidio, or Juan Street past Heritage Park in Old Town to Sunset Boulevard to see these homes. Washington Street runs up a steep hill from Interstate 8 through the center of Mission Hills. Palmier's, at the corner of Washington Street and Goldfinch, is a French cafe and charcuterie with wonderful pâtés, pastries, and wines to eat there or to go. On Goldfinch, visit the Gathering, a neighborhood restaurant with great breakfasts and outdoor tables for reading the Sunday paper in the sun.

Hillcrest, farther up Washington Street beginning at First Avenue, is San Diego's Castro Street, the center for the homosexual community and artists of all types. University Avenue and Fourth and Fifth avenues are filled with cafes, boutiques, and excellent bookstores. The Guild Theater, on Fifth Avenue between University Avenue and Robinson, shows first-run foreign films and has nice balcony seating, unusual in this age of multiplexes. The Blue Door, next to the theater, is one of San Diego's best small bookstores, with a great collection of books on art, philosophy, and other erudite matters. The Corvette Diner, on Fourth Avenue between University Avenue and Washington Street, is an outrageous fifties-diner sort of place, with burgers and shakes and campy waitresses. Quel Fromage, a coffeehouse on University Avenue between Fourth and Fifth streets, has long been the place to go to discuss philosophical or romantic matters over espresso. Washington Street eventually becomes Adams Avenue, San Diego's Antiques Row, with shops displaying an odd array of antiques and collectibles. Adams Avenue leads into Kensington and Talmadge, two lovely old neighborhoods overlooking Mission Valley. The Ken Cinema, at 4066 Adams Avenue, shows older cult movies and current art films.

Shopping

Most San Diego shops are open daily 10–6; department stores and shops within the larger malls stay open until 9 PM on weekdays. Almost every store will accept traveler's checks, with proper identification (driver's license, passport). Aside from their own credit cards, major department stores usually accept American Express, MasterCard, and Visa. Sales are advertised in the daily *San Diego Union* and San Diego edition of the *Los Angeles Times* and in the *Reader,* a free weekly that comes out on Thursday.

Shopping Distircts   San Diego's shopping areas are a mélange of self-contained mega-malls, historic districts, quaint villages, funky neighborhoods, and chic suburbs.

Coronado. Across the bay, Coronado is accessible by car or ferry. **Orange Avenue,** in the center of town, has six blocks of ritzy boutiques and galleries. The elegant Hotel Del Coronado, also on Orange Avenue, houses exclusive (and costly) specialty shops. **Old Ferry Landing,** where the new ferry lands, is a waterfront center similar to Seaport Village.

Downtown. Horton Plaza, in the heart of center city, is a shopper's Disneyland—visually exciting, multilevels of department stores, one-of-a-kind shops, fast-food counters, classy restaurants, a farmer's market, live theater, and cinemas. Surrounding Horton Plaza is the 16-block Gaslamp Quarter, a redevelopment area that features art galleries and antiques and specialty shops, housed in Victorian buildings and renovated warehouses.

Hotel Circle. The Hotel Circle area, northeast of downtown near I–8 and Freeway 163, has two major shopping centers.

Fashion Valley and **Mission Valley Center** contain hundreds of shops, as well as restaurants, cinemas, and branches of almost every San Diego department store.

Kensington/Hillcrest. These are two of San Diego's older, established neighborhoods, situated several miles north and east of downtown. **Adams Avenue,** in Kensington, is Antiques Row. More than 20 dealers sell everything from postcards and kitchen utensils to cut glass and porcelain. **Park Boulevard,** in Hillcrest, is the city's center for nostalgia. Small shops, on either side of University Avenue, stock clothing, accessories, furnishings, and bric-a-brac of the 1920s–1960s. **Uptown District,** a new shopping center on University Avenue has the neighborhood's massive Ralph's grocery store, and several specialty shops.

La Jolla/Golden Triangle. La Jolla, about 15 miles northwest of downtown, on the coast, is an ultrachic, ultraexclusive resort community. High-end and trendy boutiques line Girard Avenue and Prospect Street. Coast Walk, nestled along the cliffside of Prospect Street, offers several levels of sophisticated shops, galleries, and restaurants, as well as a spectacular ocean view. The Golden Triangle area, several miles east of coastal La Jolla, is served by two malls. **La Jolla Village Square,** just west of I–5, is an indoor shopping complex; **University Towne Centre,** farther inland, between I–5 and Highway 805, is an open-air village. Both centers feature the usual range of department stores, specialty shops, sportswear chains, restaurants, and cinemas.

Old Town. North of downtown, off I–5, this popular historic district is reminiscent of a colorful Mexican marketplace. Adobe architecture, flower-filled plazas, fountains, and courtyards highlight the shopping areas of **Bazaar del Mundo, La Esplanade,** and **Old Town Mercado,** where you will find international goods, toys, souvenirs, and arts and crafts.

Seaport Village. On the waterfront, a few minutes from downtown, **Seaport Village** offers quaint theme shops, restaurants, arts and crafts galleries, and commanding views of Coronado, the bridge, and passing ships.

Beaches

Overnight camping is not allowed on any of the beaches, but there are campgrounds at some state beaches. Lifeguards are stationed at city beaches (from Sunset Cliffs to Black's Beach) in the summertime, but coverage in winter is erratic. It should be noted that few beaches in San Diego are ideal for dogs, although exceptions are noted below and it is rarely a problem on unpatrolled, isolated beaches, especially during the winter. Glass is prohibited on all beaches, and fires are allowed only in fire rings or barbecues. A year-long ban on alcoholic beverages—including beer—on all city beaches went into effect in April 1991. For a general beach and weather report, call 619/225–9494.

Beaches are listed from south to north. For information on Mission Bay, *see* Exploring, above.

Border Field State Beach. The southernmost San Diego beach is different from most California beaches. Located just north of the Mexican border, it is a marshy area with wide chaparrals and wildflowers, a favorite of horse riders and hikers. Frequent sewage contamination from Tijuana makes the water unpleasant—if not downright dangerous—for swimming. There is ample parking and there are rest rooms and fire rings. *Exit I–5 at Dairy Mart Rd. and head west along Monument Rd.*

South Beach. One of the few beaches where dogs are free to romp, this is a good beach for long, isolated walks. The often-contaminated water and rocky beach tend to keep away crowds. The downside: There are few facilities, such as rest rooms. *Located at the end of Seacoast Dr. Take I–5 to Coronado Ave. and head west on Imperial Beach Ave. Turn left onto Seacoast Dr.*

Imperial Beach. A classic Southern California beach, where surfers and swimmers congregate to enjoy the water and waves, the Imperial Beach Municipal Pier provides a pleasant backdrop for the Frisbee games of the predominantly young crowd. Imperial Beach is also the site of the U.S. Open Sand Castle Competition every July. There are lifeguards on duty during the summer, parking lots, food vendors nearby, and rest room facilities. *Take Palm Ave. west from I–5 until it hits water.*

Silver Strand State Beach. Farther north on the isthmus of Coronado (commonly mislabeled an island), Silver Strand was set aside as a state beach in 1932. The name is derived from the tiny silver seashells found in abundance near the water. The water is relatively calm, making it ideal for families. Four parking lots provide room for more than 1,500 cars. Parking costs $6 per car. There is also an RV campground and a wide array of facilities. *Take the Palm Ave. exit from I–5 west to State Hwy. 75; turn right and follow the signs.*

Coronado Beach. With the famous Hotel Del Coronado as a backdrop, this wide stretch of sandy beach is one of the largest in the county. It is surprisingly uncrowded on most days, since the locals go to the less touristy areas to the south or north. It's a perfect beach for sunbathing or games of Frisbee and Smash Ball (played with paddles and a small ball). Parking can be a little difficult on the busiest days, but there are plenty of rest rooms and service facilities, as well as fire rings. The view (even for a brief moment) as you drive over the Coronado Bridge makes it a worthwhile excursion. *From the bridge, turn left on Orange Ave. and follow the signs.*

Sunset Cliffs. Back on the mainland, beneath the jagged cliffs on the west side of Point Loma peninsula, is one of the more secluded beaches in the area, popular primarily with surfers and locals. The tide goes out each day to reveal tide pools teeming with life at the south end of the peninsula, near Cabrillo Point. Farther north, the waves attract surfers and the lonely coves attract sunbathers. Stairs are available at the foot of Bermuda and Santa Cruz avenues, but much of the access is limited to treacherous cliff trails. Another negative: There are no available facilities. *Take I–8 west to Sunset Cliffs Blvd. and head south.*

Ocean Beach. The northern end of this beach, past the second jetty, is known as Dog Beach, the only beach within San Diego city limits that allows dogs to romp around without a leash. The southern end of Ocean Beach, near the pier, is a hangout for surfers and transients. Much of the area, though, is a haven for local volleyball players, sunbathers, and swimmers. Limited parking, fire rings, and food vendors are available. *Reach Ocean Beach by taking I–8 west to Sunset Cliffs Blvd. and heading south. Turn right on Voltaire St., West Point Loma Blvd., or Newport Ave.*

Mission Beach. It's not Atlantic City, but the boardwalk stretching along Mission Beach is a popular spot for strollers, roller skaters, and bicyclists. The south end is a popular spot for surfers, swimmers, and volleyball players. It tends to get extremely crowded, especially on hot summer days. Toward the north end, near the old Belmont Park roller coaster, the beach narrows and the water grows rougher—and the crowd gets even thicker. The newly refurbished Belmont Park is now a shopping and dining complex. Parking can be a challenge, but there are plenty of rest rooms and restaurants in the area. *Exit I–5 at Garnet Ave. and head west to Mission Blvd. Turn south and look for parking.*

Pacific Beach. The boardwalk turns into a sidewalk, but there are still bike paths and picnic tables running along the beachfront. The beach is a favorite for local teens, and the blare of rock music can be annoying. Parking, too, can be a problem, although there is a small lot at the foot of Ventura Place. *Same directions as for Mission Beach, except go north on Mission Blvd.*

Tourmaline Surfing Park and **Windansea Beach.** Immortalized in Tom Wolfe's 1965 book, *The Pumphouse Gang*, these La Jolla beaches are two of the top surfing spots in the area. Tourmaline has the better parking area. *Take Mission Blvd. north (it turns into La Jolla Blvd.) and turn west on Tourmaline St. (for the surfing park) or Nautilus St. (for Windansea Beach).*

Marine Street Beach. This is a classic stretch of sand for sunbathing and Frisbee games. *Accessible from Marine St. off La Jolla Blvd.*

Children's Pool. For the tikes, a shallow lagoon with small waves and no riptide provides a safe, if crowded, haven. *It can be reached by following La Jolla Blvd. north. When it forks, take the left choice, Coast Blvd.*

La Jolla Cove. Just north of the Children's Pool is La Jolla Cove, simply one of the prettiest spots in the world. A beautiful, palm-tree-lined park sits on top of cliffs formed by the incessant pounding of the waves. At low tide the tidal pools and cliff caves provide a goal for explorers. Seals sun themselves on the rocks. Divers explore the underwater delights of the San Diego–La Jolla Underwater Park, an ecological reserve. The cove also is a favorite of rough-water swimmers. Buoys mark distances for them. The beach below the cove is almost nonexistent at high tide, but the cove is still a must-see. *Follow Coast Blvd. north to the signs, or take the La Jolla Village Dr. exit from I–5, head west to Torrey Pines Rd., turn left and drive down the hill to Girard Ave. Turn right and follow the signs.*

La Jolla Shores. This is one of the most popular and overcrowded beaches in the county. On holidays such as Memorial Day, all access routes are usually closed. The lures are a wide sandy beach, relatively calm surf, and a concrete boardwalk paralleling the beach. There are also a wide variety of facilities, from posh restaurants to snack shops, within easy walking distance. Go early to get a parking spot. *From I–5 take La Jolla Village Dr. west and turn left onto La Jolla Shores Dr. Head west to Camino del Oro or Vallecitos St. Turn right and look for parking.*

Black's Beach. Once this was the only legal nude beach in the country, before nudity was outlawed in the late 1970s. But that doesn't stop people from braving the treacherous cliff trails for a chance to take off their clothes. Above the beach, hang gliders and sail-plane enthusiasts launch from the Torrey Pines Glider Port. Because of the difficult access, the beach is always relatively uncrowded. The waves make it a favorite haunt for surfers. *Take Genessee Ave. west from I–5 and follow the signs to the glider port.*

Participant Sports

At least one stereotype of San Diego is true—it is an active, outdoors-oriented community. People recreate more than spectate. It is hard not to, with such a wide variety of choices available.

Bicycling On any given summer day, Old Highway 101, from La Jolla to Oceanside, looks like a freeway for cyclists. Never straying more than a quarter-mile from the beach, it is easily the most popular and scenic ride around. Although the roads are narrow and windy, experienced cyclists like to follow Lomas Santa Fe Drive in Solana Beach east into beautiful Rancho Santa Fe, perhaps even continuing east on Del Dios Highway, past Lake Hodges, to Escondido. For more leisurely rides, Mission Bay, San Diego Harbor, and the Mission Beach boardwalk are all flat and scenic. San Diego even has a velodrome in Balboa Park, for those who like to race on a track. Call the Velodrome Office at 619/296–3345 for more information.

Bikes can be rented at any number of bike stores, including **Alpine Rent A Bike** in Pacific Beach (tel. 619/273–0440), **Hamel's Action Sports Center** in Mission Beach (tel. 619/488–5050), and **California Bicycle** in La Jolla (tel. 619/454–0316). A free comprehensive map of all county bike paths is available from the local office of the **California Department of Transportation** (tel. 619/688–6699).

Diving Enthusiasts from all over the world flock to La Jolla to skin-dive and scuba dive in the areas off the La Jolla Cove that are rich in ocean creatures and flora. The area marks the south end of the **San Diego–La Jolla Underwater Park,** an ecological preserve. Farther north, off the south end of Black's Beach, **Scripps Canyon** lies in about 60 feet of water. Accessible by boat, the canyon plummets to more than 175 feet in some sections. Another popular diving spot is off Sunset Cliffs in Point Loma, where lobster and a wide variety of sea life are relatively close to shore, although the strong rip currents make it an area best enjoyed by experienced divers.

Diving equipment and boat trips can be arranged through **San Diego Divers** (tel. 619/224–3439), **Ocean Enterprises** (tel. 619/565–6054), or at the several **Diving Locker** locations throughout the area. It is illegal to take any wildlife from the ecological preserves in La Jolla or near Cabrillo Point. Spearfishing requires a license (available at most dive stores), and it is illegal to take out-of-season lobster and game fish out of the water.

For general diving information, contact the San Diego City Lifeguards' office at 619/221–8884).

Fishing Variety is the key. The Pacific Ocean is full of corbina, croaker, and halibut just itching to be your dinner. No license is required to fish from a public pier, such as the Ocean Beach pier. A fishing license from the state Department of Fish and Game, available at most bait and tackle stores, is required for fishing from the shoreline, although children under 15 won't need one.

Several companies offer half-day, day, or multiday fishing expeditions in search of marlin, tuna, albacore, and other deepwater fish. **Fisherman's Landing** (tel. 619/229–0391), **H & M Landing** (tel. 619/222–1144), and **Seaforth Boat Rentals** (tel. 619/223–1681) are among the companies operating from San Diego. **Helgren's Sportfishing** (tel. 619/722–2133) offers trips from Oceanside Harbor.

Fitness Why let a gluttonous vacation or strenuous business trip interrupt your training schedule? Several hotels offer full health clubs, at least with weight machines, stationary bicycles, and spas, including, in the downtown area, the **Omni San Diego** (910 Broadway Circle, tel. 619/239–2200) and the **U.S. Grant Hotel** (326 Broadway, tel. 619/232–3121). Other hotels with health clubs include: the **Hotel Del Coronado** (1500 Orange Ave., Coronado, tel. 619/435–6611), **Sheraton Grand** (1580 Harbor Island Dr., Harbor Island, tel. 619/291–2900), **Le Meridien** (2000 Second St., Coronado, tel. 619/435–3000), the **San Diego Hilton Beach and Tennis Resort** (1775 E. Mission Bay Dr., Mission Bay, tel. 619/276–4010), the **La Costa Hotel and Spa** (Costa del Mar Rd., Carlsbad, tel. 619/438–9111), and the **Olympic Resort Hotel** (6111 El Camino Real, Carlsbad, tel. 619/438–3330). Guests of the **Town and Country Hotel** (500 Hotel Circle, tel. 619/291–7131) and the **Hanalei Hotel** (2770 Hotel Circle, tel. 619/297–1101) have access to the tennis and racquetball courts, weight room, saunas, and other facilities of the nearby **Atlas Health Club** (901 Hotel Circle S., tel. 619/298–9321), in Mission Valley. The dozen **Family Fitness Centers** in the area (including centers in Mission Valley, tel. 619/281–5543; Sports Arena area, tel. 619/224–2902; and La Jolla, tel. 619/457–3930) allow nonmembers to use the facilities for a small fee. A company called **Sweat 'N Smile Inc.** (320 Upas St., tel. 619/296–6776) offers fitness and recreation programs, including classes, volleyball, and baseball, geared toward travelers.

Golf To list the more than 70 golf courses in San Diego County requires more space than we have here. Suffice it to say, the following is merely a sampling of the public courses hereabouts.

Balboa Park Municipal Golf Course (Golf Course Dr., San Diego, tel. 619/232–2470), with 18 holes, 5,900 yards, has a neighboring nine-hole course, driving range, equipment rentals, clubhouse, and restaurant.
Coronado Golf Course (2000 Visalia Row, Coronado, tel. 619/435–3121), with 18 holes, 6,700 yards, honors other memberships, and reservations are required; it has a driving range, equipment rentals, and a clubhouse.
Mission Bay Golf Course (2702 N. Mission Bay Dr., San Diego, tel. 619/273–1221), with 18 holes, 3,175 yards, honors other memberships, and reservations are required; it has a driving range and equipment rentals.
Rancho Bernardo Inn and Country Club (17550 Bernardo Oaks

Dr., tel. 800/487–0700) has 18 holes, 6,329 yards; reservations
are required, and it offers a driving range, equipment rentals,
and lodging.
Singing Hills Country Club (3007 Dehesa Rd., El Cajon, tel.
619/442–3425), with 54 holes, honors other memberships; reservations are required, and it offers a driving range, equipment rentals, and lodging.
Torrey Pines Municipal Golf Course (11480 N. Torrey Pines
Rd., La Jolla, tel. 619/453–0380) has 36 holes; reservations are
not required (but suggested), and it offers a driving range,
equipment rentals, and lodging.
Whispering Palms Country Club (Via de la Valle, Rancho Santa
Fe, tel. 619/756–2471), with 27 holes, honors other memberships; reservations are required, and it offers lodging.

Horseback Riding   Expensive insurance has severely cut the number of stables offering horses for rent in San Diego County. The businesses
that remain offer a wide variety of organized excursions. **Holidays on Horseback** (tel. 619/445–3997) in the East County town
of Descanso leads rides ranging from a few hours to a few days
in the Cuyamaca Mountains. It rents special, easy-to-ride fox
trotters to make it a little easier for beginners. **Rancho San
Diego Stables** (tel. 619/670–1861) is located near Spring Valley.
South of Imperial Beach, near the Mexican border, **Hilltop Stables** (tel. 619/428–5441), and **Sandi's Rental Stables** (tel. 619/
424–3124) lead rides through Border Field State Park.

Jogging   There is no truth to the rumor that San Diego was created to be
one big jogging track. But it often seems that way. From downtown, the most popular run is along the Embarcadero, which
stretches around the bay. There are nice, uncongested sidewalks through most of the area. The alternative for downtown
visitors is to head east to Balboa Park, where a labyrinth of
trails snake through the canyons. Mission Bay may be the most
popular jogging spot, renowned for its wide sidewalks and basically flat landscape. Trails head west around Fiesta Island from
Mission Bay, providing distance as well as a scenic route. The
beaches, of course, are extremely popular with runners. But
there is no reason to go where everyone else goes. Running is
one of the best ways to explore San Diego, especially along the
coast. There are organized runs almost every weekend; check
any local sporting goods store for more information. Some tips:
Don't run in bike lanes, and check the local newspaper's tide
charts before heading to the beach.

Surfing   In San Diego, surfing is a year-round sport (thanks to wet suits
in the winter) for people of all ages. Surprisingly, it's not hard
to learn. Anyone can get on a board and paddle around. For the
hardcore, some of the most popular surfing spots are the Ocean
Beach pier, Tourmaline Surfing Park in La Jolla, Windansea
Beach in La Jolla, South Cardiff State Beach, and Swami's (Sea
Cliff Roadside Park) in Encinitas. Be aware that most public
beaches have separate areas for surfers.

Many local surf shops rent boards, including **Star Surfing Company** (tel. 619/273–7827) in Pacific Beach and **La Jolla Surf Systems** (tel. 619/456–2777) and **Hansen's Sporting Goods** (tel. 619/
753–6595) in Encinitas.

Tennis   There are more than 1,300 courts spread around the county,
most of them in private clubs. But there are a few public facilities. **Morley Field** (tel. 619/298–0920), in Balboa Park, has 25

courts, 12 of which are lighted. Nonmembers, however, cannot make reservations, so it's first come, first served. There is a nominal fee for use of the courts. The **La Jolla Recreation Center** (tel. 619/454–2071) offers nine public courts near downtown La Jolla, five of them lighted. Use of the courts is free. There are 12 lighted courts at **Robb Field** (tel. 619/224–7581) in Ocean Beach, with a small day-use fee.

The list of hotel complexes with tennis facilities includes the **Bahia Resort Hotel** (tel. 619/488–0551), the **Hotel Del Coronado** (tel. 619/435–6611), the **Kona Kai Beach and Tennis Resort** (tel. 619/222–1191), **Hilton San Diego** (tel. 619/276–4010), the **La Costa Hotel and Spa** (tel. 619/438–9111), and the **Rancho Bernardo Inn and Country Club** (tel. 619/487–1611). Intense tennis instruction is available at **John Gardiner's Rancho Valencia Resort** (tel. 619/756–1123 or 800/548–3664) in Rancho Santa Fe. Some of the larger private clubs are **Atlas Health Club** (tel. 619/298–9321), **San Diego Country Estates** (tel. 619/789–3826), **San Diego Tennis and Racquet Club** (tel. 619/275–3270), and **Tennis La Jolla** (tel. 619/459–0869).

Waterskiing   Mission Bay is one of the most popular waterskiing areas in Southern California. It is best to get out early when the water is smooth and the crowds are small. In Carlsbad, the **Snug Harbor Marina** (tel. 619/434–3089) is small, but off the beaten path. Boats and equipment can be rented from **Seaforth Boat Rentals** (1641 Quivera Rd., near Mission Bay, tel. 619/223–1681). The private **San Diego and Mission Bay Boat and Ski Club** (2606 N. Mission Bay Dr., tel. 619/276–0830) operates a slalom course and ski jump in Mission Bay's Hidden Anchorage. Permission from the club or the Mission Bay Harbor Patrol (tel. 619/224–1862) must be obtained to use the course and jump.

One of the few lakes in the county allowing waterskiing is **Lake San Vicente** (tel. 619/562–1042), located north of Lakeside off Interstate 8.

Spectator Sports

San Diego doesn't have a professional basketball franchise, ever since the Clippers left for Los Angeles, but it has just about every other type of sporting team and event, including a few exclusive to the area. For information on tickets to any event, contact **Teleseat** (tel. 619/452–7328). **San Diego Jack Murphy Stadium** is located at the intersection of interstates 8 and 805.

Baseball   From April through September, the **San Diego Padres** (tel. 619/280–4494) slug it out for bragging rights in the National League West. Matchups with such rivals as the hated Los Angeles Dodgers and San Francisco Giants usually are the highlights of the home season at San Diego Jack Murphy Stadium. Tickets range from $4 to $9.50 and usually are readily available, unless the Padres are in the thick of the pennant race.

Basketball   No pro team, but the San Diego State University Aztecs (tel. 619/283–7378) play at the San Diego Sports Arena (tel. 619/224–4171) December through March. The University of San Diego (tel. 619/260–4600) plays in the West Coast Athletic Conference and has earned trips to the NCAA national tournament and competes with the top teams in the country.

Football The **San Diego Chargers** (tel. 619/280–2111) have been one of the National Football League's most exciting teams since the merger with the American Football League. The Chargers were one of the original AFL franchises, originally based in Los Angeles. They fill San Diego Jack Murphy Stadium August through December. Games with AFC West rivals Los Angeles Raiders and Denver Broncos are always particularly intense.

Golf The La Costa Hotel and Spa (tel. 619/438–9111) hosts the prestigious **Tournament of Champions** in January, featuring the winners of the previous year's tournaments. The **Shearson-Lehman Brothers Open** brings the pros to the Torrey Pines Municipal Golf Course (tel. 619/453–0380). The Stoneridge Country Club (tel. 619/487–2117) hosts the **Ladies Professional Golf Association** in the spring.

Horse Racing Begun 50 years ago by Bing Crosby, Pat O'Brien, and their Hollywood cronies, the annual summer meeting of the **Del Mar Thoroughbred Club** (tel. 619/755–1141), located on the Del Mar Fairgrounds—"Where the Turf Meets the Surf" in Del Mar. The meeting begins in July and continues through early September, every day except Tuesday. But that is not the end of horse racing action in Del Mar. The Del Mar Fairgrounds also serves as a satellite wagering facility with betting on races on television from tracks throughout California. Take Interstate 5 north to the Via de la Valle Road exit (tel. 619/755–1161 for daily information).

Sailing The **America's Cup XXVIII** races will be held in San Diego in May 1992. A series of competitions that began in January will decide which boat will defend the cup and which of the challengers will race it in the one-on-one finals. For information call 800/922–8792.

Dining

San Diego certainly is a restaurant town in the sense that it offers one of the highest per capita ratios of dining places to population in the country; at last count, there were some 4,000 foodservice establishments in San Diego County. But it is not yet an eating capital in the style of Los Angeles and New York, where good or excellent restaurant meals are taken for granted.

The city's gastronomic reputation rests primarily on its seafood, which is so popular that even modest restaurants make a point of offering several fish specials daily. You are never more than a stone's throw from one or more seafood restaurants in San Diego. Bear in mind, though, that better restaurants offer better seafood dishes. As is true elsewhere, restaurants endowed with spectacular views—and there are many such in San Diego—often invest far more effort in washing the picture windows than in cooking. More and more good restaurants open every year, however, and a city that once stood solidly in the meat-and-potatoes camp now boasts Afghan, Thai, Vietnamese, and other exotic cuisines in addition to the more familiar French, Italian, and Chinese. Visitors naturally seek out Mexican restaurants, of which there are hundreds, but most of these serve California-style Mexican dishes, which have little to do with the excellent cuisine prepared south of the border.

The rules of dining out in San Diego are simple and pleasant. Most eateries serve lunch and dinner; breakfast is largely the province of hotels and coffee shops. Most restaurants accept reservations, but few require them, and waits are uncommon outside the beach areas. Dress codes, by and large, do not exist beyond simple shirt and shoes requirements, except at a handful of top restaurants that require men to wear jackets. City natives like to dine around 7:30 PM, and it is at that hour that restaurants will be the most crowded. Few restaurants offer seating past 9:30 or 10 PM.

The principal restaurant locations are in the renovated downtown area; in historic Old Town, site of the first settlement and close to the downtown area; in the beach neighborhoods; and in exclusive La Jolla, a lovely resort area that slopes from the top of Mt. Soledad to the sea and attracts jet-setters and trend setters from around the globe. Mission Valley, which remains a tourist center thanks to its concentration of hotels, sprouts restaurants like weeds, but is a virtual desert when it comes to high-quality cuisine. A similar caveat must be offered about the large, tourist-oriented eateries on Shelter and Harbor islands, which, in effect, rent out their enjoyable views and lively atmospheres by charging hefty prices for mediocre food.

Restaurants are grouped first by location and then by type of cuisine. The most highly recommended restaurants in each price category are indicated by a star ★.

Category	Cost*
Very Expensive	over $35
Expensive	$25–$35
Moderate	$15–$25
Inexpensive	under $15

*per person, without tax (6.5%), service, or drinks

Downtown
American
★

Dobson's. Consciously San Franciscan in style, Dobson's attracts the city's power structure during the day and well-heeled performing arts patrons at night. The menu changes daily and is uniformly excellent, beginning with the always-available mussel bisque and continuing with superb fish, veal, fowl, and beef entrees. The service and wine list also approach perfection. *956 Broadway Circle, tel. 619/231–6771. Reservations suggested. Dress: for success. AE, MC, V. No lunch Sat. Closed Sun. Very Expensive.*

Chinese
★

Panda Inn. Clean, graceful lines and fine works of art replace the paper lanterns and garish dragons that decorate most Chinese eateries, but, better yet, this is a place to which you can take visiting Chinese friends with utter confidence. Thanks to superior kitchen and service staffs, this is not only the city's best Chinese restaurant, but one of its best restaurants, period. Its location in Horton Plaza, downtown San Diego's shopping and entertainment hub, makes it a natural place to stop for "burnt" pork, sensational hot and pungent chicken and shrimp, succulent steamed dumplings, ridiculously delicious Szechuan-style green beans, and first-rate Peking duck. *506 Horton Plaza, tel. 619/233–7800. Reservations accepted. Dress: casual. AE, MC, V. Inexpensive.*

Mexican **Casa de Pico.** The centerpiece of the Bazaar del Mundo shopping and dining complex, this colorful eatery is a mecca for tourists who come to eat beans until they nearly burst. All the traditional American–Mexican foods, such as burritos, enchiladas, quesadillas, and tostadas vie for space on the menu, and if one wants "safe," moderately seasoned Mexican fare, this is one of the prime locations in which to find it. *2754 Calhoun St., tel. 619/296–3267. Reservations unnecessary. Dress: very casual. AE, DC, MC, V. Inexpensive.*

Old Town Mexican Cafe. This old standby looks a touch seedy, but the burritos, enchiladas, and *carne asada*, thin slices of grilled, marinated steak, are sufficiently satisfying that lines are common even during the middle of the afternoon. Carnitas and shredded beef tacos are two of the dishes responsible for this restaurant's popularity with locals and visitors. This restaurant serves late, which makes it a good place at which to satisfy a midnight taco craving. *2489 San Diego Ave., tel. 619/297–4330. Reservations accepted for groups. Dress: casual. AE, MC, V. Inexpensive.*

Mixed Menu **Old Columbia Brewery & Grill.** As the first microbrewery in San Diego, Old Columbia can be somewhat forgiven for paying more attention to its house brews than to its menu, a well-written but perfunctorily executed listing of snacks, burgers, salads, and entrees. The draw is the beer, tapped directly from tanks in the adjacent brewing room. The nibbles to go along with the Gaslamp Gold ale or the Downtown After Dark lager are beer-battered fish and chips, hefty onion rings, and oversize hamburgers. Downtown mingles here when the sun sets, and the action runs late. *1157 Columbia St., tel. 619/234–2739. Reservations accepted. Dress: casual. MC, V. Inexpensive.*

Seafood **Cafe Pacifica.** The menu changes daily to reflect the market availability of a globe-spanning selection of fish and shellfish, most of which presumably are very pleased to place themselves in Cafe Pacifica's competent hands. The approach is moderately nouvelle, which means that light, interesting sauces and imaginative garnishes are likely to be teamed with simply cooked fillets of salmon, sea bass, swordfish, and so forth. Consider oysters and smoked fish as good opening courses, and don't miss the indulgent crème brûlée dessert. *2414 San Diego Ave., tel. 619/291–6666. Reservations accepted. Dress: thoughtfully informal. AE, DC, MC, V. No lunch weekends. Moderate.*

Harbor House. This very popular eatery serves so much seafood that it is a wonder that the oceans have not been depleted in the years since it opened. Although the place could coast on its location in jammed Seaport Village, it turns in a good-quality performance with its shellfish appetizers, creamy chowder, and a long list of daily fish specials, the majority of which are simply grilled over mesquite. *831 W. Harbor Dr., tel. 619/232–1141. Reservations accepted. Dress: informal. AE, MC, V. Moderate.*

Southwestern–Nouvelle **Pacifica Grill.** If you've never had *canarditas* (and you probably haven't), this is the place to visit for juicy chunks of slowly cooked duck, which one garnishes with any of a dozen spicy or savory condiments and then rolls inside fresh, hot, blue corn tortillas. Since switching to the new Southwestern style of cooking, this ever-trendy restaurant has seen its popularity soar almost as high as the atrium that lights this beautifully remodeled warehouse. The place also serves superior seafood and

Dining

Avanti, **8**
The Belgian Lion, **27**
Cafe Pacifica, **39**
Casa de Pico, **37**
Dobson's, **52**
El Crab Catcher, **12**
Firehouse Beach
Cafe, **20**
Fisherman's Grill, **5**
George's at the
Cove, **3**
Harbor House, **53**
Hard Rock Cafe, **7**
Issimo, **14**
Karinya, **15**
La Gran Tapa, **51**
McCormick &
Schmick's, **17**
Old Columbia Brewery
& Grill, **48**
Old Town Mexican
Cafe, **38**
Pacifica Grill, **49**
Panda Inn, **50**
Piatti, **13**
Red Sails Inn, **32**
St. James Bar, **1**
Salmon House, **26**
Saska's, **18**
Star of India, **6**
Top O' the Cove, **4**

Lodging

Bahia Resort Hotel, **22**
Balboa Park Inn, **45**
Best Western Posada
Inn, **33**
Britt House, **47**
Colonial Inn, **3**
Coronado Motor
Inn, **61**
Dana Inn & Marina, **24**
Doubletree Hotel, **43**
Glorietta Bay Inn, **62**
Hacienda Hotel, **36**
Hanalei House, **41**
Heritage Park Bed &
Breakfast Inn, **40**
Horton Grand
Hotel, **59**
Hotel del
Coronado, **63**
Humphrey's Half
Moon Inn, **31**
Hyatt Islandia, **25**
Kona Kai Beach &
Tennis Resort, **30**
La Jolla Cove Motel, **9**
La Pensione, **60**
La Valencia, **10**
Mission Bay Motel, **16**
Ocean Manor
Apartment Hotel, **28**

San Diego Dining and Lodging

wildly imaginative pastas. *1202 Kettner Blvd., tel. 619/696–9226. Reservations accepted. Dress: to be noticed. AE, DC, MC, V. No lunch weekends. Moderate.*

Spanish **La Gran Tapa.** Carefully modeled to recall the fabled tapas bars that line the principal streets in Madrid, this noisy, busy in-spot prints up a daily menu of classic Spanish snacks and appetizers, with more substantial dishes and even an excellent hamburger thrown in for those who prefer traditional dining. The best bet is to order two or three tapas per person and let the whole table share. Choices include *empanadas* (spicy filled pies) made with pork and olives, or spinach and cheese, or whatever the chef has dreamed up; tiny fried squid; miniature shrimp croquettes; shrimp in garlic sauce; fresh, hot potato chips, and much more. A good spot for late-night dining. *611 B St., tel. 619/234–8272. Reservations suggested. Dress: casual. AE, MC, V. No lunch Sat. Closed Sun. Moderate.*

Beaches **Firehouse Beach Cafe.** The great attractions here are the casu-
American al beach ambience, the sun deck that allows a leisurely meal in full view of the nearby Pacific, and an acceptably prepared menu of sandwiches, seafood, steaks, and other simple American fare. *722 Grand Ave., tel. 619/272–1999. No reservations. Wear anything that fits reasonably well. AE, MC, V. Inexpensive.*

French **The Belgian Lion.** A somewhat fusty, ugly duckling of a restau-
★ rant, The Belgian Lion serves one of the best roast ducklings to be found in the city, along with marvelous creamy soups, excellent braised sweetbreads, poached salmon in a delicious sorrel sauce, sauerkraut braised in champagne with smoked meats and sausages, and a rich cassoulet. The service and wine list are worthy of the menu, and although the decor lacks that certain *je ne sais quoi*, the place has a great deal of charm. *2265 Bacon St., tel. 619/223–2700. Reservations suggested. Dress: casual. AE, DC, MC, V. Closed Sun. and Mon. Expensive.*

Seafood **McCormick and Schmick's.** Upon its opening in early 1988, this
★ excellent seafood house offered a serious challenge to the city's older fish eateries. The menu changes frequently and may include as many as 100 options, all uniformly well prepared and ranging from a lovely selection of fresh oysters to entire Dungeness crabs, a fine crab-and-salmon Newburg, grilled baby salmon, and just about everything else that swims, crawls, or ruminates under the waves. The service is good, the upstairs courtyard pleasant, and a few choice tables have ocean views. An especially good choice for a lazy, self-indulgent lunch. *4190 Mission Blvd., tel. 619/581–3938. Reservations suggested. Dress: casual. AE, DC, MC, V. Moderate.*

Salmon House. As the name implies, this handsome, waterfront restaurant specializes in salmon, grilled over alder wood in the style developed by the Indians of the northwest. Offerings run to other fish, prime ribs, and chicken, but the one real reason to visit this establishment is for the salmon, which *is* hard to top. *1970 Quivera Rd., tel. 619/223–2234. Reservations accepted. Dress: casual. AE, DC, MC, V. Moderate.*

Red Sails Inn. This is not technically at the beach, since it is on the San Diego Bay side of Point Loma. It's an old favorite with old salts, though, and a natural for anyone in search of good, simple seafood at a waterfront location. The restaurant is surrounded by yacht basins and thus enjoys a large following among nautical types, who especially treasure its hearty, all-

American breakfasts and late-night snacks. *2614 Shelter Island Dr., tel. 619/223–3030. Reservations for large parties only. Dress: casual. AE, DC, MC, V. Inexpensive.*

Steak and Seafood   **Saska's.** Walk through the doors and you're in the genuine heart of Old Mission Beach, whose lazy pulse still throbs here when the conversation in the bar turns to sports, especially San Diego's peculiar form of baseball called over-the-line. The food is simple but first rate; choices include shellfish cocktails, a fine crab chowder, the fresh fish offerings of the day (simply but beautifully grilled), and some of the best steaks in town. This is the only place that serves a full, quality menu until 3 AM nightly. *3768 Mission Blvd., tel. 619/488–7311. Reservations accepted. The waiters wear shorts, and you can, too. AE, DC, MC, V. No lunch weekdays. Moderate.*

Thai   **Karinya.** Designed and operated by a Thai architect, Karinya is rather soothingly pretty while still every bit as casual as the most beachy beachgoer could desire (and in San Diego, that's pretty casual). Start with the spicy salad called *larb* and the sweet noodles called *mee krob*, and then move along to the tart, savory *tom yum gai* soup. The entree list gets hot and spicy with the curries (the beef *penang nuah*, and a fiery blend of shrimp and pineapple), and turns mild with myriad noodle dishes. Everything is quite, quite good, including the service. *4475 Mission Blvd., tel. 619/270–5050. Reservations accepted. Dress: Jeans will suffice. AE, MC, V. No lunch weekends. Closed Mon. Inexpensive.*

La Jolla   **George's at the Cove.** A lovely, art-filled dining room, excellent
California   service, a good view of La Jolla Cove and an imaginative, well-
★   prepared menu make this one of the city's best restaurants. Pay special attention to the seafood, but the pasta, beef, and veal dishes and poultry specialties are also uniformly excellent. Desserts are outsized, grandiose, and irresistible. *1250 Prospect St., tel. 619/454–4244. Reservations suggested. Dress chicly because everyone else is sure to be. AE, DC, MC, V. Expensive.*

French   **St. James Bar.** A new offering from leading San Diego restaurateur Paul Dobson, the St. James Bar is a magnet for the area business folk at lunch and the glitterati at night. All are drawn by the creamy mussel bisque, the sweetbreads in truffle juice sauce, the delicate poached Norwegian salmon in saffron sauce, and other beautifully realized offerings. One of the city's top five eateries, it offers expert cuisine in a luxurious setting that includes marble floors, art from a top gallery, and an incongruous but handsome 100-year-old bar rescued from a Montana saloon. *4370 La Jolla Village Dr., tel. 619/453–6650. Reservations suggested. Dress: casual. AE, MC, V. No lunch Sat., closed Sun. Very Expensive.*

★   **Top O' the Cove.** More or less synonymous with romance, Top O' the Cove has been the scene of thousands of marriage proposals in its 35-year history. Yet another place that boasts an extravagant view of La Jolla Cove, it also boasts a competent kitchen that turns out beautifully garnished, luxury fare dressed with creamy and well-seasoned sauces. The menu hits all the bases—beef, veal, fowl, and seafood—but pay special attention to the nightly specials. The decor is lush, and the wine list, with more than 800 entries, the recipient of countless awards. *1216 Prospect St., tel. 619/454–7779. Reservations advised. Jacket and tie suggested. AE, MC, V. Very Expensive.*

Indian **Star of India.** As do so many other chic, big-city neighborhoods, La Jolla hosts a good selection of upscale ethnic eateries. The Star of India is a case in point: Grander and more expensive than the city's other Indian houses, it also offers a better selection of dishes and a more talented kitchen staff. In addition to all the typical curries and kebabs, the menu offers several tandoori meats (baked in a special, superheated oven), quite a number of vegetarian dishes, and a superb selection of freshly prepared Indian breads. *1025 Prospect St., tel. 619/459–3355. Reservations accepted. Dress: casual. DC, MC, V. Moderate.*

Italian **Issimo.** La Jolla is blessed in its restaurants, and Issimo is third
★ in its trilogy of stars. Beautifully arranged plates are served in grand style in a small jewel box of a dining room. Start with a pasta or the incredible, homemade pâté de foie gras (yes, this is an Italian place, but the foie gras is fabulous), and then move along to a dandy osso buco, a wonderful plate of baby lamb chops, a fine veal sauté, or a steak in a delicate sauce. This restaurant also speaks seafood fluently, and the desserts rival those made by the finest European pastry chefs. *5634 La Jolla Blvd., tel. 619/454–7004. Reservations advised. Jacket suggested. MC, V. Closed Sun. Very Expensive.*

Avanti. For staid, old La Jolla, this starkly modern restaurant, with its mirrored ceiling and white and black and chrome interior design, comes as a refreshing surprise. Which explains why it is such a popular meeting place for trendy, successful natives looking for some sophisticated fun, with cuisine to match. An open-to-view kitchen lets you watch Chef John Cooke prepare such appetite-arousing dishes as tiny pasta rings mixed with ricotta and pistachios; scampi sauteed in olive oil, minced garlic, and white wine; beef fillet topped with a porcini mushroom sauce; and chicken breasts grilled with radicchio. Counting calories? There's a spa menu, too. *875 Prospect Ave., tel. 619/454–4288. Reservations advised. Dress: thoughtfully informal. AE, MC, V. Closed for lunch. Expensive.*

★ **Delicias.** Upon opening in 1990, this bright and cheerful trattoria was adopted by the natives of the tiny, pastoral village of Rancho Santa Fe (just east of La Jolla) as their local clubhouse. Wolfgang Puck acted as consultant in drawing up a Spago-like menu and training the chef, and the results include excellent pizza and calzone straight from a wood-burning oven, and, of course, a wide range of pastas and salads using fresh-daily ingredients from nearby vegetable farms. The service here benefits from being so far away from Los Angeles's moonlighting-actor pool. *6106 Paseo Delicias, Rancho Santa Fe, tel. 619/759–1739. Reservations suggested. Dress: casual. Full bar. AE, MC, V. Moderate.*

Piatti. Another recent link in this very popular mini-chain of trattorias that now extends from one end of California to the other. Good pizza, calzone, pasta and an excellent selection of antipasti in a let's-have-fun setting. All in all, *molto simpatico. 2182 Avenida de La Playa. 619/454–1589. Reservations advised. Dress: casual. MC, V. Moderate.*

Mexican **El Crab Catcher.** Although this spot is just one of many along San Diego's most fashionable restaurant row, its spectacular view of La Jolla Cove and casual Hawaiian atmosphere (yes, Hawaiian) make it a favorite. Specialties include numerous crab dishes, other shell- and fin-fish, and simple beef and chicken dishes. Get here in time for the sunset. *1298 Prospect St.,* *tel. 619/454–9587. Reservations suggested. Dress: casual. AE, MC, V. Moderate.*

Mixed Menu ★ **Hard Rock Cafe.** It seems that every other city has a Hard Rock Cafe, and, of course, San Diego has one, too. The local college students and teens are rejoicing, and even their elders crack a smile when they stroll into this monument to ground chuck and Chuck Berry. Designed as a museum of rock 'n roll memorabilia, the place features Elton John's "Tutti Frutti" suit, guitars used by Def Leppard and Pink Floyd, and a pink Cadillac crashing through the ceiling. Most diners ogle all this while munching on hefty burgers and fat onion rings, but if you take a close look at the menu, you'll also find excellent grilled fish, a fine, lime-marinated chicken, and homemade apple pie that almost matches Mom's. *909 Prospect St., tel. 619/454–5101. AE, MC, V. No reservations. Dress: casual. Inexpensive.*

Seafood **Fisherman's Grill.** The oyster bar serves up an exceptional selection of raw bivalves and shellfish cocktails, and the kitchen follows suit by offering creamy chowders, clever sandwiches, mesquite-broiled fish, and good old-fashioned deep-fried shrimp coated with a zesty beer batter. *7825 Fay Ave., tel. 619/456–3733. Reservations accepted. Dress: casual. AE, MC, V. Closed lunch Sat. Closed Sun. Inexpensive.*

Lodging

When choosing lodgings in San Diego, the first thing to consider is location. The city has many neighborhoods, each one possessing unique characteristics. Consider the type of atmosphere you prefer. Do you want to be in the middle of a bustling metropolitan setting, or would you rather have a serene beach bungalow? Second, consider the hotel's proximity to attractions that you most want to see. And then, of course, there's the price.

The most highly recommended hotels in each price category are indicated by a star ★.

Category	Cost*
Very Expensive	over $140
Expensive	$100–$140
Moderate	$60–$100
Inexpensive	under $60

**for a double room, not including tax*

The following abbreviations for credit cards have been used: AE, American Express; DC, Diner's Club; MC, MasterCard; V, Visa.

Coronado **Coronado** is a quiet, out-of-the-way place to stay, but if you plan to see many of San Diego's attractions, you'll probably spend a lot of time commuting across the bridge or riding the ferry.

Very Expensive **Hotel Del Coronado.** Built in 1888, the Del is a historic and social landmark made famous by the Marilyn Monroe film *Some Like It Hot.* The rooms and suites in the original Victorian-style building are charmingly quirky; some have baths larger than the sleeping areas, while others seem downright palatial. More standardized accommodations are available in the newer high rise. *1500 Orange Ave., 92118, tel. 619/435–6611 or 800/ 468–5335. 700 rooms. Facilities: pool, tennis courts, beach. AE, DC, MC, V.*

Expensive **Glorietta Bay Inn.** Built around the mansion of the Spreckels family, who once owned most of downtown San Diego, this is now a spotlessly maintained hotel. Located adjacent to the Coronado harbor, the Del, and the Coronado village, there are many fine restaurants and quaint shops within walking distance. *1630 Glorietta Blvd., 92118, tel. 619/435–3101. 100 rooms. Facilities: tennis, golf, pool. AE, MC, V.*

Inexpensive **Coronado Motor Inn.** This motel is located away from the village toward the bay and the ferry stop. *266 Orange Ave., 92118, tel. 619/435–4121. 24 rooms. Facilities: pool. MC, V.*

Downtown Downtown San Diego is presently in the midst of a decade-long redevelopment effort. The revitalization has attracted many new hotels. There is much to be seen within walking distance of downtown accommodations—Seaport Village, the Embarcadero, the historic Gaslamp Quarter, a variety of theaters and night spots, and the spectacular Horton Plaza shopping center. The zoo and Balboa Park are also nearby. For nonstop shopping, nightlife, and entertainment, the downtown area is an excellent location.

Very Expensive **Omni San Diego Hotel.** This high rise was completed in 1987 and is lavishly decorated with marble, brass, and glass. The rooms are luxurious and modern. The lobby lounge is packed every night with local financiers and weary shoppers from the adjacent Horton Plaza. *910 Broadway Circle, 92101, tel. 619/ 239–2200 or 800/THE–OMNI. 450 rooms. Facilities: tennis courts, sauna, spa, pool, complete health club, lounge, disco, 2 restaurants. AE, MC, V.*

San Diego Marriott Hotel and Marina. This luxurious high rise consists of two 25-story towers offering panoramic views of the bay and/or city. The North Tower rooms all have balconies but only the suites in the South Tower offer balconies. The Marriott has a prime location between Seaport Village and the convention center. *333 W. Harbor Dr., 92101, tel. 619/234–1500 or 800/ 800/228–9290. 1,356 rooms. Facilities: 3 restaurants, 2 lounges with piano music, boutiques, full-service salon, jogging path, health spa, tennis courts, sauna, 2 outdoor pools, charter boat. AE, DC, MC, V.*

★ **U.S. Grant Hotel.** Originally built in 1910, this hotel, which faces the famed Horton Plaza, was renovated and reopened in 1985. The atmosphere is elegant and formal, with crystal chandeliers and marble floors. All rooms feature mahogany furnishings. Butlers and concierges serve the guests splendidly. There are two restaurants, the Garden Room and the Grant Grill, a longtime favorite of high-powered business types. The use of an associated health club is included. *326 Broadway, 92101, tel. 619/232–3121 or 800/237–5029, 800/334–6957 in CA. 280 rooms. AE, DC, MC, V.*

Westgate Hotel. This elegant high rise offers rooms uniquely furnished with genuine European antiques. Hand-cut Baccarat chandeliers adorn the lobby, which is modeled after the anteroom in the Palace of Versailles. The rooms feature Italian marble counters, oversize bathtubs, brass fixtures with 14-kt.-gold overlay, and breathtaking views of the harbor and the city (from the ninth floor up). Enjoy high tea and international coffee with piano accompaniment in the afternoon and the award-winning cuisine and white-glove service of Le Fontainebleau in the evening. The trolley can take you to Tijuana right from the hotel and complimentary transportation is available within the downtown area. *1055 Second Ave., 92101, tel. 619/238–1818 or 800/221–3802, 800/522–1564 in CA. 223 rooms. Facilities: restaurant, lounge. AE, DC, MC, V.*

Expensive   **Britt House.** This grand Victorian inn offers charming rooms, each uniquely furnished with antiques. Each room has a sitting area in which fresh baked goodies are served for breakfast. Lovely gardens surround the building, and an elaborate high tea is served in the parlor every afternoon. Keeping in the Victorian tradition, there is a bathroom for every two rooms to share. Located within walking distance of Balboa Park and the zoo. Reservations are a must. *406 Maple St., 92101, tel. 619/ 234–2926. 10 rooms. AE, MC, V.*

★   **Horton Grand Hotel.** This is San Diego's oldest Victorian hotel, built in 1886 and restored in 1986 in the fashion of an elegant, European-style tourist hotel. The charming rooms are furnished with period antiques and feature ceiling fans, gas-burning fireplaces, and diaries, which provide guests with a sense of those who came before them and an opportunity to share with those who will come later. Each room is different from the next. The choicest rooms are those overlooking the garden courtyard that twinkles with miniature lights each evening. Afternoon high tea and evening jazz are offered. *311 Island Ave., 92101, tel. 619/544–1886. 110 rooms. Facilities: Chinatown museum, restaurant, lounge. AE, DC, MC, V.*

Moderate– Expensive   **Balboa Park Inn.** Originally built in 1915, this charming European-style bed-and-breakfast inn was restored in 1982, with one- and two-bedroom suites with kitchenettes (for 2–4 people) housed in four two-story buildings that are connected by courtyards. Each suite has a different flavor—Italian, French, Spanish, or early Californian. Some suites have fireplaces, wet bars, and whirlpool tubs. Continental breakfast and the morning paper are delivered to every suite. Prices are reasonable considering all rooms are complete suites for 2–4 people. Balboa Park and the zoo are located directly across the street. *3402 Park Blvd., 92103, tel. 619/298–0823. 25 suites with baths. Facilities: outdoor bar, room service. AE, DC, MC, V.*

Moderate   **Radisson Harbor View.** This new high rise sits at the foot of the I-5 entrance ramp to downtown at Front Street. Near the courthouse and legal offices, the hotel is good for business travelers who don't mind the 10-block hike to the convention center—for those who do, there's a free shuttle. The pastel-decorated rooms are sparkling clean, with small harbor-view terraces. Business services and a health club are available. *1646 Front St., 92101, tel. 619/239–6800 or 800/333–3333. 333 rooms. Facilities: rooftop pool, health club. AE, MC, V.*

Inexpensive   **La Pensione.** At long last, a decent budget hotel downtown,
★   with daily, weekly, and monthly rates. Some rooms have harbor views, all have kitchenettes. La Pensione is in a quiet neighborhood, and has a pretty central courtyard. *1546 Second Ave., 92101, tel. 619/236–9292. 20 rooms. Facilities: kitchenettes. MC, V.*

Harbor Island/
Shelter Island

Harbor Island and Shelter Island are two man-made peninsulas located between downtown San Diego and the lovely community of Point Loma. Both islands are bordered by grassy parks, tree-lined paths, lavish hotels, and wonderful restaurants. Harbor Island is closest to the downtown area and less than five minutes from the airport. Shelter Island is on the Point Loma side. Both islands command breathtaking views of the bay and the downtown skyline. Although some lodgings we have listed are not located directly on the islands, they are in the vicinity.

Very Expensive
★

Sheraton Harbor Island East. Although less luxurious than the neighboring Sheraton Grand, this hotel has more charm and romance. For a view, ask for a room above the eighth floor, preferably facing across the water to the lights of downtown. The restaurants and lounges here are popular for fine dining and dancing. *1380 Harbor Island Dr., 92101, tel. 619/291–2900 or 800/325–3535. 725 rooms. Facilities: tennis courts, sauna, spa, 2 pools, fitness facility. AE, DC, MC, V.*

Expensive
★

Humphrey's Half Moon Inn. This sprawling South Seas—style resort has many open areas with palm trees, beautiful green grass, and tiki torches. The recently restored rooms have standard but pleasant modern decor; some have views of the pool area or the bay. The restaurant, Humphrey's, is famous with the locals for its good food and summer jazz concert series. *2303 Shelter Island Dr., 92106, tel. 619/224–3411 or 800/345–9995. 141 rooms. Facilities: putting green, pool, spa, bicycles. AE, DC, MC, V.*

Moderate

Best Western Posada Inn. One of the nicer Best Western hotels, this is not on Harbor Island but on one of the neighboring thoroughfares adjacent to Point Loma. The location is good, and many rooms have a wonderful view of the harbor. The rooms are clean, comfortable, and nicely furnished. There are many fabulous seafood eateries within walking distance. *5005 N. Harbor Dr., 92106, tel. 619/224–3254 or 800/528–1234. 112 rooms. Facilities: pool, spa, restaurant, lounge. AE, MC, V.*

Kona Kai Beach and Tennis Resort. This hotel also serves as a prestigious members-only club for locals, but all facilities are open to hotel guests. The rooms are simple and tasteful with Hawaiian decor. Rooms in the newer north wing are less expensive than the bayfront suites with lanais in the main building. *1551 Shelter Island Dr., 92106, tel. 619/222–1191. 89 rooms. Facilities: health club, tennis courts, racquetball courts, pool, spa, private beach, 2 restaurants, lounge. AE, DC, MC, V.*

Inexpensive

Outrigger Motel. Accommodations are less expensive here because the location is adjacent to the two resort peninsulas, not on them. It may be a bit noisier here, but the location is still picturesque. The sportfishing docks are across the street, and one can take a scenic walk along the bay to Harbor Island. Be sure to visit the famous Point Loma Seafoods Market and Restaurant across the street. *1370 Scott St., 92106, tel. 619/223–7105. 37 rooms with kitchens. Facilities: pool. AE, DC, MC, V.*

Hotel Circle/
Old Town

Hotel Circle, as the name implies, is headquarters to a number of hotels and motels, most of them moderately priced and catering to the individual traveler. A car is an absolute necessity here, since the "circle" consists of hotels on both sides of Interstate 8, the busiest stretch of freeway in San Diego. Although not particularly scenic or serene, Mission Valley is close to Balboa Park, the zoo, downtown, and the beaches. Atlas Hotels, which owns four hotels in this area, has a health club available to guests. Old Town, between downtown and Hotel Circle, is developing a crop of moderately priced chain hotels beside the freeway. As a general rule, try to reserve a room that doesn't face the freeway.

Expensive
★

Doubletree Hotel. One of the grandest hotels in the valley, this high rise offers three floors reserved for nonsmokers. The decor is modern Southwestern. Children stay free and small pets are accepted. *901 Camino del Rio S., 92108, tel. 619/543–9000 or 800/528–0444. 350 rooms. Facilities: restaurant, lounge, spa, pool, fitness center. AE, DC, MC, V.*

Moderate–
Expensive
★

Heritage Park Bed & Breakfast Inn. This inn is located a few minutes from Mission Valley in the Old Town area. The location is picturesque and quiet. Nine guest rooms decorated with 19th-century antiques are housed in a romantic Queen Anne mansion from 1889. Five of the rooms have private baths; the others share facilities. The rooms are quaint and furnished with Victorian antiques. Breakfast and afternoon refreshments are included. *2470 Heritage Park Row, 92110, tel. 619/ 295–7088. 9 rooms, 5 with bath. MC, V.*

★ **San Diego Marriott Mission Valley.** This new high rise sits in the middle of the San Diego River valley, where the dry riverbed is being graded and transformed into a commercial zone with sleek office towers and sprawling shopping malls. The hotel has become the valley's glamour spot, and the rooms are far more spacious and contemporary than in nearby hotels. *8757 Rio San Diego Dr., 92108, tel. 619/692–3800 or 800/228–9290. 350 rooms. Facilities: pool, tennis court, health club. AE, DC, MC, V.*

Town and Country Hotel. Although the original part of this hotel was built in the 1950s, it has been refurbished many times and two high-rise sections were added in the 1970s. The rooms are decorated in a quaint Colonial fashion. With Hotel Circle's largest convention facilities, the hotel caters to convention and meeting groups, but it is resortlike enough to appeal to tourists also. *500 Hotel Circle N, 92108, tel. 619/291–7131. 1,000 rooms. Facilities: 6 restaurants, 5 lounges, 4 pools, golf, health club. AE, DC, MC, V.*

Moderate

Hacienda Hotel. The white adobe hacienda-style buildings of this former shopping complex turned hotel spread up a steep hillside. Elevators are available, but you still have to do a bit of climbing. The reward is tranquillity above the bustle of Old Town. All rooms are suites with microwaves, refrigerators, and VCRs—all a family could need, plus tasteful Southwestern-style decor. *4041 Harney St., 92110, tel. 619/298–4707 or 800/888–1991. 150 suites. Facilities: pool, free indoor parking. AE, MC, V.*

Hanalei Hotel. If Interstate 8 were out of sight, you'd swear you were in a tropical paradise. This hotel has a definite island feel, with palm trees, waterfalls, koi ponds, and tiki torches. There is a two-story complex and a high rise. The two-story complex rooms are poolside and the high rise is built around a beautiful Hawaiian garden with ponds, palm trees, and plenty of spots to sit and take in the atmosphere. The rooms are clean and comfortable with Hawaiian decor. *2270 Hotel Circle S, 92108, tel. 619/297–1101. 425 rooms. Facilities: 2 restaurants, lounge, pool, spa. AE, MC, V.*

Inexpensive **Padre Trail Inn.** This standard, family-style motel is located slightly southwest of Mission Valley. Historic Old Town, shopping, and dining are all within walking distance. *4200 Taylor St., 92110, tel. 619/297–3291. 100 rooms. Facilities: pool, restaurant, lounge. AE, DC, MC, V.*

La Jolla La Jolla is one of the world's most beautiful, prestigious beach communities. Million-dollar homes line the beaches and cascade down the hillsides. Expensive boutiques, galleries, and restaurants make up the village—the heart of La Jolla. La Jolla is also a popular vacation spot and has many lodging possibilities even for those on a budget.

Very Expensive **Sea Lodge.** This hidden gem faces the ocean between La Jolla Beach and Tennis Club and La Jolla Shores, one of the best beaches in the county. Three-story buildings with red tile rooves form a low-lying compound on the beachfront, backed by the hills of La Jolla. The rooms have the sort of yellow, orange, and green decor popular in the 60s, and wooden balconies that look out on lush landscaping and the sea. Early reservations are a must here, and families will find plenty of room and distractions for both kids and parents. *8110 Camino del Oro, La Jolla, 92037, tel. 619/459–8271. 128 rooms, 19 with kitchenettes. Facilities: heated pool, hot tub, beach, 2 tennis courts, pitch-and-putt golf course, restaurant, lounge. AE, DC, MC, V.*

Expensive– **La Valencia.** This European-style, pink-stucco hotel is a La
Very Expensive Jolla landmark. A haven for the movie stars in the '30s and '40s,
★ it has a courtyard for patio dining and an elegant lobby where guests congregate in the evenings to enjoy the spectacular view of the ocean while sipping cocktails. The clientele tends to be older, except in the Whaling Bar, which is a gathering spot for all ages. The restaurants have excellent food, and the hotel is ideally located for walking to the cove, shopping, and dining out. The prices are quite reasonable if you're willing to settle for a view of the village. For a view of the ocean, the prices almost double, but on a clear, sunny day, it might be worth every penny. *1132 Prospect St., La Jolla 92037, tel. 619/454–0771. 100 rooms. AE, MC, V.*

Expensive **Colonial Inn.** A tastefully restored Victorian-style building, this hotel offers turn-of-the-century elegance with features such as fan windows and a mahogany-paneled elevator. You can get a view of the village or of the ocean, but the ocean view will cost considerably more. Located in the center of La Jolla, the hotel is within walking distance of boutiques, restaurants, and the cove. *910 Prospect St., La Jolla, 92037, tel. 619/454–2181 or 800/832–5525. 75 rooms. Facilities: restaurant, lounge, pool. AE, DC, MC, V.*

Moderate– **La Jolla Cove Motel.** Offering studios and suites, some with
Expensive spacious oceanfront balconies, this motel overlooks the famous
★ La Jolla Cove beach. *1155 Coast Blvd., La Jolla, 92037, tel. 619/459–2621 or 800/248–COVE. 130 rooms. Facilities: solarium, sun deck, fresh-water pool, spa. AE, MC, V.*

Moderate **Torrey Pines Inn.** Located on a bluff between La Jolla and Del Mar, this hotel commands a view of miles and miles of coastline. The hotel stands adjacent to the Torrey Pines Golf Course, site of the San Diego Open PGA golf tournament every January. Nearby is scenic Torrey Pines State Beach. Downtown La Jolla is a 10-minute drive away. The inn is a nice, reasonable, out-of-the-way place to stay. *11480 Torrey Pines Rd., La Jolla, 92037, tel. 619/453–4420. 75 rooms. AE, DC, MC, V.*

Mission Bay and Beaches Most people who come to San Diego would like to stay close to the water. Mission and Pacific beaches have the highest concentration of small hotels and motels. Both these areas have a casual atmosphere and a busy coastal thoroughfare offering endless shopping, dining, and nightlife possibilities. Mission Bay Park, with its beaches, bike trails, boat-launching ramps, golf course, and grassy parks is also a hotel haven. You can't go wrong with any of these locations, as long as the frenzy of hundreds at play doesn't bother you.

Very Expensive **Hyatt Islandia.** Located in one of San Diego's most beautiful seashore areas, Mission Bay Park, the Islandia has lanai-style units and a high rise. The landscaping is lush and tropical in flavor, and the room decor is tastefully modern with dramatic views of the bay area. This hotel is famous for its lavish Sunday buffet brunch. *1441 Quivira Rd., 92109, tel. 619/224–1234. 423 rooms. Facilities: pool, spa, 2 restaurants. AE, DC, MC, V.*

★ **San Diego Princess Resort.** This resort resembles a self-sufficient village with a wide range of amenities. Perhaps its greatest features are the marina and beaches. The grounds are so beautifully landscaped that this resort has been the setting for many movies. Accommodations consist of individual cottages. Kitchens and bay views are available. With something for everyone, this hotel is favored by families, particularly during the summer. *1404 W. Vacation Rd., 92109, tel. 619/274–4630. 450 cottages. Facilities: 3 restaurants, 8 tennis courts, 5 pools, bicycle and boat rentals. AE, DC, MC, V.*

Moderate–Expensive **Bahia Resort Hotel.** This huge complex is located on a 14-acre peninsula in Mission Bay Park. The ocean is also within walking distance. The rooms are studios and suites with kitchens, tastefully furnished. The price is good, considering the location and amenities. *998 W. Mission Bay Dr., 92109, tel. 619/488–0551. 300 rooms. Facilities: tennis courts, water-sport rentals, spa, pool, evening bay cruises. AE, DC, MC, V.*

Dana Inn & Marina. This hotel, which has an adjoining marina, offers a bargain in the Mission Bay Park area. The accommodations are not as grand as in the other hotels in the area but they're perfectly fine if you're not going to stay cooped up in your room. *1710 W. Mission Bay Blvd., 92109, tel. 619/222–6440. 196 rooms. Facilities: pool, spa. AE, DC, MC, V.*

Moderate **Surfer Motor Lodge.** This hotel is located right on the beach and directly behind a new shopping center with many restaurants and boutiques. The rooms are plain, but the view from the upper floors of this high rise is very nice. *711 Pacific Beach Dr., 92109, tel. 619/483–7070. 52 rooms. Facilities: restaurant, cocktail lounge, swimming pool. AE, DC, MC, V.*

Inexpensive–Moderate **Ocean Manor Apartment Hotel.** Units rent by the day (with a 3-day minimum), week, or month, and the owner says that some people have been coming every year for 20 years! This hotel is located in Ocean Beach, a community south of Mission Beach that doesn't have many lodging facilities. This is a charming place with a lovely view, located right on Sunset Cliffs. The beach below has long since washed away, but there are beaches within walking distance. The rooms are studios or one- or two-bedroom suites with kitchens and living rooms. They are furnished plainly in 1950s style but are quaint and comfortable. There is no maid service but fresh towels are always provided. This is a quiet place and the owners want to keep it that way. Make reservations months in advance. *1370 Sunset Cliffs Blvd., 92107, tel. 619/222–7901 or 619/224–1379. 20 rooms. Facilities: pool. MC, V.*

Inexpensive **Mission Bay Motel.** Located one-half block from the beach, this motel offers centrally located, modest units. Great restaurants and nightlife are within walking distance, but you might find the area to be a bit noisy. *4221 Mission Blvd., 92109, tel. 619/ 483–6440. 50 rooms. Facilities: swimming pool. AE, MC, V.*

Santa Clara Motel. This is a small motel a block from the ocean and right in the middle of restaurant, nightlife, and shopping activity in Mission Beach. Location is the plus. Kitchens are available, but there are no frills. Weekly rates are available. *839 Santa Clara Pl., 92109, tel. 619/488–1193. 17 rooms. AE, MC, V.*

The Arts

Top national touring companies perform regularly at the Civic Theatre, Golden Hall, Symphony Hall, and East County Performing Arts Center. San Diego State University, the University of California at San Diego, private universities, and community colleges present a wide variety of performing arts programs, from performances by well-known artists to student recitals. The daily *San Diego Union, Evening Tribune*, and the San Diego edition of the *Los Angeles Times* list current attractions and complete movie schedules. The *Reader*, a free weekly that comes out each Thursday, devotes an entire section to upcoming cultural events, as well as current theater and film reviews. *San Diego* magazine publishes a monthly "What's Doing" column that lists arts events throughout the county and reviews of current films, plays, and concerts.

It is best to book tickets well in advance, preferably at the same time you make hotel reservations, or half-price tickets to most theater, music, and dance events can be bought on the day of performance at the **TIMES ARTS TIX Ticket Center,** Horton Plaza, downtown (tel. 619/238–3810). Only cash is accepted. Advance full-price tickets may also be purchased through ARTS TIX.

Visa and MasterCard holders may buy tickets for many scheduled performances through **Teleseat** (tel. 619/283–7328), **Ticketmaster** (tel. 619/238–3810), and **Ticketron** (tel. 619/268–9686). Service charges vary according to event, and most tickets are nonrefundable.

Theater **Coronado Playhouse** (1755 Strand Way, Coronado, tel. 619/ 435–4856). This cabaret-type theater, near the Hotel Del Coronado, stages regular dramatic and musical performances. Dinner packages are offered on Friday and Saturday.

La Jolla Playhouse (Mandell Weiss Center for the Performing Arts, University of California at San Diego, tel. 619/534–3960). Exciting and innovative presentations, early summer to fall, under the artistic direction of Tony Award-winner Des McAnuff.

Lawrence Welk Village Theatre (8860 Lawrence Welk Dr., Escondido, tel. 619/749–3448). About a 45-minute drive from downtown, this famed dinner theater puts on polished Broadway-style productions with a professional cast.

Lyceum Theatre (Horton Plaza, tel. 619/235–8025). Home to the San Diego Repertory Theatre, San Diego's first resident acting company, which performs contemporary works year-round on the 550-seat Lyceum stage and in a 225-seat theater that can be rearranged to suit the stage set.

Old Globe Theatre (Simon Edison Centre for the Performing Arts, Balboa Park, tel. 619/239–2255). The oldest professional theater in California performs classics, contemporary dramas, experimental works, and the famous summer Shakespeare Festival at the Old Globe and its sister theaters, the Cassius Carter Centre Stage and the Lowell Davies Festival Theatre.

San Diego Gilbert and Sullivan Company (Casa del Prado Theatre, Balboa Park, tel. 619/231–5714). Four different productions of Gilbert and Sullivan and similar works are performed October–July.

Concerts   **Open-Air Theatre** (San Diego State University, tel. 619/594–5200). Top-name rock, reggae, and popular artists pack in the crowds for summer concerts under the stars.

Sherwood Auditorium (700 Prospect St., La Jolla, tel. 619/280–7013). Many classical and jazz events are held in the 550-seat auditorium within San Diego Museum of Contemporary Art. La Jolla Chamber Music Society presents nine concerts, August–May, of internationally acclaimed chamber ensembles, orchestras, and soloists. San Diego Chamber Orchestra, a 35-member ensemble, performs once a month, October–April.

Sports Arena (2500 Sports Arena Blvd., tel. 619/224–4176). Big-name rock concerts play to more than 14,000 fans, using an end-stage configuration so that all seats face in one direction.

Symphony Hall (1245 Seventh Ave., tel. 619/699–4205). The San Diego Symphony is the only California symphony with its own concert hall. The performance season runs November–May, with a series of outdoor pop concerts held at Seaport Village during the summer.

Opera   **Civic Theatre** (202 C St., tel. 619/236–6510). The San Diego Opera draws international stars like Luciano Pavarotti, Joan Sutherland, and Kiri Te Kanawa. The season of four operas runs January–April in the 3,000-seat, state-of-the-art auditorium. English translations of works sung in their original languages are projected on a large screen above the stage.

Dance   **3's Company** (tel. 619/296–9523). Interpretative dance presentations, incorporating live music, are staged at major theaters and concert halls around San Diego County.

California Ballet (tel. 619/560–5676). Four high-quality contemporary and traditional works, from story ballets to Balanchine, are performed September–May. The *Nutcracker* is staged annually at the Civic Theatre; other ballets take place at Symphony Hall, East County Performing Arts Center, and Nautilus Bowl at Sea World.

Nightlife

The unbeatable variety of sun-and-surf recreational activities is considered the primary reason tourists love to visit San Diego, but most are unexpectedly delighted that the city gains new momentum after dark. The nightlife scene is one that's constantly growing and highly mercurial, given the chameleon-like character of clubs that aim to satisfy the crowd—one night it's Top 40 or contemporary; the next, reggae, pop-jazz, or strictly rock'n'roll. Live pop and fusion jazz have become especially popular—some say it's the ideal music for what is perceived as the typically laid-back lifestyle—and it can easily be found at a dozen or so venues throughout the county. Local rock clubs and nightclubs present music ranging from danceable contemporary–Top 40 to original rock and new-wave music by San Diego's finest up-and-coming groups. Discotheques and bars in Mission Valley and at the beaches tend to be the most crowded spots in the county on the weekends, but don't let that discourage you from visiting these quintessential San Diego hangouts. And should your tastes run to softer music, there are plenty of piano bars where frazzled nerves have a chance to wind down. Check the *Reader* for weekly band information or *San Diego* magazine's Restaurant & Nightlife Guide for the full range of nightlife possibilities.

California law prohibits the sale of alcoholic beverages after 2 AM. Bars and nightclubs usually stop serving at about 1:40 AM. You must be 21 to purchase and consume alcohol, and most places will insist on current identification. Be aware that California also has some of the most stringent drunk-driving laws, and roadblocks are not an uncommon sight.

Bars and Nightclubs

Diego's Loft. Downstairs is the raucous Diego's disco, while upstairs is the quieter, more sedate nightclub presenting live jazz groups and jam sessions. *860 Garnet Ave., tel. 619/272–1241. Open Thurs.–Sat. 8 PM–1 AM, Sun. 7 PM–midnight.*

The Hard Rock Cafe. A great place to dance and party amid an impressive collection of rock-and-roll memorabilia. *909 Prospect St., La Jolla, tel. 619/454–5101. Open daily 11 AM–1:30 AM. Live music Fri. and Sat. 8:30. AE, DC, MC, V.*

Mick's P.B. In this spectacular club rich with Honduran mahogany, chicly dressed singles from 25 to 45 dance to live contemporary rock and Top 40 by bands predominantly from out of town. *4190 Mission Blvd., Pacific Beach, tel. 619/581–3938. Open 8 PM–1:30 AM. Entertainment 9 PM–1:30 AM. AE, DC, MC, V.*

Old Del Mar Cafe. Offering rock to reggae, fusion jazz to oldies, and virtually every other popular style of music, this combination woodsy cafe–lounge is considered one of the best intimate venues in the North County. *2730 Via de la Valle, Del Mar, tel. 619/455–0920. Entertainment 9 PM–1:30 AM. MC, V.*

Old Pacific Beach Cafe. Certainly one of Pacific Beach's most popular after-dark spots, showcasing the broadest range of musical styles—fusion and pop jazz, R&B, rambunctious rock'n'roll, and reggae. *4287 Mission Blvd., tel. 619/270–7522. Entertainment 9:30 PM–1:30 AM. MC, V.*

Jazz Clubs   **Cargo Bar.** The San Diego Hilton Hotel's nautical-theme bar with a can't-beat view of the bay and a don't-miss lineup of jazz and contemporary bands. *1775 E. Mission Bay Dr., tel. 619/276–4010. Open 5 PM–1:30 AM. Entertainment 8:30 PM–1 AM. AE, DC, MC, V.*

Elario's. A club on the top floor of the Summer House Inn, with a sumptuous ocean view and an incomparable lineup of internationally acclaimed jazz musicians every month. *7955 La Jolla*

Shores Dr., La Jolla, tel. 619/459–0541. Entertainment 8 PM–1 AM. AE, DC, MC, V.

Humphrey's. The premier promoter of the city's best jazz, folk, and light-rock summer concert series held out on the grass. The rest of the year the music moves indoors for some first-rate jazz Sat.–Sun. *2241 Shelter Island Dr., tel. 619/224–3577, taped concert information 619/523–1010. Entertainment 8 PM– midnight. AE, DC, MC, V.*

Rock Clubs   **Bacchanal.** An all-concert venue that brings in a mixture of comedy, rock, nostalgia, jazz, R&B, and the like. *8022 Clairemont Mesa Blvd., Kearny Mesa, tel. 619/560–8022, taped concert information 619/560–8000. Entertainment 8:30– 11:30 PM. MC, V.*

Belly Up Tavern. Located in converted Quonset huts, this eclectic live-concert venue hosts critically acclaimed artists who play everything from reggae, rock, new wave, Motown, and folk to—well, you name it. *143 S. Cedros Ave., Solana Beach, tel. 619/481–9022. Open 11 AM–1:30 AM. Entertainment 9:30 PM–1:30 AM. MC, V.*

Casbah. A small club showcasing rock, reggae, funk, and every other kind of band—except top-40—every night of the week. *2812 Kettner Blvd., near downtown, tel. 619/294–9033. Live bands at 9:30 nightly. No credit cards.*

The Hype. One of San Diego's oldest bars keeps changing names but the scene stays much the same—loud top-40s from the DJs between the sets of top local bands. *3595 Sports Arena Blvd., tel. 619/223–5596. Open daily 6 PM–1:30 AM. MC, V.*

Rio's. Some of the most intriguing and innovative local rock, blues, and reggae bands like to perform here. *4258 W. Point Loma Blvd., Loma Portal, tel. 619/225–9559. Open 7 PM–1:30 AM. Entertainment 9 PM–1:30 AM. AE, MC, V.*

Country/Western Clubs

Abilene Country Saloon. An equal mix of tourists and local cowboys congregates at the Town & Country Hotel's urban version of the country dance club with live music. *500 Hotel Circle N, Mission Valley, tel. 619/291–7131. Open 4 PM–1:30 AM. Entertainment 9 PM–1:30 AM. Closed Sun. AE, DC, MC, V.*

Leo's Little Bit O' Country. The largest country/western dance floor in the county—bar none. *680 W. San Marcos Blvd., San Marcos, tel. 619/744–4120. Open 4 PM–1 AM. Entertainment 8:30 PM–1 AM. Closed Mon. MC, V.*

Pomerado Club. The rustic dance hall, formerly a Pony Express station in the last century, now showcases the two-steppin' tunes of the house band, consisting of the owners. *12237 Pomerado Rd., Poway, tel. 619/748–1135. Entertainment Fri.–Sat. 9 PM–1:30 AM. No credit cards.*

Comedy Clubs   **Comedy Isle.** Located in the Bahia Resort Hotel, this club offers the latest in local and national talent. *998 West Mission Bay Dr., tel. 619/488–6872. Shows Tues.–Thurs. 8:30, Fri.– Sat. 8:30, 10:30. AE, DC, MC, V.*

The Comedy Store. In the same tradition as the Comedy Store in West Hollywood, San Diego's version hosts some of the best national touring and local talent. *916 Pearl St., La Jolla, tel. 619/454–9176. Open Tues.–Thur. 8–10:30 PM, Fri.–Sat. 8 PM–1 AM. Closed Sun.–Mon. AE, MC, V.*

The Improv. A superb Art Deco–style club with a distinct East Coast feel, where some of the big names in comedy present their routines. *832 Garnet Ave., Pacific Beach, tel. 619/483–4520. Open 6:30 PM–midnight. Entertainment 8 PM–midnight. AE, MC, V.*

Discos **City Colors.** Colorful and ritzy, attracting a classy crowd, City Colors is downtown's premier dance spot. *910 Broadway Circle, tel. 619/239–2200. Open 8 PM–2 AM for dancing. Closed Sun. AE, DC, MC, V.*

Club Diego's. A flashy discotheque and singles scene by the beach with excellent, nonstop dance music and friendly young (25–35) dancers. *860 Garnet Ave., Pacific Beach, tel. 619/272–1241. Open 8 PM–1:30 AM. AE, MC, V.*

Confetti. A glitzy club, popular with young professionals, students, and anyone with an inclination to party. It metamorphoses into the alternative-music club **The Piranha Room** on Sunday only. *5373 Mission Center Rd., Mission Valley, tel. 619/291–8635. Open Mon.–Fri. 5 PM–2 AM, Sat. 7 PM–2 AM, Sun. 9 PM–2 AM. AE, MC, V.*

Metro. Hip to the extreme and always hopping to the latest music mixes, this dance mecca has some of the most creatively dressed patrons in San Diego. *1051 University Ave., Hillcrest, tel. 619/295–2195. Open Wed.–Sun. 9PM–2AM. Closed Mon. and Tues. No credit cards.*

Piano Bars **Top O' the Cove.** Show tunes and standards from the '40s to the '80s are the typical piano fare at this magnificent Continental restaurant in La Jolla. *1216 Prospect St., tel. 619/454–7779. Entertainment Wed.–Sun. 8 PM–midnight. AE, DC, MC, V.*

Westgate Hotel. One of the most elegant settings in San Diego offers piano music in the Plaza Bar. *1055 Second Ave., downtown, tel. 619/238–1818. Open 11 AM–1 AM. Entertainment 8:30 PM–midnight. AE, DC, MC, V.*

Excursions to the North Coast

To say the north coast area of San Diego County is different from the city of San Diego is a vast understatement. From the northern tip of La Jolla to Oceanside, a half-dozen small communities each developed separately from urban San Diego. In fact, they developed separately from each other, and each has its own flavorful history. Del Mar, for example, exists primarily because of the lure its wide beaches and Thoroughbred horse-racing facility extended to the rich and famous. Just a couple of miles away, agriculture, not paparazzi, played a major role in the development of Solana Beach and Encinitas. Up the coast, Carlsbad still reveals elements of its heritage, roots directly tied to the old Mexican rancheros and the entrepreneurial instinct of John Frazier, who told people the area's water could cure common ailments. In the late 19th century, not far from the current site of the posh La Costa Hotel and Spa, Frazier attempted to turn the area into a massive replica of a German mineral springs resort.

Today, the north coast is a booming population center. An explosion of development throughout the 1980s turned the area into a northern extension of San Diego. The freeways started to take on the typically cluttered characteristics of most Southern California freeways.

Beyond the freeways, though, the communities have maintained their charm. Some of the finest restaurants, beaches, and attractions in San Diego County can be found in the area, a true slice of So Cal heritage. From the plush estates and rolling hills of Rancho Santa Fe and the beachfront restaurants of Cardiff, to Mission San Luis Rey, a well-preserved remnant of California's first European settlers in Oceanside, the north coast is a distinctly different place.

Arriving and Departing

By Car I-5, the main freeway artery connecting San Diego to Los Angeles, follows the coastline. To the west, running parallel to it, is Old Highway 101, which never strays more than a quarter-mile from the ocean. Beginning north of La Jolla, where it is known as Torrey Pines Road, Old Highway 101 is a designated scenic route, providing access to the beauty of the coastline.

By Train **Amtrak** (tel. 619/239–9021 or 800/872–7245) operates trains daily between Los Angeles, Orange County, and San Diego. The last train leaves San Diego at approximately 9 PM each night; the last arrival is 11:30 PM. There are stops in Oceanside and Del Mar.

By Bus **The San Diego Transit District** (tel. 619/722–6283) covers the city of San Diego up to Del Mar, where the **North County Transit District** takes over, blanketing the area with efficient, ontime bus routes.

Greyhound-Trailways (tel. 619/239–9171) has regular routes connecting San Diego to points north, with stops in Del Mar, Solana Beach, Encinitas, and Oceanside.

By Taxi Several companies are based in the North County, including **Amigo Cab** (tel. 619/693–8681) and **Bill's Cab Co.** (tel. 619/755–6737).

By Plane **Palomar Airport** (tel. 619/758–6233), located in Carlsbad two miles east of I-5 on Palomar Airport Road, is a general aviation airport run by the County of San Diego and open to the public. Commuter airlines sometimes have flights from Palomar to Orange County and Los Angeles.

Guided Tours

Civic Helicopters (2192 Palomar Airport Rd., tel. 619/438–8424) offers whirlybird tours of the area from the air.

Exploring

Numbers in the margin correspond with points of interest on The San Diego North Coast map.

Any journey around the north coast area naturally begins at the beach, and this one begins at **Torrey Pines State Beach,** just south of Del Mar. At the south end of the wide beach, perched on top of the cliffs, is the **Torrey Pines State Reserve,** one of only two places (the other place is Santa Rosa Island off the coast of northern California) where the Torrey pine tree grows naturally. The park has a museum and an excellent set of hiking trails that snake through the 1,100-acre park, which is filled with exotic California shrubbery and features picturesque views from

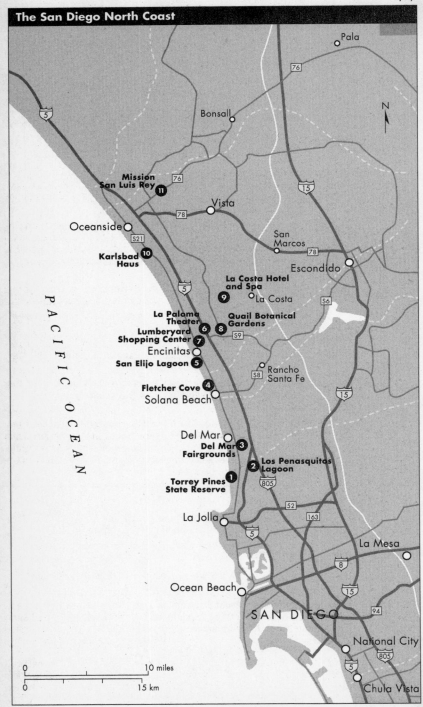

The San Diego North Coast

Pala

76

Bonsall

5

Mission
San Luis Rey **11**

76

Vista

78

Oceanside

S21

San
Marcos

Karlsbad
Haus **10**

15

78

Escondido

5

La Costa Hotel
and Spa
9 La Costa

S6

La Paloma
Theater **6** **8** Quail Botanical
Gardens

Lumberyard
Shopping Center **7**

S9

Encinitas

San Elijo Lagoon **5**

Rancho
Santa Fe

S8

Fletcher Cove **4**

Solana Beach

15

P A C I F I C   O C E A N

Del Mar

Del Mar **3**
Fairgrounds

2 Los Penasquitos
Lagoon

Torrey Pines **1**
State Reserve

805

52

163

La Jolla

5

La Mesa

8

Ocean Beach

15

SAN DIEGO

94

National City

805

0   10 miles

0   15 km

5

Chula Vista

the cliffs. *Tel. 619/755–2063. Admission: $6 per car. Open daily 9 AM–sunset.*

❷ To the east of the state beach is **Los Penasquitos Lagoon,** one of the many natural estuaries that flow inland between Del Mar and Oceanside. Following Old Highway 101, the road leads into the small village of **Del Mar,** best known for its volatile political scene, celebrity visitors, and wide beaches. Years of spats between developers and residents have resulted in the new Del Mar Plaza, hidden by boulder walls and clever landscaping at the corner of Old Highway 101 and 15th Street. The upper level has a large deck and a view out to the ocean, and the restaurants and shops are excellent barometers of the latest in Southern California style. A left turn at 15th Street leads to Seagrove Park, a small, extremely pleasant stretch of grass overlooking the ocean. A right turn on Coast Boulevard provides access to Del Mar's beautiful beaches, particularly popular with Frisbee and volleyball players.

❸ Less than a half mile north, Coast Boulevard merges with Old Highway 101. Across the road is the **Del Mar Fairgrounds,** home to more than 100 different events a year, ranging from a cat show to an auto race. *Via de la Valle Rd. exit west from I-5, tel. 619/755–1161.*

The fairgrounds also host the annual summer meeting of the **Del Mar Thoroughbred Club** (aka "Where the Turf Meets the Surf"). The track brings the top horses and jockeys to Del Mar, along with a cross section of the rich and famous, eager to bet on the ponies. Crooner Bing Crosby and his Hollywood buddies, Pat O'Brien, Gary Cooper, and Oliver Hardy, among others, organized the track in the 1930s, primarily because Crosby thought it would be fun to have a track near his Rancho Santa Fe home. Del Mar soon developed into a regular stop for the stars of stage and screen.

During the off-season, horse players can still gamble at the fairgrounds, thanks to a satellite wagering facility. Races from other California tracks are televised, and people can bet as if the races were being run right there. Times vary, depending on which tracks in the state are operating. *Tel. 619/755–1141. Racing season: July–Sept., daily except Tues. Post time 2 PM.*

Following Via de la Valle Road east from I-5 leads to the exclusive community of **Rancho Santa Fe,** one of the richest areas in the country. Groves of huge, drooping eucalyptus trees, first imported to the area by a railroad company looking to grow trees for railroad ties, cover the hills and valleys, hiding the posh estates. The little village of Rancho has some elegant and quaint—and overpriced—shops and restaurants. But it is no accident that there is little else to see or do in Rancho; the residents guard their privacy religiously. Even the challenging Rancho Santa Fe Golf Course, the original site of the Bing Crosby Pro-Am and considered one of the best courses in Southern California, is still open only to members of the Rancho Santa Fe community.

Back along the coast, along Old Highway 101 north of Del Mar, is the quiet little beach community of **Solana Beach.** A highlight **❹** of Solana Beach is **Fletcher Cove,** located at the west end of Lomas Santa Fe Drive, and called Pill Box by the locals because of a bunkerlike lifeguard station on the cliffs above the beach.

Early Solana settlers used dynamite to blast the cove out of the cliffs. It is an easy-access beach, with a large parking lot replete with a small basketball court, a favorite of local pickup game players.

⑤ North of Solana Beach, separating Solana Beach from Cardiff, is the **San Elijo Lagoon,** home to many migrating birds. Trails wind around the entire area.

As you continue along Old Highway 101, past the cluster of hillside homes that make up Cardiff, past the campgrounds of the San Elijo State Beach, the palm trees of Sea Cliff Roadside Park (Swami's to the locals) and the golden domes of the Self Realization Fellowship mark the entrance to downtown **Encinitas.** The Self Realization Fellowship was built at the turn of the century and is a retreat and place of worship for the followers of an Indian religious sect.

⑥ Another landmark of old Encinitas (which was incorporated as a city in 1986, including the communities of Cardiff, Leucadia, and Olivenhain) is the **La Paloma Theater** on the north end of town on Old Highway 101 (at the corner of Encinitas Blvd., tel. 619/436–7469). The theater was built in the Roaring '20s as a stop for traveling vaudeville troupes. It has served as a concert hall, movie theater, and meeting place for the area ever since. Plays are still being rehearsed and performed here.

⑦ A newer landmark of Encinitas is the **Lumberyard Shopping Center,** a collection of small stores and restaurants that anchors the downtown shopping area. There is a huge selection of shopping centers inland at the intersection of Encinitas Boulevard and El Camino Real.

⑧ But Encinitas is known as the "Flower Capital of the World," not the "Shopping Center Capital of the World." Although the flower industry is not as prevalent as it once was, the city is still the home of Paul Ecke Poinsettias, the largest producer of the popular Christmas flower. A sampling of the area's dedication to horticulture can be found at the **Quail Botanical Gardens,** home to thousands of different varieties of plants. *Encinitas Blvd. east from I-5 and turn left on Quail Gardens Dr., tel. 619/436–3036. Parking $1. Open daily 8–5.*

⑨ Old Highway 101 continues north through Leucadia, a small community best known for its small art galleries and stores. At the north end of Leucadia (which means "sheltered paradise" in Greek), La Costa Avenue meets Highway 101. Following La Costa Avenue east, past the Batiquitos Lagoon, leads to the famous **La Costa Hotel and Spa** (tel. 619/438–9111). It is noted for its excellent golf and tennis facilities and restaurants.

⑩ La Costa is technically part of the city of Carlsbad, which is centered farther north, west of the Tamarack Avenue and Elm Avenue exits of I-5. In Carlsbad, Old Highway 101 is called Carlsbad Boulevard. Large rancheros owned by wealthy Mexicans were the first settlements inland, while the coastal area was developed by an entrepreneur, John Frazier, who lured people to the area with talk of the healing powers of mineral water bubbling from a coastal well. The water was found to have the same properties as water from the German mineral wells of Karlsbad, hence the name of the new community. Remnants from the era, including the original well, are found at the **Alt Karlsbad Haus,** a small museum and gift shop. *2802A Carlsbad*

Blvd., tel. 619/729–6912. Admission free. Open Mon.–Sat. 10–5, Sun. 1–4:30.

North of Carlsbad is **Oceanside,** home of Camp Pendleton, the country's largest marine base, as well as a beautiful natural harbor teeming with activity. Oceanside Harbor is the north-coast center for fishing, sailing, and all ocean water sports. Oceanside Pier is a favorite hangout for fishermen. You can call for general harbor information (tel. 619/966–4570).

⑪ Oceanside is also home to **Mission San Luis Rey,** the largest and one of the best-preserved missions in the area. Built by Franciscan friars in 1798 to help educate and convert local Indians, San Luis Rey was the 18th and largest of the California missions. Today there is a picnic area, gift shop, and museum on the grounds. Self-guided tours are available through the grounds, where retreats are held. *Tel. 619/757–3651. Take Mission Ave. east from I-5. Open Mon.–Sat. 10–4, Sun. 1–4.*

Dining

Given the north-coast area's reputation as a suburban area, there is a surprisingly large selection of top-quality restaurants. In fact, San Diegans often take the drive north to enjoy the variety of cuisines offered in the North County. Prices are for one person and do not include drinks, taxes, or tip. The following credit card abbreviations are used: AE, American Express; DC, Diners Club; MC, MasterCard; V, Visa.

Cardiff
Moderate
($20–$35)

The Triton. The beach and the sunset over the Pacific are the chief attractions of this outdoor dining spot. Although the seafood is just average, and when the surf is up the waiters tend to disappear, this place is fun, especially at lunch. *2530 S. Hwy. 101, tel. 619/436–8877. Dress: casual. AE, DC, MC, V.*

Inexpensive
(under $20)

Los Olas. Funky and inexpensive Los Olas, across the street from the beach in Cardiff, serves good food, especially the chimichangas, deep-fried flour tortillas stuffed with shredded, stewed beef, and the tasty fried burritos with heaps of guacamole and sour cream. The beachside atmosphere is better suited for lunch than dinner, though. *2655 S. Hwy. 101, tel. 619/ 942–1860. Dress: casual. MC, V.*

Del Mar
Expensive
($35–$50)

Remington's. A luxurious and friendly atmosphere makes Remington's worth the high prices. The menu is exceptional and offers lobster, beef, lamb, and veal dishes. *2010 Jimmy Durante Blvd., tel. 619/755–5104. Reservations accepted. Jackets suggested. MC, V.*

Moderate
($20–$35)

The Brigantine. One of the stronger links in a chain of local fish restaurants, this one has a popular Oyster Bar. Unlucky gamblers from the nearby Del Mar Racetrack find the fair prices particularly attractive. *3263 Camino del Mar, tel. 619/481– 1166. Dress: casual. AE, MC, V.*

Cilantros. For a taste of gourmet Mexican food—creative dishes full of subtle spices—Cilantros in Del Mar offers a wide variety of unusual creations, including shark *fajitas* and chicken with a mild chile sauce. The inexpensive tapas menu, with such delicacies as crab tostadas and three-cheese quesadillas, is a little easier on the wallet. *3702 Via de la Valle, tel. 619/259– 8777. Reservations suggested. Dress: casual. AE, MC, V.*

Encinitas
Moderate
($20–$35)

Piret M. This charming, sun-dappled French bistro looks as much like a sophisticated gourmet boutique (with delicacies for sale) as it does a countryside restaurant. The menu features hearty soups, quiches that will make a man of you, crisp fresh salads, a savory lamb ragout, large but elegant sandwiches, French omelets, and the sort of rich desserts that threaten the firmest of resolves. *897 First St., tel. 619/942–5152. Reservations advised. Dress: casual. AE, MC, V.*

Portofino's. This classy little restaurant attempts to re-create the atmosphere of the posh Riviera resort from which it gets its name. Homemade pasta and the seafood dishes are popular. *1108 First St., tel. 619/942–8442. Reservations accepted. Dress: casual. Full bar. AE, DC, MC, V.*

Santa Fe Grill. Despite its Mexican-sounding name, the Santa Fe Grill offers a straightforward selection of hamburgers, prime rib, and seafood dishes. *162 S. Rancho Santa Fe Rd., tel. 619/944–7455. Reservations accepted. Dress: casual. AE, MC, V.*

La Costa
Expensive
($35–$50)

Pices. Located near the La Costa Country Club, Pices represents the upper class of north-coast seafood restaurants. Traditional seafood, such as scallops and shrimp, is served in innovative and tasty dishes. *7640 El Camino Real, tel. 619/436–9362. Reservations accepted. Jackets required. AE, DC, MC, V.*

Rancho Santa Fe
Expensive
($35–$50)
★

Mille Fleurs. This gem of a French auberge brightens a tiny village surrounded by country gentlemen estates. Just a few miles from the county's famous vegetable farms, where the chef shops daily, this is a most romantic hideaway, with tempting cuisine to help the mood. *6009 Paseo Delicias, tel. 619/756–3085. Reservations advised. Jacket and tie advised. AE, DC, MC, V.*

Solana Beach
Expensive
($35–$50)

Frederick's. This husband-and-wife-owned, friendly, relaxed bistro serves traditional French dishes with California-fresh overtones. Leave room for the freshly baked bread and one of the lush desserts. The menu changes weekly. *128 S. Acacia St., tel. 619/755–2432. Dress: casual. DC, MC, V. Closed for lunch. Closed Sun. and Mon.*

Inexpensive
(under $20)

Chung King Loh. One of the better Chinese restaurants along the coast, Chung King Loh offers an excellent variety of Mandarin and Szechuan dishes. *552 Stevens Ave., tel. 619/481–0184. Dress: casual. AE, DC, MC, V. No lunch Sun.*

Fidel's. Rich in North County tradition, both Fidel's restaurants serve a wide variety of well-prepared dishes in a low-key, pleasant atmosphere. The original restaurant in Solana Beach, a two-story building with an outdoor patio area, is particularly nice. *607 Valley Ave., tel. 619/755–5292; 3003 Carlsbad Blvd., Carlsbad, tel. 619/729–0903. Dress: casual. AE, MC, V.*

Lodging

The prices below reflect the cost of a room for two people. Many hotels offer discount rates from October to May.

Carlsbad
Very Expensive
(over $120)

The Inn L'Auberge. By far the best hotel in Del Mar, the Inn sits across the street from the Del Mar Plaza and one block from the ocean. Modeled after the Tudor-style Hotel Del Mar, playground for Hollywood's elite in the early 1900s, the Inn is filled with dark wood antiques, fireplaces, and lavish floral arrangements—a high-style ambience, and a sense of refinement that clashes somewhat with the sun-drenched Southern California scene just outside its doors. The grounds are gorgeous, with stone paths winding throughout 5.2 acres, and leading to gazebos and pools; the spa specializes in European herbal wraps and treatments. *1540 Camino Del Mar, Del Mar, 92014, tel. 619/ 259–1515 or 800/553–1336. 120 rooms. Facilities: restaurant, 2 tennis courts, 2 pools, Jacuzzi, European-style spa. AE, MC, V.*

La Costa Hotel and Spa. This famous resort has recently gone through a $100 million renovation, and the style is now mildly Southwestern. Contemporary rooms are decorated in neutral tones, or rose and turquoise. You'll find all amenities, including supervised children's activities and a movie theater. *Costa del Mar Rd., 92009, tel. 619/438–9111 or 800/854–6564. 478 rooms. Facilities: 5 restaurants, pool, exercise room, golf, tennis, theater. AE, DC, MC, V.*

Carlsbad
Expensive
(over $75)

Carlsbad Inn Beach and Tennis Resort. This hotel and time-share resort near the beach features modern amenities and rooms with an Old World feel. *3075 Carlsbad Blvd., 92008, tel. 619/434–7020. 200 rooms. Facilities: 2 restaurants, pool, health club, Jacuzzis, video room. AE, MC, V.*

Moderate
($55–$75)

Best Western Beach View Lodge. Reservations are essential at this reasonably priced hotel at the beach. Some rooms have kitchenettes; others have fireplaces. Families tend to settle in for a week or more. *3180 Carlsbad Blvd., 92008, tel. 619/729– 1151. 41 rooms. Facilities: Jacuzzi, sauna, swimming pool. AE, DC, MC, V.*

Inexpensive
(under $55)

Carlsbad Lodge. The lodge is more than an easy walk from the beach, but there is a nice park nearby. The rooms are clean and pleasant. *3570 Pio Pico Dr., 92008, tel. 619/729–2383. 66 rooms. Facilities: Jacuzzi, sauna, swimming pool. AE, DC, MC, V.*

Del Mar
Moderate
($55–$75)

Stratford Inn. The inn offers a pleasant atmosphere just outside of town and three blocks from the ocean. Rooms are clean and well maintained; some have ocean views. Suites are available. Note: Not all rooms are air-conditioned, so be sure to ask before you reserve. *710 Camino del Mar, 92014, tel. 619/ 755–1501. 110 rooms. Facilities: 2 pools, Jacuzzi. AE, DC, MC, V.*

Encinitas
Moderate
($55–$75)

Moonlight Beach Hotel. This folksy laid-back motel is a favorite with those who enjoy the area's post-hippie aura and don't mind the traffic just outside their doors. All rooms have kitchens, and the beach is a few blocks away. *233 Second St., 92024, tel. 619/753–0623. 24 rooms. AE, MC, V.*

Radisson Inn Encinitas. Formerly called the Sanderling, this hotel on the east side of Old Highway 101 sits on a slight hill near the freeway. The rooms—some with an ocean view— are efficiently designed and unobtrusively decorated. *85 Encinitas Blvd., tel. 619/942–7455 or 800/333–3333. 92 rooms. Facilities: pool, whirlpool, putting green, restaurant. AE, DC, MC, V.*

Inexpensive
(under $55)

Budget Motels of America. This motel is adjacent to the freeway and within a block of the beach. Some rooms have VCRs and in-room movies—a good deal. *133 Encinitas Blvd., 92024, tel. 619/944–0260. 124 rooms. AE, DC, MC, V.*

Leucadia *Inexpensive* *(under $55)*	**Pacific Surf Motel.** It will never be compared with The Ritz, but it is clean, comfortable, and near all the shops and restaurants of Encinitas. *1076 N. Hwy. 101, 92024, tel. 619/436–8763. 30 rooms. AE, MC, V.*
Oceanside *Inexpensive* *(under $55)*	**Oceanside TraveLodge.** Near the beach and centrally located. *1401 N. Hill St., 92054, tel. 619/722–1244. 30 rooms. AE, DC, MC, V.*
Rancho Santa Fe *Expensive* *(over $75)*	**Rancho Valencia.** This resort is so luxurious that several high-style magazines have chosen it for fashion backdrops, and have named it the most romantic hideaway in the United States. The suites are in red-tile-roofed casitas with fireplaces and private terraces. Tennis is the other draw here with 18 courts and a resident pro. *5921 Valencia Circle, tel. 619/756–1123 or 800/548–3664. 43 suites. Facilities: restaurant, 18 tennis courts, pool, 2 Jacuzzis, sauna. AE, MC, V.*

Excursions to Anza-Borrego Desert State Park

Every spring, the stark desert landscape east of the Cuyamaca Mountains explodes with color. It's the annual blooming of the wildflowers in the Anza-Borrego Desert State Park, less than a two-hour drive from central San Diego. The beauty of this annual spectacle, as well as the natural quiet and blazing climate, lures tourists and natives to the area.

The area features a desert and not much more, but it is one of the favorite parks of those Californians who travel widely in their state. People seeking bright lights and glitter should look elsewhere. The excitement in this area stems from watching a coyote scamper across a barren ridge or a brightly colored bird resting on a nearby cactus, or from a waitress delivering another cocktail to a poolside chaise longue. For hundreds of years, the only humans to linger in the area were Indians from the San Dieguito, Kamia, and Cahuilla tribes, but the extreme temperature eventually forced the tribes to leave, too. It wasn't until 1774, when Mexican explorer Captain Juan Bautista de Anza first blazed a trail through the area as a shortcut from Sonora to San Francisco, that modern civilization had its first glimpse of the oddly beautiful wasteland.

Today, more than 500,000 acres of desert are included in the Anza-Borrego Desert State Park, making it the largest state park in the United States. It is also one of the few parks in the country where people can camp anywhere. No campsite is necessary; just follow the trails and pitch a tent anywhere in the park.

Following the trails is an important point, since vehicles are prohibited from driving off the road in most areas of the park. However, there are 14,000 acres set aside in the eastern part of the desert near Ocotillo Wells for off-road enthusiasts. General George S. Patton conducted field training in the Ocotillo area to prepare for the World War II invasion of North Africa, and the area hasn't been the same since.

The little town of Borrego Springs acts as an oasis in this natural playground. Not exactly like Palm Springs—it lacks the wild crowds and preponderance of insanely wealthy residents—Borrego is basically a small retirement community, with the average age of residents about 50. For those who are uninterested in communing with the desert without a shower and pool nearby, Borrego provides several pleasant hotels and restaurants for travelers.

We recommend visiting this desert between October and May because of the extreme summer temperatures. Winter temperatures are comfortable, but nights (and sometimes days) are cold, so bring a warm jacket.

Arriving and Departing

By Car Take I-8 east to Highway 79 north. Turn east on Highway 78.

By Bus The **Northeast Rural Bus System** (NERBS) (tel. 619/765–0145) connects Julian, Borrego Springs, Oak Grove, Ocotillo Wells, Agua Caliente, Ramona, and many of the other small communities that dot the landscape with El Cajon, 15 miles east of downtown San Diego, and the East County line of the San Diego trolley, with stops at Grossmont shopping center and North County Fair.

By Plane Borrego Springs Airport (tel. 619/767–5548) has the nearest runway.

Important Addresses and Numbers

For general information about the Borrego and desert areas, contact the **Borrego Chamber of Commerce** (tel. 619/767–5555). For information on the state park, contact the Visitor Center, **Anza-Borrego Desert State Park** (Box 299, Borrego Springs 92004, tel. 619/767–5311). You can call the Visitor Center for information on when the wildflowers are blooming, or you can send a self-addressed postcard and they'll send it back when the flowers bloom. For campsite information, call **MISTIX** (tel. 800/444–7275).

Exploring

The **Anza-Borrego Desert State Park** is too vast even to consider exploring all its areas. Most people stay in the hills surrounding Borrego Springs. An excellent underground **Visitor Information Center** (tel. 619/767–5311) and museum are reachable by taking the Palm Canyon Drive spur west from the traffic circle in the center of town. The rangers are helpful and always willing to suggest areas to camp or hike. There is also a short slide show about the desert, shown throughout the day. A short, very easy trail from the Visitor Center to the campground will take you past many of the cacti illustrated in Visitor Center displays.

One of the most popular camping and hiking areas is **Palm Canyon,** just a few minutes west of the Visitor Information Center. A 1½-mile trail leads to a small oasis with a waterfall and palm trees. If you find palm trees lining city streets in San Diego and Los Angeles amusing, seeing this grove of native palms around a pool in a narrow desert valley may give you a new vision of the dignity of this tree. The Borrego Palm Canyon campground (on the desert floor a mile or so below the palm oasis) is one of only two developed campgrounds with flush toilets and showers in the park. (The other is Tamarisk Grove Campground at the intersection of Highway 78 and Yaqui Pass Road.)

Other points of interest include **Split Mountain** (take Split Mountain Rd. south from Hwy. 78 at Ocotillo Wells), a narrow gorge with 600-foot perpendicular walls. You can drive the mile from the end of the paved road to the gorge in a passenger car if you are careful (don't get stuck in the sand). Don't attempt the drive in bad weather, when the gorge can quickly fill with a torrent of water.

On the way to Split Mountain (while you are still on the paved road), you'll pass a grove of the park's unusual **elephant trees** (10 feet tall, with swollen branches and small leaves). There is a self-guided nature trail; pick up a brochure at the parking lot.

You can get a good view of the Borrego Badlands from **Font's Point,** off Borrego-Salton Seaway (S22). The badlands are a maze of steep ravines that are almost devoid of vegetation. Park rangers sometimes give guided tours of the region above the badlands. You drive your own car in a caravan behind the ranger, stopping for closer looks and detailed information.

There is little to do in **Borrego Springs** itself except lie in the sun, lie in the shade, or take advantage of the hot days and recreate in the sun. The challenging 18-hole Rams Hill Country Club course is open to the public (tel. 619/767-5000), as is the Borrego Roadrunner Club (tel. 619/767-5652), but you'll have to know a member to play the private 18 holes of the De Anza Country Club located in the north end of the valley (tel. 619/767-5105).

For tennis fans, the Borrego Tennis Club (tel. 619/767-9725) has four lighted courts open to the public. One of the best and most appreciated deals in town is the Borrego Springs High School pool, located at the intersection of Saddle and Cahuilla roads, which is open to the public during the summer.

Most people prefer to explore the desert in a motorized vehicle. While it is illegal to ride two- or four-wheel vehicles off the trails in the state park, the **Ocotillo Wells State Vehicular Recreation Area** (tel. 619/767-5391), reached by following Highway 78 east from Borrego, is a popular haven for off-road enthusiasts. The sand dunes and rock formations are challenging as well as fun. Camping is permitted throughout the area, but water is not available. The only facilities are in the small town (or, perhaps, it should be called no more than a corner) of Ocotillo Wells.

To the east of Anza-Borrego is the Salton Sink, a basin that (although not as low as Death Valley) consists of more dry land below sea level than anywhere else in the hemisphere. The Salton Sea is the most recent of a series of lakes here, divided from the Gulf of California by the delta of the Colorado River. The current lake was created in 1905-7 when the Colorado flooded north through canals meant to irrigate the Imperial Valley. The water is extremely salty, even saltier than the Pacific Ocean, and it is primarily a draw for fishermen seeking corvina, croaker, and tilapia. Some boaters and swimmers also use the lake. The state runs a pleasant park with sites for day camping, recreational vehicles, and primitive camping. *Take Hwy. 78 east to Hwy. 111 north, tel. 619/393–3052.*

Bird-watchers particularly will love the **Salton Sea National Wildlife Refuge.** A hiking trail and observation tower make it easy to spot the dozens of varieties of migratory birds stopping at Salton Sea. *At the south end of Salton Sea, off Hwy. 111, tel. 619/348–5278.*

For hunters, the **Wister Wildlife Area** (tel. 619/348–0577), off Highway 111 on the east side of Salton Sea, controls the hunting of water fowl in the area. There are campsites available.

Dining

Quality, not quantity, is the operable truism of dining in the Borrego area. Restaurants are scarce and hard to find, but the best are truly top quality. Prices are based on the cost of a complete meal for one, not including beverage, tax, or tip.

Moderate ($10–$20) **La Casa del Zorro.** An elegant Continental dining experience. The restaurant also serves Sunday brunch. *3845 Yaqui Pass Rd., tel. 619/767–5323. Reservations accepted. Dress: no shorts or jeans. AE, DC, MC, V.*

Rams Hill Country Club. An elegant, top-notch Continental restaurant in the middle of the desert. The club also serves Sunday brunch. *1881 Rams Hill Rd., tel. 619/767–5006. Reservations accepted. Dress: casual; jacket required on Sat. AE, MC, V. Closed for dinner Mon.–Wed., July–Oct. 1.*

Inexpensive **Chefs for You.** A deli located in the largest shopping center in
(under $10) Borrego. *561 The Mall, tel. 619/767–3522.*

Lodging

If camping is not your thing, there are two very nice resorts near Borrego Springs that offer fine amenities without the overdevelopment of Palm Springs. Prices are based on the cost of a room for two. In the summer months, rates drop by as much as 50%.

Expensive **Ram's Hill Country Club.** A relatively new hacienda-style coun-
(over $70) try club in the middle of the desert. Patio units are on the golf course. *Box 664, Borrego Springs, 92004, tel. 619/767–5028. 20 units. Facilities: tennis courts, Jacuzzi. AE, MC, V.*

La Casa del Zorro. A small low-key resort complex in the heart of the desert, where you need only walk a few hundred yards to be alone out under the sky and you may well see roadrunners crossing the highway. The accommodations are in comfortable 1-3 bedroom ranch-style houses complete with living rooms and kitchens. *3845 Yaqui Pass Rd., 92004, tel. 619/767–5323 or 800/325–8274. 77 suites, 94 rooms, 19 casitas. Facilities: tennis courts, golf course, horseback riding, bicycles. AE, DC, MC, V.*

Palm Canyon Resort. One of the largest facilities in the area, with a hotel, RV park, restaurant, and recreational facilities. *221 Palm Canyon Dr., 92004, tel. 619/767–5342 or 800/242–0044 in CA. 44 rooms. Facilities: 138 RV spaces, 2 pools, 2 Jacuzzis, restaurant, general store, laundromat.*

15 Palm Springs

*by Aaron
Sugarman*

What do you get when you start with dramatic scenery, add endless sunshine, mix in deluxe resorts, and spice things up with a liberal dash of celebrities? Palm Springs.

This fashionable desert resort community, nestled beneath 10,831-foot Mt. San Jacinto, sports more than 70 golf courses in a 20-mile radius, more than 300 tennis courts, 35 miles of bicycle trails, horseback riding, 7,000 or so swimming pools, and even cross-country skiing. Those inclined to less strenuous activities are attracted by such names as Gucci, I. Magnin, and Saks Fifth Avenue. The "in crowd" gathers at exclusive country clubs and openings at the city's numerous art galleries. It's often said that socializing is the top industry in Palm Springs; after a few days here, you're sure to agree.

Year-round, Palm Springs is both a vacation retreat and a residence for celebrities and famous politicians. Bob Hope is the city's honorary mayor, and Gene Autry, Frank Sinatra, Gerald Ford, and other luminaries can be spotted at charity events and restaurants and on the golf course. Carrie Fisher and Bette Midler have done stints at the Palms spa, while Donna Mills, Goldie Hawn, and Kurt Russell have been poolside stars at the Ingleside Inn. Palm Springs resorts are not new territory to celebrity visitors: Esther Williams once practiced her strokes at the El Mirador pool, Spencer Tracy played chess at the Racquet Club, and Joan Bennett pedaled her bicycle down Palm Canyon Drive.

Palm Springs became a haven for the stars in 1930, after the arrival of noted silent-film pros Charlie Farrell and Ralph Bellamy. For $30 an acre, the two actors bought 200 acres. This was the beginning of the Palm Springs Racquet Club, which soon listed Ginger Rogers, Humphrey Bogart, and Clark Gable among its members.

The desert's stunning natural beauty is a major contributor to the area's magnetism. Nature dominates the area: City buildings are restricted to a height of 30 feet; flashing, moving, and neon signs are prohibited, preserving an intimate village feeling; and 50% of the land consists of open spaces with palm trees and desert vegetation.

This beauty is particularly evident in the canyons surrounding Palm Springs. Lush Tahquitz Canyon, one of the five canyons that line the San Jacinto Mountains, was the setting for Shangri-La in the original version of *Lost Horizon*. The original inhabitants of these rock canyons were the Cahuilla Indians. Their descendants came to be known as Agua Caliente— "hot water"—Indians, named after the hot mineral springs that flowed through their reservation. The Agua Caliente still own about 30,000 acres of Palm Springs desert, making them one of the richest tribes in the country.

Despite the building restrictions, Palm Springs has a suitable array of sophisticated spots, from the outstanding Desert Museum and Annenberg Theatre to the chic shops and galleries along the palm tree-lined Palm Canyon Drive. The trendy El Paseo Drive, 10 miles south of Palm Springs in neighboring Palm Desert, is often compared to Rodeo Drive in Beverly Hills.

One brief comment on the weather: While daytime temperatures average a pleasantly warm 88° Fahrenheit, you are still in the desert. And that means during the middle of the day in the summer it is going to be very hot—sometimes uncomfortably hot. You're bound to be told that "it is a dry heat." It is. But it is still desert hot: Plan activities in the morning and late afternoon, and wear a hat and plenty of sunscreen if you're out for a midday stroll.

Arriving and Departing

By Plane Major airlines serving Palm Springs Municipal Airport include Alaska Airlines, American Airlines, American Eagle, America West, Continental Airlines, Skywest/Delta Connection, Trans World Airlines, United Airlines, and United Express. The airport is about 2 miles east of the city's main downtown intersection; most hotels provide service to and from the airport.

By Train **Amtrak** passenger trains service the Indio area, 20 miles east of Palm Springs. For information and reservations call 800/USA–RAIL. From Indio, **Greyhound/Trailways** bus service is available to Palm Springs.

By Bus **Greyhound/Trailways** Bus Lines (311 N. Indian Ave., tel. 619/325–2053).

By Car Palm Springs is about a two-hour drive east of Los Angeles and a three-hour drive northeast of San Diego. Highway 111 brings you right onto Palm Canyon Drive, the main thoroughfare in Palm Springs. From Los Angeles take the San Bernardino Freeway (I–10E) to Highway 111. From San Diego, I–15N connects with the Pomona Freeway (I–60E), leading to the San Bernardino Freeway (I–10E). If you're coming from the Riverside area, you might want to try the scenic Palms-to-Pines Highway (Hwy. 74). This 130-mile route begins in Hemet and connects directly with Highway 111; the trek from snowcapped peaks to open desert valley is breathtaking.

Getting Around

Downtown Palm Springs is distinctly walkable. Beyond that, you will find that having a car is the easiest way to get around and take in nearby attractions like the Aerial Tramway and El Paseo Drive.

By Bus **SunBus** serves the entire Coachella Valley from Desert Hot Springs to Coachella with regular routes. Call 619/323–4010 or 619/323–4058 for route and schedule information. **The Village Shuttle** is an open-air trolley that shuttles between major Palm Springs hotels. The cost is $1 per round-trip; $5 for an all-day pass. Call 619/778–1733.

By Taxi **Desert Cab** (tel. 619/325–2868) and **Caravan Yellow Cab** (tel. 619/346–2981).

By Car The easiest way to get around Palm Springs is by automobile. If you're not driving to Palm Springs, you might do well to check with one of the many rental agencies, all of which offer fairly competitive rates. Agencies include Avis (tel. 619/327–1353), Aztec (tel. 619/325–2294), Budget (tel. 619/327–1404), Dollar (tel. 619/325–7334), Enterprise (tel. 619/328–9393), Hertz (tel. 619/778–5120), and National (tel. 619/327–4100).

Important Addresses and Numbers

Tourist Information	The City of **Palm Springs Tourism Division** (2781 N. Palm Canyon Dr., Palm Springs 92262, tel. 800/347–7746) provides tourist information and maintains an information desk in the airport's main terminal. **Desert Resorts Bureau** (tel. 619/770–9000) is located at 69930 Highway 111, Suite 210, Rancho Mirage 92270.
Emergencies	Dial 911 for **police** and **ambulance** in an emergency.
Doctor	**Desert Hospital** (tel. 619/323–6511).
Dentist	Dental emergency service is available from R. Turnage D.D.S. (tel. 619/327–8448 or 619/325–1377) 24 hours a day.

Guided Tours

Orientation Tours	**Gray Line Tours** (tel. 619/325–0974) offers several good general bus tours, from the hour-long Palm Springs Special highlight tour to the Palm Springs and Living Desert tour through Palm Springs, Cathedral City, Rancho Mirage, and Palm Desert, with stops at a date shop and the Living Desert. Prices are $14.25 for adults, $8.25 for children. Most departures are in the morning; call for reservations. Pick-up and drop-off service is available to most hotels.
Special-Interest Tours	In Palm Springs, special-interest tours mean one thing: celebrity homes. **Gray Line** and **Palm Springs Celebrity Tours** (tel. 619/325–2682) both cover this turf well. Prices range from $10 to $14 for adults. **Desert Off Road Adventures** (tel. 619/773–3187) takes to the wilds with jeep tours of Indian canyons, unexpected waterfalls, and other off-the-beaten-track desert highlights. Customized helicopter tours are available from **Sunrise Balloons:** 40-minute trips start at $270 for two people.

Exploring

Numbers in the margin correspond with points of interest on the Palm Springs map.

Palm Springs proper is pretty easy to understand. Palm Canyon Drive runs north–south through the heart of downtown; the intersection with Tahquitz-McCallum is pretty much the center of the main drag. Heading south, Palm Canyon Drive splits: South Palm Canyon Drive leads you to the Indian Canyons and East Palm Canyon takes you through the growing satellite resort areas of Cathedral City, Rancho Mirage, and Palm Desert. The Aerial Tramway is at the northern limits of Palm Springs. Joshua Trees National Monument is about an hour's drive north.

Most Palm Springs attractions can be seen in anywhere from an hour or two to an entire day. Do you want to take the tram up Mt. San Jacinto, see the view, and come right back down, or spend the day hiking? Would you rather linger for a picnic lunch in one of the Indian Canyons, or double back for a snack and people-watching at Hyatt's sidewalk cafe? Your best bet is to look at the list of sights and activities as if it were an à la carte menu and pick and choose according to your appetite. To help you organize your outings, we will start in the north and work our way south and southeast. A separate tour of Joshua Trees follows.

Palm Springs and Environs

1 The **Palm Springs Aerial Tramway** is the place for a real over-view of the desert. The 2½-mile ascent brings you to an eleva-tion of 8,516 feet in under 20 minutes. On clear days, which are common, the view stretches some 75 miles from the peak of Mt. San Gorgonio to the north to the Salton Sea in the southeast. Mt. San Jacinto State Park offers 54 miles of hiking trails and camping and picnic areas; the Nordic Ski Center is open for cross-country skiing November 15 to April 15, snow permit-ting. *Tram cars depart at least every 30 min from 10 AM week-days and 8 AM weekends. Last car up is at 8 PM, last car down 9:45 PM; May–Labor Day, last car up is at 9 PM, last car down at 10:45 PM. Cost: $13.95 adults, $8.95 children 3–12. Closed for 2–4 wks after Labor Day for maintenance. Call 619/325–1391 for information; 619/325–4227 for ski and weather condi-tions.*

Strolling down **Palm Canyon Drive,** Palm Springs' version of Main Street, should satisfy even the most avid shopper. With a good pair of comfortable walking shoes you should be able to walk from one end of the drive to the other in a couple of hours. Some exceptional art galleries, such as the **Jeanette C. McIn-tyre Gallery of Fine Art,** have taken root along the route and are well worth the browsing time. The Jeanette C. McIntyre Gal-lery (447 N. Palm Canyon Dr., tel. 619/322–0966), features Ori-ental pieces and desert oils and is the dealer for P. Buckley Moss collective prints.

Downtown **horse-drawn carriages** promenade the city streets to the narrative of their guide/drivers. Their Star House Tour is especially fun. *Carriage Trade LTD, tel. 619/327–3214. $60 for 1 to 4 people. Rides start at the corner of Taquitz Way and Palm Canyon Dr.*

2 Downtown Palm Springs is not without its historical treasures. The **Village Green Heritage Center** comprises two 19th-century pioneer homes. The adobe house built by "Judge" John Mc-Callum in 1885 is now a museum housing the major portion of the collection of the Palm Springs Historical Society. Next door is the Cornelia White House, built in 1894 from railroad ties. Inside are such historical tidbits as the first telephone in Palm Springs. *221 and 223 S. Palm Canyon Dr. Nominal admis-sion. Both open Wed.–Sun. noon–3, Thurs.–Sat. 10–4. Closed June–mid-Oct.*

3 If further evidence is needed to prove that the desert is no bar-ren wasteland, there is the **Desert Museum.** Art exhibits here tend to favor a Western flavor, from California Contemporary to shows like "Art and Treasures of the Old West" from the Buf-falo Bill Historical Center. But it is not unusual to catch the likes of a Matisse exhibition or works from the impressive Armand Hammer Collection that toured the region last year. Natural-history and science exhibits illuminate aspects of the surrounding desert. The museum's Annenberg Theatre has featured Liza Minnelli and Frank Sinatra in concert. *Museum Dr., just north of Tahquitz Way (on the south side of the Desert Fashion Plaza), tel. 619/325–7186. Admission: $4 adults, $2 children under 17. (Admission free the first Tuesday of every month.) Open Tues.–Fri. 10–4, weekends until 5. Closed Mon. and June 5–Sept. 22.*

4 A short drive or distinctly long walk farther south on Palm Canyon is the **Moorten Botanical Garden.** More than 2,000 plant

Palm Springs

Desert Museum, **3**
Indian Canyons, **5**
Joshua Tree National
Monument, **7**
Living Desert
Reserve, **6**

Moorten Botanical
Garden, **4**
Palm Springs Aerial
Tramway, **1**
Village Green
Heritage Center, **2**

varieties cover the 4-acre site in settings that simulate the plants' original environments. Indian artifacts and rock, crystal, and wood forms are exhibited. *1701 S. Palm Canyon Dr., tel. 619/327-6555. Nominal admission fee. Open daily 9-4:30 Sat. 10-4.*

⑤ The **Indian Canyons** begin 5 miles south of downtown Palm Springs. Inside this Indian-owned sanctuary, visitors can gaze at pictographs, bedrock mortar holes for grinding grain, and stone houses and shelters built atop high cliff walls—all relics of ancient Indian history. Streams of icy mountain water wind through the dense growth of willows, sycamores, and mesquite and groves of stately Washingtonia palms. Bands of wild ponies roam through Murray Canyon, and Andreas Canyon has towering rock faces and mysterious crevices and caves. Desert wildlife scampers around the more than 3,000 palm trees in Palm Canyon. Experiencing the canyons leaves visitors with the sensation of slipping through a time warp into a prehistoric era. *End of S. Palm Canyon Dr., tel. 619/327-2714. Admission: $3.25 adults, 75¢ children. Open Sept.–June daily 8-5.*

⑥ Bighorn sheep, coyotes, eagles, and other desert wildlife roam in naturalistic settings at the **Living Desert Reserve,** in Palm Desert. There is a 6-mile nature walk, a walk through an aviary, a coyote grotto, a desert reptile exhibit, and regularly scheduled animal shows. This is a particularly enjoyable learning experience for children. *47-900 Portola Ave., less than 2 mi south of Hwy. 111, tel. 619/346-5694. Admission: $5.50 adults, $2.50 children 6-15. Open daily 9-5, closed mid-June-Aug.*

Time Out Tired from all your hiking around? Then sample the healing waters that have made Palm Springs famous for centuries. The Cahuilla Indians have leased 8 acres of land to form the site of the **Palm Springs Spa Hotel.** Visit the inhalation room with its soothing menthol vapors and, of course, the mineral baths. Facials and massage are also available. *100 N. Indian Ave., tel. 619/325-1461. Prices begin at $25. Open daily 10-5.*

Joshua Tree National Monument ⑦ **Joshua Tree National Monument** is about a one-hour drive from Palm Springs, whether you take I-10 north to Highway 62 to the Oasis Visitor Center or I-10 south to the Cottonwood Visitor Center. The northern part of the park is in the Mojave (or high) Desert and has the Joshua trees. The southern part is Colorado (or low) Desert; you'll see fine displays of wildflowers here in the spring. It is possible to drive through the monument and come back to Palm Springs from the other direction. This would be a good long day's exploring, but you would travel through the two major California deserts.

On the northern route to the national monument, you may want to consider stopping at the **Big Morongo Wildlife Reserve.** Once an Indian village, then a cattle ranch, and now a regional park, the reserve is a serene natural oasis supporting a wide variety of plants, birds, and animals. There is a shaded meadow for picnics and choice hiking trails. *From I-10 or Indian Ave., take Hwy. 62 east to East Dr. Admission free. Open 8-sunset.*

The monument itself is immense, complex, and ruggedly beautiful. It marks the meeting place of the Mojave and Colorado deserts with mountains of twisted rock and exposed granite monoliths, lush oases shaded by tall, elegant fan palms, and natural cactus gardens. Extensive stands of Joshua trees give the monument its name. The trees were named by early white settlers who felt their unusual forms resembled Joshua raising his arms toward heaven. With so much to see—the monument covers more than half a million acres—the **Oasis Visitor Center** is probably the best place to start. The center has an excellent selection of free and low-cost brochures, books, posters, and maps as well as several educational exhibits. Knowledgeable and helpful rangers are on hand to answer questions and offer advice. *Hwy. 62 to the town of 29 Palms, follow the signs a short distance south to the Visitor Center. There is a $5-per-vehicle entry fee to the monument.*

Right at the Visitor Center is the **Oasis of Mara.** Inhabited first by Indians and later by prospectors and homesteaders, the oasis now provides a good home for birds, small mammals, and other wildlife. Once inside the monument, you will find nine campgrounds with tables, fireplaces, and rest rooms and several picnic areas for day use. Beyond those basics, sights range from the Hidden Valley, a legendary cattle rustlers' hideout reached by a trail winding through massive boulders; and the Lost Horse Mine, a remnant of the gold-mining days; to Keys View, an outstanding scenic point commanding a superb sweep of valley, mountain, and desert. Sunrise and sunset are magic times to be at the monument, when the light throws rocks and trees into high relief before (or after) bathing the hills in brilliant shades of red, orange, and gold. The National Parks Service map available at the Visitor Center tells you where to find these and other impressive sights within the monument.

Palm Springs for Free

The North Palm Canyon Gallery Association (tel. 619/322–0966) regularly offers a free "art stroll" touring the area galleries.

There are two dozen or so municipal and school **tennis courts** scattered throughout Palm Springs that are absolutely free. Check the "Courts and Courses" listing in *Desert Guide*, available at most hotels, at the Convention and Visitors Bureau, and at the Palm Springs Tourism Division.

What to See and Do with Children

The Dinosaur Gardens are a must-see. Claude Bell designed and built the 150-foot-long brontosaurus and matching Tyrannosaurus rex right off the main highway. The dinosaurs starred in the movie *Pee-wee's Big Adventure. 5800 Seminole Dr., Cabazon, just off I–10, just before Hwy. 111, 18 mi northwest of Palm Springs, no phone. Open Wed.–Mon. 9–5.*

At the **Palm Springs Swim Center,** an Olympic-size swimming pool has a separate swimming section for children only. Swimming instruction is available for all ages. *405 S. Pavilion, adjacent to the corner of Sunrise Way and Ramon Rd., tel. 619/323–8278. Hours and admission vary by season.*

Children can also make a splash at the **Oasis Water Resort.** Tubing, water slides, "Squirt City," and other watery delights will entertain a wide range of age groups. *1500 Gene Autry Trail, between Hwy. 111 and Ramon Rd., tel. 619/325–7873. Hours and admission prices vary by season.*

California Angels spring-training baseball games, with a requisite autograph hunt, makes for a fun afternoon.

Aerial Tramway (*see* Exploring, above).

The Living Desert (*see* Exploring, above).

Indian Canyons. Hiking and picnic areas, Indian cultural remains (*see* Exploring, above).

Off the Beaten Track

Dog sled races in Palm Springs? Why not . . . ? The **Moosehead Championship Sled Dog Races** are held in January, contingent, of course, on snow conditions, atop Mt. San Jacinto. Take the Aerial Tramway up. Call 619/325–1391 for more information.

The Eldorado Polo Club (50-950 Madison Blvd., Indio, tel. 619/342–2223) is known as the "Winter Polo Capital of the West." Pack a picnic hamper and hobnob with the elite from November to April. Admission is free except for a $6 charge on Sundays.

Shopping

The Palm Springs area is full of custom boutiques and lively art galleries. The resort community also has several large air-conditioned indoor malls with major department stores and chic boutiques. El Paseo in nearby Palm Desert is the desert's other shopping mecca, with its own collection of upscale and elegant galleries and shops. Most stores are open 10–5 or 6, Monday–Saturday. A fair number are open on Sunday, typically noon–5. The sales tax in Palm Springs is 6½%.

Shopping Districts **Palm Canyon Drive** is Palm Springs' main shopping destination. It began as a dusty two-way dirt road and is now a one-way, three-lane thoroughfare with parking on both sides. Its shopping core extends from Alejo Road on the north to Ramon Road on the south. Expect to find everything your heart desires—though your wallet may have a tough time keeping up. Furs, jewelry, sportswear, home furnishings, books, shoes, and crafts will tempt you on this busy street. Anchoring the center of the drive is the Desert Fashion Plaza, sporting such big names as Saks Fifth Avenue, I. Magnin, Gucci, The Hyatt Regency Suites, and many smaller surprises.

The Courtyard at the Bank of Palm Springs Center brings Paris to Palm Springs. Expect to be dazzled by the high fashion of Rodier and Yves St. Laurent. There's also a six-screen movie theater.

El Paseo Village is touted as a true shopping experience rather than a shopping center. Unique stores, architecturally designed with a Spanish motif, are clustered among flower-lined paths and fountained courtyards. Don't miss Polo/Ralph Lauren (73-111 El Paseo, tel. 619/340–1414), featuring Lauren's classic fashions and accessories for men and women, and Cabale Cachet (73-111 El Paseo, tel. 619/346–5805) for a collection of European haute couture.

The Palm Desert Town Center is the desert's latest major addition to convenient and stylish shopping. Five major department stores anchor the center, including Bullocks and The May Co. There are also seven movie theaters and a skating rink.

Rancho las Palmas at Highway 111 and Bob Hope Drive, Rancho Mirage, offers gourmet kitchenware, antiques, imported chocolate and confections, and fine restaurants.

Department Stores The exclusive **Saks Fifth Avenue** (201 N. Palm Canyon Dr., tel. 619/327–4126) is a department store with class, so do expect cutting-edge fashions, but don't expect flea market prices. Other major department stores can be found in the various malls listed above.

Participant Sports

The *Desert Guide* from Palm Springs Life, available at most hotels and the Convention and Visitors Bureau, lists "Courts and Courses," with a map showing all of the city's golf courses and tennis courts and information on whether the facilities are public or private.

Bicycling There are more than 35 miles of bike trails, with six mapped-out city tours. Trail maps are available at the **Palm Springs Recreation Department** (401 S. Pavilion, tel. 619/323–8276) and bike-rental shops. You can rent a bike at **Mac's Bike Rental** (70–155 Highway 111, tel. 619/327–5721) and **Burnett's Bicycle Barn** (429 S. Sunrise Way, tel. 619/325–7844).

Golf Palm Springs is known as the "Winter Golf Capital of the World." The area has more than 70 golf courses within its limits, a number of which are open to the public. Among these are the **Palm Springs Municipal Golf Course** (1885 Golf Club Dr., tel. 619/328–1005) and **Fairchilds Bel Aire Greens** (1001 El Cielo Rd., tel. 619/327–0332). Don't be surprised to spy well-known politicians and Hollywood stars on the greens.

Hiking Nature trails abound in the Indian Canyons, Mt. San Jacinto State Park and Wilderness, and Living Desert Reserve (*see* Exploring, above).

Physical Fitness The **Clark Hatch Physical Fitness Center** (Hyatt Regency Suites Hotel, 285 N. Palm Canyon Dr., tel. 619/322–2778) is the latest in a worldwide chain of Hatch health clubs. The facilities are high-quality and low-key. Fees are $10 daily, $60 monthly.

Tennis Of the 350 or so tennis courts in the area, you'll find these open to the public: the **Palm Springs Tennis Center** (1300 Baristo Rd., tel. 619/320–0020), nine lighted courts; **Ruth Hardy Park** (Tamarisk and Caballeros, no phone), eight lighted courts, with no court fee; and **Demuth Park** (4375 Mesquite Ave., tel. 619/325–8265), four lighted courts.

Dining

So many L.A. natives have second homes or condos "down in the Springs" that local restaurateurs are outdoing themselves to match the Big City's standards—and more and more are succeeding. Most of the restaurants listed below can be found on or near Highway 111 running from Palm Springs to Palm Desert.

Category	Cost*
Expensive	over $35
Moderate	$15–$30
Inexpensive	under $15

* *per person, without tax (6%), service, or drinks*

Palm Springs
Expensive

Melvyn's Restaurant. "Lifestyles of the Rich and Famous" calls this Old World–style spot "one of the 10 best." Snugly nestled in the gardens of the Ingleside Inn, weekend brunch here is a Palm Springs tradition. Nightly piano bar. *200 W. Ramon Rd., tel. 619/325–2323. Reservations advised. Jacket required. AE, MC, V.*

Le Vallauris. Formerly a private club, this stylish, rather romantic setting is now open to the public. The cuisine ranges from classic French to nouvelle dessert. *385 W. Tahquitz-McCallum Way, tel. 619/325–5059. Reservations advised. Jacket and tie required. Valet parking. AE, DC, MC, V.*

Moderate–Expensive
★

SILVIO. Two of Los Angeles's most successful restaurateurs, Silvio de Mori and Robert Morris, decided it was time for Palm Springs residents to enjoy the lusty, full-flavored pleasures of simple trattoria cooking. The natives couldn't be happier. Try the osso buco, pasta, or pizza, and you'll understand why. *2665 E. Palm Canyon, tel. 619/322–0990. Reservations suggested. Dress: casual. AE, V, MC. Dinner only.*

Lyon's English Grille. When was the last time you had real honest-to-goodness roast beef and Yorkshire pudding the way only the Brits can make it? Lyon's has it and other old-country favorites. Good value and good food make this a popular stop for the locals. *233 E. Palm Canyon Dr., tel. 619/327–1551. Reservations suggested. Dress: casual. AE, DC, MC, V. Closed summer. Closed for lunch.*

Moderate

Bono. Palm Springs' mayor, Sonny Bono, serves the southern Italian dishes his mother used to make. It's a favorite feeding station for show-biz folk and the curious, and a good place for pasta, chicken, veal, and scampi dishes. Outdoor dining is available. *1700 N. Indian Ave., tel. 619/322–6200. Reservations advised. Dress: casual. Valet parking. AE, MC, V. Closed lunch.*

Brussels Cafe. The best spot in town for people-watching is this sidewalk cafe in the heart of Palm Canyon Drive. Try the Belgian waffles or homemade pâté. Beers from around the world are featured, and there's nightly entertainment. *109 S. Palm Canyon Dr., tel. 619/320–4177. Reservations required. Dress: casual. AE, DC, MC, V.*

Cafe St. James. Dine while seated on a plant-filled balcony, and watch the passing parade below. The lunch menu features excellent salads and thick, imaginative sandwiches. *254 N. Palm Canyon Dr., tel. 619/320–8041. Reservations advised. Dress: casual. AE, DC, MC, V. Closed Mon.*

Las Casuelas Original. A longtime favorite among natives and visitors alike, this restaurant offers great (in size and taste) margaritas and average Mexican dishes: crab enchilada, carne asada, lobster Ensenada. It gets very, very crowded during winter months. *368 N. Palm Canyon Dr., tel. 619/325–3213. Reservations advised. Dress: casual. AE, DC, MC, V.*

Flower Drum. Related to highly popular New York Flower Drum, this health-conscious Chinese restaurant features Hunan, Peking, Shanghai, Canton, and Szechuan cuisines in a Chinese village setting. *424 S. Indian Ave., tel. 619/323–3020. Reservations advised. Dress: casual. AE, MC, V. Lunch and dinner.*

Rennick's. This local landmark recently celebrated its silver anniversary. The health-conscious chef watches calorie and cholesterol counts. Fresh fish and grilled items are recommended. *100 N. Indian Ave., tel. 619/325–1461. Reservations suggested. Jacket required. AE, DC, MC, V.*

Riccio's. Tony Riccio, formerly of the Marquis and Martoni's, in Hollywood, knows the old-fashioned Italian food that comforts his steady patrons: fettuccine Alfredo, veal piccata, chicken Vesuvio, and a luscious Italian cheesecake. *2155 N. Palm Canyon Dr., tel. 619/325–2369. Reservations advised. Jacket required. No lunch weekends.*

Inexpensive **Di Amico's Steak House.** Hearty eaters will enjoy this early California–style restaurant. Prime Eastern corn-fed beef, liver steak vaquero, and son-of-a-gun stew are featured. *500 E. Palm Canyon Dr., tel. 619/325–9191. Reservations advised. Dress: casual. MC, V. Closed Sun. lunch.*

Elmer's Pancake and Steak House. Forget about Aunt Jemima. Elmer's offers 25 varieties of pancakes and waffles. There are steaks, chicken, and seafood on the dinner menu. A children's menu is available, too. *1030 E. Palm Canyon Dr., tel. 619/327–8419. Dress: casual. MC, V.*

Louise's Pantry. Another local landmark, in the center of downtown Palm Springs for almost 40 years, its down-home cooking 1940s-style features chicken and dumplings and short ribs of beef. You can get soup, salad, entree, beverage, and dessert for under $15. There's usually a line to get in. *124 S. Palm Canyon Dr., tel. 619/325–5124. Dress: casual. No credit cards.*

Cathedral City, Rancho Mirage, Palm Desert
Expensive **Dominick's.** An old favorite of Frank Sinatra's and what's left of his "rat pack." Steaks, pasta, and veal dishes are the order of the day. *70-030 Hwy. 111, tel. 619/324–1711. Reservations advised. Dress: casual. AE, DC, MC, V. Closed lunch.*

Mama Gina's. Generally considered the best Italian food in the Palm Springs area, this attractive, simply furnished trattoria was opened by the son of the original Mama Gina in Florence, Italy. There is an open kitchen where you can watch the chef from Tuscany prepare such specialties as deep-fried artichokes, fettuccine with porcini mushrooms, and prawns with artichoke and zucchini. The soups are excellently robust. *73-705 El Paseo, tel. 619/568–9898. Reservations required. Dress: casual. AE, DC, MC, V. Closed lunch.*

Wally's Desert Turtle. If price is no object and you like plush, gilded decor, then this is where you'll be surrounded by the golden names of Palm Springs and Hollywood society. Old-fashioned French cooking is served: rack of lamb, imported Dover sole, braised sea bass, veal Oscar, chicken Normande, and dessert souffles. *71-775 Hwy. 111, tel. 619/568–9321. Valet parking. Reservations required. Jacket required. AE, MC, V. Closed lunch except Friday.*

Moderate **The Rusty Pelican.** Fresh seafood is flown in from both coasts and served in a nautical atmosphere. The Oyster Bar shucks to order. There's live entertainment and dancing. *72-191 Hwy. 111, Palm Desert, tel. 619/346–8065. Dress: casual. Reservations suggested. AE, DC, MC, V.*

The Wilde Goose. The award-winning restaurant is popular with celebrities for its beef and lamb Wellington and five varieties of duck. A specialty of the house is duck with apricot and triple sec sauce. Dependable food and service. *67-938 Hwy. 111, Cathedral City, tel. 619/328–5775. Dress: casual. Reservations recommended. AE, MC, V. Closed for lunch.*

Inexpensive **Stuft Pizza.** What would any listing be without at least one pizza parlor? This one is popular for its thick, Chicago-style crusts and generous heaps of fresh toppings. *67-555 Hwy. 111, Cathedral City, tel. 619/321–2583. MC, V.*

La Quinta **Cunard's.** Robert Cunard converted his French-style villa to a
Expensive restaurant in 1988, and hired chef Jay Trubee to devise a
★ Franco-Italian menu. Today, the warm atmosphere and inventive cuisine have made it the area's biggest hit. *73-045 Calle Cadiz, tel. 619/564–4443. Reservations advised. Closed for lunch. Jacket and tie requested. MC, V. Closed July and Aug.*

Lodging

One of the reasons Palm Springs attracts so many celebrities, entertainment-industry honchos, and other notables is its stock of luxurious hotels. There is a full array of resorts, inns, clubs, spas, lodges, and condos, from small and private to big and bustling. Room rates cover an enormous range—from $20 to $1,600 a night—and also vary widely from summer to winter season. It is not unusual for a hotel to drop its rates from 50% to 60% during the summer (June through early Sept.). For a growing number of off-season travelers, the chance to stay in a $180 room for $60 is an offer they just can't refuse.

Don't even think of visiting here during winter and spring holiday seasons without advance reservations. The Palm Springs Chamber of Commerce (tel. 619/325–1577), Desert Resorts Bureau (tel. 619/770–9000), and Palm Springs Tourism (tel. 800/347–7746) can help you with hotel reservations and information. For a more comprehensive hotel guide complete with prices, pick up a copy of the *Convention and Visitors Bureau Accommodations Guide (tel. 800/347–7746)*.

The most highly recommended lodgings are indicated by a star ★.

Category	Cost*
Very Expensive	over $150
Expensive	$100–$150
Moderate	$70–$100
Inexpensive	under $70

**double occupancy*

Palm Springs **Doubletree Resort at Desert Princess.** This two-year-old luxu-
Very Expensive ry resort hotel has a full slate of amenities: 18-hole championship golf course, tennis and racquetball courts, pools, spas, and health club. Three restaurants, including gourmet dining room. *Vista Chino at Desert Princess Dr., Box 1644, 92263, tel. 619/322–7000. 300 rooms and suites. AE, DC, MC, V.*
Hyatt Regency Suites. Located stage center in the heart of downtown shopping at the Desert Fashion Plaza. Striking six-story asymmetrical lobby, three restaurants, including a popu-

lar sidewalk cafe, called Cafe 285. Health club and pool. *285 N. Palm Canyon Dr., 92262, tel. 619/322–9000. 194 suites. AE, DC, MC, V.*

La Mancha Private Pool Villas and Court Club. Only four blocks from downtown Palm Springs, this Hollywood-style retreat blocks out the rest of the world with plenty of panache. Villas are oversized and opulent; one is even equipped with a screening room and private pool. *444 N. Avenida Cabilleros, tel. 619/ 323–1773. Facilities: tennis courts, paddle tennis courts, pool, croquet lawns. AE, DC, MC, V.*

Palm Springs Hilton Resort and Racquet Club. The cool, white marble elegance of this plant-filled resort hotel just off Palm Canyon Drive and its two superb restaurants make it a top choice for the city. Tennis, body spa, swimming pool, Jacuzzi. *400 E. Tahquitz Way, 92262, tel. 619/320–6868 or 800/522–6900. 257 units. AE, DC, MC, V.*

The Palm Springs Marquis. Posh, desert-modern style marks this centrally located hotel, featuring gourmet restaurant and cafe, two pools, Jacuzzis, health spa, tennis courts, plus extensive meeting and convention facilities. *150 S. Indian Ave., 92262, tel. 619/322–2121. 262 units. AE, DC, MC, V.*

★ **Spa Hotel and Mineral Springs.** Therapeutic mineral springs, outdoor pool, 35 swirlpool tubs, gym, and tennis are the big attractions here. A coffee shop, restaurant, and cocktail lounge with entertainment round out the features. *100 N. Indian Ave., 92262, tel. 619/325–1461. 230 units. AE, DC, MC, V.*

Sundance Villas. Beautifully decorated, spacious villas include fireplace, wet bar, kitchen, and private patio for dining or sunning. Each villa has a private pool or Jacuzzi. The hotel also has tennis courts. Not for the weak of pocketbook. *303 Cabrillo Rd., 92262, tel. 619/325–3888. 19 villas. AE, MC, V.*

Expensive **Autry Resort.** Well decked out for activities with six tennis courts, three swimming pools, two therapy spas, horseback riding, hiking, and desert tours. Dining and entertainment are offered nightly. *4200 E. Palm Canyon Dr., 92262, tel. 619/328– 1171. 187 units. AE, DC, MC, V.*

★ **Ingleside Inn.** A hacienda-style inn furnished with antiques. Each room is equipped with a steam shower and whirlpool. Swimming pool, Jacuzzi, sauna. *200 W. Ramon Rd., 92262, tel. 619/325–0046. 29 units. AE, MC, V.*

Racquet Club of Palm Springs. Built by Charlie Farrell and Ralph Bellamy in 1933, the Racquet Club marked the beginning of Palm Spring's glamour era. Four swimming pools, therapy pool, sauna, tennis courts (where, it is said, Marilyn Monroe was "discovered"), cocktail lounge. *2743 N. Indian Ave., 92262, tel. 619/325–1281. 120 units. AE, DC, MC, V.*

Moderate **Courtyard by Marriott.** This new property represents the Marriott chain's effort to expand into comfortable, smaller hotels offering a good value. The concept works nicely. Pool, weight room, restaurant. *1300 Tahquitz Way, tel. 619/322–6100. 149 rooms. AE, MC, V.*

Mira Loma Hotel. Small, friendly family atmosphere with rooms and suites decorated in 1940s Hollywood Art Deco style. Marilyn Monroe slept here! Swimming pool. *1420 N. Indian Ave., 92262, tel. 619/320–1178. 12 units. AE, MC, V.*

Mt. View Inn. A friendly atmosphere and convenient location make this small inn a great favorite. The inn has a swimming pool. *200 S. Cahuilla Rd., 92262, tel. 619/325–5281. 11 units. No credit cards.*

Tuscany Manor Apartment-Hotel. Lovely apartments. Pool, therapeutic pool. Esther Williams shot her first movie here. *350 Chino Canyon Rd., 92262, tel. 619/325–2349. 24 units. MC, V.*

Villa Royale. Charming bed-and-breakfast, each unit individually decorated in an international theme. Some rooms with private Jacuzzis, fireplaces. *1620 Indian Trail, 92262, tel. 619/ 327–2314. 34 units. AE, MC, V.*

Inexpensive **Monte Vista Hotel.** Boasting a prime Palm Canyon Drive location, this hotel is replete with swimming pool and comfortable accommodations. *414 N. Palm Canyon Dr., 92262, tel. 619/ 325–5641. 32 units. AE, MC, V.*

Westward Ho Seven Seas Hotel. A swimming pool, therapy pool, and cocktail lounge grace this modest property. *701 E. Palm Canyon Dr., 92262, tel. 619/320–2700. 209 units. AE, MC, V.*

Outside of Palm Springs
Very Expensive **Hyatt Grand Champions Resort.** This elegant resort takes its fun seriously with two 18-hole golf courses, tennis courts featuring three court surfaces, the largest tennis stadium in the West, and a health club with a full complement of workout equipment and pampering treatments. Jasmine's nouvelle American menu is getting raves; the more casual Trattoria mixes Italian and Californian cuisines with delightful results. *44-600 Indian Wells La., Indian Wells, 92210, tel. 619/341– 1000. 334 units. AE, DC, MC, V.*

Marriott's Desert Springs Resort and Spa. The most luxurious spa facilities in the desert, two 18-hole golf courses, and a complex of waterways with boat transport around the resort let you know this is no run-of-the-mill resort. There are 16 tennis courts, five restaurants, and a European spa. *74855 Country Club Dr., Palm Desert, 92260, tel. 619/341–2211. 891 rooms. AE, DC, MC, V.*

★ **The Ritz Carlton Rancho Mirage.** The poshest gem in the desert collection is located on a 650-foot-high plateau in the foothills of the Santa Rosas, adjacent to a reserve for bighorn sheep. Needless to say, it has all the amenities you would expect from one of the world's classiest hotel chains: restaurants, entertainment, pools, bar, fitness center, and tennis. *68-900 Frank Sinatra Dr., Rancho Mirage, 92270, tel. 619/321–8282. 240 rooms including 19 suites. AE, DC, MC, V.*

Expensive **Two Bunch Palms.** Reputedly built by Al Capone to escape the pressures of gangsterdom in 1920s Chicago, this collection of white-walled villas is still something of a secret hideaway. Antiques recapture the flavor of the pre–World War II years. *67-425 Two Bunch Palms Trail, Desert Hot Springs, CA 92240, tel. 619/329–8791 or 800/472–4334. 44 villas. Facilities: tennis courts, thermal pools, restaurant. AE, MC, V.*

The Arts

For complete listings of upcoming events, pick up a copy of *Palm Springs Life* magazine or Palm Springs Life's *Desert Guide*, a free monthly publication found in any hotel.

The McCallum Theatre (73-000 Fred Waring Dr., Palm Desert, tel. 619/340–2787) in the Bob Hope Cultural Center is probably the desert's premier venue for the performing arts. Since opening in January 1988 with a tribute to Bob Hope, the theater has hosted such varied artists as Rudolf Nureyev and the Paris

Ballet, the Los Angeles Philharmonic, pantomimist Marcel Marceau, and a rock-and-roll revival starring Fabian.

The Annenberg Theatre (Museum Dr., just north of Tahquitz Way, on the south side of the Desert Fashion Plaza, tel. 619/325–7186 or 619/325–4490) of the Palm Springs Desert Museum is the area's other major arts center. Featured performers have ranged from the Second City improv troupe to Liza Minnelli, Frank Sinatra, and a slew of international musicians in its Sunday Afternoon Concerts series.

Concerts **The College of the Desert** (43-500 Monterey Ave., Palm Desert, tel. 619/346–8041). This is home to the annual Joanna Hodges Piano Conference and Competition.

Theater **VPG Theatre** (225 S. El Cielo Rd., tel. 619/320–9898). Home of the Valley Players Guild, the VPG offers a lively mix of theater fare.

Nightlife

Two good sources for finding current nightlife attractions are the *Desert Sun* (the local newspaper) and *Guide* magazine, a monthly publication distributed free at most downtown merchants' counters.

Live entertainment, ranging from soft dinner music to song-and-dance numbers, is frequently found in the city's hotels and restaurants. The piano bars at **Rennick's** and **Melvyn's Ingleside Inn** are popular. **Celebrity Supper Club** (123 N. Palm Canyon Dr., tel. 619/323–1806) has an inviting party atmosphere, and you can hear everything from Puccini to pops.

Jazz **Hank's Fish House** (in the Holiday Inn, 155 S. Belardo, Palm Springs, tel. 619/778–7171) is a cool place for light jazz every evening, followed by more serious jamming mixed with dancing after 9 PM. For refreshments, look to Hank's oyster bar—the talk of the desert.

Discos Between the flashing lights of its Top 40 disco and the retro-memorabilia in its new '50s–'60s room, **Cecil's** (1775 E. Palm Canyon Dr., tel. 619/320–4202) is bound to keep you dancing. Dance to live country music at the **Cactus Corral** (67–501 E. Palm Canyon Dr., Cathedral City, tel. 619/321–8558).

Pompeii (67–399 Highway 111, tel. 619/328–5800) is a large disco playing Top 40 music. To find this lively joint, just look for the fiery torches out front.
Zelda's (169 N. Indian Ave., tel. 619/325–2375) is another nightclub that regularly attracts a full house and a young crowd.

Comedy Clubs **The Comedy Haven.** Stand-up comics and improv groups dished up with American/Italian fare. *Desert Fashion Plaza (enter parking lot from Tahquitz Way), tel. 619/320–7855. Shows start at 9 PM.*
The Laff Stop. Stand-up comedy shows are the nightly attraction, interspersed with live and recorded music of the '50s, '60s, and '70s. *72990 El Paseo, Palm Desert, tel. 619/568–2426.*

16 The Mojave Desert and Death Valley

by Aaron
Sugarman

When most people put together their "must-see" list of California attractions, the desert is not usually jockeying for position with the top contenders. What with the heat and the vast, seemingly empty tracts of land, the desert is certainly no Disneyland. But then, that's precisely why it deserves a closer look. The desert is truly one of our last frontiers. It offers an overwhelming richness of natural beauty: rolling waves of sand dunes, black cinder cones thrusting up hundreds of feet into the air from a blistered desert floor, riotous sheets of wildflowers, the bizarre shape of the Joshua tree basking in an orange glow at sunset, unspoiled valleys surrounded by rings of mountains, and a silence both dramatic and startling in its abundance.

Unlike cities, which regularly tear down and build over their history, the progress of man is preserved with striking clarity in the desert. An archaeological site in Calico was determined to be approximately 200,000 years old; stone tools and other artifacts uncovered there are believed to be the oldest evidence of man's activity in the Americas. Petroglyphs—prehistoric rock art—are scattered throughout the California deserts. There is a bewildering array of images, deer and mountain sheep, human figures, spears and shields, and seemingly abstract geometric patterns, carved from 2,000 to 10,000 years ago. The more recent, and romanticized, past is on display, too. Ghost towns, gold mills, old rail stations, and other pieces of the Old West dot the countryside. At times it is easy to feel you would do anything to trade your car in for a horse.

What is probably most surprising about the desert is its accessibility. The days of the 20-mule team and the railroad, which brought prosperity to the towns it reached in the late 1800s and early 1900s, are long gone. A surprisingly large amount of the desert can be seen from the comfort of your air-conditioned car. And don't despair if you are without air-conditioning—just avoid the middle of the day and the middle of the summer, good advice for all desert travel. Believe everything you've ever heard about desert heat; it can be brutal. A temperature of 134° was once recorded at Furnace Creek in Death Valley, the hottest place on the planet. But during mornings and evenings, particularly in the spring and fall, the temperature ranges from cool and crisp to pleasantly warm and dry: perfect for hiking and driving. And while the air at Death Valley can certainly be quite still, much of the desert is breezy, if not downright windy.

The Mojave desert begins just north of the San Bernardino Mountains along the northern edge of Los Angeles and extends north 150 miles into the Eureka Valley and east 200 miles to the Colorado River. Death Valley lies north and east of the Mojave, bordering Nevada. Mojave, with elevations ranging from 3,000 to 5,000 feet above sea level, is known as the High Desert; Death Valley, with points at almost 300 feet below sea level, is the lowest spot in the United States.

Due to the vast size of California's deserts, an area about as big as Ohio, and the weather, careful planning is essential for an enjoyable desert adventure. Conveniences, facilities, trails, gas stations, and supermarkets do not lurk just around the corner from many desert sights. Different pieces of the desert can be easily handled in day trips, more extensive exploring will require overnight stays; it's a good idea to know in advance which approach you will be taking. Reliable maps are a must—signage is limited, and occasionally completely nonexistent. The Automobile Club of America (AAA) is probably the best source for maps. Other important accessories include: a compass, extra food and water, sunglasses, extra clothes (for wind or cool nights), a hat (if you're going to do any walking around in the sun), and plenty of sunscreen. Other than that, a pair of binoculars can come in handy, and don't forget your camera. You're likely to see things you've never seen before.

Getting Around

By Car The vast Mojave Desert is shaped like a giant *L*, with one leg north and the other east. To travel north through the Mojave, take I–10 east out of Los Angeles to I–15 north. Just through the Cajon Pass, pick up U.S. 395, which runs north through Victor Valley, Boron, the Rand Mining District, and China Lake. To travel east, continue on I–15 to Barstow. From Barstow there are two routes: I–40, which passes through the mountainous areas of San Bernardino County, whisks by the Providence Mountains and enters Arizona at Needles (noted for being the home town of Snoopy's brother Spike in the "Peanuts" cartoons); or the more northerly I–15, which passes south of Calico, near Devil's Playground and the Kelso Sand Dunes, and then veers northeast toward Las Vegas.

Death Valley National Monument can be entered from the southeast or the west. Exit U.S. 395 at either State Highway 190 or 178 to enter from the west. From the southeast: Take Highway 127 north from I–15 and then link up with either Highway 178, which travels west into the valley and then cuts north past Funeral Peak, Badwater, Dante's View, and Zabriskie Point before meeting up with Highway 190 at Furnace Creek, or continue on Highway 127 north for 28 miles and then take Highway 190 west straight into the middle of Death Valley.

Guided Tours

The following organizations regularly sponsor hikes, tours, and outings in the California deserts. Call or write them for more information.

The Audubon Society (Western Division, 555 Audubon Pl., Sacramento, CA 95825, tel. 916/481–5332).

The California Native Plant Society (909 12th St., Suite 116, Sacramento, CA 95814, tel. 916/447–CNPS).

The Nature Conservancy (785 Market St., San Francisco, CA 94103, tel. 415/777–0487).

The Sierra Club (730 Polk St., San Francisco, CA 94109, tel. 415/776–2211).

Important Addresses and Numbers

Tourist Information **Bureau of Land Management** (BLM) (California Desert District Office, 6221 Box Spring Blvd., Riverside 92507, tel. 714/276–6394) can also provide information on BLM campgrounds.

Emergencies **BLM Rangers** (tel. 714/276–6419). **Police:** *San Bernardino County Sheriff* (tel. 619/256–1796). **Hospital:** *Community Hospital* (Barstow, tel. 619/256–1761).

Exploring

Numbers in the margin correspond with points of interest on the Mojave Desert map.

Though the Mojave desert is a vast, sprawling space, many of its visitable attractions are conveniently laid out on a north–south axis along U.S. 395 and Highway 178, and an east–west axis that runs between I–15 and I–40. We'll describe tours stretching roughly 120 miles along each axis, and a third tour that winds its way through Death Valley, which lies between the two routes. Keep in mind that there are a very limited number of hotels in the desert, so if you plan to spend the night somewhere, make sure your tour leaves you time to get to places like Furnace Creek in Death Valley, or Barstow, where there are some rooms to be found.

The Western Mojave
❶ On I–15, just before you reach U.S. 395 on the northbound tour, you cross Cajon Pass, riding over the infamous **San Andreas Fault**—an apocalyptic way to start a desert trip.

❷ About 70 miles later you enter the **Rand Mining District,** consisting of the towns of Randsburg, Red Mountain, and Johannesburg. Randsburg is one of the very few authentic gold-mining communities that hasn't become a ghost town. The town first boomed with the discovery of gold in the Rand Mountains in 1895, and along with the neighboring towns, grew to support the successful Yellow Aster Mine. Rich tungsten ore was discovered during World War I and silver in 1919. All told, the total money brought in by these precious metals is estimated at more than $35 million. Thankfully, Randsburg still sports its authentic Old West heritage. The picturesque town has some original gold-rush buildings, plus a few antiques shops, a general store, and the **Randsburg Desert Museum,** which is crammed with mining and frontier life memorabilia. *U.S. 395 to Johannesburg, then follow the signs 1 mi southwest to Randsburg. The museum, tel. 619/374–2111, is open weekends, 10–5.*

❸ Just to the northwest of the Rand Mining District is **Red Rock Canyon State Park.** Red Rock Canyon is a feast for the eyes with its layers of pink, white, red, rust, and brown rocks. Entering the park from the south, you pass through a narrow, steep-walled gorge and enter a wide bowl tinted pink by what was once hot volcanic ash. The human history of this area goes back some 20,000 years to the ancient canyon dwellers known only as the Old People. Mojave Indians roamed the land for several hundred years until Gold-Rush fever hit the region in the mid-to late 1800s; remains of mining operations dot the countryside. The canyon was later invaded by filmmakers, and it has starred in numerous Westerns. The state park can be found on either side of Highway 14 about 10 miles south of where it meets U.S. 395. You can reach the informative ranger station by heading northwest on Abbott Drive from Highway 14.

❹ The nearby **Petroglyph Canyons** provide one of the desert's most amazing spectacles. The two canyons, commonly called Big and Little Petroglyph, contain what is probably the greatest concentration of rock art in the country. Scratched or pecked into the shiny desert varnish (oxidized minerals) that coats the canyon's dark basaltic rocks are thousands of images. Some are figures of animals and people, some seemingly abstract—maybe just the doodles of ancient man! All are excep-

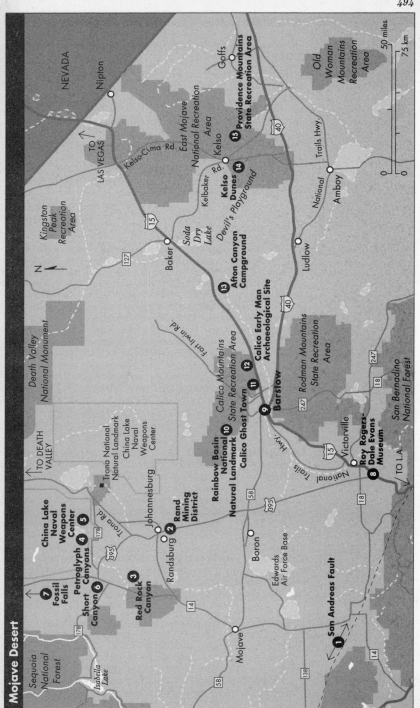

Mojave Desert

NEVADA

Nipton

TO LAS VEGAS

Death Valley National Monument

Kingston Peak Recreation Area

127

15

Baker

Soda Dry Lake

Kelso-Cima Rd.

East Mojave National Recreation Area

Goffs

Old Woman Mountains Recreation Area

15 Providence Mountains State Recreation Area

Kelbaker Rd.

14 Kelso

Kelso

Kelso Dunes

40

Devil's Playground

Trails Hwy.

National

Amboy

13 Afton Canyon Campground

Ludlow

40

Fort Irwin Rd.

TO DEATH VALLEY

Trona National Natural Landmark

China Lake Naval Weapons Center

Calico Mountains State Recreation Area

12 Calico Early Man Archaeological Site

Rodman Mountains State Recreation Area

247

N

50 miles

75 km

11

Calico Ghost Town

9 Barstow

247

18

Johannesburg

China Lake Naval Weapons Center

4 China Lake Naval Weapons Center

5

178

Trona Rd.

Petroglyph Canyons

Fossil Falls 7

Short Canyons 6

Red Rock Canyon 3

395

Randsburg

2 Rand Mining District

10 Rainbow Basin National Natural Landmark

San Bernadino National Forest

Victorville

15

Roy Rogers-Dale Evans Museum

8

TO L.A.

18

58

395

58

National Trails Hwy.

Sequoia National Forest

Isabella Lake

178

14

Boron

Edwards Air Force Base

Mojave

58

San Andreas Fault

1

14

138

247

tionally preserved and protected. The feeling of living history

⑤ is incredible. The canyons are in the **U.S. Naval Weapons Center at China Lake,** and access is limited. Weekend tours must be arranged in advance through the **Maturango Museum** (China Lake Blvd. and Las Flores Ave., Ridgecrest, tel. 619/375–6900), which will also provide you with background on what you will see.

⑥ Heading northwest, you will find **Short Canyon** about ½-mile from the intersection of Hwy. 14 and U.S. 395. Sierra snows and natural springs feed the stream that flows down the rocky canyon, spills over a falls, and then sinks into the sand. In good years, there are large beds of wildflowers; in very dry years there are still some splashes of color. In the spring, a ½-mile hike along the stream brings you to a 20-foot waterfall. Head west on the canyon road you'll find just south of Brady's Cafe on U.S. 395, but only after checking on current road conditions with the BLM (tel. 714/276–6394) or Red Rock Canyon State Park (tel. 805/942–0662).

⑦ **Fossil Falls** is another 20 miles up 395. On the way you'll pass Little Lake, a good place to see migrating waterfowl in the spring and fall, including several varieties of ducks and geese and probably pelicans as well. The area just north of the lake is often covered with wildflowers. As you pass the lake, **Red Hill** comes into view ahead of you. The hill is a small volcano that was active in the neighborhood of 20,000 years ago. Approaching the falls you cross a large volcanic field; the falls themselves drop an impressive distance along the channel cut by the Owens River through the hardened lava flows. Mammoth bones and human tools dating back 10,000 to 20,000 years ago have been found in the area. *The falls are about 20 mi north of the intersection of Hwy. 14 and U.S. 395, then a ½-mi east on Cinder Cone Rd. A dirt road leads south to a parking area. There are usually BLM signs directing the way.*

The Eastern Mojave We'll start the eastward tour in **Victorville,** less than 20 miles from Cajon Pass. First off, notice the bit of river you see flowing along the eastern side of the freeway, near Mojave Narrows Regional Park—this is one of the few places where the Mojave River runs above ground. For the most part, the 150-mile-long river flows from the San Bernardino Mountains north and east under the desert floor. The park itself offers boat rentals, an

⑧ equestrian center, fishing, and camping. Then there is the **Roy Rogers-Dale Evans Museum,** exhibiting the personal and professional memorabilia of the famous Western stars. Yes, Roy's faithful horse Trigger is there, too. *Mojave Narrows Park, 18000 Yates Rd., tel. 619/245–2226, is open daily 7:30 AM– dusk; there is a $3 per vehicle entry fee. Camping is $9 a night. The Roy Rogers-Dale Evans Museum, 15650 Seneca Rd., tel. 619/243–4547, is open daily 9–5; admission: $3 adults, $2 ages 13–16 and senior citizens, $1 ages 6–12. Closed Thanksgiving and Christmas.*

⑨ Continue along I–15 to **Barstow.** Barstow was established in 1886 when a subsidiary of the Atchison, Topeka and Santa Fe Railroad began construction of a depot and hotel at this junction of its tracks and the 35th-parallel transcontinental lines. The **Desert Information Center** (831 Barstow Rd., tel. 619/256–8313) contains exhibits about desert ecology, wildflowers, wildlife, and other features of the desert environment; a help-

ful and knowledgeable staff is on hand to answer any questions
you may have.

There is a natural impulse to describe many areas of the desert
as seemingly belonging to another planet. **Rainbow Basin,** 8
miles north of Barstow, looks just as you would expect Mars to
look like (maybe it's because some of those old Martian movies
were actually filmed there). There is a tremendous sense of upheaval; huge slabs of red, orange, white, and green stone tilt at
crazy angles like ships about to capsize. At points along the
spectacularly scenic 6-mile drive it is easy to imagine you are
alone in the world, hidden among the colorful badlands that
give the basin its name. Hike the many washes and you are likely to see the fossilized remains of creatures that roamed the basin 12 to 16 million years ago: mastodons, large and small
camels, rhinos, dog-bears, birds, and insects. Do leave any
fossils you find where they are—they are protected by Federal
law. *Take Fort Irwin Rd. about 5 mi north to Fossil Bed Rd., a
graded dirt road, and head west 3 mi. Call the Desert Information Center in Barstow (tel. 619/256–8313) for more information.*

After a 10-mile drive northeast from Barstow, you can slip into
the more recent past at **Calico Ghost Town.** Calico became a
wild—and rich—mining town after a rich deposit of silver was
found around 1881. In 1886, after more than $85 million worth
of silver, gold, and other precious metals were harvested from
the multicolored "calico" hills, the price of silver fell and the
town slipped into decline. "Borax" Smith helped revive the
town in 1889 when he started mining the unglamorous but prof-
itable mineral borax there, but that boom busted by the turn of
the century. The effort to restore the ghost town was started
by Walter Knott of Knott's Berry Farm fame in 1960. Knott
handed the land over to San Bernardino County in 1966 and it
became a regional park. Today, the 1880s come back to life as
you stroll the wooden sidewalks of Main Street, browse
through several Western shops, roam the tunnels of Maggie's
Mine, and take a ride on the Calico-Odessa Railroad. Special
festivals in March, May, October, and November add to Calico's Old West flavor. *Ghost Town Rd., 3 mi north of I-15, tel.
619/254–2122. There is a $4 per vehicle entry fee. The town is
open 9–5 daily.*

If you're at all curious about life 200,000 years ago, the **Calico
Early Man Archeological Site** is a must-see. Nearly 12,000
tools—scrapers, cutting tools, choppers, hand picks, stone
saws, and the like—have been excavated from the site since
1964. Prior to finding the site, many archaeologists believed
the first humans came to North America "only" 10,000 to
20,000 years ago. Dr. Louis Leakey, the noted archaeologist,
was so impressed with the findings that he became the Calico
Project director from 1963 to his death in 1972; his old camp is
now a visitor's center and museum. The Calico excavations provide a rare opportunity to see artifacts, buried in the walls and
floors of the excavated pits, fashioned by the earliest known
Americans. *15 mi northeast of Barstow via I-15; take
Minneola Rd. north for 3 mi. The site is open Wed.–Sun.
8–4:30, closed Mon. and Tues. Guided tours of the dig are offered Wed. at 1:30 and 3:30, Thurs.–Sun. at 9:30, 11:30, 1:30
and 3:30. Trail maps are available for self-guided tours.*

⑬ Thanks to its colorful, steep walls, **Afton Canyon** is often called the Grand Canyon of the Mojave. The canyon was carved out over many thousands of years by the rushing waters of the Mojave River, which makes another of its rare above-ground appearances here. And where you find water in the desert, you'll find trees, grasses, and wildlife. The canyon has been a popular spot for a long time; Indians and later white settlers following the Mojave Trail from the Colorado River to the Pacific coast, often set up camp here, near the welcomed presence of water. *About 38 mi from Barstow on I–15; take the Afton turnoff and follow a good dirt road about 3 mi southwest.*

Although there is a broad range of terrain that qualifies as desert, nothing says "desert" quite like graceful, wind-blown ⑭ sand dunes. And the white sand **Kelso Dunes,** located about 40 miles southeast of Baker, are perfect, pristine desert dunes. The dunes cover 70 square miles, often at heights of 500–600 feet, and they can be reached in an easy ½-mile walk from where you have to leave your car. When you reach the top of one of the dunes, kick a little bit of sand down the lee side and find out why they say the sand "sings." In Kelso, there is a Mission Revival depot dating from 1925, one of the very few of its kind still standing. *I–15 to Baker, then take Kelbaker Rd. south for 35 mi to the town of Kelso. The dunes are another 7 mi ahead.*

⑮ Our last stops in the Eastern Mojave are the **Providence Mountains State Recreation Area** and the **Mitchell Caverns Natural Preserve.** The recreation area's visitor center, at an elevation of 4,300 feet, offers spectacular views of mountain peaks, dunes, buttes, rocky crags, and desert valleys. The caves, known as El Pakiva and Tecopa, offer a rare opportunity to see all three types of cave formations—dripstone, flowstone, and erratics—in one place. The year-round 65° temperature is also a nice break from the heat. *Take I–40 east from Barstow 100 mi to Essex Rd., then head northwest for 16 mi to the state recreation area. If you have a 4-wheel-drive vehicle, you can continue south from Kelso on Kelbaker Rd. about 3 mi to the poleline road; bear left and drive about 12 mi over Foshay Pass to Essex Rd. Guided tours of the caves are offered Sept.–June, weekdays at 1:30 PM, weekends and holidays at 1:30 and 3; weekends only during the summer. Tours gather at the visitor center.*

Death Valley *Numbers in the margin correspond with points of interest on the Death Valley map.*

The topography of Death Valley National Monument is like a mini-lesson in geology. Two hundred million years ago seas covered the area, depositing layers of sediment and fossils. Between 5 million and 35 million years ago, faults in the earth's crust and volcanic activity pushed and folded the ground, causing mountain ranges to rise and the valley floor to drop. Later the valley was filled periodically by lakes, which eroded the surrounding rocks into fantastic formations and deposited the salts that now cover the floor of the basin. Today, the area sports an astounding variety of physical features: 14 square miles of sand dunes, 200 square miles of crusty salt flats, 11,000-foot mountains, hills and canyons of many colors. There are more than 1,000 species of plants and trees—21 of which are unique to the valley, like the yellow Panamint Daisy, and the blue-flowered Death Valley sage.

❶ Starting from the northernmost tip of the monument, **Scotty's Castle** is an odd apparition rising out of a desert canyon. This $2.5-million Moorish mansion, begun in 1924 and never completed, takes its name from Walter Scott, better known as Death Valley Scotty. An ex-cowboy, prospector, and performer in Buffalo Bill's Wild West Show, Scotty always told people the castle was his, financed by gold from a secret mine. That secret mine was, in fact, a Chicago millionaire named Albert Johnson, who was advised by doctors to spend time in a warm, dry climate. The house sports works of art, imported carpets, handmade European furniture, and a tremendous pipe organ. While it would probably all look perfectly normal in Beverly Hills, in Death Valley it is the wildest of mirages. *Located on the North Hwy. 190N. Admission: $6 adults, $3 children 6–11. Grounds open 7 AM to 6 PM daily; tours 9–5.*

❷ Following Highway 190 south, you'll come to the remains of the famed **Harmony Borax Works,** from which the renowned 20-mule teams hauled borax to the railroad town of Mojave. Those teams were a sight to behold: 20 mules hitched up to a single massive wagon, carrying a load of 10 tons of borax to a town 165 miles away through burning desert. The teams plied the route between 1884 and 1907, when the railroad finally arrived in Zabriskie. You can visit the ruins of the Harmony Borax Works. The Borax Museum, 2 miles farther south, houses original mining machinery and historical displays in a building that used to serve as a boarding house for miners; the adjacent structure is the original mule-team barn. *Look for the Harmony Borax Works Rd. on Hwy. 190, about 50 mi south of Scotty's Castle; take the road west a short distance to the ruins.*

❸ Between the ruins and the museum you will see a sign for the **Visitor's Center** at Furnace Creek. The center provides guided walks, exhibits, helpful publications, and more helpful rangers. *Open 8–8. Call the National Park Service in Death Valley (tel. 619/786–2331) for more information on visitor's center services.*

❹ **Zabriskie Point,** about 4 miles south of the visitor's center, is one of the monument's most scenic spots. Not particularly high—only about 710 feet—it overlooks a striking badlands panorama with wrinkled, cinammon-color hills. You might recognize it from the film *Zabriskie Point* by the Italian director Antonioni. When Highway 178 splits off from Highway 190, follow
❺ low it south about 13 miles to **Dante's View.** This viewpoint is more than 5,000 feet up in the Black Mountains. In the dry desert air, you can see most of the 110 miles the valley is stretched across. The oasis of Furnace Creek is a green spot to the north. The view up and down is equally astounding: The tiny blackish patch far below you is Badwater, the lowest point in the country at 280 feet below sea level; on the western horizon is Mt. Whitney, the highest spot in the continental United States at 14,495 feet. Those of you in great shape may want to try the 14-mile hike up to Telescope Peak. The view, not surprisingly, is breathtaking; so is the 3,000-foot elevation gain of the hike. The best time to visit any of these viewpoints is early morning or late afternoon when the light highlights the colors and shapes of the surrounding desert.

❻ Just outside the monument, at Death Valley Junction, is an unexpected pleasure to rival Scotty's Castle—**Marta Becket's**

Death Valley

Amargosa Opera House. Marta Becket is an artist and dancer
from New York who first saw the town of Amargosa when she
was on tour in 1964. Three years later she came back and had a
flat tire in the same place, and on impulse she decided to buy a
boarded-up theater amid a complex of run-down Spanish colonial buildings. Today, the population of the town is still two people and a dozen cats, but three nights a week, cars, motor
homes, and buses roll in to catch the show she has been presenting for more than 20 years. To compensate for the sparse
crowds her show attracted in the early days, Becket painted
herself an audience, making the theater a masterpiece of
trompe l'oeil painting. Now she often performs her blend of
classical ballet, mime, and 19th-century melodrama to sell-out
crowds. After the show, you can meet her in the adjacent art
gallery, where she sells her paintings and autographs her posters and books. *Amargosa Opera House, Box 8, Death Valley
Junction, CA 92328, tel. 619/852–4316. Call ahead for reservations. Performances Nov.–Apr., Fri., Sat., and Mon. at 8:15
AM; May and Oct., shows Sat. only. The opera house is closed
during the summer. Admission is by donation: $8 adults, $5
children.*

What to See and Do with Children

Many of the desert's attractions should delight children. The
following are of particular interest; for more information, *see*
the Exploring section, above.

The Rand Mining District
The Roy Rogers-Dale Evans Museum, Victorville
Calico Ghost Town
Mitchell Caverns
Marta Becket's Amargosa Opera House

Off the Beaten Track

The desert is not a particularly well-beaten track to begin with, but some spots are a bit farther out of the way, or more difficult to reach. **Trona Pinnacles National Natural Landmark,** just west of the China Lake Naval Weapons Center, is not easy to get to. There are several dirt roads leading to the "tufa" area— where towering spires of calcium carbonate reach heights of up to 140 feet. Unfortunately, the best road to the area changes depending on the weather; you either have to be lucky enough to follow someone who knows the best way, or keep trying until you get there. And forget about it if the roads are wet. Still, the pinnacles are considered the best examples of tufa towers in the country, and the area is probably a great place to film a science-fiction flick. *Take Hwy. 178 north from U.S. 395 for 29 mi. There you will find a dirt intersection; turn southeast and go ½-mi to a fork. Continue south via the right fork, cross some railroad tracks, and continue about 5 mi to the pinnacles.*

Lodging

Death Valley **Furnace Creek Inn.** The rambling stone structure tumbling down the side of a hill is something of a desert oasis. There are pleasantly cool dining rooms, a heated pool, tennis courts, golf, riding, and a cocktail lounge with entertainment. *Box 1, Death Valley 92328, tel. 619/786–2345. 67 rooms and suites. AE, DC, MC, V. Closed mid-May–mid-Oct. Double rooms range from $218 to $300, with breakfast and dinner.*

Furnace Creek Ranch. An annex of the inn, about 1 mile away on the valley floor. Originally crew headquarters for a borax company, the newer section has very good rooms. The ranch also features a coffee shop, steak house, cocktail lounge, and a general store. *Box 1, Death Valley 92328, tel. 619/786–2345. 225 rooms. AE, DC, MC, V. Double rooms start at $65 for rooms with TV and telephone.*

Stove Pipe Wells Village. A landing strip for light aircraft is an unusual touch for a motel, as is a heated mineral pool, but the rest is pretty basic. The property includes a dining room, grocery store, pool, and cocktail lounge. *Hwy. 190, tel. 619/786–2387. 82 rooms. MC, V. $50 and up.*

Barstow **Best Western Desert Villa.** A slightly above-average AAA-approved motel with a pool and whirlpool. *1984 E. Main St., tel. 619/256–1781. 79 units. AE, DC, MC, V. $52 and up.*

Camping

The Mojave Desert and Death Valley have about two dozen campgrounds in a variety of desert settings. Listed below is a sampling of what is available. For further information the following booklets are useful: *High Desert Recreation Resource Guide,* from the Mojave Chamber of Commerce (15836 Sierra Hwy., Mojave, CA 93591); *San Bernardino County Regional*

Parks, from the Regional Parks Department (825 E. 3rd St., San Bernardino, CA 92415); and *California Desert Camping*, from the Bureau of Land Management (California Desert District Office, 1695 Spruce St., Riverside, CA 92507).

Death Valley **Mahogany Flat** (east of Hwy. 178). Ten well-shaded tent spaces in a forest of juniper and piñon pine. Tables, pit toilets; no water. Open Apr.–Nov.

Mesquite Springs (Hwy. 190 near Scotty's Castle). Sixty tent or RV spaces, some shaded, with stoves or fireplaces, tables, flush toilets, water.

Wildrose (west of Hwy. 178). Thirty-nine tent or RV sites, some shaded, in a canyon. Stoves or fireplaces, tables, water, pit toilets.

Mojave Desert **Mid-Hills Campground** (123 mi east of Barstow via I–40). Hiking, horseback riding, in a wooded setting. Thirty campsites, pit toilets, water.

Mojave Narrows (I–15). Eighty-seven camping units, hot showers. Secluded picnic areas and two lakes surrounded by cottonwoods and cattails. Fishing, rowboat rentals, bait shop, specially designed trail for the handicapped.

Owl Canyon Campground (12 mi north of Barstow and 1 mi east of Rainbow Basin). Thirty-one camping units, cooking grills, vault toilets, water.

Index

Personal Itinerary

Departure *Date*

Time

Transportation

Arrival *Date*   *Time*

Departure *Date*   *Time*

Transportation

Accommodations

Arrival *Date*   *Time*

Departure *Date*   *Time*

Transportation

Accommodations

Arrival *Date*   *Time*

Departure *Date*   *Time*

Transportation

Accommodations

Personal Itinerary

Arrival   *Date*   *Time*

Departure   *Date*   *Time*

Transportation

Accommodations

Arrival   *Date*   *Time*

Departure   *Date*   *Time*

Transportation

Accommodations

Arrival   *Date*   *Time*

Departure   *Date*   *Time*

Transportation

Accommodations

Arrival   *Date*   *Time*

Departure   *Date*   *Time*

Transportation

Accommodations

Personal Itinerary

Arrival *Date*   *Time*

Departure *Date*   *Time*

Transportation

Accommodations

Arrival *Date*   *Time*

Departure *Date*   *Time*

Transportation

Accommodations

Arrival *Date*   *Time*

Departure *Date*   *Time*

Transportation

Accommodations

Arrival *Date*   *Time*

Departure *Date*   *Time*

Transportation

Accommodations

Personal Itinerary

Arrival   *Date*   *Time*

Departure   *Date*   *Time*

Transportation

Accommodations

Arrival   *Date*   *Time*

Departure   *Date*   *Time*

Transportation

Accommodations

Arrival   *Date*   *Time*

Departure   *Date*   *Time*

Transportation

Accommodations

Arrival   *Date*   *Time*

Departure   *Date*   *Time*

Transportation

Accommodations

Addresses

Name	*Name*
Address	*Address*
Telephone	*Telephone*
Name	*Name*
Address	*Address*
Telephone	*Telephone*
Name	*Name*
Address	*Address*
Telephone	*Telephone*
Name	*Name*
Address	*Address*
Telephone	*Telephone*
Name	*Name*
Address	*Address*
Telephone	*Telephone*
Name	*Name*
Address	*Address*
Telephone	*Telephone*
Name	*Name*
Address	*Address*
Telephone	*Telephone*
Name	*Name*
Address	*Address*
Telephone	*Telephone*

Fodor's Travel Guides

U.S. Guides

Alaska
Arizona
Boston
California
Cape Cod, Martha's
  Vineyard, Nantucket
The Carolinas & the
  Georgia Coast
The Chesapeake
  Region
Chicago
Colorado
Disney World & the
  Orlando Area
Florida
Hawaii

Las Vegas, Reno,
  Tahoe
Los Angeles
Maine, Vermont,
  New Hampshire
Maui
Miami & the
  Keys
National Parks
  of the West
New England
New Mexico
New Orleans
New York City
New York City
  (Pocket Guide)

Pacific North Coast
Philadelphia & the
  Pennsylvania
  Dutch Country
Puerto Rico
  (Pocket Guide)
The Rockies
San Diego
San Francisco
San Francisco
  (Pocket Guide)
The South
Santa Fe, Taos,
  Albuquerque
Seattle &
  Vancouver

Texas
USA
The U. S. & British
  Virgin Islands
The Upper Great
  Lakes Region
Vacations in
  New York State
Vacations on the
  Jersey Shore
Virginia & Maryland
Waikiki
Washington, D.C.
Washington, D.C.
  (Pocket Guide)

Foreign Guides

Acapulco
Amsterdam
Australia
Austria
The Bahamas
The Bahamas
  (Pocket Guide)
Baja & Mexico's Pacific
  Coast Resorts
Barbados
Barcelona, Madrid,
  Seville
Belgium &
  Luxembourg
Berlin
Bermuda
Brazil
Budapest
Budget Europe
Canada
Canada's Atlantic
  Provinces

Cancun, Cozumel,
  Yucatan Peninsula
Caribbean
Central America
China
Czechoslovakia
Eastern Europe
Egypt
Europe
Europe's Great Cities
France
Germany
Great Britain
Greece
The Himalayan
  Countries
Holland
Hong Kong
India
Ireland
Israel
Italy

Italy 's Great Cities
Jamaica
Japan
Kenya, Tanzania,
  Seychelles
Korea
London
London
  (Pocket Guide)
London Companion
Mexico
Mexico City
Montreal &
  Quebec City
Morocco
New Zealand
Norway
Nova Scotia,
  New Brunswick,
  Prince Edward
  Island
Paris

Paris (Pocket Guide)
Portugal
Rome
Scandinavia
Scandinavian Cities
Scotland
Singapore
South America
South Pacific
Southeast Asia
Soviet Union
Spain
Sweden
Switzerland
Sydney
Thailand
Tokyo
Toronto
Turkey
Vienna & the Danube
  Valley
Yugoslavia

Wall Street Journal Guides to Business Travel

Europe   International Cities   Pacific Rim   USA & Canada

Special-Interest Guides

Bed & Breakfast and
  Country Inn Guides:
  Mid-Atlantic Region
New England
The South
The West

Cruises and Ports
  of Call
Healthy Escapes
Fodor's Flashmaps
  New York

Fodor's Flashmaps
  Washington, D.C.
Shopping in Europe
Skiing in the USA &
  Canada

Smart Shopper's
  Guide to London
Sunday in New York
Touring Europe
Touring USA